Frommer's®

ROAD ATLAS
ATLANTE STRADALE
ATLAS DE CARRETERAS
ATLAS ROUTIER
STRASSENATLAS

EUROPE
EUROPA

Contents

II-III   Legend
IV-V   Central-northern Europe 1: 8 000 000
VI-VII   Central-southern Europe 1: 8 000 000
VIII   Useful information
1-207   **Road atlas**
208-280   Index of names
            Principal urban areas plans

Sommario

II-III   Legenda
IV-V   Europa centro-settentrionale 1: 8 000 000
VI-VII   Europa centro-meridionale 1: 8 000 000
VIII   Numeri utili
1-207   **Atlante stradale**
208-280   Indice dei nomi
            Piante delle principali aree urbane

Sumario

II-III   Leyenda
IV-V   Europa centro-norte 1: 8 000 000
VI-VII   Europa centro-sur 1: 8 000 000
VIII   Direcciones útiles
1-207   **Atlas de carreteras**
208-280   Índice de topónimos
            Planos de las principales áreas urbanas

Sommaire

II-III   Légende
IV-V   Europe centre-nord 1: 8 000 000
VI-VII   Europe centre-sud 1: 8 000 000
VIII   Informations utiles
1-207   **Atlas routier**
208-280   Index des noms
            Plans des principales aires urbaines

Inhaltsverzeichnis

II-III   Zeichenerklärung
IV-V   Mittelnördliche Europa 1: 8 000 000
VI-VII   Mittelsüdliche Europa 1: 8 000 000
VIII   Nützliche Auskünfte
1-207   **Straßenatlas**
208-280   Namenverzeichnis
            Wichtigste Stadtpläne

(GB) Legend   (I) Legenda

GB Legend	I Legenda
Toll motorway, dual carriageway	Autostrada a pedaggio a doppia carreggiata
Toll motorway, single carriageway	Autostrada a pedaggio a singola carreggiata
Non-toll motorway, dual carriageway	Autostrada senza pedaggio a doppia carreggiata
Non-toll motorway, single carriageway	Autostrada senza pedaggio a singola carreggiata
Interchange; restricted interchange; service area	Svincolo; svincolo con limitazione; area di servizio
Motorway under construction	Autostrada in costruzione
Motorway in tunnel	Autostrada in galleria
Number of motorway; european road; national road; regional or local road	Numero di autostrada; itinerario europeo; strada nazionale; strada regionale o locale
National road, dual carriageway	Strada nazionale a doppia carreggiata
National road, single carriageway	Strada nazionale a singola carreggiata
Regional road, dual carriageway	Strada regionale a doppia carreggiata
Regional road, single carriageway	Strada regionale a singola carreggiata
Local road, dual carriageway	Strada locale a doppia carreggiata
Local road, single carriageway	Strada locale a singola carreggiata
Secondary road	Strada secondaria
Road under construction	Strada in costruzione
Road in tunnel	Strada in galleria
Motorway distances in kilometres (miles in United Kingdom and Ireland)	Distanze in chilometri (miglia nel Regno Unito e Irlanda) sulle autostrade
Road distances in kilometres (miles in United Kingdom and Ireland)	Distanze in chilometri (miglia nel Regno Unito e Irlanda) sulle strade
Gradient 14% and over; gradient 6%–13%	Pendenza maggiore del 14%; pendenza dal 6% al 13%
Panoramic routes	Percorsi panoramici
Pass with height and winter closure	Passo di montagna, quota e periodo di chiusura invernale
Toll point	Barriera di pedaggio
Ferry route (with car transportation) and destination	Linea di traghetto (con trasporto auto) e destinazione
Transport of cars by rail	Trasporto auto per ferrovia
National park, natural reserve	Parco nazionale, riserva naturale
International boundary	Confine internazionale
International boundary in the sea	Confine internazionale nel mare
International airport	Aeroporto internazionale
Religious building	Edificio religioso
Castle, fortress	Castello, fortezza
Isolated monument	Monumento isolato
Ruins, archaeological area	Rovine, area archeologica
Cave	Grotta
Natural curiosity	Curiosità naturale
Panoramic view	Punto panoramico
Other curiosities (botanical garden, zoo, amusement parks etc.)	Altre curiosità (giardino botanico, zoo, parco divertimenti ecc.)
Town or place of great tourist interest	Città o luogo di grande interesse turistico
Interesting town or place	Città o luogo interessante

	E Leyenda	F Légende	D Zeichenerklärung
	Autopista de doble vía de peaje	Autoroute à péage et chaussées séparées	Zweibahnige Autobahn mit Gebühr
	Autopista de una vía de peaje	Autoroute à péage et chaussée unique	Einbahnige Autobahn mit Gebühr
	Autopista de doble vía sin peaje	Autoroute sans péage à chaussées séparées	Zweibahnige Autobahn ohne Gebühr
	Autopista de una vía sin peaje	Autoroute sans péage à chaussée unique	Einbahnige Autobahn ohne Gebühr
	Acceso; acceso parcial; estación de servicio	Échangeur; échangeur partiel; aire de service	Anschlußstelle; Autobahnein- und/oder -ausfahrt; Tankstelle
	Autopista en construcción	Autoroute en construction	Autobahn in Bau
	Túnel en autopista	Tunnel autoroutier	Autobahntunnel
A11 E50 N13 D951	Número de autopista; carretera europea; carretera nacional;	Numéro d'autoroute; route européenne; route nationale; route régionale ou locale	Straßennummer: Autobahn; Europastraße; Nationalstraße; Regional- oder Lokalstraße
	Carretera nacional de doble vía	Route nationale à chaussées séparées	Zweibahnige Nationalstraße
	Carretera nacional de vía unica	Route nationale à chaussée unique	Einbahnige Nationalstraße
	Carretera regional de doble vía	Route régionale à chaussées séparées	Zweibahnige Regionalstraße
	Carretera regional de vía unica	Route régionale à chaussée unique	Einbahnige Regionalstraße
	Carretera local de doble vía	Route locale à chaussées séparées	Zweibahnige Lokalstraße
	Carretera local de vía unica	Route locale à chaussée unique	Einbahnige Lokalstraße
	Carretera secundaria	Route secondaire	Nebenstraße
	Carretera en construcción	Route en construction	Straße in Bau
	Túnel en carretera	Tunnel routier	Straßentunnel
63	Distancias en kilómetros (millas en Gran Bretaña e Irlanda) en autopista	Distances autoroutières en kilomètres (miles en Royaume-Uni et Irlande)	Autobahnentfernungen in Kilometern (Meilen in Großbritannien und Irland)
23	Distancias en kilómetros (millas en Gran Bretaña e Irlanda) en carretera	Distances routières en kilomètres (miles en Royaume-Uni et Irlande)	Straßenentfernungen in Kilometern (Meilen in Großbritannien und Irland)
≫ →	Pendientes superiores al 14%; pendientes entre 6%–13%	Pente 14% et outre; pente 6%–13%	Steigungen über 14%; Steigungen 6%–13%
	Rutas panorámicas	Routes panoramiques	Aussichtsstraßen
Col d'Izoard 2360 10-6	Puerto de montaña con altura y cierre invernal	Col avec altitude et fermeture en hiver	Paß mit Höhe und Wintersperre
	Peaje	Barrière de péage	Gebübhrenstelle
Bastia	Línea marítima (con transporte de coches) y destino	Ligne de navigation (bac pour voitures) et destination	Schiffahrtslinie (Autofähre) und Ziel
	Transporte de coches por ferrocarril	Transport de voitures par chemin de fer	Autoverladung per Bahn
	Parque nacional, reserva natural	Parc national, réserve naturelle	Nationalpark, Naturschutzgebiet
	Límite internacional	Frontière internationale	Staatsgrenze
	Límite internacional en el mar	Frontière internationale dans la mer	Staatsgrenze im Meeresgebiet
⊕	Aeropuerto internacional	Aéroport international	Internationaler Flughafen
♘	Edificio religioso	Édifice religieux	Religiösgebäude
♜	Castillo, fortaleza	Château, château-fort	Schloß, Festung
⚑	Monumento aislado	Monument isolé	Alleinstehendes Denkmal
∴	Ruinas, zona arqueológica	Ruines, site archéologique	Ruinen, archäologisches Ausgrabungsgebiet
⌒	Cueva	Grotte	Höhle
✳	Paraje de interés natural	Curiosité naturelle	Natursehenswürdigkeit
☼	Vista panorámica	Vue panoramique	Rundblick
★	Otras curiosidades (jardín botánico, zoo, parque de atracciones etc.)	Autres curiosités (jardin botanique, zoo, parc d'attractions etc.)	Andere Sehenswürdigkeiten (Botanische Gärten, Zoo, Freizeitparks usw.)
LONDON	Ciudad o lugar de gran interés turístico	Localité ou site de grand intérêt touristique	Ortschaft oder Platz von großem touristichen Interesse
BIRMINGHAM	Ciudad o lugar interesante	Localité ou site remarquable	Sehenswerte Ortschaft oder Platz

LEGEND - SEGNI CONVENZIONALI - LEYENDA- LÉGENDE - ZEICHENERKLÄRUNG

Motorway and road with motorway characteristics
Autostrada e strada con caratteristiche autostradali
Autopista y autovía con calzadas separadas
Autoroute et route de type autoroutier
Autobahn und Schnellstraße mit getrennten Fahrbahnen

Other roads
Altre strade
Otras carreteras
Autres routes
Sonstige Straßen

E15
European road number
Numero di strada europea
Número de carretera europea
Numéro de route européenne
Europastraßennummer

169
Distances in kilometres
Distanze in chilometri
Distancias en kilómetros
Distances en kilomètres
Distanzen in Kilometern

Distances in Great Britain and Ireland are expressed in miles.
Nel Regno Unito e in Irlanda le distanze sono espresse in miglia.
Las distancias en Gran Bretaña e Irlanda son expresas en millas.
Les distances en Grande-Bretagne et Irlande sont exprimées en miles.
Entfernungsangaben in Großbritannien und Irland sind in Meilen wiedergegeben.

Scale - Scala - Escala - Échelle - Maßstab
1 : 8 000 000 (1 cm = 80 km)

0   100   200   300   400   500 km

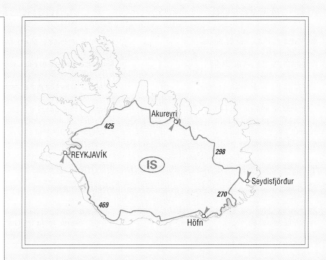

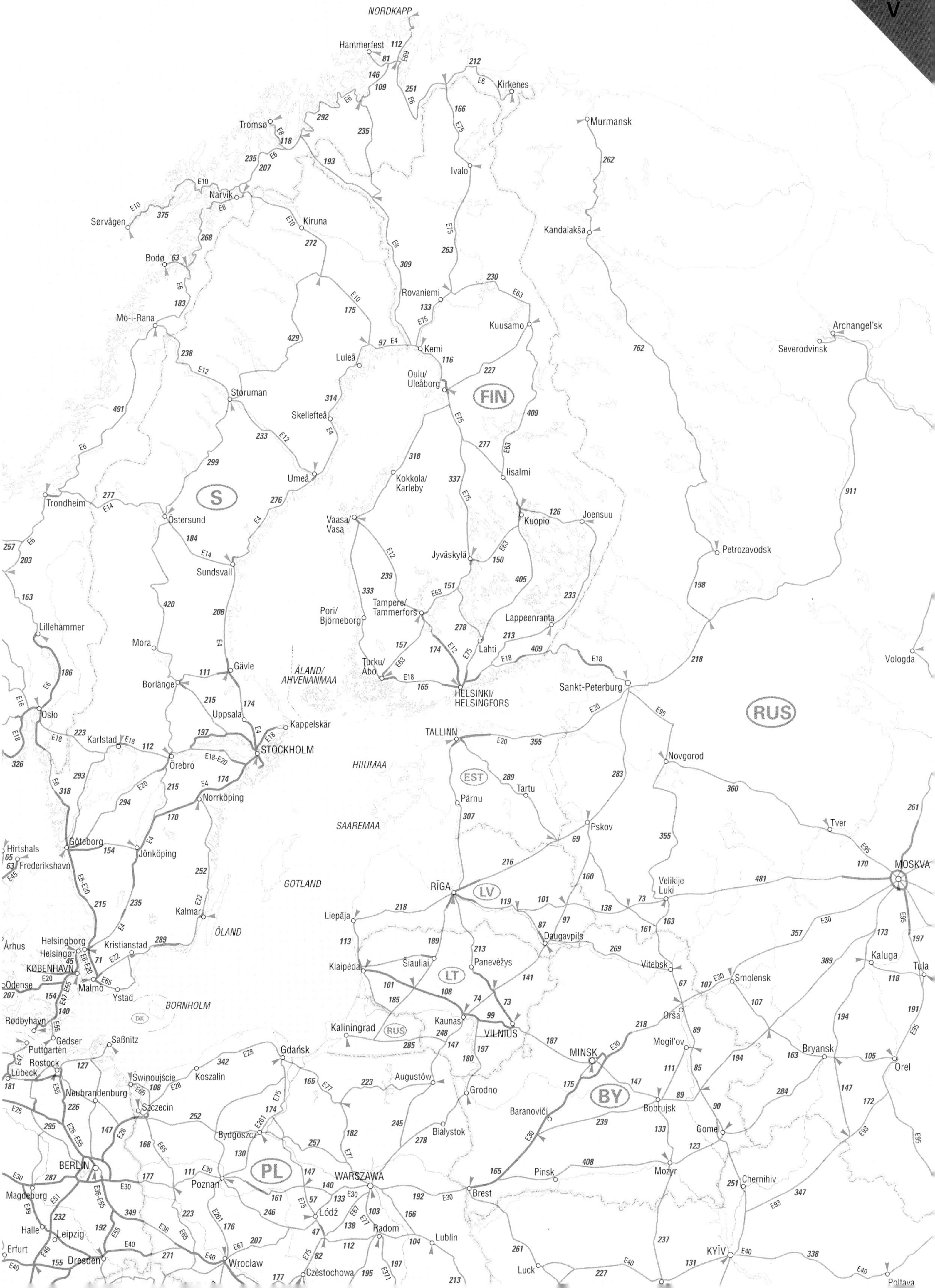

NORDKAPP

Hammerfest 112 E69
81
146
109 251 E6 Kirkenes
E6 212
166 Murmansk
Tromsø 292
E8 118 235
E6 235 193 Ivalo 262
207
E10 263 Kandalakša
Narvik E6 E8
Sørvågen E10 375 Kiruna 309 230 Archangel'sk
Bodø 63 268 E10 272 Rovaniemi E63 Severodvinsk
E6 175 133 Kuusamo
183 E10 97 E4 Kemi 227 762
Mo-i-Rana 429 Luleå 116
238 Oulu/Uleåborg FIN
E12 Storuman 314 409
491 Skellefteå 277 E63 Iisalmi 911
233 E12 318 337
E6 299 Umeå E4 Kokkola/Karleby Kuopio 126 Joensuu
Trondheim 277 Östersund 276 Vaasa/Vasa 150 Petrozavodsk
E14 184 Jyväskylä 405 233 198
E14 Sundsvall 239 151 Lappeenranta
420 208 333 Tampere/Tammerfors 278 213 409 E18 Vologda
Lillehammer 157 174 Lahti 218
186 Mora Pori/Björneborg E63 E75 E18
E6 111 Gävle Turku/Åbo 165 HELSINKI/HELSINGFORS Sankt-Peterburg
Borlänge 215 174 E18 E20 E95 RUS
Oslo Uppsala ÅLAND/AHVENANMAA Novgorod
223 112 197 TALLINN E20 355 360 261
Karlstad E18 Örebro STOCKHOLM HIIUMAA 289 283 Tver
326 293 E18-E20 EST Tartu
318 294 215 E4 174 Pärnu Pskov 355 MOSKVA
170 Norrköping 307 69 E95
Göteborg 154 SAAREMAA 216 160 Velikije Luki 481 173 197
Hirtshals 65 Jönköping 252 GOTLAND RĪGA LV 138 73 163 357 Kaluga
63 Frederikshavn E6-E20 218 119 101 87 97 161 389 118
E45 215 235 Kalmar Liepāja 113 189 Daugavpils 269 Vitebsk 67 107 Smolensk 194 191
Århus ÖLAND Klaipėda Šiauliai 213 Panevėžys 141 107 Orša 89 Bryansk
Helsingborg Kristianstad 289 LT 101 108 74 73 218 Mogil'ov 89 Orel
KØBENHAVN 71 E22 185 Kaliningrad Kaunas 99 187 MINSK 111 85 105
Odense Malmö RUS 248 VILNIUS 175 BY 147 Bobrujsk 284 147
207 154 Ystad 285 147 Grodno 89 90 172
Rødbyhavn 140 BORNHOLM 180 197 Baranoviči 239 133 Gomel
Gedser Gdańsk 342 Augustów 123
Puttgarten Saßnitz Koszalin 165 223 Białystok 408 Pinsk Mozyr 251 Chernihiv
Lübeck 127 Świnoujście 108 174 245 278 165 Brest 237 347
181 Neubrandenburg 252 Bydgoszcz 182 192 KYÏV E40 338
E26 226 Szczecin 130 257 Luck 261 227
295 147 168 PL 147 Poltava
BERLIN Poznan 111 WARSZAWA
287 177 161 140 133 Lublin
Magdeburg 232 349 223 176 246 57 Łódź 103 166 104
Halle Leipzig 192 E36 207 138 Radom 112
Erfurt Dresden 271 Wrocław 47 195 197
155 177 Częstochowa 213

Galway/ Gaillimh — IRL — 134
136
102
Limerick/ Luimneach — 65 — 124 — DUBLIN/ BAILE ÁTHA CLIATH
E20 — 161 — 102
124 — E201 — E1 — Holyhead — Liverpool — 58 — Leeds — 55 — E20 — Kingston-upon-Hull
124 — E30 — Waterford/ Port Lairge — Rosslare — E1 — 108 — Manchester — 75 — E13 — E15 — E22
Fishguard — 167 — Birmingham — 144 — E24 — 197 — 167
E30 — 84 — E5 — E24 — Cambridge — 79 — Norwich
Cardiff — 146 — E30 — Bristol — 127 — Oxford — E13 — E15 — 125 — E24 — Ipswich
124 — 117 — E30 — LONDON — 72 — E32 — Harwich
Penzance — 76 — Plymouth — 149 — Southampton — 80 — 75 — E15 — Dover
Portsmouth — 147 — Calais

upon-Tyne
116 — E5 — 96 — E15
GB

Groningen — Emden — 200
197 — E22
NL
AMSTERDAM — 226 — E37
204 — E30 — Arnhem — 172
Den Haag — 208 — 215 — E34 — Duisburg — Dortmund — 243
Rotterdam — Antwerpen — E313 — Düsseldorf
Oostende — E40 — 197 — E40 — 69 — Köln — E41
Lille — BRUSSEL/ BRUXELLES — B — Liège — 198 — Bonn — 209 — E35
170 — 287 — E42 — 215 — 198 — E40 — Koblenz
Amiens — E19 — E42 — 215 — L — 289 — E44
CHANNEL ISLANDS — GB — Cherbourg — 120 — Le Havre — E44 — 242 — 295 — E17 — Luxembourg — E50 — 265
Brest — E50 — 230 — Caen — E46 — 239 — Rouen — 123 — E46 — Mannheim — 55 — E25 — Saarbrücken
237 — E401 — St-Malo — 183 — E401 — 215 — E5 — Reims — 323 — Metz — E50 — 168 — Karlsruhe — 102
296 — E50 — Rennes — 144 — E50 — PARIS — E50 — Troyes — 316 — E54 — 283 — Nancy — 134 — E35-E52
107 — E60 — Le Mans — 120 — Orléans — E511 — E54 — 314 — Strasbourg — 192 — E57
182 — E60 — E502 — Tours — 208 — E604 — Bourges — Dijon — 247 — E54 — 211
Nantes — 179 — E62 — E601 — Poitiers — E62 — 346 — E607 — 193 — Besançon — Basel — Zürich
319 — E603 — 254 — 214 — F — E11 — 304 — E62 — 195 — BERN — 264 — CH — 360
La Rochelle — E603 — Limoges — Clermont-Ferrand — 184 — Genève — 148 — Lausanne — E62
E602 — E606 — 70 — 191 — Lyon — E611 — E712 — 296 — 254 — 328
Bordeaux — E70 — 186 — Brive-la-Gaillarde — E70 — Grenoble — E612 — 139 — E64
337 — E5-E70 — 243 — 399 — 251 — 294 — Torino — 145
Donostia-San Sebastián — E80 — Pau — 188 — Toulouse — 394 — Nîmes — Sisteron — 185 — Genova
Pamplona/ Iruñea — 257 — 146 — E80 — 128 — 130 — Nice — MC — 195
E804 — 270 — E9 — 137 — Marseille — 211
Zaragoza — AND — 349 — Perpignan
Lleida/ Lérida — 254 — Girona/ Gerona
317 — E90 — Barcelona
378 — E15

A Coruña/ La Coruña — E70 — 321 — E70 — Gijón — 305 — Santander
Santiago de Compostela — E1 — Oviedo — E70 — Bilbo/ Bilbao — E804 — E70
158 — Orense — León — 260 — Burgos — 312 — E5-E80
Vigo — E1 — 140 — E82 — 427 — E82 — Valladolid — E804 — 306
158 — Porto — E82 — Salamanca — 214 — E5 — Zaragoza — E7 — 349
120 — E802 — 429 — 370 — E803 — MADRID — 314 — E90 — 370 — E15
Coimbra — E1-E80 — P — 345 — E90 — Toledo — 378
Óbidos — 192 — Abrantes — E803 — E5 — E901 — 370
LISBOA — 279 — Badajoz — E90 — 266 — 358 — 317 — E90
E90 — E802 — Mérida — E102 — E5 — 294 — E901 — Valencia
Sines — 270 — E803 — 200 — Albacete — 145 — 260 — E15
Lagos — 249 — E1 — Córdoba — E5 — 245 — Alicante/ Alacant
Faro — Huelva — Sevilla — 243 — 135 — E92 — 273 — Murcia — Cartagena
258 — E92 — Granada — E15
Cádiz — 256 — E5 — 250 — E15 — Almería
Algeciras — Málaga — E15
Gibraltar — GB
Ceuta — E

CORSE
Bastia — 155
Ajaccio — 159
Bonifacio
Porto Torres — 122 — Olbia
229 — 285
SARDEGNA
Cagliari

Palma — Cala Rajada
ILLES BALEARS / ISLAS BALEARES

Melilla — E

USEFUL INFORMATION
NUMERI UTILI
DIRECCIONES ÚTILES
INFORMATIONS UTILES
NÜTZLICHE AUSKÜNFTE

		⊘	🏭	✚	🔥	ℹ	🚗
A	Österreich	0043	133	144	122	(43) 1 5872000	ÖAMTC (43) 1 711990
AL	Shqiperia	00355	24445*	22235*	23333*	(355) 42 4853	—
AND	Andorra, Andorre	00376	110	116	118	(376) 820214	ACA (376) 8 20890
B	België, Belgique	0032	101	100	100	(32) 2 5040200	RACB (32) 2 2870911
BG	Bǎlgarija	00359	166	150	160	(359) 2 885313	UAB (359) 2 86151
BIH	Bosna i Hercegovina	00387	92	94	93	(387) 71 532281	ACNAIT (387) 71 664374
BY	Belarus'	00375	02	03	01	(375) 17 2269840	ADAS (375) 17 2231055
CH	Schweiz, Suisse, Svizzera	0041	117	144	118	(41) 900 552000	TCS (41) 22 4172424
CZ	Česko	00420	158	155	150	(420) 2 2127111	ÚAMK ČR (420) 2 24210266
D	Deutschland	0049	110	110	112	(49) 69974640	ADAC (49) 8976760
DK	Danmark	0045	112	112	112	(45) 33111415	FDM (45) 45270707
E	España	0034	091	061	080	(34) 91 3433710	RACE (34) 91 5947400
EST	Eesti	00372	02	03	01	(372) 2 641120	EAK (372) 2 237533
F	France	0033	17	15	18	(33) 1 49556700	ACF (33) 1 43124312
FIN	Suomi, Finland	00358	10022	10022	10022	(358) 0 403011	ATCF (358) 0 774761
FL	Liechtenstein	0041	117	144	118	(41) 75 21443	ACFL (41) 75 2326767
GB	United Kingdom	0044	999	999	999	(44) 171 7303400	AA (44) 1256 320123
GR	Hellas	0030	100	100	100	(30) 1 3223111	ELPA (30) 1 7488800
H	Magyar	0036	107	104	105	(36) 1 1179800	MAK (36) 1 2122938
HR	Hrvatska	00385	92	94	93	(385) 1 4556455	HAK (385) 1 454433
I	Italia	0039	113	118	115	(39) 06 49711	ACI (39) 06 4477
IRL	Éire, Ireland	00353	999	999	999	(353) 1 747733	AA (353) 1 2833555
IS	Ísland	00354	112	112	112	(354) 1 5227488	FIB (354) 5 629999
L	Luxembourg, Lëtzebuerg	00352	113	113	113	(352) 400808	ACL (352) 450045
LT	Lietuva	00370	02	03	01	(370) 2 622610	LAS (370) 2 250556
LV	Latvija	00371	02	03	01	(371) 2229945	LAMB (371) 2566222
M	Malta	00356	191	196	199	(356) 238282	TCM (356) 241665
MC	Principauté de Monaco	00377	112	112	112	(377) 93 92166116	—
MD	Moldova	00373	902	903	901	(373) 2 262569	AITA (373) 2 735290
MK	Makedonija	00389	92	94	93	(389) 91 114359	AMSM (389) 91 116011
N	Norge	0047	112	113	110	(47) 82060100	KNA (47) 22 561900
NL	Nederland	0031	112	112	112	(31) 70 3705705	ANWB (31) 70 3147147
P	Portugal	00351	112	112	112	(351) 1 3463643	ACP (351) 1 3563931
PL	Polska	0048	997	999	998	(48) 22 260271	PZM (48) 22 6293541
RO	România	0040	055	061	055	(40) 1 6145160	ACR (40) 1 6593910
RUS	Rossija	007	02	03	01	(7) 95 2922260	RAS (7) 95 2297540
S	Sverige	0046	112	112	112	(46) 8 7892490	M (46) 8 6903800
SK	Slovensko	00421	158	155	150	(421) 7 212828	UAMK ŠR (421) 7 43413915
SLO	Slovenija	00386	113	112	112	(386) 61 1881165	AMZS (386) 61 1681111
TR	Türkiye Cumhuriyeti	0090	155	112	110	(90) 312 2128300	TTOK (90) 212 2828140
UA	Ukrajina	00380	02	03	01	(380) 44 2943111	FAU (380) 322 339332
YU	Jugoslavija	00381	92	94	93	—	AMSJ (381) 11 401699

Tiranë

ROAD ATLAS
ATLANTE STRADALE
ATLAS DE CARRETERAS
ATLAS ROUTIER
STRASSENATLAS

Legend
Legenda
Leyenda
Légende
Zeichenerklärung

International code
Prefisso internazionale
Prefijo telefónico internacional
Indicatif international
Internationale Vorwahl

Police
Polizia
Policía
Police
Polizei

Ambulance
Ambulanza
Ambulancia
Ambulance
Ambulanz

Fire-brigade
Vigili del fuoco
Bomberos
Pompiers
Feuerwehr

Tourist offices
Uffici turistici
Oficinas de turismo
Bureaux de tourisme
Touristenämter

Automobile associations
Automobil club
Clubes automovilísticos
Automobile-clubs
Automobilclubs

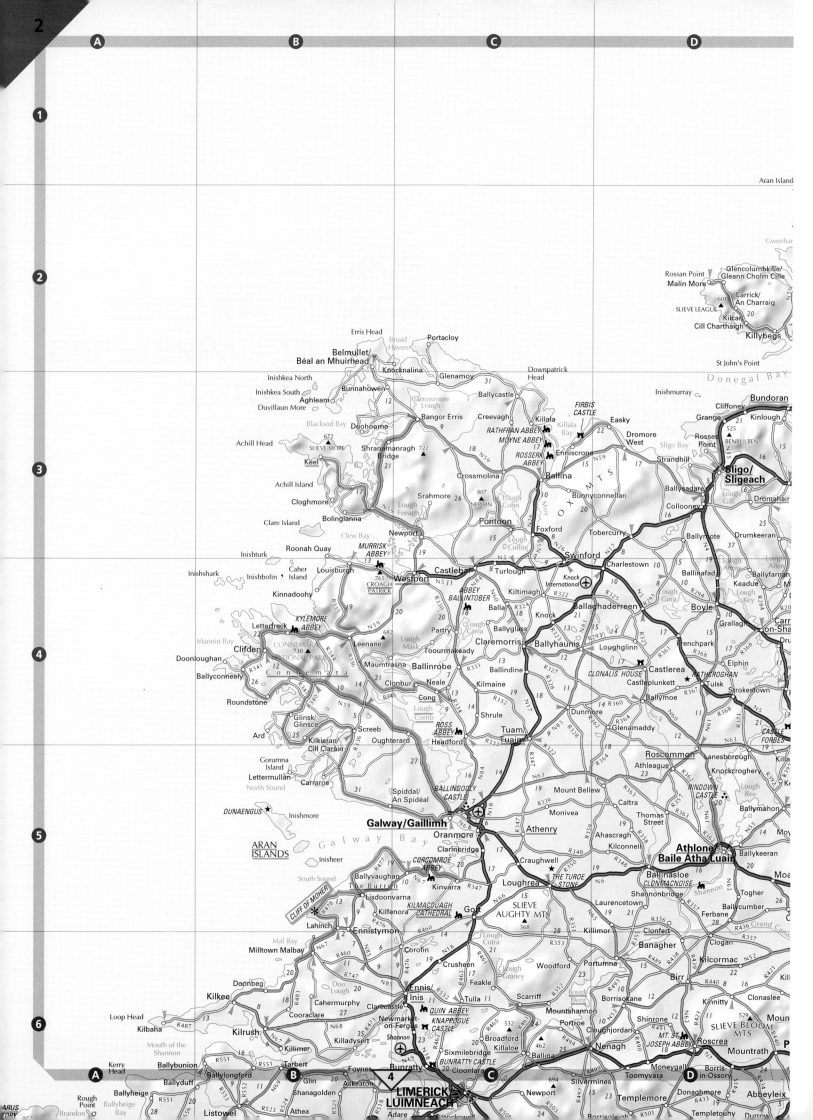

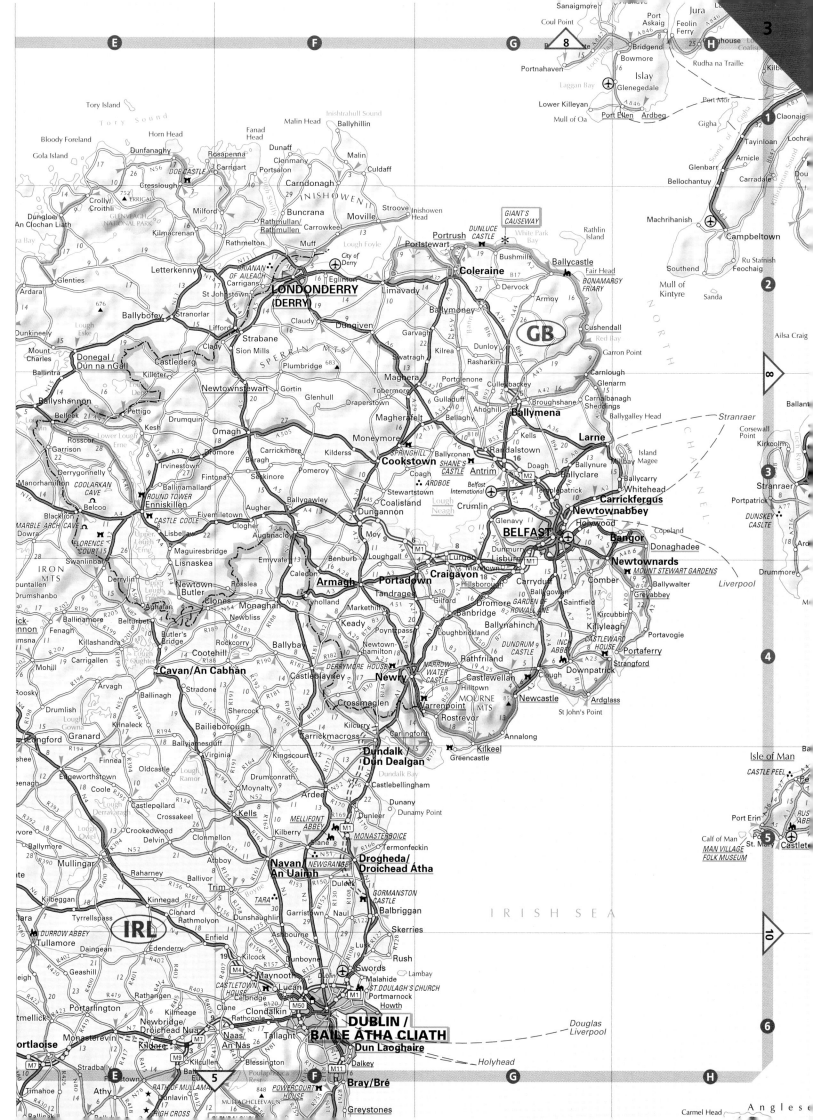

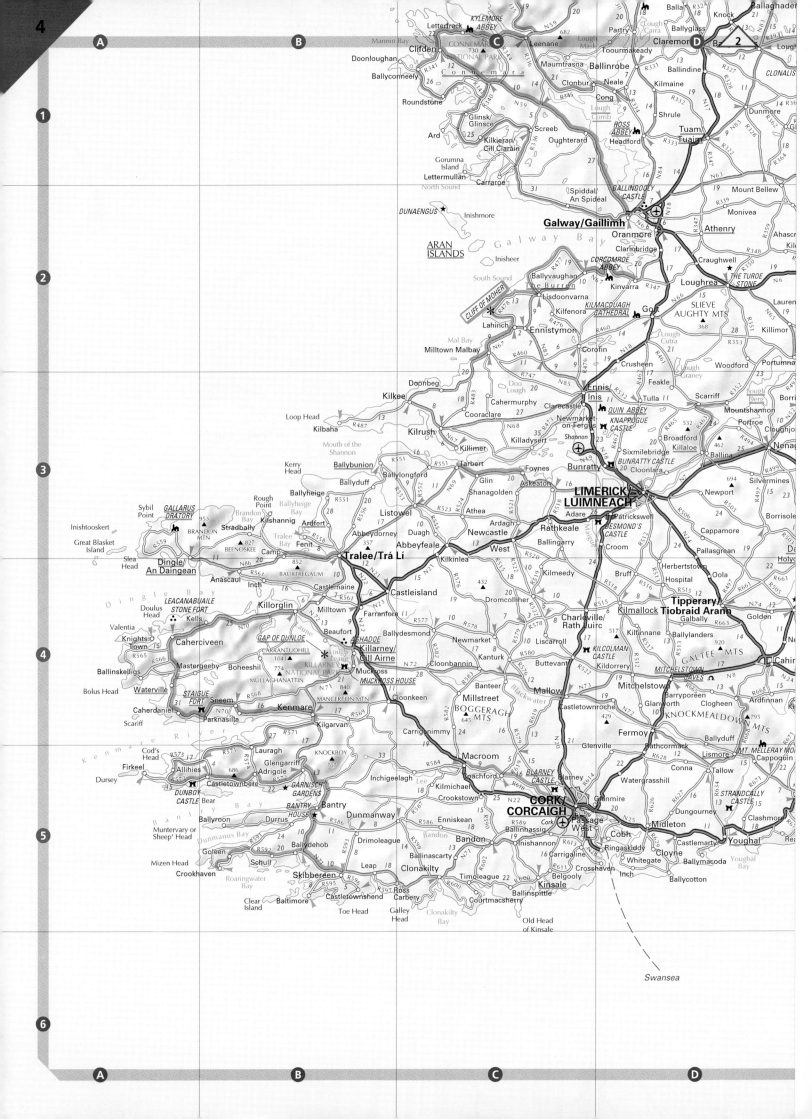

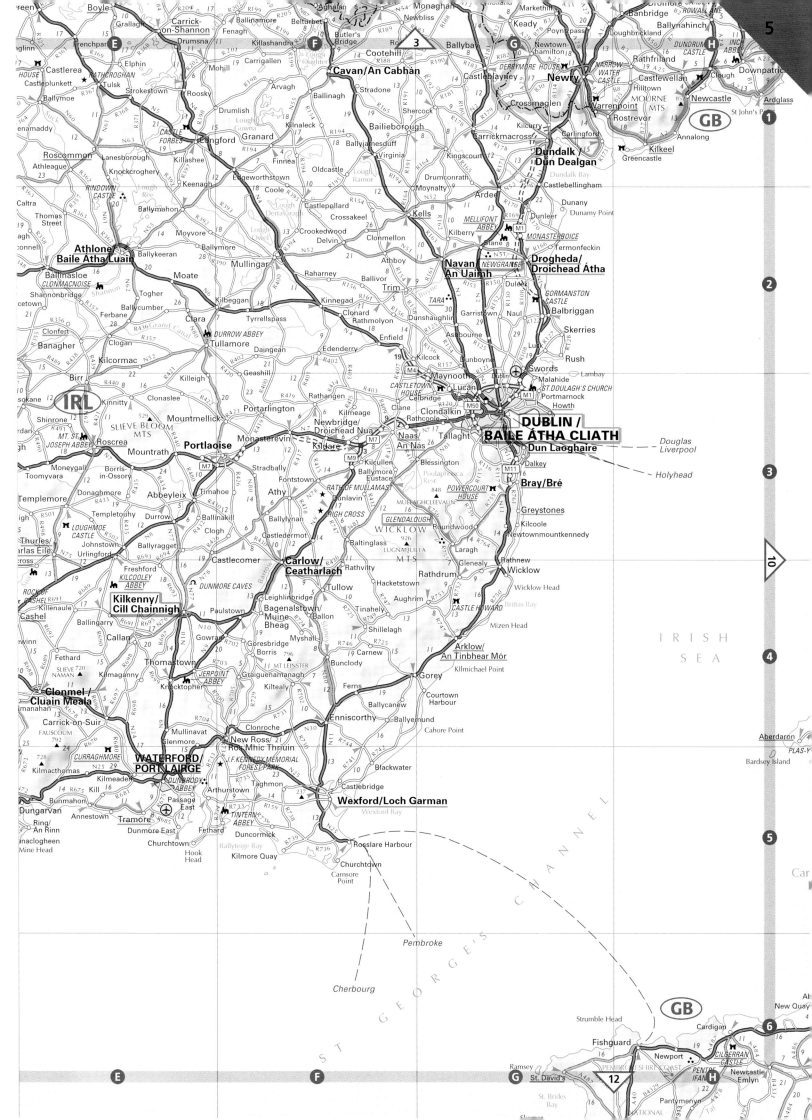

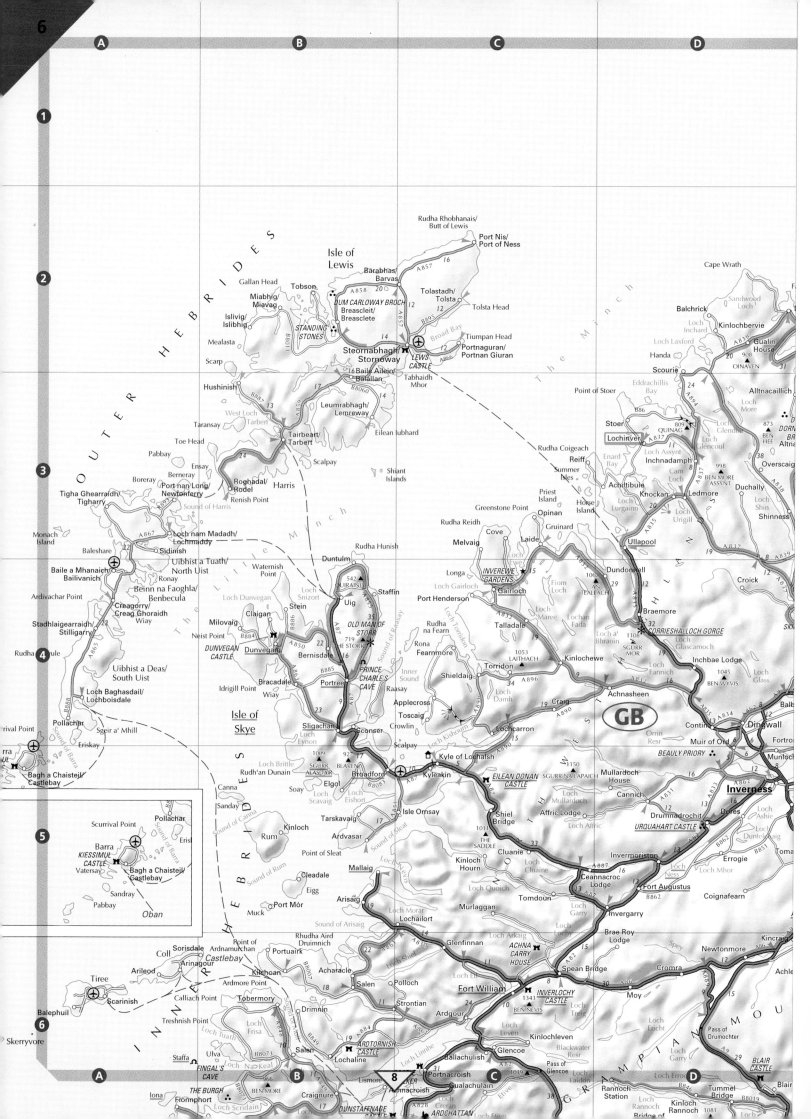

A   B   C   D

1

2

3

4

5

6

OUTER HEBRIDES

Isle of
Lewis

Rudha Rhobhanais/
Butt of Lewis

Port Nis/
Port of Ness

Gallan Head

Tobson

Barabhas/
Barvas

A857

16

Miabhig/
Miavag

A858   20

Tolastadh/
Tolsta

Cape Wrath

Sandwood
Loch

Balchrick

Loch
Inchard

Kinlochbervie

Islivig/
Islibhig

DUM CARLOWAY BROCH
Breascleit/
Breasclete

12

A857

Tolsta Head

Loch Laxford

A838

Gualin
House

Mealasta

STANDING
STONES

B8011

14

A857

B895

12

Broad Bay

Tiumpan Head

20

908

Handa

Scourie

OINAVEN

31

Scarp

Steornabhagh/
Stornoway

LEWS
CASTLE

12

Portnaguran/
Portnan Giuran

Point of Stoer

B86

Loch
Inver

873

Eddrachillis
Bay

24

Alltnacaillich

BEN
HEE

DORN
BR

Hushinish

Baile Ailein/
Balallan

B8060

Tabhaidh
Mhor

Stoer

809

QUINAG

Loch
Glendhu

Altna

B887

13

B850

17

Leumrabhagh/
Lemreway

14

Eilean Iubhard

Lochinver

A837

11

Loch
Glencoul

Overscaig

Taransay

West Loch
Tarbert

A859

Tairbeart/
Tarbert

24

Toe Head

Pabbay

Ensay

Scalpay

Shiant
Islands

Reiff

Summer
Isles

Enard
Bay

Inchnadamph

Achiltibule

Cam
Loch

8

998

BEN MORE
ASSYNT

Knockan

Loch
Urigill

Ledmore

20

Duchally

A838

Loch
Shin

Shinness

Boreray

Berneray

Roghadal/
Rodel   Harris

Priest
Island

Greenstone Point

Horse
Island

Tigha Ghearraidh/
Tigharry

Port nan Long/
Newtonferry

A867

Renish Point

Sound of Harris

Rudha Coigeach

Rudha Reidh

Cove

Opinan

Gruinard

Ullapool

A835

A837

19

A839

8

Monach
Island

Baleshare

Sidinish

Loch nam Madadh/
Lochmaddy

12

Melvaig

Laide

Loch
Ewe

INVEREWE
GARDENS

15

Croick

A837

Baile a Mhanaich/
Bailivanich

Uibhist a Tuath/
North Uist

Duntulm

Waternish
Point

Rudha Hunish

Longa

Loch Gairloch

Gairloch

Fiom
Loch

AN
TEALLACH

1062

29

Loch
Broom

12

Braemore

SKI

Ardivachar Point

Beinn na Faoghla/
Benbecula

Loch Snizort

QUIRAING

542

Staffin

Port Henderson

A832

1105

SGURR
MOR

CORRIESHALLOCH GORGE

32

Creagorry/
Creag Ghoraidh
Wiay

Claigan

Stein

Uig

35

A855

Loch
Maree

Lochan
Fada

Loch a'
Bhraoin

19

Loch
Fannich

Inchbae Lodge

Loch
Glass

Stadhlaigearraidh/
Stilligarry   22

Milovaig

Neist Point

B884

DUNVEGAN
CASTLE

22

Dunvegan

A850

OLD MAN OF
STORR   719
THE STORR

1053
LAITHACH

Talladale

A896

34

Torridon

9

Kinlochewe

Achnasheen

A832

1045
BEN WYVIS

Loch
Fannich

16

A835

A834

Rudha n'Iule

Uibhist a Deas/
South Uist

B888

Bracadale

Idrigill Point
Wiay

B885

Bernisdale

Portree

PRINCE
CHARLES'S
CAVE

Rona
Fearnmore

Rudha
na Fearn

Shieldaig

Loch
Damh

Craig

19

A890

Lochcarron

15

A835

Achanasheen

Muir of Ord

A832

Dingwall

Loch Baghasdail/
Lochboisdale

Sligachan

Sconser

23

A87

Applecross

Toscaig

Crowlin

Inner
Sound

Raasay

Sound of Raasay

GB

Orrin
Resr

Contin

Pollachar

Sound of Barra

Eriskay

Sgeir a' Mhill

Isle of
Skye

Loch
Eynon

Scalpay

Loch Kishorn

Kyle of Lochalsh

A890

BEAULY PRIORY

12

Munloch

arra
UL

Bagh a Chaisteil/
Castlebay

1009
SGURR
ALASDAIR

927
BLAVEN

17

Loch Brittle

Broadford

10

Kyleakin

B8083

A87

5

EILEAN DONAN
CASTLE

1150

SGURR NA LAPAICH

Mullardoch
House

Cannich

A831

A862

Inverness

Rudh'an Dunain

Soay

Elgol

Loch
Eishort

Isle Ornsay

A87

Affric Lodge

Loch Affric

13

Dores

A862

B851

Toma

Canna

Sanday

Tarskavaig

Ardvasar

17

Shiel
Bridge

1011
THE
SADDLE

Cluanie

33

A887

URQUHART CASTLE

Drumnadrochit

Loch
Ashie

Loch
Duntelchaig

Errogie

Kinloch

Rum

Kinloch
Hourn

Loch
Cluanie

Invermoriston

Loch
Ness

Point of Sleat

Mallaig

Loch Nevis

Kinloch
Hourn

Ceannacroc
Lodge

A887

13 A87

Fort Augustus

B862

Coignafearn

Cleadale

Eigg

Arisaig

19

Loch Morar

Lochailort

Murlaggan

Loch Quoich

Tomdoun

Loch
Garry

Invergarry

ACHNA
CARRY
HOUSE

Loch
Lochy

15

Brae Roy
Lodge

Spey

Kincraig

Muck

Port Mór

Sound of Arisaig

A830

Rhudha Aird
Druimnich

Glenfinnan

Loch Arkaig

Loch Shiel

A82

Spean Bridge

30

A86

Cromra

Newtonmore

A86

Achle

Point of
Ardnamurchan

Sorisdale

Coll

Castlebay

Portuairk

Kilchoan

B8007

Acharacle

22

A861

A830

11

8

1343
BEN NEVIS

Fort William

INVERLOCHY
CASTLE

Loch
Treig

Moy

15

Arinagour

Arileod

Ardmore Point

Salen

18

Polloch

Strontian

11

Ardgour

24

10

Kinlochleven

31

Loch
Ericht

Pass of
Drumochter

Tiree

Calliach Point

Tobermory

Drimnin

Loch Eil

Ben Nevis

Loch
Leven

Glencoe

Blackwater
Resr

Loch
Garry

BLAIR
CASTLE

Scarinish

Treshnish Point

Loch
Frisa

B849

19

A884

Lochaline

ARDTORNISH
CASTLE

Ballachulish

Pass of
Glencoe

A82

Loch
Laidon

Loch
Ericht

Balephuil

Ulva

Staffa

B8073

Salen

10

B

Portnacroish

8

Loch Linnhe

C

Gualachulain

Rannoch
Station

B846

Kinloch
Rannoch

Tummel
Bridge

B8019

Skerryvore

THE BURGH
BEN MORE
Iona
Fionnphort

666

FINGAL'S
CAVE

Loch Scridain

Craignure

17

DUNSTAFFNAGE

A828
Loch Creran

ARDCHATTAN

Loch Etive

38

GRAMPIAN MOU

Blai

Bridge of

A   B   C   D

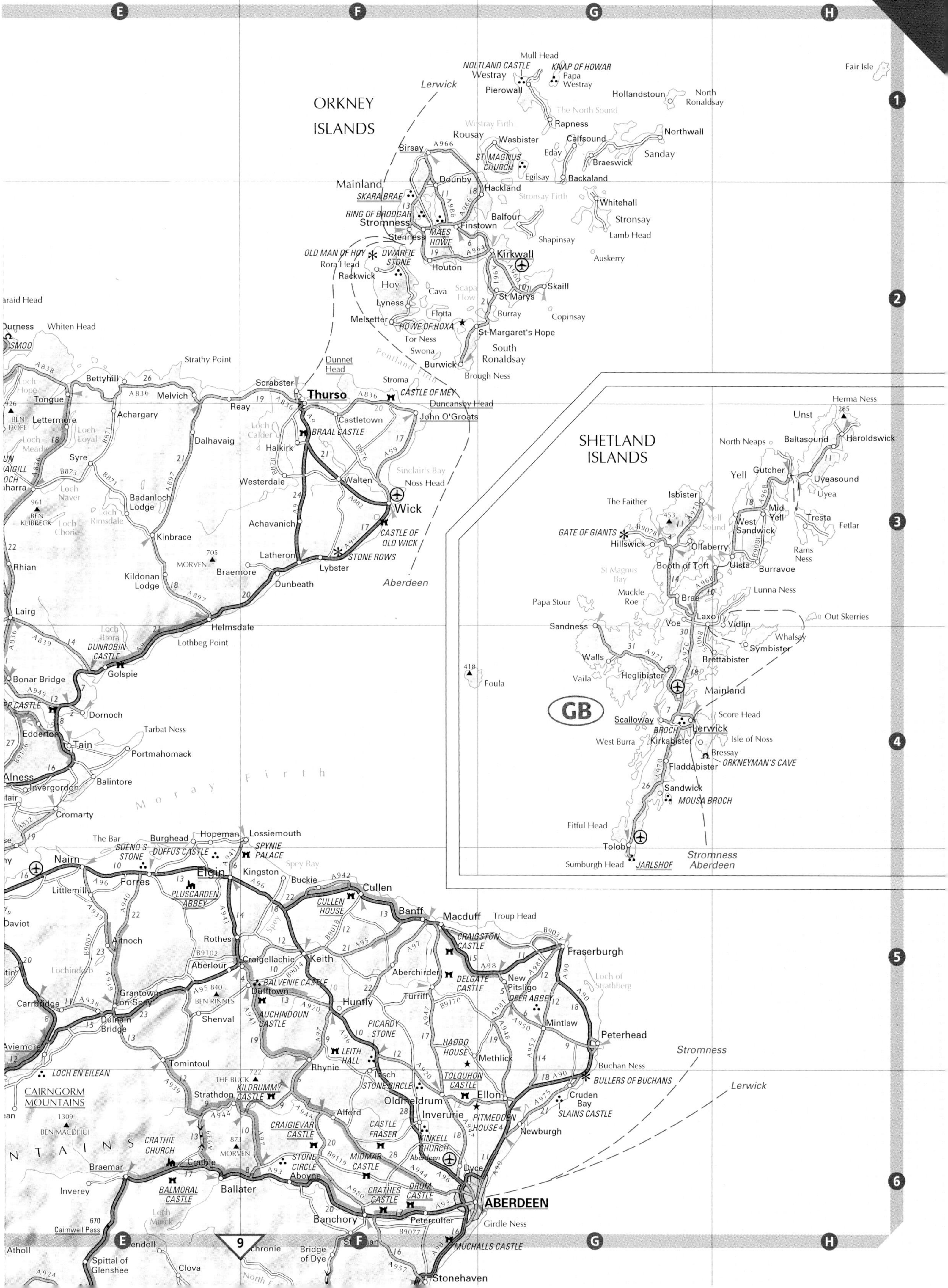

ORKNEY ISLANDS

Lerwick

Mull Head
NOLTLAND CASTLE Westray KNAP OF HOWAR
Papa Westray
Pierowall
Hollandstoun North Ronaldsay
Fair Isle

Rousay Wasbister Rapness Calfsound Northwall
Birsay A966 ST MAGNUS CHURCH Eday Braeswick Sanday
The North Sound

Mainland Dounby Hackland Egilsay Backaland
SKARA BRAE A986 Whitehall Stronsay
RING OF BRODGAR Stromness Finstown Balfour Lamb Head
Stenness MAES HOWE Shapinsay
A965 Kirkwall
OLD MAN OF HOY DWARFIE STONE Auskerry
Rora Head Rackwick Houton Copinsay
Hoy Cava Scapa Flow Skaill St Marys
Lyness Burray
Melsetter Flotta St Margaret's Hope
HOWE OF HOXA Tor Ness South Ronaldsay
Swona Burwick
Brough Ness

araid Head
Durness Whiten Head
SMOO
Loch Hope Dunnet Head
Tongue Bettyhill Strathy Point Scrabster Stroma
Lettermore Melvich Reay Thurso CASTLE OF MEY
Achargary Castletown Duncansby Head
Syre Dalhavaig John O'Groats
Loch Loyal Halkirk BRAAL CASTLE
Loch Calder Westerdale Walten Sinclair's Bay
Badanloch Lodge Noss Head
Loch Naver Achavanich Wick
BEN KLIBRECK Loch Choire CASTLE OF OLD WICK
Rhian Kinbrace Latheron STONE ROWS
MORVEN Braemore Lybster
Kildonan Lodge Dunbeath Aberdeen
Lairg Helmsdale
Loch Brora Lothbeg Point
DUNROBIN CASTLE
Bonar Bridge Golspie
CASTLE Dornoch
Edderton Tarbat Ness
Tain
Alness Portmahomack
Invergordon Balintore
Cromarty
Moray Firth

SHETLAND ISLANDS

Herma Ness
Unst
North Neaps Baltasound Haroldswick
Isbister Gutcher Uyeasound
The Faither Yell Uyea
GATE OF GIANTS Mid Yell Tresta
Hillswick Ollaberry West Sandwick Rams Ness Fetlar
Booth of Toft Burravoe
St Magnus Bay Ulsta
Papa Stour Muckle Roe Brae Lunna Ness
Sandness Voe Laxo Out Skerries
Walls Vidlin
Vaila Heglibister Symbister
Foula Brettabister Whalsay
Mainland
GB
Scalloway Score Head
BROCH Lerwick
West Burra Kirkabister Isle of Noss
Bressay
Fladdabister ORKNEYMAN'S CAVE
Sandwick
MOUSA BROCH
Fitful Head
Tolob Stromness Aberdeen
Sumburgh Head JARLSHOF

The Bar Burghead Hopeman Lossiemouth
Nairn SUENO'S STONE SPYNIE PALACE
DUFFUS CASTLE Kingston Spey Bay Buckie Cullen
Forres Elgin Buckie
Littlemill PLUSCARDEN ABBEY CULLEN HOUSE Banff Macduff Troup Head
Daviot Rothes Keith Aberchirder CRAIGSTON CASTLE Fraserburgh
Aitnoch Craigellachie DELGATE CASTLE Loch of Strathbeg
Lochindorb Aberlour New Pitsligo
Carrbridge BALVENIE CASTLE Huntly Turriff DEER ABBEY
Grantown-on-Spey Dufftown PICARDY STONE Mintlaw
BEN RINNES AUCHINDOUN CASTLE Peterhead
Dulnain Bridge Shenval HADDO HOUSE
Aviemore Tomintoul LEITH HALL Methlick Stromness
LOCH EN EILEAN THE BUCK Rhynie Insch TOLQUHON CASTLE Buchan Ness
CAIRNGORM MOUNTAINS KILDRUMMY CASTLE STONE CIRCLE BULLERS OF BUCHANS
Strathdon Oldmeldrum Ellon Lerwick
BEN MACDHUI Alford Inverurie Cruden Bay
CRAIGIEVAR CASTLE CASTLE FRASER PITMEDDEN HOUSE SLAINS CASTLE
MORVEN KINKELL CHURCH Newburgh
CRATHIE CHURCH Crathie STONE CIRCLE MIDMAR CASTLE Dyce
Braemar Aboyne CRATHES CASTLE Aberdeen
Inverey Ballater BALMORAL CASTLE DRUM CASTLE ABERDEEN
Loch Muick Banchory Peterculter Girdle Ness
Cairnwell Pass MUCHALLS CASTLE
Atholl Bridge of Dye Stonehaven
Spittal of Glenshee Clova

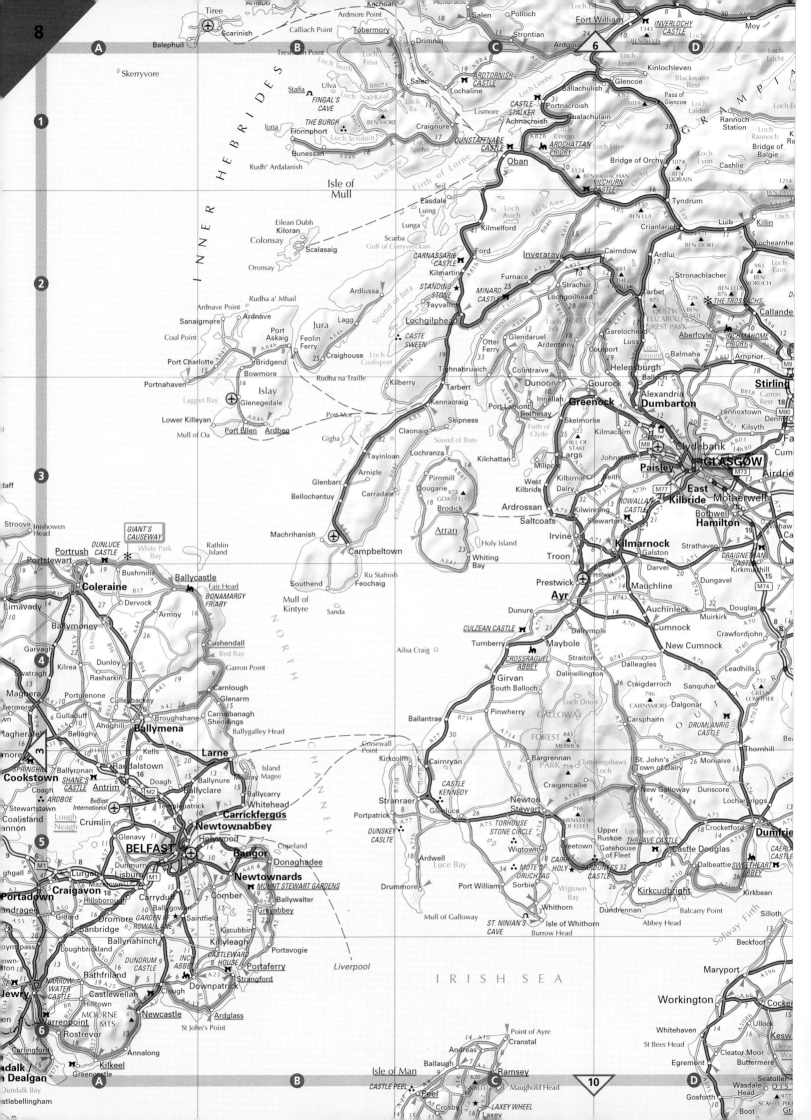

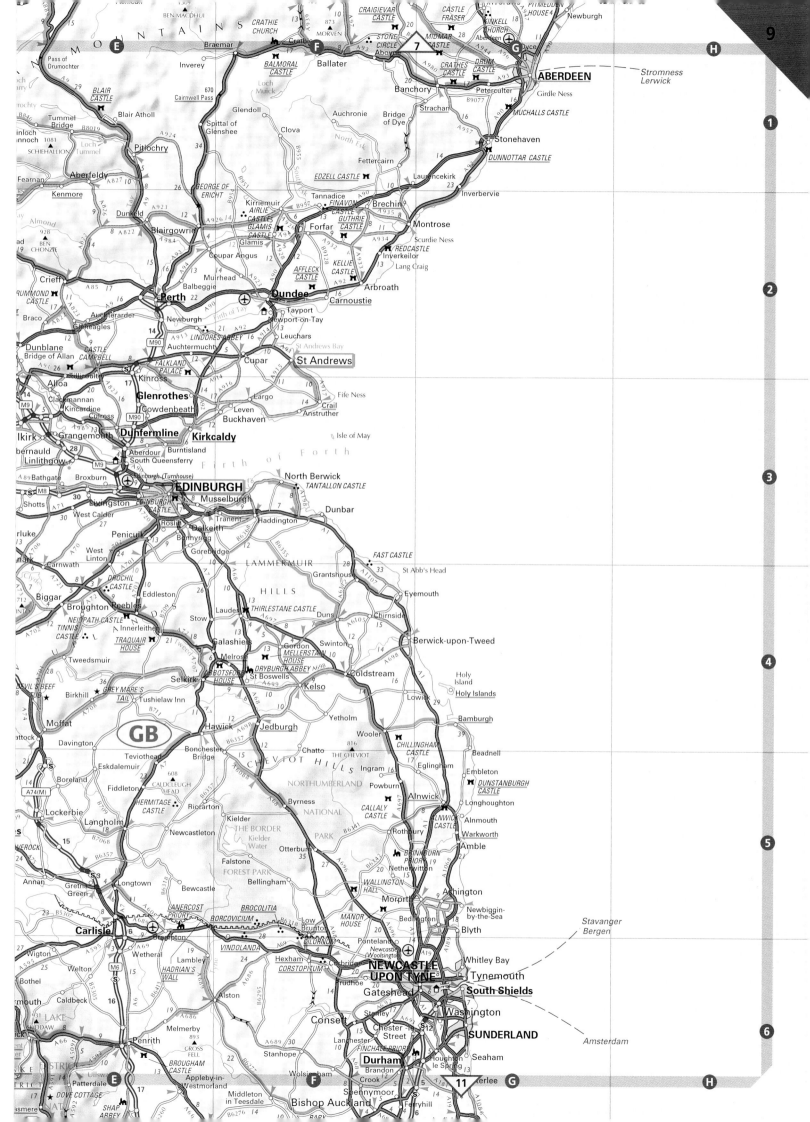

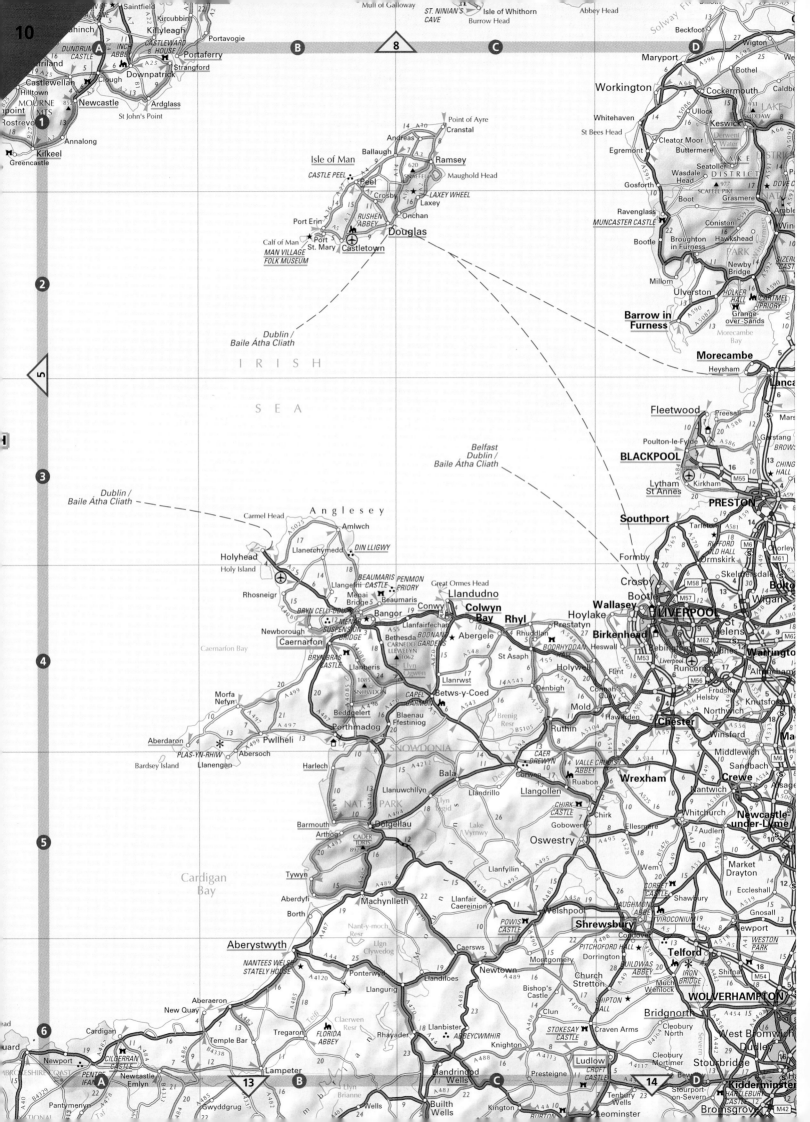

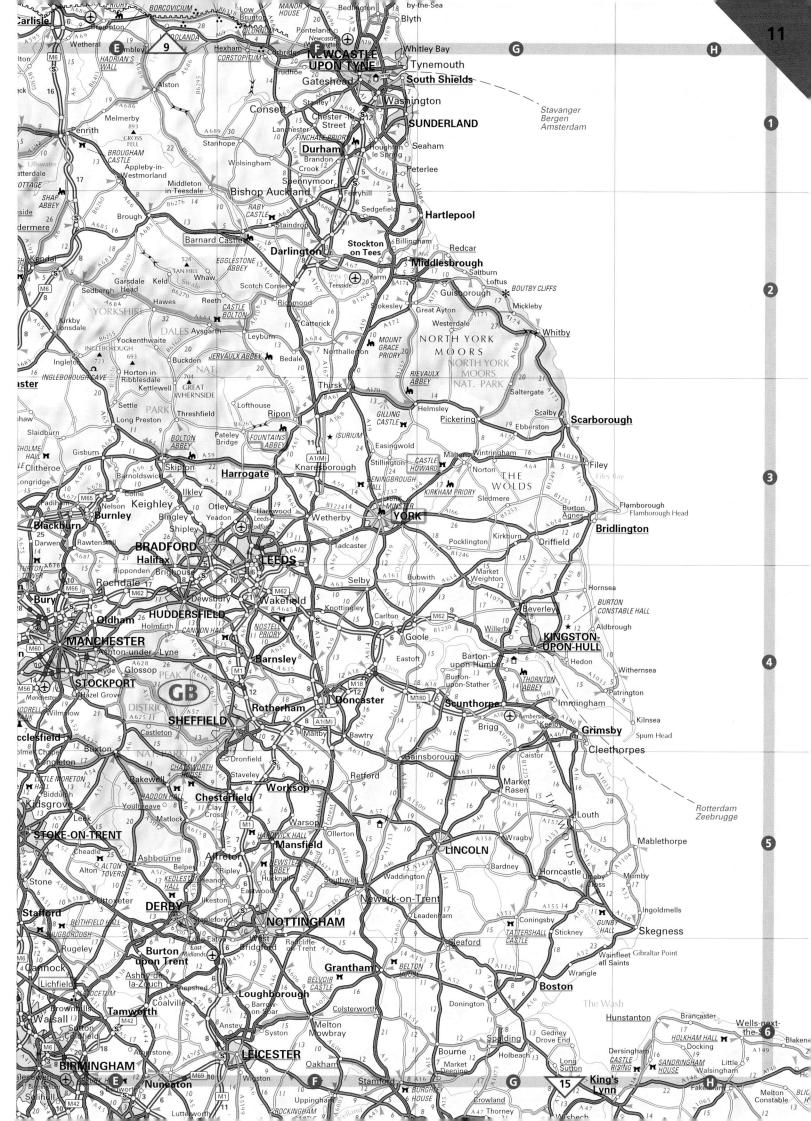

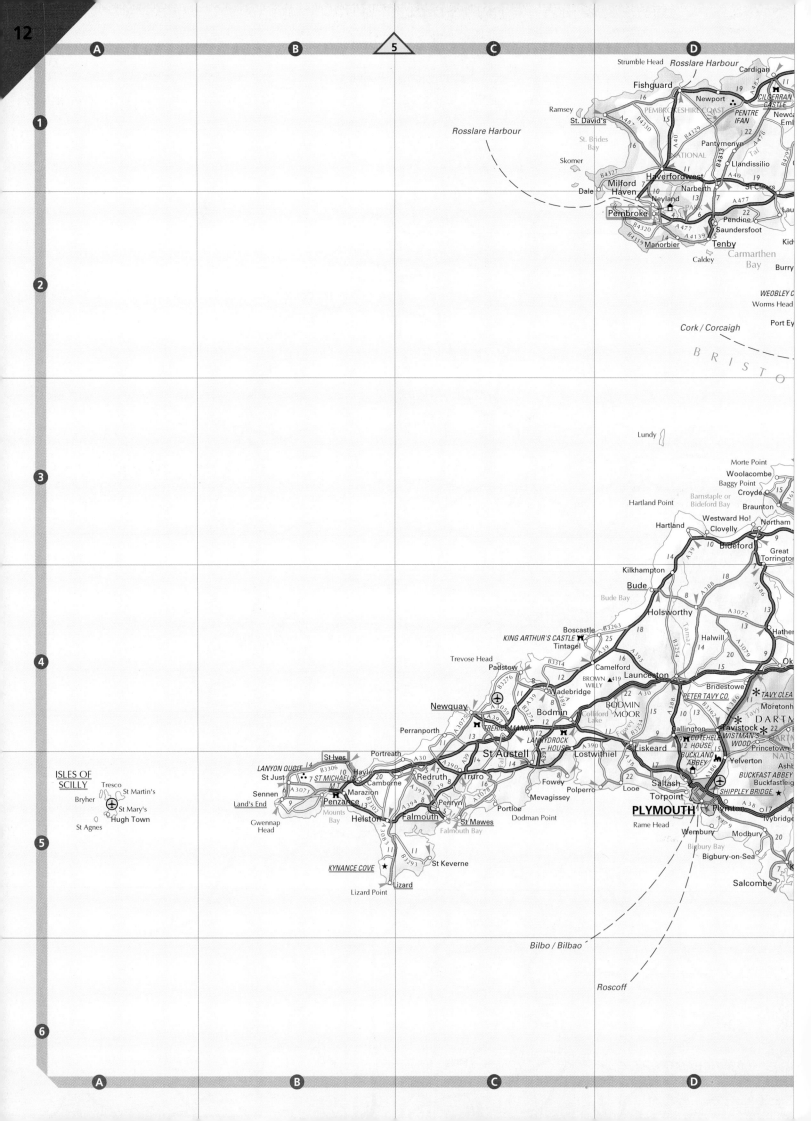

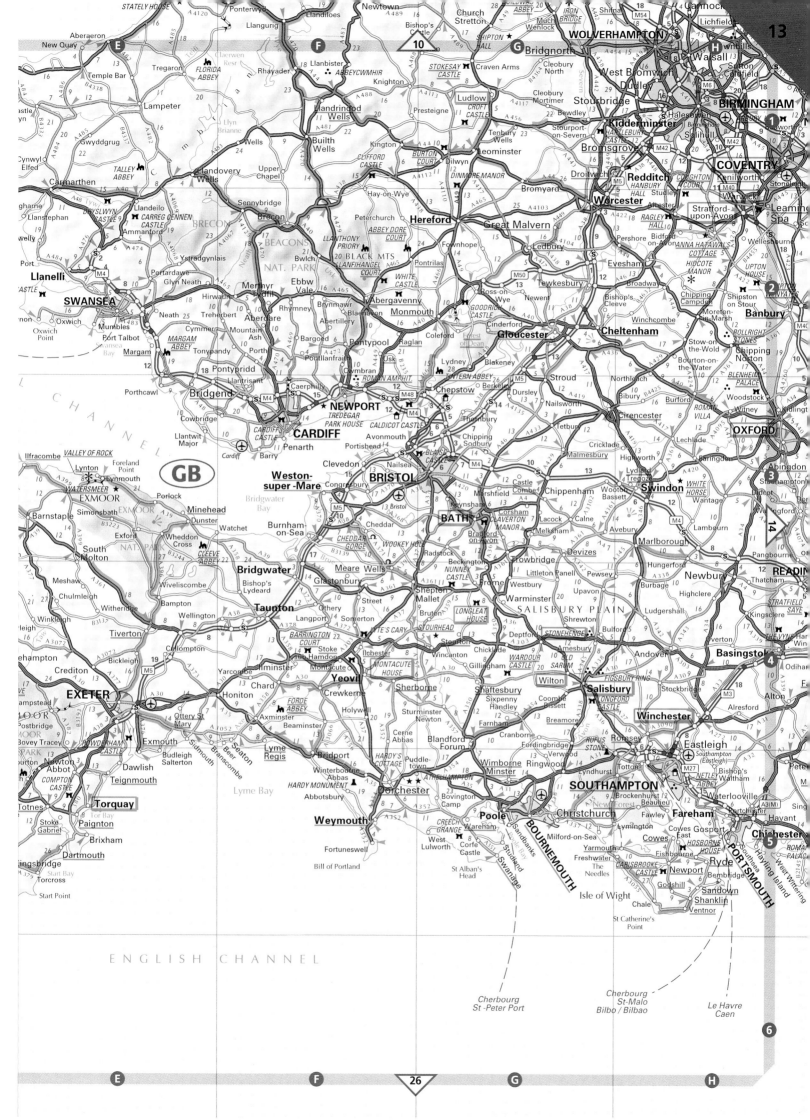

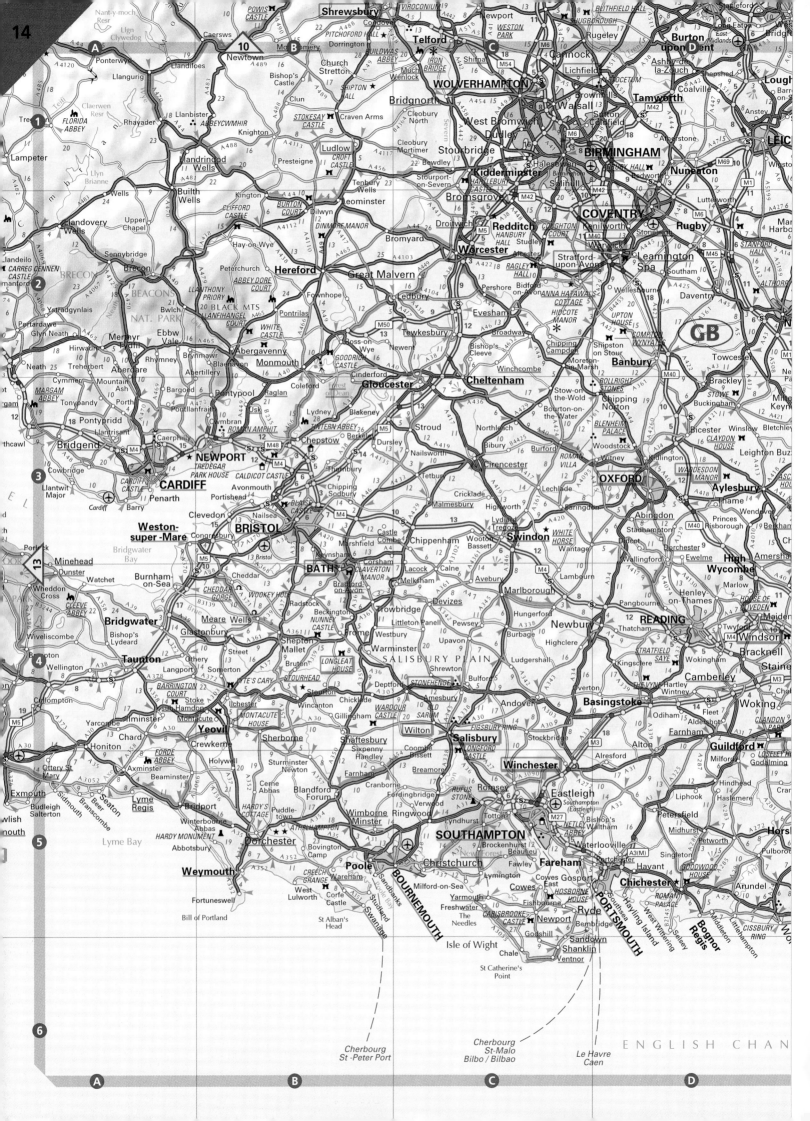

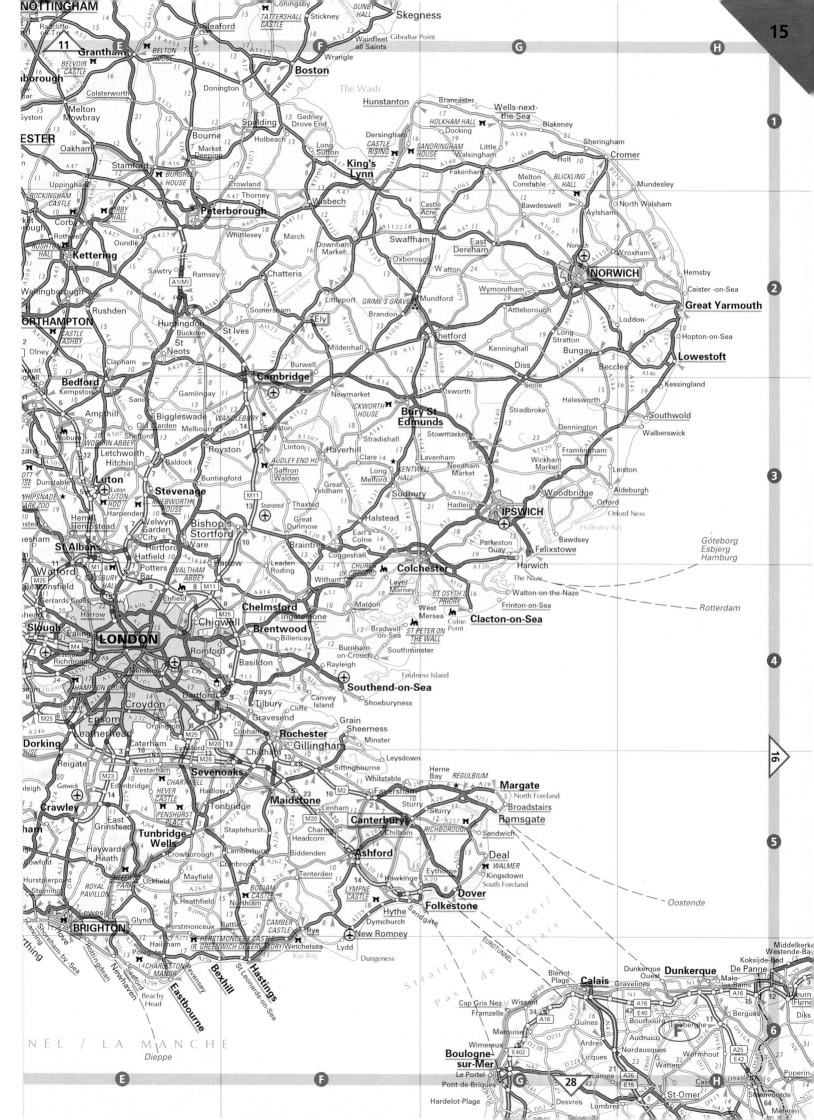

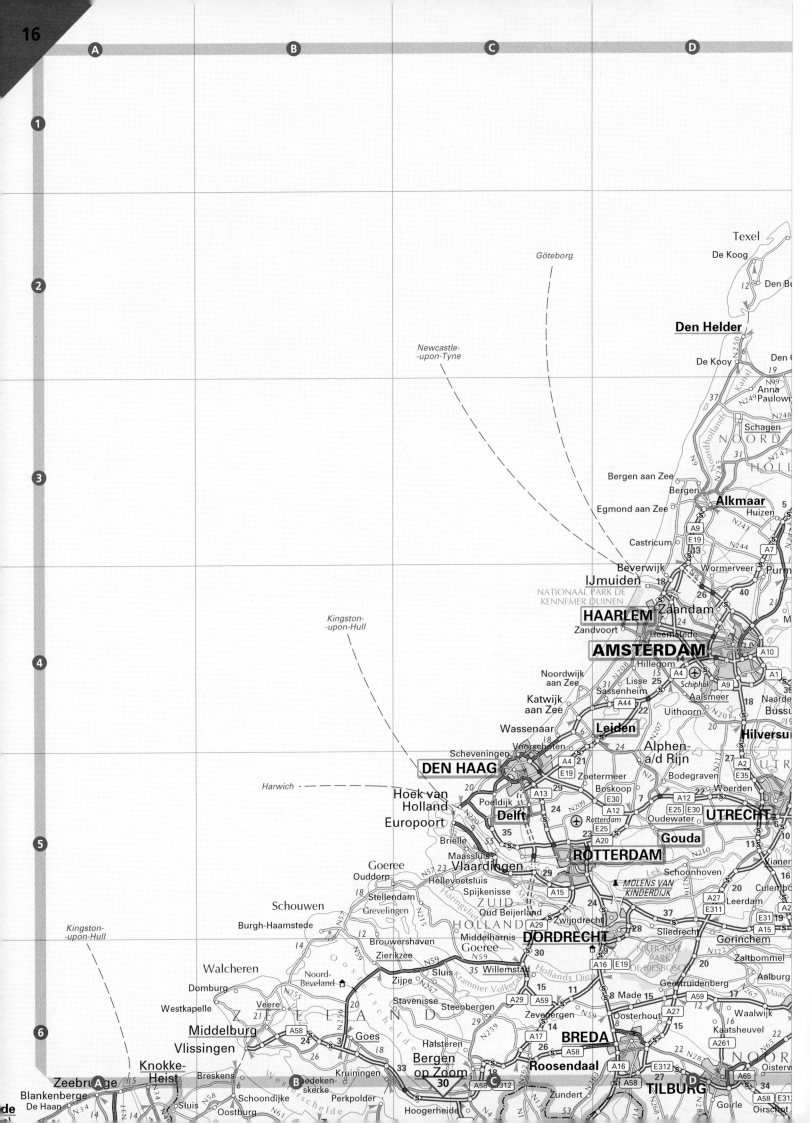

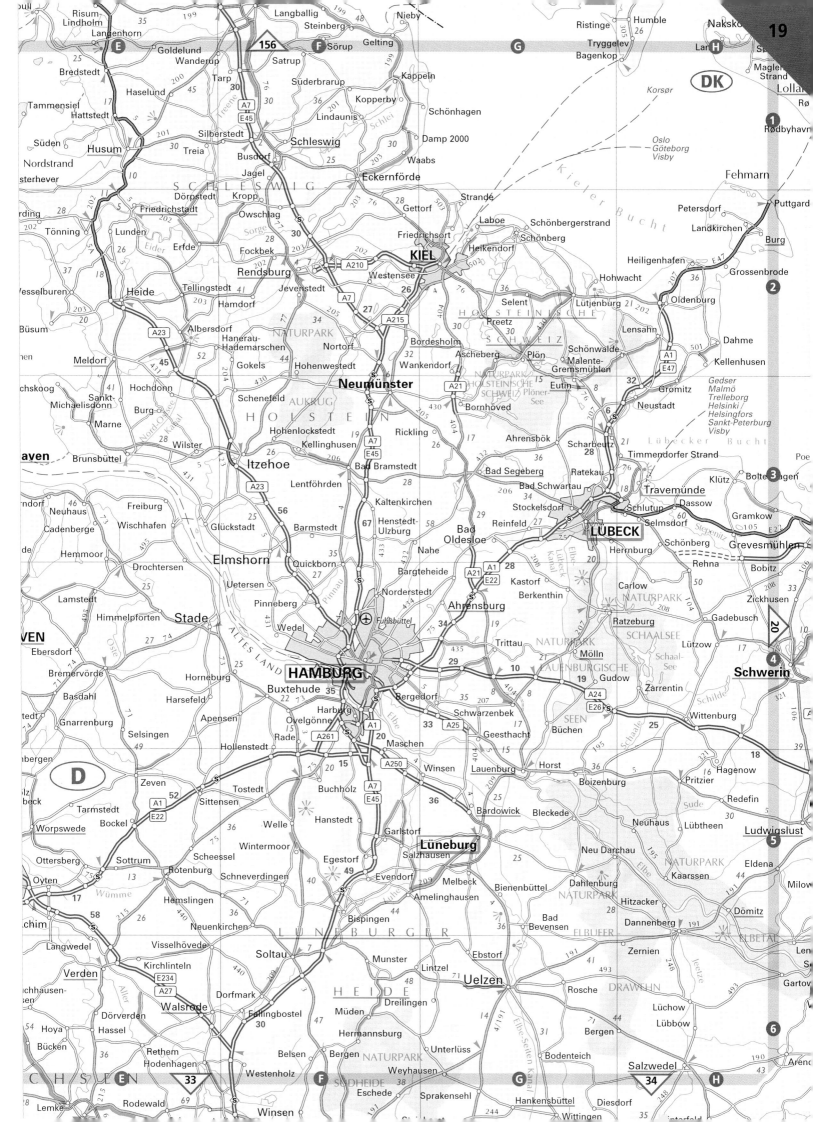

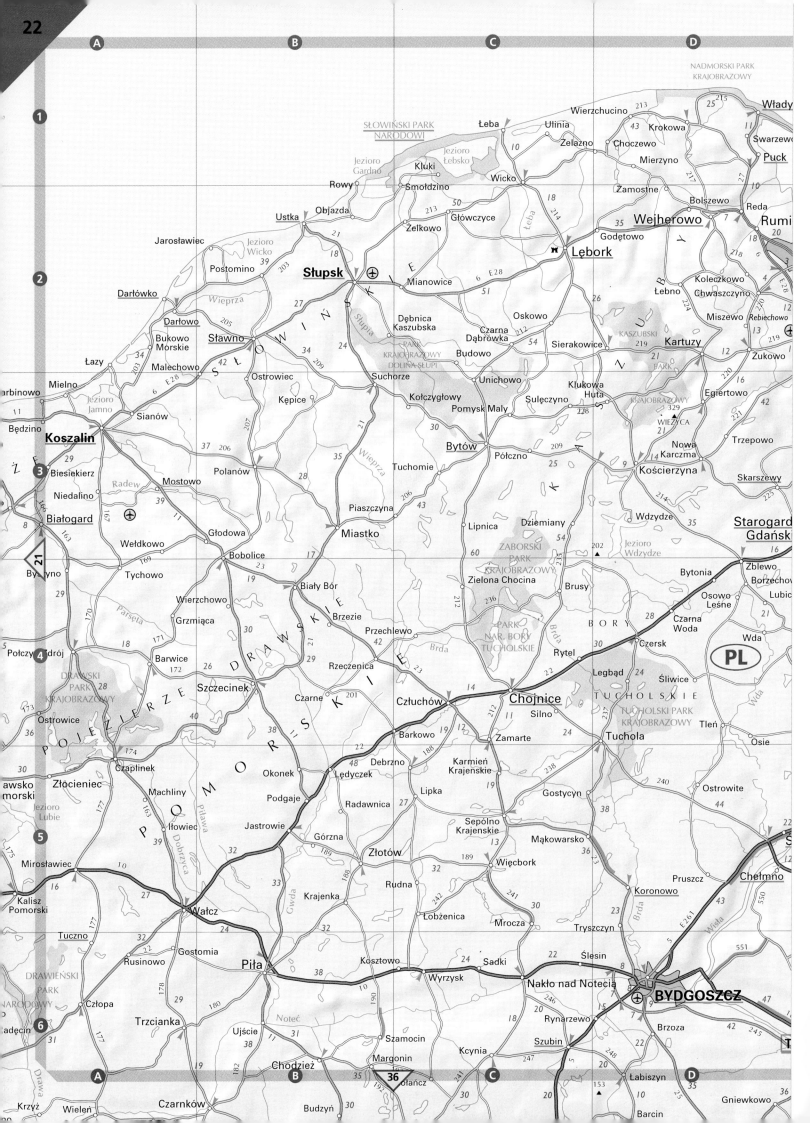

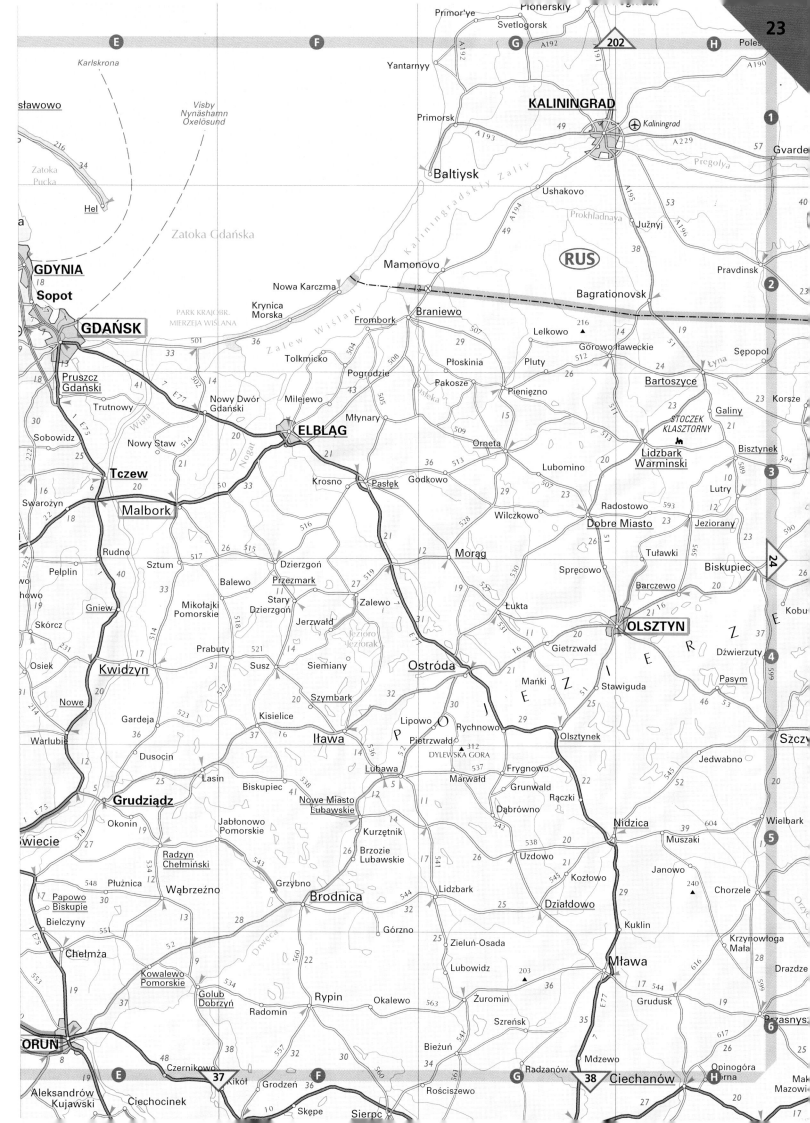

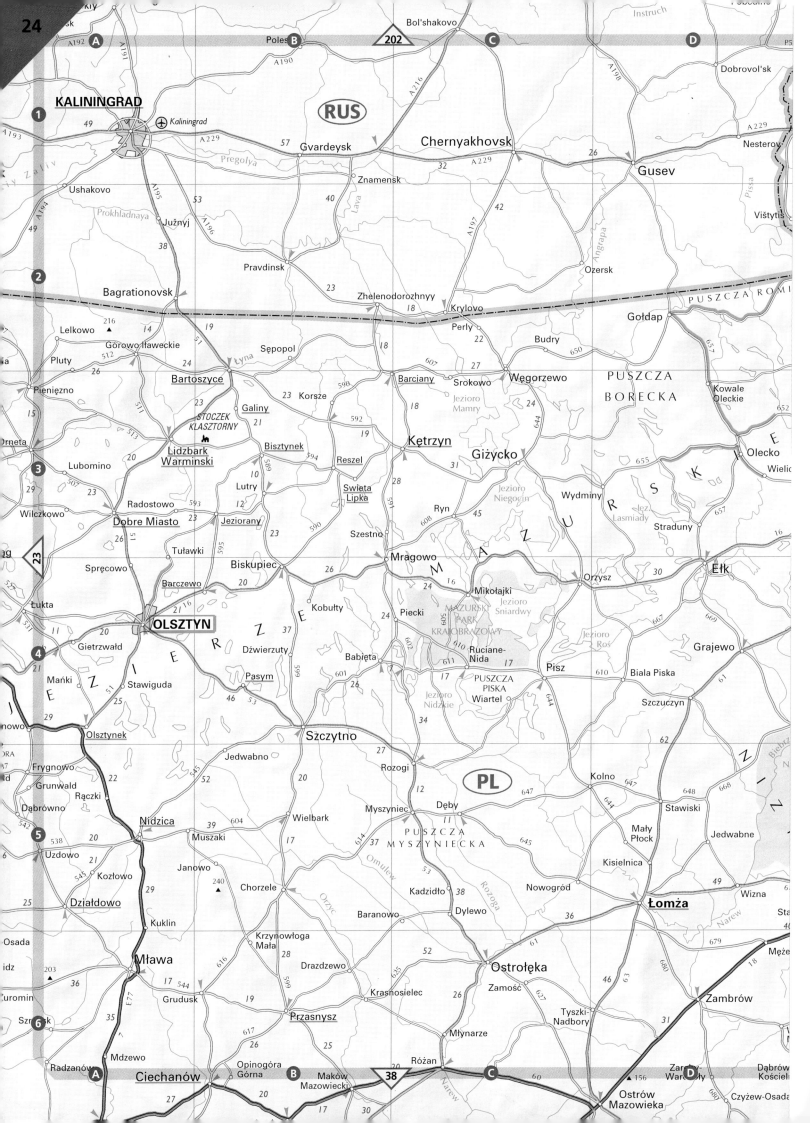

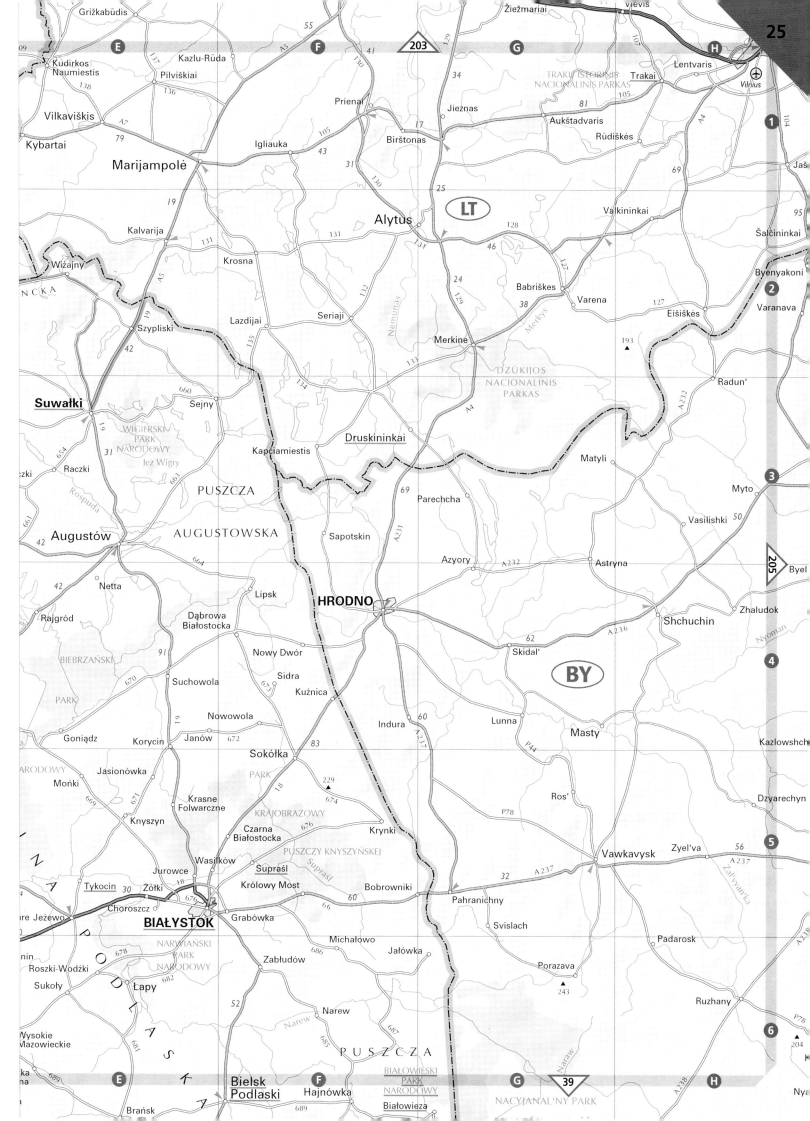

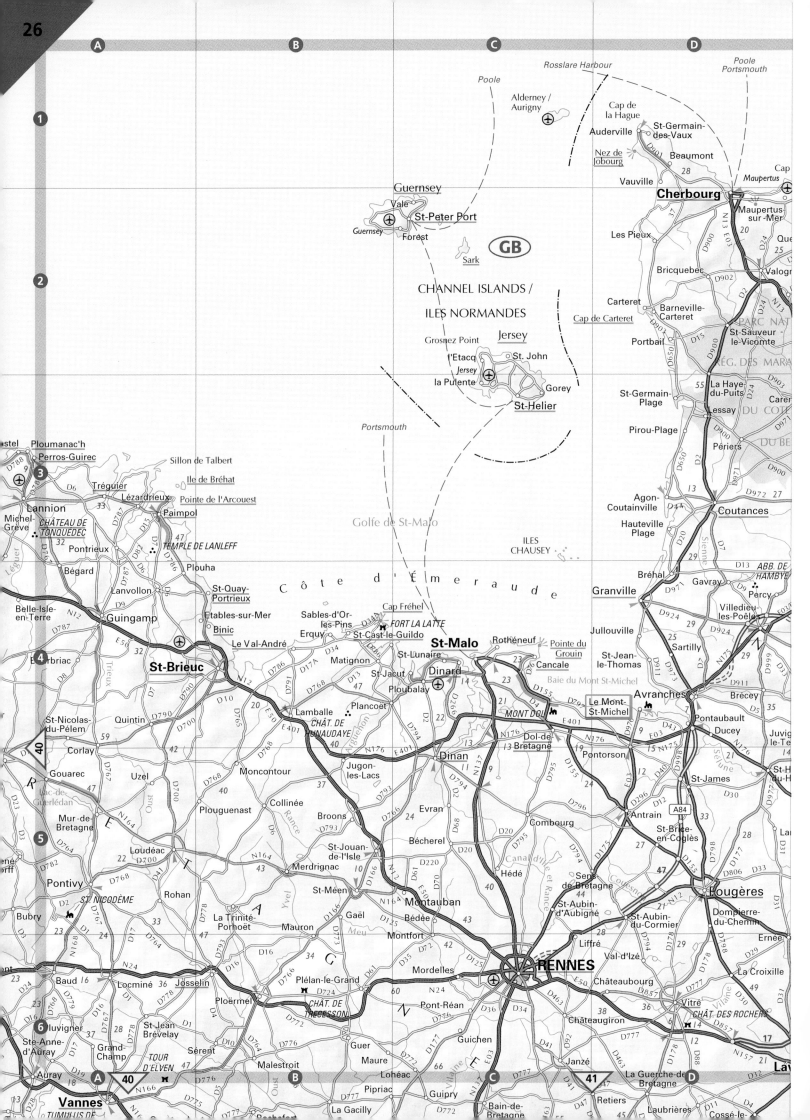

A   B   C   D

1

2

3

4

5

6

Poole

Rosslare Harbour

Poole
Portsmouth

Alderney /
Aurigny

Cap de
la Hague
St-Germain-
des-Vaux
Auderville
Nez de
Jobourg
Beaumont
D901
Cap
Maupertus
28
Vauville

Guernsey
Vale
St-Peter Port
Guernsey
Forest

Cherbourg
N13 E03
20
Maupertus-
sur-Mer
37
D24
Que

GB

Sark

Les Pieux
D900
24
25

Bricquebec
D902
Valogn
D2
N13

CHANNEL ISLANDS /
ILES NORMANDES

Carteret
Barneville-
Carteret
PARC NAT
D24
N13
D903

Cap de Carteret

Portbail
D15
St-Sauveur -
le-Vicomte

Grosnez Point
Jersey
l'Etacq
St. John
Jersey
la Pulente
Gorey
St-Helier

RÉG. DES MARA
D650
55
La Haye-
du-Puits
D24
D903
Carer
DU COTE

St-Germain-
Plage
Lessay
DU BE

Portsmouth
Pirou-Plage
D900
Périers
D971

Golfe de St-Malo

Agon-
Coutainville
D650
D2
D44
13
Coutances
D972
27
D7

ILES
CHAUSEY
29
D13
ABB. DE
HAMBYE

Côte d' Émeraude
Bréhal
D971
Gavray
D9
Percy

Granville
D924
29
Villedieu-
les-Poêles
E0

Michel-
Grève
CHÂTEAU DE
TONQUÉDEC
32
Ploumanac'h
Perros-Guirec
D788
Tréguier
D6
33
Lézardrieux
Paimpol
D787
D15
Pontrieux
D786
D7
TEMPLE DE LANLEFF
47
Plouha
Ile de Bréhat
Pointe de l'Arcouest
Lannion
Sillon de Talbert

Jullouville
Sartilly
D973
D911
St-Jean-
le-Thomas
25

N175
29
D924
D911

Bégard
D787
Plouha
St-Quay-
Portrieux
Cap Fréhel
D34
FORT LA LATTE
Rothéneuf
Pointe du
Grouin
N

Belle-Isle-
en-Terre
N12
D9
Lanvollon
Etables-sur-Mer
Binic
Sables-d'Or-
les-Pins
Erquy
St-Cast-le-Guildo
St-Malo
Cancale
Baie du Mont St-Michel
23
Brécey
Avranches
D5
35

Guingamp
E50
32
Le Val-André
Matignon
St-Lunaire
Dinard
23
D155
Le Mont-
St-Michel
D43
Pontaubault
Ducey

Barbriac
D8
D787
St-Brieuc
D786
D17A
D34
St-Jacut
Ploubalay
14
21
MONT DOL
E401
D79
N176
15 N175
Pontorson
12
D40
Juvig
le-Te

St-Nicolas-
du-Pélem
Quintin
D790
D700
D765
20
E50 E401
Lamballe
Plancoët
D266
D2
22
13
Dol-de-
Bretagne
N176
19
St-James
E03
St-H
du-H

40

Corlay
Uzel
D768
CHÂT. DE
HUNAUDAYE
40
D794
Dinan
11
N137
9
D155
24
D296
D12
Antrain
D30
D97

R
Lac de
Guerlédan
D23
Gouarec
D767
47
Moncontour
37
Jugon-
les-Lacs
D793
D794
D2
Evran
D6
D796
Combourg
D795
St-Brice-
en-Coglès
A84
D806
28
33
La

E
Mur-de-
Bretagne
N164
Plouguenast
Collinée
Broons
24
Bécherel
D20
D794
47
D175
27
D798
D177
D33
D31

Pontivy
D764
D782
Loudéac
D700
40
N164
43
Merdrignac
10
D166
D61
D220
Hédé
40
Sens-
de-Bretagne
44
Liffré
D178
29
D798
D29
Ernée

T
ST NICODÈME
D2
Rohan
St-Jouan-
de-l'Isle
N164
St-Méen
Montauban
St-Aubin-
d'Aubigné
St-Aubin-
du-Cormier
D806
Fougères
N12
Dompierre-
du-Chemin

Bubry
D767
La Trinité-
Porhoët
Gaël
Bédée
43
E50
Val-d'Izé
D794
36
La Croixille

A

Baud
Locminé
Josselin
D778
Mauron
D773
Montfort
D125
Mordelles
N24
RENNES
Châteaubourg
E50
38
Vitré
D30
CHÂT. DES ROCHERS

G
Grand-
Champ
St-Jean-
Brévelay
Ploërmel
CHÂT. DE
TRECESSON
Plélan-le-Grand
D724
60
Pont-Réan
D36
D34
D463
Châteaugiron
D777
14
D857

40

Vannes
TUMULUS DE
Ste-Anne-
d'Auray
Auray
D19
N166
Sérent
Malestroit
Guer
Maure
Lohéac
D177
Guichen
Janzé
D463
La Guerche-
de-Bretagne
Lav

41

A   B   C   D

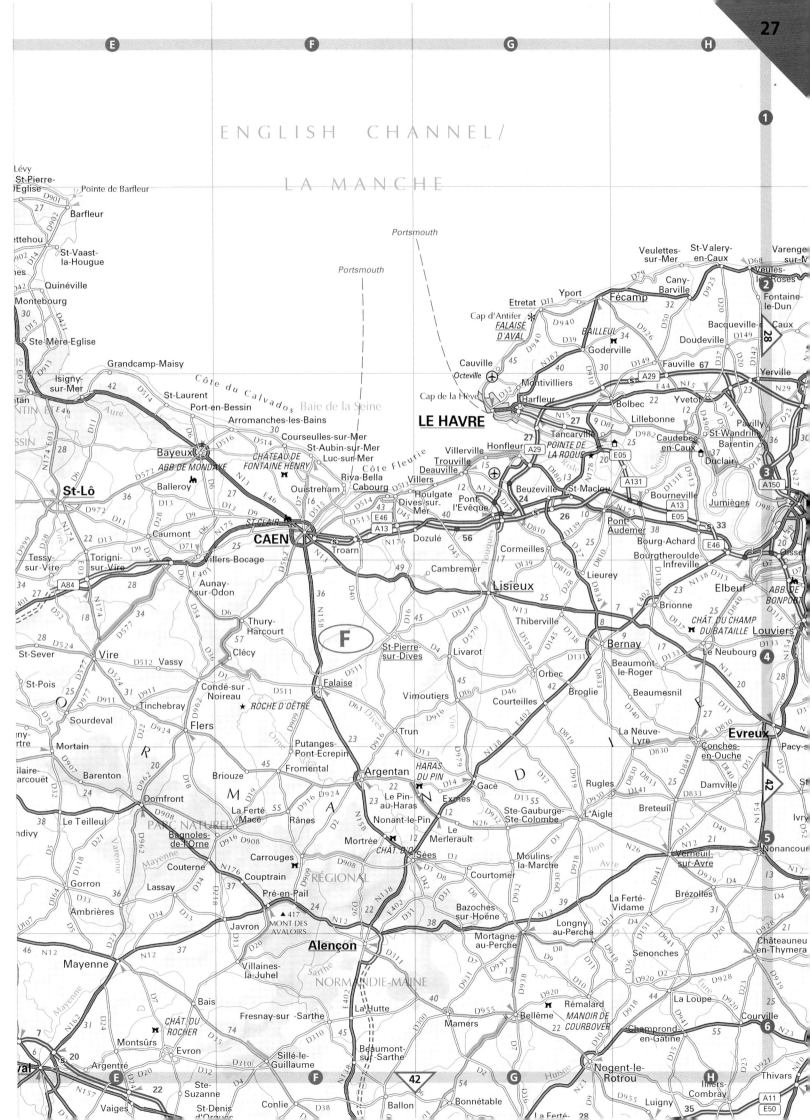

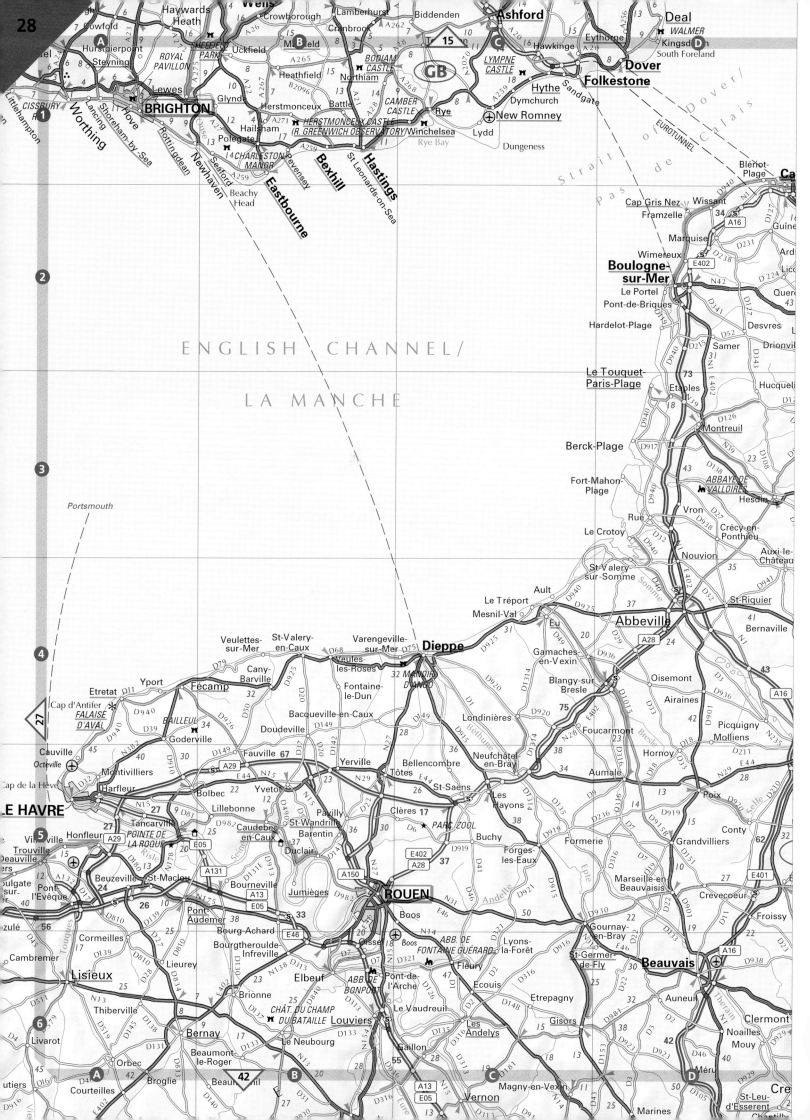

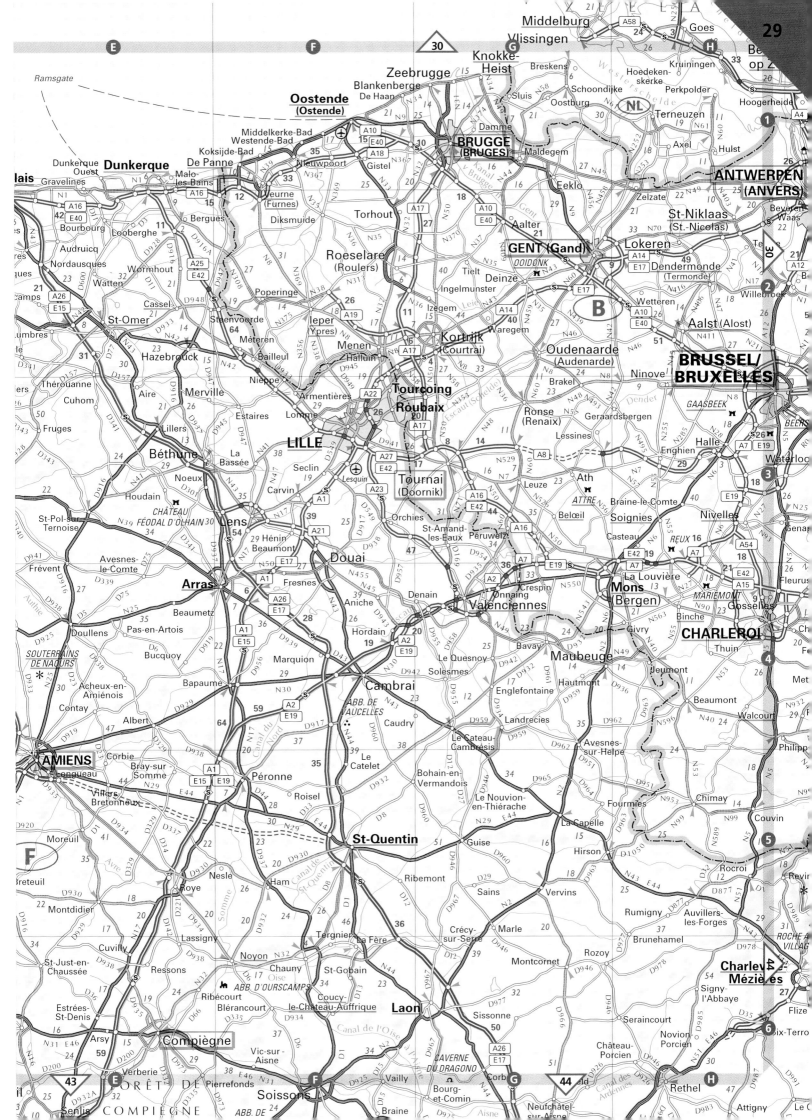

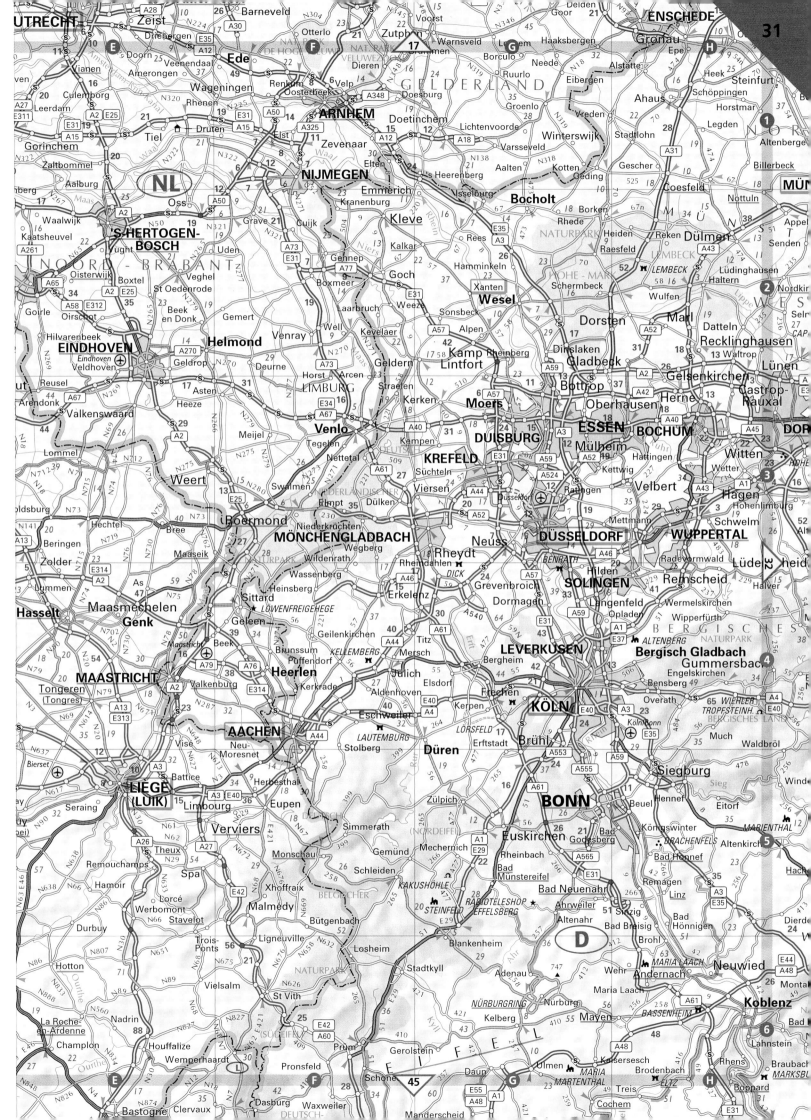

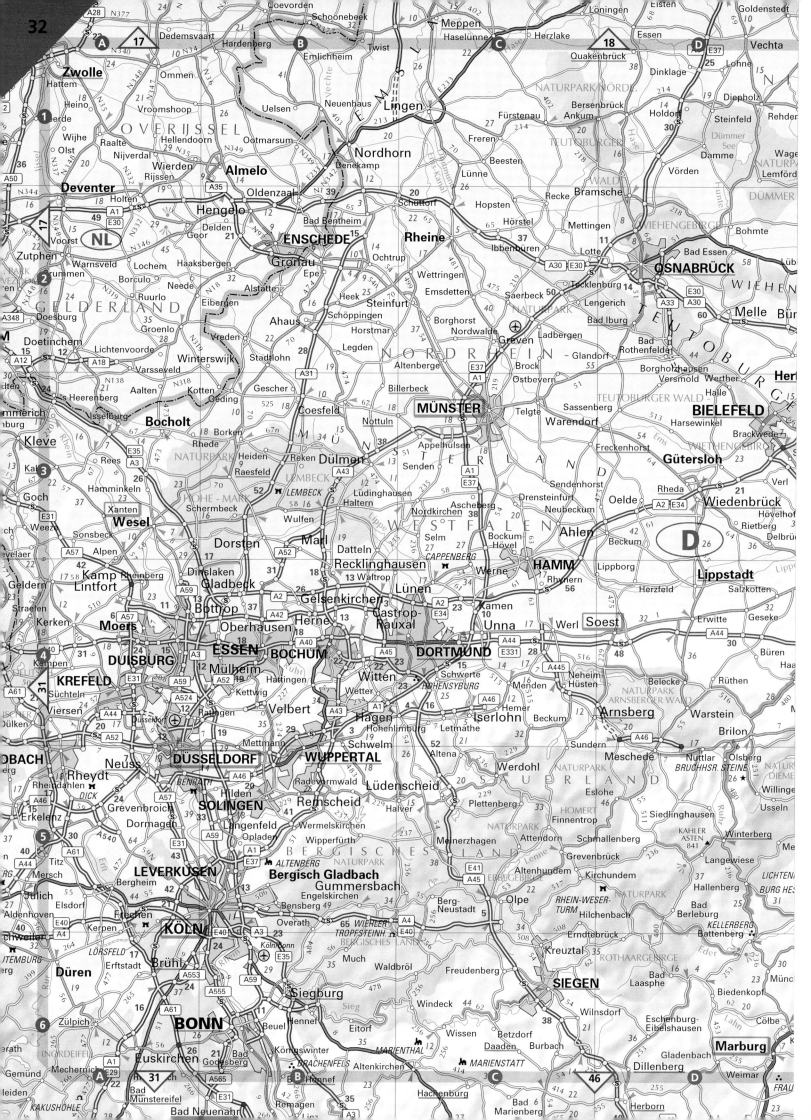

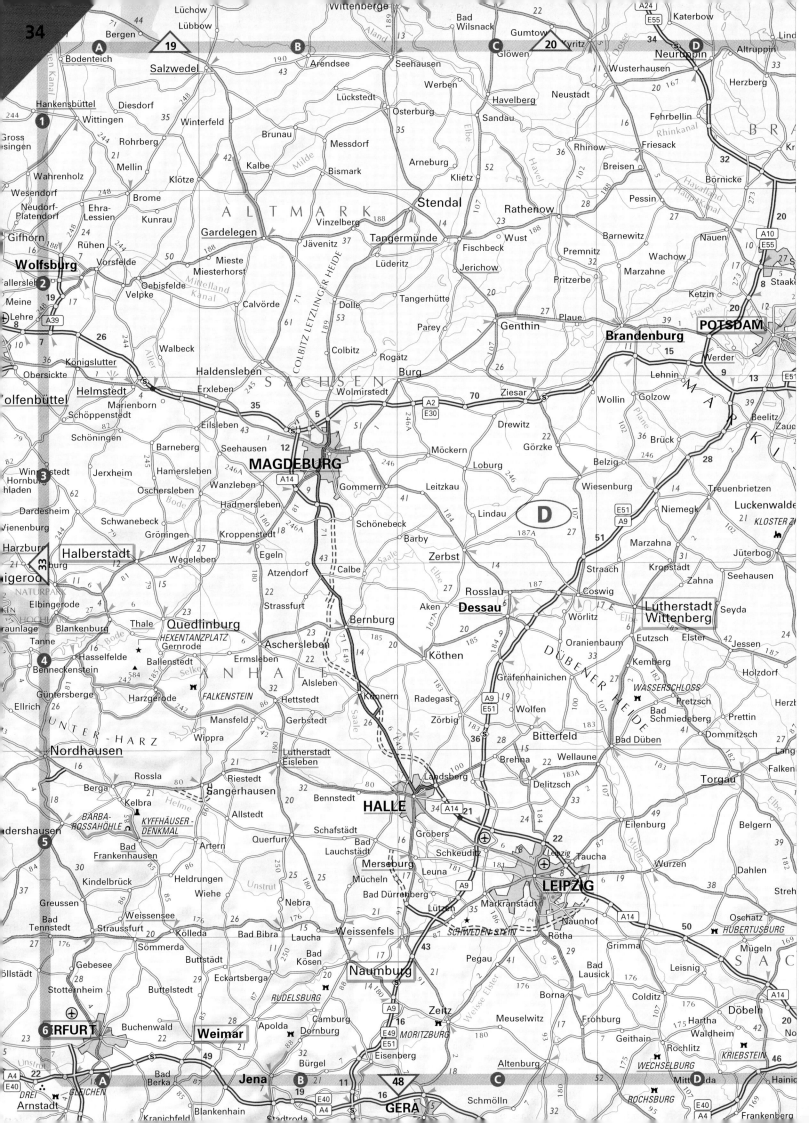

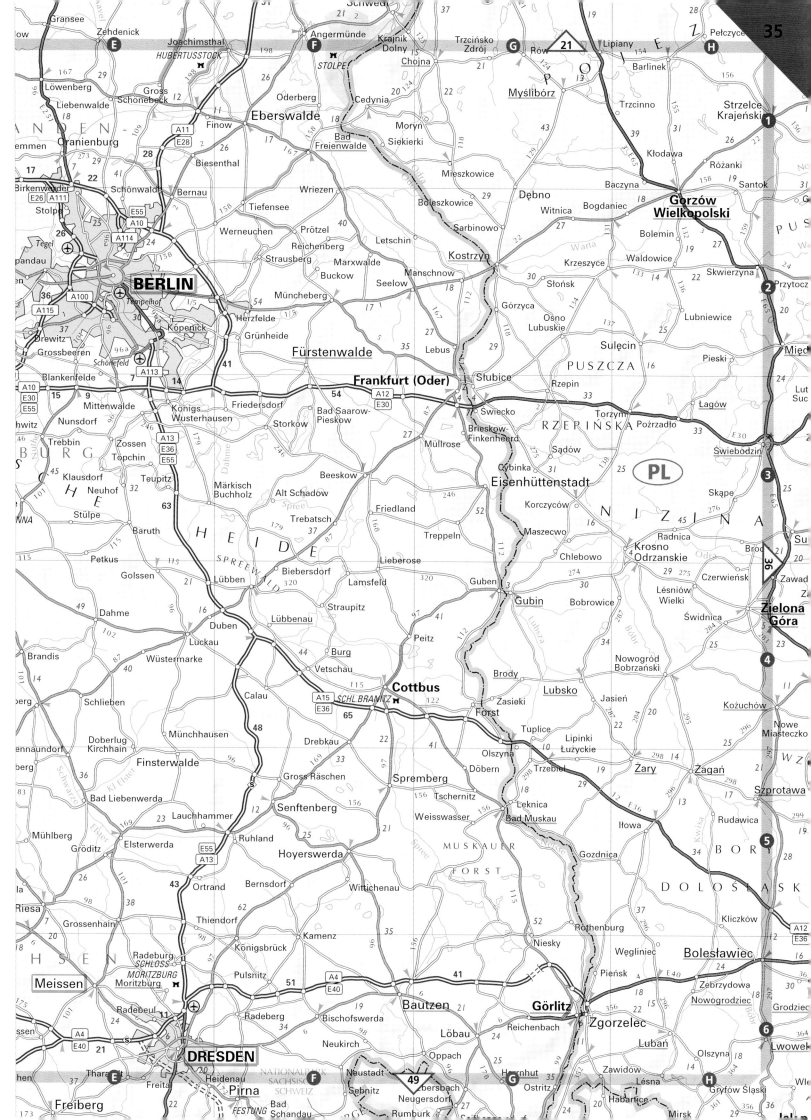

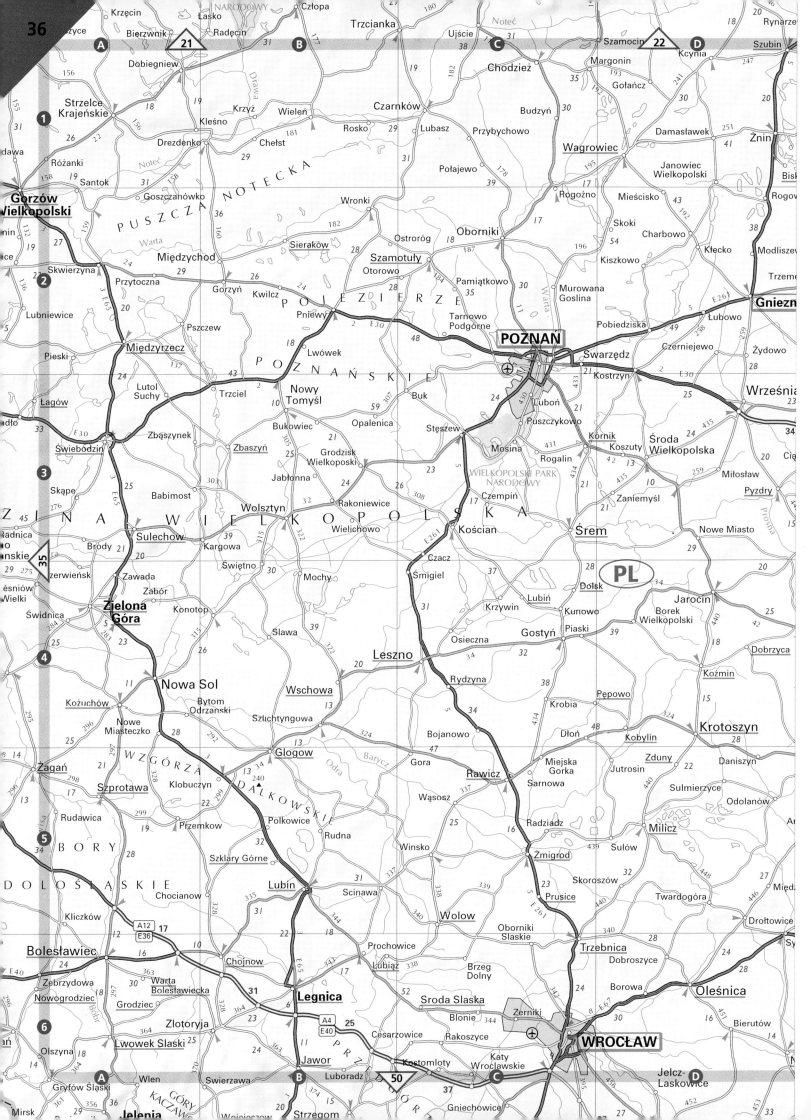

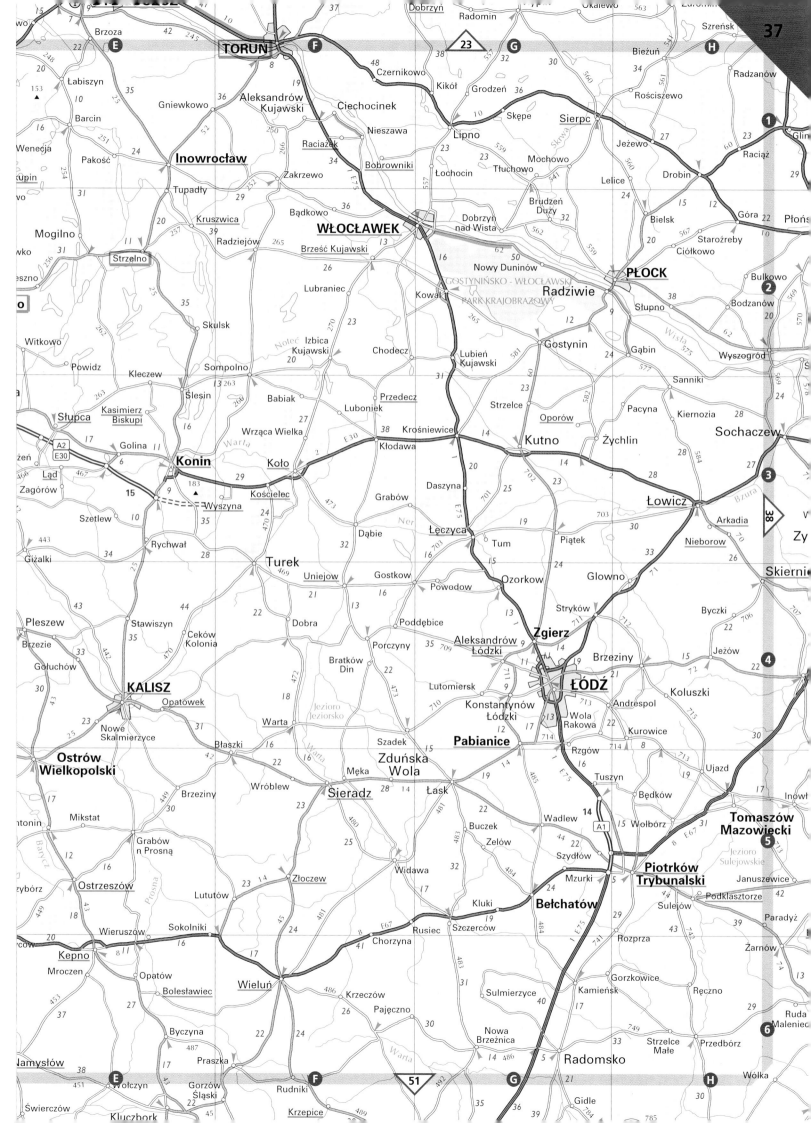

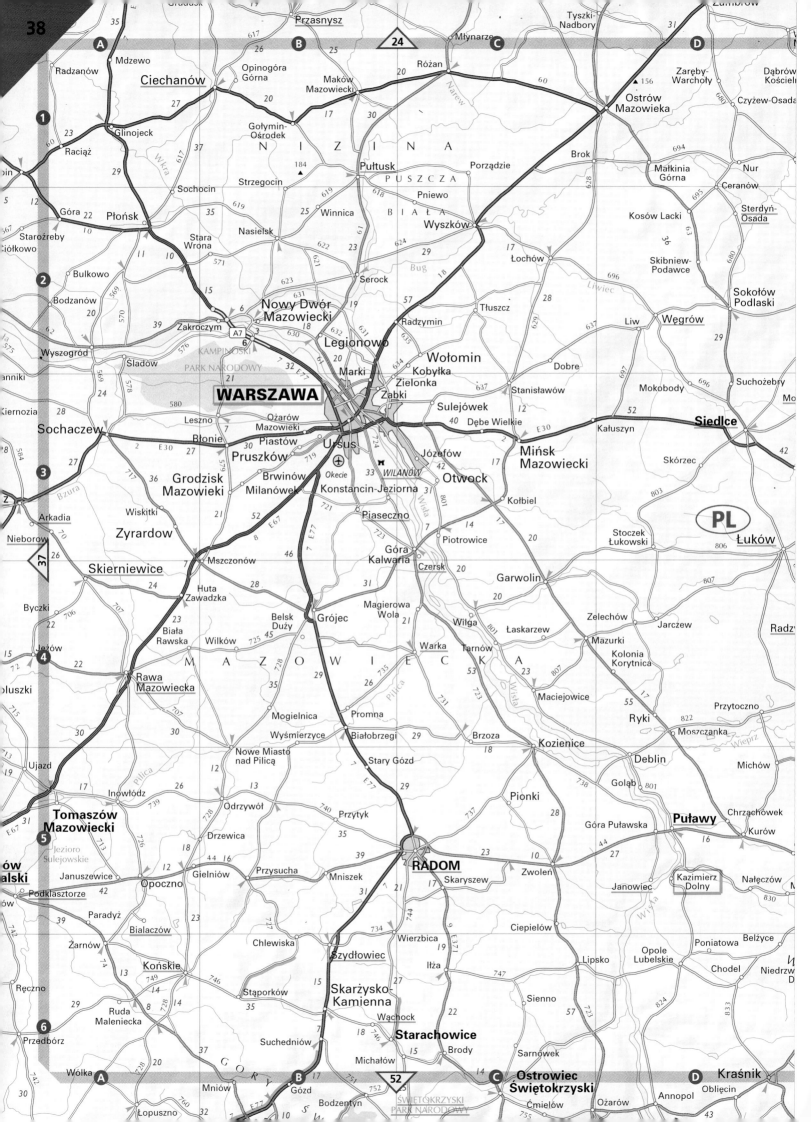

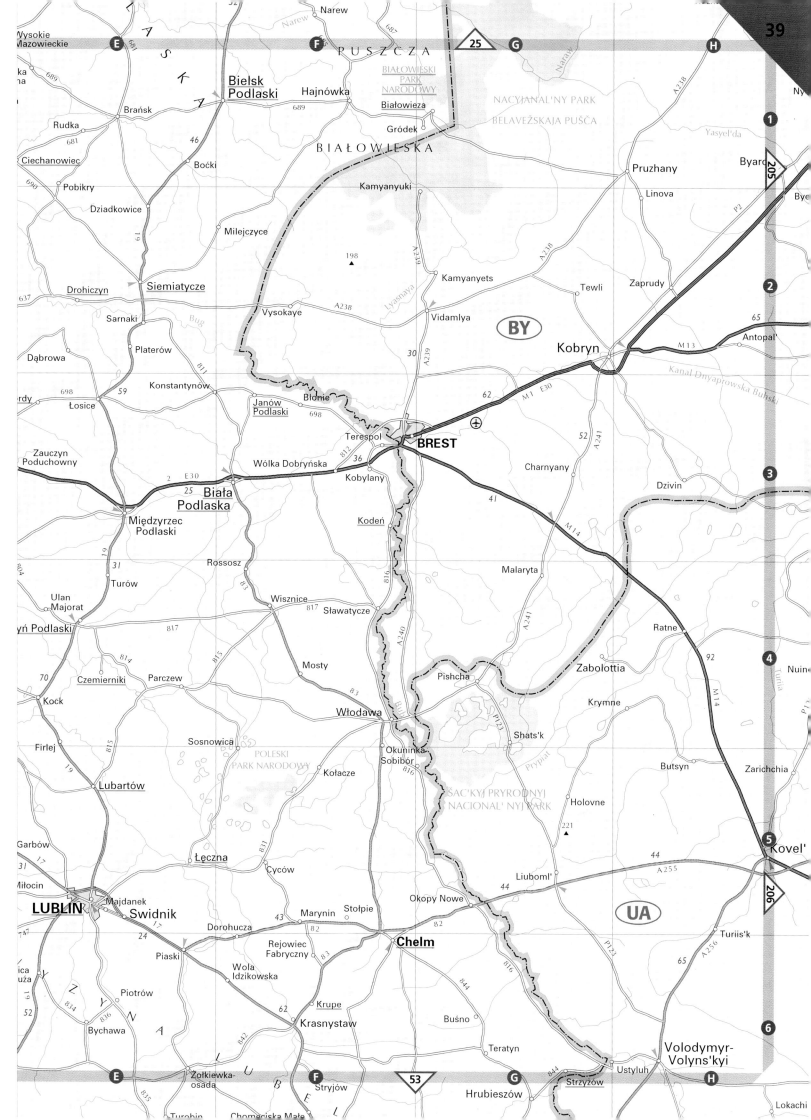

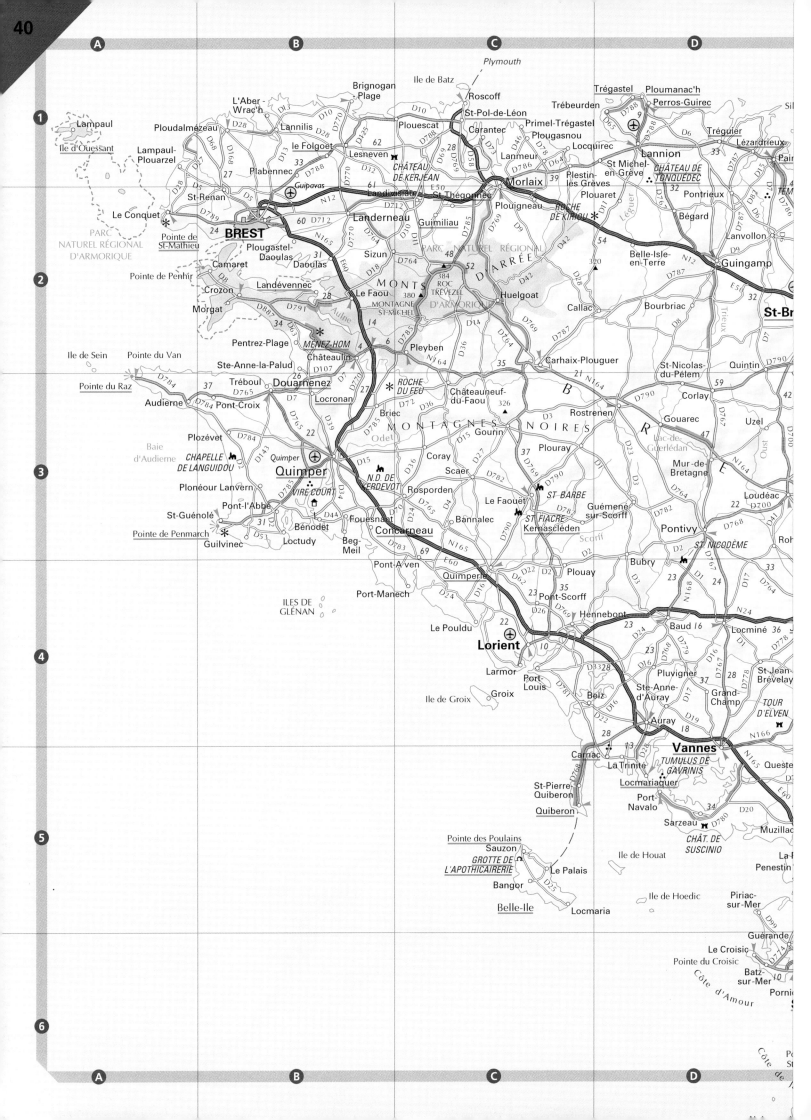

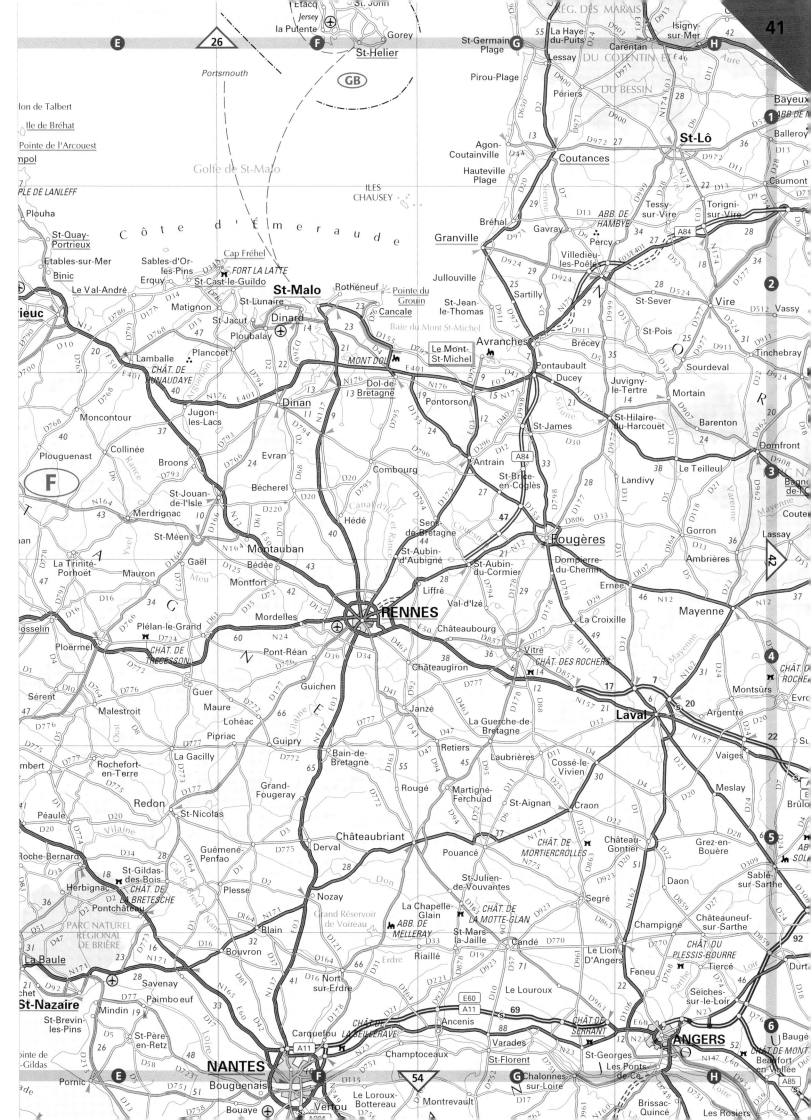

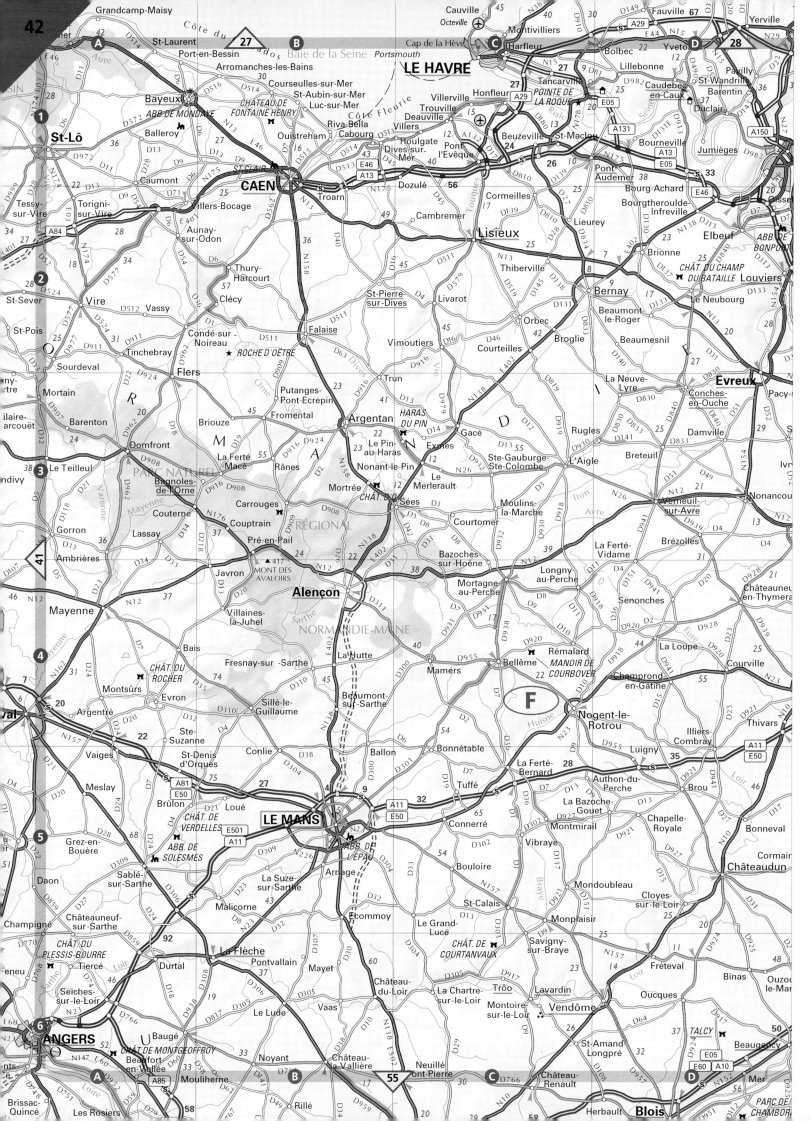

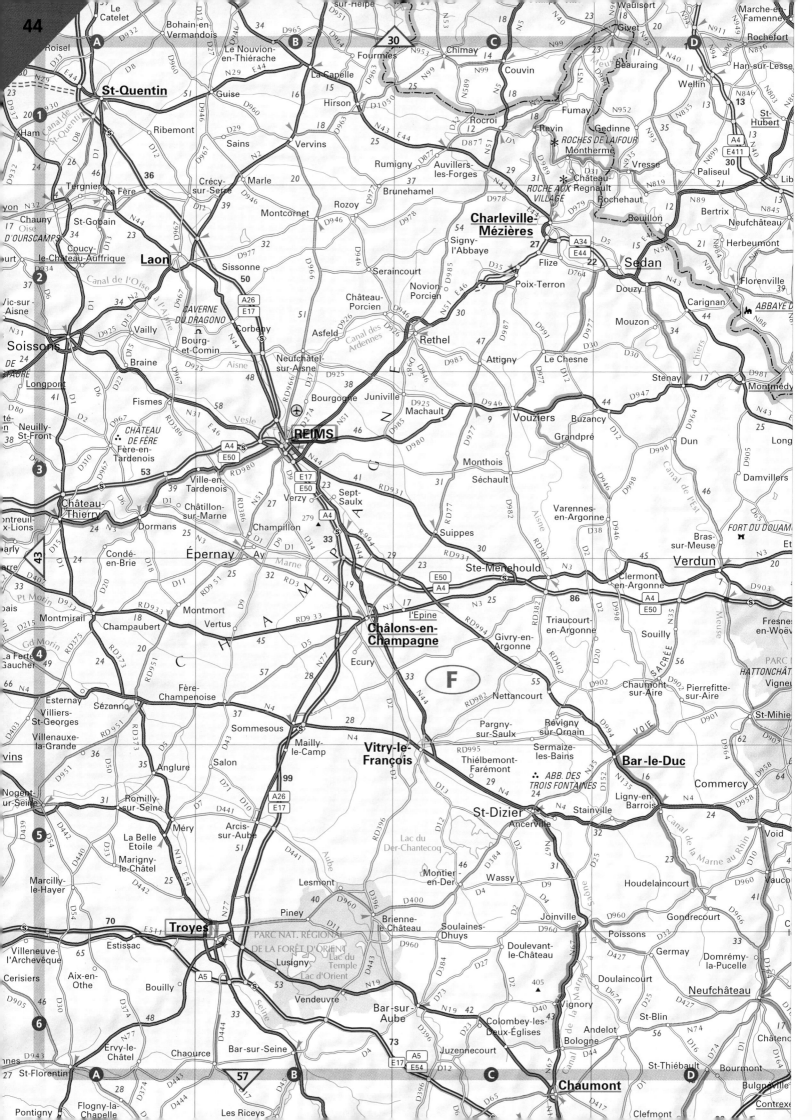

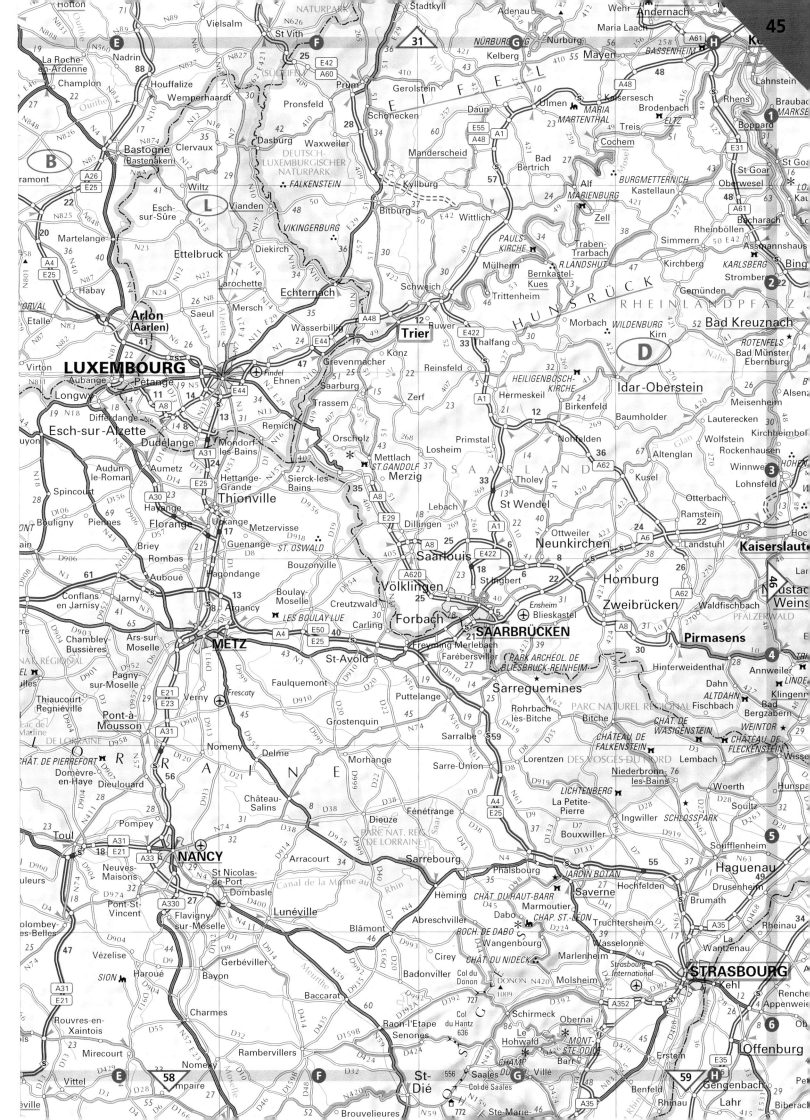

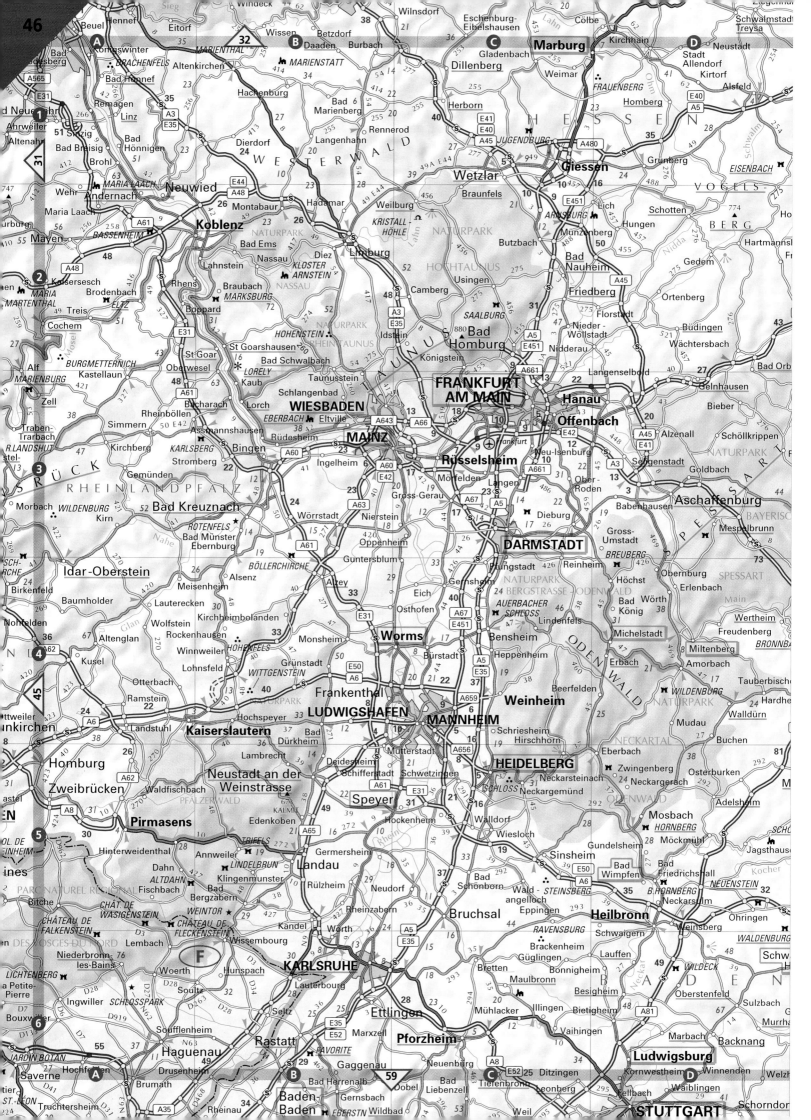

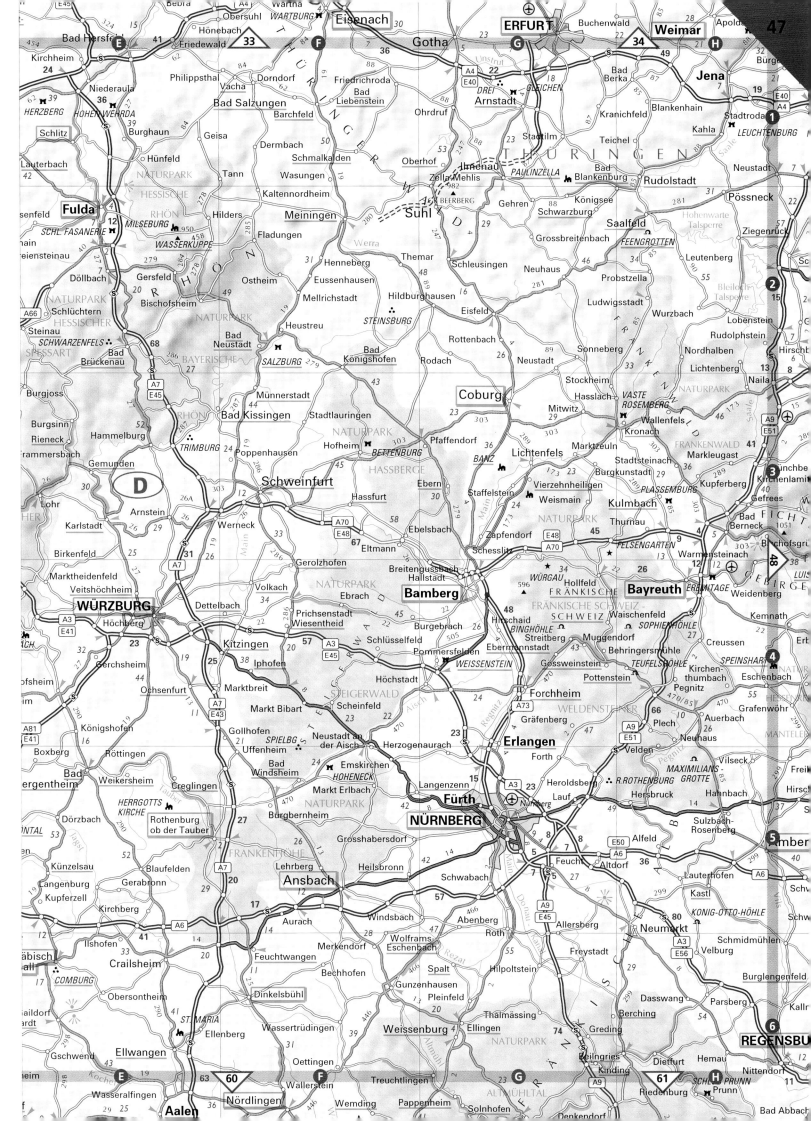

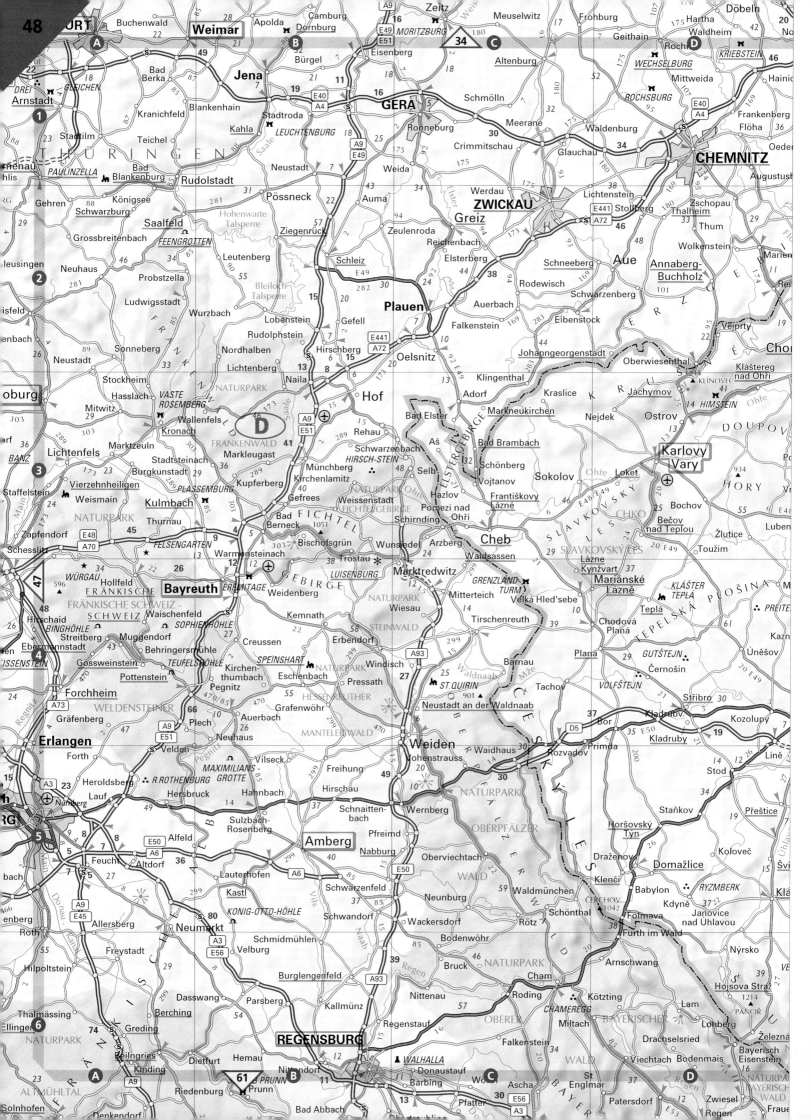

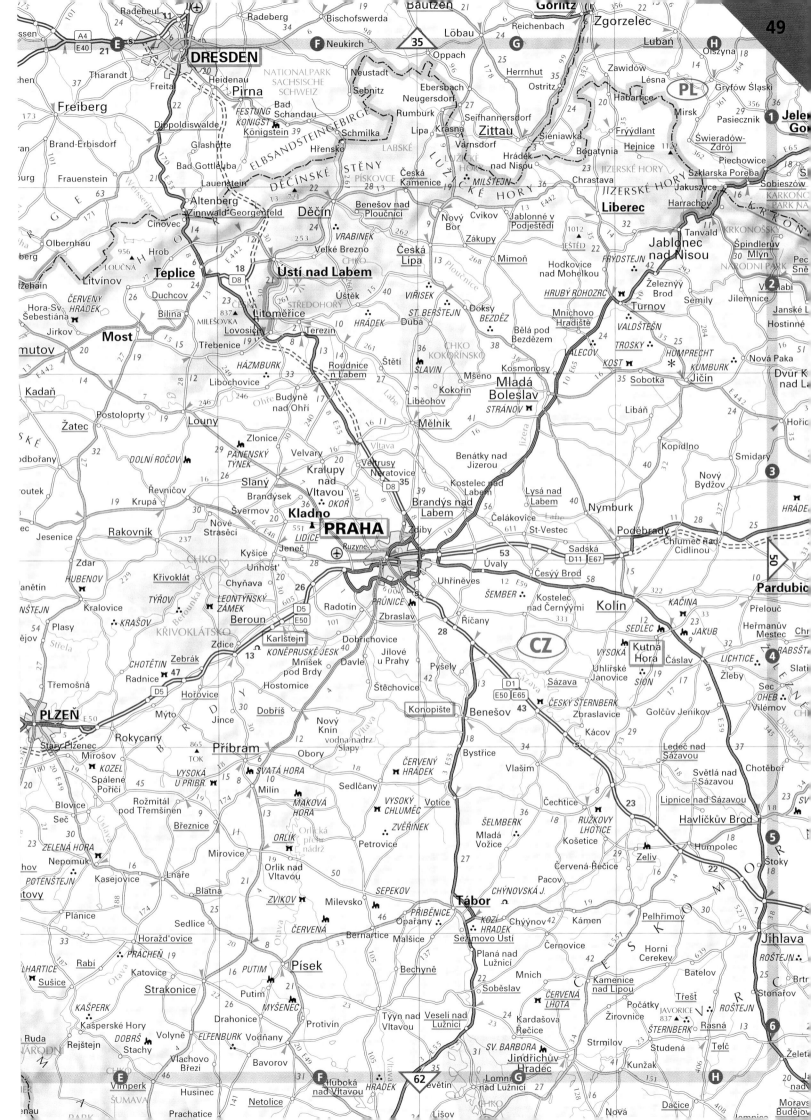

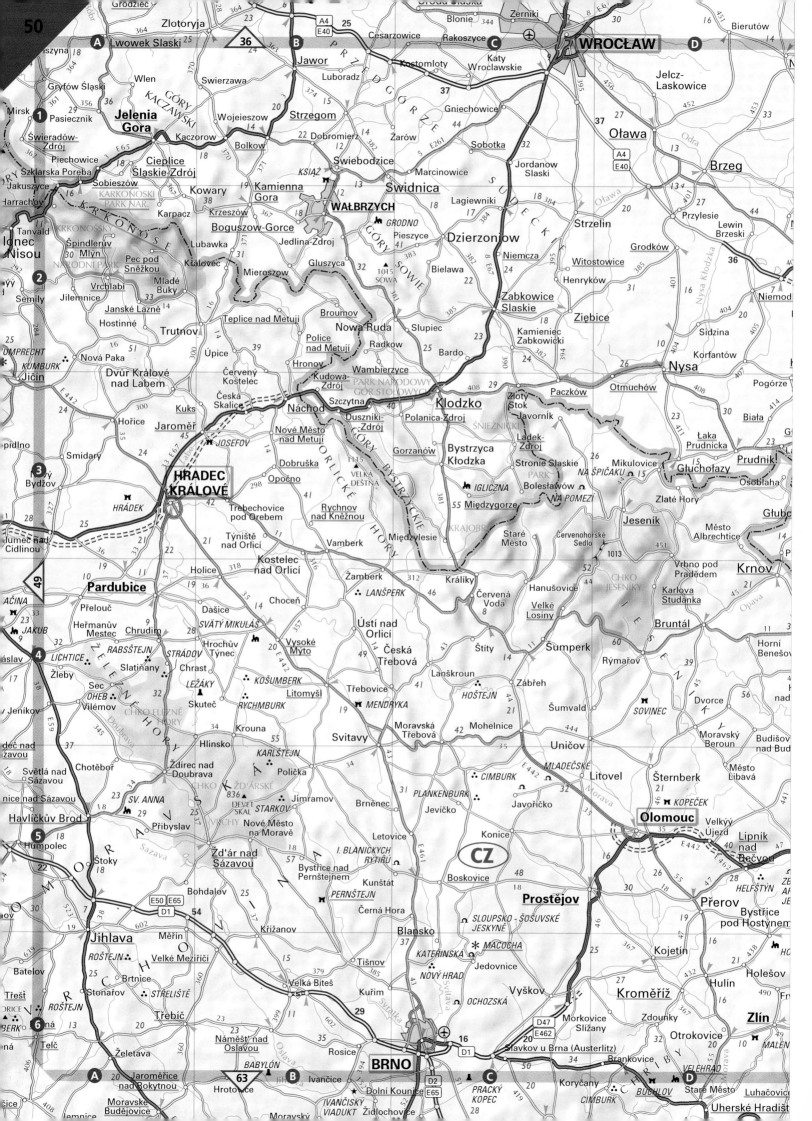

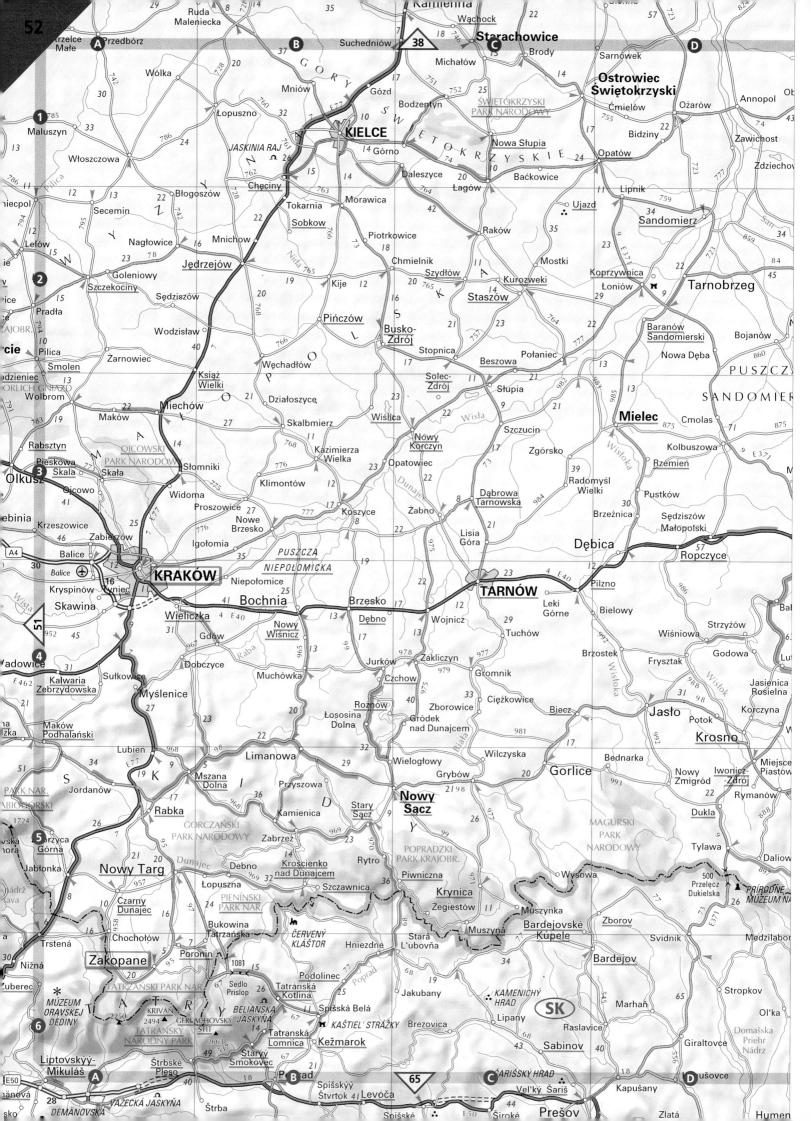

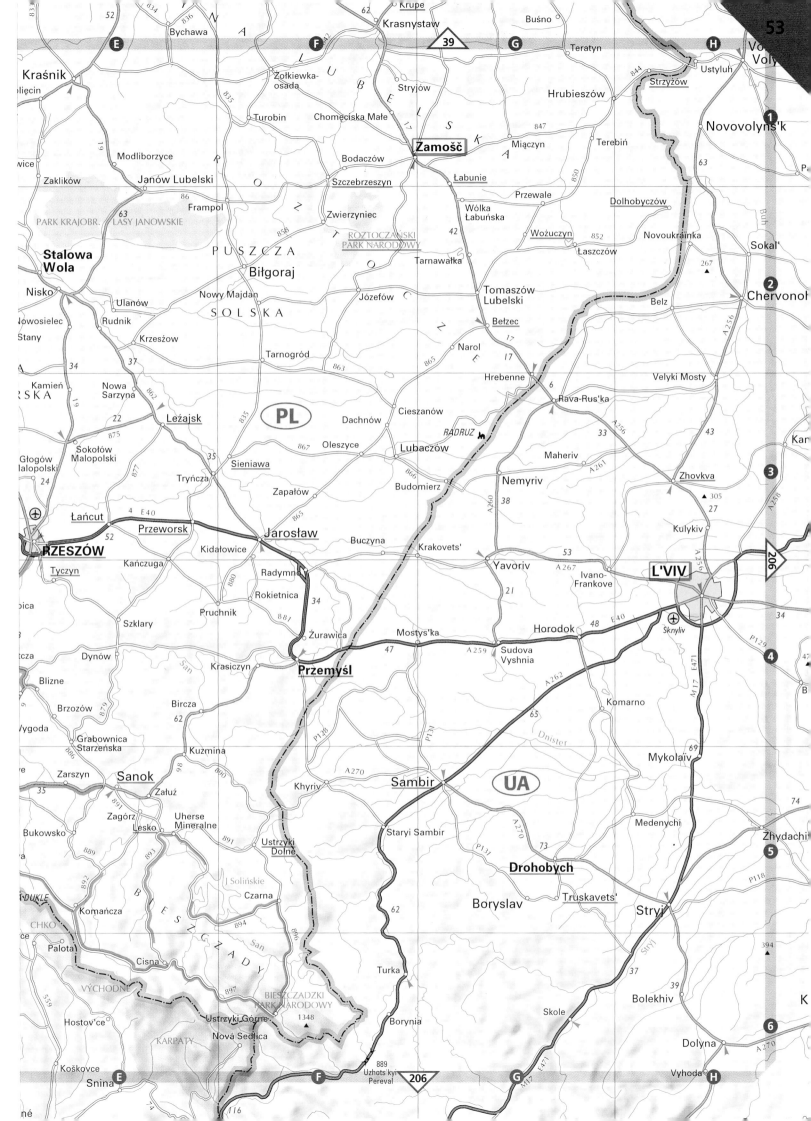

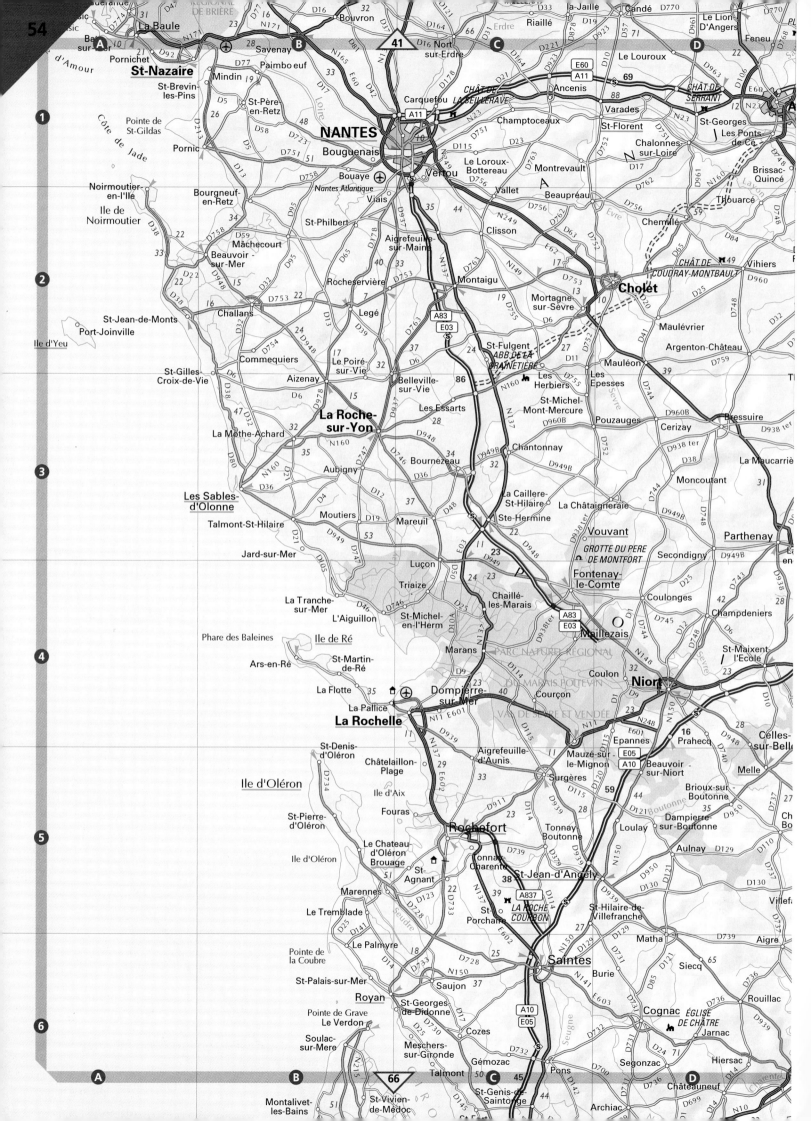

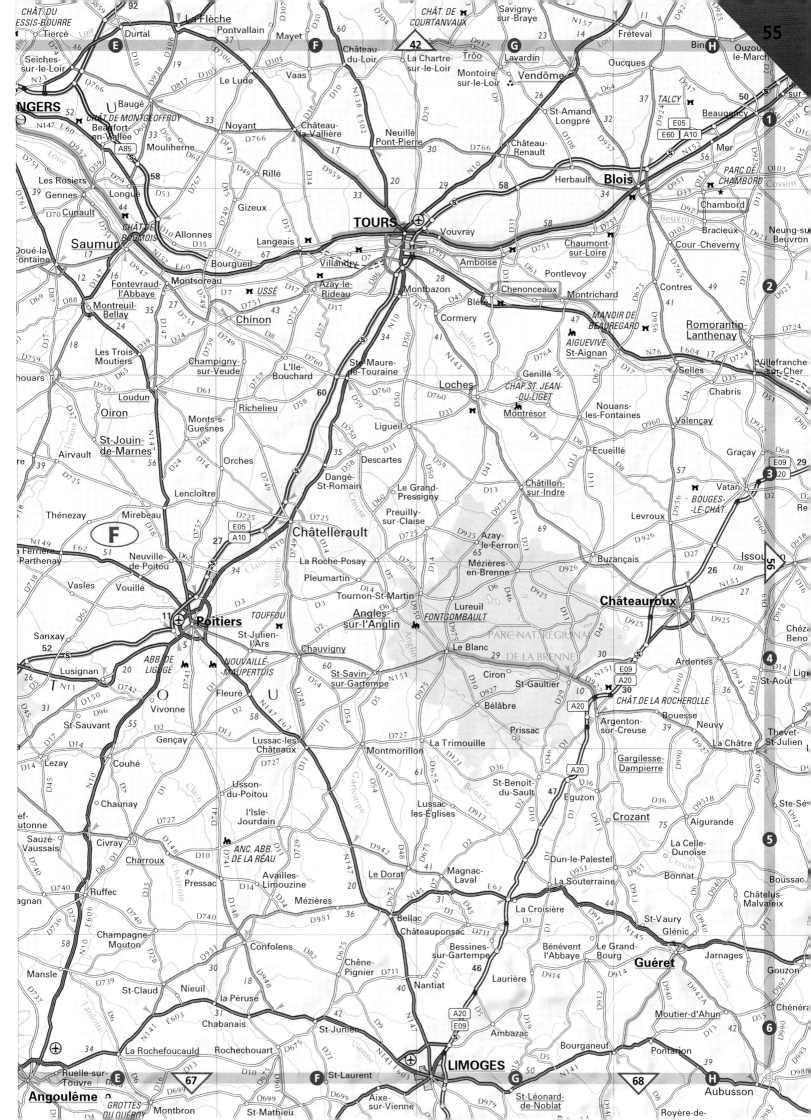

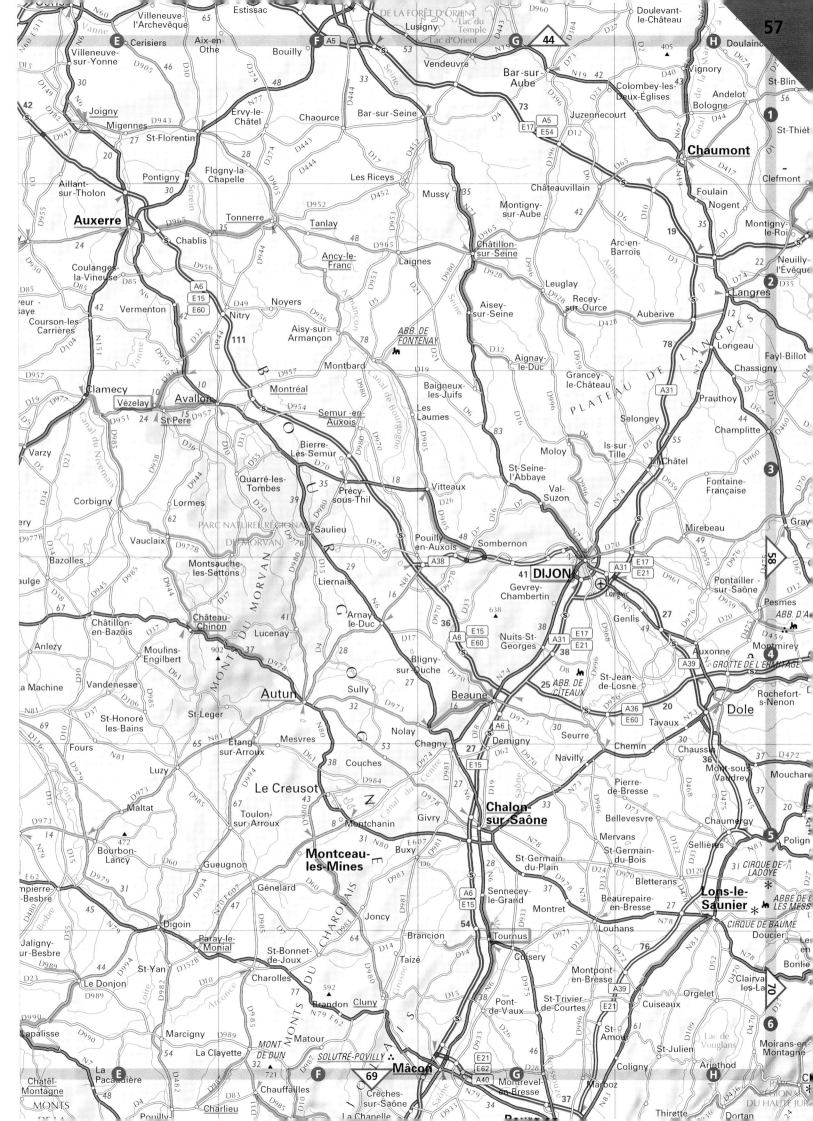

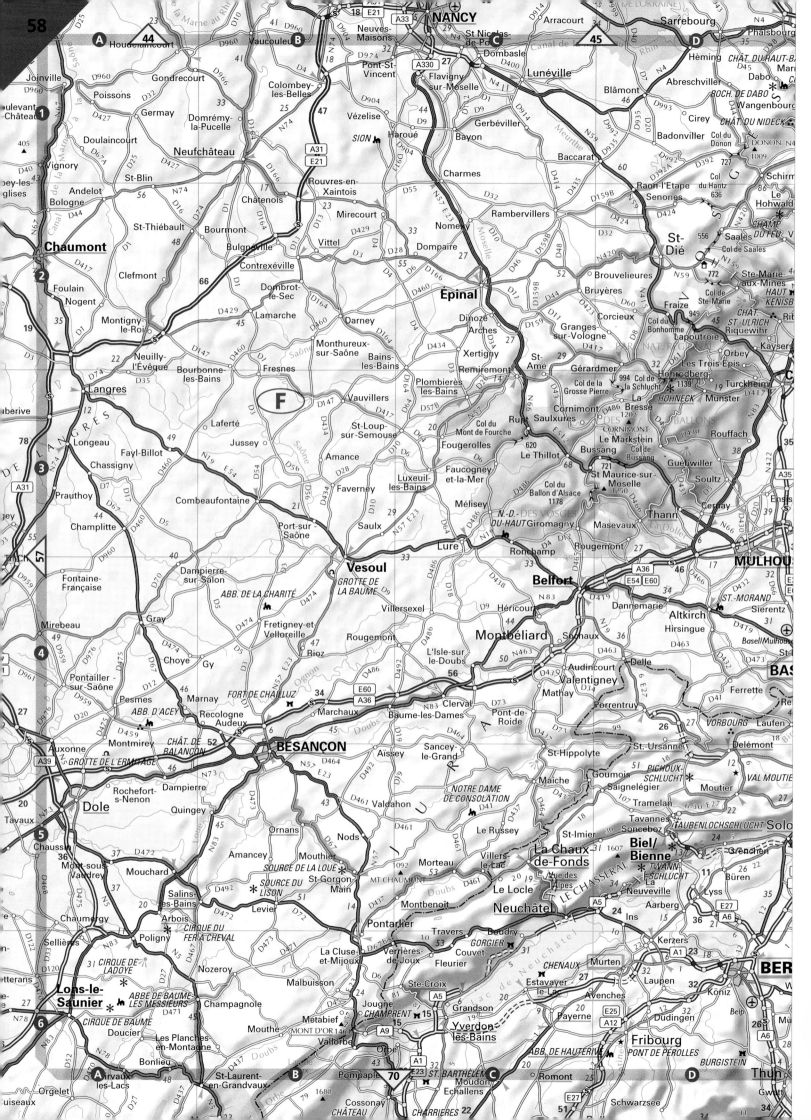

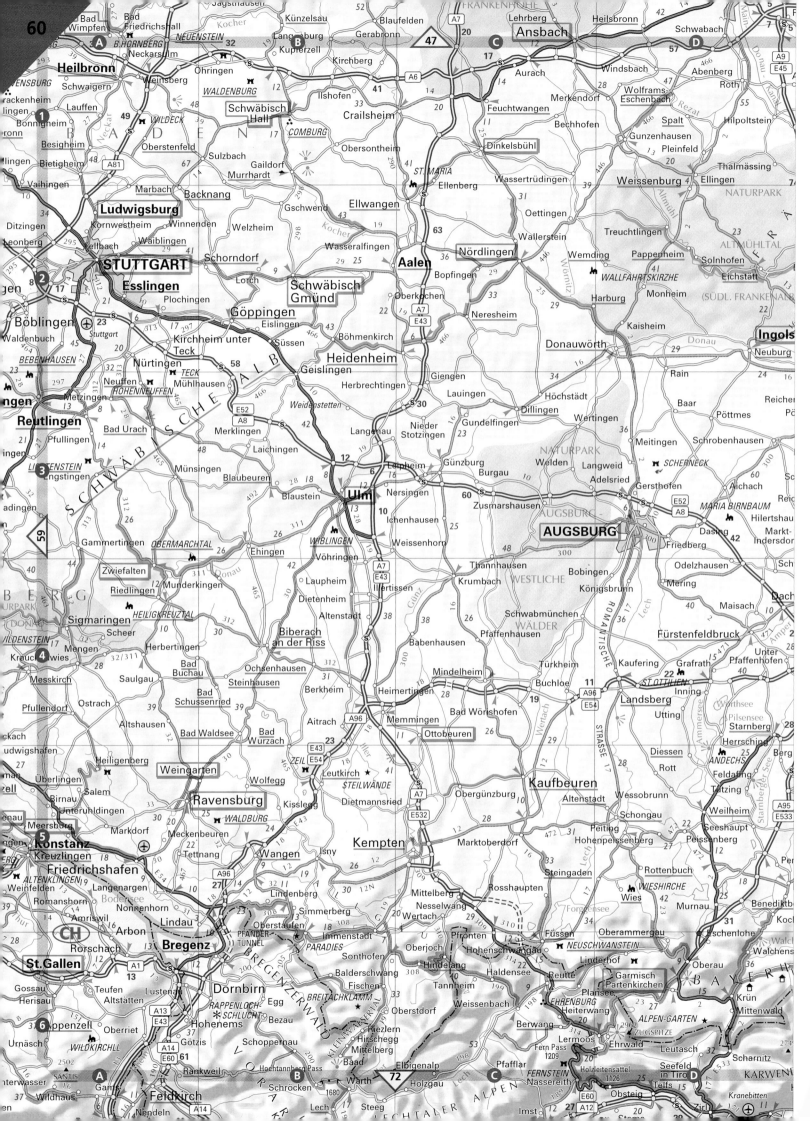

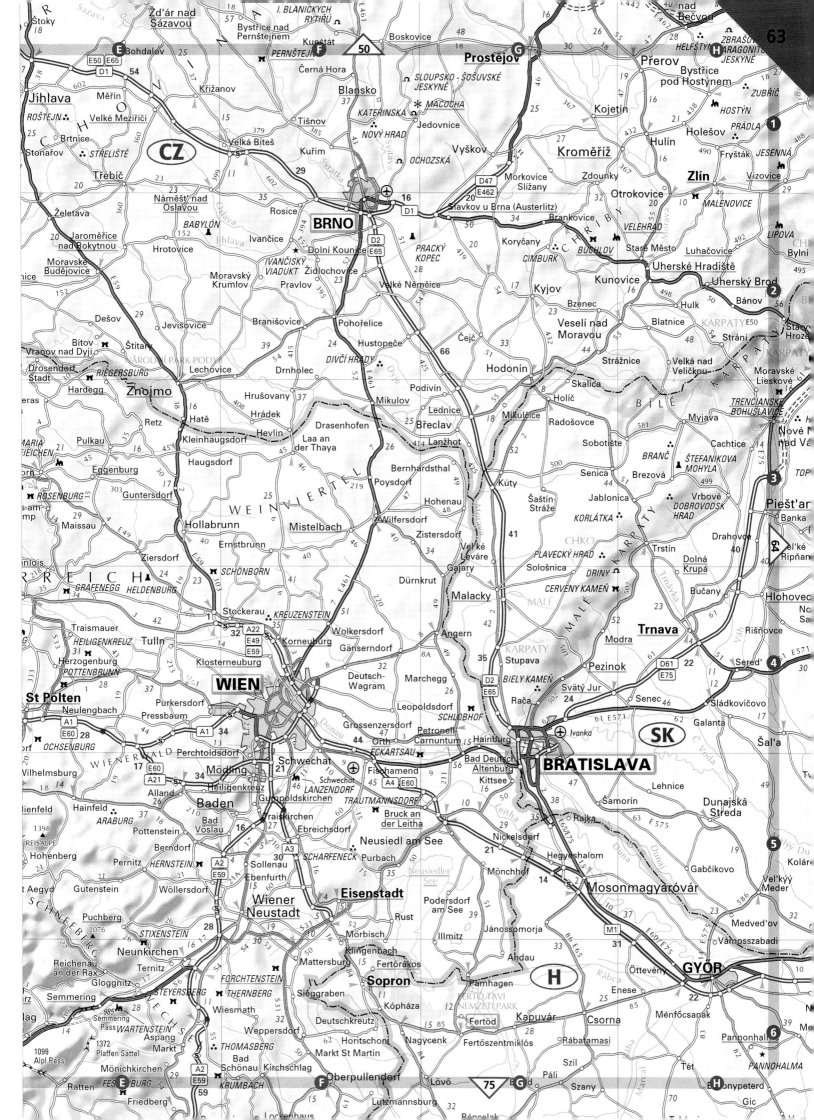

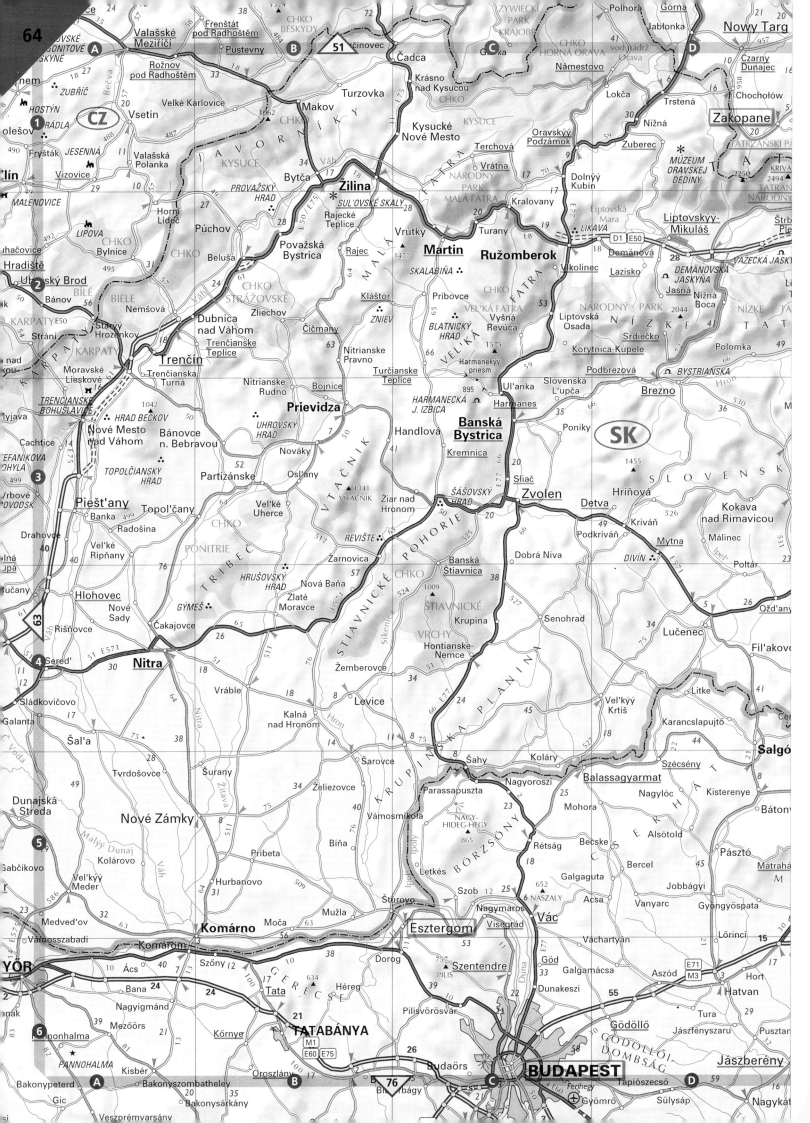

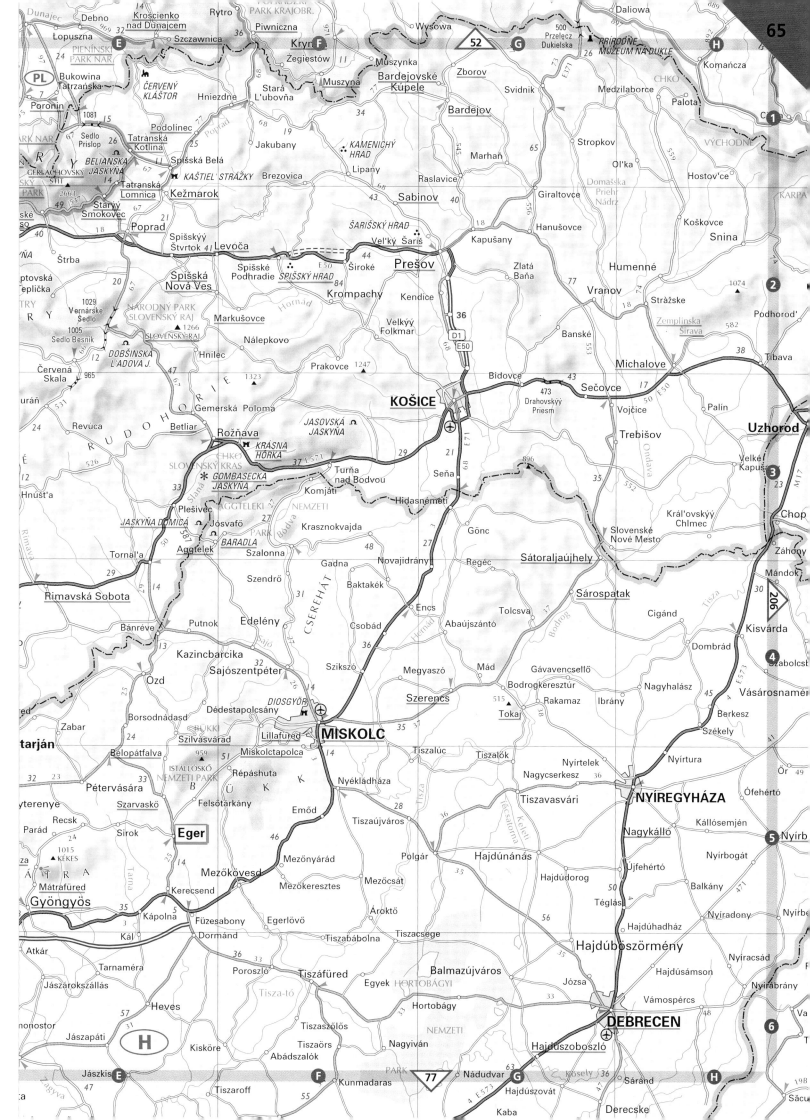

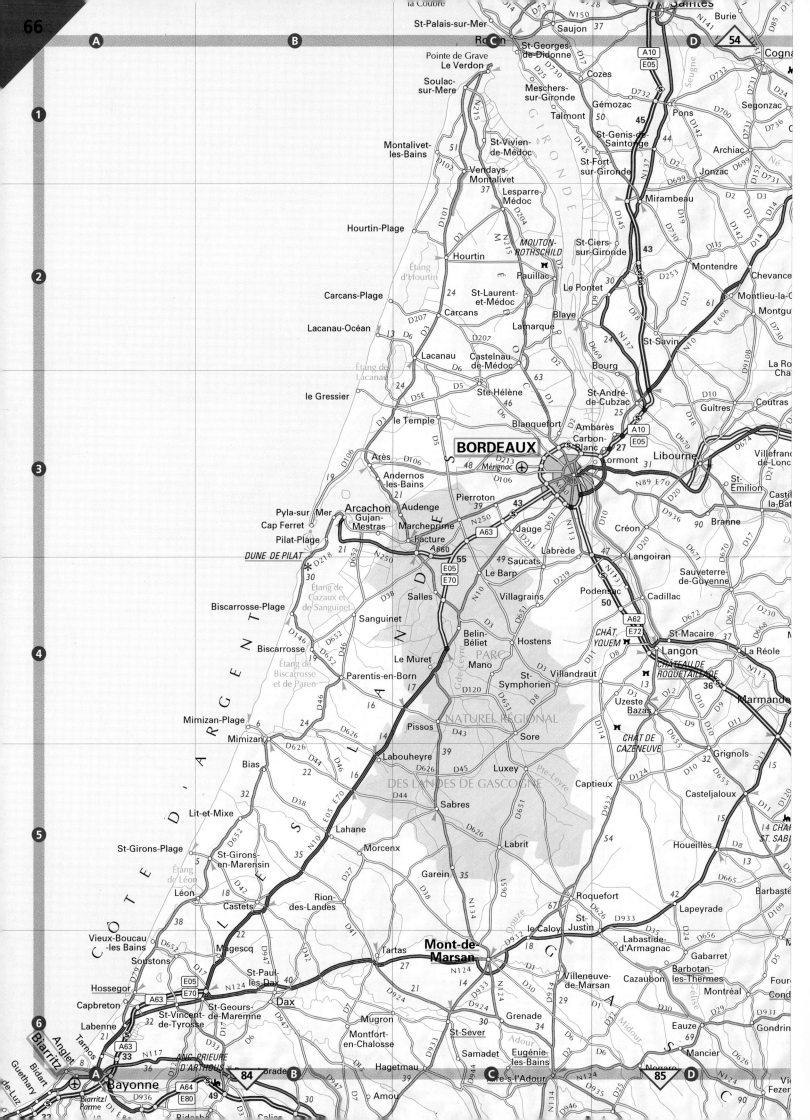

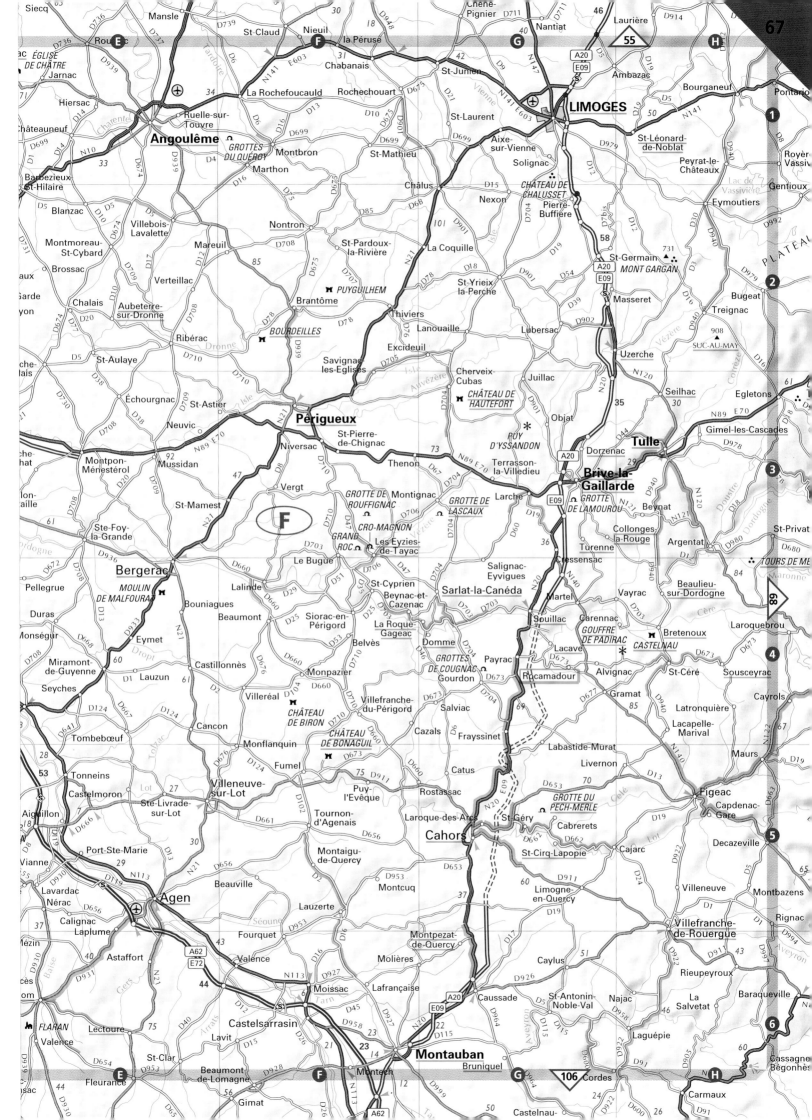

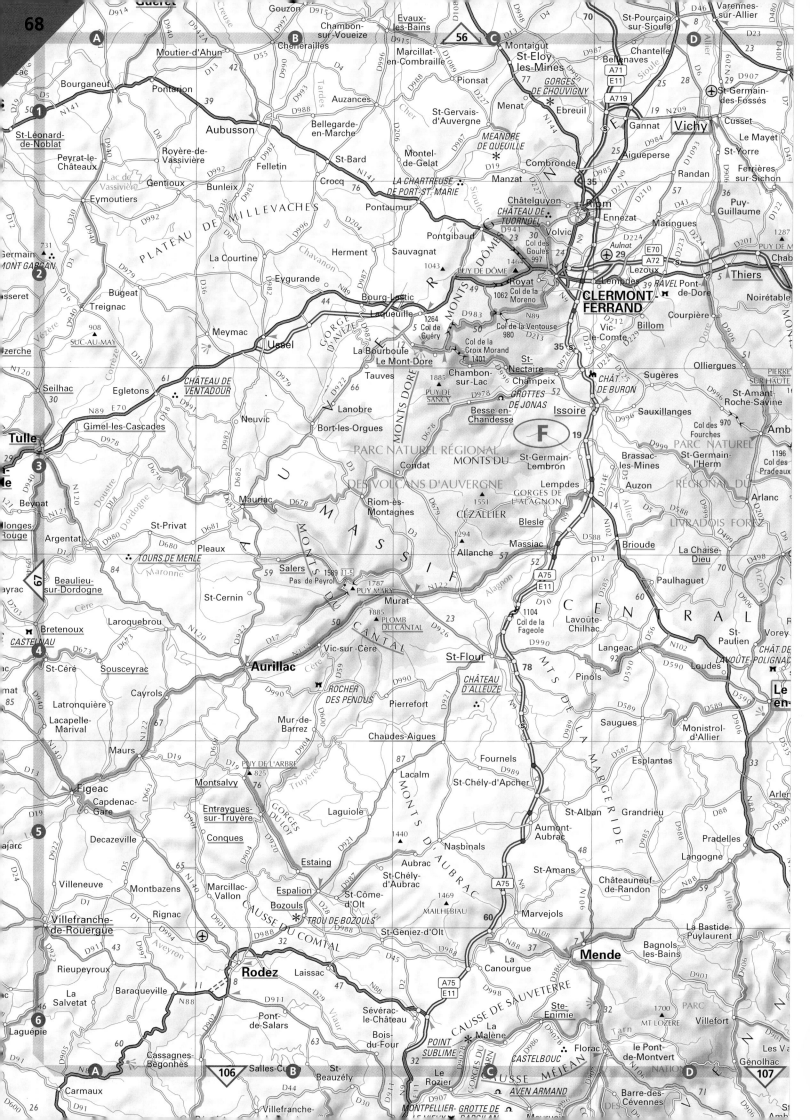

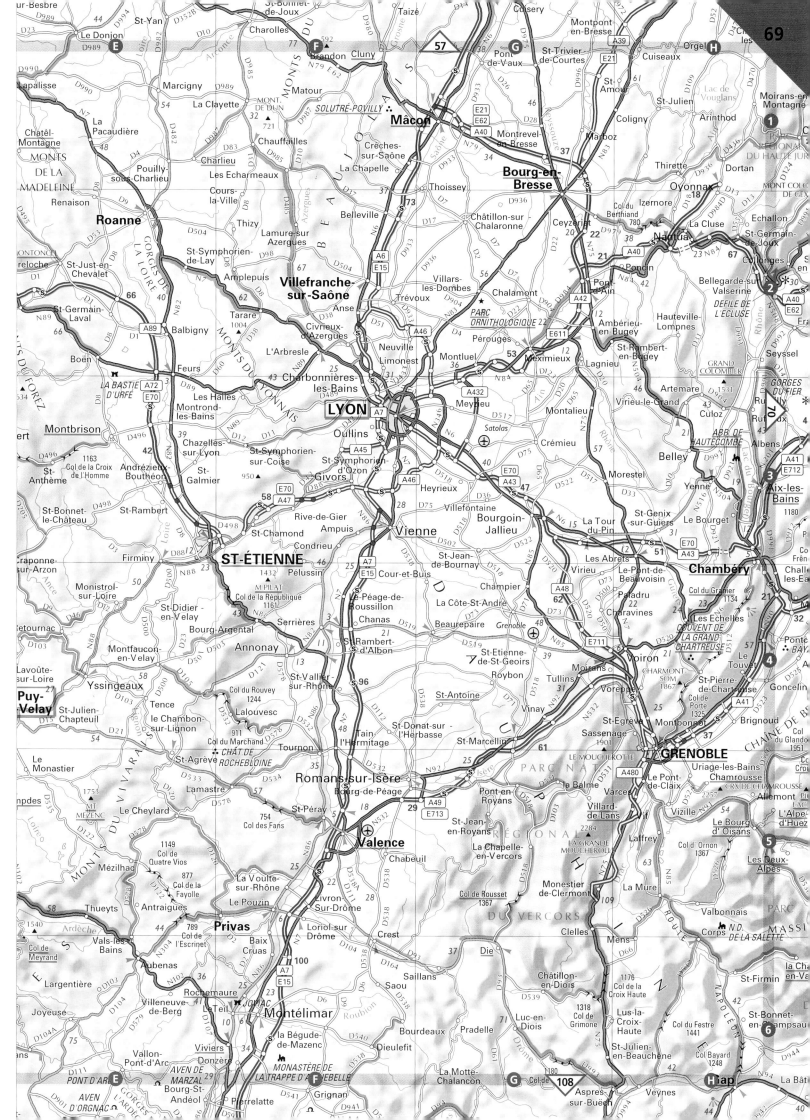

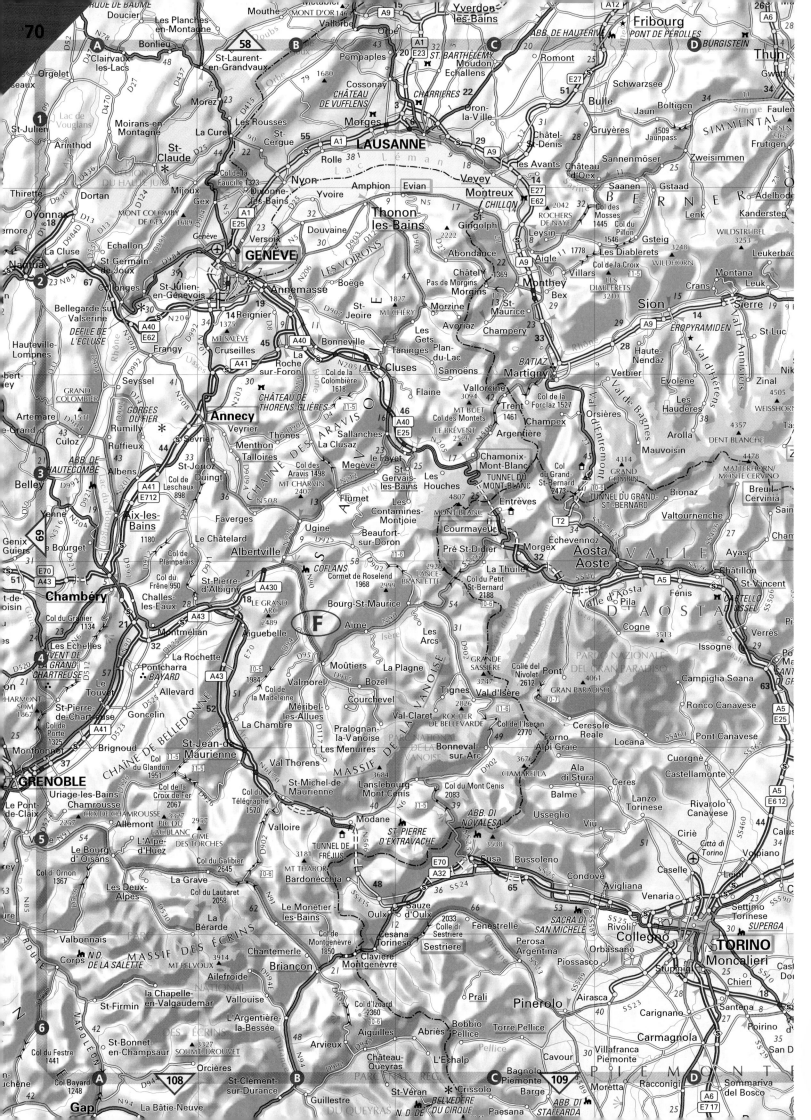

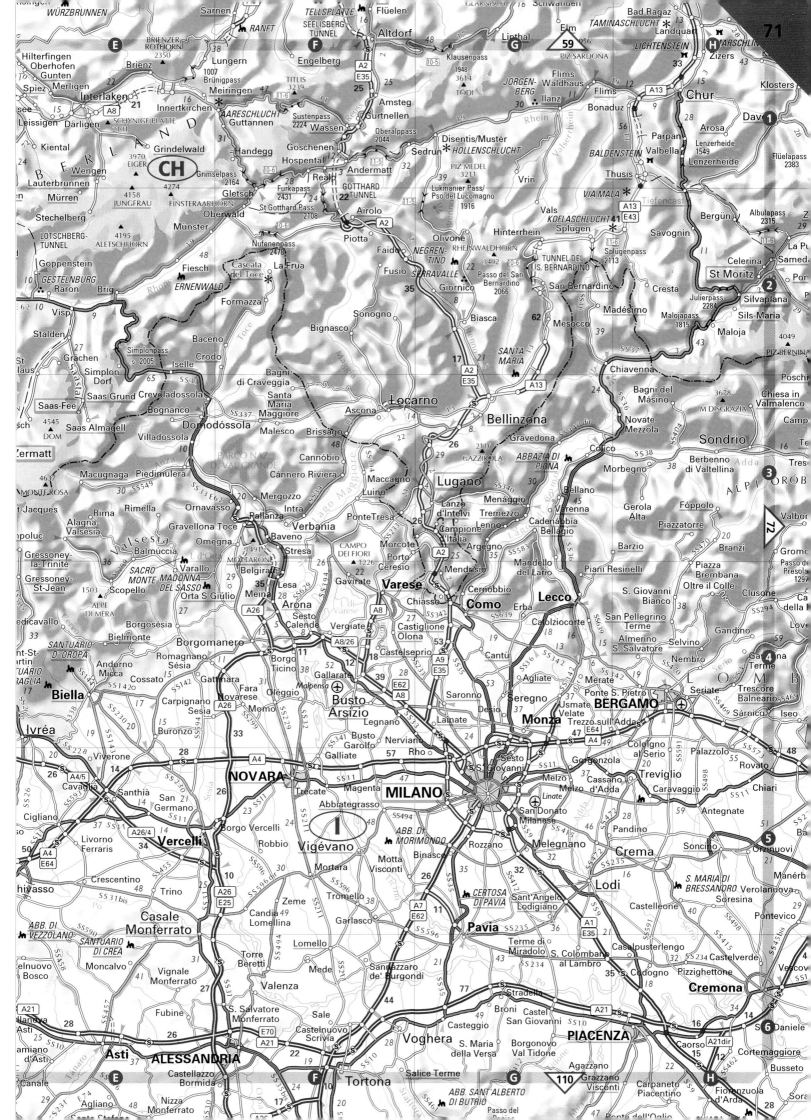

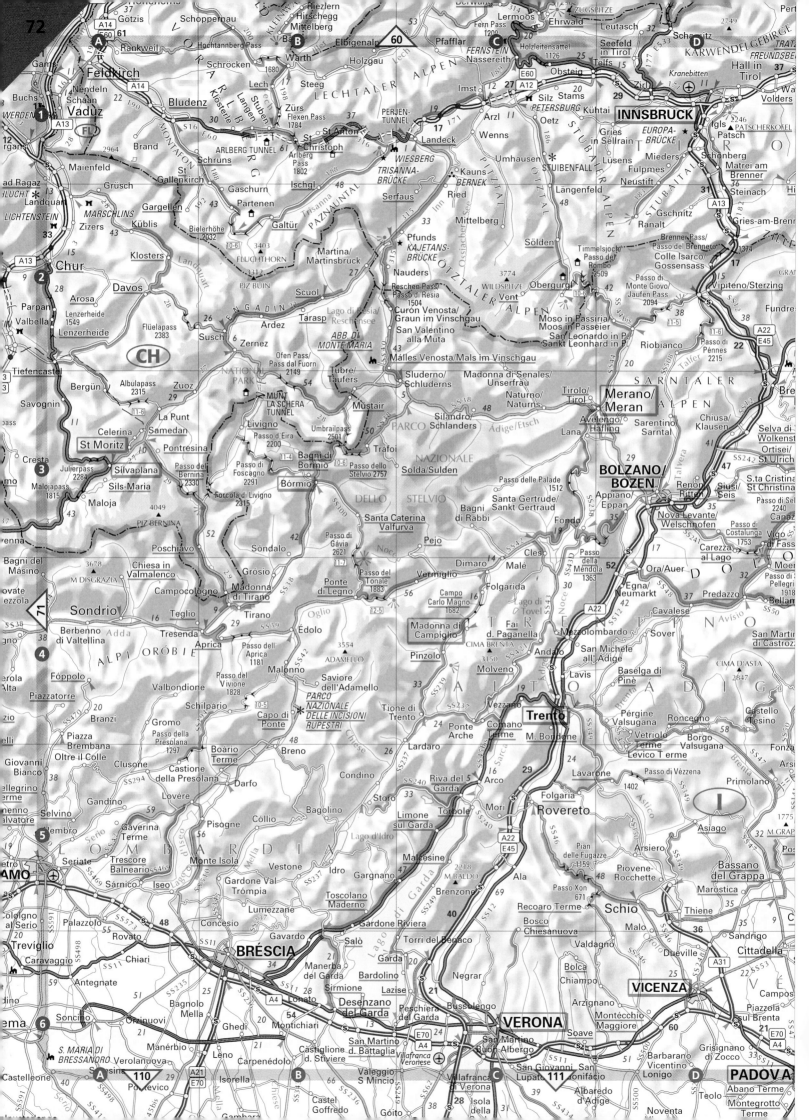

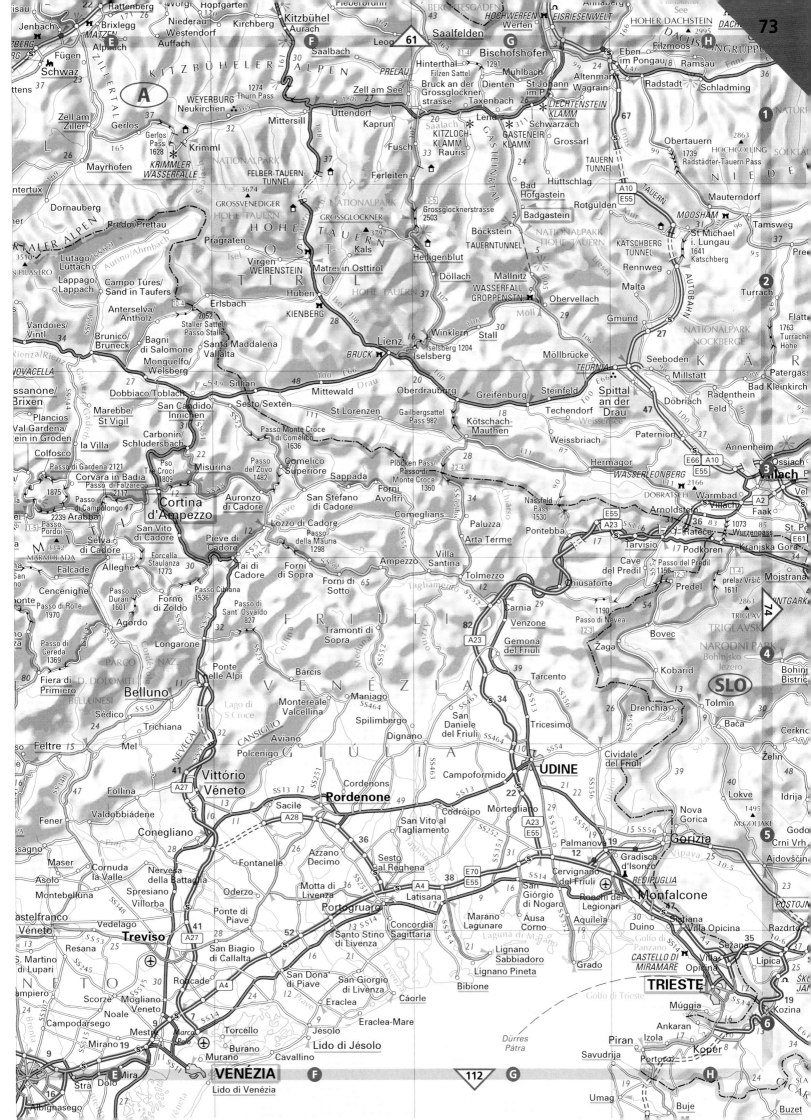

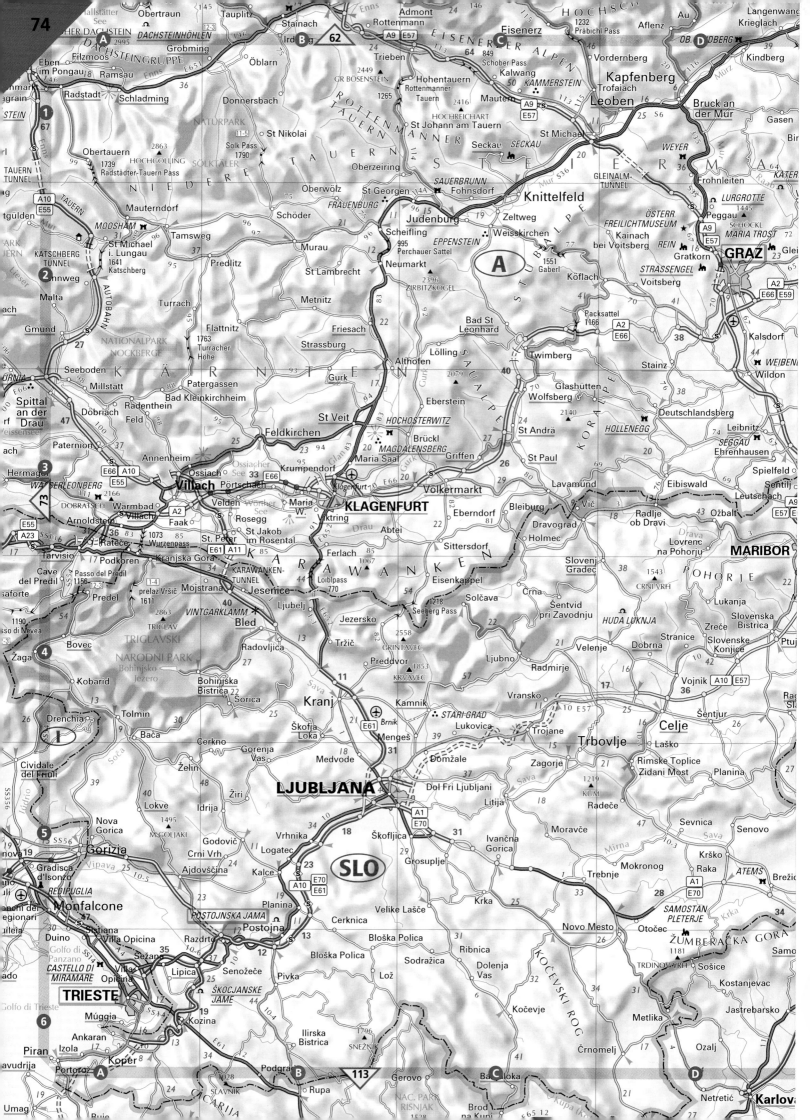

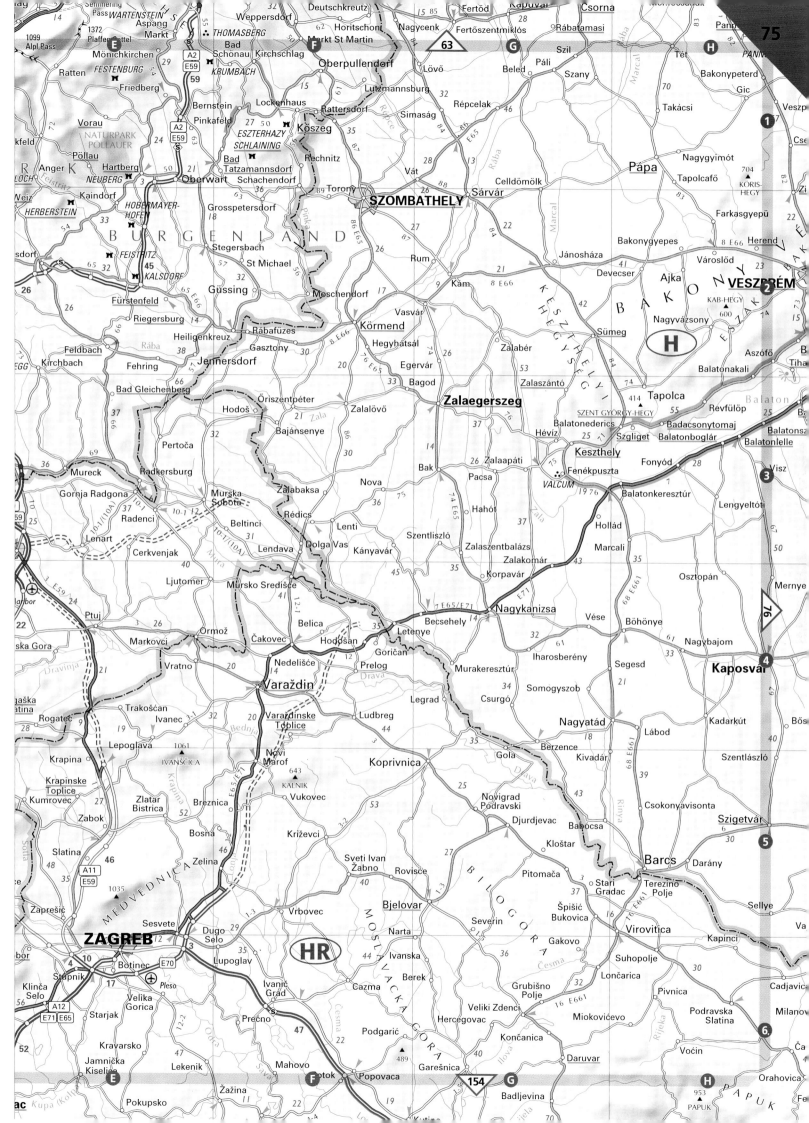

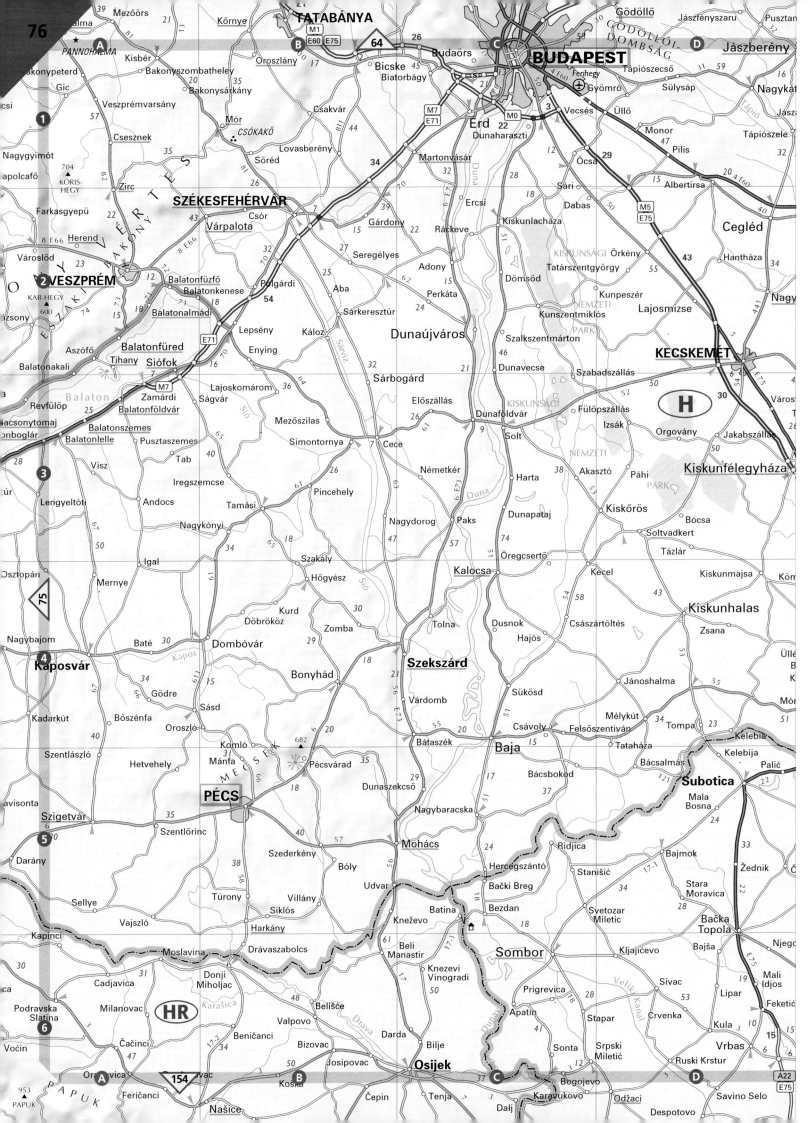

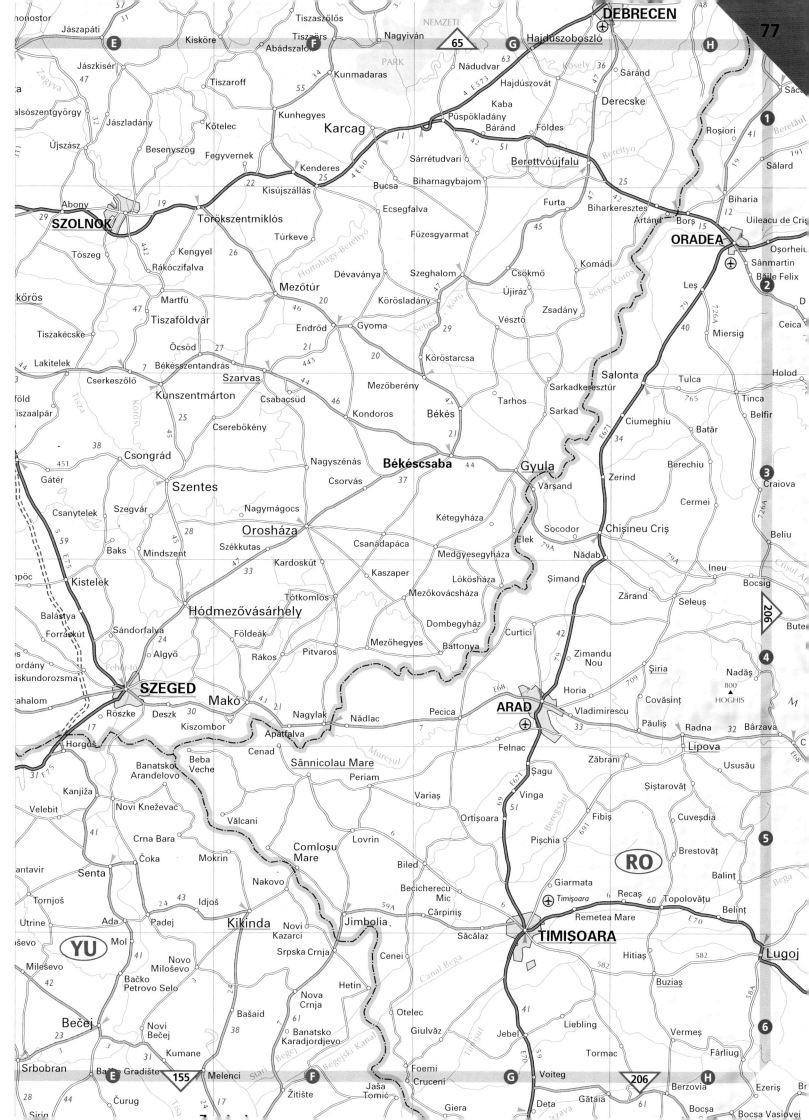

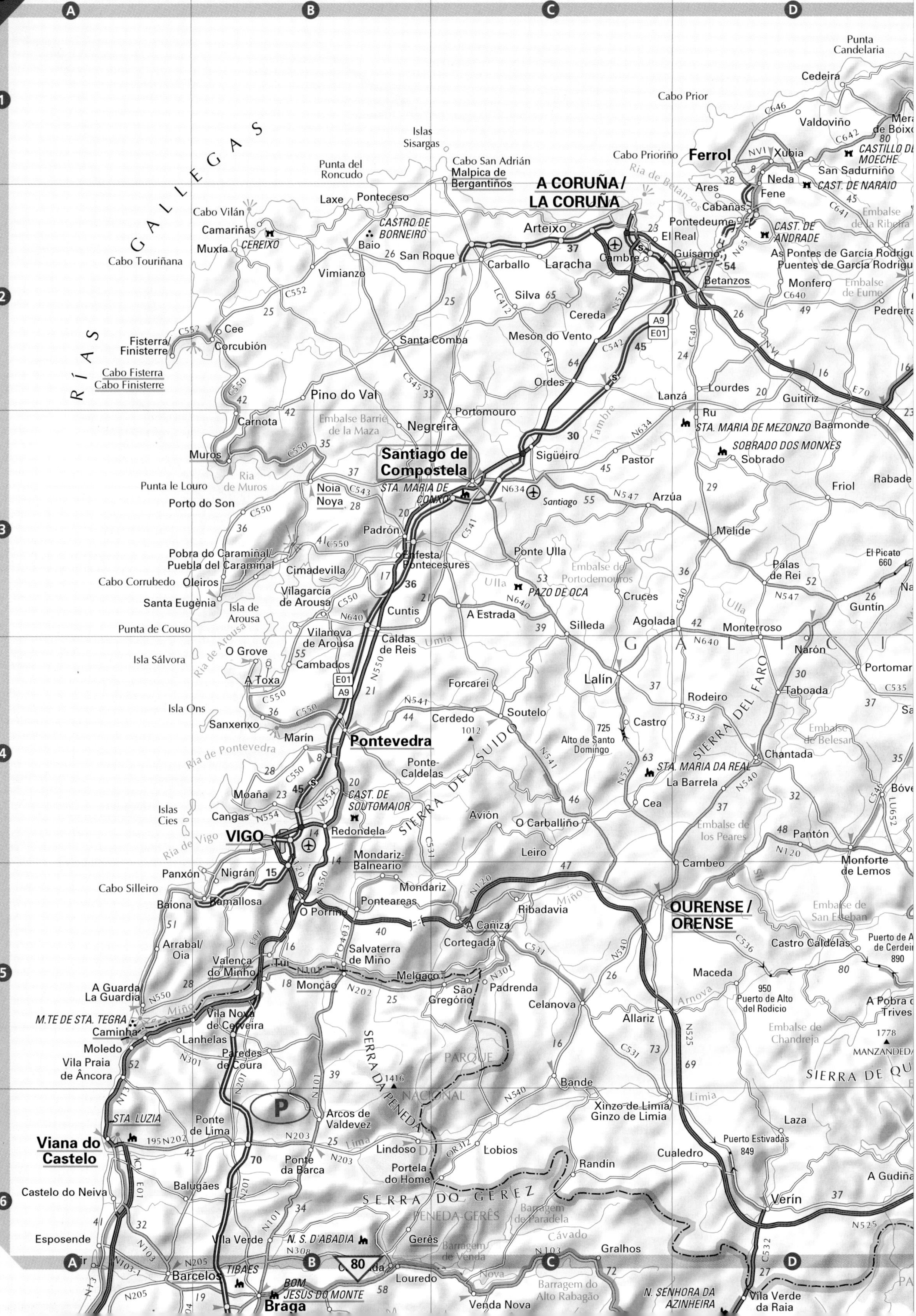

A   B   C   D

1   2   3   4   5   6

RÍAS GALLEGAS

A CORUÑA / LA CORUÑA

Ferrol

Punta Candelaria
Cedeira
Valdoviño
Mera de Boixo
CASTILLO DE MOECHE
Cabo Prior
Xubia
Neda
Fene
San Sadurniño
CAST. DE NARAIO
Cabo Prioriño
Ría de Betanzos
Ares
Cabañas
Pontedeume
El Real
Guísamo
Betanzos
As Pontes de García Rodrígu
Puentes de García Rodrígu
Monfero
CAST. DE ANDRADE
Pedreira
Embalse de la Ribeira
Embalse de Eume

Islas Sisargas
Cabo San Adrián
Malpica de Bergantiños
Punta del Roncudo
Laxe
Ponteceso
Arteixo
Cambre
Carballo
Laracha
San Roque
Baio
CASTRO DE BORNEIRO
CEREIXO
Cabo Vilán
Camariñas
Muxía
Cabo Touriñana
Vimianzo
Silva
Cereda
Santa Comba
Mesón do Vento
Ordes
Lanzá
Lourdes
Guitiriz
Ru
STA. MARIA DE MEZONZO
Baamonde
SOBRADO DOS MONXES
Sobrado
Friol
Rabade

Cee
Corcubión
Fisterra/ Finisterre
Cabo Fisterra
Cabo Finisterre
Pino do Val
Portomouro
Negreira
Sigüeiro
Santiago de Compostela
STA. MARIA DE CONXO
Santiago
Pastor
Arzúa
Melide
Pálas de Rei
El Picato
Carnota
Embalse Barrié de la Maza
Muros
Punta le Louro
Ría de Muros
Noia
Porto do Son
Padrón
Enfesta/ Pontecesures
Ponte Ulla
Embalse de Portodemouros
Cruces
Agolada
Monterroso
Narón
Portomar

Pobra do Caramiñal/ Puebla del Caramiñal
Cabo Corrubedo
Oleiros
Santa Eugènia
Cimadevilla
Vilagarcía de Arousa
Isla de Arousa
Cuntis
A Estrada
Silleda
PAZO DE OCA
Lalín
Rodeiro
Taboada
Chantada
Punta de Couso
O Grove
Vilanova de Arousa
Caldas de Reis
Cambados
A Toxa
Isla Sálvora
Isla Ons
Sanxenxo
Marín
Forcarei
Cerdedo
Soutelo
Alto de Santo Domingo
Castro
STA. MARIA DA REAL
La Barrela
Cea
GALICIA
SIERRA DEL SUIDO

Islas Cies
Moaña
Cangas
Pontevedra
Ponte-Caldelas
CAST. DE SOUTOMAIOR
Avión
O Carballiño
Leiro
Cambeo
Pantón
Monforte de Lemos
Bóve
Embalse de los Peares
SERRA DEL FARO
VIGO
Redondela
Mondariz-Balneario
Ría de Vigo
Panxón
Nigrán
Cabo Silleiro
Baiona
Ramallosa
O Porriño
Mondariz
Ponteareas
A Cañiza
Ribadavia
Cortegada
OURENSE / ORENSE
Castro Caldelas
Puerto de A de Cerdeir
Embalse de San Esteban
Arrabal/ Oia
Valença do Minho
Tui
Salvaterra de Miño
Melgaço
São Gregório
Padrenda
Celanova
Allariz
Maceda
Puerto de Alto del Rodicio
A Pobra d Trives
A Guarda La Guardia
M.TE DE STA. TEGRA
Caminha
Vila Nova de Cerveira
Monção
Lanhelas
Paredes de Coura
SERRA DA PENEDA
PARQUE NACIONAL
Bande
Xinzo de Limia/ Ginzo de Limia
Laza
Embalse de Chandreja
MANZANEDA
SIERRA DE QU
Moledo
Vila Praia de Âncora
STA. LUZIA
Ponte de Lima
Arcos de Valdevez
Lindoso
Portela do Home
Lobios
Randín
Cualedro
Verín
Puerto Estivadas
A Gudiña
Viana do Castelo
Castelo do Neiva
Esposende
Balugães
Ponte da Barca
Vila Verde
N. S. D'ABADIA
SERRA DO GEREZ
PENEDA-GERÊS
Gerês
Barragem de Paradela
Barragem de Venda
Cávado
Gralhos
Barcelos
TIBAES
BOM JESUS DO MONTE
Braga
Louredo
Venda Nova
Barragem do Alto Rabagão
N. SENHORA DA AZINHEIRA
Vila Verde da Raia

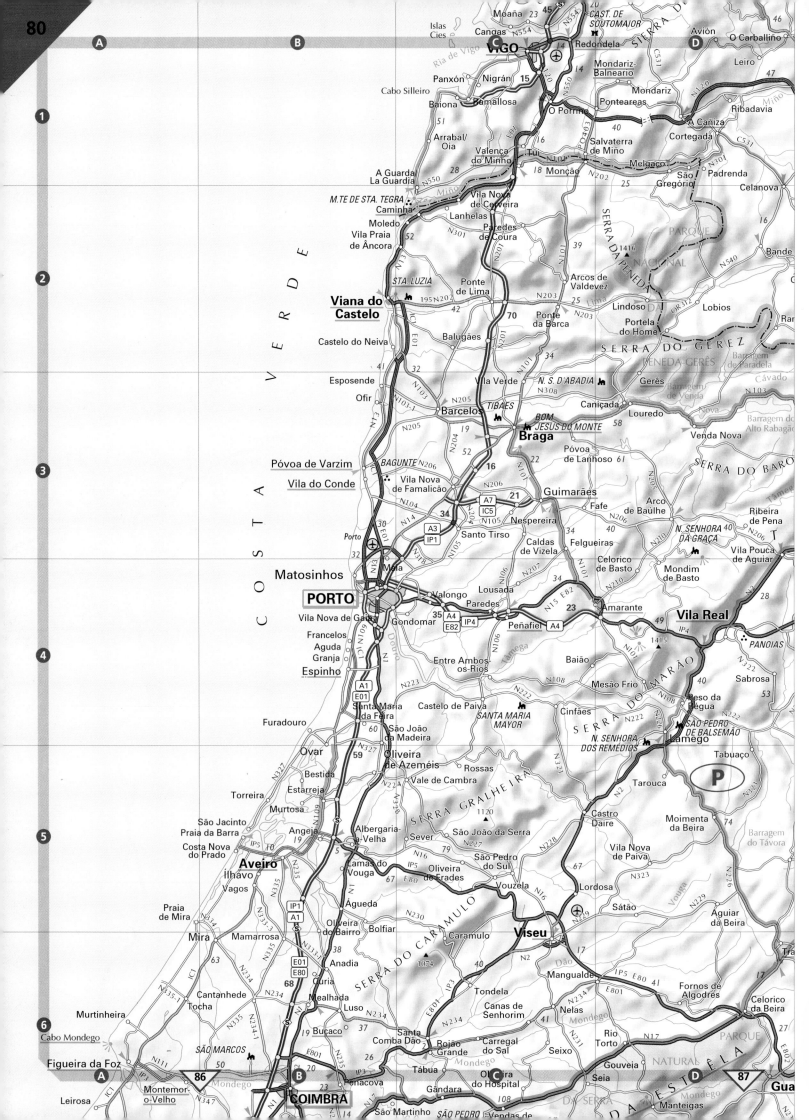

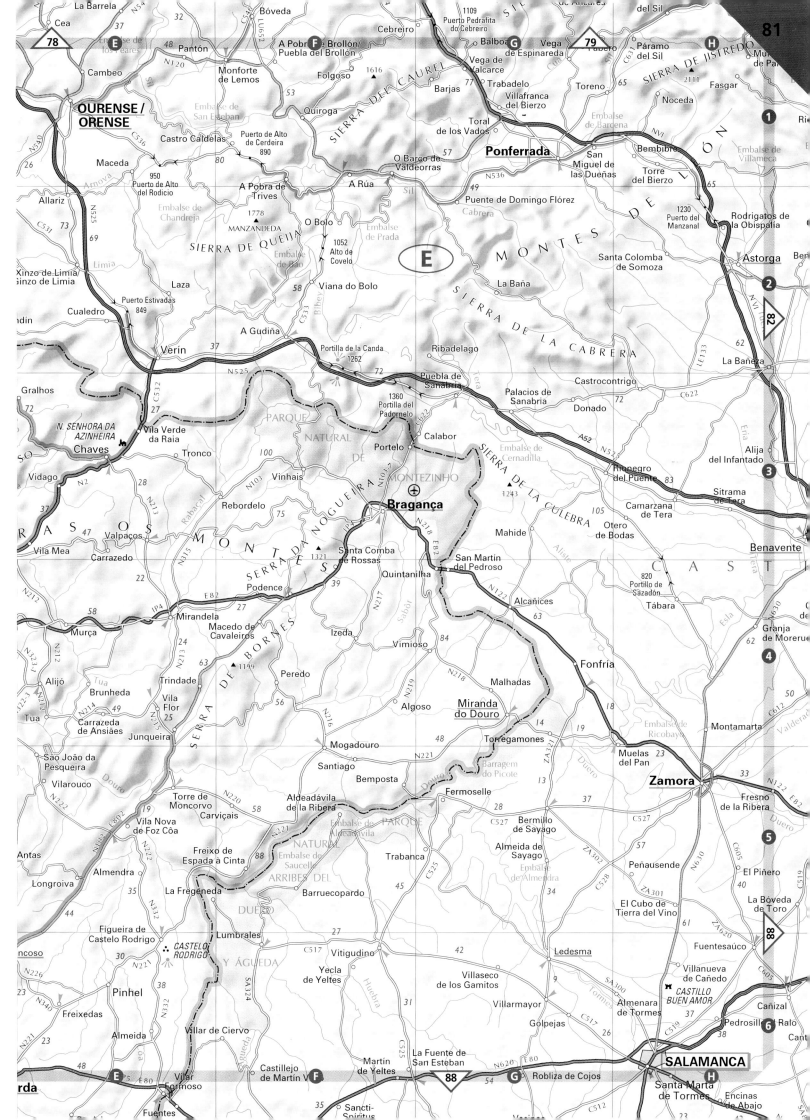

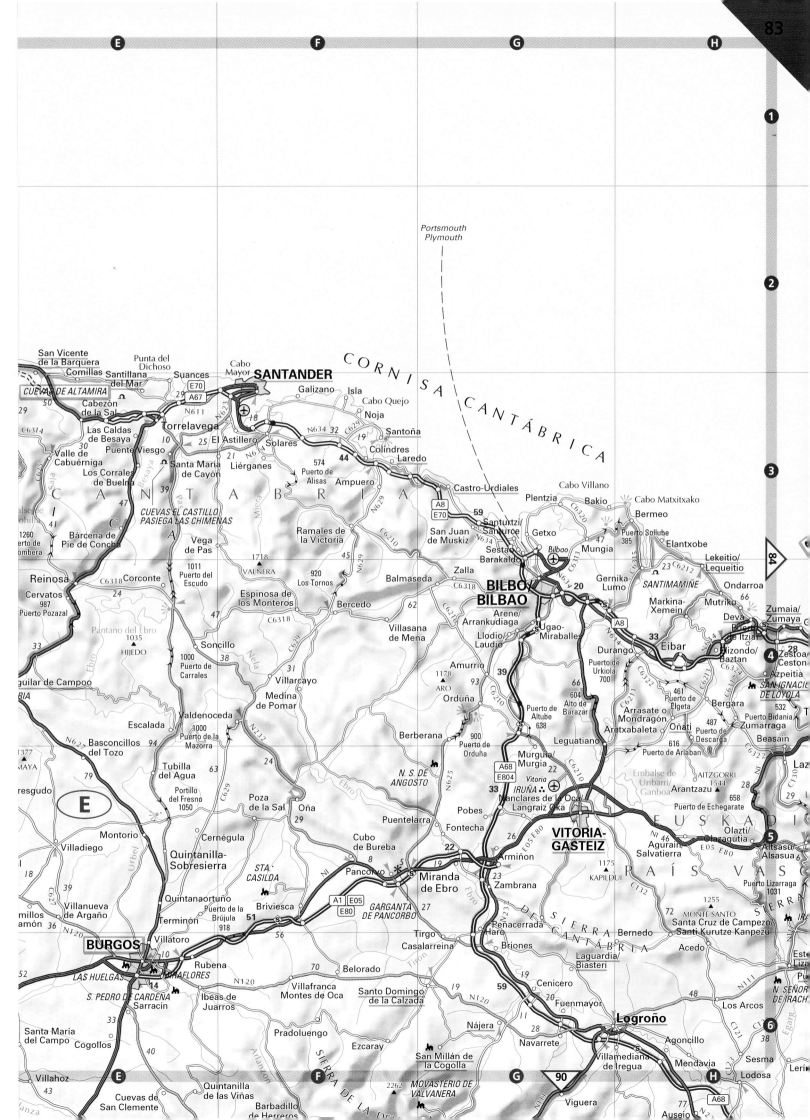

E · F · G · H

1

2

Portsmouth
Plymouth

3

84

San Vicente
de la Barquera
Comillas
Santillana
del Mar
Punta del
Dichoso
Suances
Cabo
Mayor
SANTANDER
CORNISA CANTÁBRICA
CUEVAS DE ALTAMIRA
50
29
Cabezón
de la Sal
E70
A67
29
N611
N623
Galizano
Isla
Cabo Quejo
Noja
Torrelavega
18
N634
32
C629
Santoña
Las Caldas
de Besaya
30
Puente Viesgo
10
25
El Astillero
Solares
N634
19
Colindres
Laredo
Castro-Urdiales
Valle de
Cabuérniga
Los Corrales
de Buelna
Santa María
de Cayón
Liérganes
21
N634
574
Puerto de
Alisas
Ampuero
44
A8
E70
59
San Juan
de Muskiz
Santurtzi
Santurce
Plentzia
Bakio
Cabo Villano
Cabo Matxitxako
Bermeo
C6320
CUEVAS EL CASTILLO
PASIEGA LAS CHIMENAS
47
Bárcena de
Pie de Concha
41
Vega
de Pas
Ramales de
la Victoria
C6210
Sestao
Barakaldo
Getxo
Bilbao
Mungia
Puerto Sollube
385
47
Elantxobe
Lekeitio/
Lequeitio
Ondarroa
SANTIMAMIÑE
C6215
C6212
23
Reinosa
Cervatos
987
Puerto Pozazal
1260
Puerto de
Pombera
C6318
Corconte
24
1011
Puerto del
Escudo
1718
VALNERA
45
920
Los Tornos
C629
Zalla
Balmaseda
C6318
BILBAO
BILBAO
20
Gernika-
Lumo
Markina-
Xemein
Mutriku
Deva
Puerto de
Itziar
Zumaia/
Zumaya
66
Pantano del Ebro
1035
HIJEDO
Espinosa de
los Monteros
C6318
Bercedo
62
Villasana
de Mena
C621
Arene/
Arrankudiaga
Llodio/
Laudio
Ugao-
Miraballes
A8
Durango
Puerto de
Urkiola
700
Eibar
33
C6213
Plizondo/
Baztan
28
Zestoa/
Ceston
4
33
Soncillo
1000
Puerto de
Carrales
38
C629
31
Villarcayo
Medina
de Pomar
Amurrio
1178
ARO
93
Orduña
39
C6210
604
Alto de
Barazar
66
Puerto de
Altube
638
Arrasate o
Mondragón
Aretxabaleta
461
Puerto de
Elgeta
Oñati
Bergara
487
Puerto de
Descarga
Zumarraga
616
Puerto de Arlabán
SAN IGNACIO
DE LOYOLA
532
Beasain
C6322
Valdenoceda
1000
Puerto de la
Mazorra
Escalada
94
N232
N627
1377
MAYA
Basconcillos
del Tozo
79
Berberana
900
Puerto de
Orduña
Murguía/
Murgia
N625
22
C6210
Embalse de
Uribarri/
Ganboa
AITZGORRI
1544
Arantzazu
658
Laz
N
Tubilla
del Agua
63
24
N. S. DE
ANGOSTO
A68
E804
Vitoria
33
Nanclares de la Oca/
Langraiz Oka
Puerto de Echegarate
Puerto de Arlabán
EUSKADI
Aguilar de Campoo
RIA
resgudo
Portillo
del Fresno
1050
C629
Poza
de la Sal
Oña
29
Puentelarra
Pobes
Fontecha
Armiñón
26
E05 E80
**VITORIA-
GASTEIZ**
1175
KAPILDUI
Olazti/
Olazagutia
46
NI
E05 E80
Altsasu/
Alsasua
5
PAÍS VASCO
SIERRA
Montorio
Villadiego
Cernégula
Quintanilla-
Sobresierra
STA.
CASILDA
Cubo
de Bureba
8
Pancorbo
22
5
19
Miranda
de Ebro
23
Zambrana
Puerto Lizarraga
1031
C132
SIE
18
C627
39
Quintanaortuño
Villanueva
de Argaño
millos
amón
36
N120
Quintanaortuño
Terminón
Puerto de la
Brújula
918
51
Briviesca
A1
E05
E80
GARGANTA
DE PANCORBO
27
Peñacerrada
Haro
SIERRA
DE
CANTÁBRIA
Bernedo
Aceo
1255
72
MONTE SANTO
Santa Cruz de Campezo/
Santi Kurutze Kanpezu
N111
N. SEÑORA
DE IRACHE
6
52
BURGOS
LAS HUELGAS
10
Rubena
70
56
Belorado
Tirgo
Casalarreina
Briones
Cenicero
Laguardia/
Biasteri
48
Los Arcos
C121
S. PEDRO DE CARDEÑA
MIRAFLORES
14
Villatoro
Ibeas de
Juarros
Villafranca
Montes de Oca
N120
Santo Domingo
de la Calzada
19
59
20
Fuenmayor
Navarrete
Logroño
Agoncillo
Mendavia
Sarracín
33
Pradoluengo
Ezcaray
N120
Nájera
11
28
Villamediana
de Iregua
Sesma
Villahoz
43
Santa María
del Campo
Cogollos
40
SIERRA DE LA DE
San Millán de
la Cogolla
2262
MONASTERIO DE
VALVANERA
90
Lérín
Lodosa
N111
Viguera
77
A68
Aus
Cuevas de
San Clemente
Quintanilla
de las Viñas
Barbadillo
de Herreros

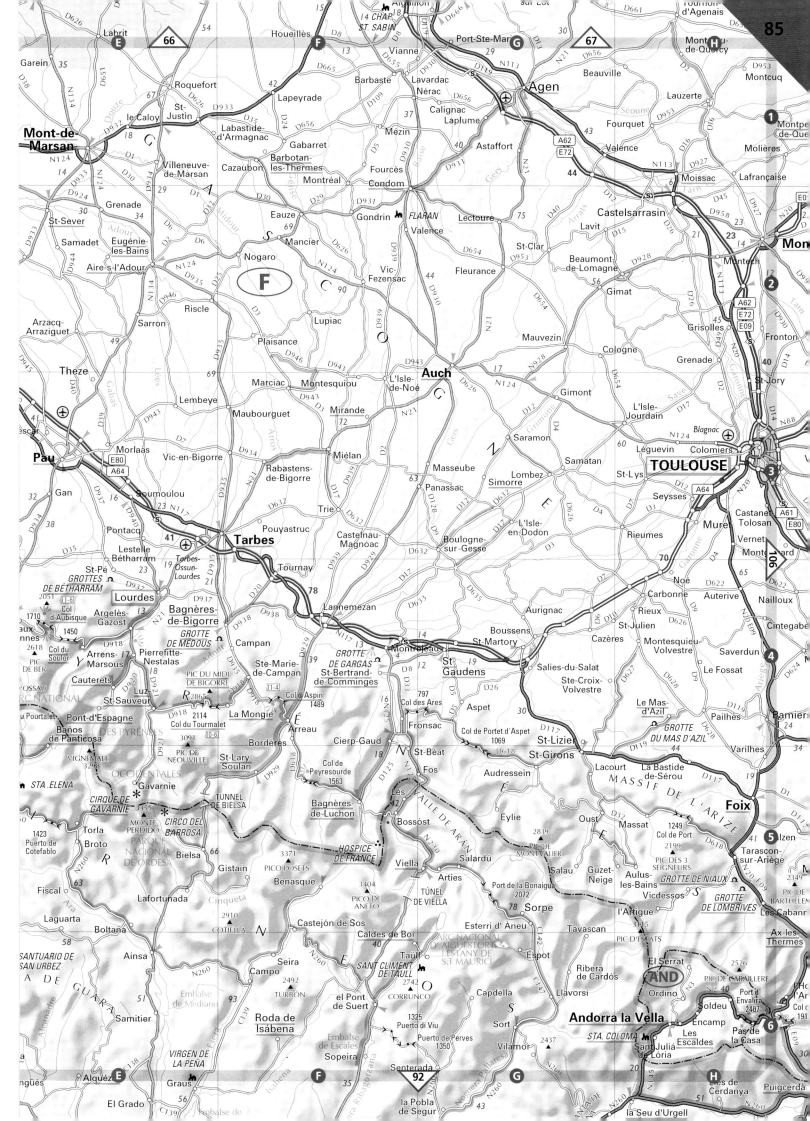

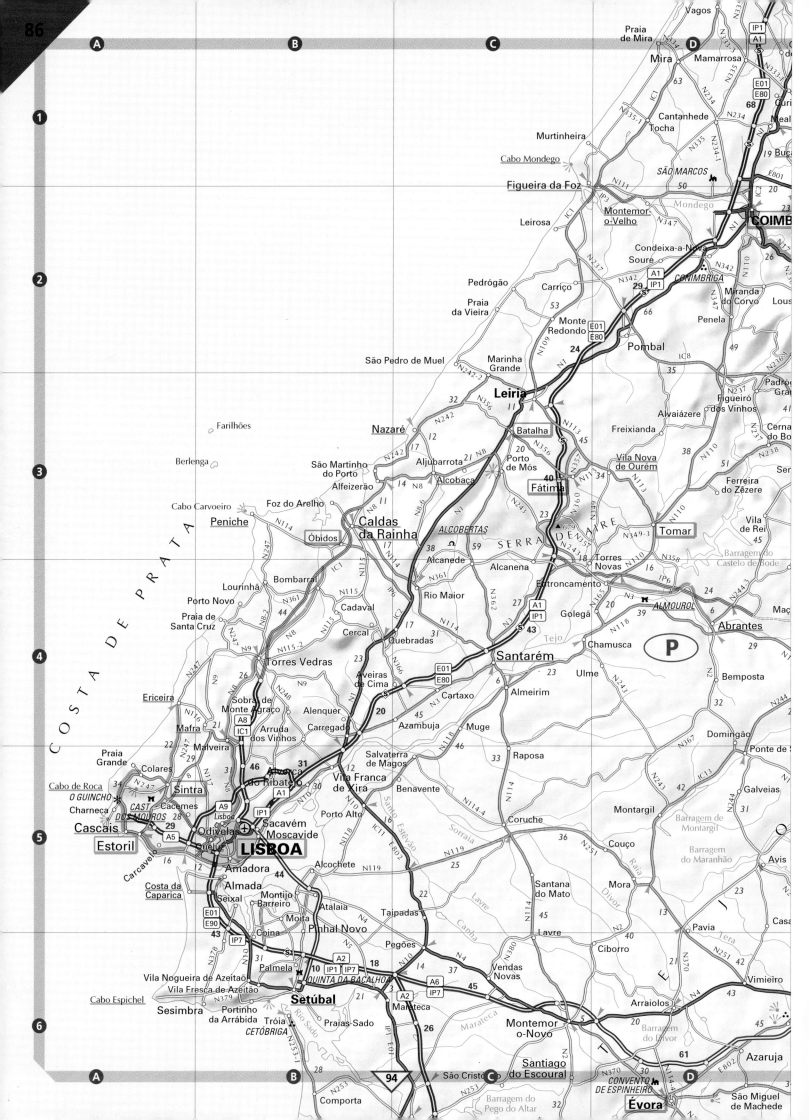

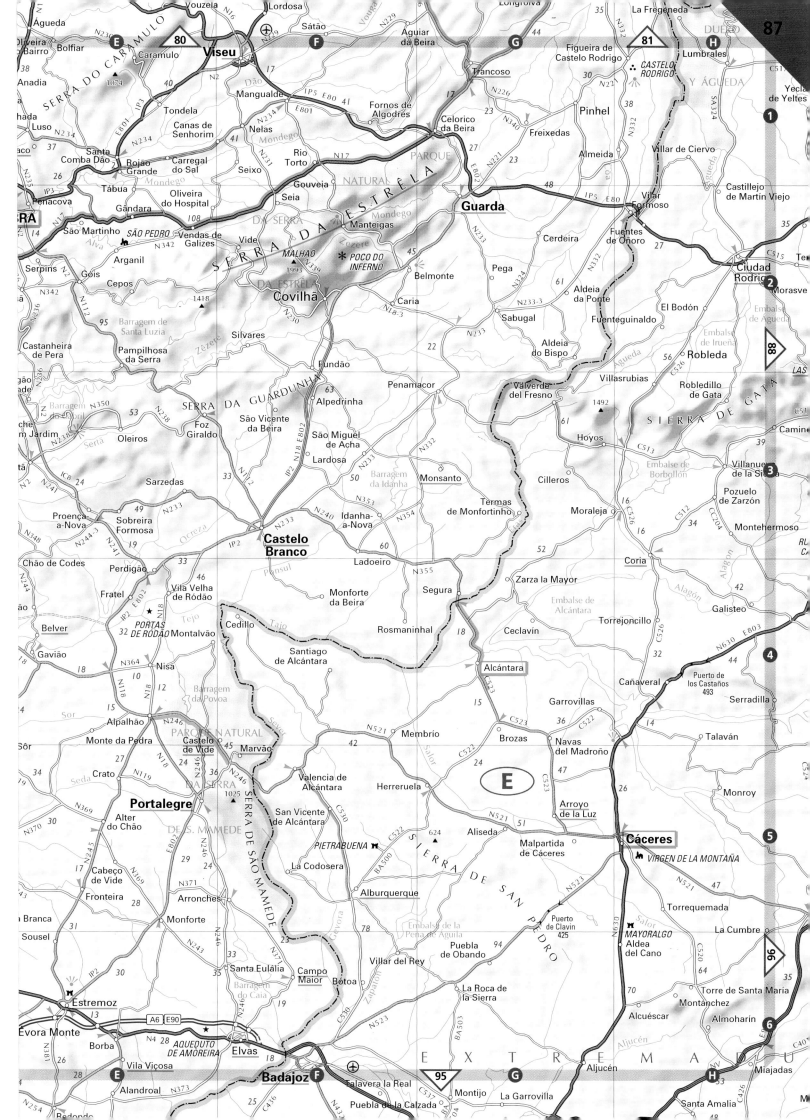

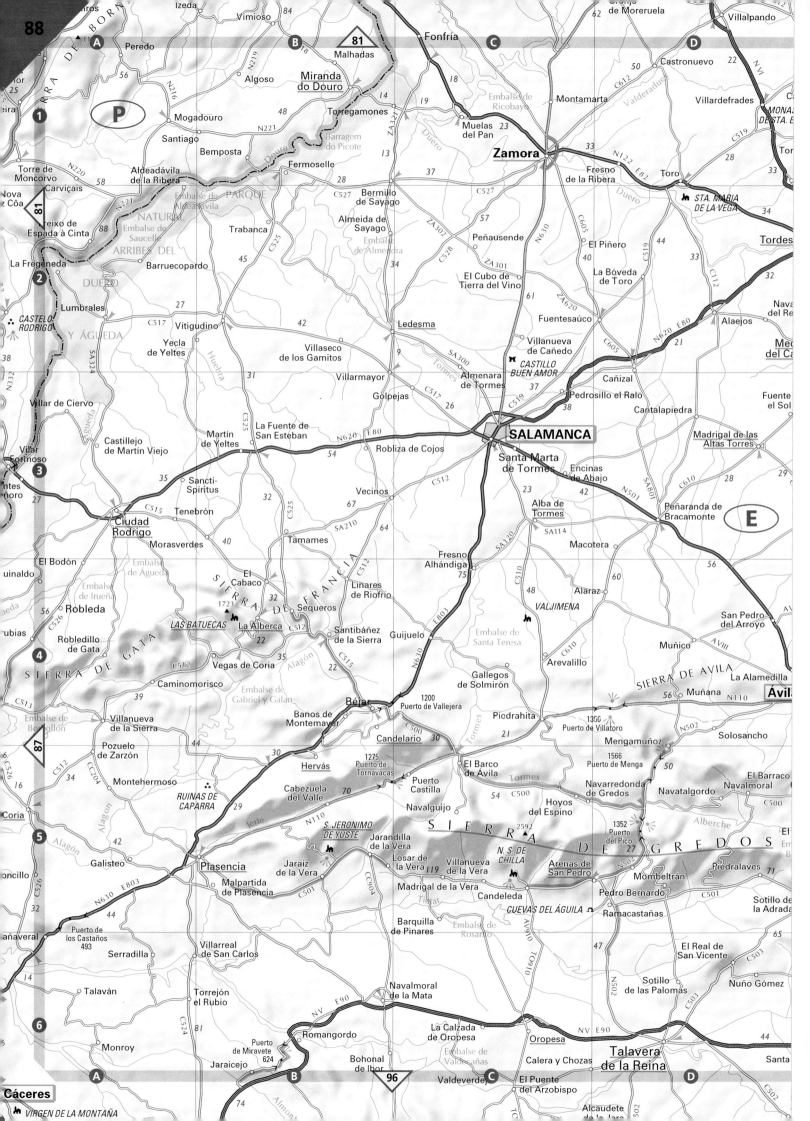

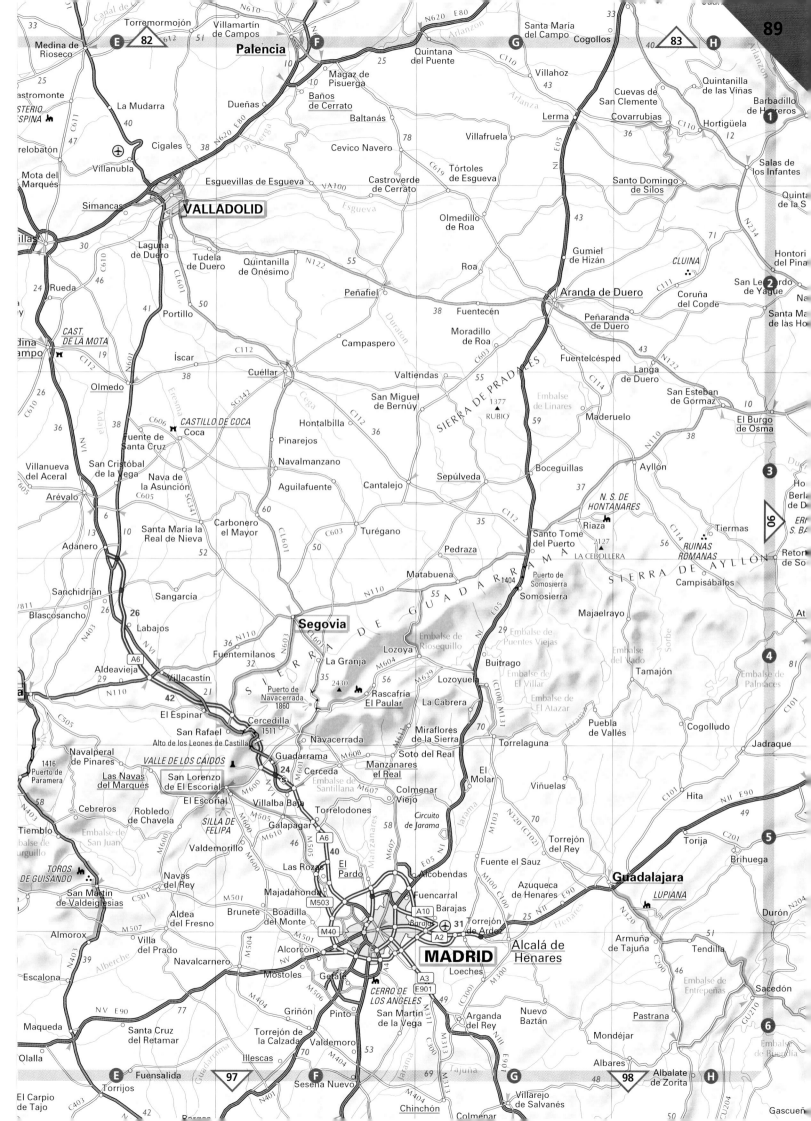

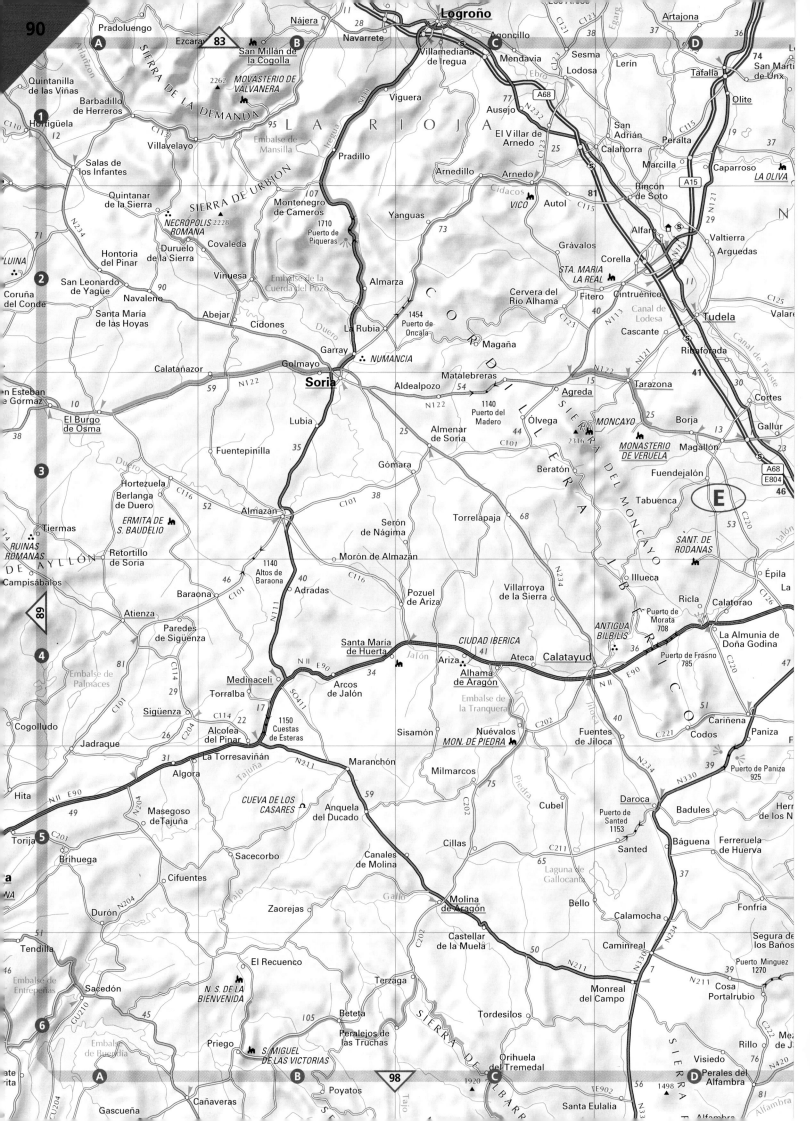

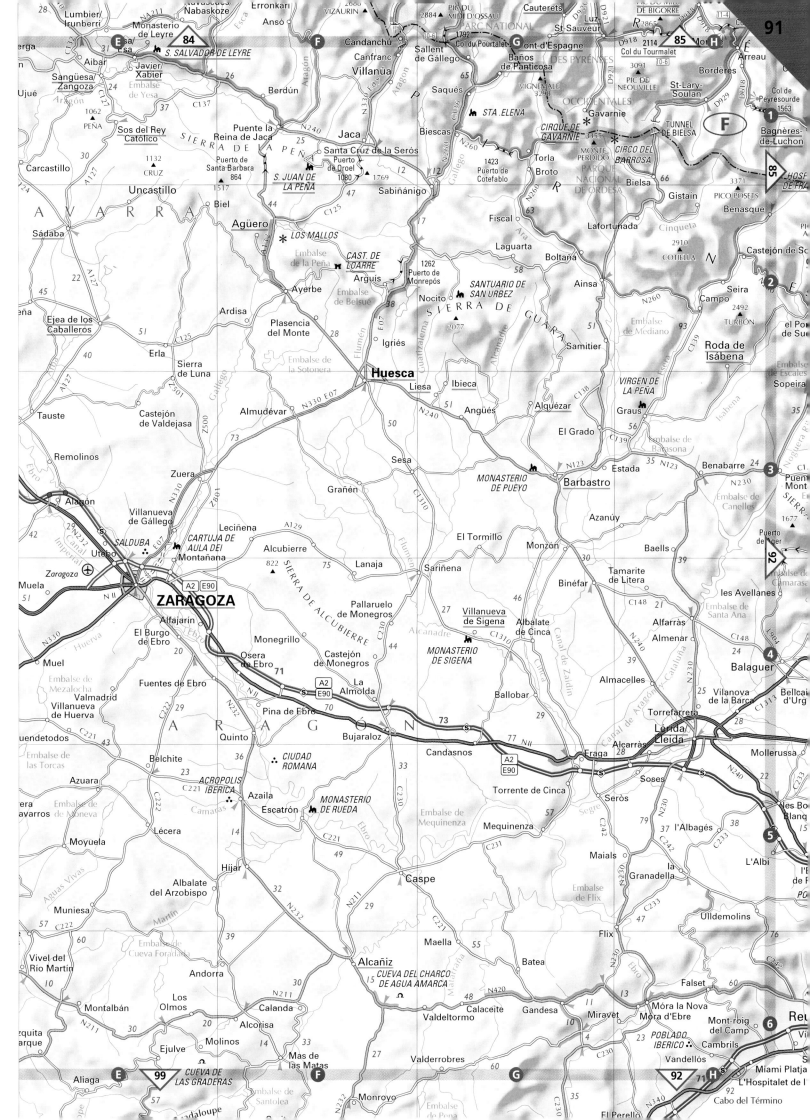

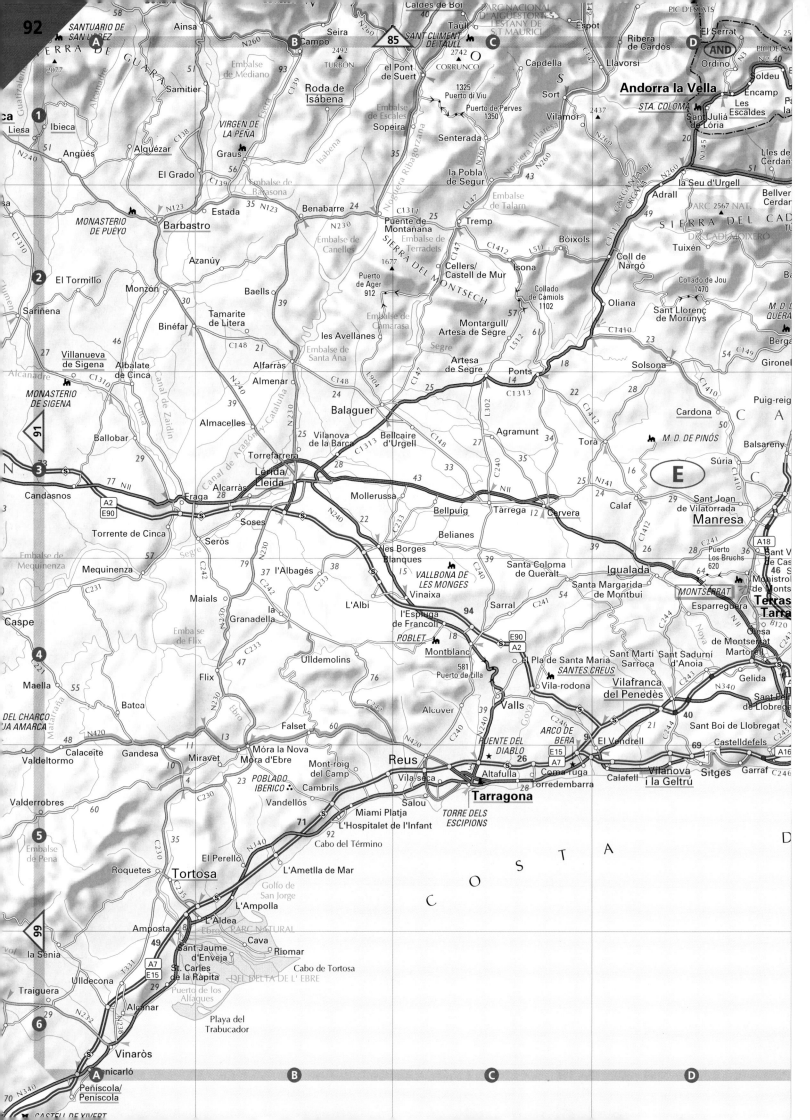

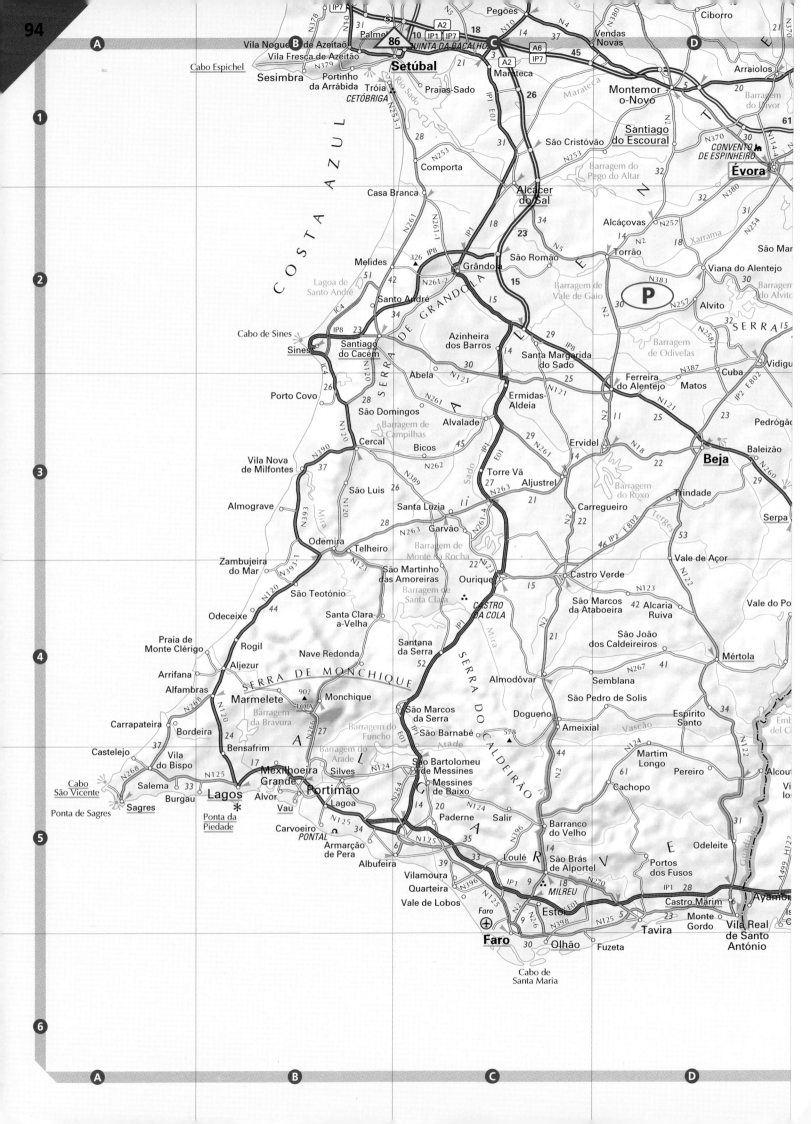

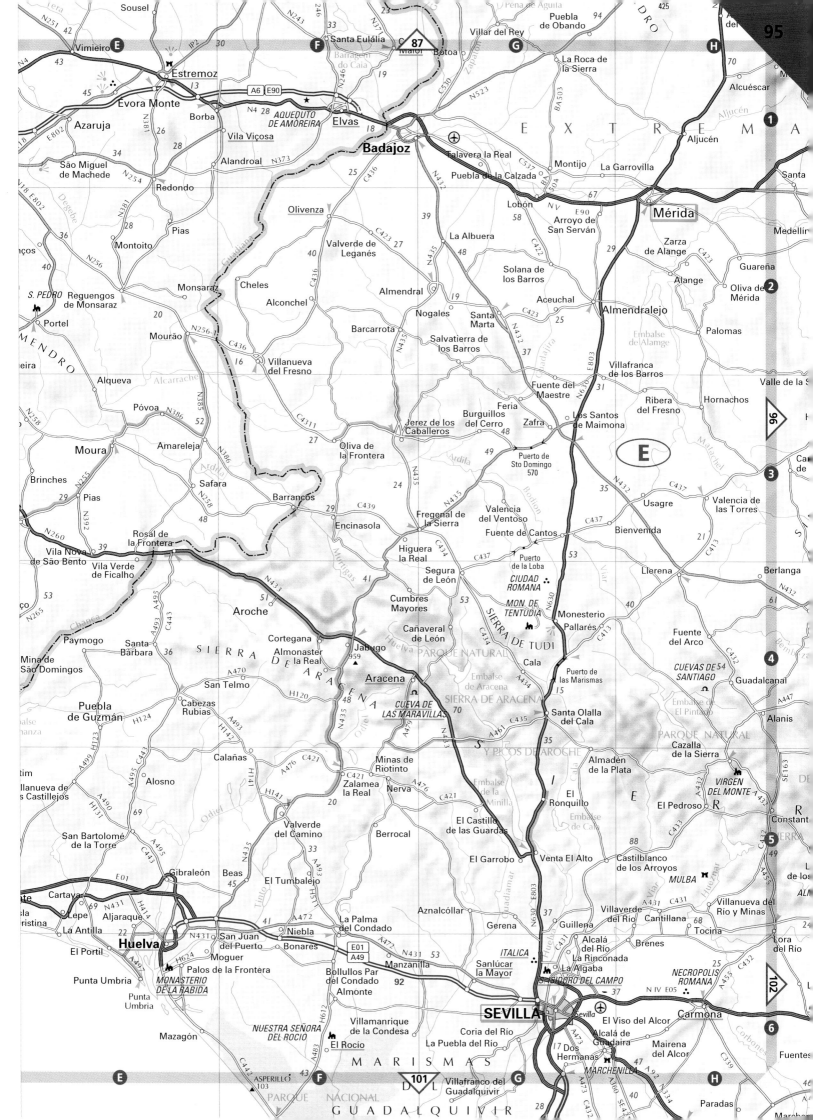

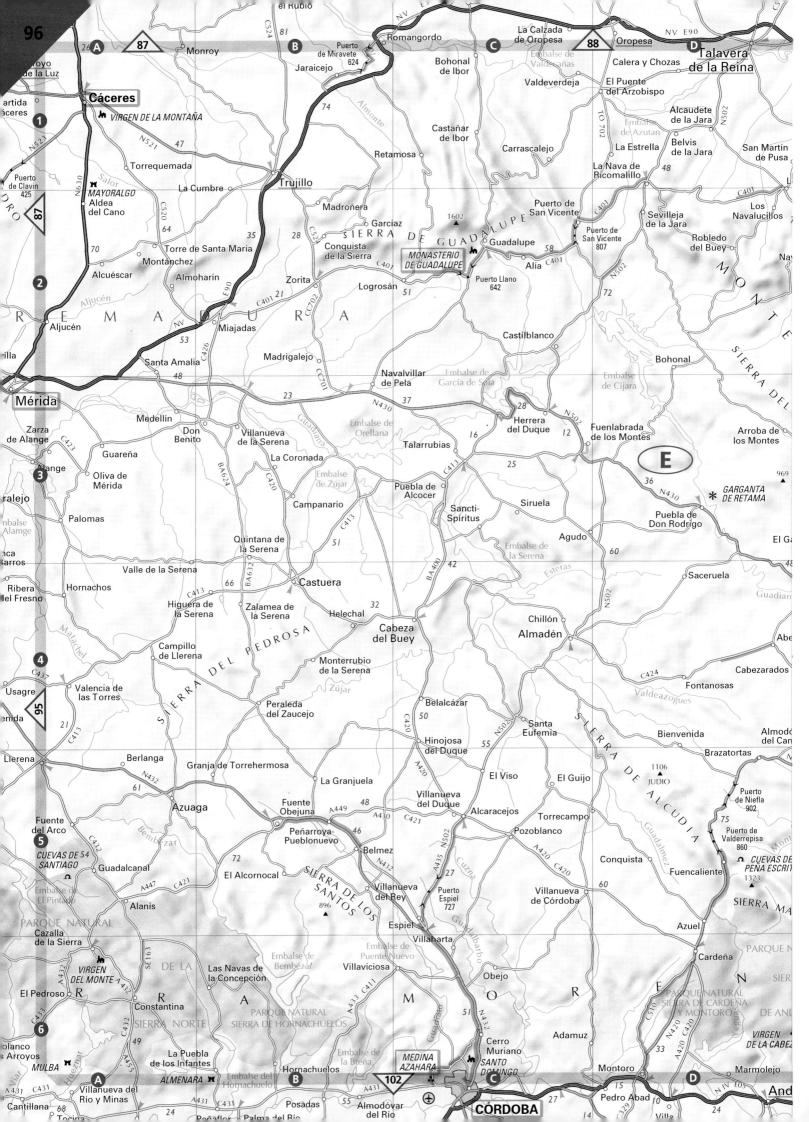

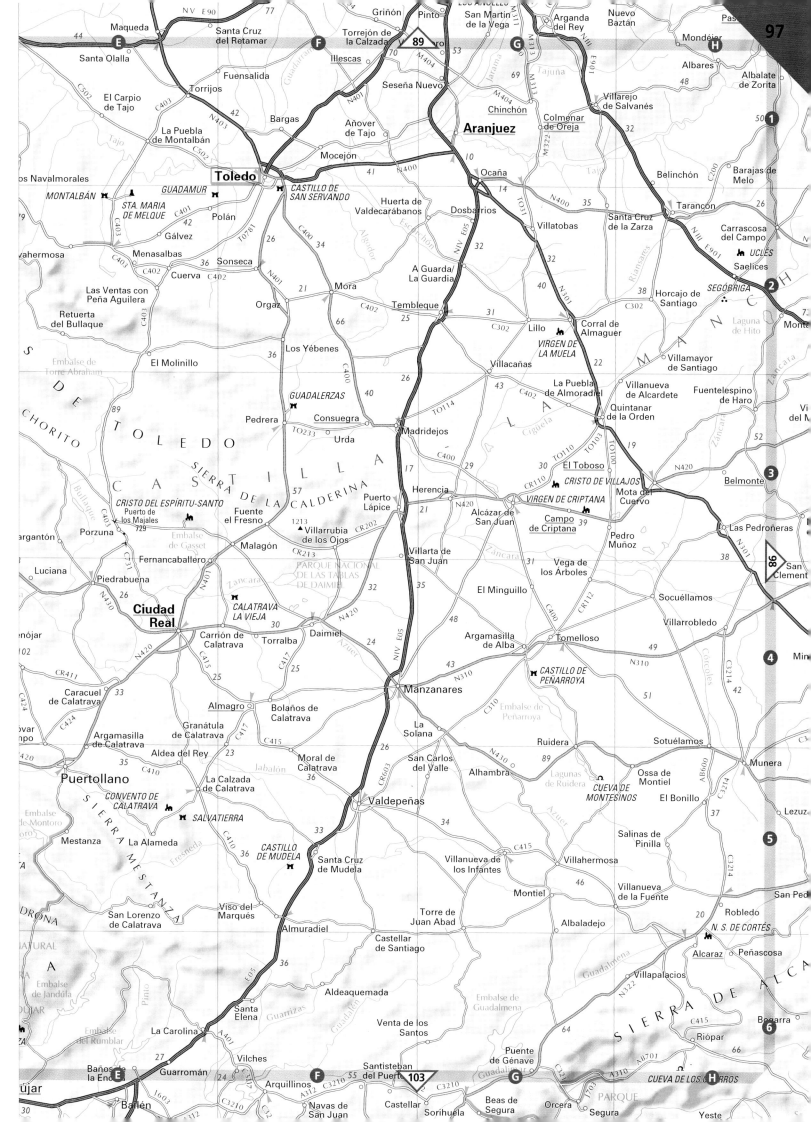

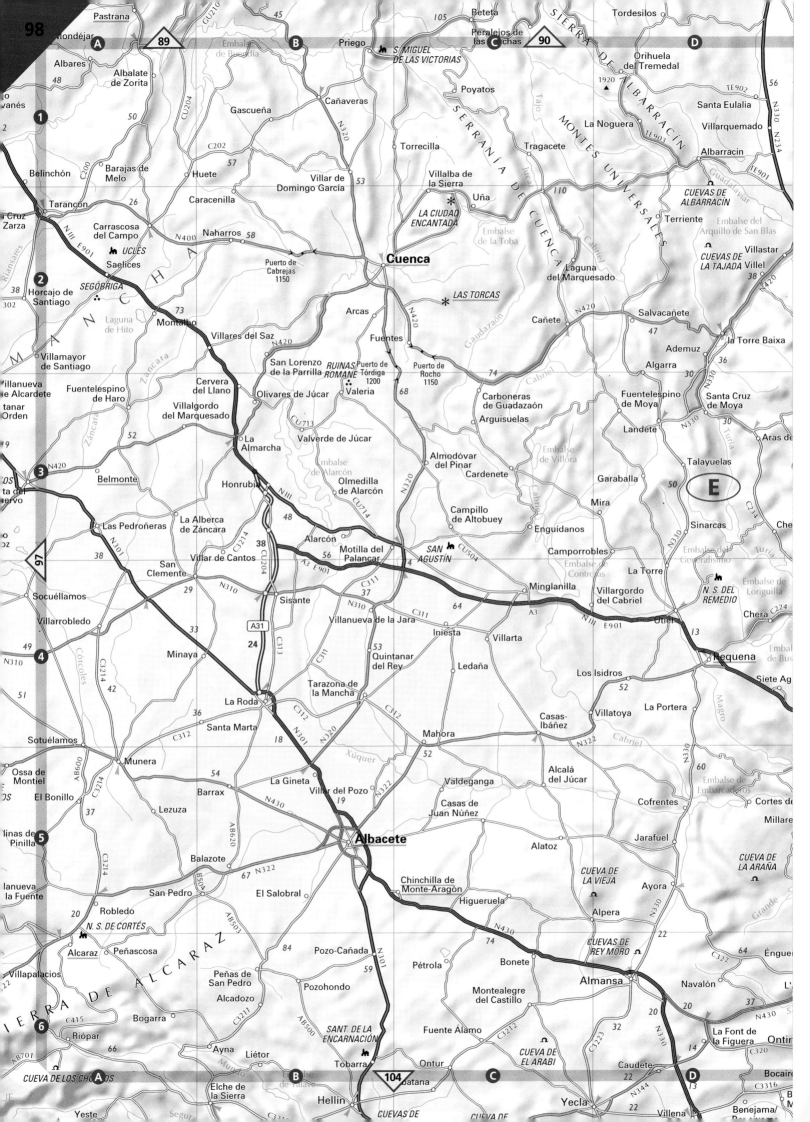

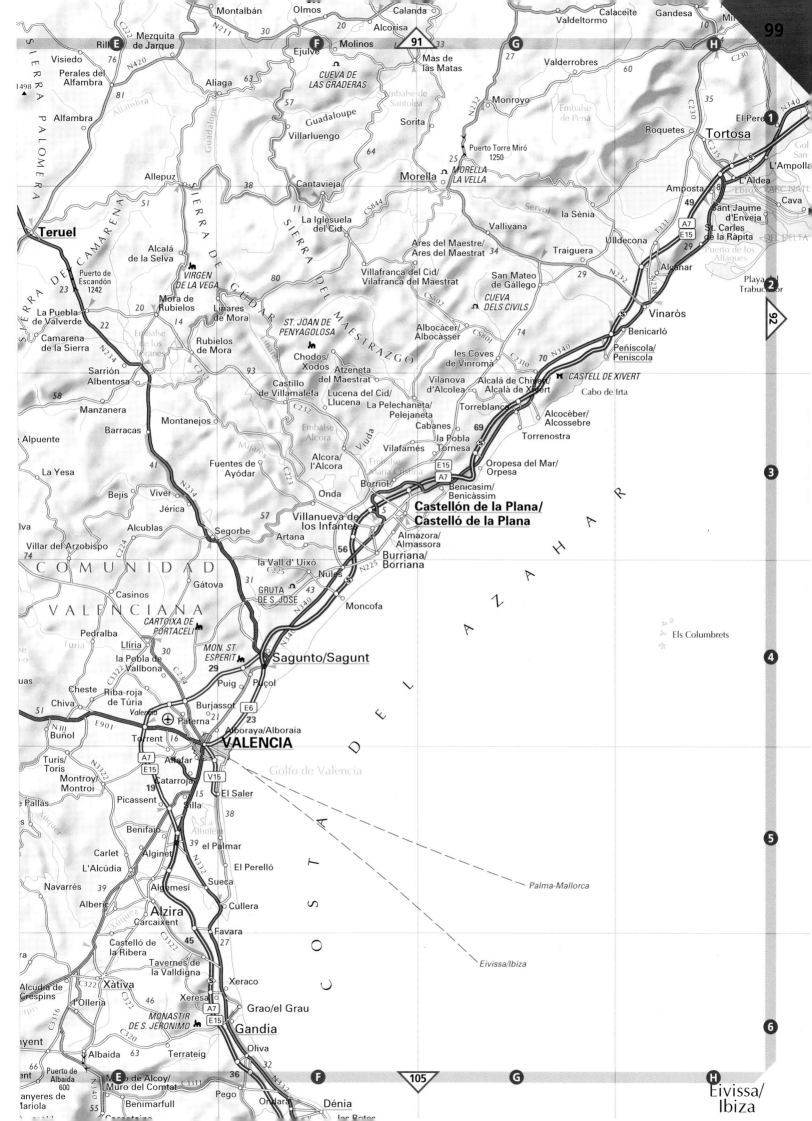

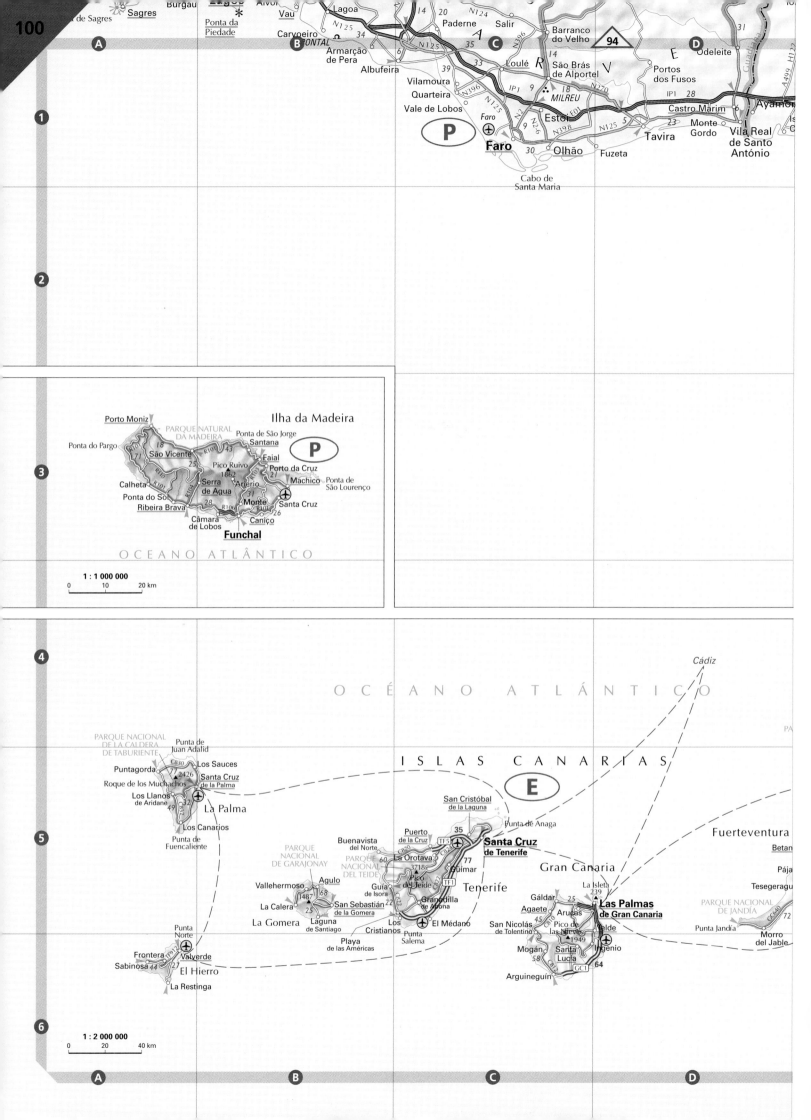

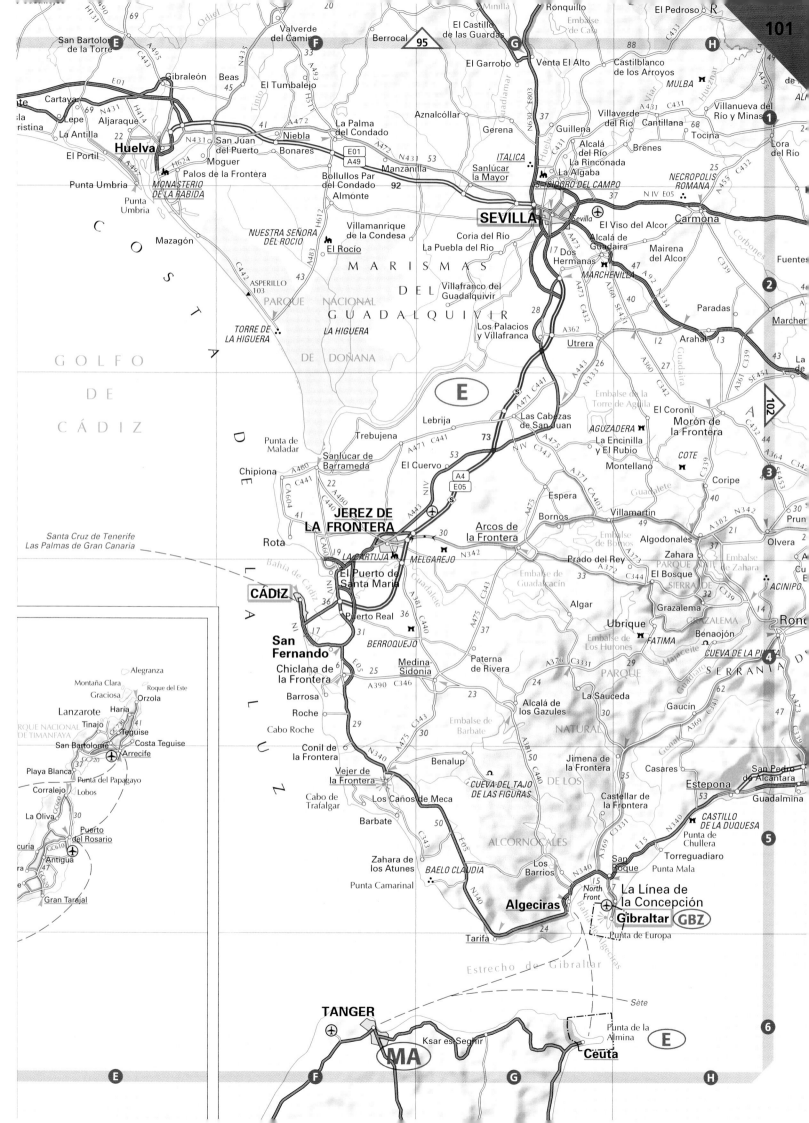

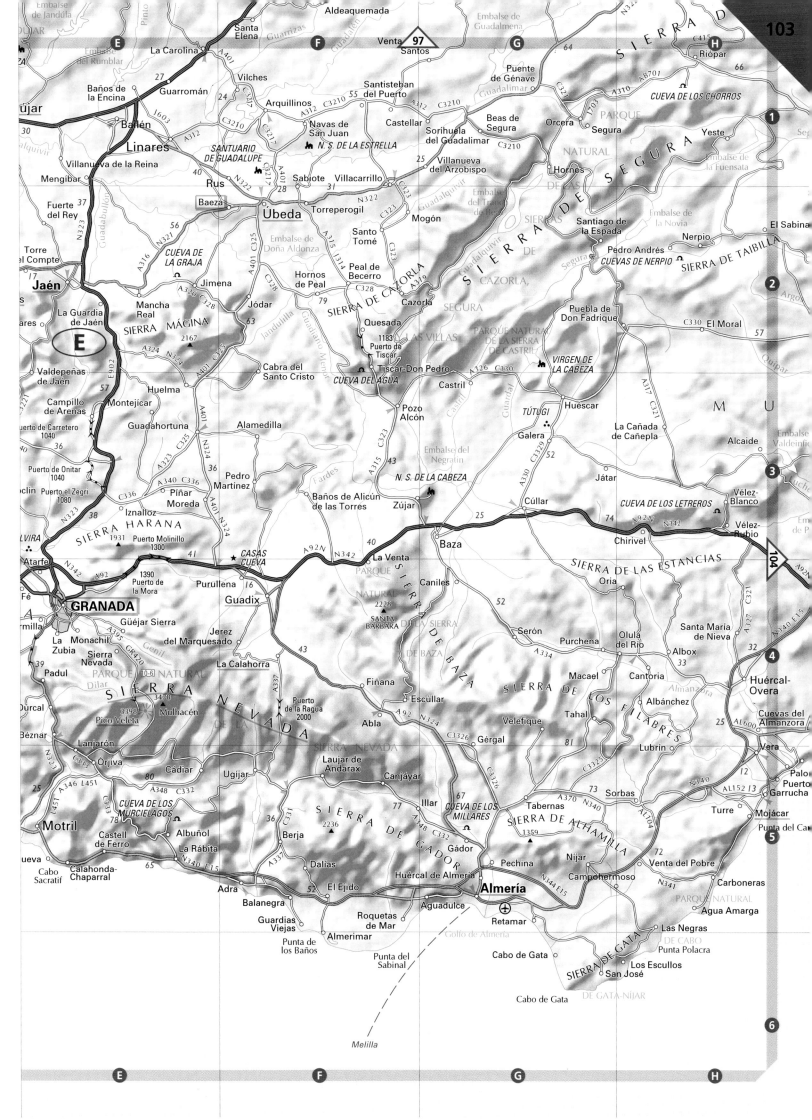

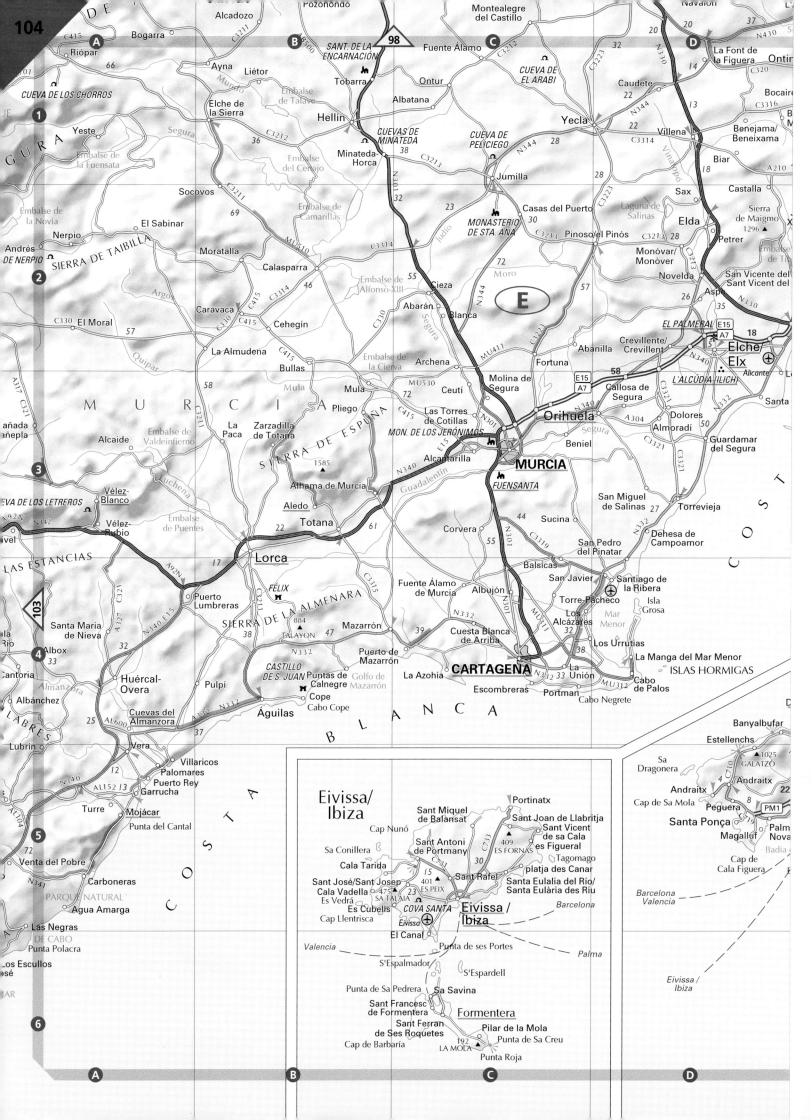

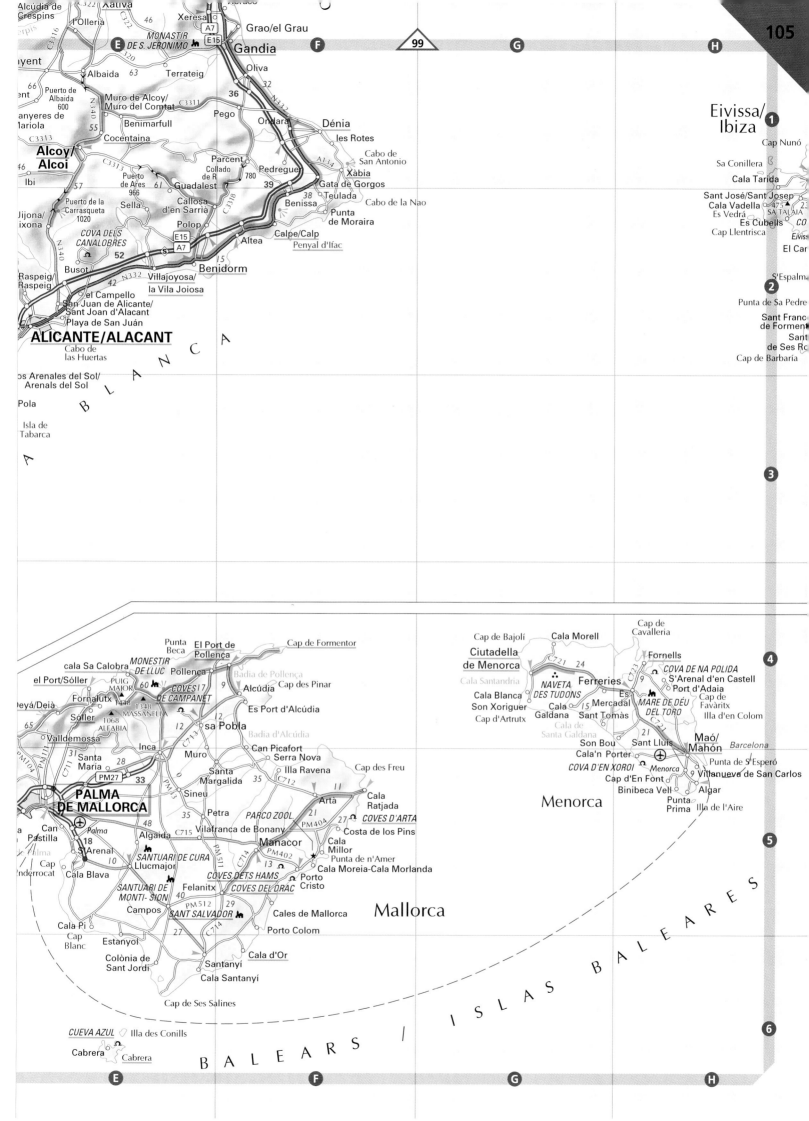

Alcúdia de Crespins
l'Olleria
C316
C322
Xàtiva
46
C222
Xeresa
A7
E15
Grao/el Grau
ayent
MONASTIR DE S. JERONIMO
E
99
F
G
Gandia
H
Albaida
63
Terrateig
Oliva
Puerto de Albaida 600
Muro de Alcoy/ Muro del Comtat
C3311
36
N332
32
Eivissa/ Ibiza
1
anyeres de Mariola
Benimarfull
C3313
55
Cocentaina
N340
Pego
Ondara
Dénia
les Rotes
Cap Nunó
Sa Conillera
Alcoy/ Alcoi
C3313
Parcent
Collado de R
780
Cabo de San Antonio
Cala Tarida
Sant José/Sant Josep
46
Ibi
57
Puerto de Ares 966
61
Guadalest
Pedreguer
A134
Xàbia
39
Gata de Gorgos
Cala Vadella
475
SA TALAIA
Jijona/ ixona
Puerto de la Carrasqueta 1020
Sella
Callosa d'en Sarrià
C3318
38
Teulada
Benissa
Cabo de la Nao
Es Vedrá
Es Cubells
Eiviss
CO
Polop
E15
Punta de Moraira
Cap Llentrisca
El Car
Raspeig/ Raspeig
COVA DELS CANALOBRES
52
A7
Altea
Calpe/Calp
Penyal d'Ifac
S'Espalm
2
Busot
N332
15
Benidorm
Punta de Sa Pedre
42
Villajoyosa/ la Vila Joiosa
Sant Franc de Formen
el Campello
San Juan de Alicante/ Sant Joan d'Alacant
Playa de San Juán
Sant de Ses Ro
ALICANTE/ALACANT
B
L
A
N
C
A
Cap de Barbaría
Cabo de las Huertas
os Arenales del Sol/ Arenals del Sol
3
Pola
A
Isla de Tabarca
A

Punta Beca
El Port de Pollença
Cap de Formentor
MONESTIR DE LLUC
cala Sa Calobra
Pollença
Badia de Pollença
Cap de Bajolí
Cala Morell
Cap de Cavalleria
4
el Port/Sóller
PUIG MAJOR
60
COVES 17 DE CAMPANET
9
Alcúdia
Cap des Pinar
Ciutadella de Menorca
C721
24
Fornells
C723
COVA DE NA POLIDA
Fornalutx
1448 1348
MASSANELLA
Es Port d'Alcúdia
Cala Santandria
NAVETA DES TUDONS
Ferreries
S'Arenal d'en Castell
Port d'Adaia
Deyá/Deià
Sóller
1068 ALFABIA
12
sa Pobla
Badia d'Alcúdia
Cala Blanca
Son Xoriguer
Mercadal
9
Es
Cala
15
Sant Tomàs
MARE DE DÉU DEL TORO
Cap de Favàritx
Illa d'en Colom
65
Valldemossa
Inca
C713
12
Muro
Can Picafort
Serra Nova
Cap d'Artrutx
Galdana
Cala de Santa Galdana
21
C722
PM111
31
Santa Maria
28
Santa Margalida
Illa Ravena
Son Bou
Sant Lluis
Maó/ Mahón
Barcelona
C711
PM27
33
Sineu
35
C712
Cap des Freu
Cala'n Porter
Menorca
Punta de S'Esperó
Villanueva de San Carlos
PM104
PALMA DE MALLORCA
Petra
Artà
Cala Ratjada
COVA D'EN XOROI
Cap d'En Font
Binibeca Vell
Algar
Can Pastilla
Palma
48
35
PARCO ZOOL.
Vilafranca de Bonany
PM404
21
27
COVES D'ARTA
Costa de los Pins
Punta Prima
Illa de l'Aire
Menorca
Algaida
C715
PM402
Manacor
Cala Millor
18
S'Arenal
SANTUARI DE CURA
10
Llucmajor
PM714
13
Punta de n'Amer
Cala Moreia-Cala Morlanda
Cala Blava
SANTUARI DE MONTI-SION
Felanitx
PM511
40
COVES DETS HAMS
COVES DEL DRAC
Porto Cristo
Cap Anderrocat
Cala Pi
Campos
PM512
29
SANT SALVADOR
Cales de Mallorca
Mallorca
27
C714
Porto Colom
Cap Blanc
Estanyol
Colònia de Sant Jordi
Santanyí
Cala d'Or
ISLAS BALEARES
Cala Santanyí
Cap de Ses Salines
CUEVA AZUL
Illa des Conills
6
Cabrera
Cabrera
B
A
L
E
A
R
S
E
F
G
H

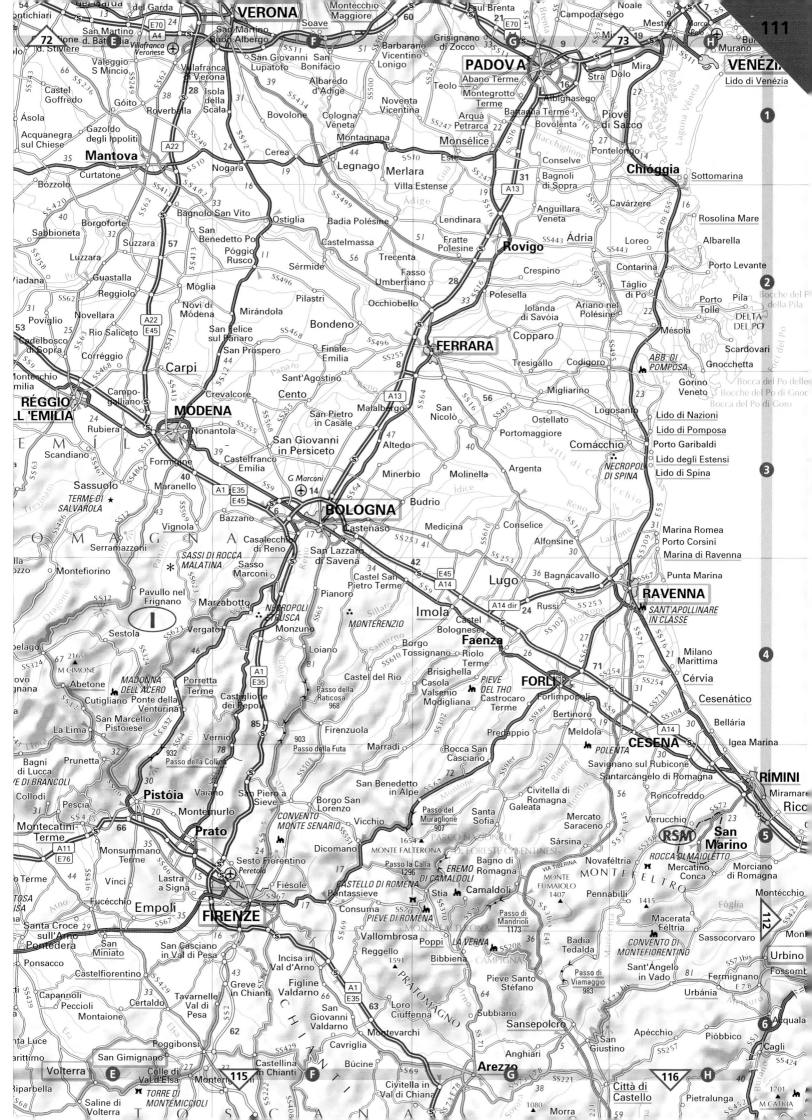

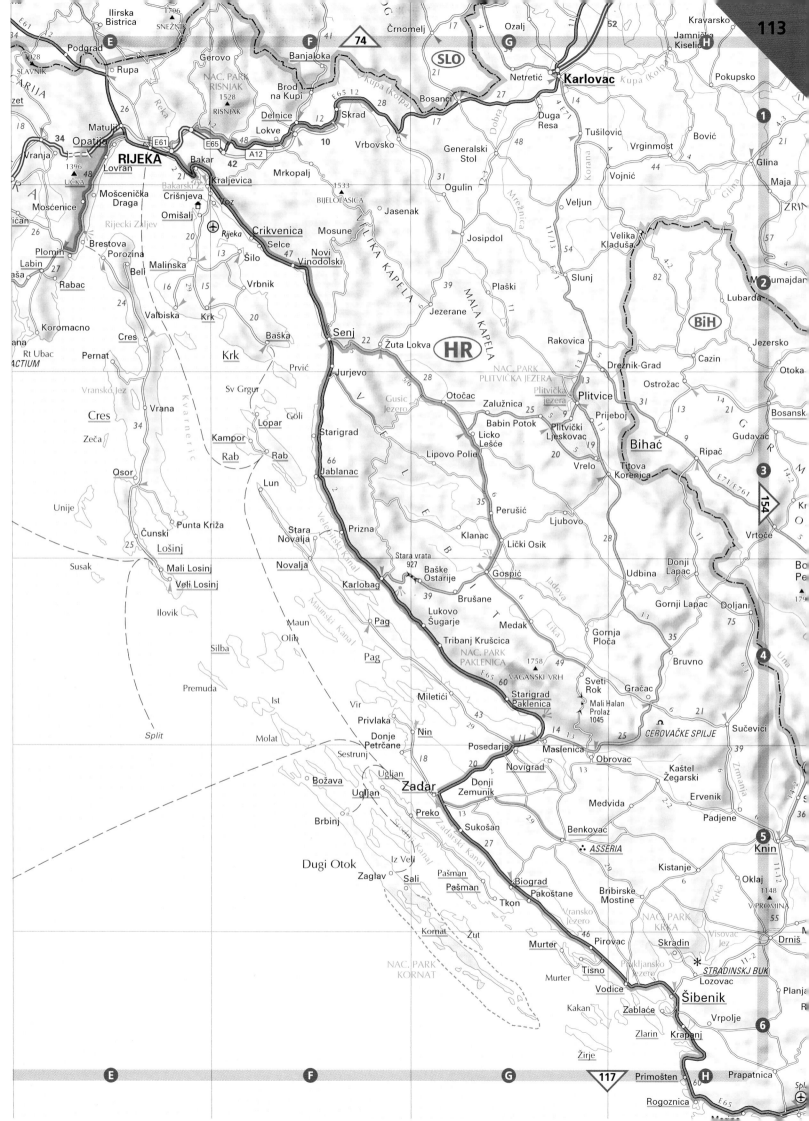

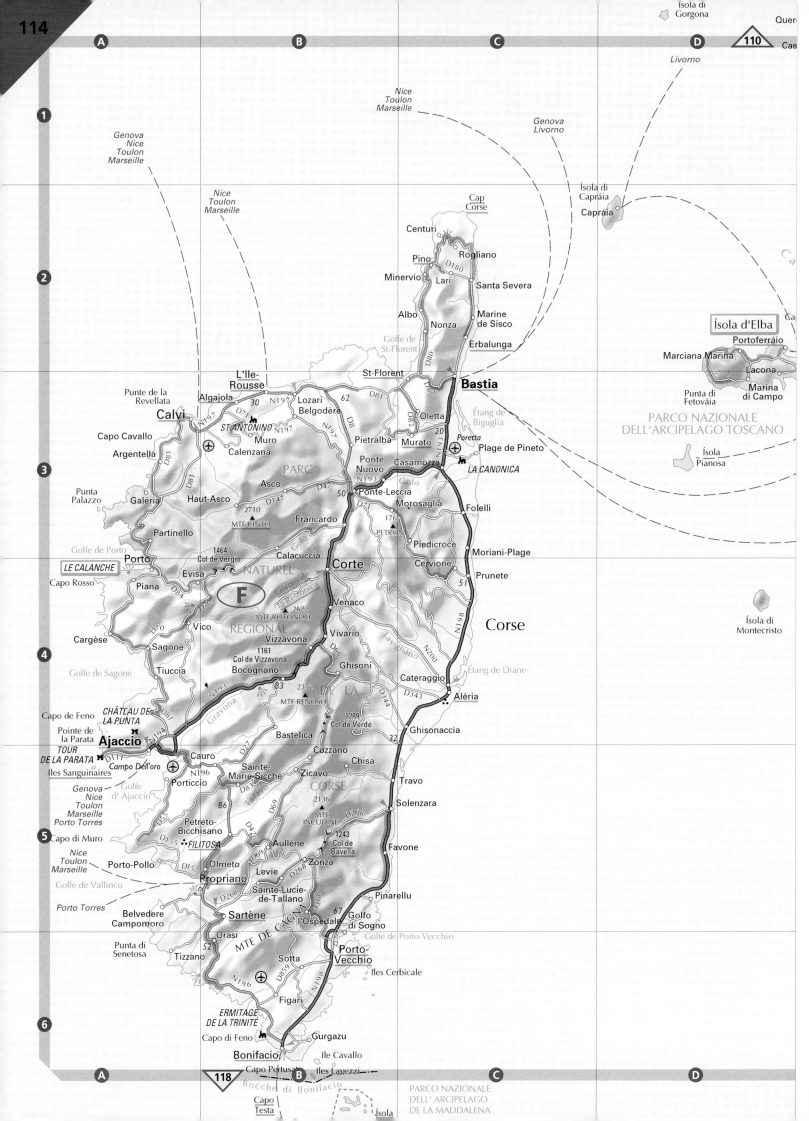

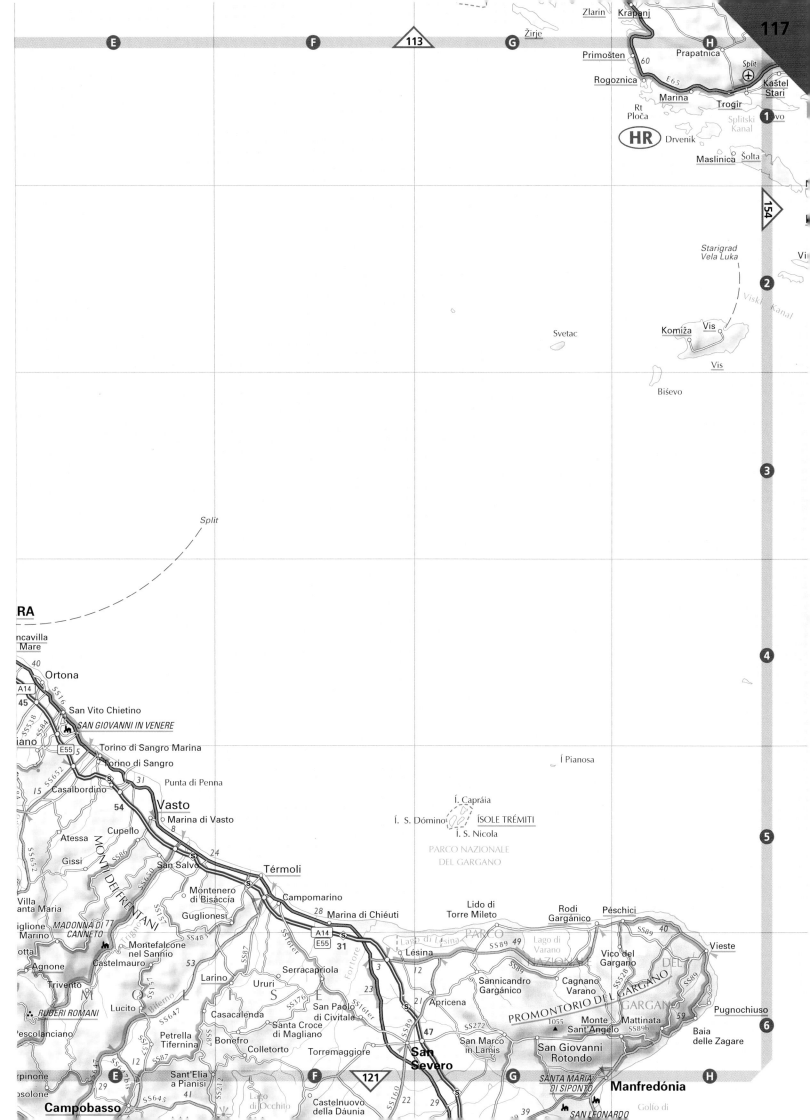

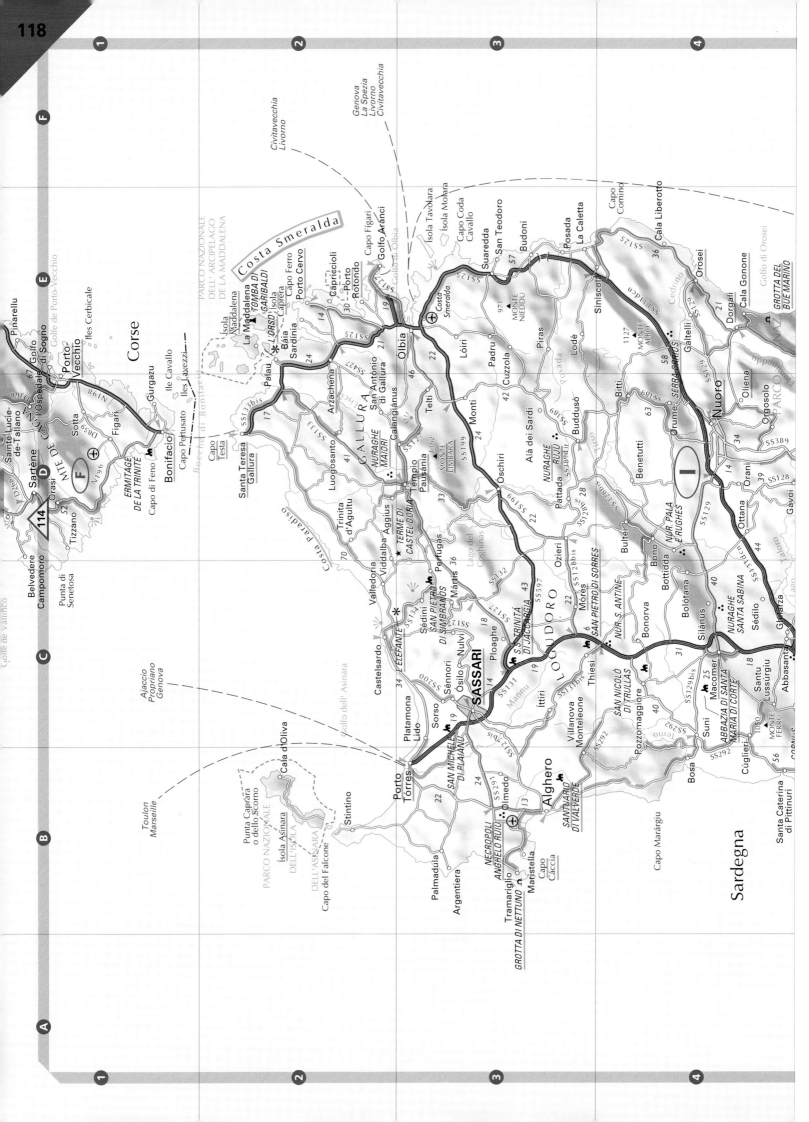

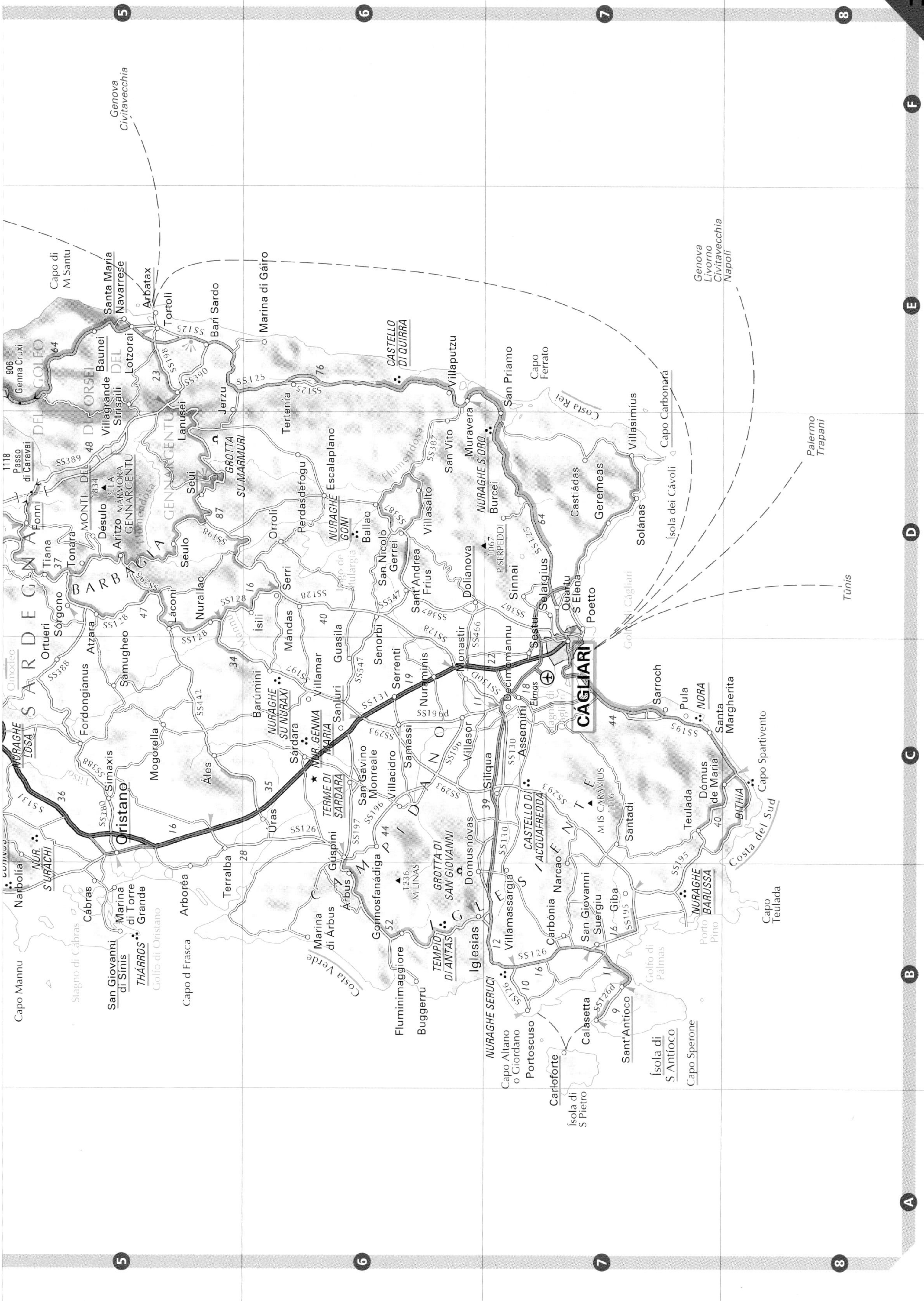

SARDEGNA

BARBÀGIA

GENNARGENTU

MONTI DEL GENNARGENTU

GOLFO DI ORSEI

Genova Civitavecchia
Genova Livorno Civitavecchia Napoli
Palermo Trapani
Tunis

Capo di M Santu
Santa Maria Navarrese
Arbatax
Tortolì
Bari Sardo
Marina di Gàiro
Baunei
Lotzorai
Villagrande Strisàili
Lanusei
Jerzu
Tertenia
Séui
Seulo
Seulo
Orroli
Perdasdefogu
Escalaplano
Ballao
San Nicolò Gerrei
San Vito
Villasalto
Muravera
Villaputzu
San Priamo
Capo Ferrato
Costa Rei
Villasimius
Capo Carbonara
Ìsola dei Càvoli
Solánas
Geremeas
Castiádas
Búrcei
Sinnai
Selárgius
S Elena
Poetto
Quartu
Sestu
CAGLIARI
Golfo di Cágliari
Sarroch
Pula
NORA
Santa Margherita
Capo Spartivento
Dómus de Maria
BITHIA
Costa del Sud
Capo Teulada
Teulada
Santadi
Capo di Pula
Fonni
Tiana
Sòrgono
Tonara
Désulo
Aritzo
Gadoni
Orroli
Serri
Làconi
Nurallao
Ìsili
Mándas
Barúmini
NURAGHE SU NURAXI
Sárdara
NUR GENNA MARIA
TERME DI SÁRDARA
Sanluri
Sanluri
Villamar
Guasila
Senórbi
Serrenti
Nuramínis
Monastir
Samatzai
Samássi
Villasor
Villacidro
San Gavino Monreale
Serramanna
Decimomannu
Assémini
Elmas
Uta
Siliqua
Villamassárgia
Narcao
Carbónia
San Giovanni Suergiu
Giba
Sant'Antioco
Ìsola di S Antioco
Calasetta
Carloforte
Ìsola di S Pietro
Portoscuso
Capo Altano o Giordano
Capo Sperone
NURAGHE SERUCI
Gonnesa
Iglésias
TEMPIO DI ANTAS
GROTTA DI SAN GIOVANNI
Domusnóvas
CASTELLO DI ACQUAFREDDA
M IS CARÁVIUS 1116
SÚLCIS
IGLESIENTE
Buggerru
Fluminimaggiore
Arbus
Marina di Árbus
Costa Verde
Guspini
Gonnosfanádiga
M LINAS 1236
ARBUREI
Terralba
Arboréa
Uras
Mogorella
Áles
Simaxis
Fordongianus
Oristano
Marina di Torre Grande
Cábras
San Giovanni di Sinis
THÁRROS
Golfo di Oristano
Capo Mannu
Capo d Frasca
Capo San Marco
Narbolia
NUR S'URÁCHI
Stagno di Cábras
Ortueri
Atzara
Samugheo
NURAGHE LOSA
Ohnodéo
Sámagheo
Passo di Caravai 1118
Genna Cruxi 906
M IS CARÁVIUS
CAMPIDANO
Villasor
GROTTA SU MARMURI
NURAGHE GONI
NURAGHE S'ORO
P LA MARMORA 1834
CASTELLO DI QUIRRA
P SERPEDDI 1067
Flumendosa
Lago de Mulárgia
SS125
SS131
SS197
SS196
SS128
SS293
SS547
SS387
SS466
SS130
SS125
SS195
SS126
SS389
SS388
SS442
SS198
SS390

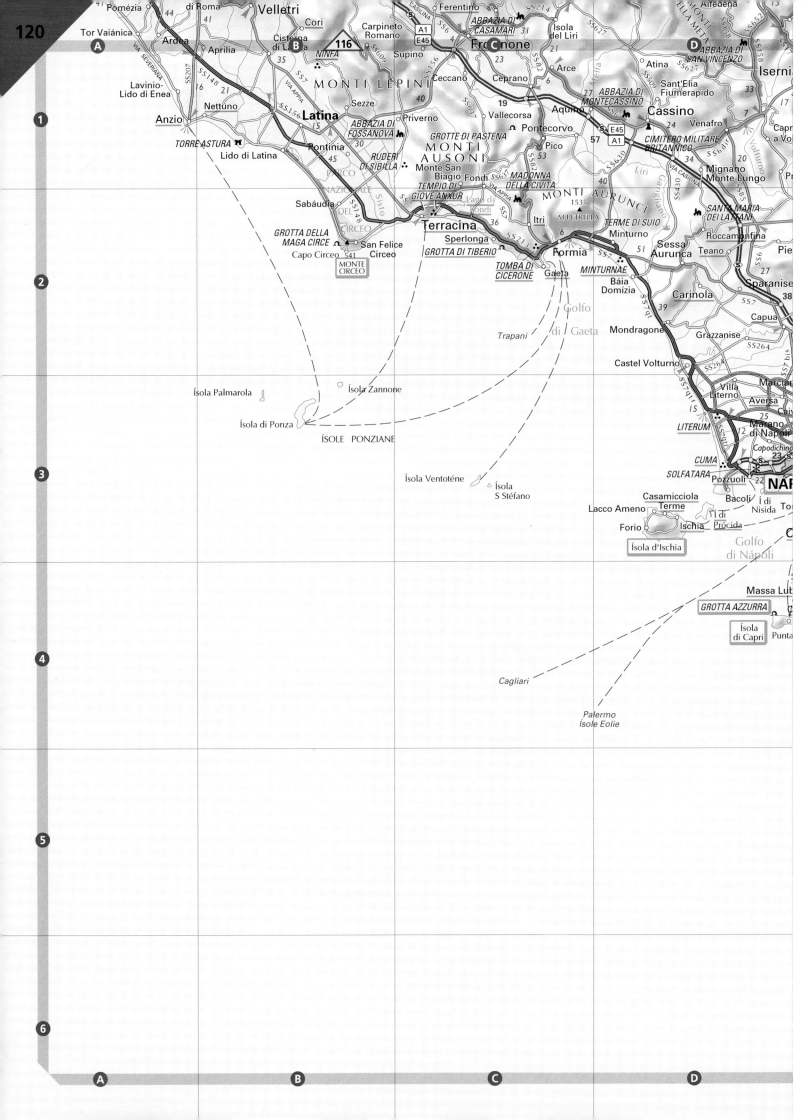

E F G H

1

2

3

4

5

6

Kérkyra
Igoumenitsa
Pátra
Durrës
Bar

BARI
FEENICE
BALSIGNANO
SS96 35 SS16
Mola
di Bari
Capurso
Rutigliano
SS634
Polignano a Mare
Casamássima
SS16
SS55
Monopoli
Conversano
37
38 Turi
GROTTE DI Castellana
CASTELLANA Grotte
18
SS379
Savelletri
SS100
SS377
SS172
Putignano
SS172
Fasano
Torre Canne
VILLAGGIO
APULO
GROTTA DI
PUTIGNANO
SS172
Alberobello
SS379
Villanova
Gióia
del Colle
Noci
13
52
SS604
37
SS377
SS172
Cisternino
26
A14
ZONA
DEI TRULLI
Locorotondo
Ostuni
SS379 E55
SS100
Martina Franca
24
San Vito
dei Normanni
Papola Casale
Kérkyra
Igoumenitsa
Pátra
28
llaneta
E843
SS581
SS581
35
SS16
Brindisi
34
34
Móttola
SS581
36
Céglie
Messápica
Ω
GROTTA
S. GIOVANNI
SS7
Palagianello
Crispiano
San Michele
Salentino
SS605
SS613
za
SS106
Massafra
SS172
37
Mesagne
39
Palagiano
10
21
Grottaglie
15
SS7
Latiano
San Pietro
Vernotico
40
SS106 E90
29
18
22
E90
SS603
Oria
Casalabate
TÁRANTO
SS7 13
Francavilla
Fontana
San
Dónaci
Squinzano
Marina
di Ginosa
San Giorgio
Iónico
Carosino
Torre
Santa Susanna
SS7ter
METAPONTIUM
23 SS7ter
Santa
Sava
San Pancrazio
Salentino
49
Campi
Salentina
San Cataldo
Capo
San Vito
Manduria
Veglie
12
LECCE
do di
etaponto
Torricella
Avetrana
SS174
47
Monteroni
di Lecce
SS16
Rocca Vecchia
anzano
co
Lido
Silvana
Campomarino
Copertino
24
SS16
SS101
SS661
Calimera
Durrës
Vlorë
Porto
Cesareo
SS664
28
35
Nardo
Galatina
SS476
Martano
SS497
17
5
Galatone
SS16
Otranto
Capo d'Ótranto
13
SS101
SS497
Máglie
SS497
Gallípoli
SS459
Parábita
SS459
SS16
Santa Cesarea
Terme
Casarano
SS476
39
SS275
Ω
GROTTA ZINZULUSA
Taviano
Ruffano
SS474
50
Ugento
Taurisano
SS275
AUSENTUM
45
SS274
Gagliano
del Capo
G O L F O   D I
T Á R A N T O
Marina di
Léuca
*Capo S Maria
di Léuca*

E F G H

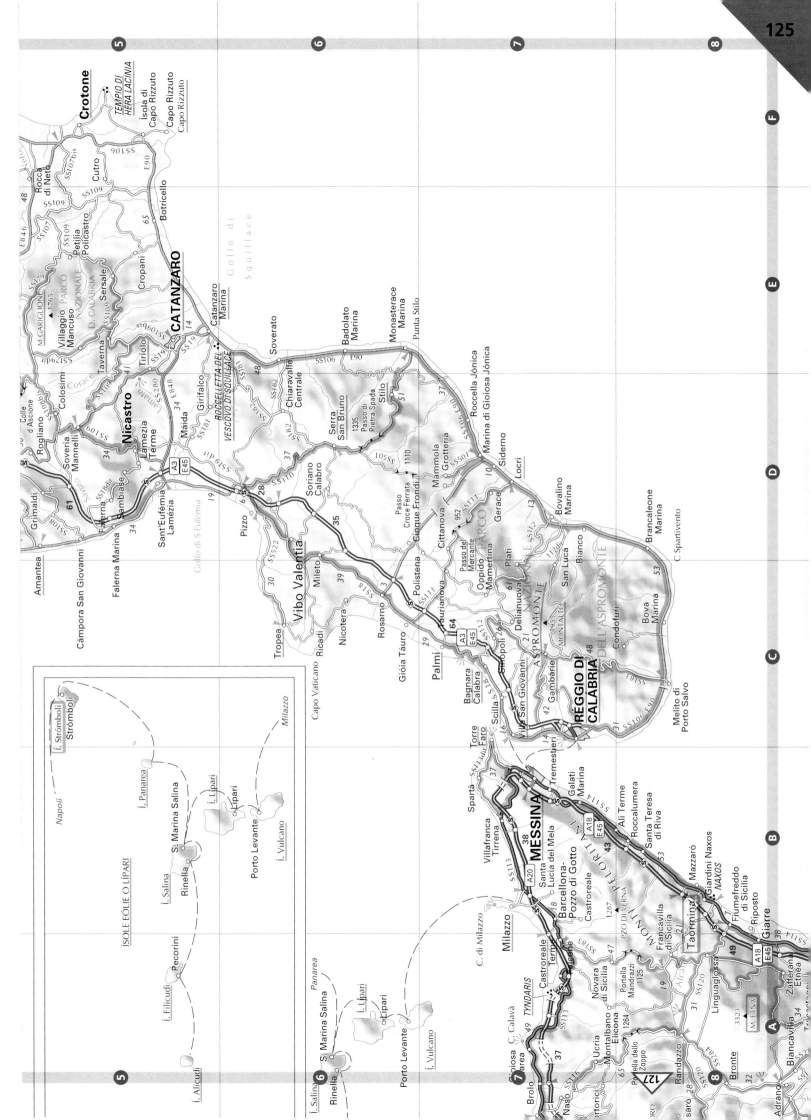

Crotone

TEMPIO DI HERA LACINIA
Isola di Capo Rizzuto
Capo Rizzuto
Capo Rizzuto

Rocca di Neto
Cutro
Petilia Policastro
Botricello

CATANZARO
Catanzaro Marina

Golfo di Squillace

Villaggio Mancuso
M. GARIGLIONE ▲ 1765
PARCO NAZIONALE D. CALABRIA

Sersale
Cropani

Taverna
Tiriolo

Nicastro
Soveria Mannelli
Lamèzia Terme
Girifalco
Màida
ROCCELLETTA DEL VESCOVO DI SQUILLACE

Soverato

Badolato Marina
Monasterace Marina
Punta Stilo

Colle d'Ascione
Rogliano
Colosimi

Sant'Eufémia Lamèzia
Falerna
Sambiase

Chiaravalle Centrale

Serra San Bruno
1335 Passo di Pietra Spada
Stilo

Roccella Jonica
Marina di Gioiosa Jónica

Grimaldi
Falerna Marina
61

Pizzo

Soriano Calabro
Cinque Frondi

Passo Croce Ferrata
1110
Mammola
Grotteria
Siderno
Locri

Amantea
Càmpora San Giovanni

Vibo Valentia
Mileto

Tropea
Ricadi
Nicotera

Rosarno
Cittanova
952
Passo del Mercante
Oppido Mamertina
Platì

Gerace
Bovalino Marina

Brancaleone Marina
C. Spartivento

Gióia Táuro
Taurianova
64

Palmi
Bagnara Calabra
Scilla

Delianuova
San Luca
Bianco
Bova Marina
Condofuri

Capo Vaticano

REGGIO DI CALABRIA
Gàmbarie
Villa San Giovanni

Melito di Porto Salvo

ISOLE EÓLIE O LÍPARI

í. Strómboli
Strómboli

í. Panarea

í. Filicudi
Pecorini

í. Salina
S. Marina Salina
Rinella

í. Lípari
Lípari

Porto Levante
í. Vulcano

Milazzo

Torre Faro
Tremestieri

Spartà
MESSINA
Galati Marina

Ali Terme
Roccalumera
Santa Teresa di Riva

Villafranca Tirrena

Santa Lucia del Mela
Barcellona-Pozzo di Gotto
Castroreale

Mazzaró
Giardini Naxos
NAXOS

í. Vulcano
Porto Levante

í. Alicudi

S. Marina Salina
Rinella

Brolo

Gióiosa Marea
C. Calavà

Castroreale Terme
TYNDARIS

Novara di Sicilia
Francavilla di Sicilia
Taormina
Fiumefreddo di Sicilia
Riposto
Giarre

Gióiosa Marea

Ucrìa
Montalbano Elicona

Portella Mandrazzi 1125
Linguaglossa

M. ETNA ▲ 3323

Bronte
Zafferana Etnea

Adrano

Napoli

Milazzo

Panarea

A   B   C   D

Cágliari
Gaeta

Valletta-Malta

Ústica
Cágliari

Génova
Livorno
Nápoli

1

Capo S. Vito

Ísola delle
Fémmine

Capo
Gallo

Mondello

San Vito lo Capo

P Ráisi

MONTE PELLEGRINO

Punta Ráisi

6

12

600

Golfo di
Palermo

Cínisi

Capaci

PALERMO

C. Zafferano

Golfo di
Castellammare

SS113

49

SS113

39

SOLUNTO

Custonaci

SAN MARTINO
DELLE SCALE

17

Monreale

Bagheria

Erice

E90

A29

Castellammare
del Golfo

Partinico

29

48

A19

Trápani

Valderice

20

SS187

42

7

29

SS121

E90

Términi
Imerese

Í. di Lévanzo

38

SS187

SS113

17

Piana degli
Albanesi

Misilmeri

58

Trabia

ÍSOLE ÉGADI

Paceco

32

Álcamo

23

Cáccamo

Buonfornello

13

12

Calatafimi

San Cipirello

Marineo

A1

Í. Favignana

31

A29dir

SEGESTA

SS188a

Camporeale

MADONNA DEL
ROSARIO

41

SS118

Villafrati

35

M

MOZIA

SS115

31

10

A29

SS119

1613

41

Í. dello Stagnone

Freddo

47

SS624

20

R BUSAMBRA

Roccapalúmba

SS120

Marsala

SS188

38

Salemi

12

Gibellina

Bélice Destro

Corleone

6

Alia

Caltavu

22

14

RUDERI
DI GIBELLINA

44

17

Lercara
Friddi

68

Petrosino

SS119

Santa
Ninfa

Bélice Sin.

Santa Margherita
di Bélice

22

24

Prizzi

SS188

SS121

Mázaro

Partanna

SS188

35

Sambuca
di Sicília

30

17

SS188

SS189

Mazara del Vallo

E90

31

Castelvetrano

SS115

35

18

34

Chiusa Scláfani

Bivona

SS118

Santo Stéfano
Quisquina

Mussòmeli

A29

Campobello
di Mazara

Menfi

Lago
Aráncio

Búrgio

64

ROCCHE DI CUSA

21

43

Caltabellotta

44

Alessándria
della Rocca

Casteltérmini

C. Granítola

SELINUNTE

Marinella

SS386

San Biágio
Plátani

Milena

Serradifalco

SAN CALOGERO

16

85

Verdura

Sciacca

Ribera

Cattólica
Eraclea

Arágona

Racalmuto

3

C. S. Marco

ERACLEA MINOA

Raffadali

SS640

35

Car

Sicilia

61

SS115

SS118

SS189

SS410

Agrigento

SS122

Favara

SS410

Porto
Empedocle

VALLE
DEI TEMPLI

Naro

SS410D

Campobello
di Licata

4

CASTELLO DI
MONTECHIARO

44

Palma di
Montechiaro

Trápani
Marsala

Pantelleria

Pantelleria

836

I

Ísola di
Pantelleria

Pantelleria
Túnis

Linosa

5

Porto
Empedocle

Ísola di Linosa

Gozo

Palermo

Victoria

Mgarr

M

ÍSOLE
PELÁGIE

I

Mellieha

Mosta

Sliema

Valletta

Ísola di Lampione

Rabat

Dingli

Vittoriosa

Luqa

Zurrieq

6

Malta

Ísola di Lampedusa

Birzebbuga

A   B   C   D

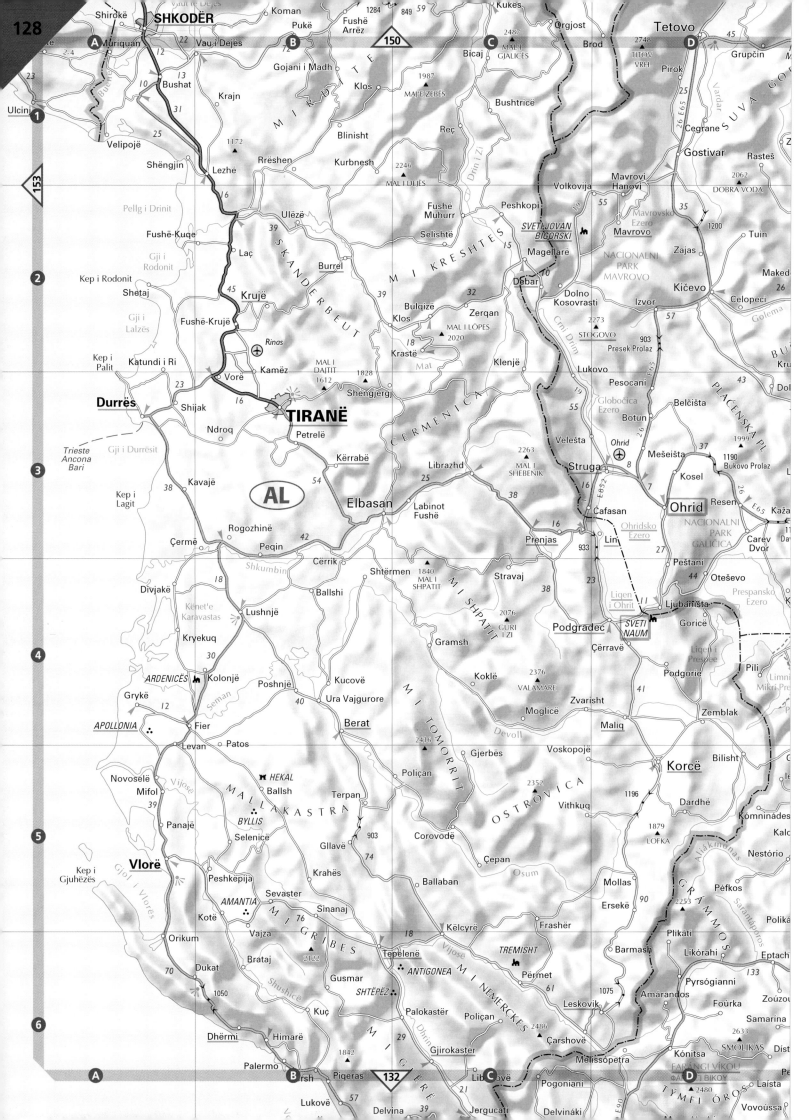

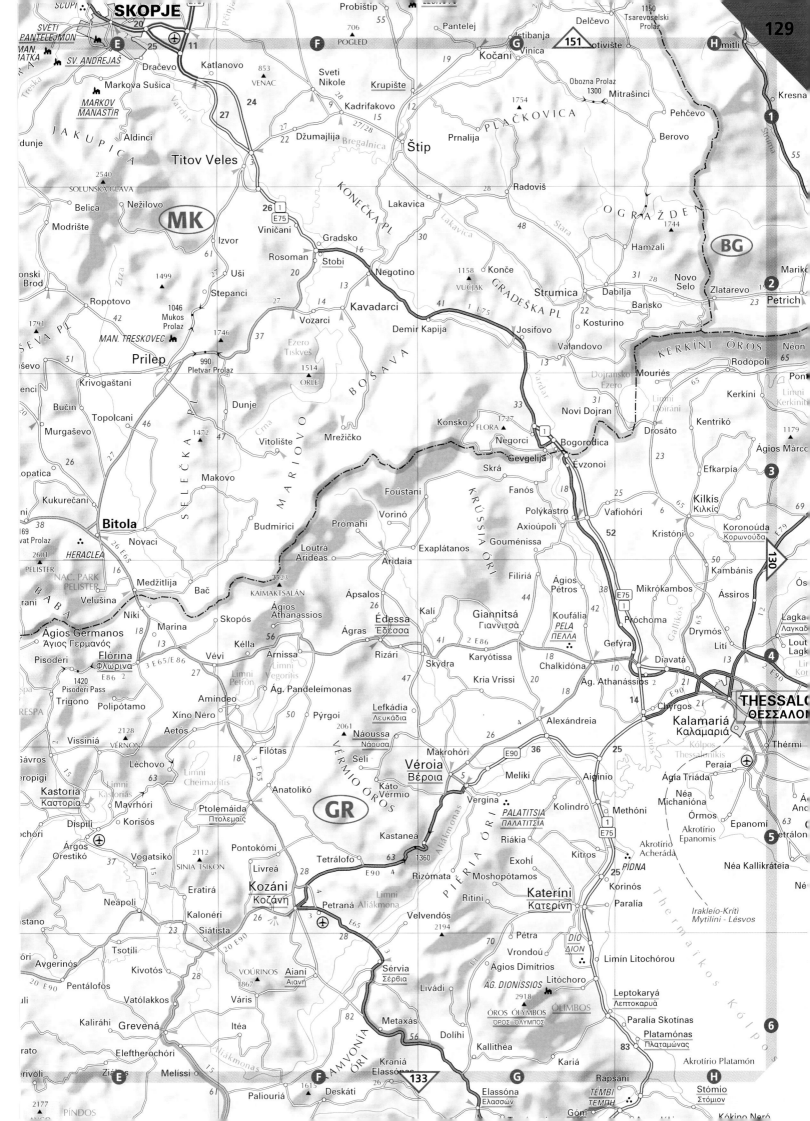

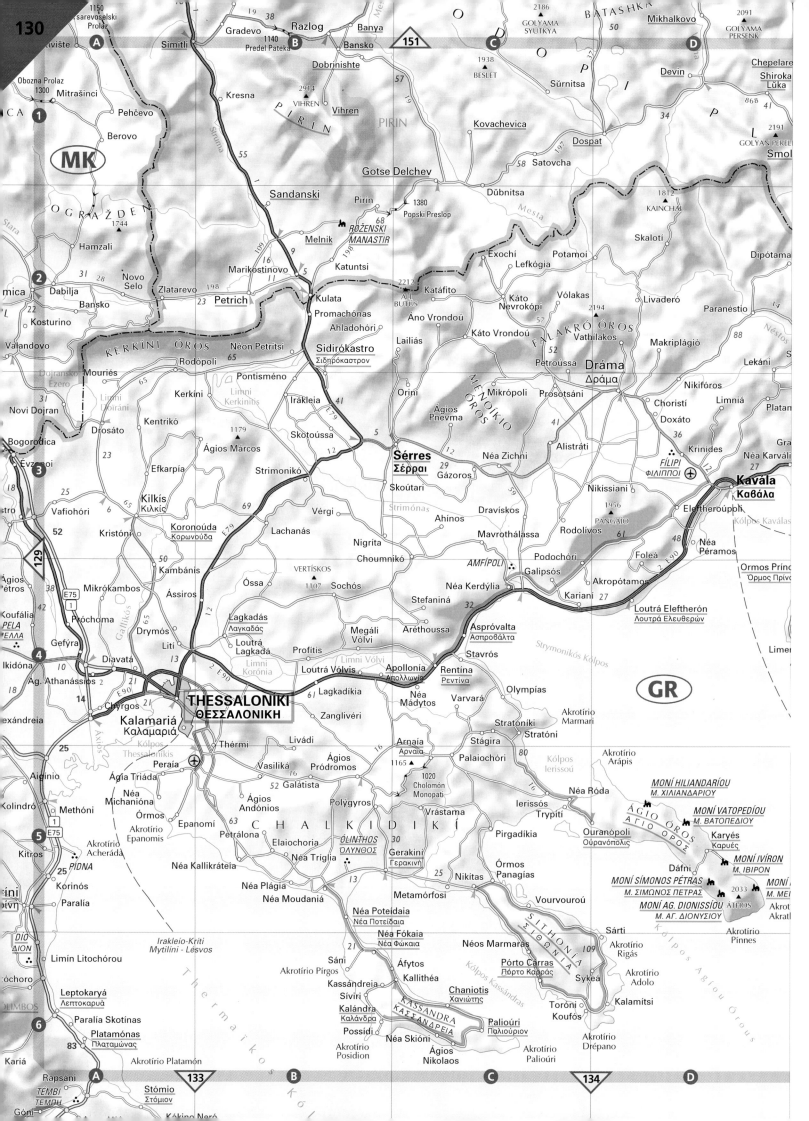

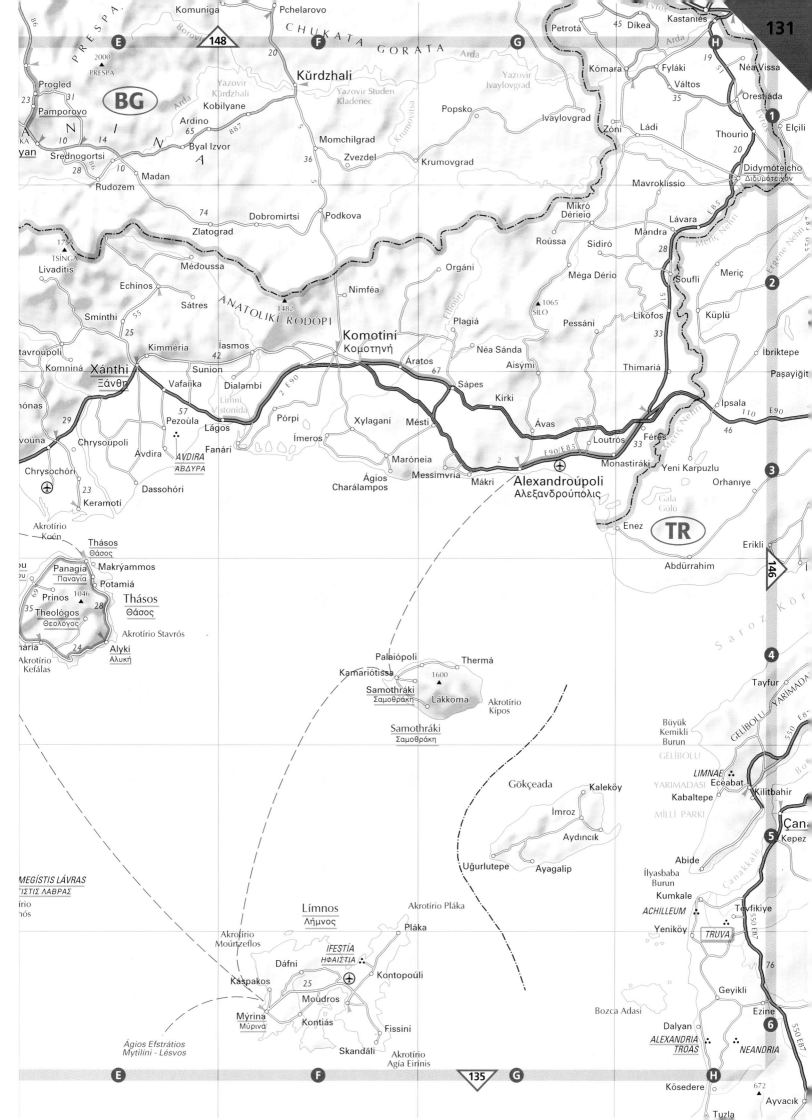

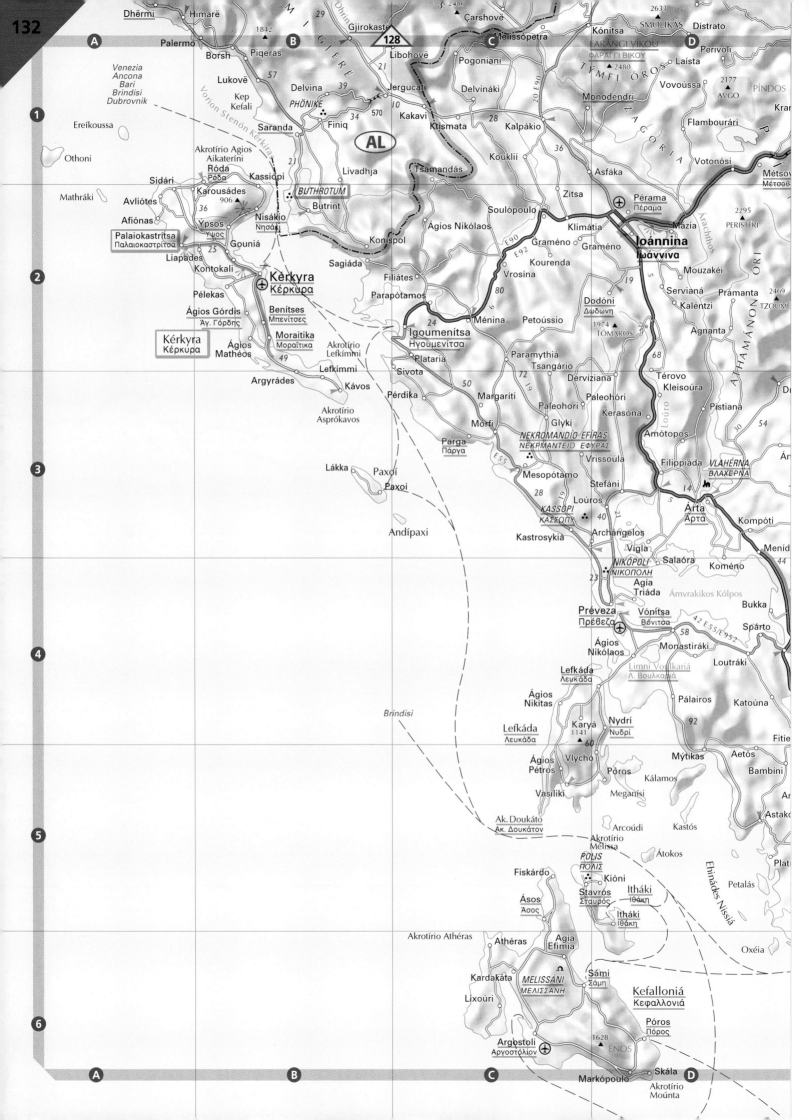

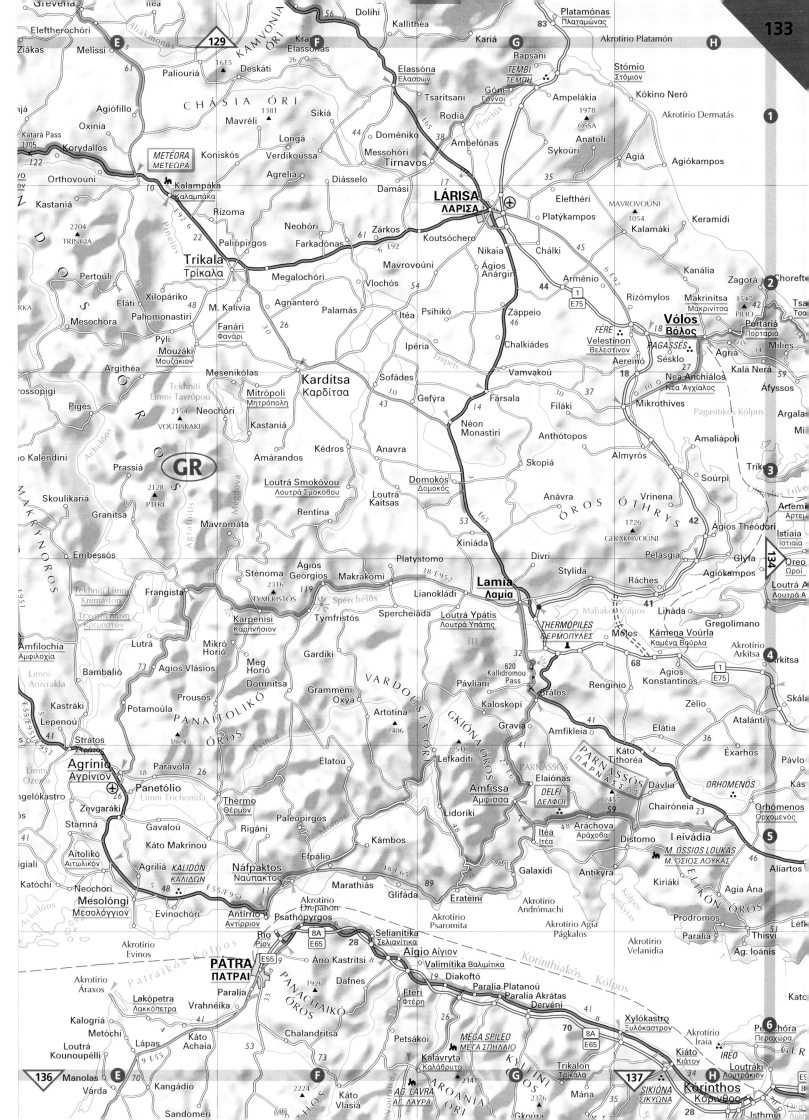

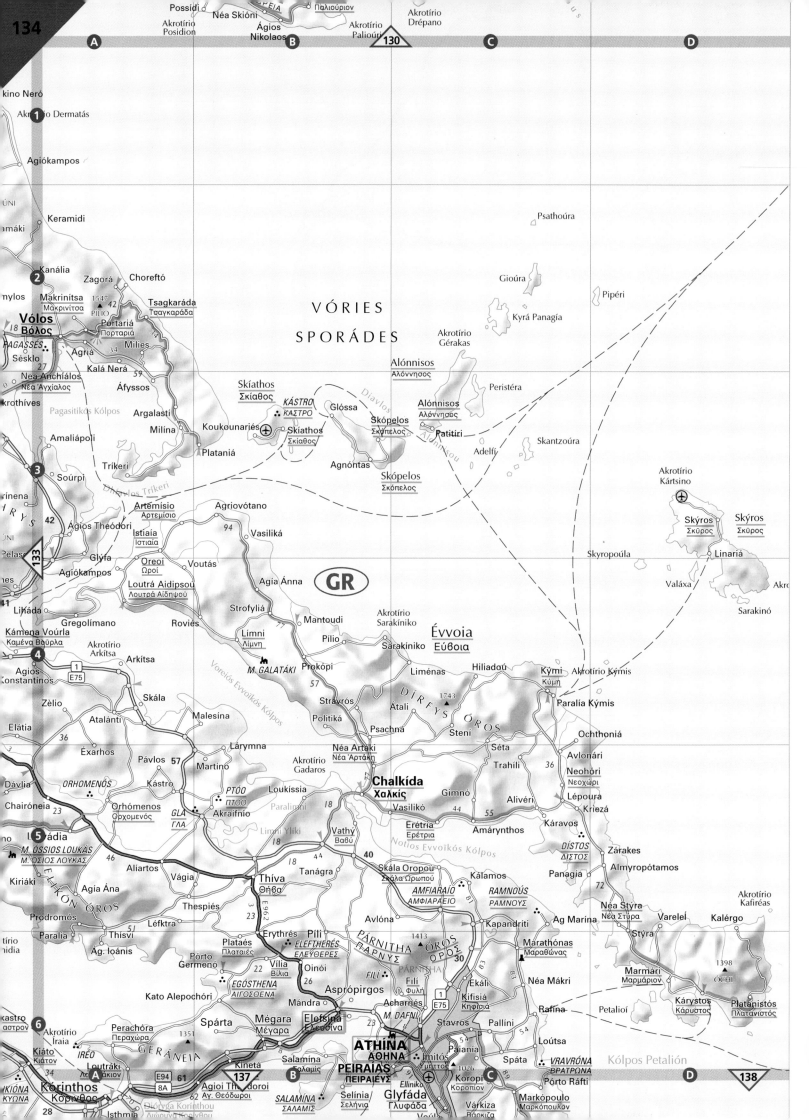

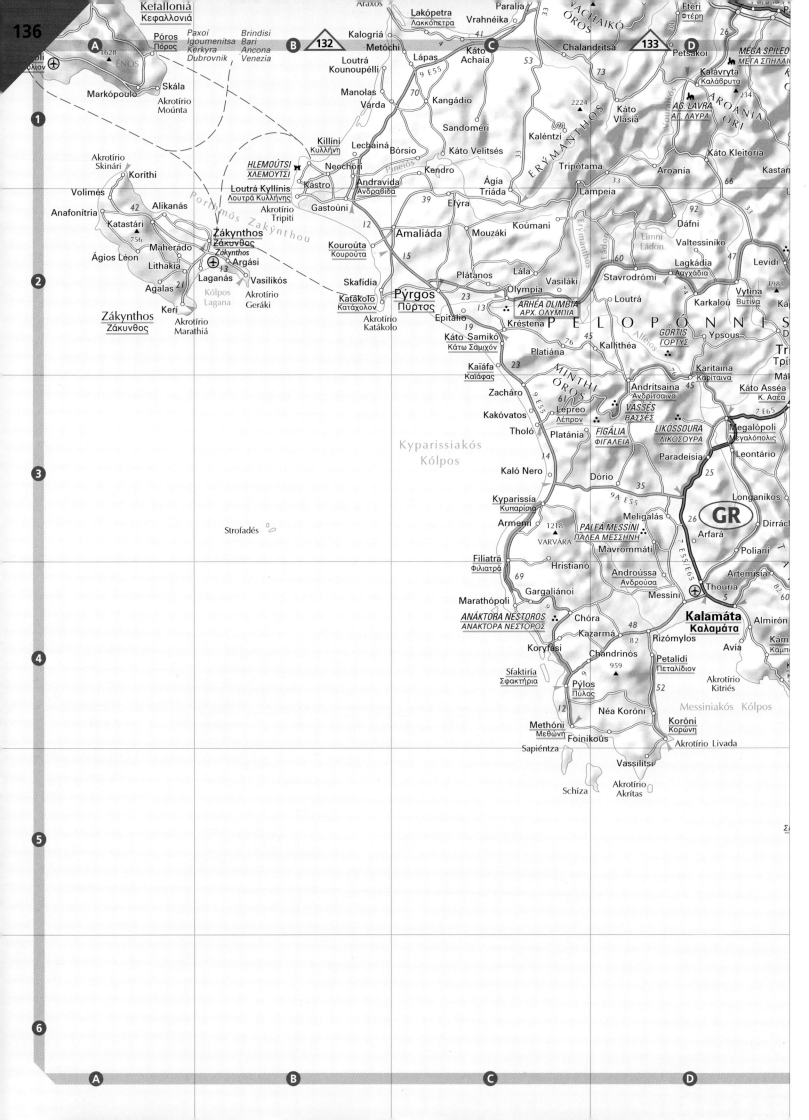

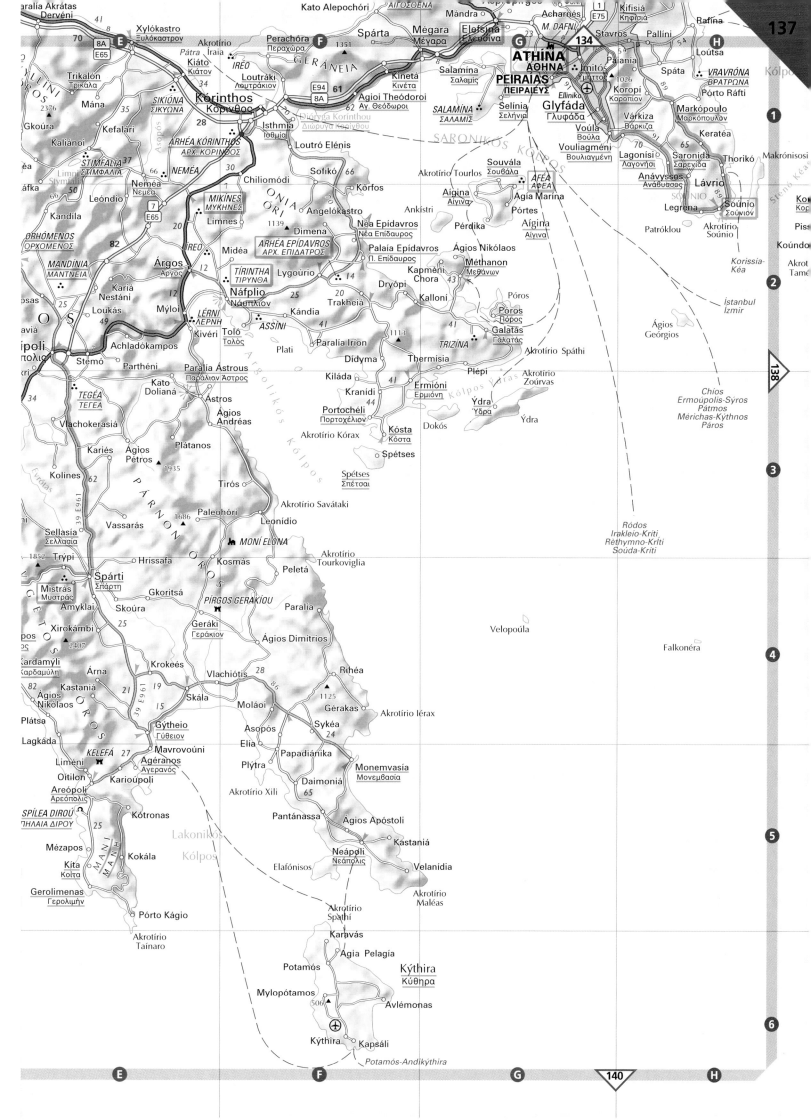

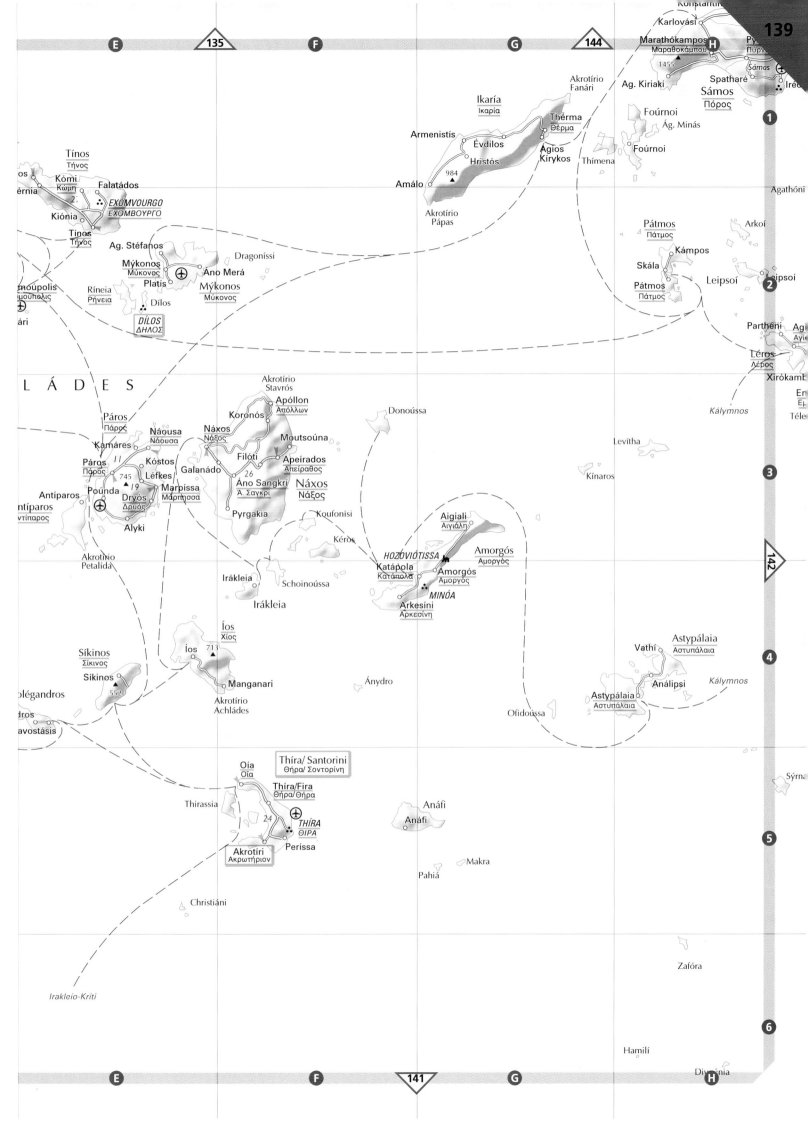

Αδάμας Zefyría
761 ▲

138

Akrotírio
Psálidi

Mílos
Μήλος

Folégandros
Folégandros
Karavostásis

Mílos -

A   B   C   D

ασία
ασία

1

óstoli

Kastaniá

Velanídia

Akrotírio
Maléas

137

2

Kýthira
Κύθηρα

αγία

Avlémonas

áli

Peiraías
Venezia

Peiraías

Kýthira

3

Potamós

Andikíthira

Akrotírio
Spánta

DIKTINÉON
ΔΙΚΤΥΝΑΙΟΝ

Stavrós

Akrotírio
Meleghas

Kólpos Chanión

Soúda

GR

GONIÁ
ΓΟΝΙΑ

Akrotírio
Voúxa

Kolymvári

Chaniá
Χανιά

Stérnes

4

FALÁSSARNA
ΦΑΛΑΣΑΡΝΑ
762

Kólpos
Kissámou

Plataniás

Soúda

K. Soúdas

Akrotírio
Drápano

Pánormos
Ράνορμος

Balí

Maleme

23

90 E75

Kalámi

Órmos Almyroú

78   90

Kastélli
Καστέλλι

90 E65

21

Voukoliés

Fournés

ÁPTERA
ΑΠΤΕΡΑ

Vámos

Réthymno
Ρέθυμνον

Platanés
Pérama

Plátanos

Topólia

Néa
Roúmata

Lákkoi

Mesklá

Vrýses

Georgioúpoli

Prassiés

Margarites

ARKÁDI
ΑΡΚΑΔΙ

IDI (

POLIRINÍA
ΠΟΛΥΡΡΗΝΙΑ

Kámbos

Élos

Strovlés

Omalós

Alikampós

Kournás

Episkopí

Armémoi

Amári

Fourfourás
2456 ▲

1182

45

Kántanos

LEFKÁ ÓRI

72

Askífou

Argiroupoli

Spíli

HRISSOSKALÍTISSA

ELIRÓS
ΕΛΙΡΟΣ

2452

Anópoli

Sellía

79

1776

VALSAM
ΒΑΛΣΑΜ

Soúgia

Ag.Roúmeli

Skalotí

Plakiás

Akoúmia

Mélampes

Tympá

Akrotírio
Kríos

Palaiochóra
Παλαιοχώρα

FARÁNGI SAMARIÁS
ΦΑΡΑΓΓΙ ΣΑΜΑΡΙΑΣ

Sfákia
Σφάκια

FRANGOKÁSTELO
ΦΡΑΓΚΟΚΑΣΤΕΛΛΟ

MONÍ PRÉVELI

Agia Galini
Άγ. Γαλήνη

AG. TRIÁDA
ΑΓ. ΤΡΙΑΔΑ

5

Paximádia

Mátala
Μάταλα

FESTÓS
ΦΑΙΣΤΟΣ

Akrotírio
Líthino

Gavdopoúla

6

Gávdos

A   B   C   D

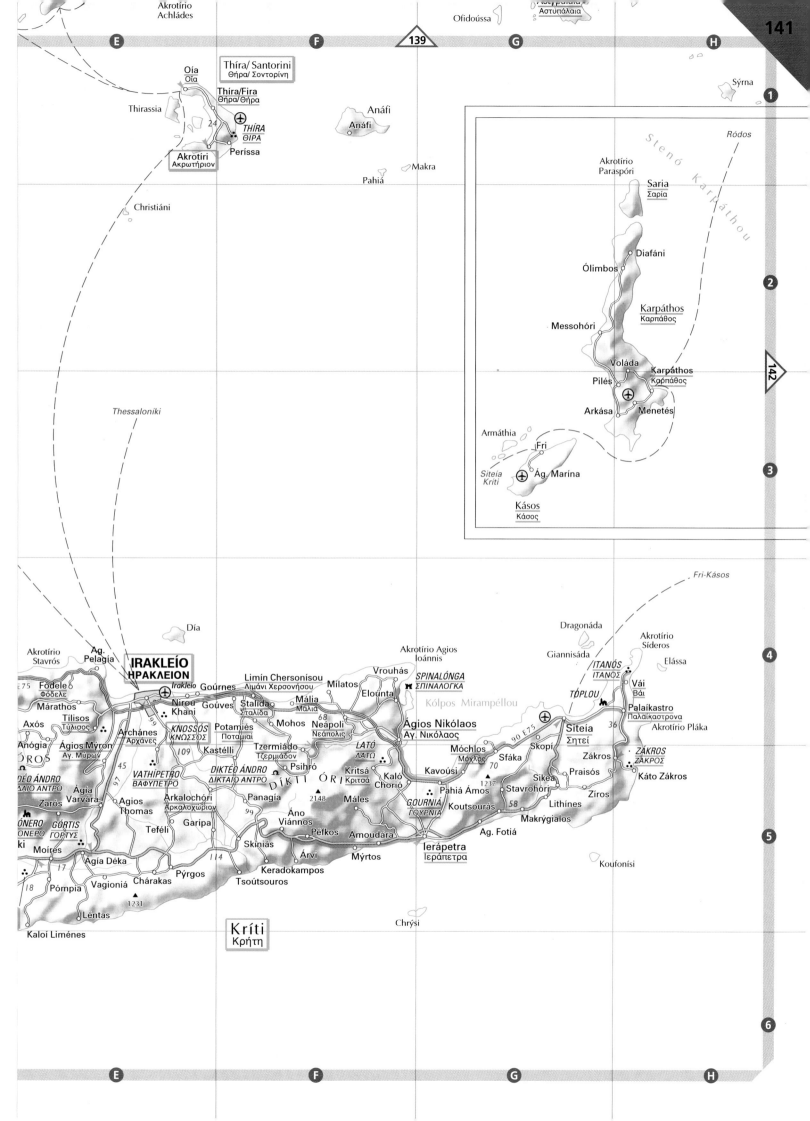

Akrotírio
Achládes

Ofidoússa

Astypálaia
Αστυπάλαια

Sýrna

Thíra/ Santorini
Θήρα/ Σαντορίνη

Oía
Οία

Anáfi

Thirassia

Thíra/Fira
Θήρα/Θήρα

24

Anáfi

⊕ THÍRA
ΘΙΡΑ

Período

Períssa

Akrotíri
Ακρωτήριον

Makra

Pahiá

Christiáni

Akrotírio
Paraspóri

Saria
Σαρία

Steno Karpáthou

Ródos

1

Diafáni

Ólimbos

Messohóri

Karpáthos
Κάρπαθος

Thessaloníki

Voláda

Karpáthos
Κάρπαθος

2

△142

Pilés

⊕

Arkása

Menetés

Armáthia

Fri

Siteia
Kríti

⊕ Ág. Marína

3

Kásos
Κάσος

Fri-Kásos

Dragonáda

Día

Giannisáda

Akrotírio
Síderos

Elássa

4

Akrotírio
Stavrós

Ag.
Pelagía

IRAKLEÍO
ΗΡΑΚΛΕΙΟΝ

Akrotírio Agios
Ioánnis

Vrouhás

ITANÓS
ΙΤΑΝΟΣ

Vái
Βάι

Fódele
Φόδελε

Gournes

⊕ Irakleío

Limín Chersonísou
Λιμάνι Χερσονήσου

Mílatos

SPINALÓNGA
ΣΠΙΝΑΛΟΓΚΑ

TÓPLOU

Palaíkastro
Παλαίκαστρο

E75

Nírou
Kháni

Goúves

Stalída
Σταλίδα

Mália
Μάλια

Eloúnta

Kólpos Mirampéllou

Akrotírio Pláka

Márathos

68

90 E75

Siteia
Σητεί

36

Áxos

Tílisos
Τύλισος

Archánes
Αρχάνες

99

Potamiés
Ποταμιαι

Mohos

Neápoli
Νεάπολις

Ágios Nikólaos
Αγ. Νικόλαος

Skopí

Zákros

ZÁKROS
ΖΑΚΡΟΣ

Anógia

Ágios Mýron
Αγ. Μύρων

KNOSSÓS
ΚΝΩΣΣΟΣ

Kastélli

109

Tzermiádo
Τζερμιάδων

Psihró

LATÓ
ΛΑΤΩ

Móchlos
Μόχλος

Sfáka

Praisós

Káto Zákros

ÁIO ANTRO

45

VATHIPETRO
ΒΑΘΥΠΕΤΡΟ

DIKTÉO ÁNDRO
ΔΙΚΤΑΙΟ ΑΝΤΡΟ

D I K T I   Ó R I

Kritsá
Κριτσά

Kavoúsi

Sikea

Zíros

Ágia
Varvára

97

Arkalochóri
Αρκαλοχωρίου

Panagía

2148

Kaló
Chorió

Pahiá Ámos

1237

Stavrohóri

Lithínes

Zarós

Agios
Thomas

Garipa

Máles

GOURNIÁ
ΓΟΥΡΝΙΑ

Koutsourás

58

Makrýgialos

ONERO
ΟΝΕΡΟ

GÓRTIS
ΓΟΡΤΥΣ

Teféli

99

Áno
Viánnos

Amoudára

Ag. Fotiá

Moíres

Agía Déka

17

Skiniás

Péfkos

Ierápetra
Ιεράπετρα

Koufonísi

5

18

Pómpia

Vagioniá

Chárakas

Pýrgos

114

Keradokampos

Tsoútsouros

Árvi

Mýrtos

1231

Léntas

Chrýsi

Kaloí Liménes

Kríti
Κρήτη

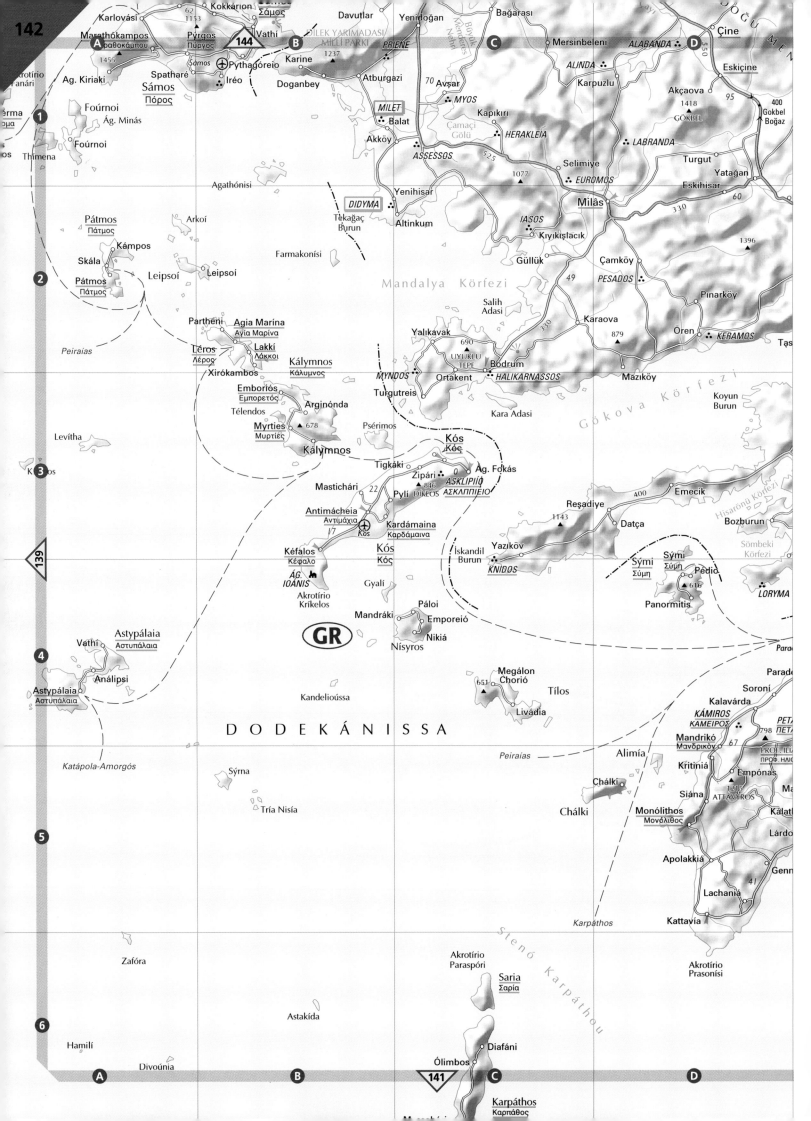

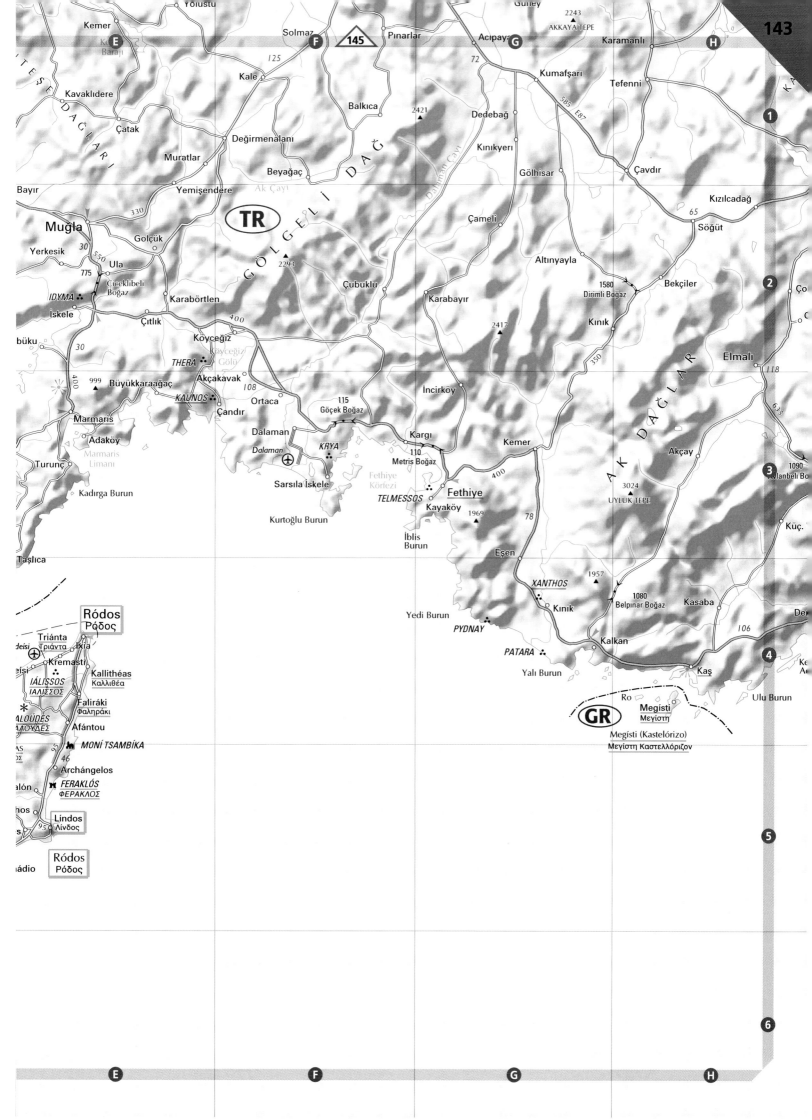

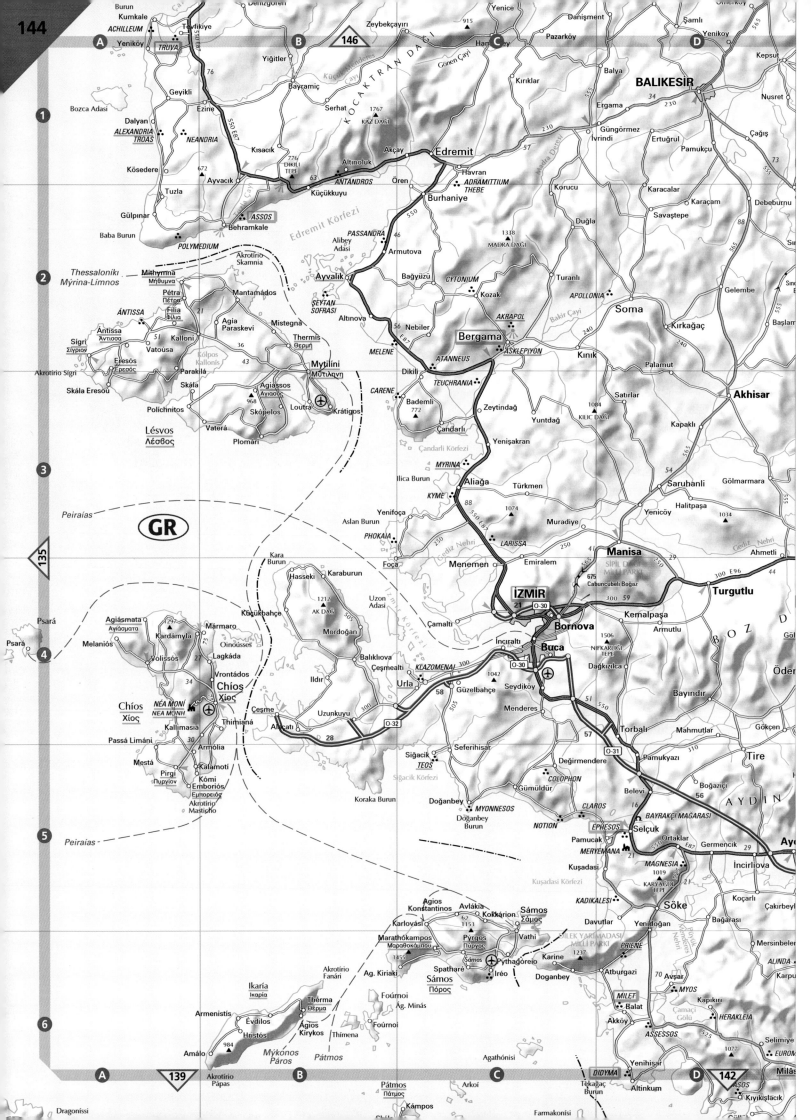

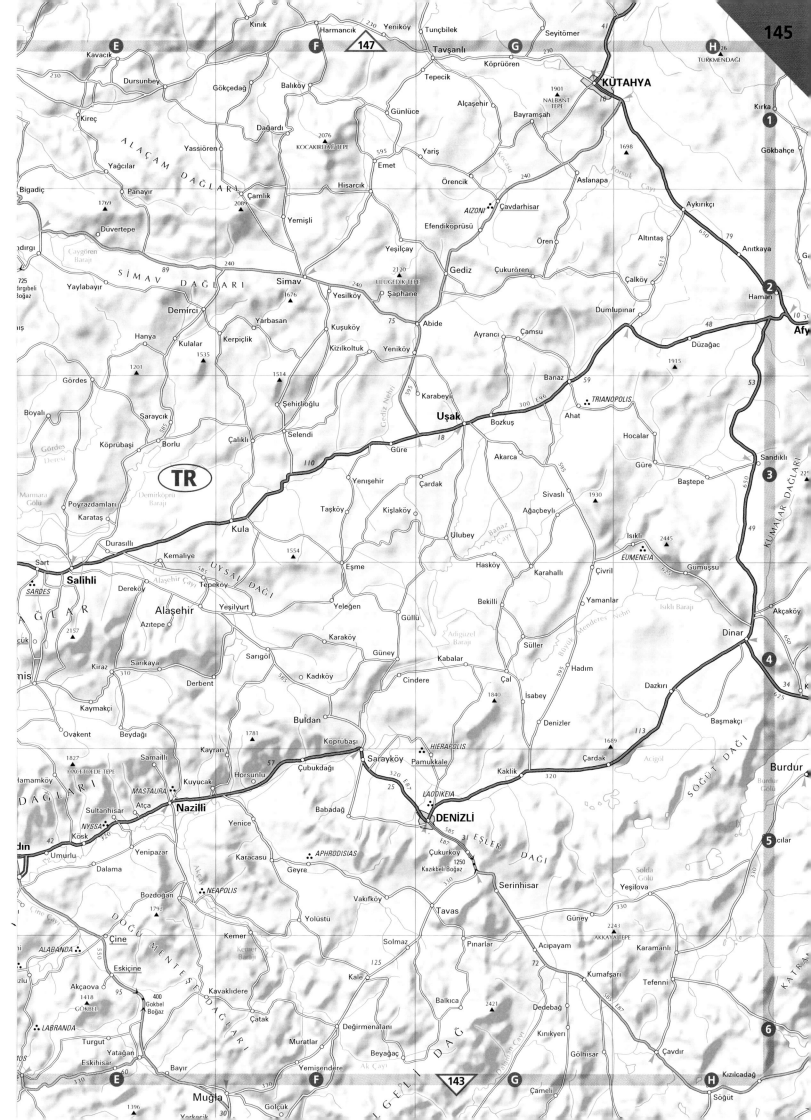

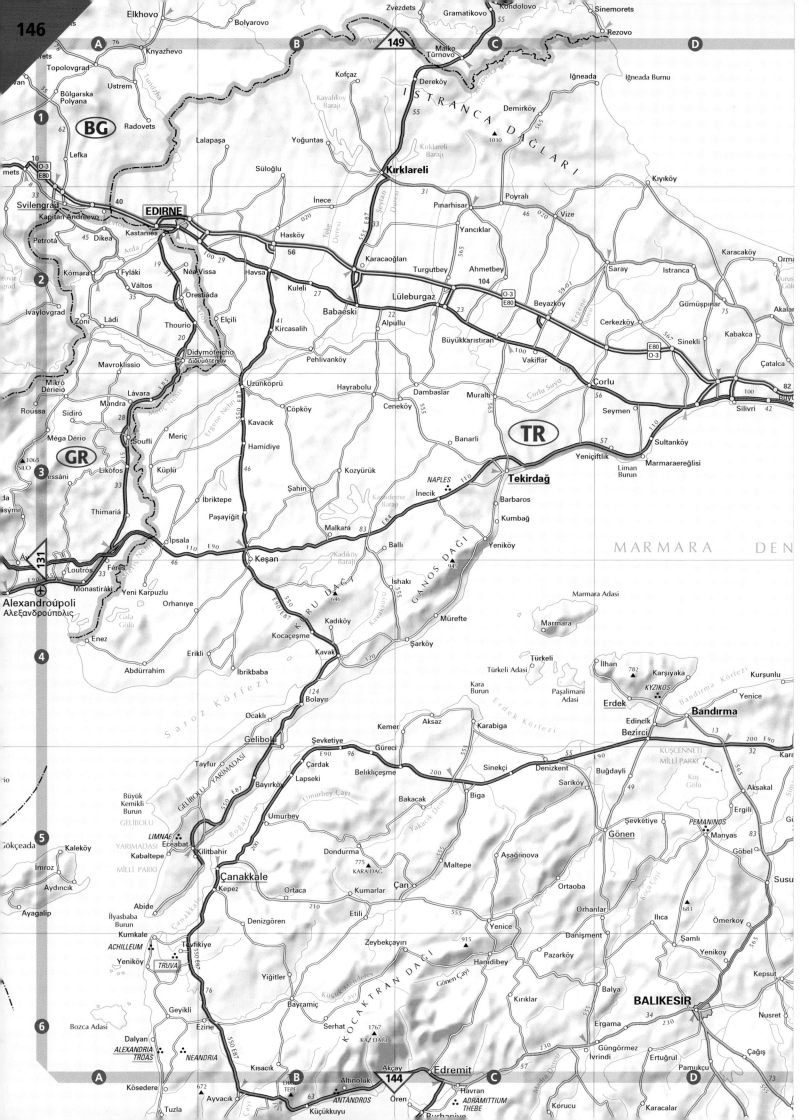

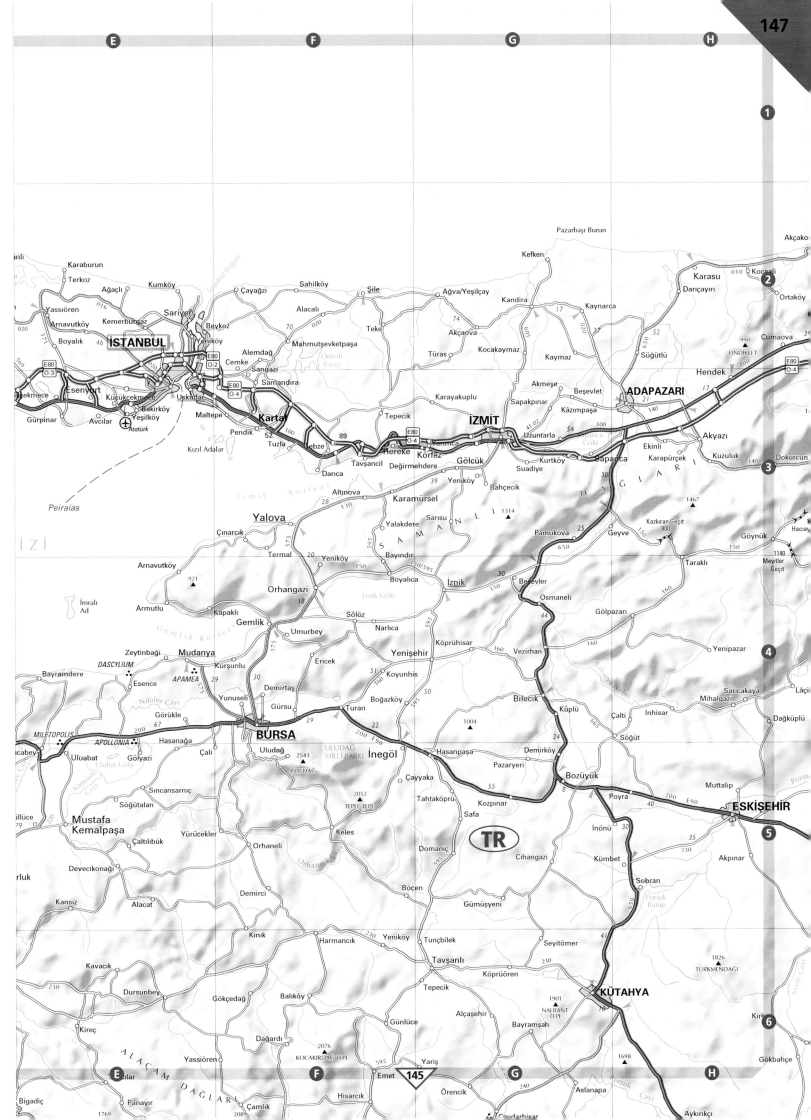

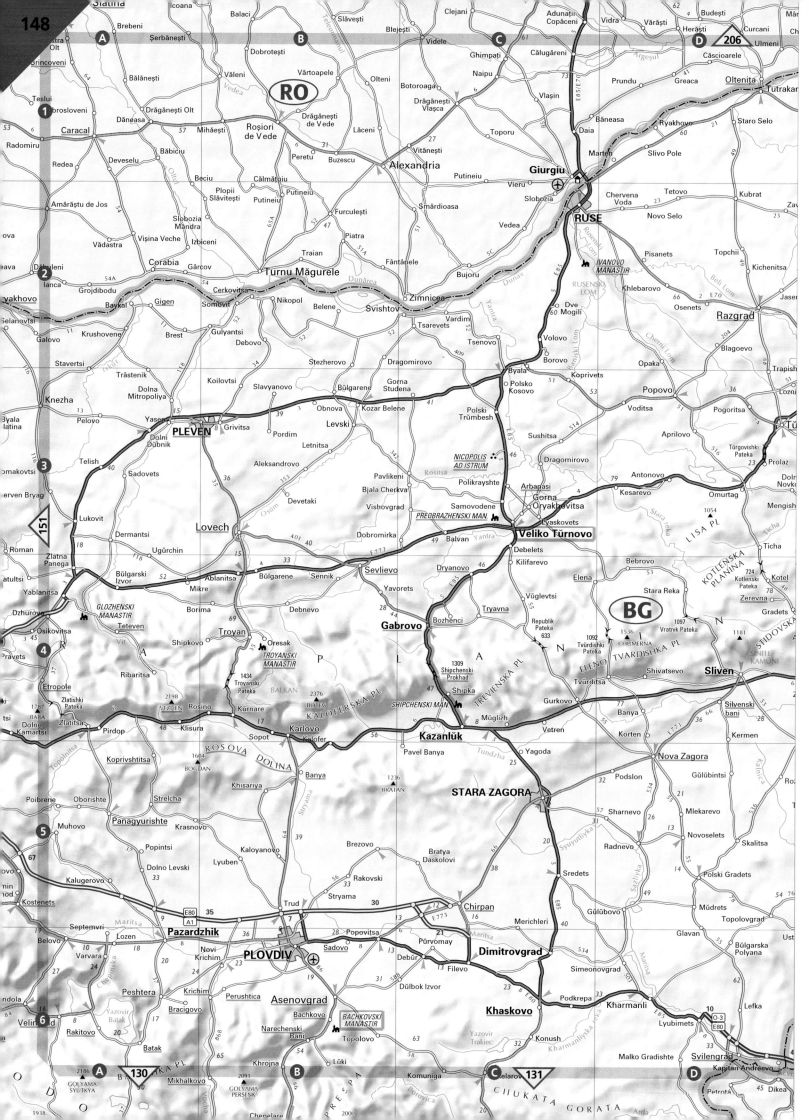

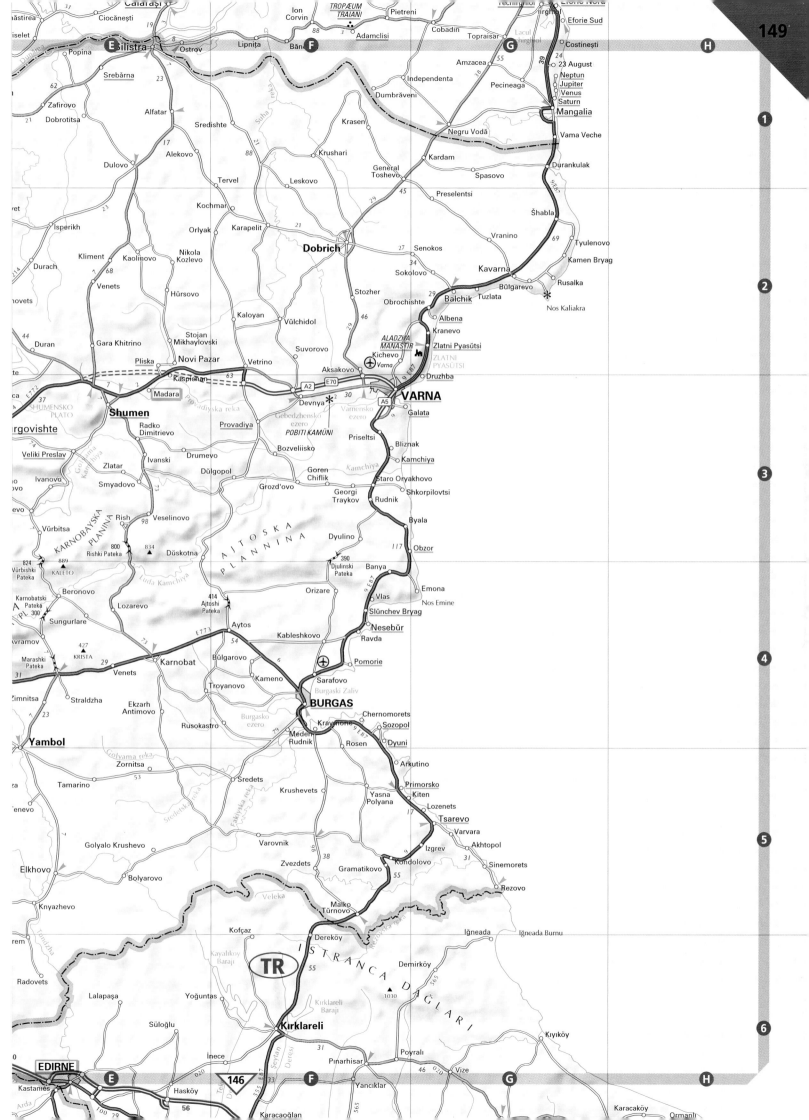

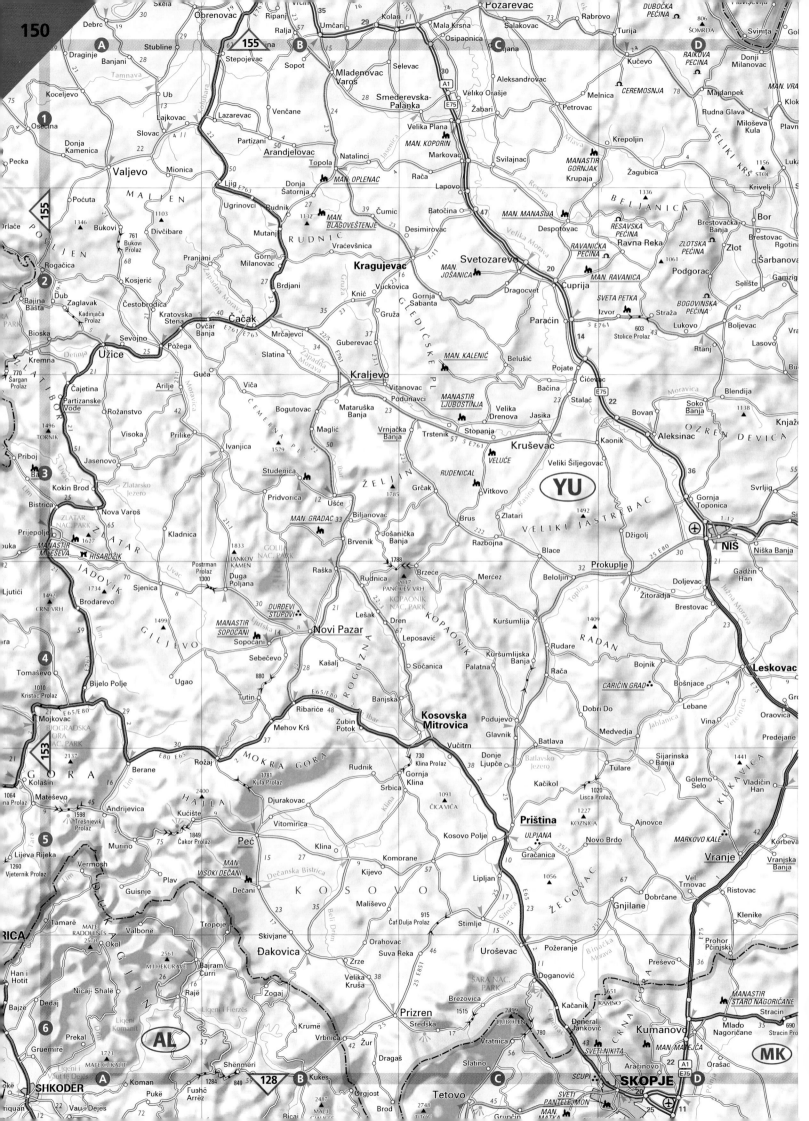

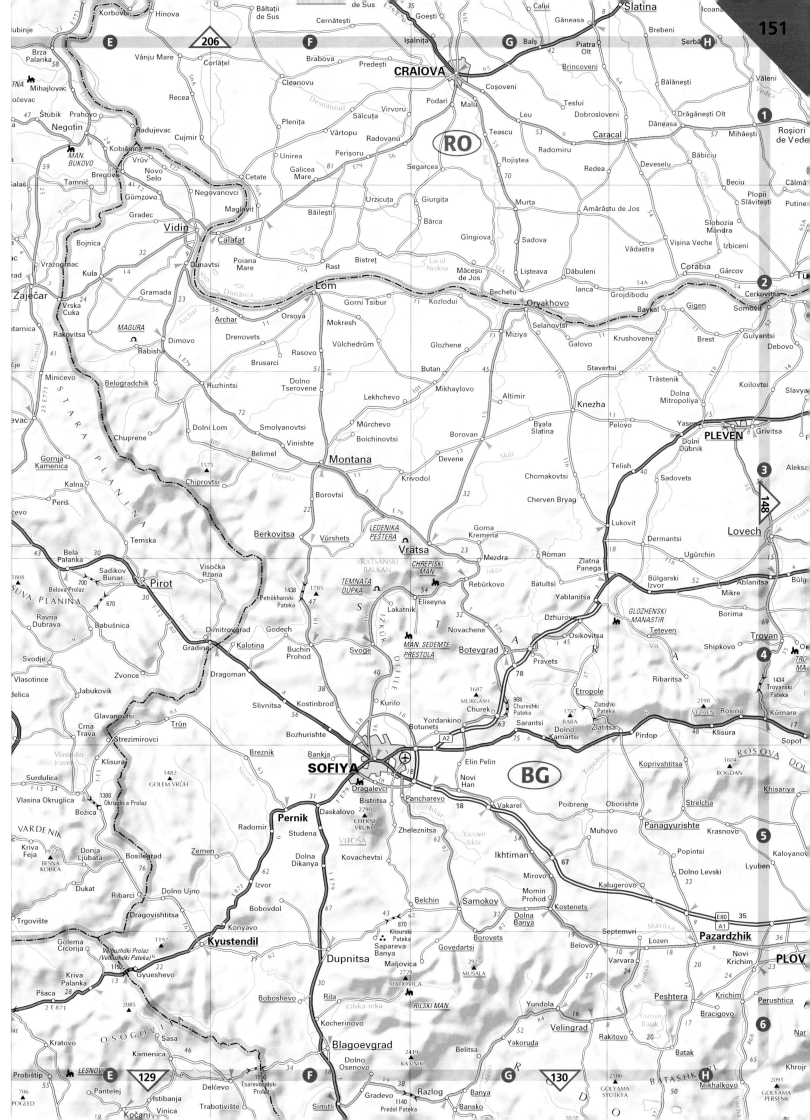

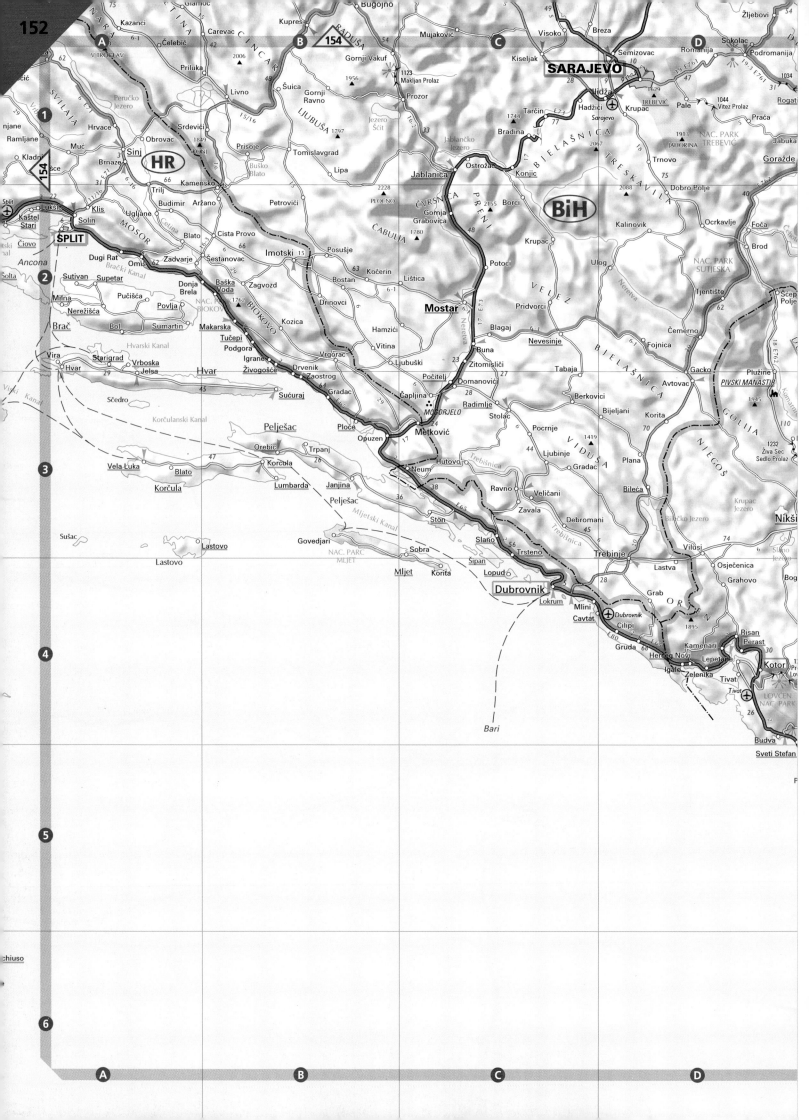

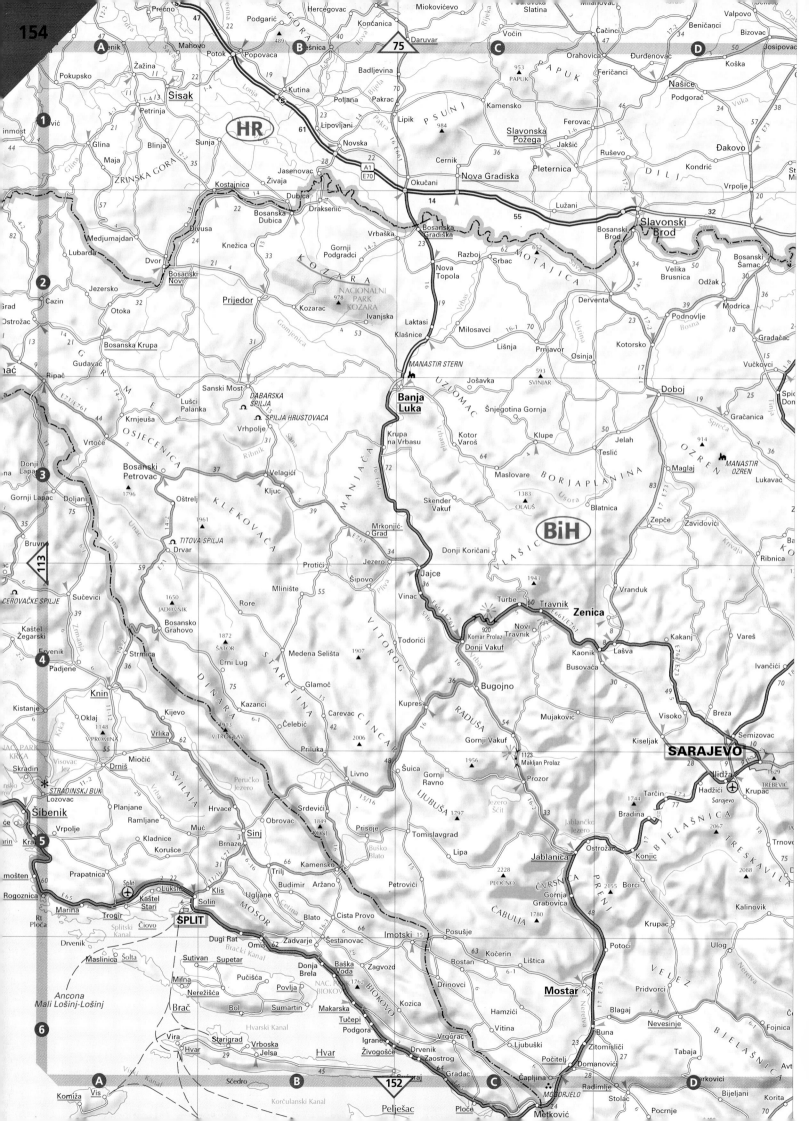

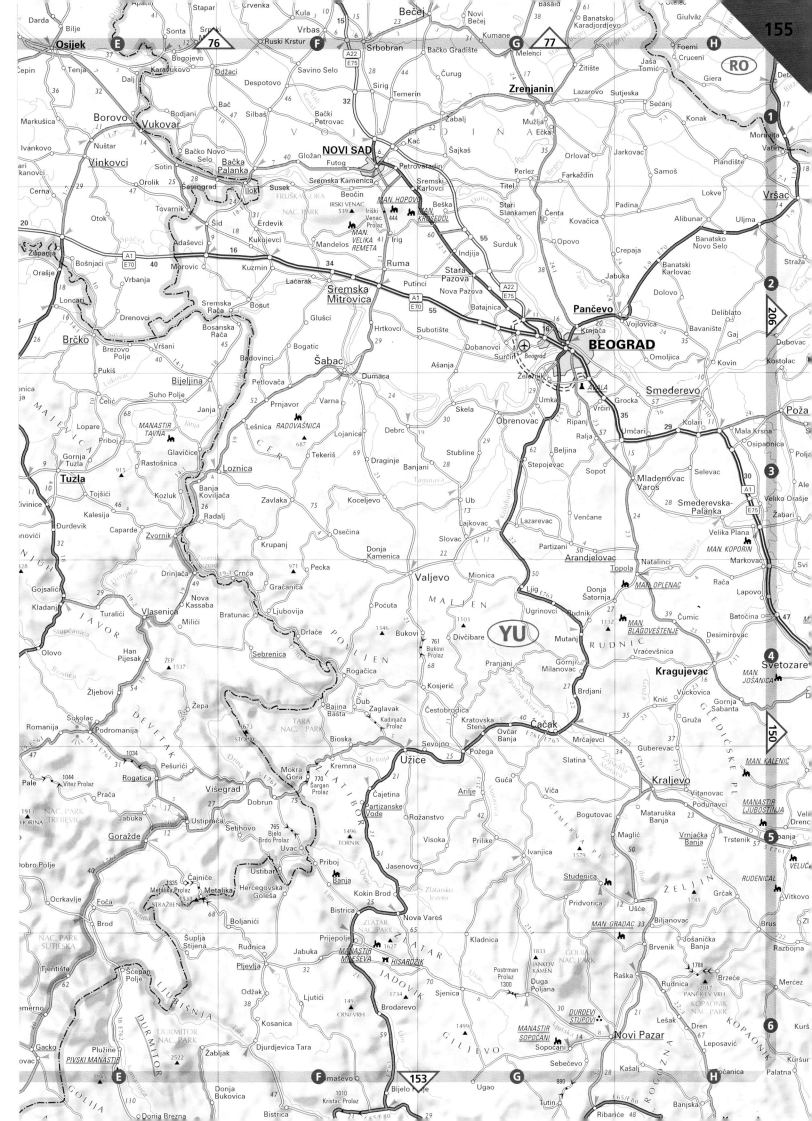

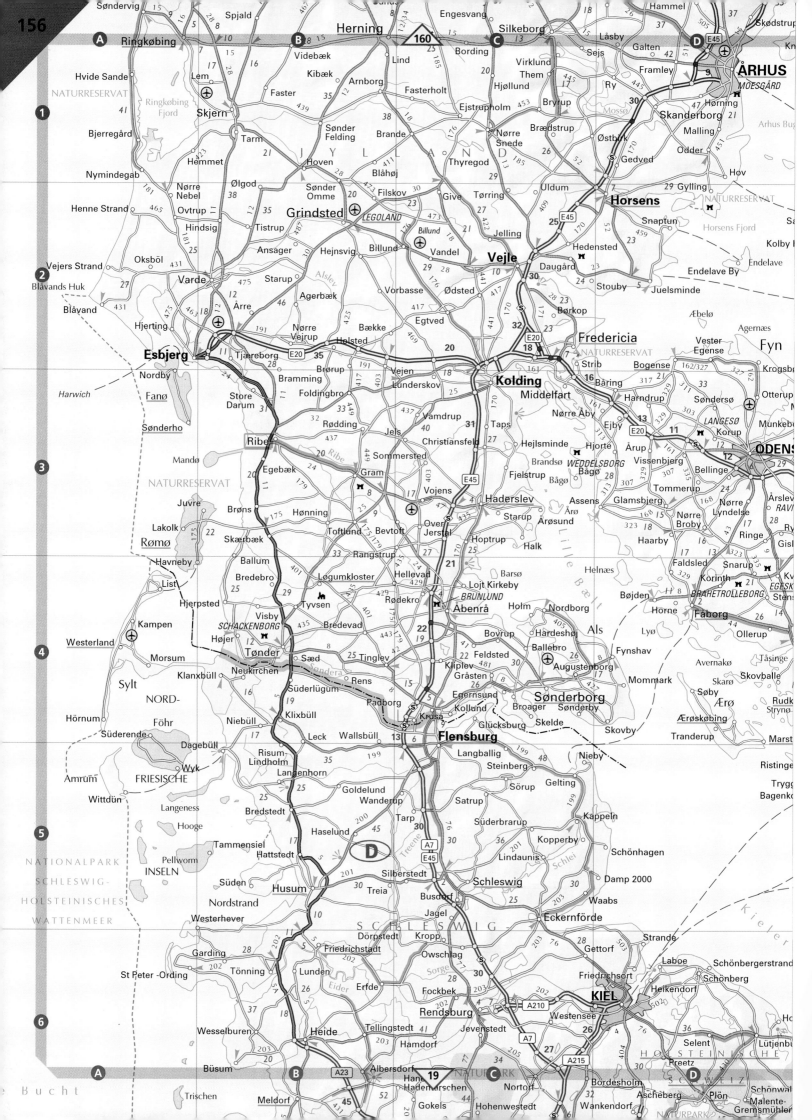

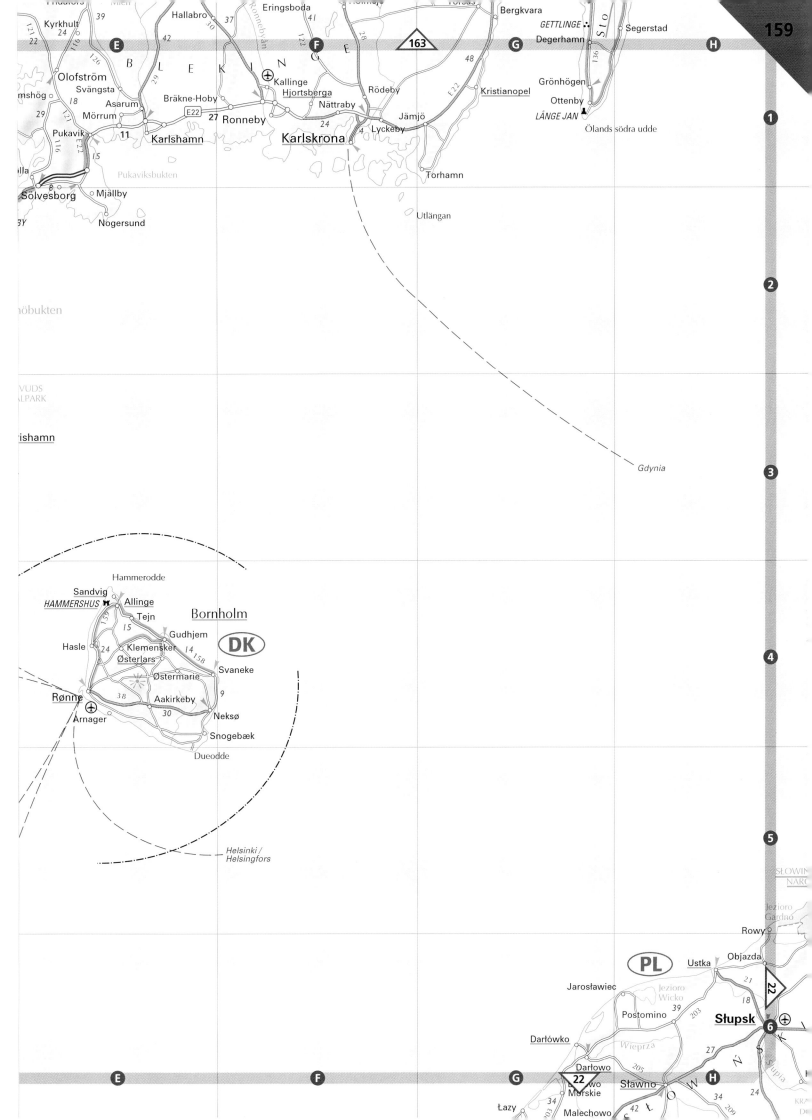

Kyrkhult
39
Hallabro
37
Eringsboda
41
Bergkvara
GETTLINGE
Segerstad
121
22
24
42
30
122
28
163
Degerhamn
Sto
E

E
F
G
G
H

B
L
E
K
I
N
G
48
Grönhögen
Olofström
Kallinge
Rödeby
Kristianopel
136
Svängsta
126
Hjortsberga
Ottenby
shög
Asarum
Bräkne-Hoby
Nättraby
E22
LÅNGE JAN
18
121
E22
29
Mörrum
27 Ronneby
24
Jämjö
Ölands södra udde
Pukavik
11
Lyckeby
116
15
Karlshamn
Karlskrona
4
lla
8
Torhamn
Sölvesborg
Mjällby
BY
Nogersund
Pukaviksbukten
Utlängan

nöbukten

VUDS
LPARK

shamn
Gdynia
3

Hammerodde
Sandvig
Allinge
HAMMERSHUS
Tejn
Bornholm
15
Gudhjem
DK
Hasle
24
Klemensker
14 158
Österlars
Svaneke
Østermarie
9
Rønne
38
Aakirkeby
Arnager
30
Neksø
Snogebæk
Dueodde
Helsinki /
Helsingfors

SŁOWIN
NARC
Jezioro
Gardno
Rowy
PL
Ustka
Objazda
Jarosławiec
Jezioro
Wicko
21
39
203
18
Postomino
Słupsk
Darłówko
Wieprza
6
Darłowo
27
205
N
22
Sławno
34
Łazy
34
42
Malechowo
209

E
F
G
22
H

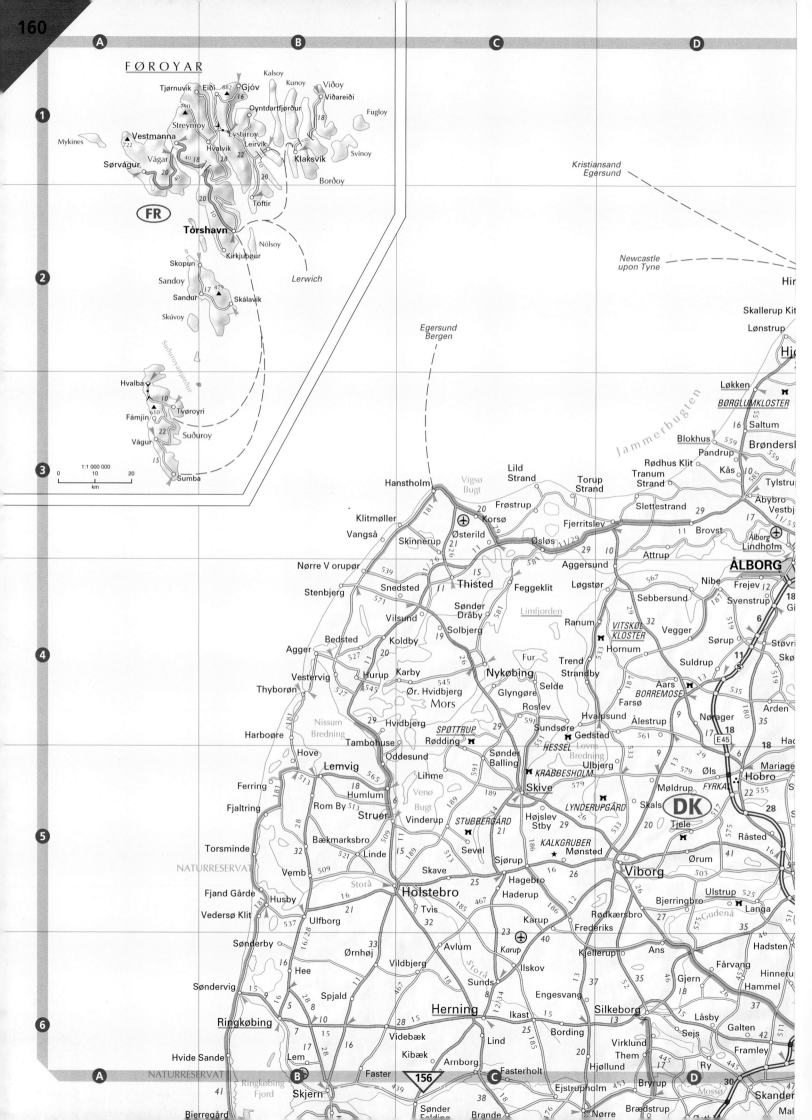

FØROYAR

A

Tjørnuvik Eiði 882 Gjógv
790 16
Streymoy
Vestmanna Hvalvík
722 Leirvik
Sørvágur Vágar
20 40 18 28
20
FR
10
Tórshavn Nólsoy
Kirkjubøur
Skopun
Sandoy Lerwich
Sandur 17 479
Skálavik
Skúvoy

Kalsoy Kunoy Viðoy
Oyndarfjørður Viðareiði
18
Eysturoy Fugloy
Leirvik
22
Klaksvík Svínoy
Borðoy
Toftir

Mykines

Suðuroyarfjørður
Hvalba
610 10
Fámjin Tvøroyri
22
Vágur Suðuroy
15
Sumba

1:1 000 000
0 10 20
km

Kristiansand
Egersund

Newcastle
upon Tyne

Egersund
Bergen

Skallerup Kit
Lønstrup

Hio

Løkken
BØRGLUMKLOSTER 55
16 Saltum
Blokhus 559 Brøndersl
Rødhus Klit Pandrup 559
Tranum Kås 105
Strand Tylstru
Slettestrand
29
Åbybro
Vestbj
17
Brovst
11 Ålborg 11/55
Lindholm

ÅLBORG
Nibe Frejev 12
181 Svenstrup
Sebbersund 6
519 Støvri
VITSKØL 32 Vegger Sørup Skø
KLOSTER Hornum 11
533 187 Suldrup
Aars 13
BORREMOSE 535
Farsø 9 Nørager
Hvalpsund Ålestrup 180 Arden
HESSEL 561 35
Gedsted E45 18 Ha
Lovns Ols Mariage
Bredning 579
Ulbjerg 13 579
KRABBESHOLM 9 Hobro
Møldrup FYRKA
579 Skals 22 555
DK 517 28
LYNDERUPGÅRD 20 Tiele
186 575 Råsted
KALKGRUBER Ørum 41 16
Mønsted Viborg 503
25 Ulstrup 525
Bjerringbro Langa
Rødkærsbro 27 575 511
Frederiks 186 35
Kjellerup 46
Ans Hadsten
Fårvang Hinneru
Gjern Hammel
52 18
Engesvang Silkeborg 37
15 Låsby Galten 42
Bording 13 Sejs 511
Virklund Them 445 Ry Skander
Hjøllund 17 445
Bryrup 30
Sønder Ejstrupholm 453 Mosso
Brande 38 Nørre Skander
Bierregård Brædstrup

Hanstholm
Vigsø
Bugt
Lild
Strand Torup
Strand
Klitmøller Frøstrup
20
Vangså Korsø Fjerritslev
Skinnerup Østerild Øsløs 11/29
21 226 11
Nørre V orupør 539 1/26 29 10
11 15 581 Aggersund Attrup
Stenbjerg Snedted 11 Thisted 567
571 Feggeklit Løgstør
Vilsund Sønder Limfjorden
Dråby 581 Ranum
Bedsted Koldby Solbjerg Fur Trend
Agger 527 11 20 19 26 Strandby
Vestervig Hurup Karby Nykøbing
Thyborøn 545 Ør. Hvidbjerg 545 Selde
527 Mors Glyngøre Roslev
Nissum 29 Hvidbjerg Sundsøre
Harboøre Bredning Tambohuse SPØTTRUP Sønder
Hove Rødding Balling
Lemvig Oddesund 591
Ferring 513 Lihme 189 Skive
Humlum Venø 189 Højslev
Fjaltring Rom By 513 Bugt Vinderup Stby 29
Struer STUBBERGÅRD 186
Torsminde 28 Bækmarksbro 509 21 Sjørup
32 Linde 15 189 Sevel Hagebro
Vemb 521 513 Skave 25
509 Storå Haderup
Fjand Gårde Holstebro 467
Husby 16 Tvis 185 Karup
Vederssø Klit 21 32 Frederiks
Ulfborg 537 Avlum Karup 40
Sønderby 16/28 23
Ørnhøj Ilskov
Hee 33 Vildbjerg Sunds
Søndervig 16 Spjald 467 Engesvang
15 28 8 Herning
Ringkøbing 5 10 Ikast 15
7 15 Videbæk 28 15 Lind Bording
Hvide Sande Lem 17 Kibæk 185
28 16 Arnborg Easterholt
Skjern Faster 156 Hjøllund

NATURRESERVAT

NATURRESERVAT
Ringkøbing
Fjord
Skjern Sønder Brande
Folding
Bierregård

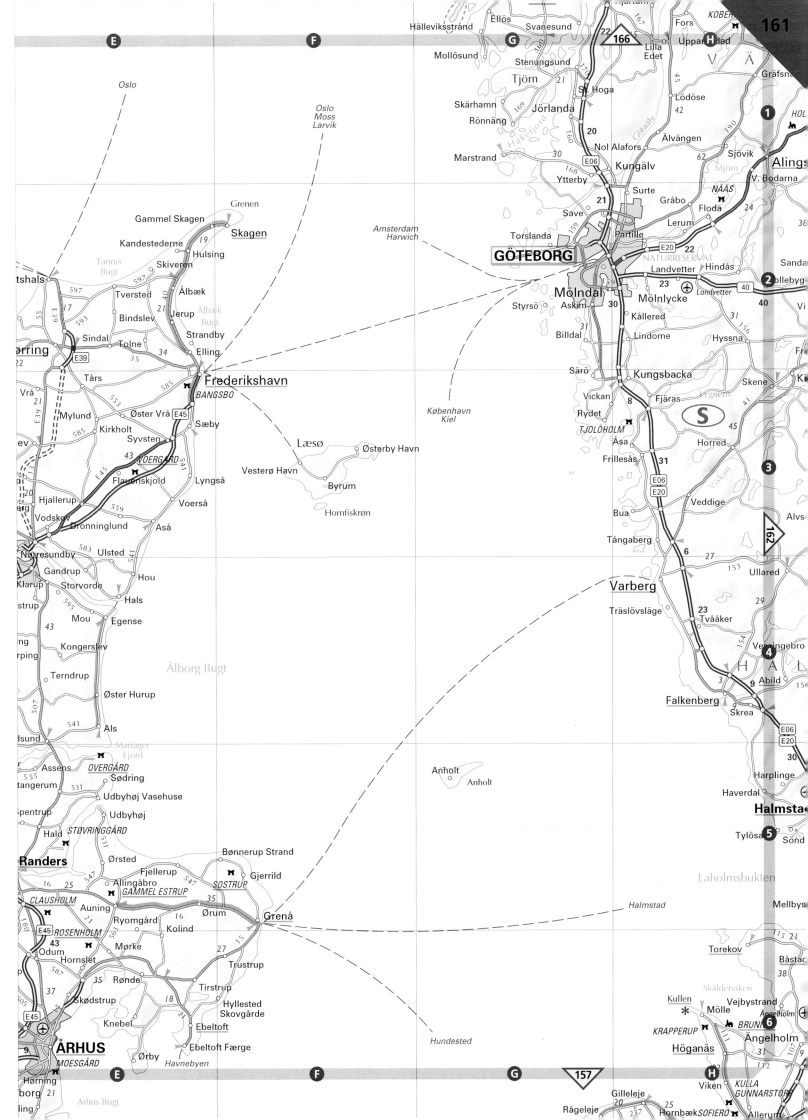

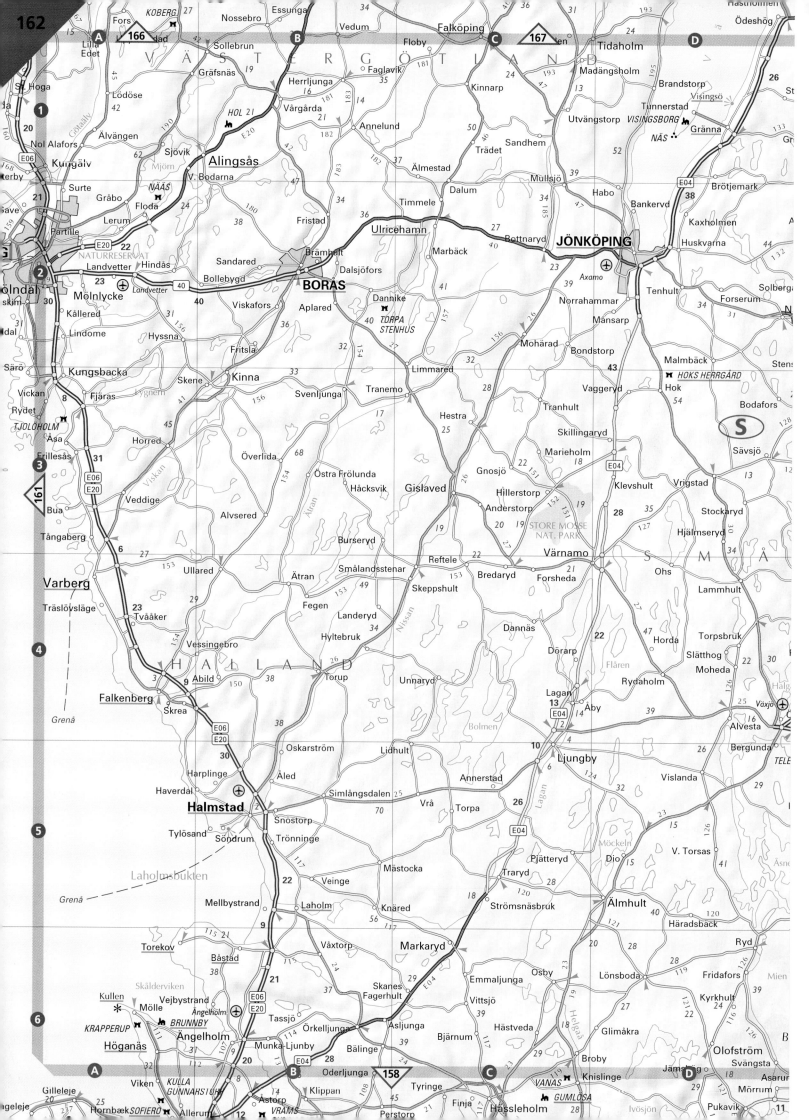

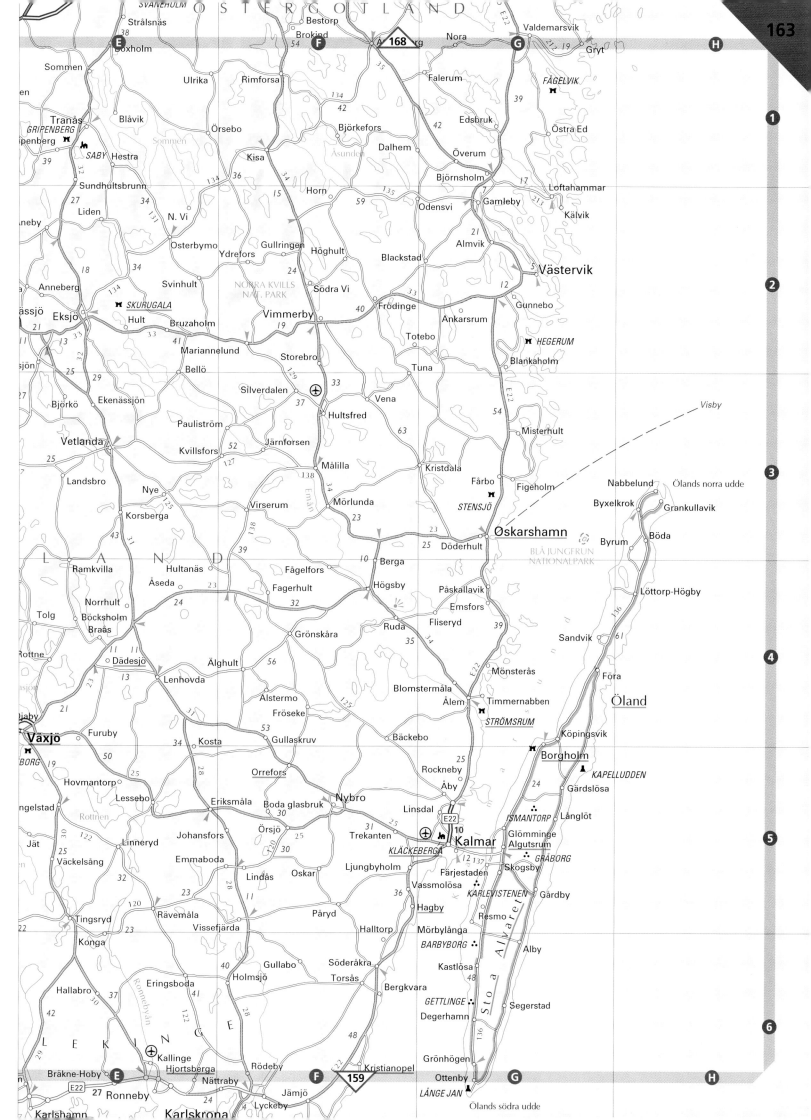

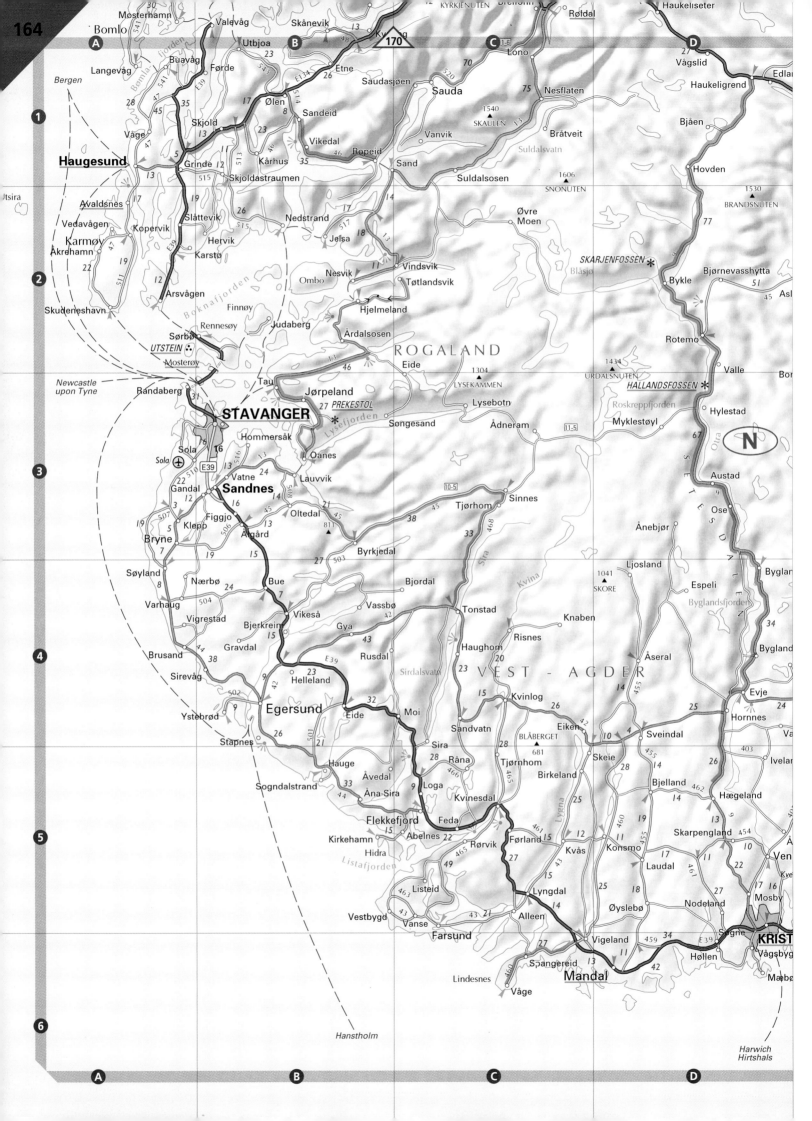

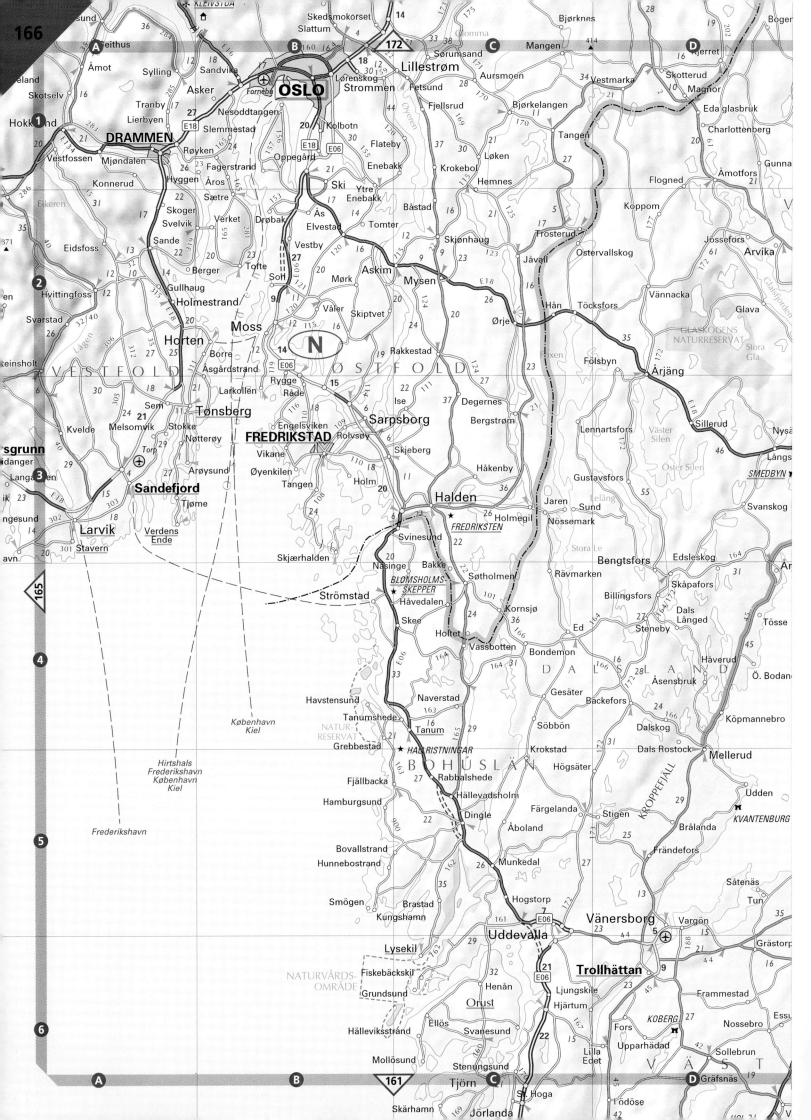

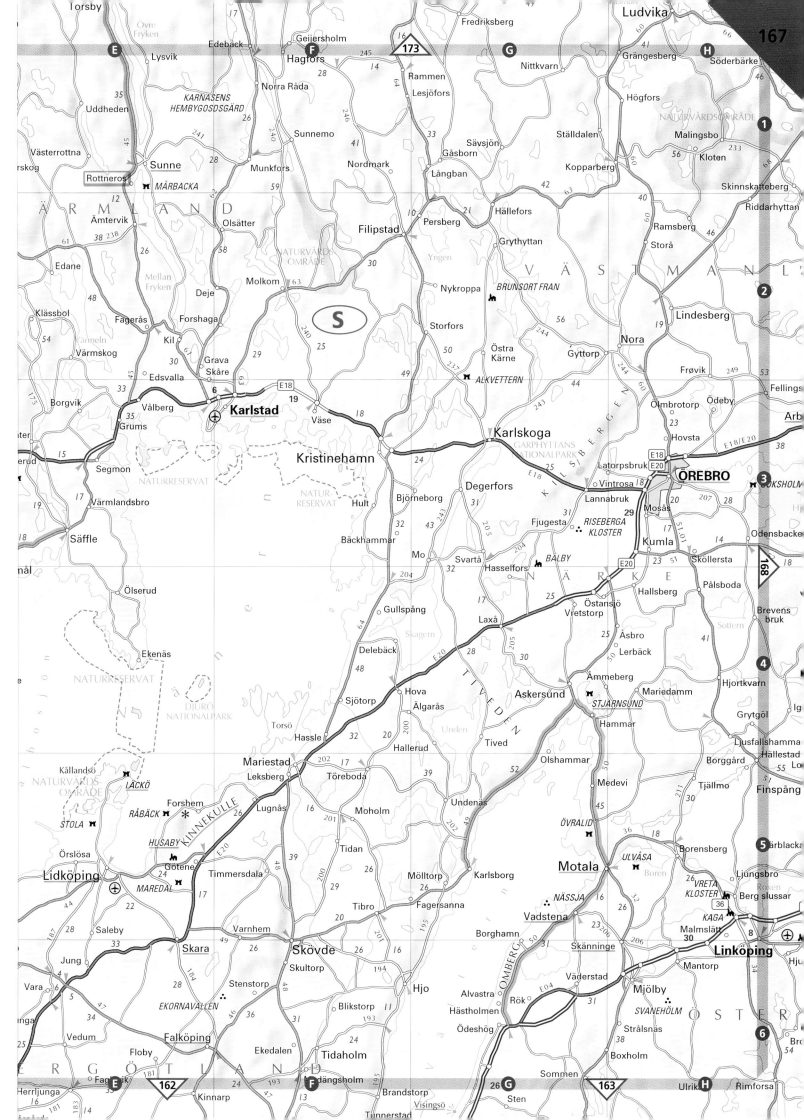

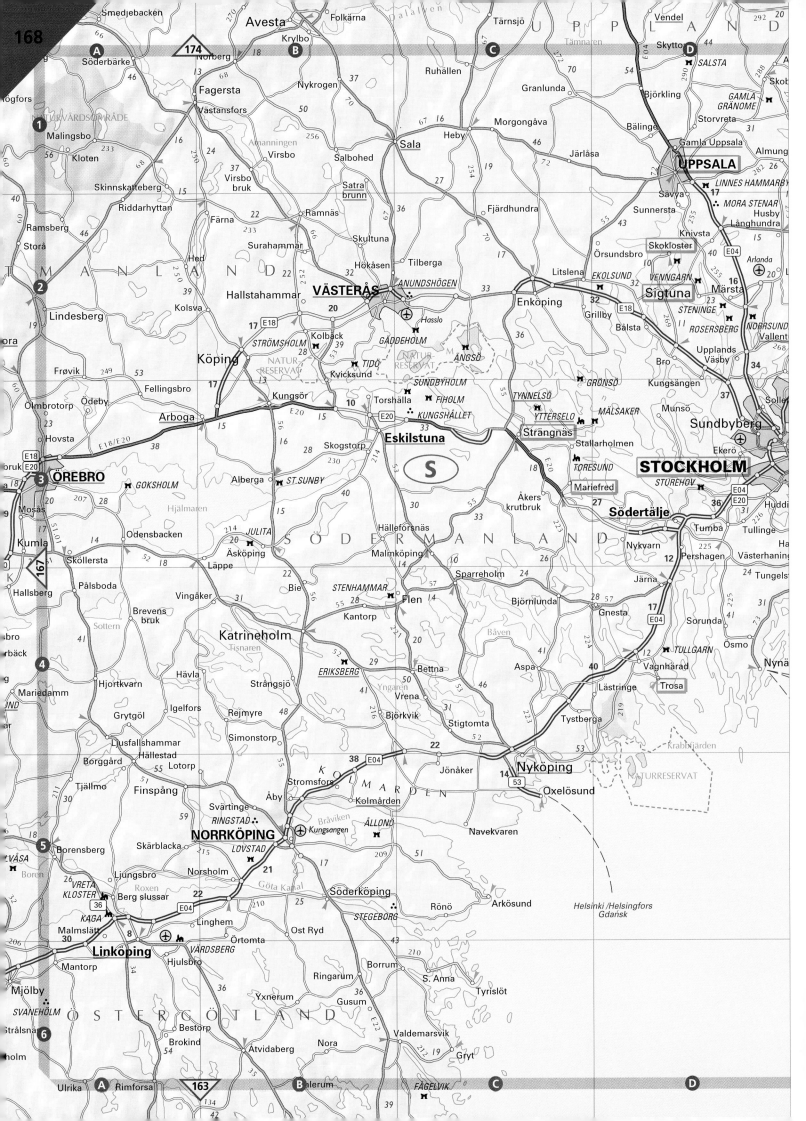

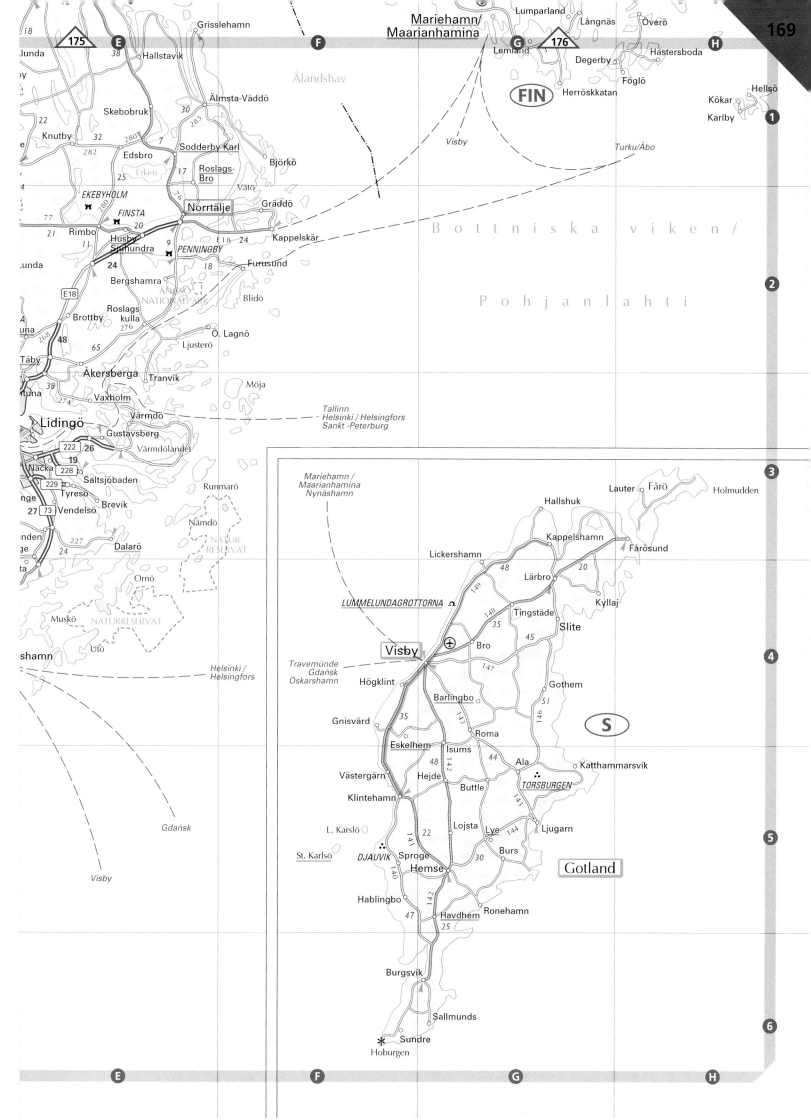

Lumparland
Långnäs
Överö
Mariehamn/
Maarianhamina
E 175 38
F
G 176
Lemland
H
Grisslehamn
18
Hallstavik
Degerby
Hastersboda

Älandshav
Föglö
Hellsö
Älmsta-Väddö
FIN
Herrösskkatan
Kökar
Karlby
1
Skebobruk
30
283
22
Knutby
32
280
7
Sodderby Karl
17
282
Edsbro
Björkö
Roslags-
Bro
25
Erken
Visby
Turku/Åbo
76
Vätö
EKEBYHOLM
280
Gräddö
B o t t n i s k a   v i k e n /
77
FINSTA
Norrtälje
21
Rimbo
20
11
Husby
Sjuhundra
9
Kappelskär
PENNINGBY
E18
24
2
24
Furusund
P o h j a n l a h t i
Bergshamra
18
E18
Blidö
ÄNGSÖ
NATIONALPARK
Brottby
Roslags-
kulla
268
48
276
65
Ö. Lagnö
Täby
Ljusterö
Åkersberga
Tranvik
Möja
38
274
Vaxholm
Värmdö
Tallinn
Helsinki / Helsingfors
Sankt -Peterburg
Lidingö
222 26
Gustavsberg
3
Värmdölandet
Mariehamn /
Maarianhamina
Nynäshamn
Lauter
Fårö
Holmudden
19
Nacka
228
Hallshuk
229
Saltsjöbaden
Kappelshamn
27 73
Tyresö
Brevik
Lickershamn
Fårösund
Vendelsö
Runmarö
48
Lärbro
20
227
Dalarö
Nämdö
LUMMELUNDAGROTTORNA
149
Kyllaj
NATUR-
RESERVAT
148
Tingstäde
Ornö
35
Slite
Visby
Bro
Muskö
NATURRESERVAT
45
Travemünde
Gdańsk
Oskarshamn
Högklint
147
Utö
Gothem
shamn
Helsinki /
Helsingfors
Barlingbo
51
Gnisvärd
35
143
141
S
Roma
Eskelhem
Isums
44
Ala
Katthammarsvik
48
142
Gdańsk
Västergärn
Hejde
Buttle
TORSBURGEN
Klintehamn
143
L. Karslö
Lojsta
Lye
144
Visby
141
22
Ljugarn
St. Karlsö
DJAUVIK
Sproge
30
Burs
Hemse
Gotland
5
140
Hablingbo
142
Ronehamn
47
Havdhem
25
Burgsvik
6
Sallmunds
Sundre
Hoburgen
E
F
G
H

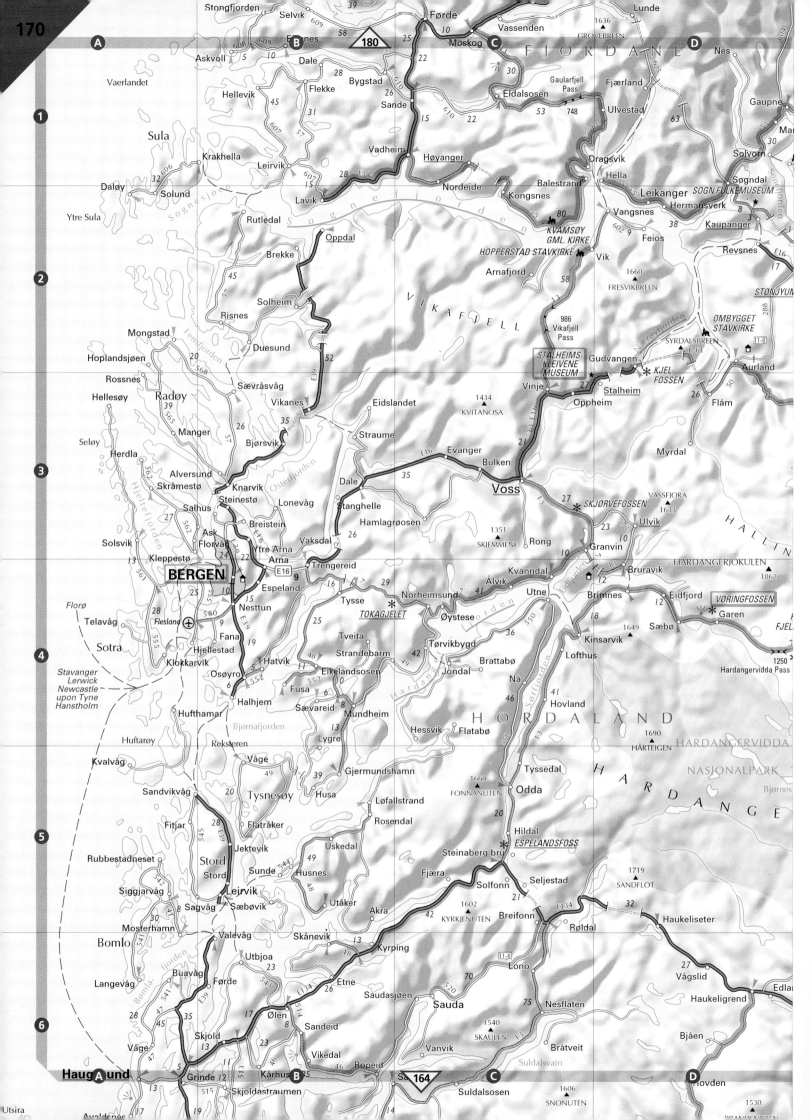

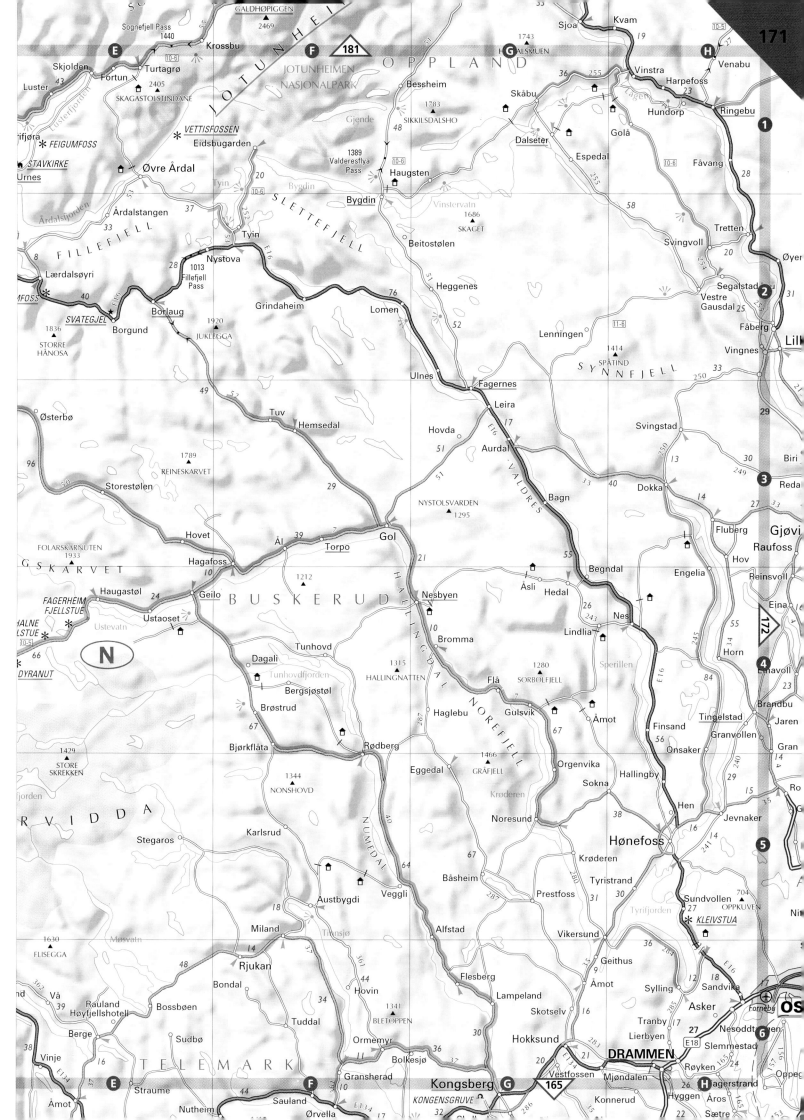

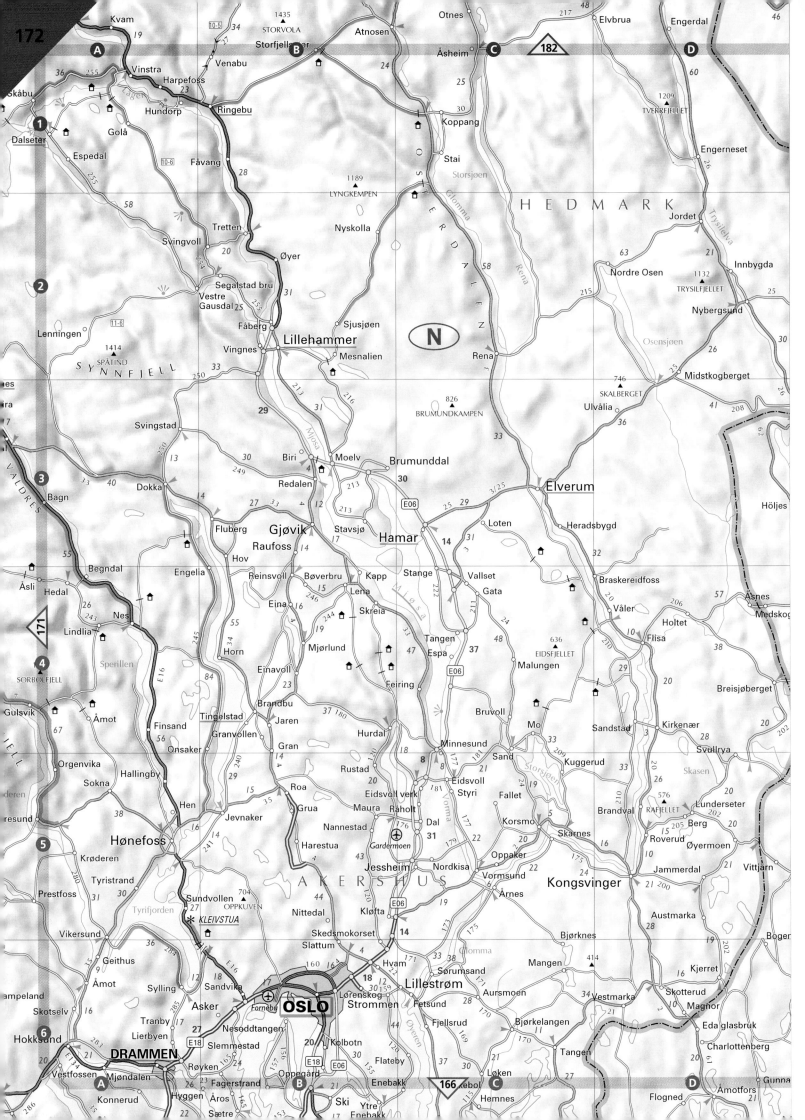

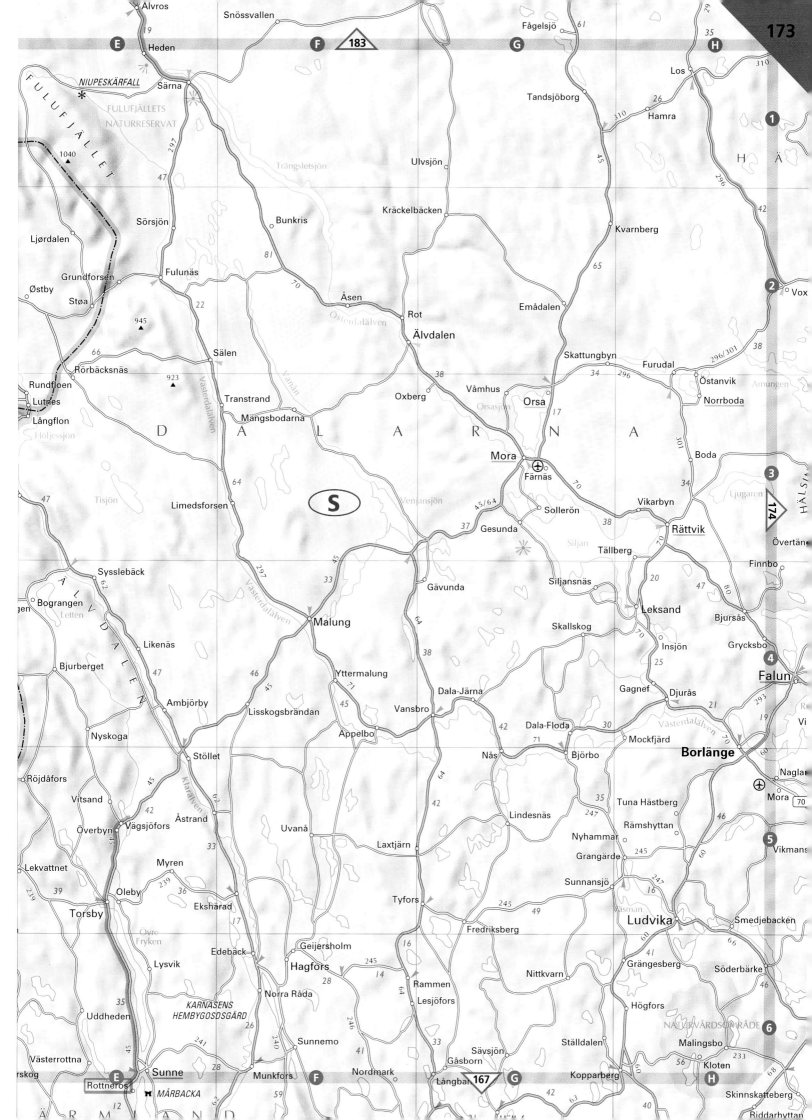

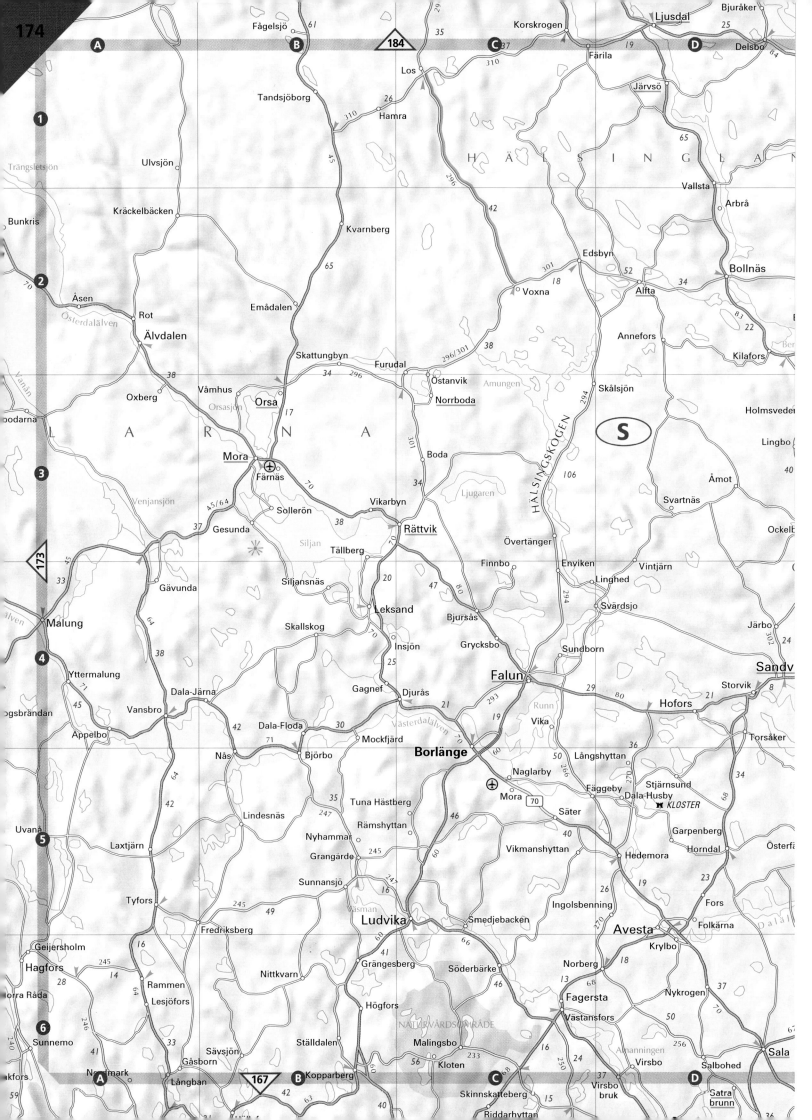

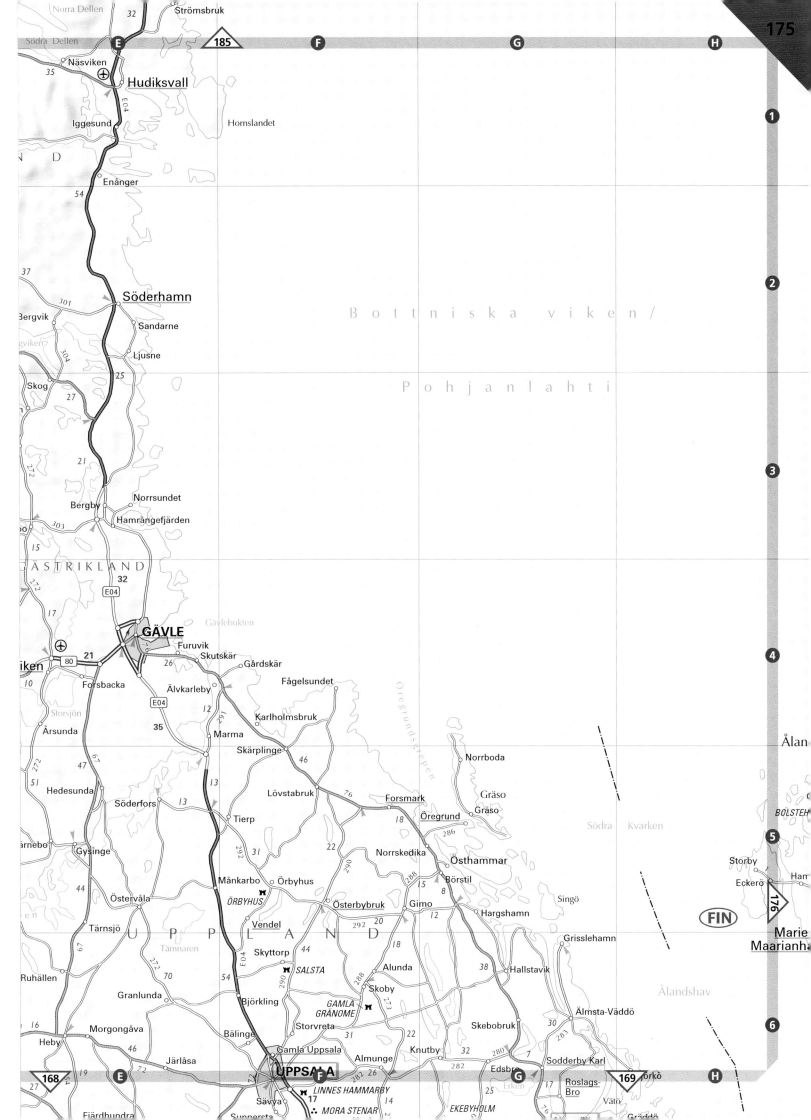

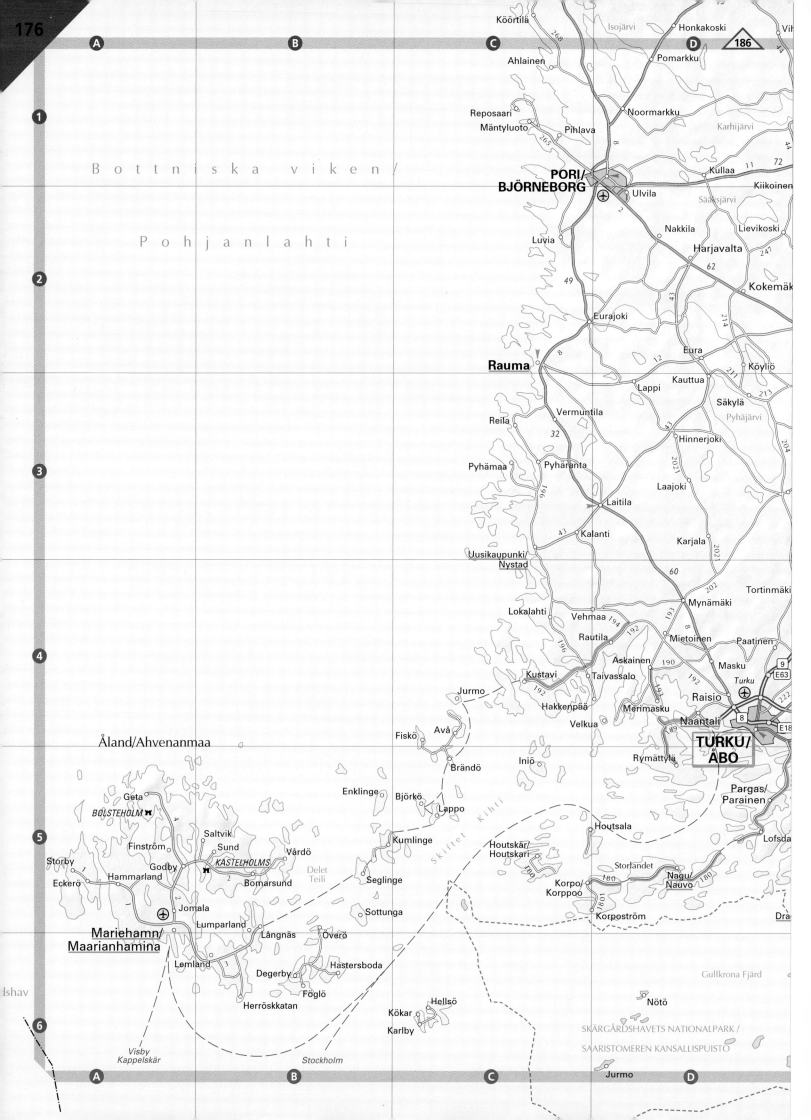

Köörtilä
Honkakoski
Isojärvi
Vih
Ahlainen
Pomarkku
268
44
Reposaari
Noormarkku
Karhijärvi
Mäntyluoto
Pihlava
265
Kullaa
11
72
PORI/
BJÖRNEBORG
Ulvila
Kiikoinen
8
2
Luvia
Nakkila
Lievikoski
Harjavalta
247
49
62
Kokemäk
Eurajoki
214
43
Eura
Rauma
Köyliö
8
12
211
Lappi
Kauttua
Säkylä
213
Vermuntila
Pyhäjärvi
Reila
43
32
Hinnerjoki
204
Pyhämaa
Pyhäranta
Laajoki
2021
196
Laitila
43
Kalanti
Karjala
2021
Uusikaupunki/
Nystad
60
202
Tortinmäki
Lokalahti
Mynämäki
Vehmaa
194
193
8
192
Rautila
Mietoinen
Paatinen
196
Askainen
190
Masku
9
Kustavi
Taivassalo
192
E63
Jurmo
192
Turku
Hakkenpää
193
Raisio
222
Velkua
8
Fiskö
Avå
Iniö
Naantali
E18
189
TURKU/
Åland/Ahvenanmaa
Brändö
Rymättylä
ÅBO
Enklinge
Björkö
Pargas/
Geta
Lappo
Parainen
BOLSTEHOLM
Houtsala
Kumlinge
Skiftet Kihti
Houtskär/
Houtskari
Lofsda
Saltvik
Finström
Sund
Vårdö
Storlandet
Nagu/
Storby
KASTELHOLMS
Delet
Seglinge
Korpo/
Nauvo
180
Godby
Teili
180
Korppoo
Eckerö
Hammarland
2
Bomarsund
180
1801
1
Jomala
Sottunga
Korpoström
Drå
Lumparland
Gullkrona Fjärd
Mariehamn/
Långnäs
Överö
Maarianhamina
Lemland
3
Hastersboda
Nötö
Degerby
Hellsö
SKÄRGÅRDSHAVETS NATIONALPARK /
Föglö
Kökar
Herröskkatan
SAARISTOMEREN KANSALLISPUISTO
lshav
Karlby
Visby
Kappelskär
Stockholm
Jurmo

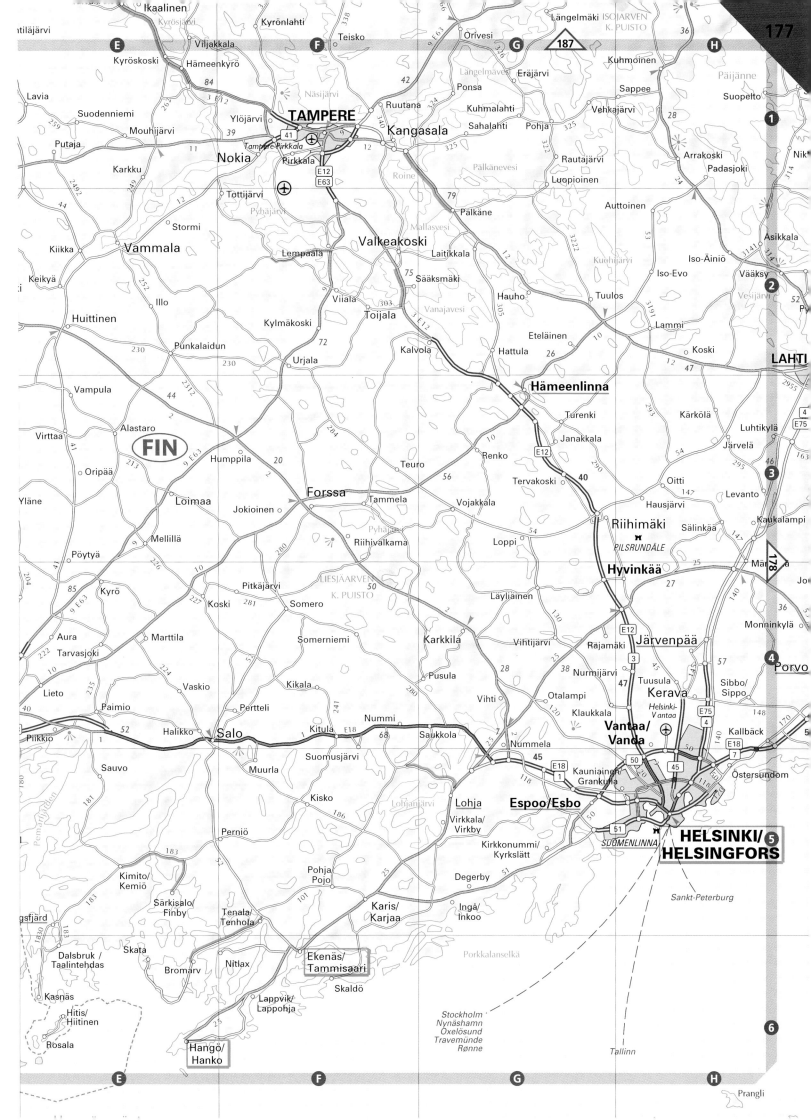

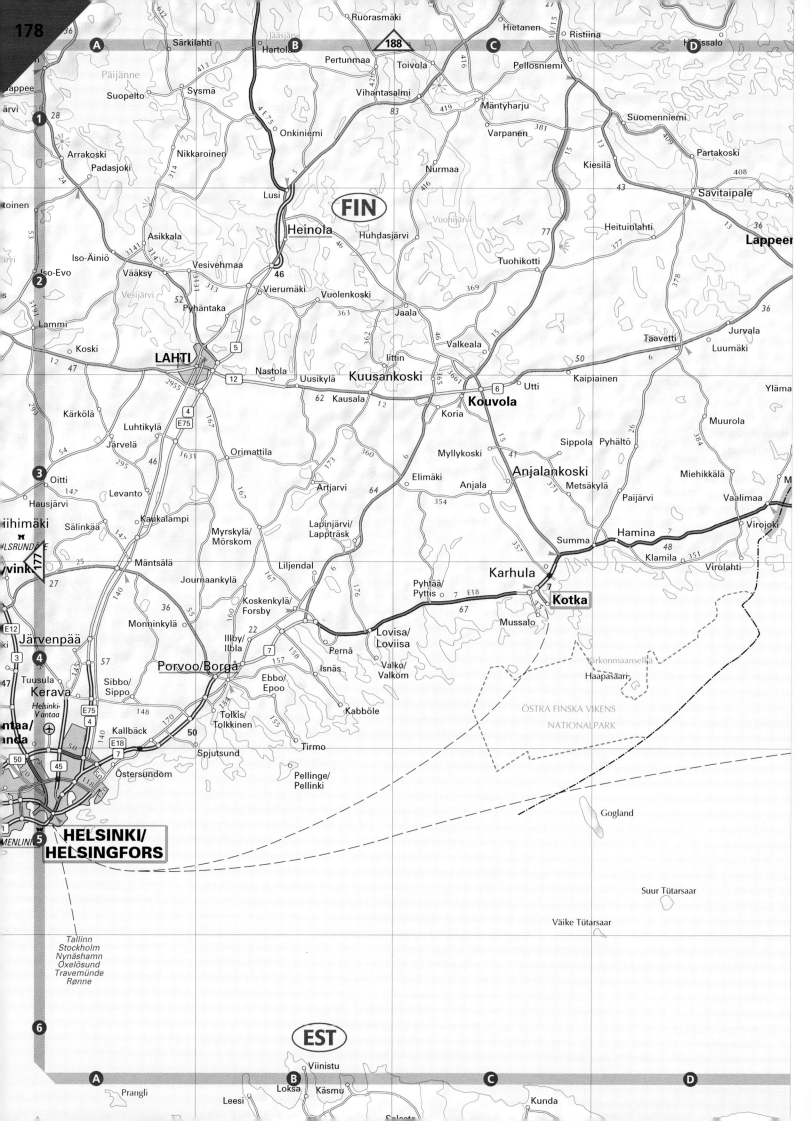

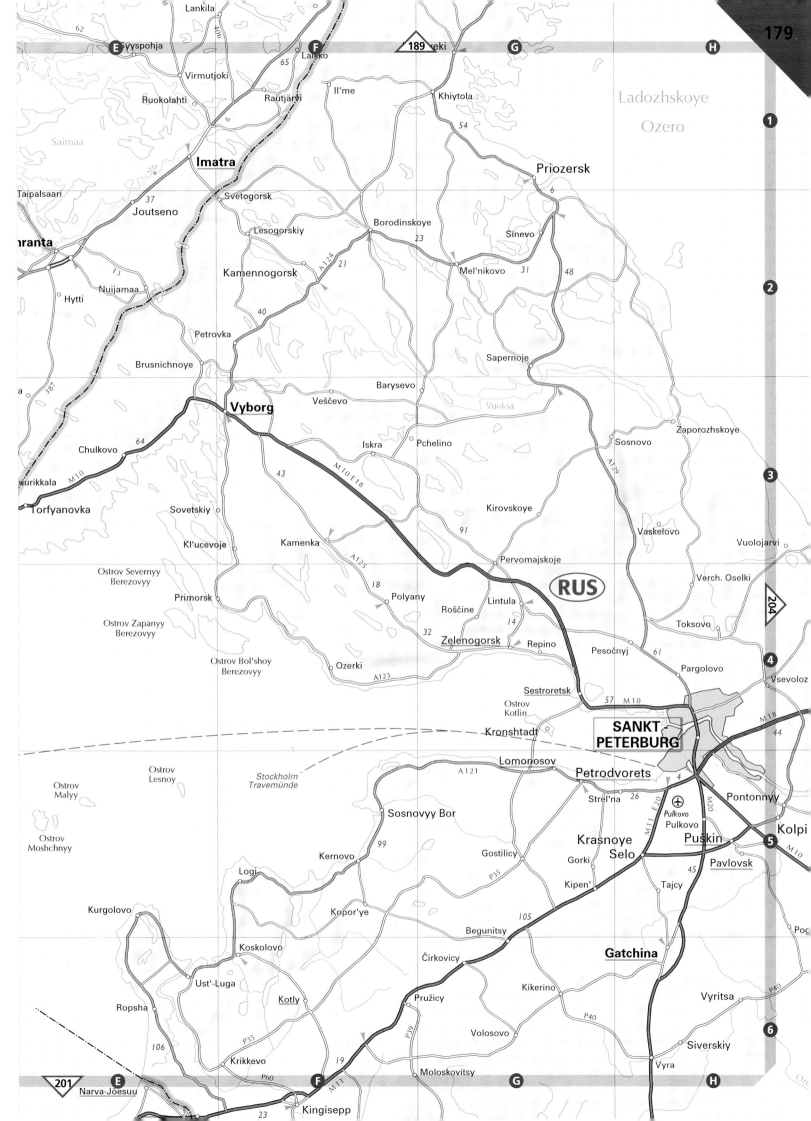

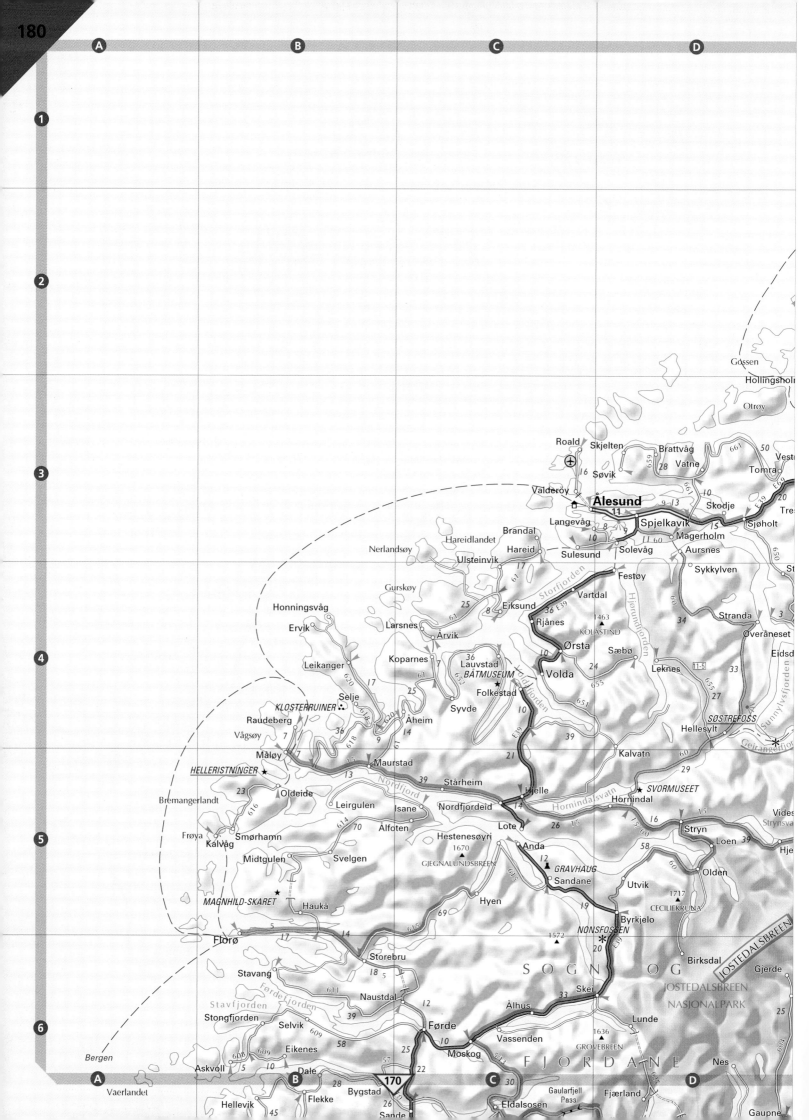

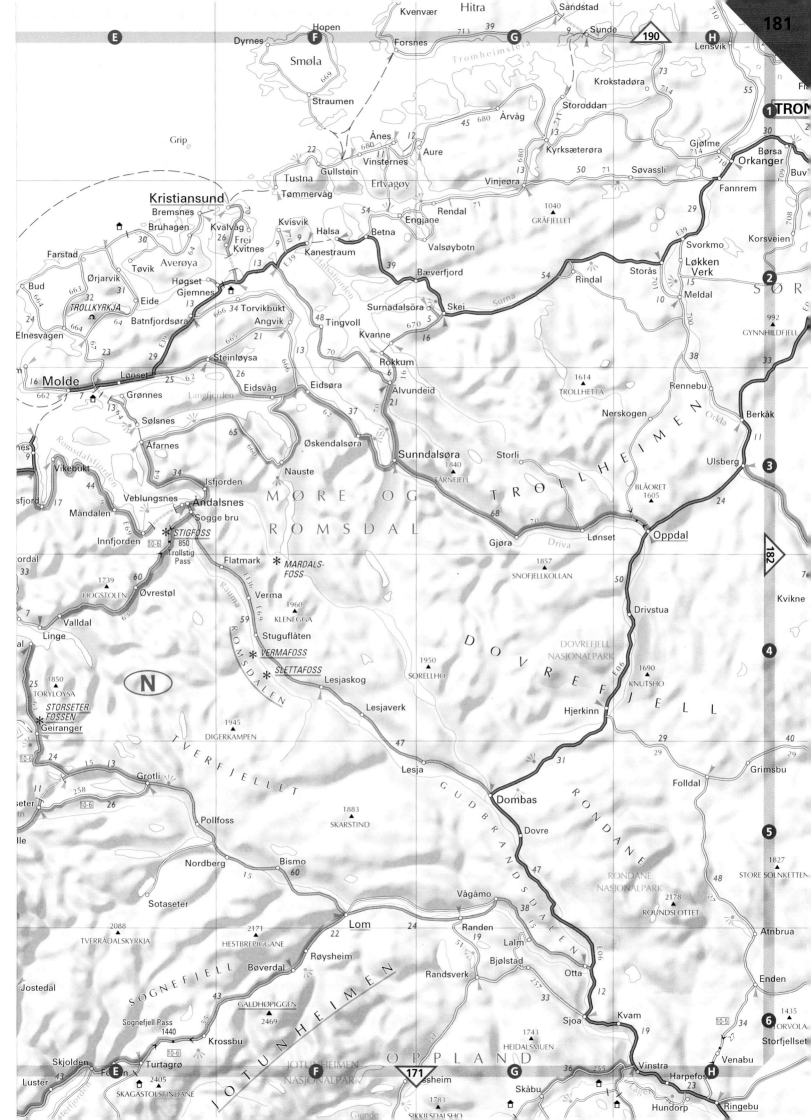

Kvenvær Hitra Sandstad
Hopen Sunde
E Dyrnes F Forsnes 713 39 G 9 6 190 H Lensvik
Smøla Tromheimsleia

Straumen 710 55
1 TROM
45 680 Årvåg 714 30
Krokstadøra 73
Storoddan
Grip Ånes 12 Aure 211 Gjølme 714 Børsa
22 680 11 Kyrksæterøra Orkanger
Vinsternes 680 Søvassli 710
Kristiansund Tustna Gullstein Ertvagøy Vinjeøra 13 50 71 Fannrem
Bremsnes Tømmervåg
Bruhagen Kvalvåg Kvisvik 54 Rendal 71 709
Frei Halsa Betna Engjane 1040 29 708
30 26 Kvitnes 9 Kanestraum GRÅFJELLET E39 Korsveien
Farstad 64 13 E39 Valsøybotn Svorkmo SØR
Tøvik Averøya Bæverfjord 2
Ørjarvik Høgset 39 Svorkmo Løkken
Bud 663 31 Gjemnes 13 Surnadalsøra Storås Verk
664 32 666 34 Torvikbukt Skei 54 Rindal 701 Meldal
24 664 TROLLKYRKJA Batnfjordsøra Angvik 48 Tingvoll Surna 10 38
Elnesvågen 664 23 29 665 21 Kvanne 670 5 1614 Rennebu
16 Molde Lønset Steinløysa 666 13 70 Røkkum 16 TROLLHETTA Orkla Berkåk
662 7 25 62 26 Eidsvåg 6 Alvundeid 1840 Nerskogen 11
13 Grønnes Eidsøra 21 TÄRNEFJELL Storli
Sølsnes Langfjorden 62 37 70 Sunndalsøra 992
65 Øskendalsøra Nauste GYNNHILDFJELL
Åfarnes 660 Storli Ulsberg
Vikebukt 64 34 Isfjorden MØRE OG 68 BLÅORET 3
44 9 Veblungsnes Andalsnes ROMSDAL 70 1605 24
sfjord 17 Sogge bru Gjøra Lønset Oppdal
Måndalen STIGFOSS Driva
Innfjorden 10-6 850 Flatmark MARDALS- 1857 182
ordal Trollstig FOSS SNOFJELLKOLLAN 50
33 Pass Verma 1960 Drivstua Kvikne
1739 60 Øvrestøl E136 KLENEGGA DOVREFJELL
HOGSTOLEN 63 E69 NASJONALPARK 4
7 Valldal 59 Stuguflåten DO 1690
Linge 1950 KNUTSHO
25 1850 VERMAFOSS SORELLHO VR E06
TORYLØYSA SLETTAFOSS Lesjaskog Hjerkinn EFJELL
STORSETER- Lesjaverk 29
FOSSEN N 1945 40
Geiranger DIGERKAMPEN 47 31 Folldal Grimsbu
10-6 24 Lesja RO 29
15 13 DOVRE 29
Grotli Dombas NDANE
11 258 TVERFJELLET GU Dovre 5
eter 10-6 26 1883 DB 1827
Pollfoss SKARSTIND RA 47 STORE SOLNKETTEN
NDS 2178
Nordberg Bismo DA RONDANE 48
15 60 Vågåmo LE NASJONALPARK ROUNDSLOTTET
Sotaseter T 38 Atnbrua
2088 2171 Lom 24 Randen 15
TVERRÅDALSKYRKJA HESTBREPIGGANE 22 19 Lalm E06
Bøverdal Røysheim 51 Bjølstad Enden
GALDHØPIGGEN Randsverk Otta 257 12 1435
43 2469 SOGNEFJELL JO Sjoa 10-5 34 TORVOLA 6
Sognefjell Pass TU 1743 19 Storfjellset
1440 Krossbu NH 51 HEIDALSMUEN Kvam Venabu
Skjolden 10-6 E EI Vinstra H
Luster 43 E Turtagrø F ME 171 G 36 255 Harpefos
2405 JOTUNHEIMEN sheim Skåbu 23 Ringebu
SKAGASTOLSTINDANE NASJONALPARK OPPLAND Hundorp
1783
SIKKILSDALSHO

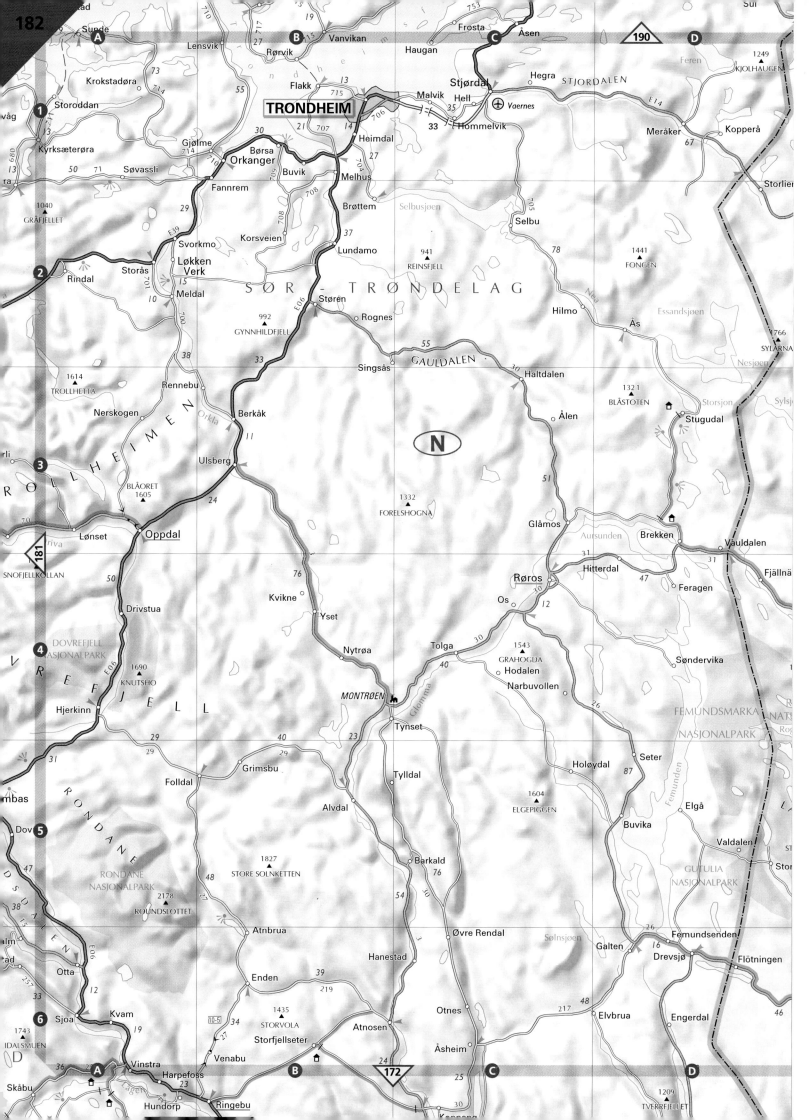

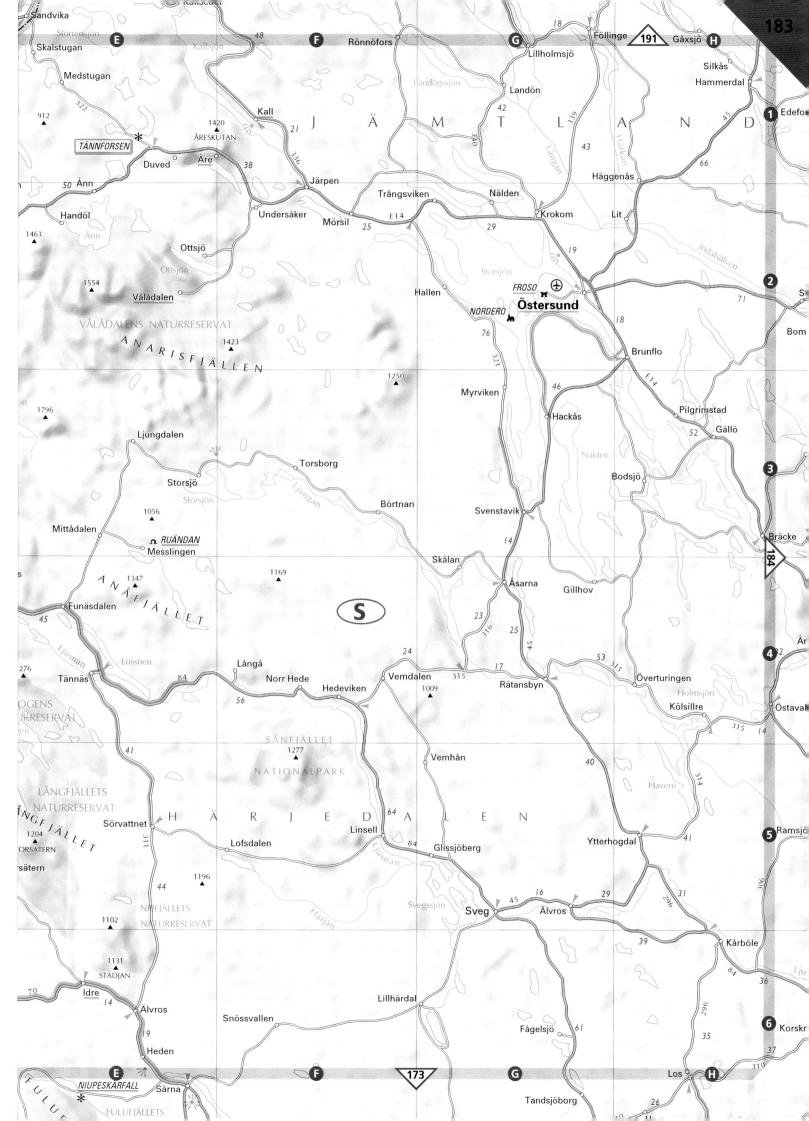

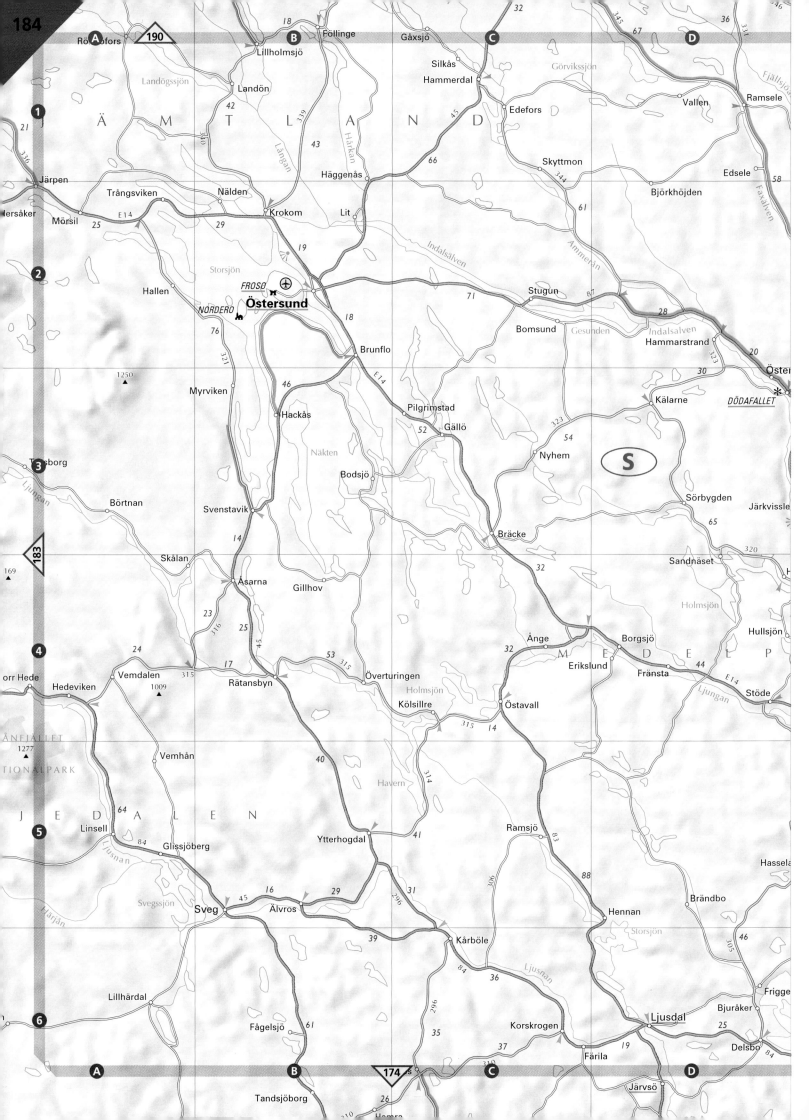

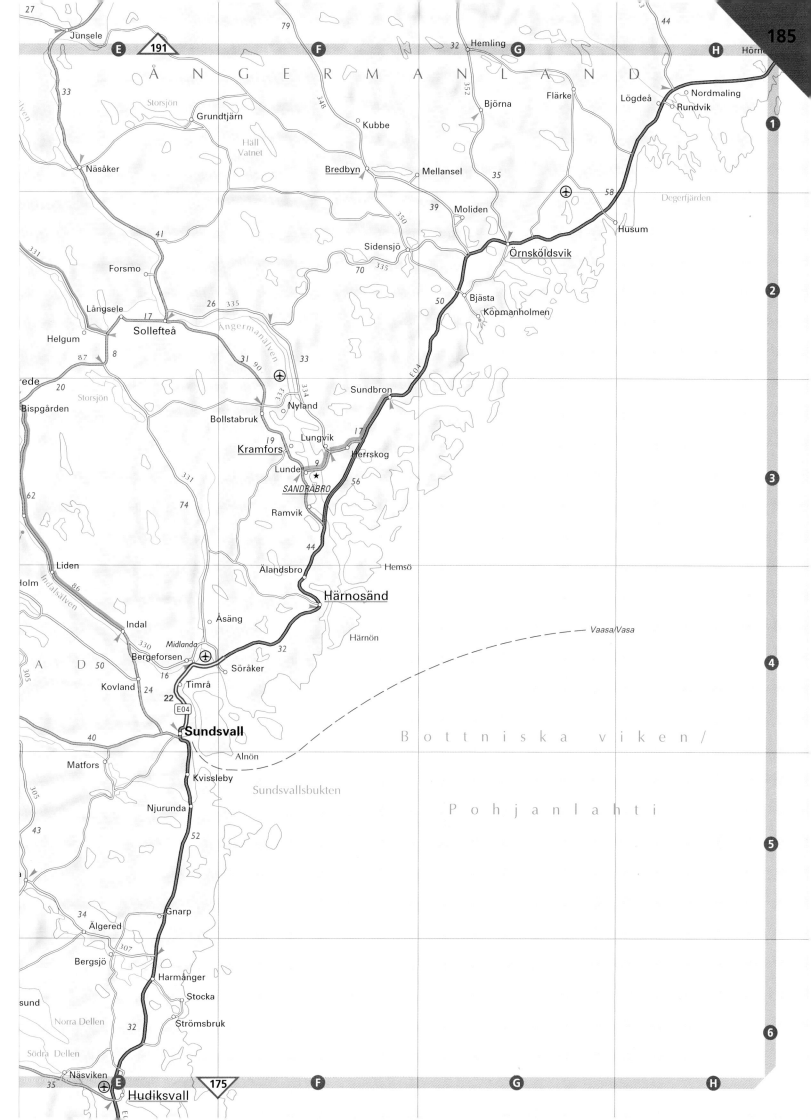

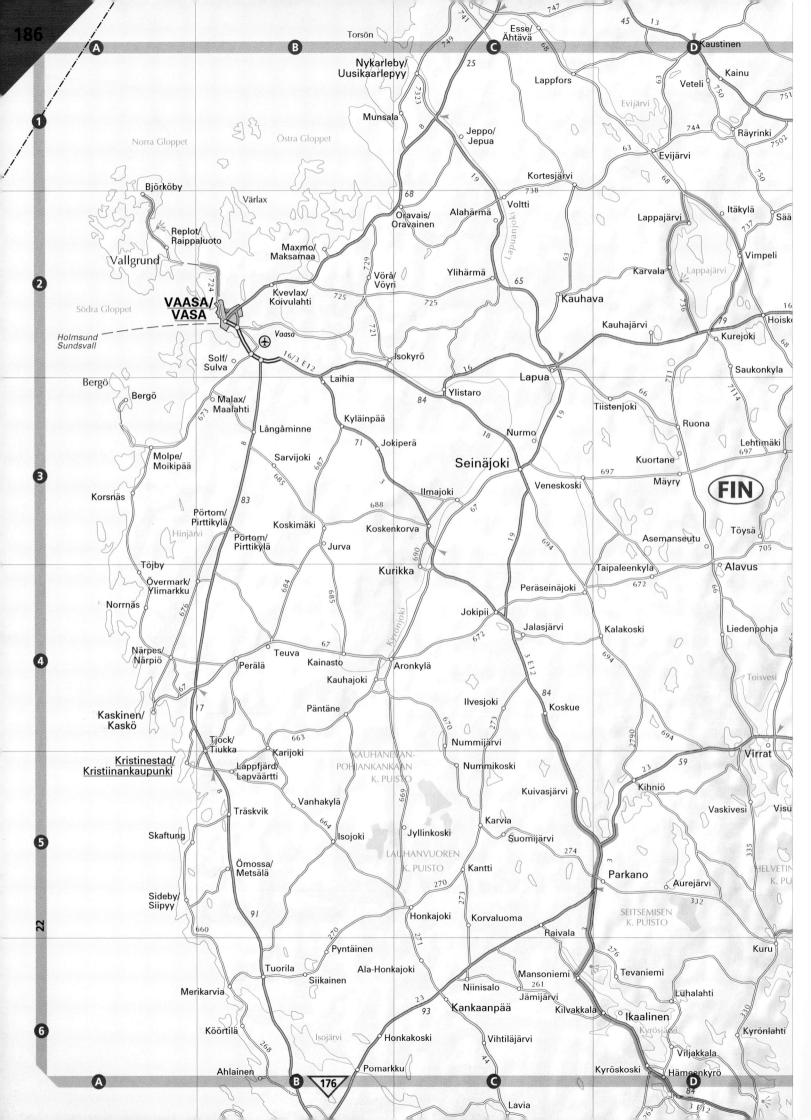

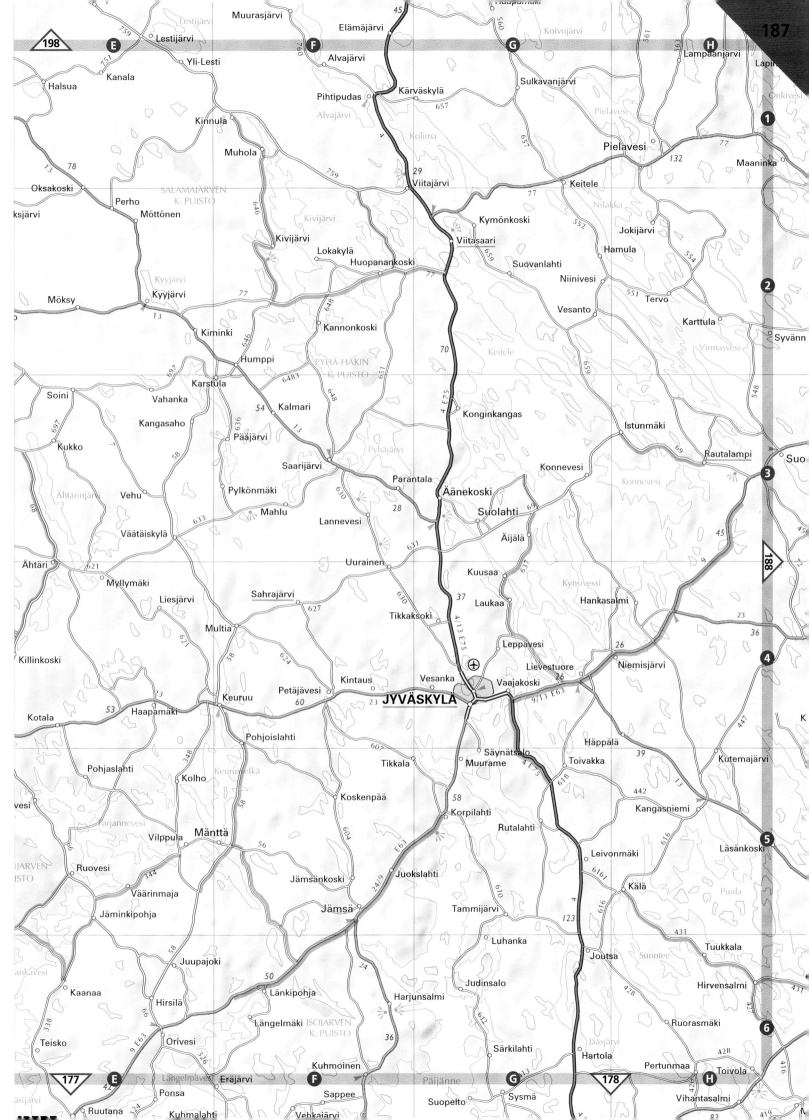

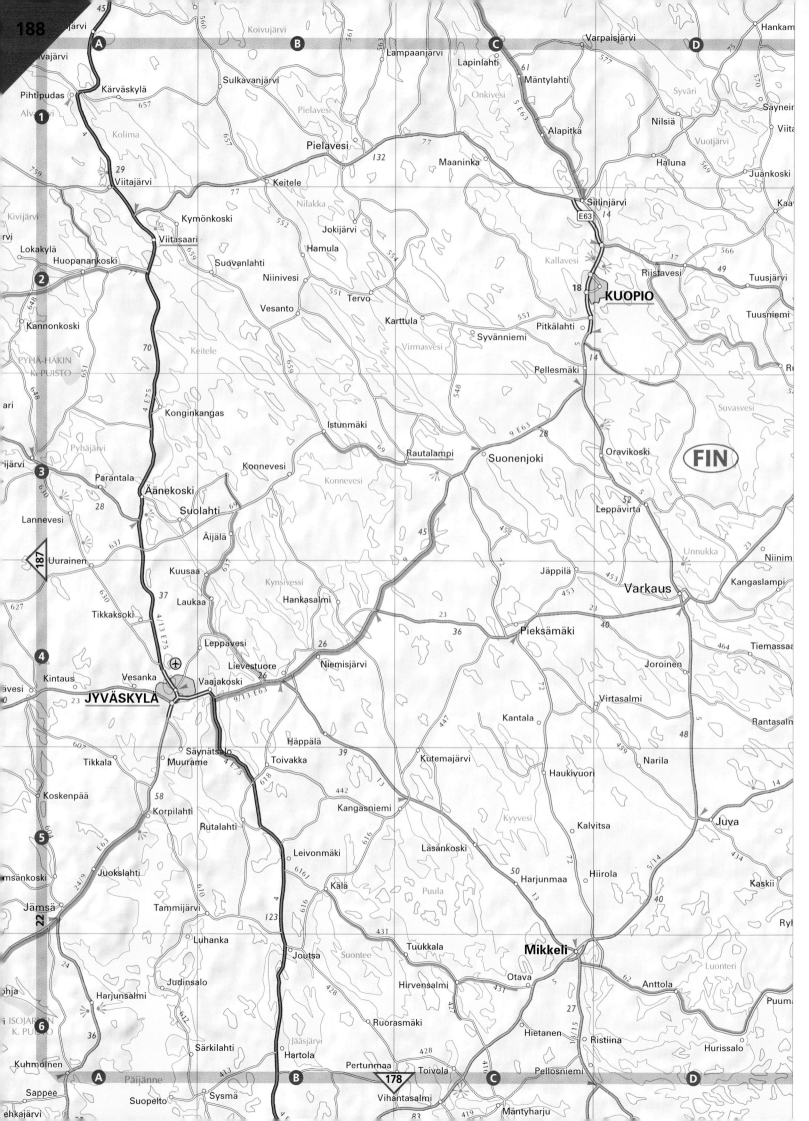

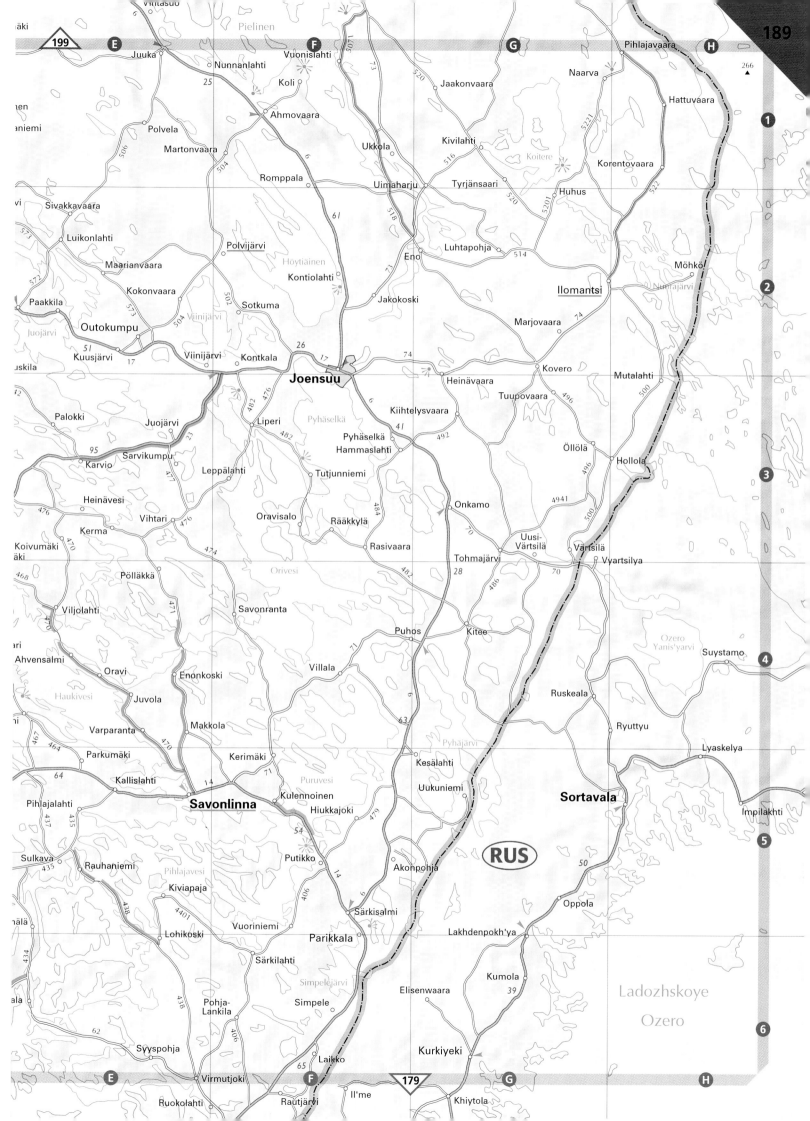

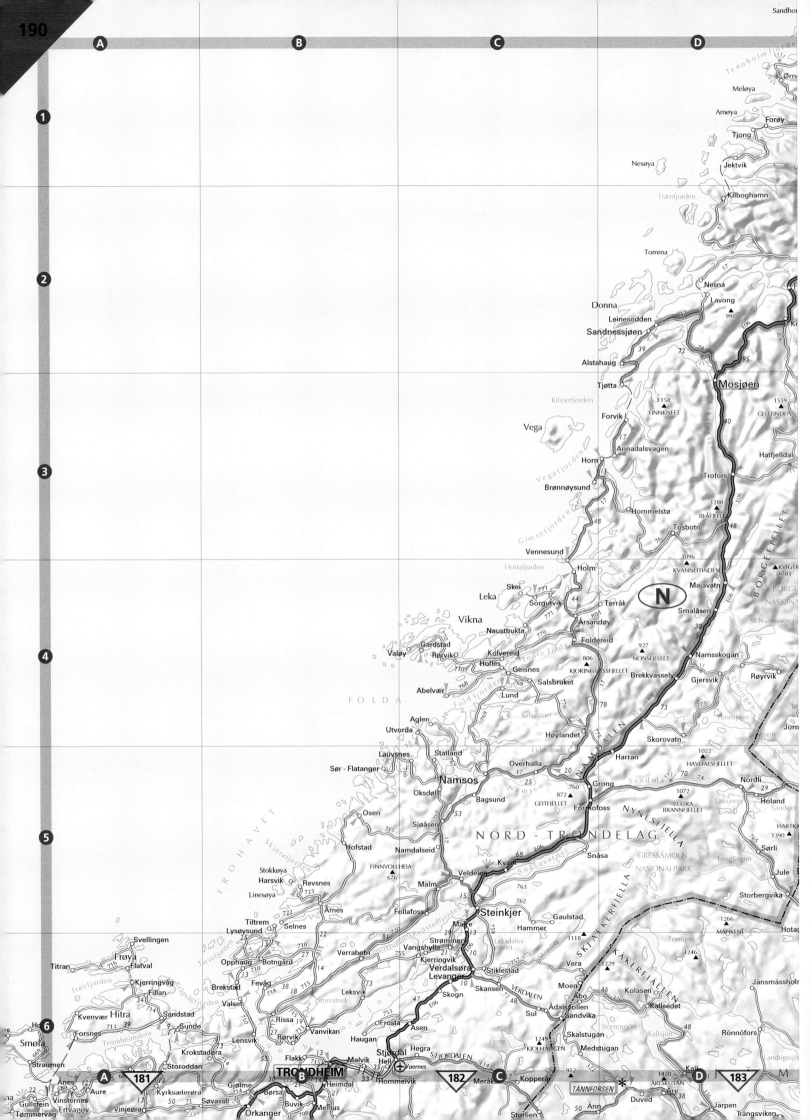

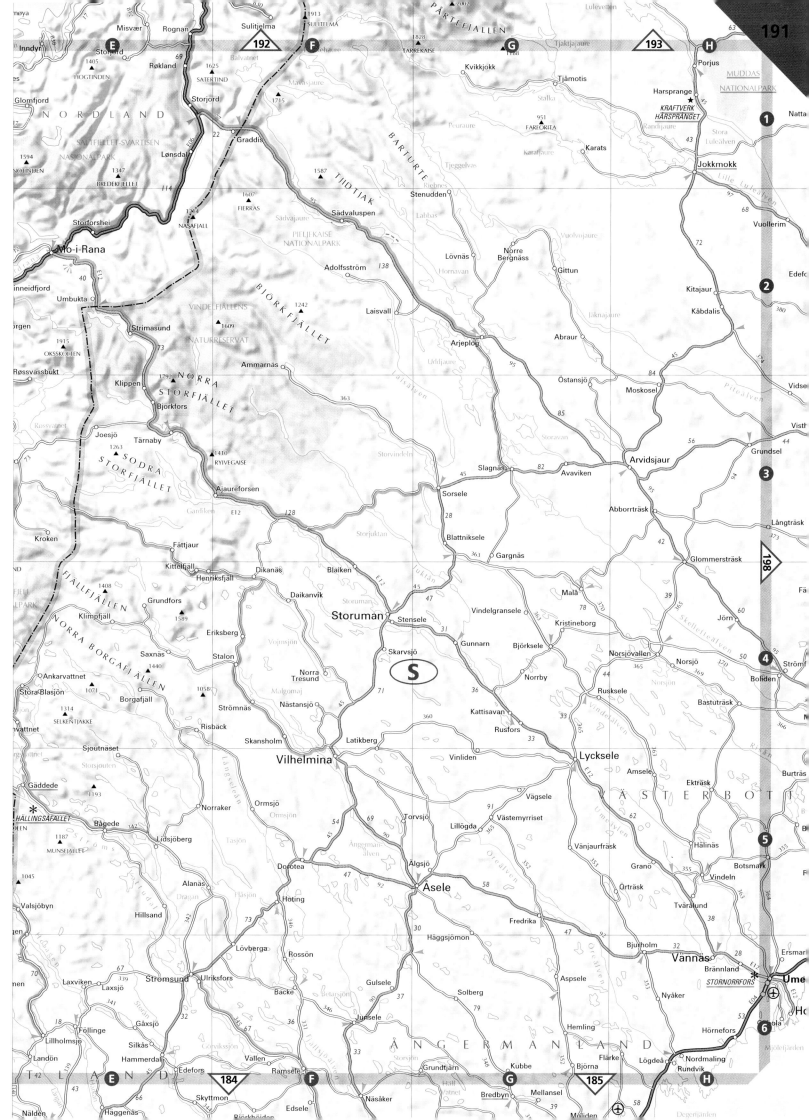

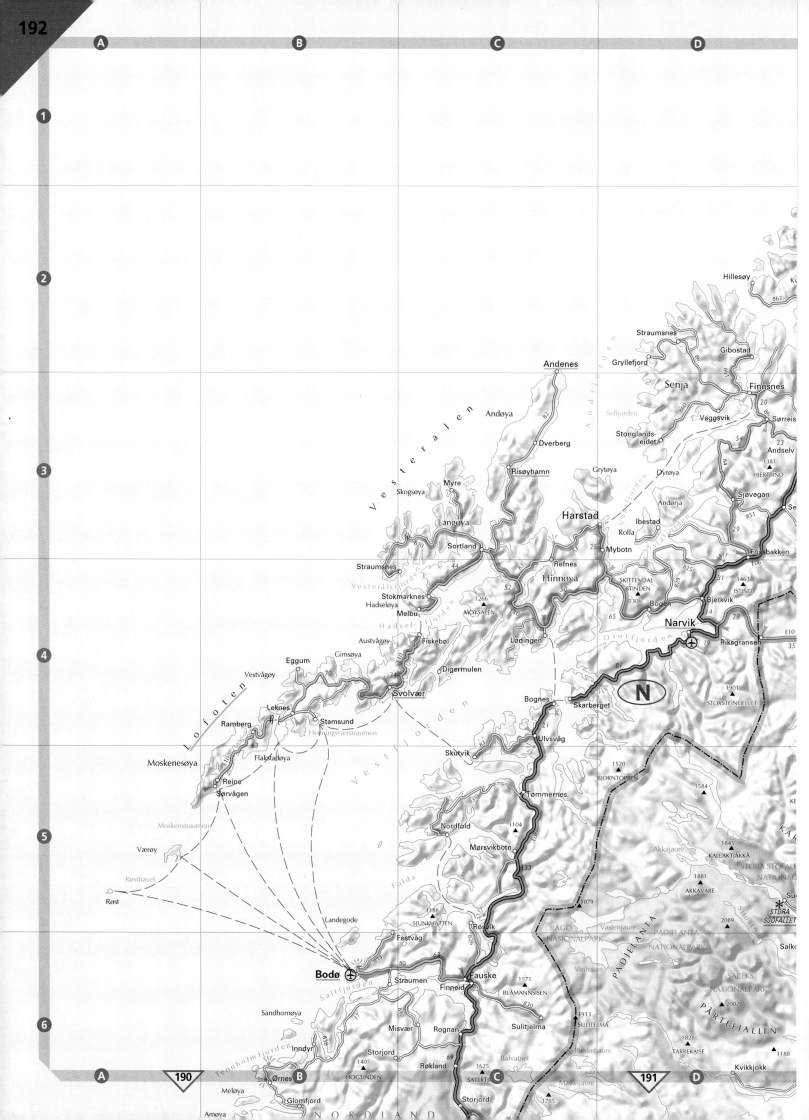

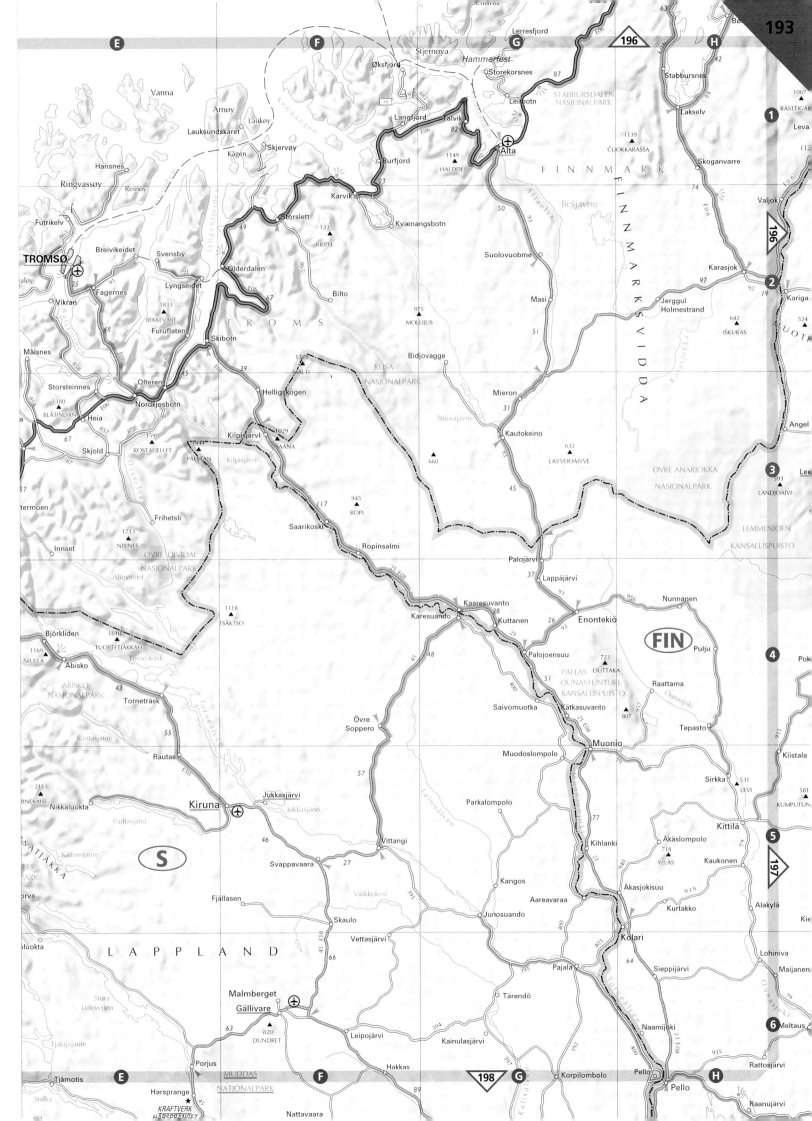

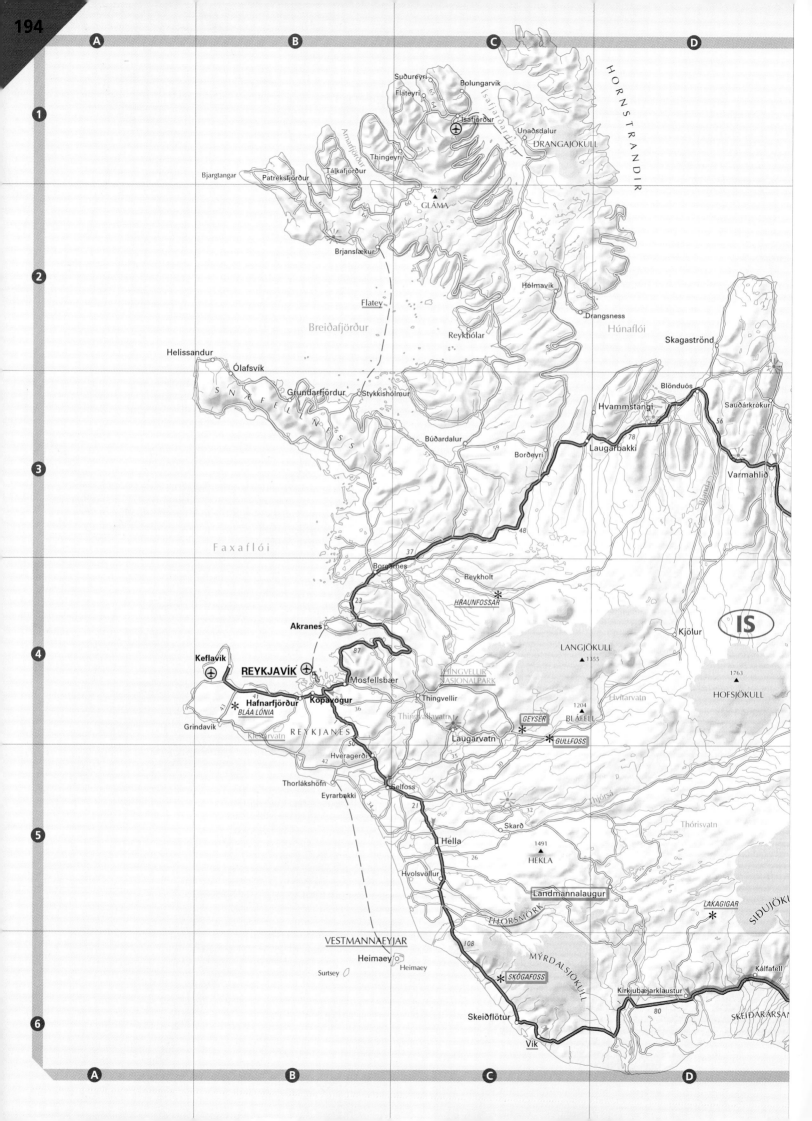

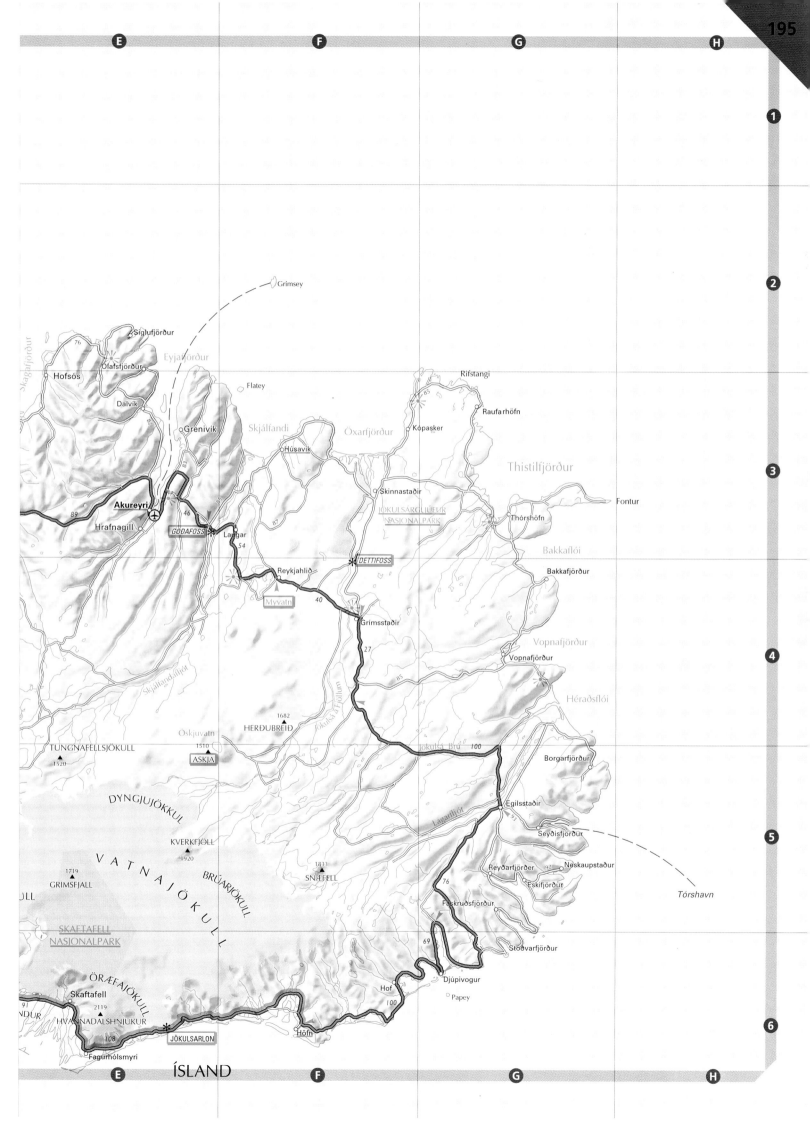

ÍSLAND

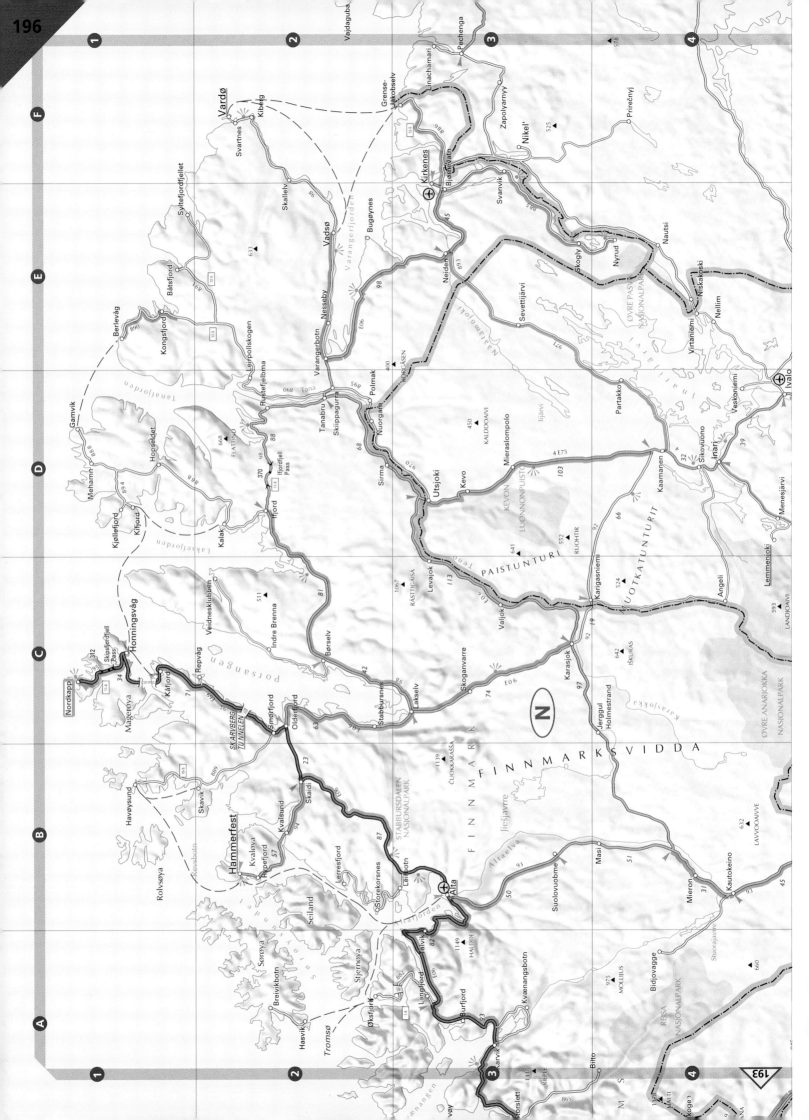

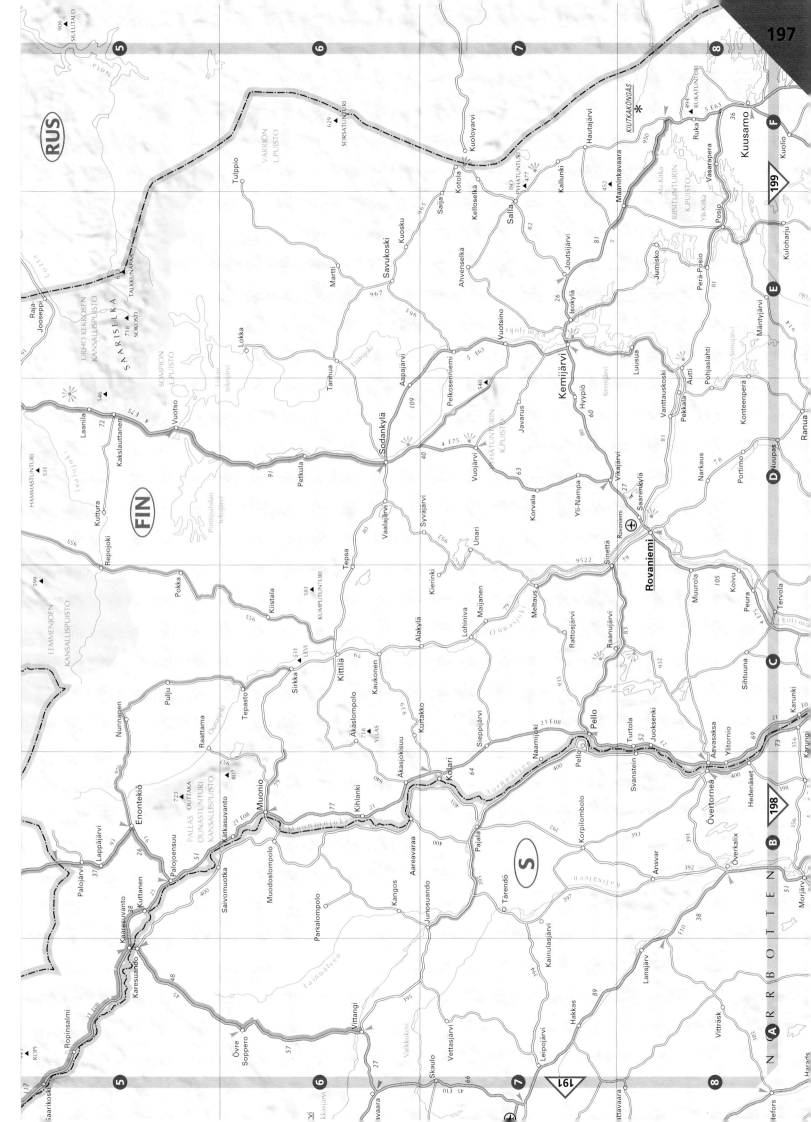

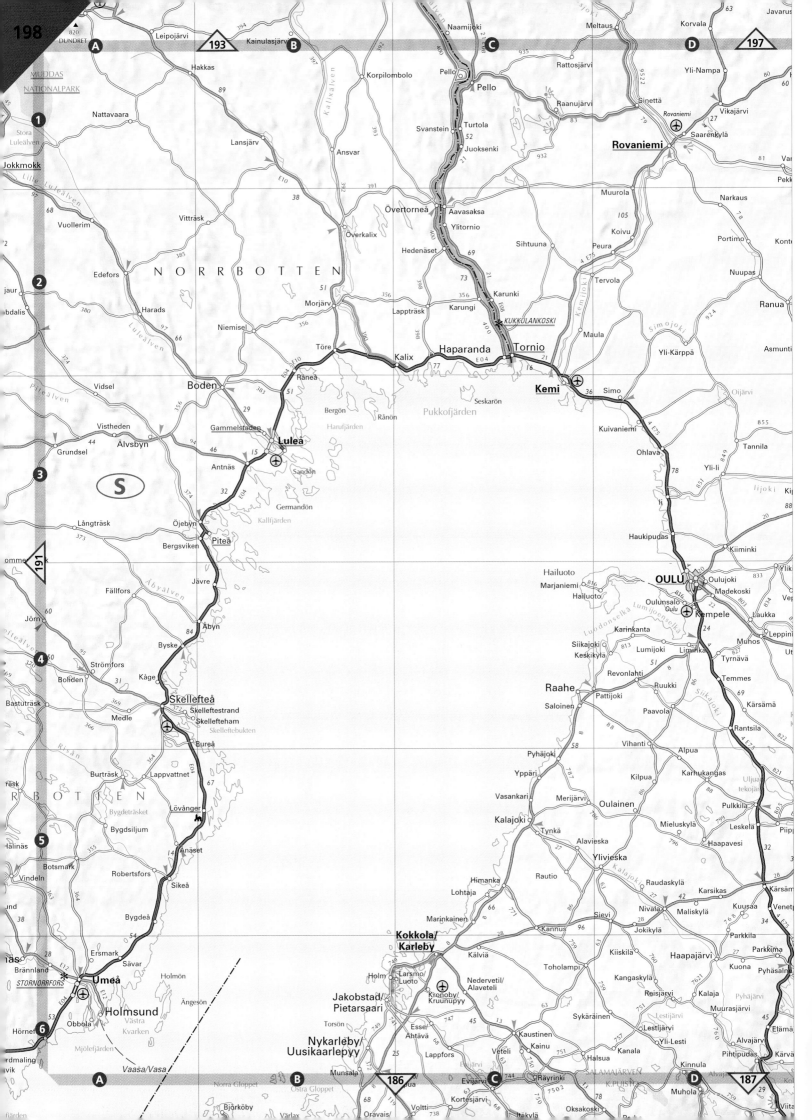

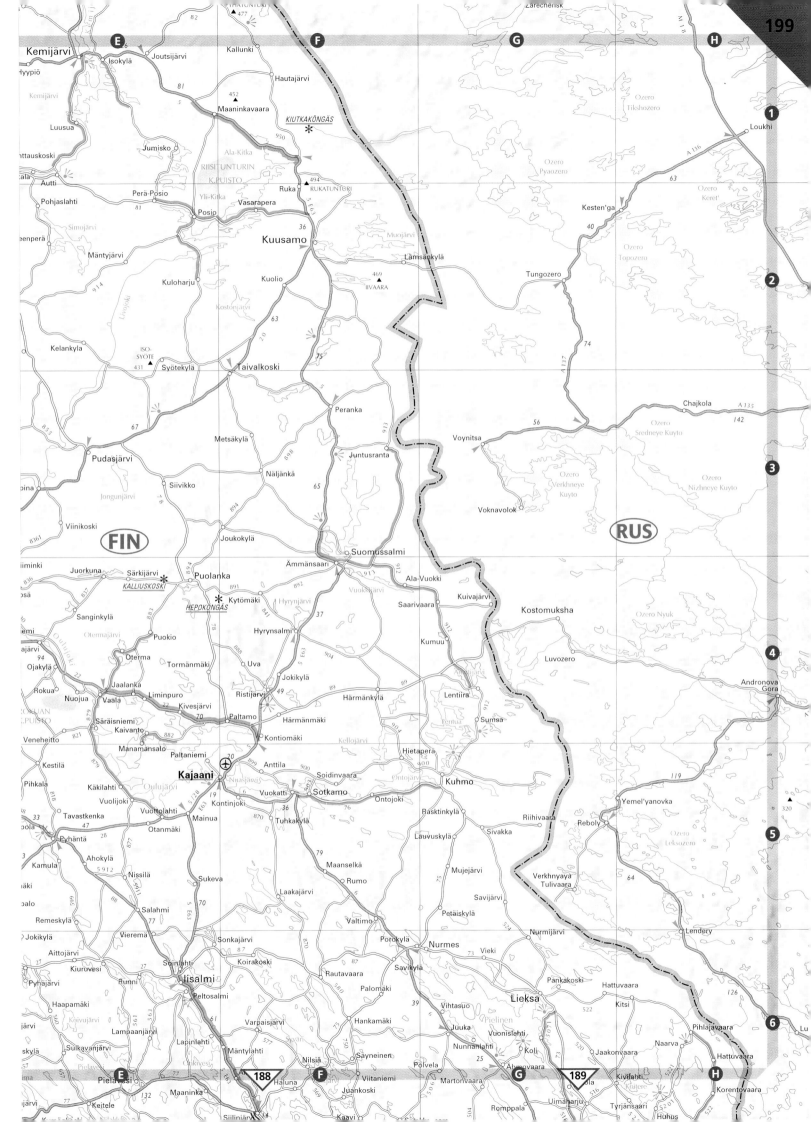

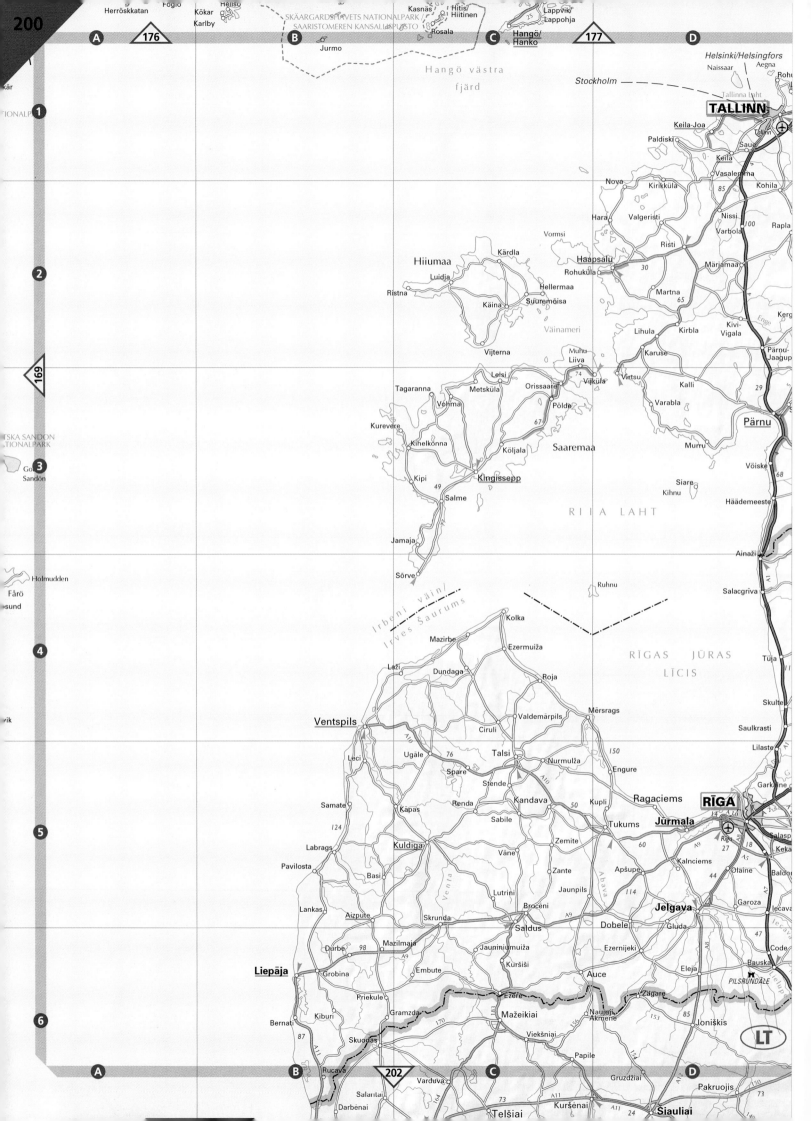

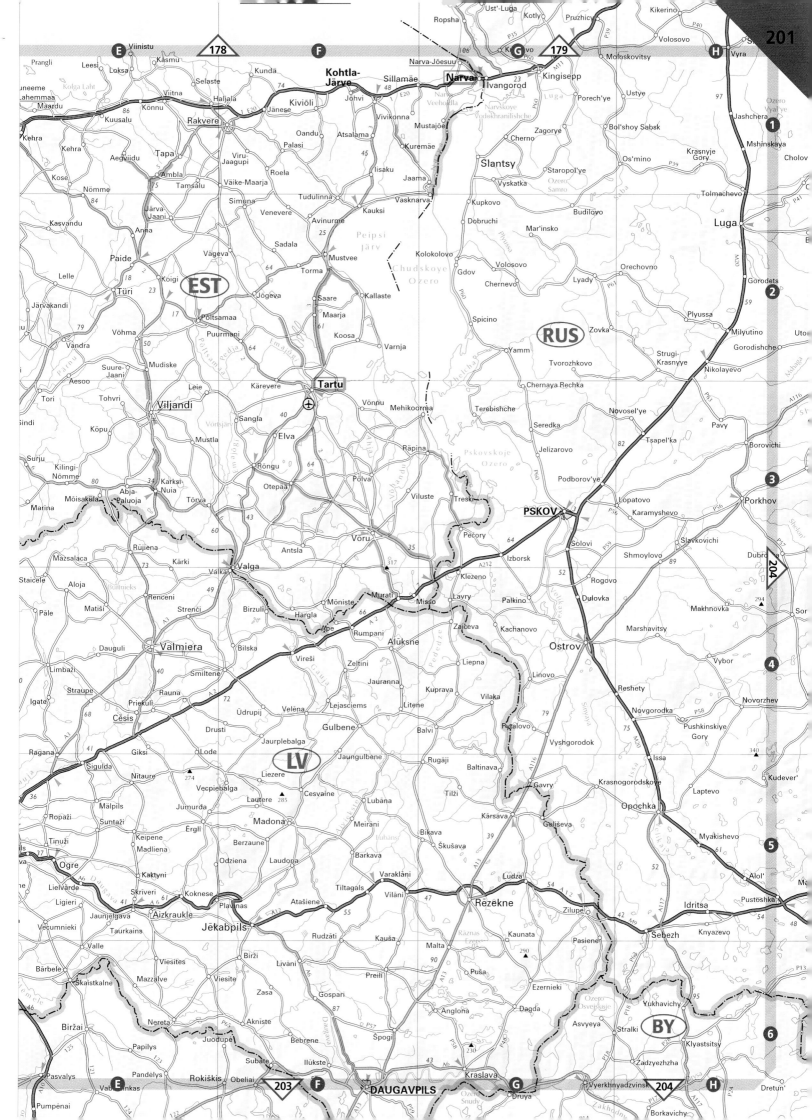

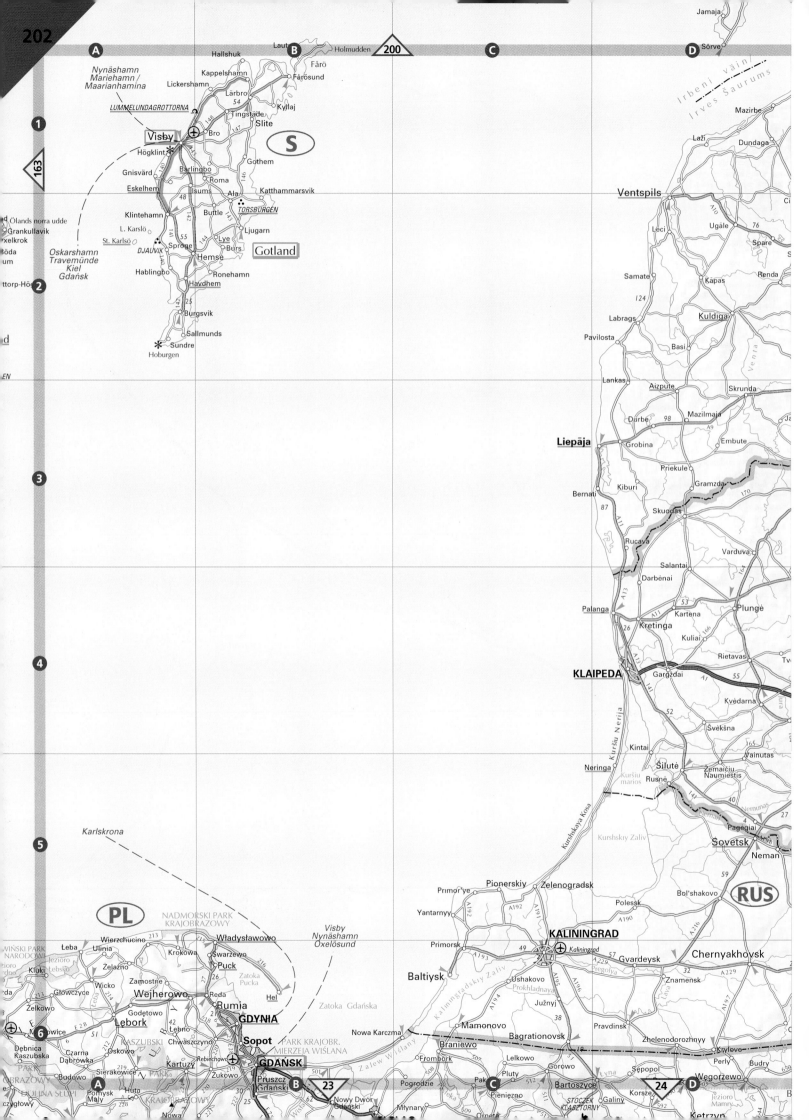

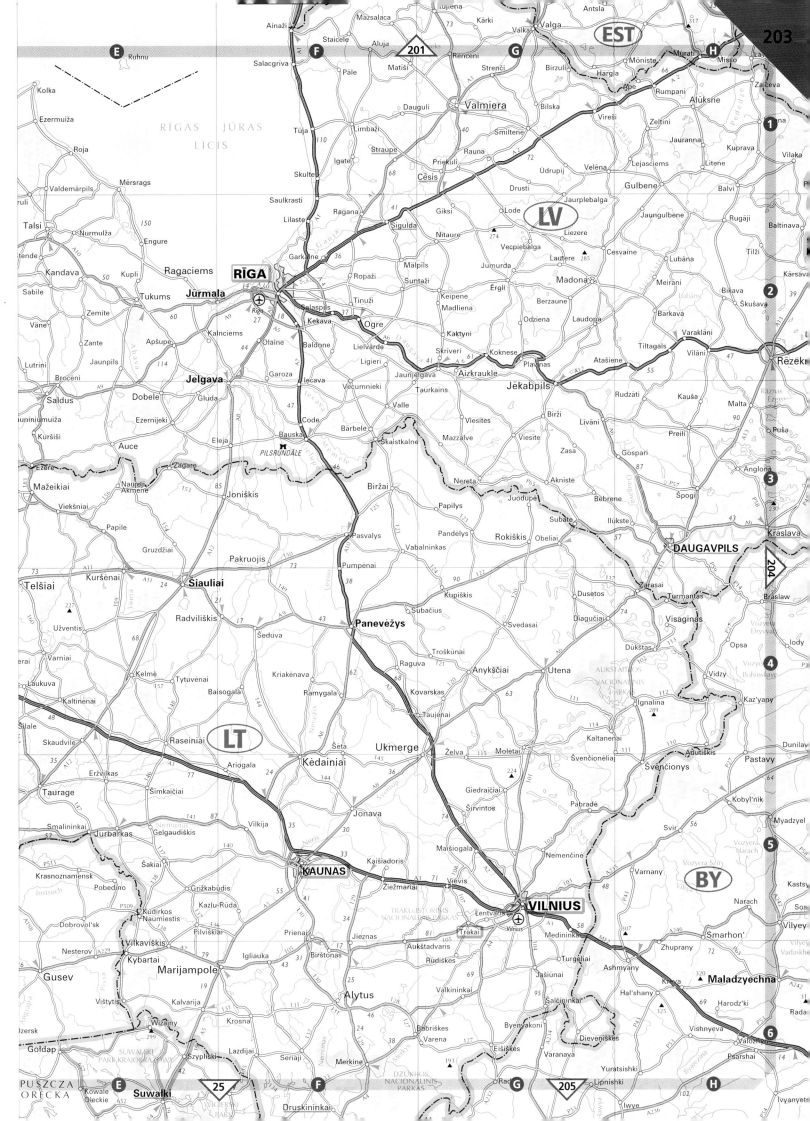

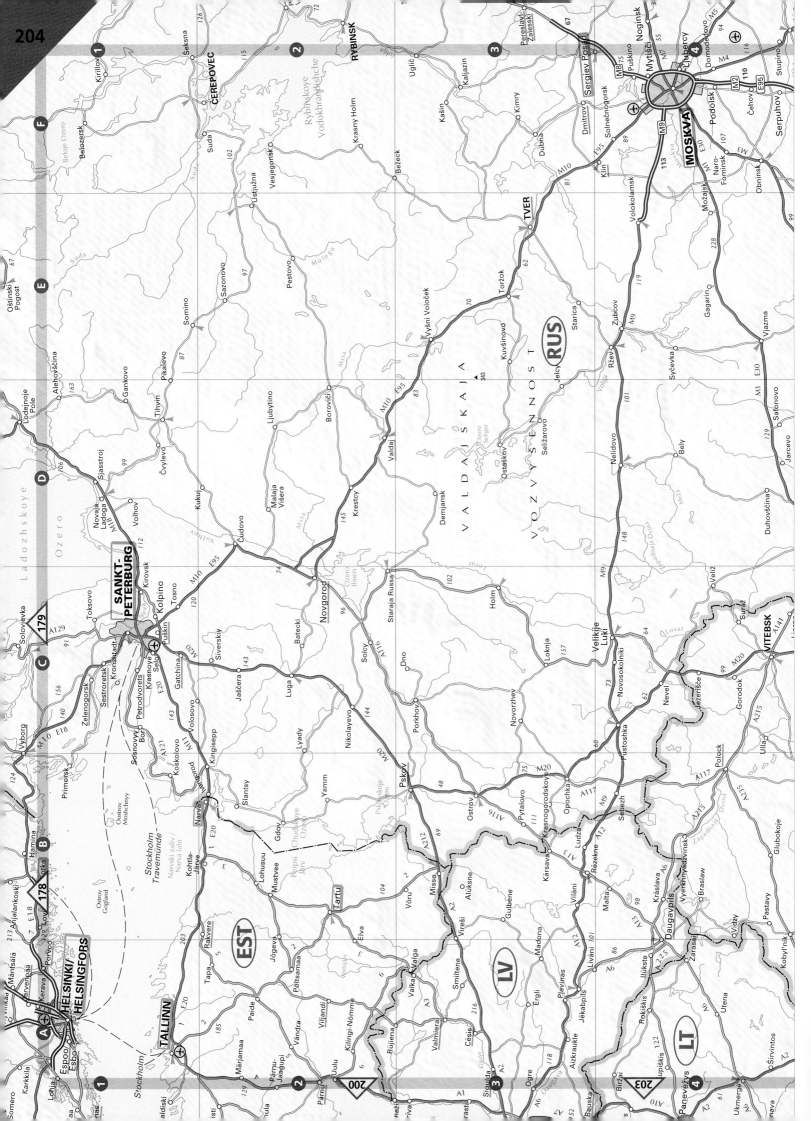

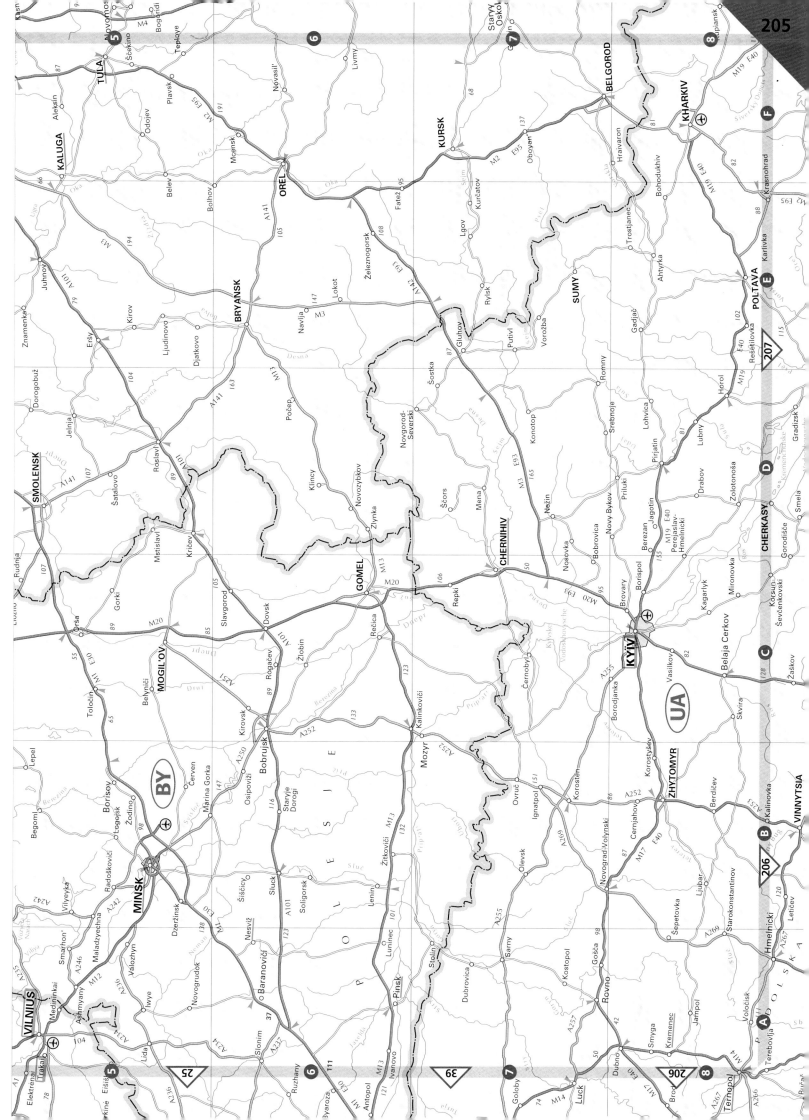

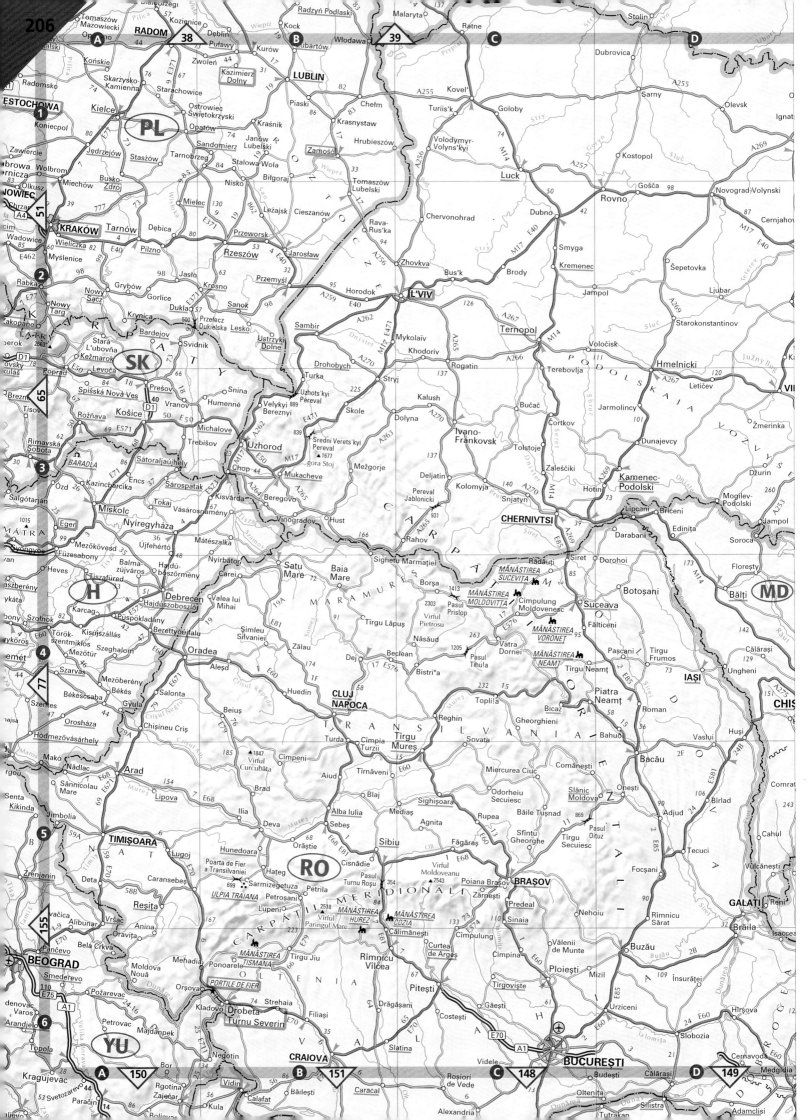

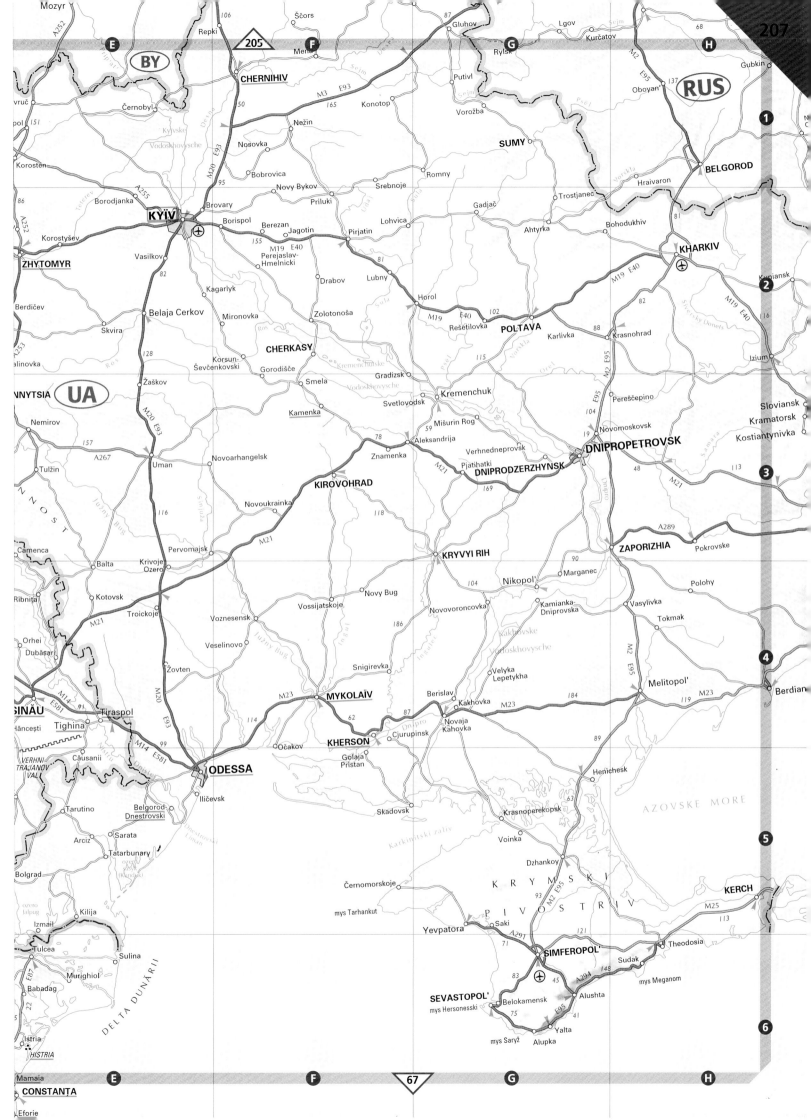

INDEX OF NAMES
INDICE DEI NOMI
ÍNDICE DE TOPÓNIMOS
INDEX DES NOMS
NAMENVERZEICHNIS

How to use the index • Avvertenze per la ricerca
Instrucciones para la consulta • Notices pour la recherche
Erläuterungen des Suchsystems

The index lists the place names and the main tunnels and passes contained in the map, followed by the abbreviation of the country name to which they belong. For easiness all names contained in two adjoining pages are referred to the even page number.

L'indice elenca i toponimi dei centri abitati e dei principali tunnel e passi presenti in cartografia accompagnati dalla sigla della nazione di appartenenza. Per semplicità tutti i nomi contenuti in due pagine affiancate sono riferiti alla pagina di numero pari.

El índice presenta los topónimos de las localidades y de los principales túneles y puertos de montaña que figuran en el mapa, seguidos de la sigla que indica el País de pertenencia. Para simplicidad todos los nombres contenidos en dos páginas juntas éstan referidos a la página de número par.

L'index récense les noms des localités et des principales tunnels et cols contenus dans la carte, suivis par le sigle qui indique le Pays d'appartenance. Pour simplicité tous les noms contenus dans deux pages l'une à côté de l'autre sont rap-portés à la page avec nombre pair.

Der Index enthält die in der Karte vorhandenen Namen von Ortschaften und wichtigsten Tunneln und Pässe, von dem zugehörigen Staatskennzeichen gefolgt. Zur Einfachheit sind alle in zwei nebeneinanderen Seiten enthaltenen Namen auf die Seite mit gerader Zahl bezogen.

PRINCIPAL URBAN AREAS PLANS
PIANTE DELLE PRINCIPALI AREE URBANE
PLANOS DE LAS PRINCIPALES ÁREAS URBANAS
PLANS DES PRINCIPALES AIRES URBAINES
WICHTIGSTE STADTPLÄNE

Amsterdam	Genève	Napoli
Antwerpen/Anvers	Göteborg	Oslo
Athína	Helsinki/Helsingfors	Paris
Barcelona	İstanbul	Porto
Beograd	København	Praha
Berlin	Köln	Roma
Bern	Lisboa	Rotterdam
Birmingham	Liverpool-Manchester	Salzburg
Bratislava	London	Sevilla
Brussel/Bruxelles	Luxembourg	Sofiya
Bucureşti	Lyon	Stockholm
Budapest	Madrid	Strasbourg
Den Haag	Marseille	Venezia
Edinburgh	Milano	Warszawa
Firenze	Moskva	Wien
Frankfurt am Main	München	Zürich

A

Aabenraa [DK] 156 C4
Aachen [D] 30 F4
Aakirkeby [DK] 158 E4
Aalborg [DK] 160 D4
Aalburg [NL] 16 D6
Aalen [D] 60 B2
Aalsmeer [NL] 16 D4
Aalst (Alost) [B] 28 H2
Aalten [NL] 16 G6
Aalter [B] 28 G2
Äänekoski [FIN] 186 G3
Aapajärvi [FIN] 196 D6
Aarau [CH] 58 E5
Aarberg [CH] 58 D5
Aarburg [CH] 58 E5
Aareavaara [S] 192 G5
Aars [DK] 160 D4
Aarschot [B] 30 D4
Aavasaksa [FIN] 196 B8
Aba [H] 76 B2
Abadín [E] 78 E2
Abádszalók [H] 64 F6
Abanilla [E] 104 C2
Abano Terme [I] 110 G1
Abarán [E] 104 C2
Abaújszántó [H] 64 G4
Abbadia San Salvatore [I] 114 G2
Abbasanta [I] 118 C4
Abbekås [S] 158 C3
Abbeville [F] 28 D4
Abbeydorney [IRL] 4 B3
Abbeyfeale [IRL] 4 C3
Abbeyleix [IRL] 4 E3
Abbiategrasso [I] 70 F5
Abborrträsk [S] 190 H3
Abbotsbury [GB] 12 F5
Abdürrahim [TR] 130 H3
Abejar [E] 90 B2
Abela [P] 94 C2
Abelnes [N] 164 C5
Abelvær [N] 190 C4
Abenberg [D] 46 G5
Abenójar [E] 96 D4
Abensberg [D] 60 E2
Aberaeron [GB] 10 B6
Aberchirder [GB] 6 F5
Aberdare [GB] 12 F2
Aberdaron [GB] 10 A4
Aberdeen [GB] 6 F6
Aberdour [GB] 8 E3
Aberdyfi [GB] 10 B5
Aberfeldy [GB] 8 E1
Aberfoyle [GB] 8 D2
Abergavenny [GB] 12 F2
Abergele [GB] 10 C4
Aberlour [GB] 6 E5
Abersoch [GB] 10 B4
Abertillery [GB] 12 F2
Aberystwyth [GB] 10 B6
Abetone [I] 110 E4

Abide [TR] 130 H5
Abide [TR] 144 G2
Abild [S] 162 B4
Abingdon [GB] 12 H3
Abisko [S] 192 E4
Abja–Paluoja [EST] 200 E3
Abla [E] 102 F4
Ablanitsa [BG] 148 B4
Ablis [F] 42 E4
Åbo [S] 190 C6
Åbo / Turku [FIN] 176 D4
Åboland [S] 166 C5
Abondance [F] 70 C2
Abony [H] 76 E2
Aboyne [GB] 6 F6
Abrantes [P] 86 D4
Abraur [S] 190 G2
Abreschviller [F] 44 G5
Abriès [F] 70 C6
Abtei [A] 74 B3
Abtenau [A] 60 H6
Abtshagen [D] 20 D3
Åby [S] 168 B5
Åby [S] 162 C4
Åby [S] 162 G5
Åbybro [DK] 160 D3
Åbyn [S] 198 B4
A Cañiza [E] 78 C5
Acate [I] 126 F5
Accadia [I] 120 G2
Acceglio [I] 108 E2
Accettura [I] 120 H4
Acciaroli [I] 120 F5
Accous [F] 84 D4
Accumoli [I] 116 B3
Acedo [E] 82 H6
Aceuchal [E] 94 G2
Acerno [I] 120 F3
Acerra [I] 120 E3
Aceuchal [E] 94 G2
Acharacle [GB] 6 B6
Achargary [GB] 6 E3
Acharnés [GR] 134 C6
Achavanich [GB] 6 F3
Achenkirch [A] 60 E6
Achern [D] 58 F1
Acheux–en–Amiénois [F] 28 E4
Achiltibuie [GB] 6 D3
Achim [D] 18 E5
Achladókampos [GR] 136 E2
Achlean [GB] 6 E6
Achnacroish [GB] 8 C1
Achnasheen [GB] 6 D4
Aci Castello [I] 126 G3
Acıpayam [TR] 144 G6
Acireale [I] 126 G3
Aci Trezza [I] 126 G3
A Coruña / La Coruña [E] 78 C2
Acqualagna [I] 112 B6
Acquanegra sul Chiese [I] 110 E1
Acquapendente [I] 114 G3

Acquasanta Terme [I] 116 C3
Acquasparta [I] 116 A3
Acquaviva delle Fonti [I] 122 D3
Acqui Terme [I] 108 H2
Acri [I] 124 D4
Ács [H] 64 A6
Acsa [H] 64 D5
Ada [YU] 76 E5
Adaköy [TR] 142 E3
Ådalsvollen [N] 190 C6
Adámas [GR] 138 D4
Adamclisi [RO] 206 D6
Adamuz [E] 96 C6
Adanero [E] 88 E3
Adapazari [TR] 146 H3
Adare [IRL] 4 C3
Adaševci [YU] 154 E2
Adelboden [CH] 70 D2
Adelebsen [D] 32 F4
Adelfi [GR] 134 C3
Adelfia [I] 122 E3
Adelsheim [D] 46 D5
Adelsried [D] 60 C3
Ademuz [E] 98 D2
Adenau [D] 30 G6
Adjud [RO] 206 D3
Admont [A] 62 C6
Ådneram [N] 164 C3
Adolfsström [S] 190 F2
Adony [H] 76 C2
Adorf [D] 48 C3
Adra [E] 102 F5
Adradas [E] 90 B4
Adrall [E] 92 D1
Adrano [I] 126 F3
Ádria [I] 110 G2
Adrigole [IRL] 4 B5
Adutiškis [LT] 202 H4
Ærøskobing [DK] 156 D4
Aegviidu [EST] 200 E1
Aereinó [GR] 132 H2
Aerzen [D] 32 F3
Aesoo [EST] 200 E2
A Estrada [E] 78 C3
Aetós [GR] 132 D5
Aetós [GR] 128 E4
Afántou [GR] 142 E4
Åfarnes [N] 180 E3
Affric Lodge [GB] 6 C5
Afiónas [GR] 132 A2
Aflenz [A] 62 D6
A Fonsagrada [E] 78 F3
Afoss [N] 164 G3
Áfyssos [GR] 134 A3
Áfytos [GR] 130 B6
Ağaçbeyli [TR] 144 G3
Ağaçlı [TR] 146 E2
Agaete [E] 100 C5
Agalas [GR] 136 A2
Agaró, S'– [E] 92 G4
Ág. Athanássios [GR] 128 H4

Agay [F] 108 E5
Agazzano [I] 110 C2
Agde [F] 106 E5
Agen [F] 66 E5
Agéranos [GR] 136 E5
Agerbæk [DK] 156 B2
Ag. Fotiá [GR] 140 G5
Agger [DK] 160 B4
Aggersund [DK] 160 D4
Ággíus [I] 118 D2
Aggsbach-Dorf [A] 62 D4
Aggsbach-Markt [A] 62 D4
Aggtelek [H] 64 E3
Aghalan [GB] 2 E4
Aghleam [IRL] 2 B3
Agiá [GR] 132 H1
Agía Ána [GR] 132 H5
Agía Ánna [GR] 134 B4
Ágía Déka [GR] 140 E5
Agía Efímía [GR] 132 C6
Agía Galíni [GR] 140 D5
Agía Marína [GR] 136 G1
Agia Marína [GR] 142 B2
Agía Paraskeví [GR] 134 G2
Agía Pelagía [GR] 136 F6
Agiásmata [GR] 134 G4
Agiássos [GR] 134 H2
Agía Triáda [GR] 132 D4
Ágía Triáda [GR] 136 C1
Ágía Triáda [GR] 128 H5
Ágía Varvára [GR] 140 E5
Ág. Ioánis [GR] 132 H6
Agiófillo [GR] 132 E1
Agioi Theódoroi [GR] 136 F1
Agiókampos [GR] 132 H4
Agiókampos [GR] 132 H1
Ágios Anárgiri [GR] 132 G2
Ágios Andónios [GR] 130 B5
Ágios Andréas [GR] 136 E3
Ágios Apóstoli [GR] 136 F5
Ágios Athanassios [GR] 128 F4
Ágios Charálampos [GR] 130 F3
Ágios Dimítrios [GR] 128 G6
Ágios Dimítrios [GR] 136 F4
Ágios Efstrátios [GR] 134 E1
Ágios Geórgios [GR] 132 F4
Ágios Germanos [GR] 128 E4
Ágios Górdis [GR] 132 B2
Ágios Kírykos [GR] 138 G1
Agios Konstantinos [GR] 144 C5
Agios Konstantínos [GR] 132 H4
Ágios Léon [GR] 136 A2
Ágios Márcos [GR] 128 H3
Ágios Mathéos [GR] 132 B2
Ágios Mýron [GR] 140 E5
Ágios Nikítas [GR] 132 C4
Ágios Nikólaos [GR] 136 G2
Ágios Nikólaos [GR] 132 C2
Ágios Nikólaos [GR] 136 E4
Ágios Nikólaos [GR] 140 F4
Ágios Nikólaos [GR] 132 D4
Ágios Nikólaos [GR] 130 C6
Ágios Pétros [GR] 136 E3
Ágios Pétros [GR] 132 C5
Ágios Pétros [GR] 128 G4
Ágios Pnevma [GR] 130 C3
Ágios Pródromos [GR] 130 B5
Ágios Theódori [GR] 132 H3
Agios Vlásios [GR] 132 E4
Agira [I] 126 F3
Ag. Kiriakí [GR] 138 H1
Aglen [N] 190 C4

Agliano [I] 108 H2
Agliate [I] 70 G4
Ag. Marína [GR] 134 C5
Ágnanta [GR] 132 D2
Agnanteró [GR] 132 F2
Agnita [RO] 206 C5
Agnone [I] 116 E6
Agnóntas [GR] 134 B3
Agolada [E] 78 C3
Agoncillo [E] 82 H6
Agon-Coutainville [F] 26 D3
Agordo [I] 72 E4
Ág. Pandeleímonas [GR] 128 F4
Ag. Pelagía [GR] 140 E4
Agramunt [E] 92 C3
Ágras [GR] 128 F4
Agreda [E] 84 A6
Agreliá [GR] 132 F1
Agriá [GR] 132 H2
Agriliá [GR] 132 E5
Agrínio [GR] 132 E5
Agriovótano [GR] 134 B3
Agropoli [I] 120 F4
Ag.Rouméli [GR] 140 C5
Ágskaret [N] 190 D1
Ag. Stéfanos [GR] 138 C2
Agua Amarga [E] 102 H5
Aguadulce [E] 102 G5
A Guarda / La Guardia [E] 78 A5
A Guarda / La Guardia [E] 96 G2
Aguda [P] 80 B4
A Gudiña [E] 78 D6
Agudo [E] 96 C3
Águeda [P] 80 B5
Agüero [E] 84 C5
Aguiar da Beira [P] 80 D5
Aguilafuente [E] 88 F3
Aguilar de Campoo [E] 82 D4
Aguilar de la Frontera [E] 102 C2
Águilas [E] 104 B4
Agulo [E] 100 B5
Agurain / Salvatierra [E] 82 H5
Ağva / Yeşilçay [TR] 146 G2
Ag. Varvára [GR] 140 E5
Ahascragh [IRL] 2 D5
Ahat [TR] 144 G3
Ahaus [D] 16 G5
Åheim [N] 180 C4
Ahínos [GR] 132 G2
Ahladohóri [GR] 130 B2
Ahlainen [FIN] 176 C1
Ahlbeck [D] 20 E4
Ahlbeck [D] 20 E3
Ahlen [D] 32 C3
Ahlhorn [D] 18 C6
Ahmetbey [TR] 146 C2
Ahmetli [TR] 144 D3
Ahmovaara [FIN] 188 F1
Ahoghill [GB] 2 G3
Ahokylä [FIN] 198 E5
Ahrensbök [D] 18 G3
Ahrensburg [D] 18 G4
Ahrweiler [D] 30 G5
Ähtäri [FIN] 186 E4
Ähtävä / Esse [FIN] 198 C6
Ahtyrka [UA] 206 G2
Ahun [F] 54 H6
Åhus [S] 158 D2
Ahvensalmi [FIN] 188 E4
Ahvenselkä [FIN] 196 E7
Aianí [GR] 128 F6
Aibar [E] 84 C4
Aicha [D] 60 H3
Aichach [D] 60 D3
Aiddejavrre [N] 192 G3
Aidenbach [D] 60 G3
Aidone [I] 126 F4
Aigen [A] 62 B3
Aigiali [GR] 138 G3
Aigina [GR] 136 G2
Aigínio [GR] 128 G5
Aígio [GR] 132 F6

Aigle [CH] 70 C2
Aiglsbach [D] 60 E3
Aignay-le-Duc [F] 56 G2
Aigre [F] 54 D6
Aigrefeuille [F] 54 C5
Aigrefeuille-sur-Maine [F] 54 C2
Aiguablava [E] 92 G3
Aiguebelle [F] 108 D6
Aiguebelle [F] 70 B4
Aigueperse [F] 68 D1
Aigues-Mortes [F] 106 F4
Aiguilles [F] 70 B6
Aiguillon [F] 66 E5
Aigurande [F] 54 H5
Äijälä [FIN] 186 G3
Ailefroide [F] 70 B6
Aillant-sur-Tholon [F] 56 E1
Aime [F] 70 B4
Ainaži [LV] 200 D4
Ainhoa [F] 84 C2
Ainsa [E] 84 E6
Airaines [F] 28 D4
Airasca [I] 70 D6
Airdrie [GB] 8 D3
Aire [F] 28 E3
Aire-sur-l'Adour [F] 84 E2
Aisey-sur-Seine [F] 56 G2
Aïssey [F] 58 B5
Aisými [GR] 130 G3
Aisy-sur-Armançon [F] 56 F2
Aiterhofen [D] 60 G2
Aitnoch [GB] 6 E5
Aitolikó [GR] 132 E5
Aitrach [D] 60 B4
Aittojärvi [FIN] 198 E6
Aittojärvi [FIN] 198 E3
Aiud [RO] 206 B5
Aix-en-Othe [F] 42 H6
Aix-en-Provence [F] 108 B4
Aixe-sur-Vienne [F] 66 G1
Aix-les-Bains [F] 68 H3
Aizenay [F] 54 B3
Aizkraukle [LV] 200 E5
Aizpute [LV] 200 B5
Ajaccio [F] 114 A5
Ajaureforsen [S] 190 F3
Ajdovščina [SLO] 74 A5
Ajka [H] 74 H2
Ajnovce [YU] 150 D5
Ajos [FIN] 198 C3
Akalan [TR] 146 D2
Akarca [TR] 144 G3
Akarp [S] 158 C3
Äkasjokisuu [FIN] 192 H5
Äkäslompolo [FIN] 192 H5
Akasztó [H] 76 C3
Akçakavak [TR] 142 F3
Akçakoca [TR] 146 H5
Akçaova [TR] 142 D1
Akçaova [TR] 146 G2
Akçay [TR] 142 H3
Akçay [TR] 144 C1
Aken [D] 34 C4
Åker [S] 168 C3
Åkersberga [S] 168 E2
Åkers krutbruk [S] 168 C3
Akhisar [TR] 144 D3
Akhtopol [BG] 148 G5
Akköy [TR] 142 C1
Akland [N] 164 F4
Akmeşe [TR] 146 G3
Akníste [LV] 200 F6
Akonpohja [FIN] 188 F5
Akoúmia [GR] 140 D5
Akpınar [TR] 146 H5
Åkra [N] 170 B5
Akraifnio [GR] 134 B5
Akranes [IS] 194 B4
Åkrehamn [N] 164 A2
Akropótamos [GR] 130 C4
Akrotíri [GR] 138 F5
Aksakal [TR] 146 D5
Aksakovo [BG] 148 F2
Aksaz [TR] 146 C4
Akujärvi [FIN] 196 D4
Akureyri [IS] 194 E3
Akyazı [TR] 146 H3

Ål [N] 170 F3
Ala [I] 72 C5
Ala [S] 168 G5
Alacalı [TR] 146 F2
Alacant / Alicante [E] 104 E2
Alacat [TR] 146 E5
Alaçatı [TR] 134 H5
Alà dei Sardi [I] 118 D3
Ala di Stura [I] 70 C5
Alaejos [E] 88 D2
Alagón [E] 90 E3
Alahärmä [FIN] 186 C2
Ala-Honkajoki [FIN] 186 C6
Alakylä [FIN] 192 H5
Alameda [E] 102 C3
Alamedilla [E] 102 F3
Ala-Nampa [FIN] 196 D7
Alanäs [S] 190 E5
Alandroal [P] 94 E1
Alange [E] 94 H2
Alaniemi [FIN] 198 D2
Alanís [E] 94 H4
Ala-Paakkola [FIN] 198 C2
Alapitkä [FIN] 188 C1
Alaraz [E] 88 D4
Alarcón [E] 98 B3
Alaşehir [TR] 144 E4
Alássio [I] 108 G4
Alastaro [FIN] 176 E3
Alatoz [E] 98 C5
Alatri [I] 116 C6
Alaveteli / Nedervetil [FIN] 198 C6
Alavieska [FIN] 198 C5
Ala-Vuokki [FIN] 198 F4
Alavus [FIN] 186 D4
Alba [I] 108 G2
Alba Adriatica [I] 116 D3
Albacete [E] 98 B5
Alba de Tormes [E] 88 C3
Ålbæk [DK] 160 E2
Albaida [E] 98 E6
Alba Iulia [RO] 206 B5
Albaladejo [E] 96 G5
Albalate de Cinca [E] 90 G4
Albalate del Arzobispo [E] 90 E5
Albalate de Zorita [E] 98 A1
Alban [F] 106 C3
Albánchez [E] 102 H4
Albano Laziale [I] 116 A6
Albaredo d'Adige [I] 110 F1
Albarella [I] 110 H2
Albares [E] 88 H6
Albarracín [E] 98 D1
Albatana [E] 104 C1
Albena [BG] 148 G2
Albenga [I] 108 G4
Albens [F] 70 A3
Albentosa [E] 98 E3
Alberga [S] 168 B3
Albergaria-a-Velha [P] 80 B5
Alberic [E] 98 E5
Alberobello [I] 122 E3
Albersdorf [D] 18 E2
Albert [F] 28 E4
Albertirsa [H] 76 D1
Albertville [F] 70 B3
Albi [F] 106 B2
Albignasego [I] 110 G1
Albisola Marina [I] 108 H3
Albo [F] 114 C2
Albocácer / Albocàsser [E] 98 G2
Albocàsser / Albocácer [E] 98 G2
Alboraia / Alboraya [E] 98 E4
Alboraya / Alboraia [E] 98 E4
Albox [E] 102 H4
Albufeira [P] 94 C5
Albujón [E] 104 C4
Albuñol [E] 102 E5
Albuñuelas [E] 102 D4
Alburquerque [E] 86 F5

Alby [S] 162 G6
Alcáoor do Sal [P] 94 C1
Alcáçovas [P] 94 D2
Alcadozo [E] 98 B6
Alcaide [E] 102 H3
Alcalá de Chivert / Alcalà de Xivert [E] 98 G2
Alcalá de Guadaira [E] 94 G6
Alcalá de Henares [E] 88 G6
Alcalá de la Selva [E] 98 E2
Alcalá del Júcar [E] 98 C5
Alcalá de los Gazules [E] 100 G4
Alcalá del Río [E] 94 G6
Alcalá del Valle [E] 102 A3
Alcalà de Xivert / Alcalá de Chivert [E] 98 G2
Alcalá la Real [E] 102 D3
Álcamo [I] 126 C2
Alcanar [E] 92 A6
Alcanede [P] 86 C4
Alcanena [P] 86 C4
Alcañices [E] 80 G4
Alcañiz [E] 90 F6
Alcántara [E] 86 G4
Alcantarilla [E] 104 C3
Alcaracejos [E] 96 C5
Alcaraz [E] 96 H6
Alcaria Ruiva [P] 94 D4
Alcarràs [E] 90 H5
Alçaşehir [TR] 144 G1
Alcaudete [E] 102 D2
Alcaudete de la Jara [E] 96 D1
Alcázar de San Juan [E] 96 G3
Alcester [GB] 12 H2
Alcobaça [P] 86 C3
Alcobendas [E] 88 F5
Alcocéber / Alcossebre [E] 98 G3
Alcochete [P] 86 B5
Alcoi / Alcoy [E] 104 E1
Alcolea del Pinar [E] 90 B4
Alconchel [E] 94 F2
Alcora / l'Alcora [E] 98 F3
Alcorcón [E] 88 F6
Alcorisa [E] 90 F6
Alcossebre / Alcocéber [E] 98 G3
Alcoutim [P] 94 D5
Alcover [E] 92 C4
Alcoy / Alcoi [E] 104 E1
Alcubierre [E] 90 F3
Alcublas [E] 98 E3
Alcúdia [E] 104 F4
Alcuéscar [E] 86 H6
Aldbrough [GB] 10 G4
Aldeadávila de la Ribera [E] 80 F5
Aldea del Cano [E] 86 H6
Aldea del Fresno [E] 88 E5
Aldea del Rey [E] 96 E5
Aldealpozo [E] 90 C3
Aldeaquemada [E] 96 F6
Aldeavieja [E] 88 E4
Aldeburgh [GB] 14 G3
Aldeia da Ponte [P] 86 G2
Aldeia do Bispo [P] 86 G2
Aldenhoven [D] 30 F4
Aldershot [GB] 14 D4
Aldinci [MK] 128 E1
Åled [S] 162 B5
Aledo [E] 104 B3
Alehovščina [RUS] 204 D1
Alekovo [BG] 148 E1
Aleksandrija [UA] 206 F3
Aleksandrovac [YU] 150 C1
Aleksandrovo [BG] 148 B3
Aleksandrów Kujawski [PL] 36 F1
Aleksandrów Łódzki [PL] 36 G4
Aleksin [RUS] 204 F5
Aleksinac [YU] 150 D3
Ålem [S] 162 G4
Alemdağ [TR] 146 F2
Ålen [N] 182 C3
Alençon [F] 26 F6

Alenquer [P] 86 B4
Aléria [F] 114 C4
Alés [F] 106 F3
Áles [I] 118 C5
Alesd [RO] 206 B4
Alessándria [I] 70 F6
Alessandria del Carretto [I] 122 D6
Alessándria della Rocca [I] 126 D3
Ålestrup [DK] 160 D4
Ålesund [N] 180 C3
Alexándreia [GR] 128 G4
Alexandria [GB] 8 D3
Alexandria [RO] 148 B1
Alexandroúpoli [GR] 130 G3
Alf [D] 44 G2
Alfafar [E] 98 E5
Alfajarín [E] 90 E4
Alfambra [E] 98 E1
Alfambras [P] 94 B4
Alfaro [E] 84 B5
Alfarràs [E] 90 H4
Alfatar [BG] 148 E1
Alfedena [I] 116 D6
Alfeizerão [P] 86 B3
Alfeld [D] 46 H5
Alfeld [D] 32 F3
Alfonsine [I] 110 G3
Alford [GB] 6 F6
Ålfoten [N] 180 C5
Alfreton [GB] 10 F5
Alfstad [N] 170 G5
Alfta [S] 174 D2
Algaida [E] 104 E5
Algajola [F] 114 B3
Algar [E] 100 G4
Algar [E] 104 H5
Älgarås [S] 166 F3
Ålgård [N] 164 B3
Algarinejo [E] 102 D3
Algarra [E] 98 D3
Algeciras [E] 100 G5
Algemesí [E] 98 E5
Ålgered [S] 184 E5
Alghero [I] 118 B3
Älghult [S] 162 F4
Alginet [E] 98 E5
Algodonales [E] 100 H3
Algora [E] 90 A5
Algoso [P] 80 F4
Älgsjö [S] 190 G5
Algutsrum [S] 162 G5
Algyő [H] 76 E4
Alhama de Aragón [E] 90 C4
Alhama de Granada [E] 102 D4
Alhama de Murcia [E] 104 B3
Alhambra [E] 96 G5
Alhaurín de la Torre [E] 102 B5
Alhaurín el Grande [E] 102 B4
Ålhus [N] 180 C6
Alía [E] 96 C2
Ália [I] 126 D3
Aliaga [E] 98 F1
Aliağa [TR] 144 C3
Alíartos [GR] 134 A5
Alibunar [YU] 154 H2
Alicante / Alacant [E] 104 E2
Alija del Infantado [E] 80 H3
Alijó [P] 80 E4
Alíkampos [GR] 140 C4
Alikanás [GR] 136 A2
Alimena [I] 126 E3
Alingsås [S] 162 B1
Aliseda [E] 86 G5
Alistráti [GR] 130 C3
Ali Terme [I] 124 B7
Alivéri [GR] 134 C5
Aljaraque [E] 94 E5
Aljezur [P] 94 B4
Aljubarrota [P] 86 C3
Aljucén [E] 86 G6
Aljustrel [P] 94 C3
Alkmaar [NL] 16 D3

Alkotz [E] 84 B3
Alkoven [A] 62 B4
Allaines [F] 42 E5
Allainville [F] 42 E4
Allanche [F] 68 C3
Alland [A] 62 E5
Allariz [E] 78 C5
Allauch [F] 108 B5
Alleen [N] 164 C5
Álleghe [I] 72 E4
Allemont [F] 70 A5
Allensbach [D] 58 G4
Allentsteig [A] 62 D3
Allepuz [E] 98 E1
Allersberg [D] 46 G6
Allershausen [D] 60 E3
Allerum [S] 156 H1
Allevard [F] 70 A4
Allihies [IRL] 4 A5
Allingåbro [DK] 160 E5
Allinge [DK] 158 F4
Alloa [GB] 8 E3
Allonnes [F] 54 E2
Allos [F] 108 D3
Allstedt [D] 34 B5
Alltnacaillich [GB] 6 D3
Almacelles [E] 90 H4
Almada [P] 86 B5
Almadén [E] 96 C4
Almadén de la Plata [E] 94
  G5
Almagro [E] 96 F4
Almandoz [E] 84 B3
Almansa [E] 98 D6
Almanza [E] 82 C4
Almargen [E] 102 B3
Almarza [E] 90 B2
Almassora / Almazora [E] 98
  F3
Almazán [E] 90 B3
Almazora / Almassora [E] 98
  F3
Almeida [P] 80 E6
Almeida de Sayago [E] 80
  G5
Almelo [NL] 16 G4
Almenar [E] 90 H4
Almenara de Tormes [E] 80
  G6
Almenar de Soria [E] 90 C3
Almendra [P] 80 E5
Almendral [E] 94 G2
Almendralejo [E] 94 G2
Almenno S. Salvatore [I] 70
  H4
Almere [NL] 16 E4
Almería [E] 102 G5
Almerimar [E] 102 F6
Älmestad [S] 162 C1
Älmhult [S] 162 D5
Almirón [GR] 136 D4
Almodôvar [P] 94 C4
Almodóvar del Campo [E]
  96 E4
Almodóvar del Pinar [E] 98
  C3
Almodóvar del Río [E] 102
  B1
Almogía [E] 102 C4
Almograve [P] 94 B3
Almoharín [E] 86 H6
Almonaster la Real [E] 94
  F4
Almonte [E] 94 F6
Almoradí [E] 104 D3
Almorox [E] 88 E6
Älmsta [S] 168 E1
Älmsta–Väddö [S] 168 E1
Almudévar [E] 90 F3
Almuñécar [E] 102 D5
Almunge [S] 168 D1
Almuradiel [E] 96 F5
Almvik [S] 162 G2
Almyropótamos [GR] 134
  D5
Almyrós [GR] 132 H3
Alness [GB] 6 E4
Alnmouth [GB] 8 G5
Alnwick [GB] 8 G5
Aloja [LV] 200 E4
Alol' [RUS] 200 H5
Alónnisos [GR] 134 C3

Álora [E] 102 B4
Alosno [E] 94 E5
Alost (Aalst) [B] 28 H2
Alp [E] 92 E2
Alpalhão [P] 86 E4
Alpbach [A] 60 E6
Alpedrinha [P] 86 F3
Alpen [D] 30 G2
Alpera [E] 98 C5
Alphen–aan den Rijn [NL]
  16 D5
Alpirsbach [D] 58 F2
Alpua [FIN] 198 D5
Alpullu [TR] 146 B2
Alqueva [P] 94 E3
Alquézar [E] 90 G3
Alresford [GB] 12 H4
Als [DK] 160 E4
Alsager [GB] 10 D5
Alsasua / Altsasu [E] 82 H5
Alsenz [D] 46 B4
Alsfeld [D] 46 D1
Alsleben [D] 34 B4
Alsótold [H] 64 D5
Ålstad [N] 192 C5
Alstad [S] 158 C3
Alstahaug [N] 190 D2
Alstätte [D] 16 G5
Alstermo [S] 162 F4
Alston [GB] 8 F6
Alta [N] 192 G1
Altafulla [E] 92 C5
Altamura [I] 122 D3
Altaussee [A] 62 A4
Altavilla Silentina [I] 120 F4
Altdorf [CH] 58 F6
Altdorf [D] 46 G5
Altea [E] 104 F2
Altedo [I] 110 F3
Alteidet [N] 192 F1
Altena [D] 32 C5
Altenahr [D] 30 G5
Altenau [D] 32 G4
Altenberg [D] 48 E2
Altenberge [D] 16 H5
Altenburg [D] 34 C6
Altenglan [D] 44 H3
Altenhundem [D] 32 C5
Altenkirchen [D] 32 C6
Altenkirchen [D] 20 D1
Altenmarkt [A] 62 C6
Altenmarkt [D] 60 F5
Altenmarkt im Pongau [A]
  72 H1
Altenstadt [D] 60 B4
Altenstadt [D] 60 D5
Altensteig [D] 58 G1
Altentreptow [D] 20 D4
Altenwalde [D] 18 D3
Alter do Chão [P] 86 E5
Altheim [A] 60 H4
Althofen [A] 74 B2
Altimir [BG] 150 G3
Altinkum [TR] 142 C2
Altınoluk [TR] 144 B1
Altınova [TR] 144 B2
Altınova [TR] 146 F3
Altıntaş [TR] 144 H2
Altınyayla [TR] 142 G2
Altipiani di Arcinazzo [I] 116
  B6
Altkirch [F] 58 D4
Altmünster [A] 62 A5
Altnaharra [GB] 6 E3
Alto de los Leones de
  Castilla [E] 88 F4
Altomonte [I] 124 D3
Alton [GB] 10 E5
Alton [GB] 14 D4
Altötting [D] 60 G4
Altrincham [GB] 10 E4
Altruppin [D] 20 C6
Altsasu / Alsasua [E] 82 H5
Alt Schadow [D] 34 F3
Altshausen [D] 58 H3
Altstätten [CH] 58 H5
Alūksne [LV] 200 F4
Alunda [S] 168 D1
Alupka [UA] 206 G6
Alushta [UA] 206 G6
Alvaiázere [P] 86 D3
Alvajärvi [FIN] 186 F1

Alvalade [P] 94 C3
Älvängen [S] 160 H1
Alvastra [S] 166 G6
Alvdal [N] 182 B5
Älvdalen [S] 172 F2
Alverca do Ribatejo [P] 86
  B5
Alversund [N] 170 B3
Alvesta [S] 162 D4
Alvignac [F] 66 G4
Ålvik [N] 170 C4
Alvito [P] 94 D2
Älvkarleby [S] 174 E4
Alvor [P] 94 B5
Älvros [S] 182 E6
Älvros [S] 182 G5
Älvsbyn [S] 198 A3
Älvsered [S] 162 B3
Ålvundeid [N] 180 F3
Alyki [GR] 138 E3
Alykí [GR] 130 E4
Alytus [LT] 24 G2
Alzenau [D] 46 D3
Alzey [D] 46 B4
Alzira [E] 98 E5
Alzon [F] 106 E3
Alzonne [F] 106 B4
Amadora [P] 86 B5
Åmål [S] 166 D4
Amalfi [I] 120 E4
Amaliáda [GR] 136 C2
Amaliápoli [GR] 132 H3
Amálo [GR] 138 G1
Amance [F] 58 B3
Amancey [F] 58 B5
Amandola [I] 116 C2
Amantea [I] 124 D5
Amárandos [GR] 132 F3
Amarante [P] 80 C4
Amărăştu de Jos [RO] 150
  G2
Amareleja [P] 94 E3
Amári [GR] 140 D5
Amárynthos [GR] 134 C5
Amatrice [I] 116 C3
Amaxádes [GR] 130 E2
Amay [B] 30 E5
Ambarès [F] 66 D3
Ambazac [F] 54 G6

Ambelónas [GR] 132 G1
Amberg [D] 48 B5
Ambérieu–en–Bugey [F] 68
  G2
Ambert [F] 68 D3
Ambjörby [S] 172 E4
Ambla [EST] 200 E1
Amble [GB] 8 G5
Ambleside [GB] 10 D2
Amboise [F] 54 G2
Ambrières [F] 26 E5
Åmdal [N] 164 D5
Ameixial [P] 94 C4
Amélia [I] 116 A3
Amélie–les–Bains [F] 92 F2
Amelinghausen [D] 18 F5
Amendolara [I] 122 D6
Amerongen [NL] 16 E5
Amersfoort [NL] 16 E5
Amersham [GB] 14 E3
Amesbury [GB] 12 G4
Amfíkleia [GR] 132 G4
Amfilochía [GR] 132 D4
Ámfissa [GR] 132 G5
Amiens [F] 28 E5
Åmli [N] 164 E4
Amlwch [GB] 10 B3
Ammanford [GB] 12 E2
Ämmänsaari [FIN] 198 F4
Ammarnäs [S] 190 F2
Åmmeberg [S] 166 G4
Åmnes [N] 164 F2
Amorbach [D] 46 D4
Amorgós [GR] 138 G4
Åmot [N] 164 E1
Åmot [N] 164 G1
Åmot [N] 170 G4
Åmot [S] 174 D3
Åmotfors [S] 166 D1
Amótopos [GR] 132 D3
Amou [F] 84 D2
Amoudára [GR] 140 F5
Ampelákia [GR] 132 G1
Ampelákia [GR] 134 C5
Ampezzo [I] 72 F4
Amphion [F] 70 B2
Amplepuis [F] 68 F2
Amposta [E] 92 A6
Ampthill [GB] 14 E3

Ampuero [E] 82 F3
Ampuis [F] 68 F3
Amriswil [CH] 58 H4
Åmsele [S] 190 H5
Amsteg [CH] 70 F1
Amsterdam [NL] 16 D4
Amstetten [A] 62 C4
Ämtervik [S] 166 E2
Amurrio [E] 82 G4
Amyklai [GR] 136 E4
Amýntaio [GR] 128 F4
Amzacea [RO] 148 G1
Anadia [P] 80 B6
Anáfi [GR] 138 F5
Anagni [I] 116 B6
Análipsi [GR] 138 H4
Anascaul [IRL] 4 B4
Anatolí [GR] 132 G1
Anatolikó [GR] 128 F5
Anáviyssos [GR] 136 H1
Anávra [GR] 132 G3
Anavra [GR] 132 F3
An Cabhán / Cavan [IRL]
  2 E4
Ancenis [F] 40 G6
Ancerville [F] 44 C5
An Charraig / Carrick [IRL] 2
  D2
Ancona [I] 112 C6
Ancy–le–Franc [F] 56 F2
Anda [N] 180 C5
An Daingean / Dingle [IRL]
  4 A3
Andalo [I] 72 C4
Åndalsnes [N] 180 E3
Andau [A] 62 G6
Andelot [F] 44 D6
Andenes [N] 192 C2
Andenne [B] 30 D5
Andermatt [CH] 70 F1
Andernach [D] 30 H6
Andernos–les–Bains [F] 66
  B3
Anderslov [S] 158 C3
Anderstorp [S] 162 C3
Andijk [NL] 16 E3
Andocs [H] 76 A3

Andolsheim [F] 58 E3
Andorno Micca [I] 70 E4
Andorra [E] 90 F6
Andorra la Vella [AND] 84
  H6
Andover [GB] 12 H4
Andraitx [E] 104 D5
Andravída [GR] 136 B1
Andreas [GBM] 8 C6
Andrespol [PL] 36 G4
Andretta [I] 120 G3
Andrézieux–Bouthéon [F] 68
  E3
Ándria [I] 122 C2
Andrijevica [YU] 150 A5
Andrítsaina [GR] 136 D3
Ándros [GR] 134 E6
Androússa [GR] 136 D4
Andrychów [PL] 50 G4
Andselv [N] 192 E3
Andújar [E] 102 D1
Anduze [F] 106 F3
Ånebjør [N] 164 D3
Aneby [S] 162 E2
Ånes [N] 180 F1
Anet [F] 42 E3
Ånge [S] 184 C4
Angeja [P] 80 B5
Ängelholm [S] 156 H1
Angeli [FIN] 196 C4
Angelókastro [GR] 136 F2
Angelókastro [GR] 132
  E5
Anger [A] 74 E1
Angermünde [D] 20 E6
Angern [A] 62 G4
Angers [F] 40 H6
Angerville [F] 42 E5
Anghiari [I] 110 G6
Anglès [E] 92 F3
Angles–sur–l'Anglin [F] 54
  F4
Anglet [F] 84 C2
Anglona [LV] 200 G6
Anglure [F] 44 A5
Angoulême [F] 66 E1
Angüés [E] 90 G3
Anguillara Sabazia [I] 114
  H5

Ard [IRL] 2 B4
Ardagh [IRL] 4 C3
Ardales [E] 102 B4
Årdalsosen [N] 164 B2
Årdalstangen [N] 170 E2
Ardara [IRL] 2 E2
Ardbeg [GB] 2 H1
Ardea [I] 116 A6
Ardee [IRL] 2 F5
Arden [DK] 160 D4
Ardentes [F] 54 H4
Ardentinny [GB] 8 C2
Ardez [CH] 72 B2
Ardfert [IRL] 4 B3
Ardfinnan [IRL] 4 D4
Ardglass [GB] 2 G4
Ardgour [GB] 6 C6
Ardino [BG] 130 E1
Ardisa [E] 84 C6
Ardlui [GB] 8 D2
Ardlussa [GB] 8 B2
Ardnave [GB] 8 B2
Ardres [F] 14 G6
Ardrossan [GB] 8 C3
Ardvasar [GB] 6 B5
Ardwell [GB] 8 C5
Åre [S] 182 E1
Arenal, S'– [E] 104 E5
Arenal d'en Castell, S'– [E] 104 H4
Arenas [E] 82 D2
Arenas de San Pedro [E] 88 D5
Arendal [N] 164 F5
Arendonk [B] 30 D3
Arendsee [D] 20 A6
Arene / Arrankudiaga [E] 82 G4
Areños [E] 82 D3
Arenys de Mar [E] 92 F4
Arenzano [I] 108 H3
Areópoli [GR] 136 E5
Ares [E] 78 D2
Arès [F] 66 B3
Ares del Maestrat / Ares del Maestre [E] 98 F2
Ares del Maestre / Ares del Maestrat [E] 98 F2
Aréthoussa [GR] 130 C4
Aretxabaleta [E] 82 H4
Arevalillo [E] 88 C4
Arévalo [E] 88 E3
Arezzo [I] 114 G1
Arfará [GR] 136 D3
Argalastí [GR] 134 A3
Áratos [GR] 130 F2

Ariano Irpino [I] 120 F2
Ariano nel Polésine [I] 110 H2
Aridaía [GR] 128 F3
Arieiro [P] 100 B3
Arileod [GB] 6 A6
Arilje [YU] 150 A3
Arinagour [GB] 6 A6
Arinthod [F] 56 H6
Ariogala [LT] 202 F5
Arisaig [GB] 6 B5
Aritzo [I] 118 D5
Ariza [E] 90 C4
Årjäng [S] 166 D2
Arjeplog [S] 190 G2
Arjona [E] 102 D1
Arkadia [PL] 36 H3
Arkalochóri [GR] 140 E5
Arkása [GR] 140 H3
Arkesíni [GR] 138 F4
Arkítsa [GR] 134 A4
Arklow / An Tinbhear Mór [IRL] 4 G4
Arkösund [S] 168 C5
Arkutino [BG] 148 F5
Arlanc [F] 68 D3
Arlberg Tunnel [A] 72 B1
Arlempdes [F] 68 D5
Arles [F] 106 G4
Arles-sur-Tech [F] 92 F2
Arlon [B] 44 E2
Arlöv [S] 156 H3
Armação de Pera [P] 94 B5
Armémoi [GR] 140 D5
Arménio [GR] 132 G2
Armenistís [GR] 138 G1
Armentières [F] 28 F3
Armilla [E] 102 E4
Armiñon [E] 82 G5
Armólia [GR] 134 G5
Armoy [GB] 2 G2
Armuña de Tajuña [E] 88 H6
Armutlu [TR] 144 D4
Armutlu [TR] 146 E4
Armutova [TR] 144 B2
Árna [GR] 136 E4
Arna [N] 170 B4
Arnafjord [N] 170 C2
Arnage [F] 42 B5
Arnager [DK] 158 E4
Arnaía [GR] 130 C5
Arnavutköy [TR] 146 E2
Arnavutköy [TR] 146 E4
Arnay-le-Duc [F] 56 F4
Arnborg [DK] 156 B1
Arneburg [D] 34 C1
Arnedillo [E] 90 C1
Arnedo [E] 84 A5
Årnes [N] 172 C5
Årnes [N] 190 B5
Arnhem [NL] 16 F5
Arnicle [GB] 2 H1
Árnissa [GR] 128 F3
Arnoldstein [A] 72 H3
Arnøyhamn [N] 192 F1
Arnprior [GB] 8 D2
Arnsberg [D] 32 C4
Arnschwang [D] 48 D6
Arnstadt [D] 46 G1
Arnstein [D] 46 E3
Aroania [GR] 136 D1
Aroche [E] 94 F4
Ároktő [H] 64 F5
Arolla [CH] 70 D3
Arolsen [D] 32 E5
Arona [I] 70 F4
Aronkylä [FIN] 186 B4
Åros [N] 164 H1
Arosa [CH] 70 H1
Årøsund [DK] 156 C3
Arøysund [N] 164 H3
Arpajon [F] 42 F4
Arpela [FIN] 198 C2
Arquà Petrarca [I] 110 G1
Arquata del Tronto [I] 116 C3
Arquata Scrivia [I] 110 B2
Arrabal / Oia [E] 78 A5
Arracourt [F] 44 F5

Arraiolos [P] 86 D6
Arrakoski [FIN] 176 H1
Arras [F] 28 F4
Arrasate o Mondragón [E] 82 H4
Årre [DK] 156 B2
Arreau [F] 84 F4
Arrecife [E] 100 E5
Årrenjarka [S] 190 G1
Arrens–Marsous [F] 84 E4
Arrifana [P] 94 B4
Arriondas [E] 82 C2
Arroba de los Montes [E] 96 D3
Arromanches–les–Bains [F] 26 F3
Arronches [P] 86 F5
Arroyo de la Luz [E] 86 G5
Arroyo de la Miel–Benalmádena Costa [E] 102 B5
Arroyo de San Serván [E] 94 G2
Arruda dos Vinhos [P] 86 B4
Årsandøy [N] 190 C4
Ars–en–Ré [F] 54 B4
Arsiè [I] 72 D5
Arsiero [I] 72 D5
Årslev [DK] 156 D3
Arsoli [I] 116 B5
Ars–sur–Moselle [F] 44 E4
Årsunda [S] 174 E4
Arsvågen [N] 164 A2
Arsy [F] 28 E6
Artà [E] 104 F5
Árta [GR] 132 D3
Artajona [E] 84 B4
Artana [E] 98 F3
Ärtånd [H] 76 H2
Arta Terme [I] 72 G3
Arteixo [E] 78 C2
Artemare [F] 68 H3
Artemisía [GR] 136 D4
Artemísio [GR] 134 A3
Artemón [GR] 138 D3
Artenay [F] 42 E5
Artern [D] 34 A5
Artesa de Segre [E] 92 C3
Arth [CH] 58 F6
Arth [D] 60 F3
Arthog [GB] 10 B5
Arthurstown [IRL] 4 E5
Arties [E] 84 G5
Artix [F] 84 E3
Artjärvi [FIN] 178 B3
Artotína [GR] 132 F4
A Rúa [E] 78 E5
Arucas [E] 100 C5
Arudy [F] 84 D3
Arundel [GB] 14 D5
Årup [DK] 156 D3
Årvåg [N] 180 G1
Arvagh [IRL] 2 E4
Árvi [GR] 140 F5
Arvidsjaur [S] 190 H3
Arvieux [F] 70 B6
Årvik [N] 180 C4
Arvika [S] 166 D2
Årviksand [N] 192 F1
Arzachena [I] 118 E2
Arzacq–Arraziguet [F] 84 E2
Aržano [HR] 152 B2
Arzberg [D] 48 C3
Arzignano [I] 72 D6
Arzl [A] 72 C1
Arzúa [E] 78 C3
As [B] 30 E4
Aš [CZ] 48 C3
Ås [N] 166 B2
Ås [N] 182 D2
Åså [DK] 160 E3
Åsa [S] 160 H2
Aşağıinova [TR] 146 C5
Aşağıtefen [TR] 144 F3
Åsäng [S] 184 E4
Ašanja [YU] 154 G2
Åsarna [S] 182 G4
Asarum [S] 158 E1
Åsbro [S] 166 H4
Ascain [F] 84 C2
Ascha [D] 60 G2

Aschach [A] 62 B4
Aschaffenburg [D] 46 D3
Aschau [D] 60 F5
Aschbach Markt [A] 62 C5
Ascheberg [D] 16 H6
Ascheberg [D] 18 G2
Aschendorf [D] 16 H3
Aschersleben [D] 34 B4
Asciano [I] 114 G1
Asco [F] 114 B3
Ascoli Piceno [I] 116 C3
Ascoli Satriano [I] 120 G2
Ascona [CH] 70 F3
Åseda [S] 162 E4
Åsele [S] 190 G5
Asemanseutu [FIN] 186 D3
Åsen [N] 190 C6
Åsen [S] 172 F2
Asendorf [D] 18 E6
Asenovgrad [BG] 148 B6
Åsensbruk [S] 166 D4
Åseral [N] 164 D4
Asfáka [GR] 132 C1
Asfeld [F] 44 B2
Åsgårdstrand [N] 164 H2
Ashbourne [GB] 10 E5
Ashbourne [IRL] 2 F6
Ashburton [GB] 12 E5
Ashby–de–la–Zouch [GB] 10 E6
Åsheim [N] 182 C6
Ashford [GB] 14 F5
Ashington [GB] 8 G5
Ashmyany [BY] 202 H6
Ashton–under–Lyne [GB] 10 E4
Asiago [I] 72 D5
Asikkala [FIN] 176 H2
Asíni [GR] 136 F2
Ask [N] 170 B3
Aska [FIN] 196 D6
Askainen [FIN] 176 D4
Askeaton [IRL] 4 C3
Askeby [DK] 156 G4
Asker [N] 164 H1
Askersund [S] 166 G4
Askífou [GR] 140 C5
Askim [N] 166 C2
Askim [S] 160 G2
Asköping [S] 168 B3
Askvoll [N] 170 B1
Aslanapa [TR] 144 G1
Aslestad [N] 164 E2
Åsli [N] 170 G4
Åsljunga [S] 162 B6
Asmunti [FIN] 198 E2
Asnæs [DK] 156 F2
Åsnes [N] 172 D4
Asola [I] 110 E1
Asolo [I] 72 E5
Asopós [GR] 136 F4
Ásos [GR] 132 C5
Aspa [S] 168 C4
Aspang Markt [A] 62 E6
Aspe [E] 104 D2
Aspet [F] 84 G4
Aspres–sur–Buëch [F] 108 C2
Asprópirgos [GR] 134 B6
Asprovalta [GR] 130 C4
Aspsele [S] 190 G6
Assebakte [N] 192 H2
Assemini [I] 118 C7
Assen [NL] 16 G3
Assens [DK] 156 D3
Assens [DK] 160 E5
Asserbo [DK] 156 G1
Assergi [I] 116 C4
Ássiros [GR] 128 H4
Assisi [I] 116 A2
Assling [D] 60 F5
Assmannshausen [D] 46 B3
Assoro [I] 126 F3
Astaffort [F] 66 E6
Astakós [GR] 132 D5
Asten [A] 62 B4
Asten [NL] 30 F3
Astorga [E] 78 G6
Åstorp [S] 156 H1
Åstrand [S] 172 E5
Ástros [GR] 136 E3

Astryna [BY] 24 G3
Astudillo [E] 82 D6
Astypálaia [GR] 138 H4
Asvyeja [BY] 200 G6
Aszód [H] 64 D6
Aszófő [H] 76 A2
Atalaia [P] 86 B5
Atalánti [GR] 132 H4
Átali [GR] 134 C4
Atarfe [E] 102 E4
Atašiene [LV] 200 F5
Atburgazi [TR] 142 B1
Atça [TR] 144 E5
Ateca [E] 90 C4
Atessa [I] 116 E5
Ath [B] 28 G3
Athboy [IRL] 2 E5
Athea [IRL] 4 C3
Athenry [IRL] 2 C5
Athéras [GR] 132 C6
Atherstone [GB] 10 E6
Athína [GR] 134 C4
Athleague [IRL] 2 D5
Athlone / Baile Átha Luain [IRL] 2 D5
Athy [IRL] 4 F3
Atienza [E] 90 A4
Atina [I] 116 C6
Atkár [H] 64 E6
Atnbrua [N] 180 H6
Atnosen [N] 182 B6
Atostugan [S] 190 E3
A Toxa [E] 78 B4
Ätran [S] 162 B4
Atri [I] 116 D3
Atsalama [EST] 200 F1
Attel [D] 60 F4
Attendorn [D] 32 C5
Attersee [A] 60 H5
Attigny [F] 44 C2
Attleborough [GB] 14 G2
Attnang–Puchheim [A] 62 A5
Attrup [DK] 160 D3
Åtvidaberg [S] 168 B6
Atzara [I] 118 D5
Atzendorf [D] 34 B4
Atzeneta del Maestrat [E] 98 F3
Au [A] 62 D6
Au [D] 60 E3
Aubagne [F] 108 B5
Aubange [B] 44 E3
Aubenas [F] 68 E6
Auberive [F] 56 H2
Aubeterre–sur–Dronne [F] 66 E2
Aubigny [F] 54 B3
Aubigny–sur–Nere [F] 56 C2
Auboué [F] 44 E4
Aubrac [F] 68 C5
Aubusson [F] 68 B1
Auce [LV] 200 C6
Auch [F] 84 G2
Auchinleck [GB] 8 D4
Auchronie [GB] 8 F1
Auchterarder [GB] 8 E2
Auchtermuchty [GB] 8 E2
Audenge [F] 66 C3
Auderville [F] 26 D1
Audeux [F] 58 B4
Audierne [F] 40 A3
Audincourt [F] 58 C4
Audlem [GB] 10 D5
Audressein [F] 84 G5
Audruicq [F] 14 H6
Audun–le–Roman [F] 44 E3
Aue [D] 48 D2
Auer / Ora [I] 72 D4
Auerbach [D] 46 H4
Auerbach [D] 48 C2
Auffach [A] 60 F6
Augher [GB] 2 F3
Aughnacloy [GB] 2 F3
Aughrim [IRL] 4 G4
Augsburg [D] 60 D3
23 August [RO] 148 G1
Augusta [I] 126 G4
Augustenborg [DK] 156 C4
Augustów [PL] 24 E3
Augustusburg [D] 48 D1

Aukštadvaris [LT] 24 G1
Auktsjaur [S] 190 H3
Auletta [I] 120 G4
Aulla [I] 110 C4
Aullène [F] 114 B5
Ault [F] 28 D4
Aulus–les–Bains [F] 84 H5
Auma [D] 48 B2
Aumale [F] 28 D5
Aumetz [F] 44 E3
Aumont–Aubrac [F] 68 C5
Aunay–sur–Odon [F] 26 E4
Auneau [F] 42 E4
Auneuil [F] 28 D6
Auning [DK] 160 E5
Aups [F] 108 D4
Aura [FIN] 176 D4
Aurach [A] 60 F6
Aurach [D] 46 F5
Auray [F] 40 D4
Aurdal [N] 170 G3
Aure [N] 180 G1
Aurejärvi [FIN] 186 D5
Aurich [D] 18 B4
Aurignac [F] 84 G4
Aurillac [F] 68 B4
Auritz / Burguete [E] 84 C3
Aurland [N] 170 D2
Auron [F] 108 E3
Auronzo di Cadore [I] 72 F3
Aursmoen [N] 166 C1
Aursnes [N] 180 D3
Áusa Corno [I] 72 G5
Ausejo [E] 90 C1
Aussernbrünst [D] 60 H3
Austad [N] 164 D3
Austbygdi [N] 170 F5
Austertana [N] 196 D2
Austmarka [N] 172 D5
Autol [E] 84 A5
Autti [FIN] 196 E8
Authon [F] 108 D3
Authon–du–Perche [F] 42 C5
Autun [F] 56 F4
Auvers–s–Oise [F] 42 F3
Auvillers–les–Forges [F] 28 H5
Auxerre [F] 56 E2
Auxi–le–Château [F] 28 D4
Auxonne [F] 56 H4
Auzances [F] 56 B6
Auzon [F] 68 D3
Avå [FIN] 176 C4
Availles–Limouzine [F] 54 F5

Avaldsnes [N] 164 A2
Avallon [F] 56 E3
Ávas [GR] 130 G3
Avaviken [S] 190 G3
Avcılar [TR] 146 E3
Ávdira [GR] 130 E3
Åvedal [N] 164 B5
Aveiras de Cima [P] 86 C4
Aveiro [P] 80 B5
Avelengo / Hafling [I] 72 D3
Avellino [I] 120 F3
Avenches [CH] 58 C6
Aversa [I] 120 D3
Avesnes–le–Comte [F] 28 E4
Avesnes–sur–Helpe [F] 28 G4
Avesta [S] 174 D5
Avetrana [I] 122 F4
Avezzano [I] 116 C5
Avgerinós [GR] 128 E6
Avía [GR] 136 D4
Aviano [I] 72 F5
Aviemore [GB] 6 E5
Avigliana [I] 70 D5
Avigliano [I] 120 G3
Avignon [F] 106 G3
Ávila [E] 88 E4
Avilés [E] 78 H3
Avinurme [EST] 200 F2
Avinyó [E] 92 E3
Avión [E] 78 C4
Avis [P] 86 D5
Avlákia [GR] 144 C5
Avlémonas [GR] 136 F6
Avliótes [GR] 132 A2
Avlóna [GR] 134 C5
Avlonári [GR] 134 C5
Avlum [DK] 160 C6
Avola [I] 126 G5
Avonmouth [GB] 12 F3
Avoriaz [F] 70 C2
Avramov [BG] 148 E4
Avranches [F] 26 D4
Avşar [TR] 142 C1
Avtovac [BIH] 152 D3
Axat [F] 106 B5
Axel [NL] 28 H1
Axioúpoli [GR] 128 G3
Ax–les–Thermes [F] 106 A6
Axminster [GB] 12 F4
Axós [GR] 140 E4
Ay [F] 44 B3
Ayagalım [TR] 130 G3
Ayamonte [E] 94 D5
Ayas [I] 70 D3
Aydın [TR] 144 D5
Aydıncık [TR] 130 G5

Ayerbe [E] 84 D6
Aykırıkçı [TR] 144 H2
Aylesbury [GB] 14 D3
Ayllón [E] 88 H3
Aylsham [GB] 14 G2
Ayna [E] 98 B6
Ayora [E] 98 D5
Ayr [GB] 8 C4
Ayranci [TR] 144 G2
Aysgarth [GB] 10 E2
Aytos [BG] 148 F4
Ayvacık [TR] 134 H1
Ayvalık [TR] 144 B2
Azaila [E] 90 F5
Azambuja [P] 86 C4
Azanúy [E] 90 H3
Azaruja [P] 86 D6
Azay–le–Ferron [F] 54 G3
Azay–le–Rideau [F] 54 F2
Azinheira dos Barros [P] 94 C2
Azitepe [TR] 144 E4
Aznalcóllar [E] 94 G5
Azpeitia [E] 82 H4
Azuaga [E] 96 A5
Azuara [E] 90 E5
Azuel [E] 96 D5
Azuqueca de Henares [E] 88 G5
Azory [BY] 24 G4
Azzano Decimo [I] 72 F5

B

Baad [A] 60 B6
Baamonde [E] 78 D3
Baar [D] 60 D3
Baarle Nassau [NL] 30 D2
Baarn [N] 16 E4
Babadag [RO] 206 E6
Babadağ [TR] 144 F5
Babaeski [TR] 146 B2
Babenhausen [D] 60 C4
Babenhausen [D] 46 D3
Babiak [PL] 36 F3
Babica [PL] 52 D4
Babice [PL] 50 G4
Băbiciu [RO] 148 A1
Babięta [PL] 24 B4
Babigoszcz [PL] 20 F4
Babimost [PL] 36 A3
Babin Potok [HR] 112 G3
Babócsa [H] 74 G5
Babruysk [BY] 202 C6
Babriškes [LT] 24 G2
Babušnica [YU] 150 E4
Babylon [CZ] 48 D5
Bač [MK] 128 E4

Bač [YU] 154 E1
Bača [SLO] 72 H4
Bacău [RO] 206 D5
Baccarat [F] 44 F6
Baceno [I] 70 F2
Bacharach [D] 46 B3
Bachkovo [BG] 148 B6
Bačina [YU] 150 C3
Backaland [GB] 6 G1
Bačka Palanka [YU] 154 F1
Bačka Topola [YU] 76 D5
Backe [S] 190 F6
Bäckebo [S] 162 F4
Bäckefors [S] 166 D4
Bäckhammar [S] 166 F3
Bački Breg [YU] 76 C5
Bački Petrovac [YU] 154 F1
Backnang [D] 46 D6
Bačko Gradište [YU] 154 G1
Bačko Novo Selo [YU] 154 E1
Bačko Petrovo Selo [YU] 76 E6
Bačkowice [PL] 52 C1
Bacoli [I] 120 D3
Bacqueville-en-Caux [F] 28 B4
Bácsalmás [H] 76 D5
Bácsbokod [H] 76 C5
Baczyna [PL] 34 H1
Bad Abbach [D] 60 F2
Badacsonytomaj [H] 74 H3
Bad Aibling [D] 60 F5
Badajoz [E] 86 F6
Badalona [E] 92 E4
Badanloch Lodge [GB] 6 E3
Bad Aussee [A] 62 A6
Bad Bentheim [D] 16 H5
Bad Bergzabern [D] 46 B5
Bad Berka [D] 46 H1
Bad Berleburg [D] 32 D5
Bad Berneck [D] 46 H3
Bad Bertrich [D] 44 G1
Bad Bevensen [D] 18 G5
Bad Bibra [D] 34 B5
Bad Blankenburg [D] 46 H2
Bad Brambach [D] 48 C3
Bad Bramstedt [D] 18 F3
Bad Breisig [D] 30 H5
Bad Brückenau [D] 46 E2
Bad Buchau [D] 60 A4
Bad Deutsch-Altenburg [A] 62 G5
Bad Doberan [D] 20 B3
Bad Driburg [D] 32 E4
Bad Düben [D] 34 D4
Bad Dürkheim [D] 46 B4
Bad Dürrenberg [D] 34 C5
Bad Dürrheim [D] 58 F3
Bad Elster [D] 48 C3
Bademli [TR] 144 C3
Bad Ems [D] 46 B2
Baden [A] 62 F5
Baden [CH] 58 F4
Baden-Baden [D] 58 F1
Bad Endorf [D] 60 F5
Badenweiler [D] 58 E3
Baderna [HR] 112 D2
Bad Essen [D] 32 D2
Bad Frankenhausen [D] 34 A5
Bad Freienwalde [D] 34 F1
Bad Friedrichshall [D] 46 D5
Bad Gandersheim [D] 32 G3
Badgastein [A] 72 G2
Bad Gleichenberg [A] 74 E3
Bad Godesberg [D] 30 H5
Bad Goisern [A] 60 H6
Bad Gottleuba [D] 48 F1
Bad Grund [D] 32 G4
Bad Hall [A] 62 B5
Bad Harzburg [D] 32 H3
Bad Herrenalb [D] 58 F1
Bad Hersfeld [D] 32 F6
Bad Hofgastein [A] 72 G1
Bad Homburg [D] 46 C2
Bad Honnef [D] 30 H5

Bad Hönnigen [D] 30 H5
Badia Polésine [I] 110 F2
Badia Tedalda [I] 110 G6
Bad Iburg [D] 32 D2
Bad Ischl [A] 60 H5
Bad Kissingen [D] 46 E3
Bad Kleinen [D] 20 A4
Bad Kleinkirchheim [A] 72 H3
Bad König [D] 46 D4
Bad Königshofen [D] 46 F2
Bad Kösen [D] 34 B6
Bądkowo [PL] 36 F2
Bad Kreuznach [D] 46 B3
Bad Krozingen [D] 58 E3
Bad Laasphe [D] 32 D6
Bad Langensalza [D] 32 H6
Bad Lauchstädt [D] 34 B5
Bad Lausick [D] 34 D6
Bad Lauterburg [D] 32 G4
Bad Leonfelden [A] 62 B3
Bad Liebenstein [D] 46 F1
Bad Liebenwerda [D] 34 E5
Bad Liebenzell [D] 58 G1
Bad Lippspringe [D] 32 E3
Badljevina [HR] 154 C1
Bad Marienberg [D] 46 B1
Bad Meinberg [D] 32 E3
Bad Mergentheim [D] 46 E5
Bad Mitterndorf [A] 62 B6
Bad Münder [D] 32 F2
Bad Münster Ebernburg [D] 46 B3
Bad Münstereifel [D] 30 G5
Bad Muskau [D] 34 G5
Bad Nauheim [D] 46 C2
Bad Nenndorf [D] 32 F2
Bad Neuenahr [D] 30 G5
Bad Neustadt [D] 46 F2
Bad Oeynhausen [D] 32 E2
Badolato Marina [I] 124 E6
Bad Oldesloe [D] 18 G3
Badonviller [F] 44 F6
Bad Orb [D] 46 D2
Badovinci [YU] 154 F2
Bad Peterstal [D] 58 F2
Bad Pyrmont [D] 32 E3
Bad Ragaz [CH] 58 H6
Bad Reichenhall [D] 60 G5
Bad Rippoldsau [D] 58 F2
Bad Rothenfelde [D] 32 D2
Bad Saarow-Pieskow [D] 34 F3
Bad Sachsa [D] 32 G4
Bad Säckingen [D] 58 E4
Bad Salzdetfurth [D] 32 G3
Bad Salzuflen [D] 32 E3
Bad Salzungen [D] 46 F1
Bad Schallerbach [A] 62 B4
Bad Schandau [D] 48 F1
Bad Schmiedeberg [D] 34 D4
Bad Schönau [A] 74 F1
Bad Schönborn [D] 46 C5
Bad Schussenried [D] 60 B4
Bad Schwalbach [D] 46 B2
Bad Schwartau [D] 18 G3
Bad Segeberg [D] 18 G3
Bad Sooden-Allendorf [D] 32 F5
Bad St. Leonhard [A] 74 C2
Bad Sülze [D] 20 C3
Bad Tatzamannsdorf [A] 74 F1
Bad Tennstedt [D] 32 H5
Bad Tölz [D] 60 E5
Badules [E] 90 D5
Bad Urach [D] 58 H2
Bad Vöslau [A] 62 F5
Bad Waldsee [D] 60 B4
Bad Wiessee [D] 60 E5
Bad-Wildungen [D] 32 E5
Bad Wilsnack [D] 20 B6
Bad Wimpfen [D] 46 D5
Bad Windsheim [D] 46 F5
Bad Wörishofen [D] 60 C4
Bad Wurzach [D] 60 B5
Bad Zwischenahn [D] 18 C5

Bække [DK] 156 B2
Bækmarksbro [DK] 160 B5
Baells [E] 90 H3
Baena [E] 102 D2
Baeza [E] 102 F2
Bagà [E] 92 E2
Bağarası [TR] 144 D5
Bågede [S] 190 E5
Bagenalstown / Muine Bheag [IRL] 4 F4
Bagenkop [DK] 18 H1
Bagheria [I] 126 D2
Bagn [N] 170 G3
Bagnacavallo [I] 110 G4
Bagnara Calabra [I] 124 C7
Bagnères-de-Bigorre [F] 84 F4
Bagnères-de-Luchon [F] 84 F5
Bagni del Másino [I] 70 H3
Bagni di Bórmio [I] 72 B3
Bagni di Craveggia [I] 70 F3
Bagni di Lucca [I] 110 E5
Bagni di Rabbi [I] 72 C3
Bagni di Salomone [I] 72 E2
Bagni di Vinadio [I] 108 E3
Bagno di Romagna [I] 110 G5
Bagnoles-de-l'Orne [F] 26 F5
Bagnoli di Sopra [I] 110 G1
Bagnolo Mella [I] 72 B6
Bagnolo Piemonte [I] 108 F1
Bagnolo San Vito [I] 110 E2
Bagnols-en-Forêt [F] 108 D5
Bagnols-les-Bains [F] 68 D6
Bagnols-sur-Cèze [F] 106 G3
Bågø [DK] 156 C3
Bagod [H] 74 F3
Bagolino [I] 72 B5
Bagrationovsk [RUS] 22 H2
Bagsund [N] 190 C5
Báguena [E] 90 D5

Bağyüzü [TR] 144 C2
Bahçecik [TR] 146 G3
Bahillo [E] 82 D5
Bahuşi [RO] 206 D4
Baia delle Zagare [I] 116 H6
Báia Domízia [I] 120 D2
Baia Mare [RO] 206 B4
Baiano [I] 120 E3
Baião [P] 80 C4
Báia Sardínia [I] 118 C2
Baierbronn [D] 58 F2
Baigneux-les-Juifs [F] 56 G3
Baile Ailein / Balallan [GB] 6 B3
Baile a Mhanaich / Bailivanich [GB] 6 A4
Baile Átha Cliath / Dublin [IRL] 2 F6
Baile Átha Luain / Athlone [IRL] 2 D5
Băile Felix [RO] 76 H2
Bailén [E] 102 E1
Băile Tuşnad [RO] 206 C5
Bailieborough [IRL] 2 F4
Bailivanich / Baile a Mhanaich [GB] 6 A4
Bailleul [F] 28 F2
Bain-de-Bretagne [F] 40 F5
Bains-les-Bains [F] 58 C2
Baio [E] 78 B2
Baiona [E] 78 A5
Bais [F] 26 E6
Baisogala [LT] 202 F4
Baix [F] 68 F5
Baixas [F] 92 G1
Baja [H] 76 C4
Bajánsenye [H] 74 F3
Bajina Bašta [YU] 154 F4
Bajmok [YU] 76 D5
Bajram Curri [AL] 150 A6
Bajša [YU] 76 D6
Bajzë [AL] 152 E4
Bak [H] 74 G3
Bakacak [TR] 146 C5
Bakar [HR] 112 E1
Bakewell [GB] 10 E5
Bakio [E] 82 G3

Bakırköy [TR] 146 E3
Bakkafjörður [IS] 194 G4
Bakke [N] 166 C4
Bakkejord [N] 192 D2
Bakonygyepes [H] 74 H2
Bakonypeterd [H] 76 A1
Bakonysárkány [H] 76 A1
Bakonyszombatheley [H] 76 A1
Baks [H] 76 E3
Baktakék [H] 64 F4
Bala [GB] 10 C5
Balaguer [E] 92 B3
Balallan / Baile Ailein [GB] 6 B3
Balanegra [E] 102 F5
Bălăneşti [RO] 148 A1
Balassagyarmat [H] 64 C5
Balástya [H] 76 E4
Balat [TR] 142 B1
Balatonakali [H] 74 H2
Balatonalmádi [H] 76 A2
Balatonboglár [H] 74 H3
Balatonederics [H] 74 H3
Balatonföldvár [H] 76 A3
Balatonfüred [H] 76 A2
Balatonfüzfő [H] 76 A2
Balatonkenese [H] 76 A2
Balatonkeresztúr [H] 74 H3
Balatonlelle [H] 74 H3
Balatonszemes [H] 76 A3
Balazote [E] 98 B5
Balbeggie [GB] 8 E2
Balbigny [F] 68 E2
Balblair [GB] 6 E4
Balboa [E] 78 E4
Balbriggan [IRL] 2 F5
Balchik [BG] 148 G2
Balchrick [GB] 6 D2
Balderschwang [D] 60 B6
Baldock [GB] 14 E3
Baldone [LV] 200 E5
Bale [HR] 112 D2
Baleira [E] 78 E3
Baleizão [P] 94 D3
Balephuil [GB] 6 A6
Balestrand [N] 170 C1
Balewo [PL] 22 F4
Balfour [GB] 6 G2

Balí [GR] 140 D4
Balice [PL] 50 H3
Balıkesir [TR] 144 D1
Balıklıova [TR] 144 B4
Balıköy [TR] 144 F1
Bälinge [S] 168 D1
Bälinge [S] 158 C1
Balingen [D] 58 G2
Balinţ [RO] 76 H5
Balintore [GB] 6 E4
Balkány [H] 64 H5
Balkıca [TR] 142 F1
Balla [IRL] 2 C4
Ballaban [AL] 128 C5
Ballachulish [GB] 6 C6
Ballaghaderreen [IRL] 2 D4
Ballangen [N] 192 D4
Ballantrae [GB] 8 C4
Ballao [I] 118 D6
Ballater [GB] 6 E6
Ballaugh [GBM] 8 C6
Ballebro [DK] 156 C4
Ballen [DK] 156 E2
Ballenstedt [D] 34 A4
Balleroy [F] 26 E3
Ballerup [DK] 156 G2
Ballı [TR] 146 B3
Ballina [IRL] 2 C6
Ballina [IRL] 2 C3
Ballinafad [GB] 2 D4
Ballinagh [IRL] 2 E4
Ballinakill [IRL] 4 E3
Ballinamallard [GB] 2 E3
Ballinamore [IRL] 2 E4
Ballinascarty [IRL] 4 C5
Ballinasloe [IRL] 2 D5
Ballindine [IRL] 2 C4
Balling [DK] 160 C5
Ballingarry [IRL] 4 C3
Ballingarry [IRL] 4 E4
Ballinhassig [IRL] 4 C5
Ballinrobe [IRL] 2 C4
Ballinskelligs [IRL] 4 A4
Ballinspittle [IRL] 4 C5
Ballintra [IRL] 2 E3
Ballivor [IRL] 2 E5
Ballobar [E] 90 G4
Balloch [GB] 8 D3
Ballon [F] 42 B4

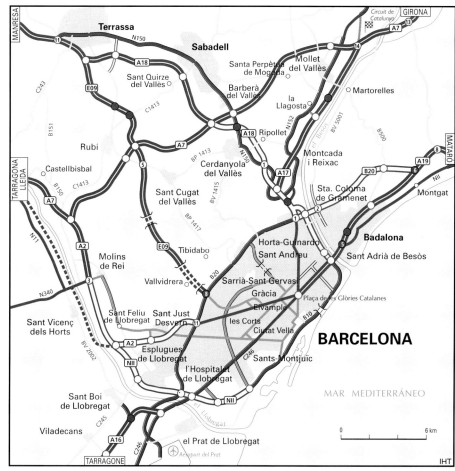

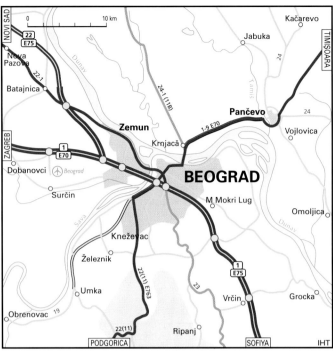

Ballon [IRL] 4 F4
Ballsh [AL] 128 B5
Ballshi [AL] 128 B4
Ballstad [N] 192 B4
Ballum [DK] 156 B3
Ballybay [IRL] 2 F4
Ballybofey [IRL] 2 E2
Ballybunion [IRL] 2 B6
Ballycanew [IRL] 4 F4
Ballycarry [GB] 2 H3
Ballycastle [GB] 2 G2
Ballycastle [IRL] 2 C3
Ballyclare [GB] 2 G3
Ballyconneely [IRL] 2 B4
Ballycotton [IRL] 4 D5
Ballycumber [IRL] 2 D5
Ballydehob [IRL] 4 B5
Ballydesmond [IRL] 4 C4
Ballyduff [IRL] 4 D4
Ballyduff [IRL] 4 B3
Ballyemund [IRL] 4 F4
Ballyfarnan [IRL] 2 D4
Ballygawley [GB] 2 F3
Ballyglass [IRL] 2 C4
Ballygowan [GB] 2 G4
Ballyhaunis [IRL] 2 C4
Ballyheige [IRL] 4 B3
Ballyhillin [IRL] 2 F1
Ballyjamesduff [IRL] 2 E4
Ballykeeran [IRL] 2 D5
Ballylanders [IRL] 4 D4
Ballylongford [IRL] 2 B6
Ballylynan [IRL] 4 F3
Ballymacoda [IRL] 4 D5
Ballymahon [IRL] 2 D5
Ballymena [GB] 2 G3
Ballymoe [IRL] 2 D4
Ballymoney [GB] 2 G2
Ballymore [IRL] 2 E5
Ballymore Eustace [IRL] 4 F3
Ballymote [IRL] 2 D3
Ballynahinch [GB] 2 G4
Ballynure [GB] 2 G3
Ballyragget [IRL] 4 E3
Ballyronan [GB] 2 G3
Ballyroon [IRL] 4 B5
Ballysadare [IRL] 2 D3
Ballyshannon [IRL] 2 E3
Ballyvaughan [IRL] 2 C5
Ballywalter [GB] 2 H4
Balmaha [GB] 8 D2
Balmaseda [E] 82 G4
Balmazújváros [H] 64 G6
Balme [I] 70 C5
Balmúccia [I] 70 E3
Balş [RO] 150 G1
Balsareny [E] 92 D3
Balsfjord [N] 192 E2
Balsicas [E] 104 C4

Balsorano [I] 116 C6
Bålsta [S] 168 D2
Balsthal [CH] 58 E5
Balta [UA] 206 E4
Baltanás [E] 88 F1
Baltasound [GB] 6 H3
Bălţi [MD] 206 D4
Baltimore [IRL] 4 B5
Baltinava [LV] 200 G5
Baltinglass [IRL] 4 F3
Baltiysk [RUS] 22 G1
Baltrum [D] 18 B3
Balugães [P] 78 A6
Balvan [BG] 148 C3
Balvi [LV] 200 G4
Balya [TR] 144 D1
Bambalió [GR] 132 E4
Bamberg [D] 46 G4
Bambíni [GR] 132 D5
Bamble [N] 164 G3
Bamburgh [GB] 8 G4
Bampton [GB] 12 E4
Bana [H] 64 A6
Banagher [IRL] 2 D6
Banarli [TR] 146 C3
Banatski Karlovac [YU] 154 H2
Banatsko Aranđelovo [YU] 76 E5
Banatsko Karadjordjevo [YU] 76 F6
Banatsko Novo Selo [YU] 154 H2
Banaz [TR] 144 G3
Banbridge [GB] 2 G4
Banbury [GB] 14 D2
Banchory [GB] 6 F6
Bande [E] 78 C5
Bandholm [DK] 156 F5
Bandırma [TR] 146 D4
Bandol [F] 108 B5
Bandon [IRL] 4 C5
Băneasa [RO] 148 C1
Banff [GB] 6 F5
Bangor [F] 40 C5
Bangor [GB] 10 B4
Bangor [GB] 2 H3
Bangor Erris [IRL] 2 C3
Bangsund [N] 190 C5
Banie [PL] 20 F6
Banja [YU] 152 E2
Banja Koviljača [YU] 154 E3
Banjaloka [SLO] 112 F1
Banja Luka [BIH] 154 C3
Banjani [YU] 150 A1
Banjska [YU] 150 A3
Banka [SK] 64 A3
Bankervd [S] 162 D2
Bankja [BG] 150 F5

Bannalec [F] 40 C3
Banon [F] 108 C3
Baños de Alicún de las Torres [E] 102 F3
Baños de Cerrato [E] 88 F1
Baños de la Encina [E] 102 E1
Baños de la Fuensanta [E] 104 A3
Baños de Montemayor [E] 88 B4
Baños de Panticosa [E] 84 E5
Bánov [CZ] 62 H2
Bánovce nad Bebravou [SK] 64 B3
Banovići [BIH] 154 D3
Bánréve [H] 64 E4
Bansin [D] 20 E3
Banská Bystrica [SK] 64 C3
Banská Štiavnica [SK] 64 C3
Bansko [BG] 130 B1
Bansko [MK] 128 H2
Banteer [IRL] 4 C4
Bantry [IRL] 4 B5
Banya [BG] 148 B5
Banya [BG] 148 F4
Banya [BG] 148 D4
Banyeres de Mariola [E] 104 D1
Banyoles [E] 92 F3
Banyuls-sur-Mer [F] 92 G2
Bapaume [F] 28 F4
Bar [YU] 152 E5
Barabhas / Barvas [GB] 6 C2
Barajas de Melo [E] 96 H1
Barakaldo [E] 82 G3
Baralla [E] 78 E4
Báránd [H] 76 G1
Baranoviči [BY] 204 A6
Baranowo [PL] 24 C5
Baranów Sandomierski [PL] 52 D2
Baraona [E] 90 B4
Baraqueville [F] 68 A6
Barbadillo de Herreros [E] 90 A1
Barban [HR] 112 D2
Barbarano Vicentino [I] 72 D6
Barbaros [TR] 146 C3
Barbaste [F] 66 E5
Barbastro [E] 90 G3
Barbate [E] 100 F5
Bärbele [LV] 200 E6
Barbezieux [F] 66 E2
Barbing [D] 60 F2
Barbizon [F] 42 F5

Barbotan-les-Thermes [F] 66 D6
Barby [D] 34 C3
Bârca [RO] 150 G2
Barcarrota [E] 94 F2
Barcellona-Pozzo di Gotto [I] 124 B7
Barcelona [E] 92 E4
Barcelonnette [F] 108 E2
Barcelos [P] 80 C3
Bárcena de Pie de Concha [E] 82 E3
Barchfeld [D] 46 F1
Barciany [PL] 24 B3
Barcin [PL] 36 E1
Bárcis [I] 72 E4
Barcs [H] 74 H5
Barczewo [PL] 22 H4
Bardejov [SK] 52 D6
Bårdesø [DK] 156 D2
Bardi [I] 110 C3
Bardney [GB] 10 G5
Bardo [PL] 50 C2
Bardolino [I] 72 C6
Bardonécchia [I] 70 B5
Bardowick [D] 18 G5
Barenburg [D] 32 E1
Barentin [F] 26 H3
Barenton [F] 26 E5
Barfleur [F] 26 E2
Barga [I] 110 D4
Bargas [E] 96 F1
Barge [I] 108 F2
Bargoed [GB] 12 F2
Bargrennan [GB] 8 C5
Bargteheide [D] 18 G4
Bari [I] 122 E2
Bari Sardo [I] 118 E5
Barisciano [I] 116 C4
Barjac [F] 106 G2
Barjas [E] 78 E5
Barjols [F] 108 C4
Barkald [N] 182 C5
Barkava [LV] 200 F5
Barkowo [PL] 22 C4
Bar-le-Duc [F] 44 D5
Barlinek [PL] 20 G6
Barlingbo [S] 168 G4
Barletta [I] 122 C2
Barmash [AL] 128 D6
Barmouth [GB] 10 B5
Barmstedt [D] 18 F3
Barnard Castle [GB] 10 F2
Bärnau [D] 48 C4
Barneberg [D] 34 A3
Barneveld [NL] 16 E5
Barneville-Carteret [F] 26 D2
Barnewitz [D] 34 D2
Barnoldswick [GB] 10 E3
Barnsley [GB] 10 F4
Barnstaple [GB] 12 E3
Barnstorf [D] 18 D6
Barntrup [D] 32 E3
Barquilla de Pinares [E] 88 C5
Barr [F] 44 G6
Barracas [E] 98 E3
Barrafranca [I] 126 E4
Barranco do Velho [P] 94 C5
Barrancos [P] 94 F3
Barrax [E] 98 B5
Barrea [I] 116 D6
Barre-des-Cévennes [F] 106 E2
Barreiro [P] 86 B5
Barrême [F] 108 D3
Barrosa [E] 100 F4
Barrow in Furness [GB] 10 D2
Barrow-on-Soar [GB] 10 F6
Barruecopardo [E] 80 F5
Barry [GB] 12 F3
Barryporeen [IRL] 4 D4
Barsinghausen [D] 32 F2
Barssel [D] 18 C5
Bar-sur-Aube [F] 44 C6
Bar-sur-Seine [F] 44 B6
Barth [D] 20 C2

Barton-upon-Humber [GB] 10 G4
Bartoszyce [PL] 22 H2
Barúmini [I] 118 C6
Baruth [D] 34 E3
Barvas / Barabhas [GB] 6 C2
Barver [D] 32 E1
Barwice [PL] 22 A4
Barysevo [RUS] 178 G3
Barzio [I] 70 G3
Bašaid [YU] 76 F6
Basconcillos del Tozo [E] 82 E5
Basdahl [D] 18 E4
Basel [CH] 58 E4
Baselga di Pinè [I] 72 D4
Båsheim [N] 170 G5
Basi [LV] 200 B5
Basildon [GB] 14 F4
Basilice [I] 120 F2
Basingstoke [GB] 14 D4
Baška [HR] 112 F2
Baška Voda [HR] 152 B2
Baške Ostarije [HR] 112 G4
Başlamış [TR] 144 D2
Başmakçı [TR] 144 H4
Bassano del Grappa [I] 72 D5
Bassella [E] 92 C2
Bassum [D] 18 D6
Båstad [N] 166 C2
Båstad [S] 162 B6
Bastelica [F] 114 B4
Basti [TR] 144 H3
Bastia [F] 114 C3
Bastia Umbra [I] 116 A2
Bastogne [B] 44 E1
Bastuträsk [S] 190 H4
Batajnica [YU] 154 G2
Batak [BG] 148 A6
Batalha [P] 86 C3
Batăr [RO] 76 H3
Bátaszék [H] 76 C4
Baté [H] 76 A4
Batea [E] 90 G6
Batecki [RUS] 204 C2
Batelov [CZ] 48 H6
Bath [GB] 12 G3
Bathgate [GB] 8 E3
Batina [HR] 76 C5
Batlava [YU] 150 C4
Batnfjordsøra [N] 180 E2
Batočina [YU] 150 C2
Bátonyterenye [H] 64 D5
Båtsfjord [N] 196 E1
Batsí [GR] 134 E6
Battaglia Terme [I] 110 G1
Battenberg [D] 32 D6
Battice [B] 30 E5
Battipáglia [I] 120 F4
Battle [GB] 14 F5
Battonya [H] 76 G4
Baud [F] 26 A6
Baugé [F] 42 A6
Baugy [F] 56 C3
Baume-les-Dames [F] 58 B4
Baumholder [D] 44 H3
Baunei [I] 118 E5
Bauska [LV] 200 D6
Bautzen [D] 34 F6
Bavanište [YU] 154 H2
Baveno [I] 70 F3
Bavorov [CZ] 48 F6
Bawdeswell [GB] 14 G2
Bawdsey [GB] 14 G3
Bawtry [GB] 10 F4
Bayerisch Eisenstein [D] 48 D6
Bayeux [F] 26 E3
Bayındır [TR] 144 D4
Bayındır [TR] 146 F4
Bayır [TR] 142 D2
Bayırköy [TR] 146 B5
Baykal [BG] 148 A2
Bayon [F] 44 E6
Bayonne [F] 84 C2
Bayramdere [TR] 146 E4

Bayramiç [TR] 144 B1
Bayramşah [TR] 144 G1
Bayreuth [D] 46 H4
Bayrischzell [D] 60 F5
Baza [E] 102 G3
Bazas [F] 66 D4
Bazoches-sur-Hoëne [F] 26 G5
Bazolles [F] 56 E4
Bazzano [I] 110 F3
Beaconsfield [GB] 14 D4
Beadnell [GB] 8 G4
Béal an Mhuirhead / Belmullet [IRL] 2 B2
Beames-de-Venise [F] 106 H3
Beaminster [GB] 12 F4
Beas [E] 94 F5
Beasain [E] 84 A3
Beas de Segura [E] 102 G1
Beattock [GB] 8 E4
Beaucaire [F] 106 G4
Beaufort [IRL] 4 B4
Beaufort-en-Vallée [F] 54 E1
Beaufort-sur-Doron [F] 70 B3
Beaugency [F] 42 D6
Beaulieu [GB] 12 H5
Beaulieu-sur-Dordogne [F] 66 H4
Beaulieu-sur-Mer [F] 108 F4
Beaumaris [GB] 10 B4
Beaumesnil [F] 26 H4
Beaumetz [F] 28 E4
Beaumont [B] 28 H4
Beaumont [F] 66 F4
Beaumont [F] 26 D1
Beaumont-de-Lomagne [F] 84 H2
Beaumont-le-Roger [F] 26 H4
Beaumont-sur-Sarthe [F] 26 F6
Beaune [F] 56 G4
Beaune-la-Rolande [F] 42 F6
Beaupréau [F] 54 C2
Beauraing [B] 30 D6
Beaurepaire [F] 68 G4
Beaurepaire-en-Bresse [F] 56 H5
Beauvais [F] 28 D6
Beauvallon [F] 108 D5
Beauvezer [F] 108 D3
Beauville [F] 66 F5
Beauvoir-sur-Mer [F] 54 B2
Beauvoir-sur-Niort [F] 54 D5
Bebington [GB] 10 D4
Bebra [D] 32 F6
Bebrene [LV] 200 F6
Bebrovo [BG] 148 D4
Beccles [GB] 14 H2
Bečej [YU] 76 E6
Becerreá [E] 78 E4
Bécherel [F] 26 C5
Bechetu [RO] 150 G2
Bechhofen [D] 46 F6
Bechyně [CZ] 48 F6
Becicherecu Mic [RO] 76 G5
Becilla de Valderaduey [E] 82 B5
Beciu [RO] 148 A2
Beckenried [CH] 58 F6
Beckfoot [GB] 8 D6
Beckington [GB] 12 G4
Beckum [D] 32 C4
Beckum [D] 32 D3
Beclean [RO] 206 B4
Becov nad Tepbu [CZ] 48 D3
Becsehely [H] 74 G4
Becske [H] 64 D5
Bedale [GB] 10 F2
Bédarieux [F] 106 D4
Beddgelert [GB] 10 B4
Beddingestrand [S] 158 C3
Bédée [F] 26 C5

Bederkesa [D] 18 D4
Bedford [GB] 14 E3
Będków [PL] 36 H5
Bedlington [GB] 8 G5
Bednarka [PL] 52 D5
Bedonia [I] 110 C3
Bedous [F] 84 D4
Bedsted [DK] 160 B4
Bedworth [GB] 14 D1
Będzin [PL] 50 G3
Będzino [PL] 20 H3
Beek [NL] 30 E4
Beek en Donk [NL] 30 E2
Beelitz [D] 34 D3
Beer [GB] 12 F4
Beerfelden [D] 46 D4
Beeskow [D] 34 F3
Beesten [D] 32 C1
Bégard [F] 26 A4
Beg-Meil [F] 40 B3
Begndal [N] 170 G4
Begoml [BY] 204 B5
Begunitsy [RUS] 178 G6
Begur [E] 92 G3
Behramkale [TR] 134 H1
Behringersmühle [D] 46 G4
Beilen [NL] 16 G3
Beilngries [D] 46 H6
Beith [GB] 8 D3
Beitostølen [N] 170 F2
Beiuş [RO] 206 B4
Beja [P] 94 D3
Béjar [E] 88 B4
Bejís [E] 98 E3
Bekçiler [TR] 142 H2
Békés [H] 76 G4
Békéscsaba [H] 76 G3
Békésszentandrás [H] 76 F2
Bekilli [TR] 144 G4
Bélâbre [F] 54 G4
Bela Crkva [YU] 206 A6
Belaja Cerkov [UA] 206 E2
Belalcázar [E] 96 C4
Bela Palanka [YU] 150 E4
Bělá pod Bezdězem [CZ] 48 G2
Belcaire [F] 106 A5
Bełchatów [PL] 36 G5
Belchin [BG] 150 G5
Belchite [E] 90 E5
Belčišta [MK] 128 D3
Belcoo [GB] 2 E3
Belecke [D] 32 D4
Beled [H] 74 G1
Belene [BG] 148 B2
Belev [RUS] 204 F5
Belevi [TR] 144 D5
Belfast [GB] 2 G3
Belfir [RO] 76 H3
Belfort [F] 58 C4
Belgern [D] 34 D5
Belgirate [I] 70 F4
Belgodère [F] 114 B3
Belgooly [IRL] 4 C5
Belgorod [RUS] 206 H1
Belgorod-Dnestrovski [UA] 206 E5
Beli [HR] 112 E2
Belianes [E] 92 C3
Belica [HR] 74 F4
Belica [MK] 128 E2
Belıklıçeşme [TR] 146 C5
Beli Manastir [HR] 76 B6
Belimel [BG] 150 F3
Belin-Béliet [F] 66 C4
Belinchón [E] 96 H1
Belinţ [RO] 76 H5
Belišće [HR] 76 B6
Belitsa [BG] 150 G6
Beljina [YU] 154 G3
Bellac [F] 54 F5
Bellaghy [GB] 2 G3
Bellágio [I] 70 G3
Bellamonte [I] 72 D4
Bellano [I] 70 G3
Bellária [I] 110 H4
Bellcaire d'Urgell [E] 92 C3
Belleek [GB] 2 E3
Bellegarde [F] 42 F6
Bellegarde [F] 106 G4

Bellegarde-en-Marche [F] 68 B1
Bellegarde-sur-Valserine [F] 70 A2
Belle-Isle-en-Terre [F] 40 D2
Bellême [F] 26 G6
Bellenaves [F] 56 D6
Bellencombre [F] 28 C5
Bellevesvre [F] 56 H5
Belleville [F] 68 F2
Belleville-sur-Vie [F] 54 B2
Belley [F] 68 H3
Bellinge [DK] 156 D3
Bellingham [GB] 8 F5
Bellinzona [CH] 70 G3
Bello [E] 90 D5
Bellö [S] 162 E2
Bellochantuy [GB] 2 H1
Bellpuig [E] 92 C3
Belluno [I] 72 E4
Bellver de Cerdanya [E] 92 E2
Belmez [E] 96 B5
Belmonte [E] 96 H3
Belmonte [E] 78 G3
Belmonte [E] 86 F2
Belmont-sur-Rance [F] 106 D3
Belmullet / Béal an Mhuirhead [IRL] 2 B2
Beloeil [B] 28 G3
Belogradchik [BG] 150 E3
Belokamensk [UA] 206 G6
Beloljin [YU] 150 C4
Bélopátfalva [H] 64 E5
Belorado [E] 82 F6
Bělotín [CZ] 50 E5
Belovo [BG] 148 A6
Belozersk [RUS] 204 F1
Belpasso [I] 126 G3
Belper [GB] 10 E5
Belsen [D] 18 F6
Belsk Duży [PL] 38 B4
Beltinci [SLO] 74 F3
Belturbet [IRL] 2 E4
Beluša [SK] 64 B2
Belušić [YU] 150 C2
BelvedereCampomoro [F] 114 A5
Belvedere Maríttimo [I] 124 C3
Belver [P] 86 E4
Belvès [F] 66 F4
Belvis de la Jara [E] 96 D1
Bely [RUS] 204 D4
Belynići [BY] 204 C5
Belz [F] 40 C4
Belz [UA] 52 H2
Bełżec [PL] 52 G2
Belzig [D] 34 D3
Bełżyce [PL] 38 D6
Bembibre [E] 78 F5
Bembridge [GB] 12 H5
Bemposta [P] 80 F5
Bemposta [P] 86 D4
Benabarre [E] 90 H3
Benalmádena [E] 102 B5
Benalup [E] 100 G5
Benaojan [E] 100 H4
Benasque [F] 84 F5
Benatsky nad Jizerou [CZ] 48 G3
Benavente [E] 82 A5
Benavente [P] 86 C5
Benavites [E] 78 G6
Benburb [GB] 2 F3
Benediktbeuern [D] 60 D5
Beneixama / Benejama [E] 104 D1
Benejama / Beneixama [E] 104 D1
Benešov [CZ] 48 G4
Benešov nad Ploučnicí [CZ] 48 F2
Bénévent l'Abbaye [F] 54 G6
Benevento [I] 120 F2
Benfeld [F] 58 E2
Bengtsfors [S] 166 D4
Beničanci [HR] 76 B6
Benicarló [E] 98 H2

Benicasim / Benicàssim [E] 98 G3
Benicàssim / Benicasim [E] 98 G3
Benidorm [E] 104 E2
Beniel [E] 104 C3
Benifaió [E] 98 E5
Benimarfull [E] 104 E1
Benissa [E] 104 F2
Benítses [GR] 132 B2
Benkovac [HR] 112 G5
Benneckenstein [D] 32 H4
Bennstedt [D] 34 B5
Bénodet [F] 40 B3
Bensafrim [P] 94 B5
Bensberg [D] 30 H4
Bensersiel [D] 18 C3
Bensheim [D] 46 C4
Beočin [YU] 154 F2
Beograd [YU] 154 G2
Bera / Vera de Bidasoa [E] 84 B2
Beragh [GB] 2 F3
Berane [YU] 150 A5
Berat [AL] 128 B4
Beratón [E] 90 C3
Berbenno di Valtellina [I] 70 H3
Berberana [E] 82 G4
Bercedo [E] 82 F4
Bercel [H] 64 D5
Berceto [I] 110 D3
Berching [D] 46 G6
Berchtesgaden [D] 60 G6
Berck-Plage [F] 28 D3
Berdiansk [UA] 206 H4
Berdičev [UA] 206 D2
Berducedo [E] 78 F3
Berdún [E] 84 C5
Berechiu [RO] 76 H3
Beregovo [UA] 206 B3
Berek [HR] 74 G6
Berettvóújfalu [H] 76 G1
Berezan [UA] 206 F2
Berg [D] 60 D5
Berg [N] 172 D5
Berg [N] 190 C3
Berga [D] 32 H5
Berga [E] 92 E2

Berga [S] 162 F4
Bergama [TR] 144 C2
Bergamo [I] 70 H4
Bergara [E] 82 H4
Bergby [S] 174 E3
Berge [N] 164 E1
Bergedorf [D] 18 G4
Bergeforsen [S] 184 E4
Bergen [D] 18 F6
Bergen [D] 18 H6
Bergen [D] 20 D2
Bergen [N] 170 B4
Bergen [N] 16 D3
Bergen (Mons) [B] 28 G4
Bergen aan Zee [NL] 16 D3
Bergen op Zoom [NL] 16 C6
Berger [N] 164 H2
Bergerac [F] 66 E4
Bergheim [D] 30 G4
Bergisch Gladbach [D] 30 H4
Bergkvara [S] 162 F6
Berglern [D] 60 E3
Bergnäset [S] 198 B3
Bergö [FIN] 186 A3
Bergshamra [S] 168 E2
Bergsjö [S] 184 E6
Berg slussar [S] 166 H5
Bergstrøm [N] 166 C3
Bergsviken [S] 198 B3
Bergues [F] 14 H6
Bergum [NL] 16 F2
Bergün [CH] 70 H2
Bergunda [S] 162 D5
Bergvik [S] 174 E2
Beringen [B] 30 E3
Berislav [UA] 206 G4
Berja [E] 102 F5
Berkåk [N] 180 H3
Berkeley [GB] 12 G3
Berkenthin [D] 18 G4
Berkesz [H] 64 H4
Berkhamsted [GB] 14 E3
Berkheim [D] 60 B4
Berkhof [D] 32 F1
Berkovici [BIH] 152 C3

Berkovitsa [BG] 150 F3
Berlanga [E] 96 A5
Berlanga de Duero [E] 90 A3
Berlevåg [N] 196 E1
Berlin [D] 34 E2
Berlingen [CH] 58 G4
Bermeo [E] 82 H3
Bermillo de Sayago [E] 80 G5
Bern [CH] 58 D6
Bernalda [I] 122 D4
Bernartice [CZ] 48 F5
Bernati [LV] 200 B6
Bernau [D] 60 F5
Bernau [D] 34 E2
Bernaville [F] 28 E4
Bernay [F] 26 G4
Bernburg [D] 34 B4
Berndorf [A] 62 E5
Berne [D] 18 D5
Beredo [E] 82 H6
Bernhardsthal [A] 62 G3
Bernisdale [GB] 6 B4
Bernkastel-Kues [D] 44 G2
Bernsdorf [D] 34 F5
Bernstein [A] 74 F1
Beromünster [CH] 58 F5
Beronovo [BG] 148 E4
Beroun [CZ] 48 F4
Berovo [MK] 128 H1
Berre-l'Etang [F] 106 H5
Berrocal [E] 94 F5
Bersenbrück [D] 32 D1
Bertinoro [I] 110 G4
Bertrix [B] 44 D2
Berwang [A] 60 C6
Berwick-upon-Tweed [GB] 8 F4
Berzaune [LV] 200 F5
Berzence [H] 74 G4
Besalú [E] 92 F2
Besançon [F] 58 B5
Besande [E] 82 C3
Besenyszög [H] 76 E1
Beşevler [TR] 146 G4
Beşevlet [TR] 146 G3
Besigheim [D] 46 D6
Beška [YU] 154 G2

Bessan [F] 106 E4
Bessay-sur-Allier [F] 56 D5
Besse-en-Chandesse [F] 68 C3
Besse-sur-Issole [F] 108 C5
Bessheim [N] 170 F1
Bessines-sur-Gartempe [F] 54 G6
Bestida [P] 80 B5
Bestorp [S] 168 A6
Beszowa [PL] 52 C2
Betancuria [E] 100 E5
Betanzos [E] 78 D2
Betelu [E] 84 B3
Beteta [E] 90 B6
Bethesda [GB] 10 B4
Betna [N] 180 F2
Bettna [S] 168 C4
Bettola [I] 110 C2
Bettyhill [GB] 6 E2
Betws-y-Coed [GB] 10 C4
Betz [F] 42 G3
Betzdorf [D] 32 C6
Beuel [D] 30 H5
Beuil [F] 108 E3
Beuron [D] 58 G3
Beuzeville [F] 26 G3
Bevagna [I] 116 A2
Beveren-Waas [B] 30 C3
Beverley [GB] 10 G4
Beverstedt [D] 18 D4
Beverungen [D] 32 F4
Beverwijk [NL] 16 D4
Bevtoft [DK] 156 C3
Bewcastle [GB] 8 E5
Bewdley [GB] 12 G1
Bex [CH] 70 C2
Bexhill [GB] 14 E6
Beyağaç [TR] 142 F1
Beyazköy [TR] 146 C2
Beydağı [TR] 144 E4
Beykoz [TR] 146 E2
Beynac-et-Cazenac [F] 66 F4
Beynat [F] 66 H3

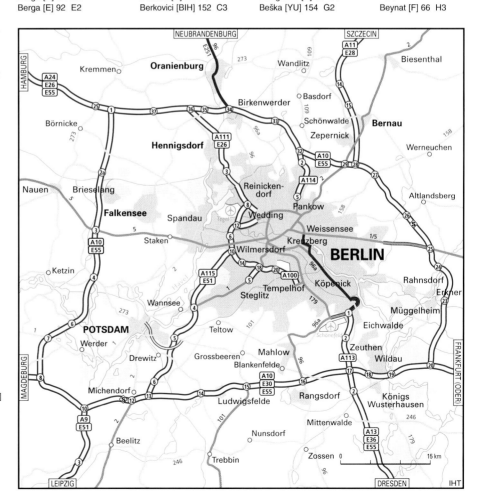

Bezau [A] 60 B6
Bezdan [YU] 76 C5
Bežeck [RUS] 204 F3
Béziers [F] 106 D4
Biała [PL] 50 D3
Bialaczów [PL] 38 A5
Biala Piska [PL] 24 D4
Biała Podlaska [PL] 38 F3
Biała Rawska [PL] 38 A4
Białobrzegi [PL] 38 B4
Białogard [PL] 20 H3
Białowieza [PL] 38 G1
Biały Bór [PL] 22 B4
Białystok [PL] 24 E5
Biancavilla [I] 126 G3
Bianco [I] 124 D7
Biar [E] 104 D1
Biarritz [F] 84 C2
Bias [F] 66 B5
Biasca [CH] 70 G2
Biasteri / Laguardia [E] 82
   G6
Biatorbágy [H] 76 C1
Bibbiena [I] 110 G6
Bibbiona [I] 114 E1
Biberach [D] 58 F2
Biberach an der Riss [D] 60
   B4
Bibione [I] 72 G6
Bibury [GB] 12 H3
Bicaj [AL] 128 C1
Bicaz [RO] 206 C4
Bicester [GB] 14 D3
Bichl [D] 60 D5
Bickleigh [GB] 12 E4
Bicos [P] 94 C3
Bicske [H] 76 B1
Bidache [F] 84 C2
Bidart [F] 84 C2
Biddenden [GB] 14 F5
Biddulph [GB] 10 E5
Bideford [GB] 12 D3
Bidford-on-Avon [GB] 12
   H2
Bidjovagge [N] 192 G2
Bidovce [SK] 64 G3
Bidziny [PL] 52 D1
Bie [S] 168 B4

Bieber [D] 46 D3
Biebersdorf [D] 34 F4
Biecz [PL] 52 C4
Biedenkopf [D] 32 D6
Biel [E] 84 C5
Biel / Bienne [CH] 58 D5
Bielawa [PL] 50 C2
Bielczyny [PL] 22 E5
Bielefeld [D] 32 D3
Biella [I] 70 E4
Bielmonte [I] 70 E4
Bielowy [PL] 52 D4
Bielsa [E] 84 E5
Bielsk [PL] 36 H2
Bielsko-Biała [PL] 50 G4
Bielsk Podlaski [PL] 38 F1
Bienenbüttel [D] 18 G5
Bienne / Biel [CH] 58 D5
Bienvenida [E] 94 G3
Bienvenida [E] 96 D4
Bierre-Lès-Semur [F] 56
   F3
Bierutów [PL] 36 D6
Bierzwnik [PL] 20 H6
Biescas [E] 84 D5
Biesenthal [D] 34 E1
Biesiekierz [PL] 20 H3
Bietigheim [D] 46 D6
Bieżuń [PL] 22 G6
Biga [TR] 146 C5
Bigadiç [TR] 144 D2
Bigbury-on-Sea [GB] 12
   D5
Biggar [GB] 8 E4
Biggleswade [GB] 14 E3
Bignasco [CH] 70 F2
Bihać [BIH] 112 H3
Biharia [RO] 76 H2
Biharkeresztes [H] 76 H2
Biharnagybajom [H] 76 G1
Bijeljani [BIH] 152 D3
Bijeljina [BIH] 154 E3
Bijelo Polje [YU] 150 A4
Bikava [LV] 200 G5
Bilbao / Bilbo [E] 82 G4
Bilbo / Bilbao [E] 82 G4
Bileča [BIH] 152 D3
Bilecik [TR] 146 G4
Biled [RO] 76 G5

Biłgoraj [PL] 52 F2
Bílina [CZ] 48 E2
Bilisht [AL] 128 D5
Biljanovac [YU] 150 B3
Bilje [HR] 76 C6
Billdal [S] 160 G2
Billefjord [N] 196 C2
Billerbeck [D] 16 H6
Billericay [GB] 14 F4
Billingham [GB] 10 F2
Billingsfors [S] 166 D4
Billom [F] 68 D2
Billund [DK] 156 C2
Bílovec [CZ] 50 E4
Bilska [LV] 200 F4
Bilto [N] 192 F2
Biňa [SK] 64 B5
Binas [F] 42 D6
Binasco [I] 70 G5
Binche [B] 28 H4
Bindslev [DK] 160 E2
Binéfar [E] 90 G4
Bingen [D] 46 B3
Bingley [GB] 10 E3
Binibeca Vell [E] 104 H5
Binic [F] 26 B4
Binz [D] 20 D2
Bioče [YU] 152 E4
Biograd [HR] 112 G5
Bionaz [I] 70 D3
Bioska [YU] 152 F1
Bircza [PL] 52 E4
Biri [N] 172 B3
Birkeland [N] 164 E5
Birkeland [N] 164 C5
Birkenfeld [D] 46 E4
Birkenfeld [D] 44 G3
Birkenhead [GB] 10 D4
Birkenwerder [D] 34 E2
Birkerød [DK] 156 G2
Birkfeld [A] 74 E1
Birkhill [GB] 8 E4
Birksdal [N] 180 D6
Bîrlad [RO] 206 D5
Birmingham [GB] 10 E6
Birnau [D] 58 H4
Birr [IRL] 2 D6
Birsay [GB] 6 F1
Birštonas [LT] 24 F1

Birtavarre [N] 192 F2
Biržai [LT] 200 E6
Birżebbuga [M] 126 C6
Birži [LV] 200 F6
Birzuli [LV] 200 F4
Bisaccia [I] 120 G3
Bisbal d'Empordà, la– [E] 92
   G3
Biscarrose [F] 66 B4
Biscarrose-Plage [F] 66
   B4
Biscéglie [I] 122 D2
Bischofsgrün [D] 46 H3
Bischofsheim [D] 46 E2
Bischofshofen [A] 72 G1
Bischofswerda [D] 34 F6
Bishop Auckland [GB] 10
   F2
Bishop's Castle [GB] 10 C6
Bishop's Cleeve [GB] 12
   G2
Bishop's Lydeard [GB] 12
   F4
Bishop's Stortford [GB] 14
   F3
Bishop's Waltham [GB] 12
   H5
Bisignano [I] 124 D4
Biskupiec [PL] 22 F5
Biskupiec [PL] 22 H4
Biskupin [PL] 36 D1
Bismark [D] 34 B1
Bismo [N] 180 F5
Bispfors [S] 184 D3
Bispgården [S] 184 D3
Bispingen [D] 18 F5
Bistret [RO] 150 F2
Bistrica [YU] 152 E3
Bistrica [YU] 150 A3
Bistriţa [RO] 206 C4
Bistritsa [BG] 150 F5
Bisztynek [PL] 22 H3
Bitburg [D] 44 F2
Bitche [F] 44 G4
Bitetto [I] 122 D3
Bitola [MK] 128 E3
Bitonto [I] 122 D2
Bítov [CZ] 62 E2
Bitterfeld [D] 34 C4

Bitti [I] 118 D4
Bivona [I] 126 D3
Bizovac [HR] 76 B6
Bjåen [N] 164 D1
Bjärnum [S] 158 D1
Bjärred [S] 156 H2
Bjästa [S] 184 G2
Bjelland [N] 164 D5
Bjelovar [HR] 74 G5
Bjerkreim [N] 164 B4
Bjerkvik [N] 192 D4
Bjerregård [DK] 156 A1
Bjerringbro [DK] 160 D5
Bjølstad [N] 180 G6
Bjørbo [S] 172 G5
Bjordal [N] 164 C4
Björkefors [S] 162 F1
Bjørkelangen [N] 166 C1
Bjørkflåta [N] 170 F4
Björkfors [S] 190 E3
Björkhöjden [S] 184 D2
Björkliden [S] 192 E4
Björkling [S] 168 D1
Bjørknes [N] 172 C6
Björkö [FIN] 176 C5
Björkö [S] 168 F1
Björkö [S] 162 E3
Björköby [FIN] 186 A2
Björksele [S] 190 G4
Björkvik [S] 168 B4
Bjørn [N] 190 D2
Björna [S] 184 G1
Björneborg [S] 166 G3
Bjørnevasshytta [N] 164
   D2
Bjørnevatn [N] 196 E3
Björnlunda [S] 168 C4
Björnsholm [S] 162 G1
Bjørsvik [N] 170 B3
Bjuråker [S] 184 D6
Bjurberget [S] 172 E4
Bjurholm [S] 190 H6
Bjursås [S] 172 H4
Bjuv [S] 156 H1
Blace [YU] 150 C3
Blachownia [PL] 50 F2
Blackburn [GB] 10 E3
Blacklion [IRL] 2 E3
Blackpool [GB] 10 D3
Blackstad [S] 162 G2
Blackwater [IRL] 4 F5
Blaenau Ffestiniog [GB] 10
   B4
Blaenavon [GB] 12 F2
Blagaj [BIH] 152 C2
Blagoevgrad [BG] 150 F6
Blagoevo [BG] 148 D2
Blåhøj [DK] 156 B1
Blaiken [S] 190 F4
Blain [F] 40 F5
Blair Atholl [GB] 8 E1
Blairgowrie [GB] 8 E2
Blaj [RO] 206 B5
Blakeney [GB] 14 G1
Blakeney [GB] 12 G2
Blakstad [N] 164 E5
Blâmont [F] 44 F6
Blanca [E] 104 C2
Blandford Forum [GB] 12
   G4
Blanes [E] 92 F4
Blangy-sur-Bresle [F] 28
   D4
Blankaholm [S] 162 G2
Blankenberge [B] 28 G1
Blankenburg [D] 32 H4
Blankenfelde [D] 34 E2
Blankenhain [D] 46 H1
Blankenheim [D] 30 G6
Blanquefort [F] 66 C3
Blanzac [F] 66 E2
Blarney [IRL] 4 C5
Blascosancho [E] 88 E4
Błaszki [PL] 36 F5
Blatná [CZ] 48 E5
Blatnica [BIH] 154 C3
Blatnice [CZ] 62 H2
Blato [HR] 152 A2
Blato [HR] 152 A3

Blattniksele [S] 190 G3
Blaubeuren [D] 60 B3
Blaufelden [D] 46 E5
Blaustein [D] 60 B3
Blåvand [DK] 156 A2
Blåvik [S] 162 E1
Blaye [F] 66 C2
Bleckede [D] 18 G5
Bled [SLO] 74 B4
Bleiburg [A] 74 C3
Bleicherode [D] 32 G5
Bleik [N] 192 C3
Blendija [YU] 150 D3
Bléneau [F] 56 D2
Blera [I] 114 H4
Blérancourt [F] 28 F6
Bléré [F] 54 G2
Blériot-Plage [F] 14 G6
Blesle [F] 68 C3
Blessington [IRL] 2 F6
Bletchley [GB] 14 E3
Bletterans [F] 56 H5
Blexen [D] 18 D4
Blieskastel [D] 44 G4
Bligny-sur-Ouche [F] 56
   G4
Blikstorp [S] 166 F6
Blinisht [AL] 128 B1
Blinja [HR] 154 A1
Bliznak [BG] 148 F3
Blizne [PL] 52 E4
Błogoszów [PL] 52 A2
Blois [F] 54 H1
Blokhus [DK] 160 D3
Blokzijl [NL] 16 F3
Blomberg [D] 32 E3
Blomstermåla [S] 162 G4
Blöndúos [IS] 194 D3
Błonie [PL] 36 C6
Błonie [PL] 38 B3
Błonie [PL] 38 C2
Bloška Polica [SLO] 74 B6
Blovice [CZ] 48 E5
Bludenz [A] 72 A1
Blumberg [D] 58 F3
Blyth [GB] 8 G5
Bø [N] 164 F2
Boadilla del Monte [E] 88
   F5
Boal [E] 78 F2
Boário Terme [I] 72 B5
Bobbio [I] 110 C2
Bobbio Pellice [I] 70 C6
Bobingen [D] 60 D4
Bobitz [D] 20 A4
Böblingen [D] 58 G1
Bobolice [PL] 22 B3
Boboshevo [BG] 150 F6
Bobovdol [BG] 150 F5
Bobrovica [UA] 206 F1
Bobrowice [PL] 34 H4
Bobrowniki [PL] 24 C5
Bobrowniki [PL] 36 F1
Bobrujsk [BY] 204 C6
Bocairent [E] 104 E1
Boceguillas [E] 88 G3
Böçen [TR] 146 F5
Bochnia [PL] 52 B4
Bocholt [D] 16 G6
Bochov [CZ] 48 D3
Bochum [D] 30 H3
Bockel [D] 18 E5
Bockenem [D] 32 G3
Boćki [PL] 38 E1
Böcksholm [S] 162 E4
Böckstein [A] 72 G2
Bockum-Hovel [D] 32 C3
Bocognano [F] 114 B4
Bócsa [H] 76 D3
Bocsig [RO] 76 H4
Böda [S] 162 H3
Boda [S] 172 H3
Bodaczów [PL] 52 F1
Bodafors [S] 162 D3
Boda glasbruk [S] 162 F5
Bodegraven [NL] 16 D5
Boden [S] 198 B3
Bodenmais [D] 48 D6
Bodenteich [D] 18 G6
Bodenwerder [D] 32 F3
Bodenwöhr [D] 48 C6
Bodjani [YU] 154 E1

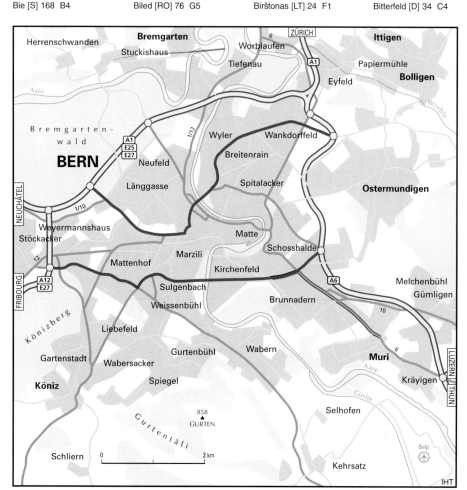

Bodman [D] 58 G4
Bodmin [GB] 12 C4
Bodø [N] 192 B6
Bodom [N] 190 C5
Bodrogkeresztúr [H] 64 G4
Bodrum [TR] 142 C2
Bodsjö [S] 182 H3
Bodträskfors [S] 198 A2
Bodzanów [PL] 36 H2
Bodzentyn [PL] 52 C1
Boëge [F] 70 B2
Boën [F] 68 E2
Bogarra [E] 98 C6
Bogatic [YU] 154 F2
Bogatynia [PL] 48 G1
Boğaziçi [TR] 144 D5
Boğazköy [TR] 146 F4
Bogdaniec [PL] 34 H2
Bogen [D] 60 G2
Bogen [N] 192 D4
Bogen [S] 172 D6
Bogense [DK] 156 D2
Bogetiči [YU] 152 E4
Bognanco [I] 70 E3
Bognelv [N] 192 F1
Bognes [N] 192 C4
Bognor Regis [GB] 14 D5
Bogojevo [YU] 154 E1
Bogoridick [RUS] 204 F5
Bogorodica [MK] 128 G3
Bogøy [N] 192 C5
Bograngen [S] 172 E4
Boguszow–Gorce [PL] 50 B2
Bogutovac [YU] 150 B3
Bohain–en–Vermandois [F] 28 F5
Bohdalov [CZ] 50 A5
Boheeshil [IRL] 4 B4
Bohinjska Bistrica [SLO] 74 A4
Böhmenkirch [D] 60 B2
Bohmte [D] 32 D2
Bohodukhiv [UA] 206 G2
Bohonal [E] 96 D2
Bohonal de Ibor [E] 88 B6
Böhönye [H] 74 H4
Boichinovtsi [BG] 150 F3
Bois–du–Four [F] 68 B6
Boitzenburg [D] 20 D5
Bóixols [E] 92 C2
Boizenburg [D] 18 G5
Bojano [I] 120 E1
Bojanów [PL] 52 D2
Bojanowo [PL] 36 C4
Bøjden [DK] 156 D4
Bojnica [BG] 150 E2
Bojnik [YU] 150 D4
Bol [HR] 152 A2
Bolaños de Calatrava [E] 96 F4
Bolayır [TR] 146 B4
Bolbec [F] 26 H3
Bolca [I] 72 C6
Bolekhiv [UA] 52 H6
Bolemin [PL] 34 H2
Bolesławiec [PL] 36 A6
Bolesławiec [PL] 36 E6
Bolesławów [PL] 50 C3
Boleszkowice [PL] 34 G2
Bolfiar [P] 80 B5
Bolgrad [UA] 206 D5
Bolhov [RUS] 204 E5
Boliden [S] 198 A4
Bolinglanna [IRL] 2 B3
Boljanići [YU] 152 E2
Boljevac [YU] 150 D2
Bolkesjø [N] 164 G1
Bolków [PL] 50 B1
Bollebygd [S] 162 B2
Bollène [F] 106 G2
Bollnäs [S] 174 D2
Bollstabruk [S] 184 F3
Bollullos Par del Condado [E] 94 F6
Bologna [I] 110 F3
Bologne [F] 44 C6
Bolótana [I] 118 C4
Bolsena [I] 114 H3
Bol'shakovo [RUS] 202 D5
Bol'shoy Sabsk [RUS] 200 G1

Bolsward [NL] 16 E2
Bolszewo [PL] 22 D2
Boltaña [E] 84 E5
Boltenhagen [D] 18 H3
Boltigen [CH] 70 D1
Bolton [GB] 10 E4
Bolungarvik [IS] 194 C1
Bóly [H] 76 B5
Bolyarovo [BG] 148 E5
Bolzano / Bozen [I] 72 D3
Bomarsund [FIN] 176 B5
Bombarral [P] 86 B4
Bominago [I] 116 C4
Bomsund [S] 184 C2
Bonaduz [CH] 70 H1
Boñar [E] 82 C3
Bonar Bridge [GB] 6 E4
Bonares [E] 94 F6
Bonassola [I] 110 C4
Bonchester Bridge [GB] 8 F5
Bondal [N] 164 F1
Bondemon [S] 166 C4
Bondeno [I] 110 F2
Bondstorp [S] 162 C2
Bonefro [I] 116 F6
Bonete [E] 98 C6
Bonifacio [F] 114 B6
Bonlieu [F] 70 A1
Bonn [D] 30 G5
Bonnåsjøen [N] 192 C5
Bonnat [F] 54 H5
Bonndorf [D] 58 F4
Bønnerup Strand [DK] 160 F5
Bonnétable [F] 42 C5
Bonneval [F] 42 D5
Bonneval–sur–Arc [F] 70 C4
Bonneville [F] 70 B2
Bonnières [F] 42 E3
Bonnieux [F] 106 H4
Bonnigheim [D] 46 D6
Bonnyrigg [GB] 8 E3
Bonny–sur–Loire [F] 56 D2
Bono [I] 118 D4
Bonorva [I] 118 C4
Bonyhád [H] 76 B4
Boom [B] 30 C3
Boos [F] 28 C5
Boot [GB] 10 D2
Booth of Toft [GB] 6 H3
Bootle [GB] 10 D4
Bootle [GB] 10 D2
Bopfingen [D] 60 C2
Boppard [D] 44 H1
Bor [CZ] 48 D4
Bor [YU] 150 D2
Borås [N] 164 F4
Borås [S] 162 B2
Borba [P] 86 E6
Borbona [I] 116 B4
Borchen [D] 32 E4
Borci [BIH] 152 C2
Borculo [NL] 16 G5
Bordány [H] 76 E4
Bordeaux [F] 66 C3
Bordeira [P] 94 A4
Bordères [F] 84 F4
Bordesholm [D] 18 F2
Borðeyri [IS] 194 C3
Bordighera [I] 108 F4
Bording [DK] 160 C6
Borek Wielkopolski [PL] 36 D4
Boreland [GB] 8 E5
Borensberg [S] 166 H5
Borgå / Porvoo [FIN] 178 B4
Borgafjäll [S] 190 E4
Borgarfjörður [IS] 194 G5
Borgarnes [IS] 194 B4
Borgen [N] 164 E3
Borgentreich [D] 32 E4
Börger [D] 32 E4
Borger [NL] 16 G3
Borggård [S] 166 H5
Borghamn [S] 166 G6
Borgholm [S] 162 G4
Borgholzhausen [D] 32 D2
Borghorst [D] 16 H5
Borgoforte [I] 110 E2

Borgomanero [I] 70 F4
Borgonovo Val Tidone [I] 70 G6
Borgorose [I] 116 B5
Borgo San Dalmazzo [I] 108 F3
Borgo San Lorenzo [I] 110 F5
Borgosésia [I] 70 E4
Borgo Ticino [I] 70 F4
Borgo Tossignano [I] 110 F4
Borgo Val di Taro [I] 110 C3
Borgo Valsugana [I] 72 D4
Borgo Vercelli [I] 70 F5
Borgsjö [S] 184 D4
Borgund [N] 170 E2
Borgvik [S] 166 E3
Borima [BG] 148 B4
Borisov [BY] 204 B5
Borispol [UA] 206 F2
Borja [E] 90 D3
Börjelslandet [S] 198 B3
Borken [D] 32 E6
Borken [D] 16 G6
Borkenes [N] 192 C3
Børkop [DK] 156 C2
Borkum [D] 16 G1
Borlänge [S] 172 H4
Borlaug [N] 170 E2
Borlu [TR] 144 E3
Bormes–les–Mimosas [F] 108 D6
Bórmio [I] 72 B3
Borna [D] 34 C6
Bornhöved [D] 18 G3
Börnicke [D] 34 D1
Bornos [E] 100 G3
Bornova [TR] 144 C4
Borodinskoye [RUS] 178 F2
Borodjanka [UA] 206 E2
Borovan [BG] 150 G3
Borovany [CZ] 62 C2
Borovets [BG] 150 G5
Borovichi [RUS] 200 H3
Boroviči [RUS] 204 D2
Borovo [HR] 154 E1
Borovtsi [BG] 150 F3
Borowa [PL] 36 D6
Borrby [S] 158 D3
Borre [DK] 156 G4
Borre [N] 164 H2
Borredà [E] 92 E2
Borriana / Burriana [E] 98 F3
Börringe [S] 158 C3
Borriol [E] 98 F3
Borris [IRL] 4 F4
Borris–in–Ossory [IRL] 2 D6
Borrisokane [IRL] 2 D6
Borrisoleigh [IRL] 4 E3
Borrum [S] 168 C6
Borş [RO] 76 H2
Børsa [N] 182 B1
Borşa [RO] 206 C4
Børselv [N] 196 C2
Borsh [AL] 132 B1
Bórsio [GR] 136 C1
Borsodnádasd [H] 64 E4
Börstil [S] 174 G5
Borth [GB] 10 B5
Bort–les–Orgues [F] 68 B3
Börtnan [S] 182 F3
Borup [DK] 156 G3
Borynia [UA] 52 F6
Boryslav [UA] 52 G5
Borzechowo [PL] 22 D4
Bosa [I] 118 B4
Bosanci [HR] 112 G1
Bosanska Dubica [BIH] 154 B2
Bosanska Gradiška [BIH] 154 C2
Bosanska Krupa [BIH] 154 A2
Bosanska Rača [BIH] 154 F2
Bosanski Brod [BIH] 154 D2
Bosanski Novi [HR] 154 A2

Bosanski Petrovac [BIH] 154 A3
Bosanski Šamac [BIH] 154 D2
Bosansko Grahovo [BIH] 154 A4
Boscastle [GB] 12 D4
Bosco Chiesanuova [I] 72 C5
Bösel [D] 18 C5
Bosilegrad [YU] 150 E5
Boskoop [NL] 16 D5
Boskovice [CZ] 50 C5
Bosna [HR] 74 F5
Bošnjace [YU] 150 D4
Bošnjaci [HR] 154 E2
Bosruck Tunnel [A] 62 B6
Bossbøen [N] 164 E1
Bossea [I] 108 G3
Bossòst [E] 84 F5
Bostan [BIH] 152 B2
Böste [S] 158 C3
Boston [GB] 10 G6
Bostrak [N] 164 F3
Bosut [YU] 154 F2
Bőszénfa [H] 76 A4
Botevgrad [BG] 150 G4
Bothel [GB] 8 D6
Bothwell [GB] 8 D3
Botinec [HR] 74 E6
Botngård [N] 190 B6
Bótoa [E] 86 F6
Botoroaga [RO] 148 C1
Botoşani [RO] 206 D4
Botricello [I] 124 E5
Botsmark [S] 198 A5
Bottidda [I] 118 D4
Bottnaryd [S] 162 C2
Bottrop [D] 30 G3
Botun [MK] 128 D3
Botunets [BG] 150 G4
Bouaye [F] 54 B1
Boudry [CH] 58 C6
Bouesse [F] 54 H4
Bouguenais [F] 54 B1
Bouillon [B] 44 D2
Bouilly [F] 44 A6
Boulay–Moselle [F] 44 F4
Bouligny [F] 44 E3
Boulogne [F] 14 G6
Boulogne–sur–Gesse [F] 84 G3
Bouloire [F] 42 C5
Bouniagues [F] 66 E4
Bourbon–Lancy [F] 56 E5
Bourbon–l'Archambault [F] 56 D5
Bourbonne–les–Bains [F] 58 B2
Bourbourg [F] 14 H6

Bourbriac [F] 40 D2
Bourdeaux [F] 68 F6
Bourg [F] 66 D3
Bourg–Achard [F] 26 H3
Bourganeuf [F] 54 H6
Bourg–Argental [F] 68 F4
Bourg–de–Péage [F] 68 F5
Bourg–en–Bresse [F] 68 G2
Bourges [F] 56 C3
Bourg–Lastic [F] 68 B2
Bourg–Madame [F] 92 E1
Bourgneuf–en–Retz [F] 54 B2
Bourgogne [F] 44 B3
Bourgoin–Jallieu [F] 68 G3
Bourg–St–Andéol [F] 106 G2
Bourg–St–Maurice [F] 70 C4
Bourg–et–Comin [F] 44 A2
Bourgtheroulde–Infreville [F] 26 H4
Bourgueil [F] 54 E2
Bourmont [F] 58 B2
Bourne [GB] 10 G6
Bournemouth [GB] 12 G5
Bourneville [F] 26 H3
Bournezeau [F] 54 C3
Bourton–on–the–Water [GB] 12 H2
Boussac [F] 56 B5
Boussens [F] 84 G4
Bouvignes [B] 30 D5
Bouvron [F] 40 F6
Bouxwiller [F] 44 G5
Bouzonville [F] 44 F3
Bovalino Marina [I] 124 D7
Bovallstrand [S] 166 C5
Bova Marina [I] 124 C8
Bovan [YU] 150 D3
Bovec [SLO] 72 H4
Bóveda [E] 78 D4
Bovense [DK] 156 E3
Bøverbru [N] 172 B4
Bøverdal [N] 180 F6
Boves [I] 108 F3
Bovey Tracey [GB] 12 E4
Bovič [HR] 112 H1
Bovington Camp [GB] 12 G5
Bovino [I] 120 G2
Bovolenta [I] 110 G1
Bovolone [I] 110 F1
Bovrup [DK] 156 C4
Bowmore [GB] 2 H1
Boxberg [D] 46 E5
Boxholm [S] 166 G6
Boxmeer [NL] 16 F6
Boxtel [NL] 30 E2

Boyalı [TR] 144 E3
Boyalıca [TR] 146 F4
Boyalık [TR] 146 E2
Boyle [IRL] 2 D4
Bøylefoss [N] 164 F4
Božaj [YU] 152 E4
Božava [HR] 112 F5
Bozburun [TR] 142 D3
Bozdoğan [TR] 144 E5
Bozel [F] 70 B4
Bozen / Bolzano [I] 72 D3
Bozhenci [BG] 148 C4
Bozhurishte [BG] 150 F4
Božica [YU] 150 E5
Bozkuş [TR] 144 G3
Bozouls [F] 68 B5
Bozüyük [TR] 146 G5
Bozveliisko [BG] 148 F3
Bózzolo [I] 110 E1
Bra [I] 108 G2
Braås [S] 162 E4
Brabova [RO] 150 F1
Bracadale [GB] 6 B4
Bracciano [I] 114 H5
Bracieux [F] 54 H2
Bracigovo [BG] 148 A6
Bräcke [S] 182 H3
Brackenheim [D] 46 C6
Brackley [GB] 14 D3
Bracknell [GB] 14 D4
Brackwede [D] 32 D3
Braco [GB] 8 E2
Brad [RO] 206 B5
Bradford [GB] 10 E3
Bradford–on–Avon [GB] 12 G3
Bradina [BIH] 152 C1
Bradwell–on–Sea [GB] 14 F4
Brae [GB] 6 G3
Brædstrup [DK] 156 C1
Braemar [GB] 6 E6
Braemore [GB] 6 D4
Braemore [GB] 6 F3
Brae Roy Lodge [GB] 6 D6
Braeswick [GB] 6 G1
Braga [P] 80 C3
Bragança [P] 80 F3
Brăila [RO] 206 D6
Braine [F] 44 A2
Braine–le–Comte [B] 28 H3
Braintree [GB] 14 F3
Brake [D] 18 D4
Brakel [B] 28 G3
Brakel [D] 32 E4
Bräkne–Hoby [S] 158 F1
Brålanda [S] 166 D5
Brálos [GR] 132 G4
Bram [F] 106 B4
Brämhult [S] 162 B2

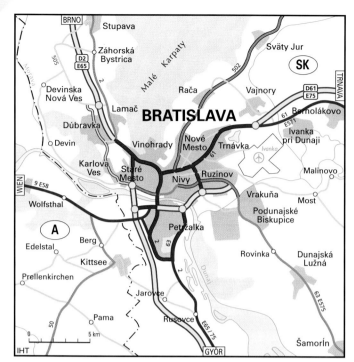

Bratislava map

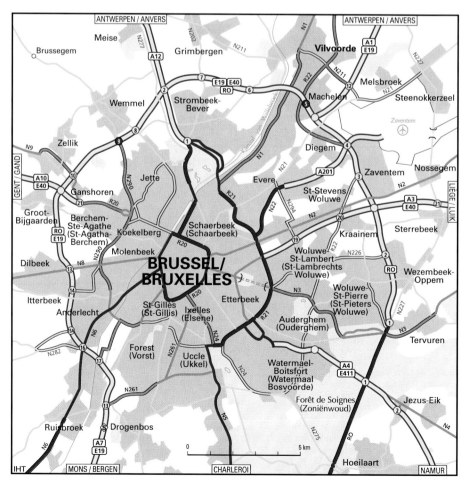

Brussel/Bruxelles map

Bramming [DK] 156 B2
Brampton [GB] 8 E5
Bramsche [D] 32 D2
Branca [I] 116 B1
Brancaleone Marina [I] 124 D8
Brancaster [GB] 10 H6
Brancion [F] 56 G6
Brand [A] 72 A1
Brandal [N] 180 C3
Brändbo [S] 184 D5
Brandbu [N] 170 H4
Brande [DK] 156 C1
Brandenberg [A] 60 E6
Brandenburg [D] 34 D2
Brand–Erbisdorf [D] 48 E1
Brandis [D] 34 E4
Brändö [FIN] 176 C5
Brandon [F] 56 F6
Brandon [GB] 14 F2
Brandon [GB] 8 F6
Brandstorp [S] 162 D1
Brandval [N] 172 D5
Brandýsek [CZ] 48 F3
Brandýs n Labem [CZ] 48 G3
Braniewo [PL] 22 F2
Branišovice [CZ] 62 F2
Brankovice [CZ] 50 D6
Branne [F] 66 D3
Brannenburg [D] 60 F5
Brännland [S] 190 H6
Branscombe [GB] 12 E4
Brańsk [PL] 38 E1
Brantôme [F] 66 F2
Branzi [I] 70 H3
Bras–d'Asse [F] 108 C3
Braskereidfoss [N] 172 D4
Braslaw [BY] 204 B4
Braslaw [BY] 202 H4
Brașov [RO] 206 C5
Brassac [F] 106 C3
Brassac–les–Mines [F] 68 D3
Brasschaat [B] 30 D2
Bras–sur–Meuse [F] 44 D3
Brastad [S] 166 C3
Brataj [AL] 128 B6
Bratislava [SK] 62 G4
Bratków Din [PL] 36 F4
Brattabø [N] 170 C4
Brattvåg [N] 180 D3
Bratunac [BIH] 154 F4
Bråtveit [N] 164 C1
Bratya Daskolovi [BG] 148 C5
Braubach [D] 46 B2
Braunau [A] 60 G4
Braunfels [D] 46 C2
Braunlage [D] 32 H4

Braunschweig [D] 32 H2
Braunton [GB] 12 D3
Bray / Bré [IRL] 4 G3
Bray–sur–Seine [F] 42 G5
Bray–sur–Somme [F] 28 E5
Brazatortas [E] 96 D5
Brbinj [HR] 112 F5
Brčko [BIH] 154 E2
Brdjani [YU] 150 B2
Bré / Bray [IRL] 4 G3
Breamore [GB] 12 G4
Breascleit / Breasclete [GB] 6 B2
Breasclete / Breascleit [GB] 6 B2
Brécey [F] 26 D4
Brechin [GB] 8 F2
Brecht [B] 30 D2
Břeclav [CZ] 62 G3
Brecon [GB] 12 F2
Breda [NL] 16 D6
Bredaryd [S] 162 C4
Bredbyn [S] 184 F1
Bredebro [DK] 156 B4
Bredelar [D] 32 E4
Bredevad [DK] 156 B4
Bredsel [S] 198 A3
Bredstedt [D] 18 E1
Bree [B] 30 E3
Bregenz [A] 60 B6
Bregovo [BG] 150 E1
Bréhal [F] 26 D4
Brehna [D] 34 C5
Breifonn [N] 170 C5
Breil–sur–Roya [F] 108 F4
Breisach [D] 58 E3
Breisen [D] 34 D1
Breisjøberget [N] 172 D4
Breistein [N] 170 B3
Breitengussbach Hallstadt [D] 46 G4
Breivikbotn [N] 196 A2
Breivikeidet [N] 192 E2
Brekke [N] 170 B2
Brekken [N] 182 D3
Brekkvasselv [N] 190 D4
Brekstad [N] 190 B6
Bremen [D] 18 D5
Bremerhaven [D] 18 D4
Bremervörde [D] 18 E4
Bremsnes [N] 180 E2
Brenes [E] 94 H6
Brenner Pass [Eur.] 72 D2
Breno [I] 72 B5
Brentwood [GB] 14 F4
Brenzone [I] 72 C5
Bréscia [I] 72 B6
Breskens [NL] 28 G1
Bressanone / Brixen [I] 72 D3

Bressuire [F] 54 D3
Brest [BG] 148 A2
Brest [F] 40 B2
Brest [BY] 38 F3
Brestova [HR] 112 E2
Brestovac [YU] 150 D4
Brestovac [YU] 150 D2
Brestovačka Banja [YU] 150 D2
Brestovăţ [RO] 76 H5
Bretenoux [F] 66 H4
Breteuil [F] 28 D5
Breteuil [F] 26 H5
Brettabister [GB] 6 H4
Bretten [D] 46 C6
Breuil–Cervínia [I] 70 D3
Breuna [D] 32 E4

Brevens Bruk [S] 166 H4
Brevik [N] 164 G3
Brevik [S] 168 E3
Breza [BIH] 154 D4
Brežice [SLO] 74 D5
Breznica [HR] 74 F5
Březnice [CZ] 48 E5
Breznik [BG] 150 F5
Brezno [SK] 64 D3
Brézolles [F] 26 H5
Brezová [SK] 62 H3
Brezovica [SK] 52 C6
Brezovica [YU] 150 C6
Brezovo [BG] 148 B5
Brezovo Polje [BIH] 154 E2
Briançon [F] 70 B6
Briare [F] 56 D2
Bribirske Mostine [HR] 112 H5
Briceni [MD] 206 D3
Bricquebec [F] 26 D2
Bridestowe [GB] 12 D4
Bridgend [GB] 8 B2
Bridge of Allan [GB] 8 E2
Bridge of Balgie [GB] 8 D1
Bridge of Dye [GB] 8 F1
Bridge of Orchy [GB] 8 D1
Bridgnorth [GB] 10 D6
Bridgwater [GB] 12 F4
Bridlington [GB] 10 G3
Bridport [GB] 12 F5
Briec [F] 40 B3
Brie–Comte–Robert [F] 42 G4
Brielle [NL] 16 C5
Brienne–le–Château [F] 44 B5
Brienz [CH] 70 E1
Brienza [I] 120 G4
Brieskow–Finkenheerd [D] 34 G3
Brieves [E] 78 G3
Briey [F] 44 E3
Brig [CH] 70 E2
Brigg [GB] 10 G4
Brighouse [GB] 10 E4
Brighton [GB] 14 E5
Brignogan–Plage [F] 40 B1
Brignoles [F] 108 C5

Brignoud [F] 68 H4
Brihuega [E] 88 H5
Brilon [D] 32 D4
Brimnes [N] 170 D4
Brinches [P] 94 E3
Brincoveni [RO] 150 G1
Bríndisi [I] 122 G4
Brinkum [D] 18 D5
Briones [E] 82 G6
Brionne [F] 26 H4
Brioude [F] 68 D3
Brioux–sur–Boutonne [F] 54 D5
Briouze [F] 26 F5
Brisighella [I] 110 G4
Brissac–Quincé [F] 54 D1
Brissago [CH] 70 F3
Bristol [GB] 12 G3
Brive–la–Gaillarde [F] 66 G3
Briviesca [E] 82 F5
Brixen / Bressanone [I] 72 D3
Brixham [GB] 12 E5
Brixlegg [A] 60 E6
Brjanslækur [IS] 194 B2
Brnaze [HR] 152 A1
Brněnec [CZ] 50 C5
Brno [CZ] 50 C6
Bro [S] 168 G4
Bro [S] 168 D2
Broadford [GB] 6 B5
Broadford [IRL] 2 C6
Broadstairs [GB] 14 G5
Broadway [GB] 12 H2
Broager [DK] 156 C4
Broby [S] 158 D1
Broceni [LV] 200 C5
Brock [D] 32 C2
Bröckel [D] 32 G2
Brockenhurst [GB] 12 G5
Brod [BIH] 152 D2
Brod [YU] 128 D1
Brodarevo [YU] 150 A4
Brodenbach [D] 44 H1
Brodick [GB] 8 C3
Brod na Kupi [HR] 112 F1
Brodnica [PL] 22 F5
Brody [PL] 34 G4
Brody [PL] 34 G4

Brody [PL] 38 C6
Brody [PL] 36 A3
Brody [UA] 206 C2
Broglie [F] 26 G4
Brohl [D] 30 H6
Brok [PL] 38 C1
Brokind [S] 168 A6
Brolo [I] 124 B6
Bromarv [FIN] 176 E6
Brome [D] 32 H2
Bromma [N] 170 G4
Bromölla [S] 158 E1
Bromsgrove [GB] 12 H1
Bromyard [GB] 12 G1
Brønderslev [DK] 160 E3
Broni [I] 70 G6
Brønnøysund [N] 190 C3
Brøns [DK] 156 B3
Bronte [I] 126 F3
Broons [F] 26 B5
Brørup [DK] 156 B2
Brösarp [S] 158 D2
Brossac [F] 66 E2
Brøstadbotn [N] 192 D3
Brøstrud [N] 170 F4
Brötjemark [S] 162 D1
Broto [E] 84 E5
Brottby [S] 168 E2
Bröttem [N] 182 B2
Brou [F] 42 D5
Brouage [F] 54 C5
Brough [GB] 10 E2
Broughshane [GB] 2 G3
Broughton [GB] 8 E4
Broughton in Furness [GB] 10 D2
Broumov [CZ] 50 B2
Brouvelieures [F] 58 C2
Brouwershaven [NL] 16 B5
Brovary [UA] 206 G2
Brovst [DK] 160 D3
Brownhills [GB] 10 E6
Broxburn [GB] 8 E3
Brozas [E] 86 G4
Brtnice [CZ] 50 A6
Bruchhausen–Vilsen [D] 18 E6
Bruchsal [D] 46 C5

Bue [N] 164 B4
Buenavista del Norte [E] 100 B5
Buğdayli [TR] 146 D5
Bugeat [F] 68 A2
Buggerru [I] 118 B6
Bugojno [BIH] 154 C4
Bugøyfjord [N] 196 E3
Bugøynes [N] 196 E2
Bühl [D] 58 F1
Büilești [RO] 150 F2
Builth Wells [GB] 12 F1
Buis–les–Baronnies [F] 108 B2
Buitenpost [NL] 16 F2
Buitrago [E] 88 G4
Bujalance [E] 102 D1
Bujaraloz [E] 90 F4
Buje [HR] 112 D1
Bujoru [RO] 148 C2
Buk [PL] 36 C3
Buk [PL] 20 E5
Bukka [GR] 132 D4
Bukovi [YU] 150 A2
Bukowiec [PL] 36 B3
Bukowina Tatrzańska [PL] 52 B6
Bukowo Morskie [PL] 22 A2
Bukowsko [PL] 52 E5
Bülach [CH] 58 F4
Buldan [TR] 144 F4
Bulford [GB] 12 G4
Bŭlgarene [BG] 148 B3
Bŭlgarene [BG] 148 B4
Bŭlgarevo [BG] 148 G2
Bŭlgarovo [BG] 148 F4
Bŭlgarska Polyana [BG] 146 A1
Bŭlgarski Izvor [BG] 148 A4
Bulgnéville [F] 58 B2
Bulken [N] 170 C3
Bulkowo [PL] 36 H2
Bullas [E] 104 B2
Bulle [CH] 70 C1
Bulqizë [AL] 128 C2
Bultei [I] 118 D4
Buna [BIH] 152 C2
Bunclody [IRL] 4 F4

Buncrana [IRL] 2 F2
Bunde [D] 16 H2
Bünde [D] 32 E2
Bundoran [IRL] 2 D3
Bunessan [GB] 8 B1
Bungay [GB] 14 G2
Bunkris [S] 172 E1
Bunleix [F] 68 B2
Bunmahon [IRL] 4 E5
Bunnahowen [IRL] 2 B3
Bunnyconnellan [IRL] 2 C3
Buñol [E] 98 E4
Bunratty [IRL] 2 C6
Buonalbergo [I] 120 F2
Buonconvento [I] 114 G2
Buonfornello [I] 126 D2
Buonvicino [I] 124 C3
Burano [I] 72 F6
Burbach [D] 32 C6
Burbage [GB] 12 H4
Burcei [I] 118 D7
Bureå [S] 198 A4
Burela [E] 78 E2
Büren [CH] 58 D5
Büren [D] 32 D4
Burfjord [N] 192 F1
Burford [GB] 12 H3
Burg [D] 34 C3
Burg [D] 18 H2
Burg [D] 18 E3
Burgas [BG] 148 F4
Burgau [D] 60 C3
Burgau [P] 94 B5
Burgbernheim [D] 46 F5
Burgdorf [CH] 58 E5
Burgdorf [D] 32 G2
Burgebrach [D] 46 F4
Bürgel [D] 34 B6
Burgelu / Elburgo [E] 102 B4
Burghaun [D] 46 E1
Burghausen [D] 60 G4
Burghead [GB] 6 E4
Burgh–Haamstede [NL] 16 B5
Búrgio [I] 126 C3
Burgjoss [D] 46 E3
Burgkunstadt [D] 46 G3

Burglengenfeld [D] 48 B6
Burgos [E] 82 E6
Burgsinn [D] 46 E3
Burg Stargard [D] 20 D5
Burgsvik [S] 168 G6
Burguete / Auritz [E] 84 C3
Burguillos del Cerro [E] 94 G3
Burg Vetschau [D] 34 F4
Burhaniye [TR] 144 C2
Burie [F] 54 D6
Burjassot [E] 98 E4
Burladingen [D] 58 G2
Burnham–on–Crouch [GB] 14 F4
Burnham–on–Sea [GB] 12 F3
Burnley [GB] 10 E3
Burntisland [GB] 8 E3
Buronzo [I] 70 E4
Burravoe [GB] 6 H3
Burrel [AL] 128 B2
Burriana / Borriana [E] 98 F3
Burry Port [GB] 12 E2
Burs [S] 168 G5
Bursa [TR] 146 F4
Burseryd [S] 162 B3
Bürstadt [D] 46 C4
Burton Agnes [GB] 10 G3
Burton–upon–Stather [GB] 10 G4
Burton upon Trent [GB] 10 E6
Burträsk [S] 198 A5
Burwell [GB] 14 F2
Burwick [GB] 6 F2
Bury [GB] 10 E4
Bury St Edmunds [GB] 14 F3
Busalla [I] 110 B3
Busana [I] 110 D4
Busca [I] 108 F2
Busdorf [D] 18 F1
Bushat [AL] 128 A1
Bushmills [GB] 2 G2
Bushtricë [AL] 128 C1
Bus'k [UA] 206 C2
Busko–Zdrój [PL] 52 B2

Bruck [D] 48 C6
Brück [D] 34 D3
Bruck an der Grossglocknerstrasse [A] 72 G1
Bruck an der Leitha [A] 62 G5
Bruck an der Mur [A] 74 D1
Brückl [A] 74 C3
Brudzeń Duży [PL] 36 G2
Brüel [D] 20 A4
Bruère–Allichamps [F] 56 C4
Bruff [IRL] 4 D4
Brugg [CH] 58 F4
Brugge [B] 28 G1
Bruhagen [N] 180 E2
Brühl [D] 30 G4
Brújula, Puerto de– [E] 82 F6
Brûlon [F] 42 A5
Brumath [F] 44 H5
Brummen [NL] 16 F5
Brumunddal [N] 172 B3
Brunau [D] 34 B1
Bruneck / Brunico [I] 72 E2
Brunehamel [F] 28 H5
Brunete [E] 88 F5
Brunflo [S] 182 H2
Brunheda [P] 80 E4
Brunico / Bruneck [I] 72 E2
Bruniquel [F] 66 G6
Brunkeberg [N] 164 E2
Brunnen [CH] 58 F6
Brunsbüttel [D] 18 E3
Brunssum [NL] 30 F4
Bruntál [CZ] 50 D4
Bruravik [N] 170 D4
Brus [YU] 150 C3
Brusand [N] 164 A4
Brušane [HR] 112 G4
Brusarci [BG] 150 F2
Brusnichnoye [RUS] 178 E2
Brussel / Bruxelles [B] 30 C4
Brüssow [D] 20 E5
Brusy [PL] 22 C4
Bruton [GB] 12 G4
Bruvno [HR] 112 H4
Bruvoll [N] 172 C4
Bruxelles / Brussel [B] 30 C4
Bruyères [F] 58 C2
Bruzaholm [S] 162 E2
Brvenik [YU] 150 B3
Brwinów [PL] 38 B3
Bryansk [RUS] 204 E6
Bryne [N] 164 A3
Brynmawr [GB] 12 F2
Bryrup [DK] 156 C1

Brza Palanka [YU] 150 E1
Brzeče [YU] 150 C4
Brzeg [PL] 50 D1
Brzeg Dolny [PL] 36 C6
Brześč Kujawski [PL] 36 F2
Brzesko [PL] 52 B4
Brzeszcze [PL] 50 G4
Brzezie [PL] 36 E4
Brzezie [PL] 22 B4
Brzeziny [PL] 36 E5
Brzeziny [PL] 36 H4
Brzeżnica [PL] 52 D3
Brzostek [PL] 52 D4
Brzoza [PL] 38 C4
Brzoza [PL] 22 D6
Brzozie Lubawskie [PL] 22 F5
Brzozów [PL] 52 E4
Bua [S] 160 H3
Buavåg [N] 164 A1
Bubry [F] 40 D3
Bubwith [GB] 10 F4
Buca [TR] 144 C4
Bučač [UA] 206 C3
Buçaco [P] 80 B6
Bučany [SK] 62 H4
Buccheri [I] 126 F4
Bucchianico [I] 116 D4
Buchen [D] 46 D4
Buchen [D] 18 G4
Buchenwald [D] 34 A6
Buchholz [D] 18 F5
Buchin Prohod [BG] 150 F4
Buchloe [D] 60 C4
Buchs [CH] 58 H6
Buchy [F] 28 C5
Bučin [MK] 128 E3
Búcine [I] 110 F6
Bučje [YU] 150 D2
Buckden [GB] 14 E2
Buckden [GB] 10 E2
Bückeburg [D] 32 E2
Bücken [D] 18 E6
Buckfastleigh [GB] 12 E5
Buckhaven [GB] 8 F3
Buckie [GB] 6 F5
Buckingham [GB] 14 D3
Buckow [D] 34 F2
Bucquoy [F] 28 E4
Bucsa [H] 76 F1
București [RO] 206 C6
Buczek [PL] 36 G5
Buczyna [PL] 52 F3
Bud [N] 180 E2
Budaörs [H] 64 C6
Budapest [H] 64 C6
Búðardalur [IS] 194 C3
Buddusò [I] 118 D3
Bude [GB] 12 D4
Budești [RO] 206 C6

Budilovo [RUS] 200 G2
Budimir [HR] 152 A2
Büdingen [D] 46 D2
Budišov nad Budišovkou [CZ] 50 D4
Budleigh Salterton [GB] 12 E5
Budmirici [MK] 128 F3
Budomierz [PL] 52 G3
Budoni [I] 118 E3
Budowo [PL] 22 C2
Budrio [I] 110 F3
Budry [PL] 24 C2
Budva [YU] 152 D4
Budyně nad Ohří [CZ] 48 F3
Budzyń [PL] 36 C1

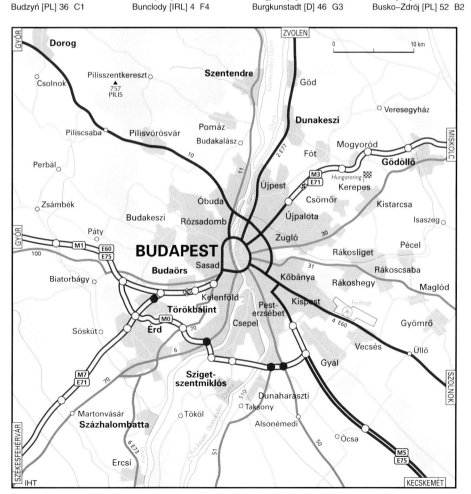

Bušno [PL] 38 G6
Busot [E] 104 E2
Busovača [BIH] 154 D4
Bussang [F] 58 D3
Busseto [I] 110 D2
Bussolengo [I] 72 C6
Bussoleno [I] 70 C5
Bussum [NL] 16 E4
Busto Arsízio [I] 70 F4
Busto Garolfo [I] 70 F4
Büsum [D] 18 E2
Butan [BG] 150 G3
Butera [I] 126 E4
Bütgenbach [B] 30 F5
Butler's Bridge [IRL] 2 E4
Butrint [AL] 132 B2
Butsyn [UA] 38 H5
Buttelstedt [D] 34 A6
Buttermere [GB] 8 D6
Buttevant [IRL] 4 C4
Buttle [S] 168 G5
Buttstädt [D] 34 B6
Butzbach [D] 46 C2
Bützow [D] 20 B3
Buvik [N] 182 B1
Buvika [N] 182 D5
Buxtehude [D] 18 F4
Buxton [GB] 10 E5
Buxy [F] 56 F5
Büyükçekmece [TR] 146 E3
Büyükkaraağaç [TR] 142 E3
Büyükkarıştıran [TR] 146 C2
Buzançais [F] 54 G3
Buzancy [F] 44 D3
Buzău [RO] 206 D6
Buzescu [RO] 148 B1
Buzet [HR] 112 D1
Buziaş [RO] 76 H6
Bwlch [GB] 12 F2
Byala [BG] 148 C2
Byala [BG] 148 F3
Byala Slatina [BG] 150 G3
Byal Izvor [BG] 130 E1
Byaroza [BY] 204 A6
Bybjerg [DK] 156 F2
Bychawa [PL] 38 E6
Byczki [PL] 36 H4
Byczyna [PL] 36 E6
Bydgoszcz [PL] 22 D6
Byenyakoni [BY] 202 G6
Bygdeå [S] 198 A5
Bygdin [N] 170 F2
Bygdsiljum [S] 198 A5
Bygland [N] 164 D4
Byglandsfjord [N] 164 D4
Bygstad [N] 170 B1
Bykle [N] 164 D2
Bylnice [CZ] 64 A2
Byrkjedal [N] 164 B3
Byrkjelo [N] 180 D5
Byrness [GB] 8 F5
Byrum [DK] 160 F3
Byrum [S] 162 H3
Byske [S] 198 A4
Bystřice [CZ] 48 G4
Bystřice nad Pernštejnem [CZ] 50 D4
Bystřice pod Hostýnem [CZ] 50 D6
Bystrzyca Kłodzka [PL] 50 C3
Byszyno [PL] 20 H4
Bytča [SK] 50 F6
Bytom [PL] 50 F3
Bytom Odrzański [PL] 36 A4
Bytonia [PL] 22 D4
Bytów [PL] 22 C3
Byxelkrok [S] 162 H3
Bzenec [CZ] 62 G2

C

Cabañaquinta [E] 78 H4
Cabañas [E] 78 D2
Cabanes [E] 98 G3
Cabeço de Vide [P] 86 E5
Cabeza del Buey [E] 96 C4
Cabezarados [E] 96 E4

Cabezas Rubias [E] 94 E4
Cabezón de la Sal [E] 82 E3
Cabezuela del Valle [E] 88 B5
Cabo de Gata [E] 102 G6
Cabo de Palos [E] 104 D4
Cabo São Vicente [P] 94 A5
Cabourg [F] 26 F3
Cabra [E] 102 C2
Cabra del Santo Cristo [E] 102 F2
Cábras [I] 118 B5
Cabreiros [E] 78 D2
Cabrera [E] 104 E6
Cabrerets [F] 66 G5
Čačak [YU] 150 B2
Cáccamo [I] 126 D2
Cacemes [P] 86 A5
Cáceres [E] 86 H5
Cachopo [E] 94 D5
Čačinci [HR] 76 A6
Cadaqués [E] 92 G2
Cadaval [P] 86 B4
Cadavedo [E] 78 G2
Čadca [SK] 50 F5
Cadelbosco di Sopra [I] 110 E2
Cadenábbia [I] 70 G3
Cadenberge [D] 18 E3
Cadenet [F] 108 B4
Cádiar [E] 102 E5
Cadillac [F] 66 D4
Cádiz [E] 100 F4
Cadjavica [HR] 76 A6
Caen [F] 26 F3
Caernarfon [GB] 10 B4
Caerphilly [GB] 12 F3
Caersws [GB] 10 C6
Ćafasan [MK] 128 C3
Çağış [TR] 144 D1
Cagli [I] 112 B6
Cágliari [I] 118 C7
Cagnano Varano [I] 116 G6
Cagnes-sur-Mer [F] 108 E4
Caherdaniel [IRL] 4 A4
Cahermurphy [IRL] 2 B6
Cahersiveen [IRL] 4 A4
Cahir [IRL] 4 D4
Cahors [F] 66 G5
Cahul [MD] 206 D5
Caiazzo [I] 120 E2
Caiolo [I] 70 H3
Cairndow [GB] 8 D2
Cairnryan [GB] 8 C5
Cairo Montenotte [I] 108 G3
Caister-on-Sea [GB] 14 H2
Caistor [GB] 10 G4
Caivano [I] 120 E3
Cajarc [F] 66 G5
Čajetina [YU] 150 A3
Čajniče [BIH] 152 E2
Čakajovce [SK] 64 A4
Cakovec [HR] 74 F4
Çal [TR] 144 G4
Cala [E] 94 G4
Cala Blanca [E] 104 G4
Cala Blava [E] 104 E5
Calabor [E] 80 F3
Calabritto [I] 120 F3
Calaceite [E] 90 G6
Calacuccia [F] 114 B3
Cala de Moral, La– [E] 102 B5
Cala d'Oliva [I] 118 B2
Cala d'Or [I] 104 F6
Calaf [E] 92 D3
Calafat [RO] 150 F2
Calafell [E] 92 D5
Cala Galdana [E] 104 G4
Cala Gonone [I] 118 E4
Calahonda [E] 102 B5
Calahonda–Chaparral [E] 102 E5
Calahorra [E] 84 A5
Cala Liberotto [I] 118 E4
Cala Millor [E] 104 F5
Calamocha [E] 90 D5

Cala Moreia–Cala Morlanda [E] 104 F5
Cala Morell [E] 104 G4
Calañas [E] 94 F5
Calanda [E] 90 F6
Calangiánus [I] 118 D3
Cala'n Porter [E] 104 H5
Cala Pi [E] 104 E5
Călăraşi [MD] 206 D4
Călăraşi [RO] 206 D6
Cala Ratjada [E] 104 F5
cala Sa Calobra [E] 104 E4
Cala Santanyí [E] 104 E6
Calasetta [I] 118 B7
Calasparra [E] 104 B2
Calatafimi [I] 126 B2
Calatañazor [E] 90 B3
Cala Tarida [E] 104 B5
Calatayud [E] 90 D4
Calatorao [E] 90 D4
Calau [D] 34 F4
Cala Vadella [E] 104 B5
Calbe [D] 34 B4
Caldarola [I] 116 C2
Caldas da Rainha [P] 86 B3
Caldas de Reis [E] 78 B3
Caldas de Vizela [P] 80 C3
Caldbeck [GB] 8 E6
Caldes de Boí [E] 84 F6
Caldes de Malavella [E] 92 F3
Caldes de Montbui [E] 92 E4
Caldes d'Estrac [E] 92 F4
Caldirola [I] 110 B2
Caledon [GB] 2 F4
Calella [E] 92 F4
Calella de Palafrugell [E] 92 G3
Calenzana [F] 114 B3
Calera y Chozas [E] 88 C6
Cales de Mallorca [E] 104 F5
Calfsound [GB] 6 G1
Calheta [P] 100 A3
Çali [TR] 146 F5
Calignac [F] 66 E5
Çalıklı [TR] 144 F3
Călimăneşti [RO] 206 B6
Calimera [I] 122 G5
Calitri [I] 120 G3
Çalköy [TR] 144 H2
Callac [F] 40 D2
Callan [IRL] 4 E4
Callander [GB] 8 D2
Callington [GB] 12 D4
Callosa d'en Sarrià [E] 104 E2
Callosa de Segura [E] 104 D3
Călmăţuiu [RO] 148 B2
Calne [GB] 12 G3
Calnegre, Puntas de– [E] 104 B4
Calolziocorte [I] 70 G4
Calonge [E] 92 G3
Calpe / Calp [E] 104 F2
Caltabellotta [I] 126 C3
Caltagirone [I] 126 F4
Caltanissetta [I] 126 E3
Caltavuturo [I] 126 E2
Çalti [TR] 146 H4
Çaltılıbük [TR] 146 E5
Caltra [IRL] 2 D5
Călugăreni [RO] 148 C1
Caluso [I] 70 D5
Calvello [I] 120 H4
Calvi [F] 114 A3
Calvörde [D] 34 B2
Calw [D] 58 G1
Calzadilla de la Cueza [E] 82 C5
Calaiore [I] 110 D5
Camaldoli [I] 110 G5
Çamaltı [TR] 144 C4
Câmara de Lobos [P] 100 B3
Camarena de la Sierra [E] 98 E2
Camarès [F] 106 D3
Camaret [F] 40 B2

Camariñas [E] 78 B2
Camarzana de Tera [E] 80 H3
Cambados [E] 78 B4
Cambeo [E] 78 C5
Camberg [D] 46 C2
Camberley [GB] 14 D4
Cambo-les-Bains [F] 84 C2
Camborne [GB] 12 C5
Cambrai [F] 28 F4
Cambre [E] 78 C2
Cambremer [F] 26 G4
Cambridge [GB] 14 F3
Cambrils [E] 92 C5
Camburg [D] 34 B6
Camelford [GB] 12 C4
Camerino [I] 116 B2
Camigliatello [I] 124 D4
Caminha [P] 78 A5
Caminomorisco [E] 88 A4
Caminreal [E] 90 D6
Camogli [I] 110 B3
Camp [IRL] 4 B3
Campan [F] 84 F4
Campana [I] 124 E4
Campanario [E] 96 B3
Campanas / Kanpaneta [E] 84 B4
Campaspero [E] 88 F2
Campbeltown [GB] 2 H2
Campiglia Soana [I] 70 D4
Campillo de Altobuey [E] 98 C3
Campillo de Arenas [E] 102 E3
Campillo de Llerena [E] 96 A4
Campillos [E] 102 B3
Campione d'Italia [I] 70 G3
Campisábalos [E] 88 H4
Campi Salentina [I] 122 G4
Campo [E] 84 F6
Campobasso [I] 120 E1
Campobello di Licata [I] 126 E4
Campobello di Mazara [I] 126 B3
Campocologno [CH] 72 B4
Campodarsego [I] 72 E6
Campo de Caso / Caso [E] 82 C2
Campo de Criptana [E] 96 G3
Campodón [E] 92 F2
Campoformido [I] 72 G5
Campogalliano [I] 110 E3
Campohermoso [E] 102 G5
Campo Ligure [I] 110 A3
Campo Maior [P] 86 F6
Campomanes [E] 78 H4
Campomarino [I] 122 F5
Campomarino [I] 116 F5
Campora San Giovanni [I] 124 D5
Camporeale [I] 126 C2
Camporrobles [E] 98 D3
Campos [E] 104 E5
Camposampiero [I] 72 E6
Campo Tures / Sand in Taufers [I] 72 E2
Çamsu [TR] 144 G2
Çan [TR] 146 C5
Çanakkale [TR] 146 B5
Canale [I] 108 G1
Canales de Molina [E] 90 C5
Canas de Senhorim [P] 80 C6
Cañaveral [E] 86 H4
Cañaveral de León [E] 94 G4
Cañaveras [E] 98 B1
Canazei [I] 72 E3
Cancale [F] 26 C4
Cancon [F] 66 E4
Candanchú [E] 84 D4
Çandarlı [TR] 144 C3

Candás [E] 78 H3
Candasnos [E] 90 G4
Candé [F] 40 G6
Candela [I] 120 G2
Candelario [E] 88 B4
Candeleda [E] 88 C5
Candia Lomellina [I] 70 F5
Canelli [I] 108 H2
Canero [E] 78 G2
Canet [F] 106 E4
Canet de Mar [E] 92 F4
Cañete [E] 98 C2
Cañete la Real [E] 102 B3
Canet–Plage [F] 92 G1
Canfranc [E] 84 D4
Cangas [E] 78 B4
Cangas del Narcea [E] 78 F3
Cangas de Onís [E] 82 C2
Caniçada [P] 80 D3
Canicattì [I] 126 D4
Canicattini Bagni [I] 126 G5
Caniço [P] 100 B3
Caniles [E] 102 G4
Canino [I] 114 G4
Cañizal [E] 88 D2
Canjáyar [E] 102 F5
Cannara [I] 116 A2
Cánnero Riviera [I] 70 F3
Cannes [F] 108 E5
Canneto [I] 114 E1
Canneto Sull' Óglio [I] 110 D1
Cannich [GB] 6 D5
Cannóbio [I] 70 F3
Cannock [GB] 10 E6
Canosa di Puglia [I] 120 H2
Canossa [I] 110 D3
Can Pastilla [E] 104 E5
Can Picafort [E] 104 F4
Cantalapiedra [E] 88 D3
Cantalejo [E] 88 F3
Cantanhede [P] 80 B6
Cantavieja [E] 98 F2
Canterbury [GB] 14 F5
Cantillana [E] 94 H5
Cantoral de la Peña [E] 82 D4
Cantoria [E] 102 H4
Cantù [I] 70 G4
Canvey Island [GB] 14 F4
Cany–Barville [F] 26 H2
Cáorle [I] 72 F6
Caorso [I] 70 H6
Capaccio [I] 120 F4
Capaci [I] 126 C1
Capalbio [I] 114 F4
Capannoli [I] 110 E6
Caparde [BIH] 154 E3
Caparroso [E] 84 B5
Capbreton [F] 66 A6
Cap–d'Ail [F] 108 F4
Capdella [F] 84 G6
Capdenac–Gare [F] 66 H5
Cap d'En Font [E] 104 H5
Capendu [F] 106 C5
Capestang [F] 106 D4
Cap Ferret [F] 66 B3
Cap Gris Nez [F] 14 G6
Capistrello [I] 116 C5
Čapljina [BIH] 152 C3
Capo Cavallo [F] 114 A3
Capodimonte [I] 114 G3
Capo di Ponte [I] 72 B4
Capo d'Orlando [I] 124 B6
Capolíveri [I] 114 E3
Capo Rizzuto [I] 124 F5
Cappamore [IRL] 4 D3
Cappoquin [IRL] 4 D5
Capracotta [I] 116 D6
Capráia [I] 114 D2
Capranica [I] 114 H4
Capri [I] 120 D4
Capriati a Volturno [I] 120 D1
Capriccioli [I] 118 E2
Captieux [F] 66 D5
Capua [I] 120 D2
Capurso [I] 122 E3
Caracal [RO] 148 A1

Caracenilla [E] 98 B2
Caracuel de Calatrava [E] 96 E4
Caraglio [I] 108 F2
Caraman [F] 106 B3
Caramulo [P] 80 C6
Caranga [E] 78 G4
Caransebeş [RO] 206 A5
Cárantec [F] 40 C1
Caravaca [E] 104 B2
Caravaggio [I] 70 H5
Carballo [E] 78 C2
Carbon–Blanc [F] 66 D3
Carboneras [E] 102 H5
Carboneras de Guadazaón [E] 98 C3
Carbonero el Mayor [E] 88 F3
Carbónia [I] 118 B7
Carbonin / Schluderbach [I] 72 E3
Carbonne [F] 84 H4
Carcabuey [E] 102 C3
Carcaixent [E] 98 E5
Carcans [F] 66 C2
Carcans–Plage [F] 66 B2
Carcare [I] 108 H3
Carcassonne [F] 106 B4
Carcastillo [E] 84 B5
Carcavelos [P] 86 A5
Carcès [F] 108 C5
Çardak [TR] 146 B5
Çardak [TR] 144 G5
Çardak [TR] 144 G3
Cardedeu [E] 92 E4
Cardeña [E] 96 D6
Cardenete [E] 98 C3
Cardiff [GB] 12 F3
Cardigan [GB] 4 H6
Cardona [E] 92 D3
Carei [RO] 206 B4
Carennac [F] 66 H4
Carentan [F] 26 E3
Carevac [BIH] 154 B4
Carev Dvor [MK] 128 D3
Carezza al Lago [I] 72 D3
Cargèse [F] 114 A4
Carhaix–Plouguer [F] 40 C2
Caria [P] 86 F2
Cariati [I] 124 E4
Carignan [F] 44 D2
Carignano [I] 70 D6
Cariñena [E] 90 D4
Cariño [E] 78 E1
Carinola [I] 120 D2
Carisbrooke [GB] 12 H5
Carlet [E] 98 E5
Carling [F] 44 F4
Carlingford [IRL] 2 G4
Carlisle [GB] 8 E6
Carloforte [I] 118 B7
Carlow [D] 18 H4
Carlow / Ceatharlach [IRL] 4 F4
Carlton [GB] 10 F4
Carluke [GB] 8 D3
Carmagnola [I] 70 D6
Carmarthen [GB] 12 E2
Carmaux [F] 106 C2
Carmona [E] 94 H6
Carnac [F] 40 D5
Carnalbanagh Sheddings [GB] 2 G3
Carndonagh [IRL] 2 F1
Carnew [IRL] 4 F4
Carnia [I] 72 G4
Carnlough [GB] 2 G3
Carnota [E] 78 B3
Carnoustie [GB] 8 F2
Carnwath [GB] 8 E4
Carolei [I] 124 D4
Carolinensiel [D] 18 C3
Carosino [I] 122 F4
Carpaneto Piacentino [I] 110 C2
Carpenédolo [I] 72 B6
Carpentras [F] 106 H3
Carpi [I] 110 E2
Carpignano Sesia [I] 70 E4
Carpineto Romano [I] 116 B6
Cărpiniş [RO] 76 G5

Carpinone [I] 120 E1
Carquefou [F] 40 F6
Carqueiranne [F] 108 C6
Carradale [GB] 8 C3
Carrapateira [P] 94 A4
Carrara [I] 110 D4
Carraroe [IRL] 2 B5
Carrascalejo [E] 96 C1
Carrascosa del Campo [E] 98 A2
Carrazeda de Ansiães [P] 80 E4
Carrazedo [P] 80 E3
Carrbridge [GB] 6 E5
Carregado [P] 86 B4
Carregal do Sal [P] 80 C6
Carregueiro [P] 94 C3
Carrick / An Charraig [IRL] 2 D2
Carrickfergus [GB] 2 G3
Carrickmacross [IRL] 2 F4
Carrickmore [GB] 2 F3
Carrick–on–Shannon [IRL] 2 D4
Carrick–on–Suir [IRL] 4 E4
Carriço [P] 86 C2
Carrigaline [IRL] 4 C5
Carrigallen [IRL] 2 E4
Carriganimmy [IRL] 4 C4
Carrigans [IRL] 2 F2
Carrigart [IRL] 2 F1
Carrión de Calatrava [E] 96 F4
Carrión de los Condes [E] 82 C5
Carrizo [E] 78 G5
Carro [F] 106 G5
Carrouges [F] 26 F5
Carrowkeel [IRL] 2 F2
Carrù [I] 108 G2
Carryduff [GB] 2 G4
Carry–le–Rouet [F] 106 H5
Çarshovë [AL] 128 C6
Carsoli [I] 116 B5
Carsphairn [GB] 8 D4
Cartagena [E] 104 C4
Cártama [E] 102 B4
Cartaxo [P] 86 C4
Cartaya [E] 94 E5
Carteret [F] 26 D2
Carviçais [P] 80 F5
Carvin [F] 28 F3
Carvoeiro [P] 94 B5
Casabermeja [E] 102 C4
Casabona [I] 124 E4
Casa Branca [P] 86 D5
Casa Branca [P] 94 C2
Casacalenda [I] 116 E6
Casalabate [I] 122 G4
Casalarreina [E] 82 G6
Casalbordino [I] 116 E5
Casalbuono [I] 120 G5
Casalecchio di Reno [I] 110 F3
Casale Monferrato [I] 70 E5
Casalmaggiore [I] 110 D2
Casalpusterlengo [I] 70 H6
Casamássima [I] 122 E3
Casamicciola Terme [I] 120 D3
Casamozza [F] 114 C3
Casamozza [F] 114 B3
Casarano [I] 122 G5
Casares [E] 100 H5
Casariche [E] 102 B3
Casas de Juan Núñez [E] 98 C4
Casas del Puerto [E] 104 C2
Casas–Ibáñez [E] 98 C4
Cascais [P] 86 A5
Cascante [E] 84 B6
Cascia [I] 116 B3
Casciana Terme [I] 110 E6
Cáscina [I] 110 D5
Căscioarele [RO] 148 D1
Casekow [D] 20 E5
Caselle [I] 70 D5
Caserta [I] 120 E2
Cashel [IRL] 4 D4
Cashlie [GB] 8 D1
Casina [I] 110 E3

Casinos [E] 98 E4
Čáslav [CZ] 48 H4
Casola Valsenio [I] 110 G4
Casoli [I] 116 D5
Casoria [I] 120 E3
Caspe [E] 90 F5
Cassà de la Selva [E] 92 F3
Cassagnes–Bégonhès [F] 68 B6
Cassano allo Ionio [I] 122 C6
Cassano d'Adda [I] 70 G5
Cassano delle Murge [I] 122 D3
Cassel [F] 28 E2
Cassine [I] 108 H2
Cassino [I] 120 D1
Cassis [F] 108 B5
Castagneto Carducci [I] 114 E1
Castalla [E] 104 D2
Castañar de Ibor [E] 96 C1
Castanet–Tolosan [F] 106 A3
Castanheira de Pera [P] 86 E2
Casteau [B] 28 H3
Casteggio [I] 70 G6
Castejón de Monegros [E] 90 F4
Castejón de Sos [E] 84 F5
Castejón de Valdejasa [E] 90 E3
Castel Bolognese [I] 110 G4
Castelbuono [I] 126 E2
Casteldelfino [I] 108 E2
Castel del Piano [I] 114 G2
Castel del Rio [I] 110 F4
Castel di Sangro [I] 116 D6
Castelejo [P] 94 A5
Castelfidardo [I] 116 C1
Castelfiorentino [I] 110 E6
Castelfranco Emilia [I] 110 F3
Castelfranco Véneto [I] 72 E6
Castel Goffredo [I] 110 E1
Casteljaloux [F] 66 D5
Castellabate [I] 120 F5
Castellammare del Golfo [I] 126 C2
Castellammare di Stábia [I] 120 E3
Castellamonte [I] 70 D5
Castellana Grotte [I] 122 E3
Castellana Sícula [I] 126 E3
Castellane [F] 108 D4
Castellaneta [I] 122 E4
Castellar [E] 102 F1
Castellar de la Frontera [E] 100 G5
Castellar de la Muela [E] 90 C5
Castellar de Santiago [E] 96 F5
Castell' Arquato [I] 110 C2
Castellazzo Bormida [I] 108 H2
Castelldefels [E] 92 D5
Castell de Ferro [E] 102 E5
Castelleone [I] 70 H5
Castelletto d'Orba [I] 110 A2
Castellfollit de la Roca [E] 92 F2
Castellina in Chianti [I] 114 G1
Castelló de la Plana / Castellón de la Plana [E] 98 F3
Castelló de la Ribera [E] 98 E6
Castelló d'Empúries [E] 92 G2
Castellón de la Plana / Castelló de la Plana [E] 98 F3
Castello Tesino [I] 72 D4
Castellúccio dei Sáuri [I] 120 G2

Castelmagno [I] 108 F2
Castelmassa [I] 110 F2
Castelmauro [I] 116 E6
Castelmoron [F] 66 E5
Castelnaudary [F] 106 B4
Castelnau–de–Médoc [F] 66 C2
Castelnau–de–Montmiral [F] 106 B2
Castelnau–Magnoac [F] 84 F3
Castelnuovo Berardenga [I] 114 G1
Castelnuovo della Dáunia [I] 120 F1
Castelnuovo di Garfagnana [I] 110 D4
Castelnuovo di Porto [I] 116 A5
Castelnuovo Don Bosco [I] 70 E6
Castelnuovo Scrívia [I] 70 F6
Castelo Branco [P] 86 F3
Castelo de Paiva [P] 80 C4
Castelo de Vide [P] 86 F4
Castelo do Neiva [P] 78 A6
Castelraimondo [I] 116 B2
Castel San Giovanni [I] 70 G6
Castel San Lorenzo [I] 120 F4
Castel San Pietro Terme [I] 110 F4
Castelsardo [I] 118 C2
Castelsarrasin [F] 66 F6
Castelseprio [I] 70 F4
Casteltérmini [I] 126 D3
Castelvecchio Subequo [I] 116 C5
Castelverde [I] 70 H6
Castelvetrano [I] 126 B3
Castel Volturno [I] 120 D2
Castenaso [I] 110 F3
Castets [F] 66 B5
Castiádas [I] 118 D7
Castigliole d'Orcia [I] 114 G2
Castiglioncello [I] 114 E1
Castiglione dei Pepoli [I] 110 F4
Castiglione del Lago [I] 114 H2
Castiglione della Pescáia [I] 114 E3
Càstiglione delle Stiviere [I] 72 B6
Castiglione Messer Marino [I] 116 E6
Castiglione Olona [I] 70 F4
Castiglion Fiorentino [I] 114 H1
Castilblanco [E] 96 C2
Castilblanco de los Arroyos [E] 94 G5
Castillejo de Martín Viejo [E] 86 H2
Castillo de Locubín [E] 102 D3
Castillo de Tajarja [E] 102 D4
Castillo de Villamalefa [E] 98 F3
Castillon–la–Bataille [F] 66 D3
Castillonnès [F] 66 E4
Castione della Presolana [I] 72 A5
Castle Acre [GB] 14 G2
Castlebar [IRL] 2 C4
Castlebay [GB] 6 A5
Castlebellingham [IRL] 2 F5
Castleblayney [IRL] 2 F4
Castlebridge [IRL] 4 F5
Castle Combe [GB] 12 G3
Castlecomer [IRL] 4 E3
Castlederg [GB] 2 E3
Castledermot [IRL] 4 F3
Castle Douglas [GB] 8 D5
Castleisland [IRL] 4 B4
Castlemaine [IRL] 4 B4
Castlemartyr [IRL] 4 D5

Castleplunkett [IRL] 2 D4
Castlepollard [IRL] 2 E5
Castlerea [IRL] 2 D4
Castleton [GB] 10 E4
Castletown [GB] 6 F3
Castletown [GBM] 10 B2
Castletownbere [IRL] 4 B5
Castletownroche [IRL] 4 D4
Castletownsend [IRL] 4 B5
Castlewellan [GB] 2 G4
Castres [F] 106 B3
Castries [F] 106 F4
Castricum [NL] 16 D3
Castril [E] 102 G3
Castro [E] 78 C4
Castro Caldelas [E] 78 D5
Castrocaro Terme [I] 110 G4
Castrocontrigo [E] 78 F6
Castro Daire [P] 80 C5
Castro del Río [E] 102 C2
Castrojeriz [E] 82 D6
Castro Marim [P] 94 D5
Castromonte [E] 88 E1
Castronuevo [E] 88 D1
Castropol [E] 78 F2
Castrop–Rauxel [D] 30 H3
Castroreale [I] 124 B7
Castroreale Terme [I] 124 A7
Castro–Urdiales [E] 82 G3
Castroverde [E] 78 E3
Castro Verde [P] 94 C4
Castroverde de Cerrato [E] 88 F2
Castrovillari [I] 122 C6
Castuera [E] 96 B4
Çatak [TR] 142 E1
Çatalca [TR] 146 D2
Catánia [I] 126 G3
Catanzaro [I] 124 E5
Catanzaro Marina [I] 124 E5
Catarroja [E] 98 E5
Catenanuova [I] 126 F3
Cateraggio [F] 114 C4
Caterham [GB] 14 E5
Catterick [GB] 10 F2
Cáttolica [I] 112 B5
Cattolica Eraclea [I] 126 C3
Catus [F] 66 G5
Caudebec [F] 26 H3
Caudete [E] 104 D1
Caudeval [F] 106 B5
Caudry [F] 28 F4
Caumont [F] 26 E3
Caunes–Minervois [F] 106 C4
Cauro [F] 114 B5
Caussade [F] 66 G6
Cauterets [F] 84 E4
Cauville [F] 26 G2
Cava [E] 92 B6
Cava de Tirreni [I] 120 E3
Cavaglia [I] 70 E5
Cavaillon [F] 106 H4
Cavalaire–sur–Mer [F] 108 D6
Cavalese [I] 72 D4
Cavalière [F] 108 D6
Cavallino [I] 72 F6
Cavárzere [I] 110 G2
Çavdarhisar [TR] 144 G2
Çavdır [TR] 142 H1
Cave del Predil [I] 72 H4
Cavo [I] 114 C2
Cavour [I] 70 C6
Cavriglia [I] 110 F6
Cavtat [HR] 152 C4
Çayağzı [TR] 146 F2
Caylus [F] 66 G6
Cayrols [F] 68 A4
Cazalla de la Sierra [E] 94 H5
Cazals [F] 66 F4
Cazaubon [F] 66 D6
Cazères [F] 84 G4
Cazin [BIH] 112 H2

Cazma [HR] 74 F6
Cazorla [E] 102 F2
Cea [E] 82 C5
Cea [E] 78 C4
Cebreiro [E] 78 E4
Cebreros [E] 88 E5
Ceccano [I] 120 C1
Cece [H] 76 B3
Cedeira [E] 78 D1
Cedillo [E] 86 F4
Cedynia [PL] 34 F1
Cee [E] 78 B2
Cefalù [I] 126 E2
Ceglie Messápica [I] 122 F4
Cegléd [H] 76 D2
Cehegín [E] 104 B2
Cehov [RUS] 204 F4
Čejč [CZ] 62 G2
Ceków Kolonia [PL] 36 E4
Čelákovice [CZ] 48 G3
Celano [I] 116 C5
Celanova [E] 78 C5
Celbridge [IRL] 2 F6
Čelebič [BIH] 154 B4
Celerina [CH] 70 H2
Čelić [BIH] 154 E3
Celico [I] 124 D4
Celje [SLO] 74 D4
Celldömölk [H] 74 G1
Celle [D] 32 G1
Celle Lígure [I] 108 H3
Cellers / Castell de Mur [E] 92 C2
Celles–sur–Belle [F] 54 D4
Celopeci [MK] 128 D2
Celorico da Beira [P] 80 D6
Celorico de Basto [P] 80 D4
Čemerno [BIH] 152 D2
Cemke [TR] 146 F2
Cencenighe [I] 72 E4
Ceneköy [TR] 146 C3
Cenicero [E] 82 G6
Čenta [YU] 154 G2
Centallo [I] 108 F2
Centelles [E] 92 E3
Cento [I] 110 F3
Centuri [F] 114 C2
Centúripe [I] 126 F3
Çepan [AL] 128 C5
Čepin [HR] 154 D1
Cepos [P] 86 E2
Ceprano [I] 120 C1
Cerami [I] 126 F2
Ceranów [PL] 38 D2
Cerbère [F] 92 G2
Cercal [P] 94 B3
Cercal [P] 86 B4
Cerceda [E] 88 F5
Cercedilla [E] 88 F4
Cerchiara di Calabria [I] 122 D6
Cerdedo [E] 78 C4
Cerdeira [P] 86 G2
Cerea [I] 110 G2
Cerecinos de Campos [E] 82 B6
Cered [H] 64 E4
Cereda [E] 78 C2
Čerepovec [RUS] 204 F2
Ceres [I] 70 D5
Ceresole Reale [I] 70 C4
Cerignola [I] 120 H2
Cerilly [F] 56 C5
Cerisay [F] 54 D3
Cerisiers [F] 42 H6
Cerizay [F] 54 D3
Cerkezköy [TR] 146 D2
Cerknica [SLO] 74 B6
Cerkno [SLO] 74 B5
Cerkovitsa [BG] 148 B2
Cerkvenjak [SLO] 74 E3
Çermë [AL] 128 B3
Cermei [RO] 76 H3

Černá [CZ] 62 B3
Cerna [HR] 154 E2
Cernache do Bom Jardim [P] 86 D3
Černá Hora [CZ] 50 C5
Cernavoda [RO] 206 D6
Cernay [F] 58 D3
Cerne Abbas [GB] 12 F4
Cernégula [E] 82 E5
Cernihiv [UA] 204 C7
Cernik [HR] 154 C1
Cernjahov [UA] 206 E2
Černóbbio [I] 70 G4
Černobyl [UA] 204 C7
Černomorskoje [UA] 206 F5
Černošin [CZ] 48 D4
Černovice [CZ] 48 G6
Çërravë [AL] 128 D4
Čërrik [AL] 128 B4
Cerro Muriano [E] 96 C6
Certaldo [I] 110 E6
Cervatos [E] 82 E4
Červen [BY] 204 B5
Červená–Řečice [CZ] 48 H5
Červená Skala [SK] 64 E2
Červená Voda [CZ] 50 C4
Červený Kostelec [CZ] 50 B2
Cervera [E] 92 C3
Cervera del Llano [E] 98 B3
Cervera del Río Alhama [E] 84 A6
Cervera de Pisuerga [E] 82 D4
Cerveteri [I] 114 H5
Cérvia [I] 110 H4
Cervignano del Friuli [I] 72 G5
Cervinara [I] 120 E3
Cervione [F] 114 C4
Cervo [E] 78 E1
Cervo [I] 108 G3
Cesana Torinese [I] 70 B6
Cesarò [I] 126 F2
Cesarzowice [PL] 36 C6
Cesena [I] 110 H4
Cesenático [I] 110 H4
Cēsis [LV] 200 E4
Česká Kamenice [CZ] 48 F2
Česká Lípa [CZ] 48 G2
Česká Skalice [CZ] 50 B3
Česká Třebová [CZ] 50 B4
České Budějovice [CZ] 62 C2
České Velenice [CZ] 62 C3
Český Brod [CZ] 48 G4
Český Krumlov [CZ] 62 B4
Český Těšín [CZ] 50 F5
Çeşme [TR] 134 H5
Çeşmealtı [TR] 144 C4
Cessenon–sur–Orb [F] 106 D4
Čestobrodica [YU] 150 A2
Cestona / Zestoa [E] 84 A2
Cesvaine [LV] 200 F5
Cetate [RO] 150 F1
Cetinje [YU] 152 E4
Cetraro [I] 124 C4
Ceuta [E] 100 G6
Ceutí [E] 104 C3
Ceva [I] 108 G3
Cevico Navero [E] 88 F1
Čevo [YU] 152 E4
Ceyzériat [F] 68 G2
Chabanais [F] 54 F6
Chabeuil [F] 68 F5
Chablis [F] 56 E2
Chabreloche [F] 68 D2
Chabris [F] 54 H3
Chagny [F] 56 G5
Chaillé–les–Marais [F] 54 C4
Chairóneia [GR] 132 H5
Chajkola [RUS] 198 H3
Chalabre [F] 106 B5
Chalais [F] 66 E2
Chalamont [F] 68 G2
Chalampé [F] 58 E3
Chalandrítsa [GR] 132 F6

Chale [GB] 12 H5
Chálki [GR] 142 D5
Chálki [GR] 132 G2
Chalkiádes [GR] 132 G2
Chalkída [GR] 134 B5
Chalkidóna [GR] 128 G4
Challans [F] 54 B2
Challes-les-Eaux [F] 70 A4
Chalonnes [F] 54 D1
Chalonnes-sur-Loire [F] 54 D1
Châlons-en-Champagne [F] 44 B4
Chalon-sur-Saône [F] 56 G5
Châlus [F] 66 G2
Cham [F] 54 F6
Cham [D] 48 C6
Chambéry [F] 68 H3
Chambley-Bussières [F] 44 E4
Chambon-sur-Lac [F] 68 C2
Chambon-sur-Voueize [F] 56 B6
Chambord [F] 54 H2
Chamonix-Mont-Blanc [F] 70 C3
Champagne-Mouton [F] 54 E5
Champagnole [F] 58 B6
Champaubert [F] 44 A4
Champdeniers [F] 54 D4
Champeix [F] 68 C3
Champéry [CH] 70 C2
Champex [CH] 70 C3
Champier [F] 68 G4
Champigné [F] 40 H6
Champigny-sur-Veude [F] 54 F2
Champillon [F] 44 B3
Champlitte [F] 58 A3
Champlon [B] 30 E6
Champoluc [I] 70 D3
Champrond-en-Gâtine [F] 26 H6
Champtoceaux [F] 40 F6
Chamrousse [F] 68 H5
Chamusca [P] 86 C4
Chanas [F] 68 F4
Chandrinós [GR] 136 C4
Chaniá [GR] 140 C4
Chaniotis [GR] 130 C6
Chantada [E] 78 D4
Chantelle [F] 56 D6
Chantemerle [F] 70 B6
Chantilly [F] 42 G3
Chantonnay [F] 54 C3
Chão de Codes [P] 86 D4
Chaource [F] 44 B6
Chapelle-Royale [F] 42 D5
Chárakas [GR] 140 E5
Charavines [F] 68 G4
Charbonnières-les-Bains [F] 68 F3
Charbowo [PL] 36 D2
Chard [GB] 12 F4
Charenton-du-Cher [F] 56 C4
Charing [GB] 14 F5
Charleroi [B] 30 C5
Charlestown [IRL] 2 D4
Charleville / Rath Luirc [IRL] 4 C4
Charleville-Mézières [F] 44 C2
Charlieu [F] 68 E1
Charlottenberg [S] 166 D1
Charly [F] 42 H3
Charmes [F] 44 E6
Charneca [P] 86 A5
Charny [F] 56 D1
Charnyany [BY] 38 G3
Charolles [F] 56 F6
Chârost [F] 56 B3
Charroux [F] 54 E5
Chartres [F] 42 E4
Chassigny [F] 56 H3
Château-Arnoux [F] 108 C3
Châteaubourg [F] 26 D6
Châteaubriant [F] 40 F5
Château-Chinon [F] 56 E4
Château d'Oex [CH] 70 D1

Château-du-Loir [F] 42 B6
Châteaudun [F] 42 D5
Châteaugiron [F] 26 C6
Château-Gontier [F] 40 H5
Château-la-Vallière [F] 42 B6
Châteaulin [F] 40 B2
Châteaumeillant [F] 56 B5
Châteauneuf [F] 66 E1
Châteauneuf-de-Randon [F] 68 D5
Châteauneuf-du-Faou [F] 40 C3
Châteauneuf-du-Pape [F] 106 G3
Châteauneuf-en-Thymerais [F] 26 H6
Chateauneuf-sur-Cher [F] 56 C4
Châteauneuf-sur-Loire [F] 42 F6
Châteauneuf-sur-Sarthe [F] 40 H6
Châteauponsac [F] 54 G5
Château-Porcien [F] 28 H6
Château-Queyras [F] 70 B6
Château-Regnault [F] 44 C1
Châteaurenard [F] 42 G6
Château-Renault [F] 54 G1
Châteauroux [F] 54 H4
Château-Salins [F] 44 F5
Château-Thierry [F] 42 H3
Châteauvillain [F] 56 G2
Châtel [F] 70 C2
Châtelaillon-Plage [F] 54 C5
Châtelet [B] 30 C5
Châtelguyon [F] 68 C2
Châtellerault [F] 54 F4
Chatêl-Montagne [F] 68 E1
Châtel-St-Denis [CH] 70 C1
Châtelus-Malvaleix [F] 54 H5
Châtenois [F] 44 E6
Chatham [GB] 14 F4
Châtillon [I] 70 D4
Châtillon-Coligny [F] 56 D1
Châtillon-en-Bazois [F] 56 E4
Châtillon-en-Diois [F] 68 G6
Châtillon-sur-Chalaronne [F] 68 G2
Châtillon-sur-Indre [F] 54 G3
Châtillon-sur-Loire [F] 56 D2
Châtillon-sur-Marne [F] 44 A3
Châtillon-sur-Seine [F] 56 G2
Chatteris [GB] 14 F2
Chatto [GB] 8 F4
Chaudes-Aigues [F] 68 C5
Chauffailles [F] 68 F1
Chaufour-lès-Bonnières [F] 42 E3
Chaumergy [F] 56 H5
Chaumont [F] 54 G2
Chaumont [F] 56 H1
Chaumont-sur-Aire [F] 44 D4
Chaumont-sur-Loire [F] 54 G2
Chaunay [F] 54 E5
Chauny [F] 28 F6
Chaussin [F] 56 H5
Chauvigny [F] 54 F4
Chaves [P] 80 E3
Chazelles [F] 68 F3
Chazelles-sur-Lyon [F] 68 F3
Cheadle [GB] 10 E5
Cheb [CZ] 48 C3
Chęciny [PL] 52 B1
Cheddar [GB] 12 F3
Chef-Boutonne [F] 54 D5
Cheles [E] 94 F2
Chelm [PL] 38 F6
Chelmek [PL] 50 G3

Chełmno [PL] 22 D5
Chelmsford [GB] 14 F4
Chełmża [PL] 22 E6
Chełst [PL] 36 B1
Cheltenham [GB] 12 G2
Chelva [E] 98 D3
Chemillé [F] 54 D2
Chemin [F] 56 H5
Chemnitz [D] 48 D1
Chêne-Pignier [F] 54 F6
Chénéraailles [F] 56 B6
Chenonceaux [F] 54 G2
Chepelare [BG] 130 E1
Chepstow [GB] 12 G3
Chera [E] 98 D4
Cherasco [I] 108 G2
Cherbourg [F] 26 D2
Cherkasy [UA] 206 F2
Chernaya Rechka [RUS] 200 G3
Chernevo [RUS] 200 G2
Chernivtsi [UA] 206 C3
Cherno [RUS] 200 G1
Chernomorets [BG] 148 F4
Chernyakhovsk [RUS] 24 C1
Chéroy [F] 42 G5
Cherveix-Cubas [F] 66 G3
Chervena Voda [BG] 148 D2
Cherven Bryag [BG] 150 G3
Chervonohrad [UA] 52 H2
Chesham [GB] 14 E3
Cheste [E] 98 E4
Chester [GB] 10 D4
Chesterfield [GB] 10 F5
Chester-le-Street [GB] 8 F6
Chevagnes [F] 56 D5
Chevanceaux [F] 66 D2
Chevreuse [F] 42 F4
Chézal-Benoît [F] 56 B4
Chiampo [I] 72 D6
Chianciano Terme [I] 114 G2
Chiaramonti Gulfi [I] 126 F5
Chiaravalle [I] 112 C6
Chiaravalle Centrale [I] 124 D6
Chiari [I] 70 H5
Chiasso [CH] 70 G4
Chiavari [I] 110 B3
Chiavenna [I] 70 G2
Chichester [GB] 14 D5
Chicklade [GB] 12 G4
Chiclana de la Frontera [E] 100 F4
Chieming [D] 60 F5
Chieri [I] 70 D6
Chiesa in Valmalenco [I] 70 H3
Chieti [I] 116 D4
Chigwell [GB] 14 E4
Chilham [GB] 14 F5
Chiliomódi [GR] 136 F1
Chillón [E] 96 C4
Chimay [B] 28 H5
Chinchilla de Monte-Aragón [E] 98 C5
Chinchón [E] 96 G1
Chinon [F] 54 F2
Chióggia [I] 110 H1
Chíos [GR] 134 G4
Chipiona [E] 100 F3
Chippenham [GB] 12 G3
Chipping Campden [GB] 12 H2
Chipping Norton [GB] 12 H2
Chipping Sodbury [GB] 12 G3
Chiprovtsi [BG] 150 F3
Chirivel [E] 102 H3
Chirk [GB] 10 C5
Chirnside [GB] 8 F4
Chirpan [BG] 148 C5
Chisa [F] 114 B5
Chişinău [MD] 206 E4
Chişineu Criş [RO] 76 G3
Chiusa / Klausen [I] 72 D3
Chiusa di Pesio [I] 108 F3
Chiusaforte [I] 72 G4
Chiusa Scláfani [I] 126 C3

Chiusi [I] 114 H2
Chiva [E] 98 E4
Chivasso [I] 70 D5
Chlebowo [PL] 34 G3
Chlewiska [PL] 38 B6
Chlumec nad Cidlinou [CZ] 48 H3
Chlum u Třeboně [CZ] 62 C2
Chmielnik [PL] 52 B2
Chobham [GB] 14 D4
Choceň [CZ] 50 B4
Chochołów [PL] 50 H5
Chocianów [PL] 36 B5
Chociwel [PL] 20 G5
Choczewo [PL] 22 D1
Chodecz [PL] 36 F2
Chodel [PL] 38 D6
Chodos / Xodos [E] 98 F2
Chodová Planá [CZ] 48 D4
Chodzież [PL] 22 B6
Chojna [PL] 20 F6
Chojnice [PL] 22 C4
Chojnów [PL] 36 B6
Cholet [F] 54 D2
Chomakovtsi [BG] 150 G3
Chomęciska Małe [PL] 52 F1
Chomutov [CZ] 48 E2
Chop [UA] 206 B3
Chóra [GR] 136 C4
Choreftó [GR] 134 A2
Chorges [F] 108 D2
Choristí [GR] 130 D3
Chorley [GB] 10 D3
Choroszcz [PL] 24 E5
Chorzele [PL] 22 H5
Chorzów [PL] 50 G3
Chorzyna [PL] 36 F5
Choszczno [PL] 20 G6
Chotěboř [CZ] 50 A5
Choumnikó [GR] 130 C3
Choye [F] 58 A4
Chrast [CZ] 50 B4
Chrastava [CZ] 48 G1
Christchurch [GB] 12 G5
Christiansfeld [DK] 156 C3
Chrudim [CZ] 50 A4
Chrysochóri [GR] 130 E3
Chrysoúpoli [GR] 130 E3
Chrzanôwek [PL] 38 D5
Chrzanów [PL] 50 G3
Chulkovo [RUS] 178 E3
Chulmleigh [GB] 12 E4
Chuprene [BG] 150 E3
Chur [CH] 70 H1
Church Stretton [GB] 10 D6
Churchtown [IRL] 4 F5
Churchtown [IRL] 4 E6
Churek [BG] 150 G4
Chwaszczyno [PL] 22 D2
Chyňava [CZ] 48 F4
Chýnov [CZ] 48 G5
Chýrgos [GR] 128 H4
Ciąże [PL] 36 E3
Ciborro [P] 86 D6
Ciboure [F] 84 B2
Cicciano [I] 120 E3
Ćićevac [YU] 150 C3
Cidones [E] 90 B2
Ciechanów [PL] 38 B1
Ciechanowiec [PL] 38 D1
Ciechocinek [PL] 36 F1
Ciepielów [PL] 38 C5
Cieplice Śląskie-Zdrój [PL] 50 A1
Cierp-Gaud [F] 84 F4
Cieszanów [PL] 52 F3
Cieszyn [PL] 50 F4
Cieza [E] 104 C2
Ciężkowice [PL] 52 C4
Cifuentes [E] 90 A5
Cigales [E] 88 E1
Cigánd [H] 64 H4
Cigliano [I] 70 E5
Cihangazi [TR] 146 G5
Cilipi [HR] 152 D4
Cill Airne / Killarney [IRL] 4 B4
Cillas [E] 90 C5
Cill Chainnigh / Kilkenny [IRL] 4 E4

Cill Charthaigh / Kilcar [IRL] 2 D2
Cill Ciaráin / Kilkieran [IRL] 2 B4
Cilleros [E] 86 G3
Cimadevilla [E] 78 B3
Cîmpeni [RO] 206 B5
Cîmpia Turzii [RO] 206 B5
Cîmpina [RO] 206 C6
Cîmpulung [RO] 206 C6
Cîmpulung Moldovenesc [RO] 206 C4
Çınarcık [TR] 146 F3
Cindere [TR] 144 F4
Çine [TR] 144 E6
Ciney [B] 30 D5
Cinfães [P] 80 C4
Cingoli [I] 116 C1
Cinigiano [I] 114 F2
Cínisi [I] 126 C1
Cínovec [CZ] 48 E2
Cinque Frondi [I] 124 D6
Cintegabelle [F] 106 A4
Cintruénigo [E] 84 A6
Ciółkowo [PL] 36 H2
Cirella [I] 124 C3
Cirencester [GB] 12 G3
Cirey [F] 44 G6
Cirò [I] 70 D5
Ciriè [I] 70 D5
Čirkovicy [RUS] 178 G6
Cirò Marina [I] 124 F4
Ciron [F] 54 G4
Ciruli [LV] 200 C4
Cisa, Passo della [I] 110 C3
Cisna [PL] 52 E6
Cisnădie [RO] 206 B5
Cisterna di Latina [I] 116 B6
Cisternino [I] 122 F3
Cistierna [E] 82 C4
Cista Provo [HR] 152 B2
Cisterna [E] 82 C4
Cisterna Provo [HR] 152 B2
Cisterna di Latina [I] 116 B6
Çıtlık [TR] 142 E2
Cittadella [I] 72 D6
Città della Pieve [I] 114 H2
Città del Vaticano [V] 116 A5
Città di Castello [I] 116 A1
Cittaducale [I] 116 B4
Cittanova [I] 124 D7
Cittá San Angelo [I] 116 D4
Ciudad Real [E] 96 E4
Ciudad Rodrigo [E] 88 A3
Ciumeghiu [RO] 76 H3
Ciutadella de Menorca [E] 104 D2
Cividale del Friuli [I] 72 G5
Cívita Castellana [I] 116 A4
Civitanova Marche [I] 116 C1
Civitavécchia [I] 114 G5
Civitella del Tronto [I] 116 C3
Civitella di Romagna [I] 110 G5
Civitella in Val di Chiana [I] 114 G1
Civitella Roveto [I] 116 C5
Civray [F] 54 E5
Civrieux-d'Azergues [F] 68 F2
Çivril [TR] 144 G4
Cjurupinsk [UA] 206 F4
Clackmannan [GB] 8 E3
Clacton-on-Sea [GB] 14 G4
Clady [GB] 2 F2
Clairvaux-les-Lacs [F] 70 A1
Clamecy [F] 56 E3
Clane [IRL] 2 F6
Claonaig [GB] 8 C3
Clapham [GB] 14 E2
Clara [IRL] 2 D5
Clare [IRL] 2 D5
Clarecastle [IRL] 2 C6
Claremorris [IRL] 2 C4
Clarinbridge [IRL] 2 C5
Clashmore [IRL] 4 D5
Claudy [GB] 2 F2
Clausthal-Zellerfeld [D] 32 G4
Clavières [I] 70 B6
Clay Cross [GB] 10 F5

Cleadale [GB] 6 B5
Cleanovu [RO] 150 F1
Cleator Moor [GB] 8 D6
Clécy [F] 26 F4
Cleethorpes [GB] 10 G4
Clefmont [F] 58 A2
Clelles [F] 68 G5
Cleobury Mortimer [GB] 10 D6
Cleobury North [GB] 10 D6
Clères [F] 28 C5
Clermont [F] 28 E6
Clermont-en-Argonne [F] 44 D4
Clermont-Ferrand [F] 68 C2
Clermont-l'Hérault [F] 106 E4
Clerval [CH] 58 C4
Clervaux [L] 44 F1
Cléry [F] 42 E6
Cles [I] 72 C3
Clevedon [GB] 12 F3
Clifden [IRL] 2 B4
Cliffe [GB] 14 F4
Cliffony [IRL] 2 D3
Clisson [F] 54 C2
Clitheroe [GB] 10 E3
Clogan [IRL] 2 D6
Clogheen [IRL] 4 D4
Clogher [GB] 2 F3
Cloghmore [IRL] 2 B3
Clonakilty [IRL] 4 C5
Clonard [IRL] 2 E5
Clonaslee [IRL] 2 D6
Clonbur [IRL] 2 C4
Clondalkin [IRL] 2 F6
Clonfert [IRL] 2 D5
Clonmany [IRL] 2 F1
Clonmel / Cluain Meala [IRL] 4 E4
Clonmellon [IRL] 2 E5
Clonroche [IRL] 4 F4
Cloonbannin [IRL] 4 C4
Cloonkeen [IRL] 4 B4
Cloonlara [IRL] 4 D3
Cloppenburg [D] 18 C6
Clough [GB] 2 G4
Cloughjordan [IRL] 2 D6
Clova [GB] 8 F1
Clovelly [GB] 12 D3
Cloyes-sur-le-Loir [F] 42 D5
Cloyne [IRL] 4 D5
Cluain Meala / Clonmel [IRL] 4 E4
Cluanie [GB] 6 C5
Cluj Napoca [RO] 206 B4
Clun [GB] 10 C6
Cluny [F] 56 F6
Cluses [F] 70 B2
Clusone [I] 72 A5
Clydebank [GB] 8 D3
Ćmielów [PL] 52 D1
Cmolas [PL] 52 D3
Coachford [IRL] 4 C5
Coagh [GB] 2 F3
Coalisland [GB] 2 F3
Coalville [GB] 10 E6
Coaña [E] 78 F2
Cobh [IRL] 4 D5
Cobham [GB] 14 F4
Coburg [D] 46 G3
Coca [E] 88 E3
Cocentaina [E] 104 E1
Cochem [D] 44 G1
Cockermouth [GB] 8 D6
Code [LV] 200 D6
Codigoro [I] 110 G2
Codogno [I] 70 H6
Codos [E] 90 D4
Codróipo [I] 72 G5
Coesfeld [D] 16 H6
Coevorden [NL] 16 G4
Cofrentes [E] 98 D5
Coggeshall [GB] 14 F3
Cognac [F] 54 D6
Cogne [I] 70 D4
Cogolin [F] 108 D5
Cogollos [E] 82 E6
Cogolludo [E] 88 H4

Coignafearn [GB] 6 D5
Coimbra [P] 86 D2
Coín [E] 102 B4
Coina [P] 86 B6
Čoka [YU] 76 E5
Colares [F] 86 A5
Cölbe [D] 32 D6
Colbitz [D] 34 B2
Colcerasa [I] 116 B1
Colchester [GB] 14 F3
Col de Braus [F] 108 F4
Col de Brouis [F] 108 F4
Col de Bussang [F] 58 D3
Col de la Croix Haute [F] 68 G6
Col de la Fageole [F] 68 C4
Col de la Faucille [F] 70 B1
Col de la Moreno [F] 68 C2
Col de la République [F] 68 F4
Col de Montgenèvre [Eur.] 70 B6
Col de Puymorens [F] 92 E1
Col des Goules [F] 68 C2
Col des Leques [F] 108 D4
Col de Toutes Aures [F] 108 D4
Colditz [D] 34 D6
Coldstream [GB] 8 F4
Col du Bonhomme [F] 58 D2
Col du Grand–St–Bernard [Eur.] 70 C3
Col du Pourtalet [Eur.] 84 D4
Col du Tourmalet [F] 84 E4
Coleford [GB] 12 G2
Coleraine [GB] 2 G2
Colfiorito [I] 116 B2
Colfosco [I] 72 E3
Colico [I] 70 G3
Coligny [F] 56 H6
Colindres [E] 82 F3
Colintraive [GB] 8 C2
Collado de Toses [E] 92 E2
Coll de Nargó [E] 92 D2
Collécchio [I] 110 D2
Colle di Tenda / Col de Tende [Eur.] 108 F3
Colle di Val d'Elsa [I] 114 F1
Colleferro [I] 116 B6
Collegno [I] 70 D6
Colle Isarco / Gossensass [I] 72 D2
Collesalvetti [I] 110 D6
Colle Sannita [I] 120 F2
Collesano [I] 126 E2
Colletorto [I] 116 F6
Collinée [F] 26 B5
Cóllio [I] 72 B5
Collioure [F] 92 G2
Collodi [I] 110 E5
Collonges [F] 70 A2
Collonges–la–Rouge [F] 66 G3
Collooney [IRL] 2 D3
Colmar [F] 58 D3
Colmars [F] 108 D3
Colmenar [E] 102 C4
Colmenar de Oreja [E] 96 G1
Colmenar Viejo [E] 88 F5
Colne [GB] 10 E3
Cologna Véneta [I] 110 F1
Cologne [F] 84 G2
Cologno al Serio [I] 70 H5
Colombey–les–Belles [F] 44 E5
Colombey–les–Deux–Églises [F] 44 C6
Colomiers [F] 84 H3
Colònia de Sant Jordi [E] 104 E6
Colorno [I] 110 D2
Colosimi [I] 124 D5
Colsterworth [GB] 10 F6
Colunga [E] 82 C2
Colwyn Bay [GB] 10 C4
Comácchio [I] 110 H3
Comăneşti [RO] 206 C5

Comano Terme [I] 72 C4
Coma–ruga [E] 92 C5
Combeaufontaine [F] 58 B3
Comber [GB] 2 G4
Combourg [F] 26 C5
Combronde [F] 68 C1
Comeglians [I] 72 G3
Comelico Superiore [I] 72 F3
Comillas [E] 82 E3
Cómiso [I] 126 F5
Commentry [F] 56 C6
Commequiers [F] 54 B2
Commercy [F] 44 D5
Como [I] 70 G4
Compiègne [F] 28 E6
Comporta [P] 94 C1
Comps–sur–Artuby [F] 108 D4
Comrat [MD] 206 E5
Concarneau [F] 40 B3
Concesio [I] 72 B5
Conches [F] 26 H4
Concordia Sagittaria [I] 72 F5
Condat [F] 68 C3
Condé–en–Brie [F] 44 A3
Condeixa–a–Nova [P] 86 D2
Condé–sur–Noireau [F] 26 E4
Condino [I] 72 B5
Condofuri [I] 124 C8
Condom [F] 66 E6
Condove [I] 70 C5
Condover [GB] 10 D6
Condrieu [F] 68 F3
Conegliano [I] 72 E5
Conflans [F] 44 E4
Conflans–en Jarnisy [F] 44 E4
Confolens [F] 54 F6
Cong [IRL] 2 C4
Congleton [GB] 10 E5
Congosto de Valdavia [E] 82 D4
Congresbury [GB] 12 F3
Conil de la Frontera [E] 100 F5
Coningsby [GB] 10 G5
Coniston [GB] 10 D2
Conlie [F] 42 B5
Conna [IRL] 4 D5
Connah's Quay [GB] 10 D4
Connerré [F] 42 C5
Conques [F] 68 B5
Conquista [E] 96 D5
Conquista de la Sierra [E] 96 B2
Conselice [I] 110 G3
Conselve [I] 110 G1
Consett [GB] 8 F6
Constanţa [RO] 206 E6
Constantina [E] 96 A6
Consuegra [E] 96 F3
Consuma [I] 110 F5
Contarina [I] 110 H2
Contay [F] 28 E4
Contigliano [I] 116 B4
Contin [GB] 6 D4
Contres [F] 54 H2
Contrexéville [F] 58 B2
Contursi Terme [I] 120 F4
Conty [F] 28 D5
Conversano [I] 122 E3
Conwy [GB] 10 C4
Cookstown [GB] 2 F3
Coole [IRL] 2 E5
Coombe Bissett [GB] 12 G4
Cooraclare [IRL] 2 B6
Cootehill [IRL] 2 F4
Cope [E] 104 B4
Copertino [I] 122 G5
Cöpköy [TR] 146 B3
Copparo [I] 110 G2
Coppenbrügge [D] 32 F3
Corabia [RO] 148 A2
Corato [I] 122 D2
Coray [F] 40 C3
Corbeil–Essonnes [F] 42 F4

Corbeny [F] 28 G6
Corbie [F] 28 E5
Corbigny [F] 56 E3
Corbridge [GB] 8 F6
Corby [GB] 14 E2
Corcaigh / Cork [IRL] 4 C5
Corciano [I] 114 H2
Corcieux [F] 58 D2
Corconte [E] 82 E4
Corcubión [E] 78 B2
Cordenons [I] 72 F5
Cordes [F] 106 B2
Corella [E] 84 A6
Corfe Castle [GB] 12 G5
Cori [I] 116 B6
Coria [E] 86 H3
Coria del Río [E] 94 G6
Corigliano Calabro [I] 124 E3
Corinaldo [I] 112 C6
Coripe [E] 100 H3
Cork / Corcaigh [IRL] 4 C5
Corlăţel [RO] 150 E1
Corlay [F] 26 A4
Corleone [I] 126 C2
Corleto Perticara [I] 120 H4
Çorlu [TR] 146 C3
Cormainville [F] 42 E5
Cormeilles [F] 26 G3
Cormery [F] 54 G2
Corniglio [I] 110 D3
Cornimont [F] 58 D3
Cornuda la Valle [I] 72 E5
Corofin [IRL] 2 C6
Corovodë [AL] 128 C5
Corps [F] 68 H6
Corral de Almaguer [E] 96 G2
Corralejo [E] 100 E5
Corréggio [I] 110 E2
Corrido [I] 116 C2
Corsham [GB] 12 G3
Corte [F] 114 B4
Cortegada [E] 78 C5
Cortegana [E] 94 F4
Cortemaggiore [I] 110 H6
Cortemília [I] 108 G2
Cortes [E] 90 D3
Cortes de Pallás [E] 98 D5
Cortina d'Ampezzo [I] 72 E3
Čortkov [UA] 206 C3
Cortona [I] 114 H1
Coruche [P] 86 C5
Coruña del Conde [E] 88 H2
Corvara in Badia [I] 72 E3
Corvera [E] 104 C3
Corwen [GB] 10 C5
Cosa [E] 90 D6
Cosenza [I] 124 D4
Cosne [F] 56 D3
Cosne d'Allier [F] 56 C5
Coşoveni [RO] 150 G1
Cossato [F] 28 E4
Cossé–le–Vivien [F] 40 G5
Cossonay [CH] 70 B1
Costa da Caparica [P] 86 A5
Costa de los Pinos [E] 104 F5
Costa Nova do Prado [P] 80 B5
Costa Teguise [E] 100 E4
Costeşti [RO] 206 C6
Costigliole Saluzzo [I] 108 F2
Coswig [D] 34 C4
Cotignac [F] 108 C5
Cottbus [D] 34 F4
Couches [F] 56 F5
Couço [P] 86 D5
Coucy [F] 28 F6
Couhé [F] 54 E5
Couilly [F] 42 G3
Couiza [F] 106 B5
Coulanges–la–Vineuse [F] 56 E2
Coulommiers [F] 42 G4

Coulon [F] 54 D4
Coulonges [F] 54 D4
Coulport [GB] 8 C2
Coupar Angus [GB] 8 E2
Couptrain [F] 26 F5
Courchevel [F] 70 B4
Cour–Cheverny [F] 54 H2
Courçon [F] 54 C4
Cour–et–Buis [F] 68 G4
Courmayeur [I] 70 C3
Courpière [F] 68 D2
Coursan [F] 106 D5
Courseulles–sur–Mer [F] 26 F3
Cours–la–Ville [F] 68 F2
Courson–les–Carrières [F] 56 E2
Courteilles [F] 26 G4
Courtenay [F] 42 G6
Courtmacsherry [IRL] 4 C5
Courtomer [F] 26 G5
Courtown Harbour [IRL] 4 G4
Courtrail (Kortrijk) [B] 28 G2
Courville [F] 26 H6
Coutances [F] 26 D3
Couterne [F] 26 E5
Coutevroult [F] 42 G4
Coutras [F] 66 D3
Couvet [CH] 58 C6
Couvin [B] 28 H5
Covadonga [E] 82 C2
Covaleda [E] 90 B2
Covarrubias [E] 88 H1
Covăsinţ [RO] 76 H4
Cove [GB] 6 C3
Coventry [GB] 14 D2
Covilhã [P] 86 F2
Cowbridge [GB] 12 F3
Cowdenbeath [GB] 8 E3
Cowes [GB] 12 H5
Cowfold [GB] 14 E5
Cozes [F] 54 C6
Cozzano [F] 114 B5
Craco [I] 122 D4
Craig [GB] 6 C4
Craigavon [GB] 2 G4
Craigdarroch [GB] 8 D4
Craigellachie [GB] 6 F5
Craigencallie [GB] 8 C5
Craighouse [GB] 8 B2
Craignure [GB] 8 C1
Crail [GB] 8 F3
Crailsheim [D] 46 E6
Craiova [RO] 150 G1
Craiova [RO] 76 H3
Cranborne [GB] 12 G4
Cranbrook [GB] 14 F5
Cranleigh [GB] 14 D5
Crans [CH] 70 D2
Cranstal [GB] 8 C6
Craon [F] 40 G5
Craponne–sur–Arzon [F] 68 D3
Crathie [GB] 6 E6
Crato [P] 86 E5
Craughwell [IRL] 2 C5
Craven Arms [GB] 10 C6
Crawfordjohn [GB] 8 D4
Crawley [GB] 14 E5
Crêches–sur–Saône [F] 68 F1
Crécy [F] 42 G4
Crécy–en–Ponthieu [F] 28 D3
Crécy–sur–Serre [F] 28 G6
Crediton [GB] 12 E4
Creetown [GB] 8 C5
Creevagh [IRL] 2 C3
Creglingen [D] 46 E5
Creil [F] 42 G2
Crema [I] 70 H5
Crémieu [F] 68 G3
Créon [F] 66 D3
Crepaja [YU] 154 G2
Crépy–en–Valois [F] 42 G3
Cres [HR] 112 E2
Crescentino [I] 70 E5
Crespin [F] 28 G4
Crespino [I] 110 G2

Cressensac [F] 66 G3
Cresslough [IRL] 2 E1
Crest [F] 68 F6
Cresta [CH] 70 H2
Creussen [D] 46 H4
Creutzwald [F] 44 F4
Creuzburg [D] 32 G6
Crevalcore [I] 110 F3
Crevecoeur [F] 28 D5
Crevillent / Crevillente [E] 104 D2
Crevillente / Crevillent [E] 104 D2
Crevoladossola [I] 70 E3
Crewe [GB] 10 D5
Crewkerne [GB] 12 F4
Crianlarich [GB] 8 D2
Cricklade [GB] 12 H3
Crieff [GB] 8 E2
Crikvenica [HR] 112 F2
Crimmitschau [D] 48 C1
Crišnjeva [HR] 112 F2
Crispiano [I] 122 E4
Crissolo [I] 108 F2
Crivitz [D] 20 A4
Crkvina Prolaz [YU] 152 E3
Črna [SLO] 74 C4
Crna Bara [YU] 76 E5
Crna Trava [YU] 150 E4
Crnča [YU] 154 F4
Crni Lug [BIH] 154 B4
Crni Vrh [SLO] 74 B5
Črnomelj [SLO] 74 D6
Crocketford [GB] 8 D5
Crocq [F] 68 B1
Crodo [I] 70 F2
Croick [GB] 6 D4
Croithli / Crolly [IRL] 2 E2
Crolly / Croithli [IRL] 2 E2
Cromarty [GB] 6 E4
Cromer [GB] 14 G1
Cromra [GB] 6 D6
Crook [GB] 10 F1
Crookedwood [IRL] 2 E5
Crookhaven [IRL] 4 B5
Crookstown [IRL] 4 C5
Croom [IRL] 4 `D3
Cropani [I] 124 E5
Crosby [GB] 10 D4
Crosby [GBM] 10 B2
Crosia [I] 124 E4
Crossakeel [IRL] 2 E5
Crosshaven [IRL] 4 D5
Crossmaglen [GB] 2 F4
Crossmolina [IRL] 2 C3
Crotone [I] 124 F5
Crowborough [GB] 14 E5
Crowland [GB] 14 F1
Croyde [GB] 12 D3
Croydon [GB] 14 E4
Crozant [F] 54 G5
Crozon [F] 40 B2
Cruas [F] 68 F6
Cruces [E] 78 C3
Cruden Bay [GB] 6 G6
Crumlin [GB] 2 G3
Cruseilles [F] 70 B2
Crusheen [IRL] 2 C6
Cruzy [F] 106 D4
Crvenka [YU] 76 D6
Csabacsüd [H] 76 F3
Csakvár [H] 76 B1
Csanádapáca [H] 76 F3
Csanytelek [H] 76 E3
Császártöltés [H] 76 C4
Csávoly [H] 76 C4
Cserebökény [H] 76 E3
Cserkeszőlő [H] 76 E2
Csesznek [H] 76 A1
Csobád [H] 64 F4
Csökmő [H] 76 G2
Csokonyavisonta [H] 74 H5
Csongrád [H] 76 E3
Csór [H] 76 B2
Csorna [H] 62 G6
Csorvás [H] 76 F3
Csurgó [H] 74 G4
Cualedro [E] 78 D6
Cuba [P] 94 D2
Cubel [E] 90 C5
Cubo de Bureba [E] 82 F5

Çubukdağı [TR] 144 F5
Çubuklu [TR] 142 F2
Cudillero [E] 78 G3
Čudovo [RUS] 204 D2
Cuéllar [E] 88 F2
Cuenca [E] 98 B2
Cuers [F] 108 C5
Cuerva [E] 96 E2
Cuesta Blanca de Arriba [E] 104 C4
Cuestas de Esteras [E] 90 B4
Cuevas del Almanzora [E] 102 H4
Cuevas del Becerro [E] 102 B4
Cuevas de San Clemente [E] 88 H1
Cuevas de San Marcos [E] 102 C3
Cúglieri [I] 118 C4
Cuhom [F] 28 E3
Cuijk [NL] 16 E6
Cuiseaux [F] 56 H6
Cuisery [F] 56 G6
Cujmir [RO] 150 E1
Çukurköy [TR] 144 G5
Çukurören [TR] 144 G2
Culan [F] 56 B5
Culdaff [IRL] 2 F1
Culemborg [NL] 16 E5
Cúllar [E] 102 G3
Cullen [GB] 6 F5
Cullera [E] 98 E5
Culleybackey [GB] 2 G3
Cullompton [GB] 12 E4
Culoz [F] 68 H3
Cumaovasi [TR] 144 C4
Cumbernauld [GB] 8 D3
Cumbres Mayores [E] 94 F4
Čumic [YU] 150 B2
Cumnock [GB] 8 D4
Cunault [F] 54 E2
Cúneo [I] 108 F3
Čunski [HR] 112 E3
Cuntis [E] 78 B3
Cuorgnè [I] 70 D5
Cupar [GB] 8 F2
Cupello [I] 116 E5
Cupra Marittima [I] 116 D2
Cupramontana [I] 116 B1
Ćuprija [YU] 150 C2
Curia [P] 80 B6
Curon Venosta / Graun im Vinschgau [I] 72 B2
Curtatone [I] 110 E1
Curtea de Argeş [RO] 206 C6
Curtici [RO] 76 G4
Čurug [YU] 154 G1
Cushendall [GB] 2 G2
Cusset [F] 68 D1
Custonaci [I] 126 B2
Cutigliano [I] 110 E4
Cutro [I] 124 F5
Cuveşdia [RO] 76 H5
Cuvilly [F] 28 E6
Cuxhaven [D] 18 D3
Cuzzola [I] 118 E3
Cvikov [CZ] 48 G2
Čvylevo [RUS] 204 D1
Cwmbran [GB] 12 F2
Cybinka [PL] 34 G3
Cyców [PL] 38 F5
Cymmer [GB] 12 E2
Cynwyl Elfed [GB] 12 E1
Czacz [PL] 36 C3
Czaplinek [PL] 22 A5
Czarna [PL] 52 F5
Czarna Białostocka [PL] 24 F5
Czarna Dąbrówka [PL] 22 C2
Czarna Woda [PL] 22 D4
Czarne [PL] 22 B4
Czarnków [PL] 36 C1
Czarny Dunajec [PL] 50 H5
Czchów [PL] 52 B4
Czechowice–Dziedzice [PL] 50 G4
Czemierniki [PL] 38 E4

Czempiń [PL] 36 C3
Czerniejewo [PL] 36 D2
Czernikowo [PL] 36 F1
Czersk [PL] 22 D4
Czersk [PL] 38 C3
Czerwieńsk [PL] 34 H4
Częstochowa [PL] 50 G1
Człopa [PL] 20 H6
Człuchów [PL] 22 C4
Czyżew–Osada [PL] 38 D1

D

Daaden [D] 32 C6
Dabas [H] 76 C2
Dąbie [PL] 20 F5
Dąbie [PL] 36 F3
Dabilja [MK] 128 G2
Dabo [F] 44 G5
Dąbrowa [PL] 50 E2
Dąbrowa Białostocka [PL] 24 F4
Dąbrowa Górnicza [PL] 50 G3
Dąbrowa Tarnowska [PL] 52 C3
Dąbrówka Košcielna [PL] 24 E6
Dąbrówno [PL] 22 G5
Dăbuleni [RO] 150 G2
Dachau [D] 60 E4
Dachnow [PL] 52 F3
Dačice [CZ] 62 D2
Dädesjö [S] 162 E4
Dáfnes [GR] 132 F6
Dáfni [GR] 136 D2
Dáfni [GR] 130 D5
Dagali [N] 170 F4
Dağardı [TR] 144 F1
Dagda [LV] 200 G6
Dağkızılca [TR] 144 D4
Dahlen [D] 34 D5
Dahlenburg [D] 18 G5
Dahme [D] 34 E4
Dahme [D] 18 H2
Dahmen [D] 20 C4
Dahn [D] 44 H4
Daia [RO] 148 C1
Daikanvik [S] 190 F4
Daimiel [E] 96 F4
Daimoniá [GR] 136 F5
Daingean [IRL] 2 E6
Đakovica [YU] 150 B6
Đakovo [HR] 154 D1
Dal [TR] 172 C5
Dala–Floda [S] 172 G4
Dala–Husby [S] 174 D5
Dala–Järna [S] 172 G4
Dalama [TR] 144 E5
Dalaman [TR] 142 F3
Dalarö [S] 168 E3
Dalbeattie [GB] 8 D5
Dalby [DK] 156 G3
Dalby [S] 158 C3
Dale [GB] 12 D1
Dale [N] 170 B3
Dale [N] 170 B1
Dale [N] 164 E3
Dalen [N] 164 E2
Daleszyce [PL] 52 C1
Dalgonar [GB] 8 D4
Dalhavaig [GB] 6 E3
Dalhem [S] 162 F1
Dalías [E] 102 F5
Daliowa [PL] 52 D5
Dalj [HR] 154 E1
Dalkeith [GB] 8 E3
Dalkey [IRL] 2 F6
Dalleagles [GB] 8 D4
Dalmellington [GB] 8 D4
Dalmose [DK] 156 F3
Daløy [N] 170 A2
Dalry [GB] 8 C3
Dalrymple [GB] 8 C4
Dalsbruk / Taalintehdas [FIN] 176 E6
Dalseter [N] 170 G1
Dalsjöfors [S] 162 B2
Dalskog [S] 166 D4

Dals Långed [S] 166 D4
Dals Rostock [S] 166 D4
Dalum [S] 162 C1
Dalvík [IS] 194 E3
Dalyan [TR] 130 H6
Damási [GR] 132 F1
Damasławek [PL] 36 D1
Dambaslar [TR] 146 C3
Dammartin–en–Goële [F] 42 G3
Damme [D] 32 D1
Dammen [N] 164 G2
Dampierre [F] 58 A5
Dampierre [F] 42 F4
Dampierre–sur–Boutonne [F] 54 D5
Dampierre–sur–Salon [F] 58 A4
Damp ŒO [D] 18 F1
Damville [F] 26 H5
Damvillers [F] 44 D3
Dăneasa [RO] 148 A1
Dangé–St–Romain [F] 54 F3
Danilovgrad [YU] 152 E4
Danişment [TR] 146 D5
Daniszyn [PL] 36 D5
Dannäs [S] 162 C4
Dannemarie [F] 58 D4
Dannenberg [D] 18 H5
Dannike [S] 162 B2
Daon [F] 40 H5
Daoulas [F] 40 B2
Darabani [RO] 206 D3
Darány [H] 74 H5
Darbėnai [LT] 202 D4
Darda [HR] 76 C6
Dardesheim [D] 32 H3
Dardhë [AL] 128 D5
Darfo [I] 72 B5
Dargun [D] 20 C3
Darıca [TR] 146 F3
Darıçayırı [TR] 146 H2
Darlas Eile / Thurles [IRL] 4 E3
Därligen [CH] 70 E1
Darlington [GB] 10 F2
Darłówko [PL] 22 A2
Darłowo [PL] 22 A2
Darmstadt [D] 46 C3
Darney [F] 58 B2
Darnius [E] 92 G2
Daroca [E] 90 D5
Dąrowa [PL] 38 E2
Dartford [GB] 14 E4
Dartmouth [GB] 12 E5
Daruvar [HR] 74 G6
Darvel [GB] 8 D3
Darwen [GB] 10 E3
Dasburg [D] 44 F1
Dašice [CZ] 50 B4
Dasing [D] 60 D3
Daskalovo [BG] 150 F5
Dassel [D] 32 F4
Dassohóri [GR] 130 E3
Dassow [D] 18 H3
Dasswang [D] 46 H6
Daszyna [PL] 36 G3
Datça [TR] 142 D3
Datteln [D] 30 H2
Daugård [DK] 156 C2
Daugavpils [LV] 202 H3
Dauguli [LV] 200 E4
Daun [D] 30 G6
Daventry [GB] 14 D2
Daviá [GR] 136 D2
Davington [GB] 8 E4
Daviot [GB] 6 D5
Davle [CZ] 48 F4
Dávlia [GR] 132 H5
Davos [CH] 72 A2
Davutlar [TR] 144 D5
Dawlish [GB] 12 E5
Dax [F] 66 B6
Dazkırı [TR] 144 H4
Deal [GB] 14 G5
Deauville [F] 26 G3
Debar [MK] 128 C2
Debeburnu [TR] 144 D2
Debelets [BG] 148 C3
Dębe Wielkie [PL] 38 C3
Dębica [PL] 52 D3

Dębina [PL] 50 E3
Deblin [PL] 38 D5
Debnevo [BG] 148 B4
Dębnica Kaszubska [PL] 22 B2
Dębno [PL] 34 G1
Dębno [PL] 52 B4
Debno [PL] 52 B5
Debovo [BG] 148 B2
Debrc [YU] 154 F3
Debrecen [H] 64 G6
Debromani [BIH] 152 C3
Debrzno [PL] 22 C5
Debür [BG] 148 C6
Dęby [PL] 24 C5
Dečani [YU] 150 B5
Decazeville [F] 68 A5
Decimomannu [I] 118 C7
Děčín [CZ] 48 F2
Decize [F] 56 D4
De Cocksdorp [NL] 16 D2
Dedaj [AL] 152 E4
Dedebağ [TR] 142 G1
Dedemsvaart [NL] 16 G4
Dédestapolcsány [H] 64 E4
Degaña [E] 78 F4
Degebüll [D] 156 B5
Degerby [FIN] 168 G1
Degerby [FIN] 176 G5
Degerfors [S] 166 G3
Degerhamn [S] 162 G6
Degerndorf [D] 60 F5
Degernes [N] 166 C3
Deggendorf [D] 60 G2
Değirmenalanı [TR] 142 F1
Değirmendere [TR] 144 C5
Değirmendere [TR] 146 G3
De Haan [B] 28 F1
Dehesa de Campoamor [E] 104 A3
Deià / Deyá [E] 104 E4
Deidesheim [D] 46 B5
Deinze [B] 28 G2
Dej [RO] 206 B4
Deje [S] 166 F2
De Koog [NL] 16 D2
De Kooy [NL] 16 D2
Delbrück [D] 32 D3
Delčevo [MK] 128 G1
Delden [NL] 16 G5
Delebäck [S] 166 F4
Delémont [CH] 58 D5
Delft [NL] 16 C5
Delfzijl [NL] 16 H2
Délia [I] 126 E4
Delianuova [I] 124 C7
Deliblato [YU] 154 H2
Delitzsch [D] 34 C5
Deljatin [UA] 206 C3
Delle [F] 58 D4
Delme [F] 44 F5
Delmenhorst [D] 18 D5
Delnice [HR] 112 F1
Delsbo [S] 184 D6
Delvin [IRL] 2 E5
Delvina [AL] 132 B1
Delvináki [GR] 132 C1
Demandice [SK] 64 C4
Demigny [F] 56 G5
Demirci [TR] 144 E2
Demirci [TR] 146 F5
Demir Kapija [MK] 128 G2
Demirköy [TR] 146 C1
Demirköy [TR] 146 G5
Demirtaş [TR] 146 F4
Demjansk [RUS] 204 D3
Demmin [D] 20 C3
Denain [F] 28 G4
Denbigh [GB] 10 C4
Den Burg [NL] 16 D2
Dendermonde [B] 28 H2
Denekamp [NL] 16 G4
Đeneral Jankovič [YU] 150 C6
Den Haag [NL] 16 C5
Den Helder [NL] 16 D2
Dénia [E] 104 F1
Denizgören [TR] 146 B5
Denizkent [TR] 146 C5
Denizler [TR] 144 G4
Denizli [TR] 144 G5
Denkendorf [D] 60 E2

Dennington [GB] 14 G3
Denny [GB] 8 D3
Den Oever [NL] 16 E2
Denzlingen [D] 58 E3
De Panne [B] 28 F1
Deptford [GB] 12 G4
Derbent [TR] 144 E4
Derby [GB] 10 E5
Derecske [H] 76 G1
Dereköy [TR] 146 C1
Dereköy [TR] 144 E4
Dermantsi [BG] 148 A3
Dermbach [D] 46 F1
Derneburg [D] 32 G3
Derrygonnelly [GB] 2 E3
Derrylin [GB] 2 E4
Derval [F] 40 F5
Dervéni [GR] 132 G6
Derventa [BIH] 154 D2
Dervock [GB] 2 G2
Descartes [F] 54 F3
Desenzano del Garda [I] 72 B6
Desimirovac [YU] 150 C2
Desio [I] 70 G4
Dešov [CZ] 62 E2
Despotovac [YU] 150 C2
Despotovo [YU] 154 F1
Dessau [D] 34 C4
Désulo [I] 118 D5
Desvres [F] 28 D2
Deszk [H] 76 E4
Deta [RO] 206 A5
Detmold [D] 32 E3
Dettelbach [D] 46 F4
Deurne [NL] 30 F2
Deutschkreutz [A] 62 F6
Deutschlandsberg [A] 74 D3
Deutsch–Wagram [A] 62 F4
Deva [E] 82 H4
Deva [RO] 206 B5
Dévaványa [H] 76 F2
Devecser [H] 74 H2
Devecikonağı [TR] 146 E5
Devene [BG] 150 G3
Deventer [NL] 16 F5
Deveselu [RO] 148 A1
Devetaki [BG] 148 B3
Devin [BG] 130 D1
Devizes [GB] 12 G3
Devnya [BG] 148 F3
Dewsbury [GB] 10 F4
Deyá / Deià [E] 104 E4
Dhërmi [AL] 128 B6
Dheskáti [GR] 132 F1
Diafáni [GR] 140 H2
Diagúčiai [LT] 202 G4

Diakoftó [GR] 132 G6
Dialambí [GR] 130 F3
Diamante [I] 124 C3
Dianalund [DK] 156 F3
Diano Marina [I] 108 G4
Diásselo [GR] 132 F1
Diavatá [GR] 128 H4
Dicomano [I] 110 F5
Didcot [GB] 14 D3
Dídyma [GR] 136 F2
Didymóteicho [GR] 130 H1
Die [F] 68 G6
Dieburg [D] 46 C3
Diekirch [L] 44 F2
Diemelstadt [D] 32 E4
Dienten [A] 72 G1
Diepholz [D] 32 D1
Dieppe [F] 28 C4
Dierdorf [D] 46 B1
Dieren [NL] 16 F5
Diesdorf [D] 32 H1
Diessen [D] 60 D5
Diest [B] 30 D4
Dietenheim [D] 60 B4
Dietikon [CH] 58 F5
Dietmannsried [D] 60 C5
Dieulefit [F] 68 F6
Dieulouard [F] 44 E5
Dieuze [F] 44 F5
Dievenišķes [LT] 202 G6
Diever [NL] 16 G3
Diez [D] 46 B2
Differdange [L] 44 E3
Digermulen [N] 192 C4
Dignano [I] 72 G4
Digne–les–Bains [F] 108 D3
Digoin [F] 56 E5
Dijon [F] 56 G4
Dikänas [S] 190 F4
Díkea [GR] 146 A2
Dikili [TR] 144 C3
Diksmuide [B] 28 F2
Dillenberg [D] 32 D6
Dillingen [D] 60 C3
Dillingen [D] 44 F3
Dilwyn [GB] 12 G1
Dimaro [I] 72 C4
Dimena [GR] 136 F2
Dimitrovgrad [BG] 148 C6
Dimitrovgrad [YU] 150 E4
Dimovo [BG] 150 E2
Dinan [F] 26 C5
Dinant [B] 30 D6
Dinar [TR] 144 H4
Dinard [F] 26 C4
Dingelstädt [D] 32 G5
Dingle [S] 166 C5
Dingle / An Daingean [IRL] 4 A3

Dingli [M] 126 C6
Dingolfing [D] 60 F3
Dingwall [GB] 6 D4
Dinkelsbühl [D] 46 F6
Dinklage [D] 32 D1
Dinozé [F] 58 C2
Dinslaken [D] 30 G2
Dio [S] 162 D5
Dipótama [GR] 130 D2
Dippoldiswalde [D] 48 E1
Dirráchi [GR] 136 D3
Disentis / Mustér [CH] 70 G1
Dispíli [GR] 128 E5
Diss [GB] 14 G2
Dístomo [GR] 132 H5
Dístrato [GR] 128 D6
Ditzingen [D] 58 G1
Divčibare [YU] 150 A2
Dives–sur–Mer [F] 26 F3
Divjakë [AL] 128 A4
Divonne–les–Bains [F] 70 B2
Dívri [GR] 132 G4
Divusa [HR] 154 A2
Djatkovo [RUS] 204 E5
Djúpivogur [IS] 194 G6
Djupvik [N] 192 F2
Djurakovac [YU] 150 B5
Djurås [S] 172 H4
Djurdjevac [HR] 74 G5
Djurdjevica Tara [YU] 152 E2
Dłoń [PL] 36 C4
Dmitrov [RUS] 204 F3
Dniprodzerzhynsk [UA] 206 G3
Dnipropetrovsk [UA] 206 G3
Dno [RUS] 204 C3
Doagh [GB] 2 G3
Dobanovci [YU] 154 G2
Dobbiaco / Toblach [I] 72 E3
Dobczyce [PL] 52 A4
Dobel [D] 58 G1
Dobele [LV] 200 D5
Doberlug Kirchhain [D] 34 E4
Döbern [D] 34 G5
Dobersberg [A] 62 D2
Dobiegniew [PL] 20 H6
Doboj [BIH] 154 D3
Dobra [PL] 36 F3
Dobra [PL] 20 G4
Dobrá Niva [SK] 64 C3
Dobrčane [YU] 150 D5
Dobre [PL] 38 C2
Dobre Miasto [PL] 22 G3

Döbriach [A] 72 H3
Dobrich [BG] 148 F2
Dobřichovice [CZ] 48 F4
Dobri Do [YU] 150 C4
Dobrinishte [BG] 130 B1
Dobříš [CZ] 48 F4
Dobrodzień [PL] 50 F2
Döbrököz [H] 76 B4
Dobromierz [PL] 50 B1
Dobromirka [BG] 148 C3
Dobromirtsi [BG] 130 F2
Dobro Polje [BIH] 152 D2
Dobrosloveni [RO] 150 H1
Dobroszyce [PL] 36 D6
Dobroteşti [RO] 148 B1
Dobrotitsa [BG] 148 E1
Dobrovol'sk [RUS] 24 D1
Dobruchi [RUS] 200 G2
Dobrun [BIH] 152 E1
Dobruška [CZ] 50 B3
Dobrzany [PL] 20 G5
Dobrzyca [PL] 36 D4
Dobrzyń nad Wisła [PL] 36 G2
Docking [GB] 10 H6
Döderhult [S] 162 G3
Dodóni [GR] 132 D2
Doesburg [NL] 16 F5
Doetinchem [NL] 16 F5
Doganbey [TR] 142 B1
Doğanbey [TR] 144 C5
Doganović [YU] 150 C6
Dogliani [I] 108 G2
Dogueno [P] 94 C4
Dokka [N] 170 H3
Dokkas [S] 192 F6
Dokkum [NL] 16 F2
Doksy [CZ] 48 G2
Dolceácqua [I] 108 F4
Dol-de-Bretagne [F] 26 C4
Dole [F] 56 H4
Dølemo [N] 164 E4
Dolenci [MK] 128 D3
Dolenja Vas [SLO] 74 C6
Dolga Vas [SLO] 74 F3
Dolgellau [GB] 10 B5
Dolhobyczów [PL] 52 H2
Dolianova [I] 118 D6
Dolice [PL] 20 G6
Dolíhi [GR] 128 G6
Doljani [HR] 112 H4
Doljevac [YU] 150 D4
Döllach [A] 72 G2
Döllbach [D] 46 E2
Dolle [D] 34 B2
Döllstädt [D] 32 H6
Dolna Banya [BG] 150 G5
Dolna Dikanya [BG] 150 F5
Dolna Mitropoliya [BG] 148 A3
Dolni Dŭbnik [BG] 148 A3
Dolní Dvonste [CZ] 62 C3
Dolní Kounice [CZ] 62 F2
Dolni Lom [BG] 148 E3
Dolno Kamartsi [BG] 150 G4
Dolno Kosovrasti [MK] 128 C2
Dolno Levski [BG] 148 A5
Dolno Novkovo [BG] 148 D3
Dolno Tserovene [BG] 150 F3
Dolno Ujno [BG] 150 E5
Dolný Kubín [SK] 50 G6
Dolo [I] 110 H1
Dolores [E] 104 D3
Dolovo [YU] 154 H2
Dolsk [PL] 36 C4
Dolyna [UA] 52 H6
Domaniç [TR] 146 G5
Domanovići [BIH] 152 C3
Domažlice [CZ] 48 D5
Dombås [N] 180 G5
Dombasle [F] 44 F5
Dombegyház [H] 76 G4
Dombóvár [H] 76 B4
Dombrád [H] 64 H4
Dombrot-le-Sec [F] 58 B2
Domburg [NL] 16 B6
Doméniko [GR] 132 F1
Domèvre-en-Haye [F] 44 E5

Domfront [F] 26 E5
Domingão [P] 86 D4
Dömitz [D] 18 H5
Domme [F] 66 G4
Dommitzsch [D] 34 D4
Domnítsa [GR] 132 F4
Domodedovo [RUS] 204 F4
Domodóssola [I] 70 E3
Domokós [GR] 132 G3
Dompaire [F] 58 C2
Dompierre [F] 56 E5
Dompierre-du-Chemin [F] 26 D5
Dompierre-sur-Besbre [F] 56 E5
Dompierre-sur-Mer [F] 54 C4
Domrémy-la-Pucelle [F] 44 D6
Dömsöd [H] 76 C2
Dómus de Maria [I] 118 C8
Domusnóvas [I] 118 B6
Domžale [SLO] 74 C5
Donado [E] 80 G3
Donaghadee [GB] 2 H3
Donaghmore [IRL] 4 E3
Doña Mencía [E] 102 C2
Donaueschingen [D] 58 F3
Donaustauf [D] 60 F2
Donauwörth [D] 60 D2
Don Benito [E] 96 B3
Doncaster [GB] 10 F4
Dondurma [TR] 146 B5
Donegal / Dún na nGall [IRL] 2 E2
Donington [GB] 10 G6
Donja Brela [HR] 152 B2
Donja Brezna [YU] 152 D3
Donja Bukovica [YU] 152 E3
Donja Kamenica [YU] 150 A1
Donja Ljubata [YU] 150 E5
Donja Šatornja [YU] 150 B2
Donje Ljupče [YU] 150 C5
Donje Petrčane [HR] 112 F5
Donji Koričani [BIH] 154 C3
Donji Lapac [HR] 112 H4
Donji Miholjac [HR] 76 B6
Donji Milanovac [YU] 150 D1
Donji Vakuf [BIH] 154 C4
Donji Zemunik [HR] 112 G5
Donnersbach [A] 74 B1
Dønnes [N] 190 D2
Donostia–San Sebastián [E] 84 B2
Dontilly [F] 42 G5
Donzenac [F] 66 G3
Donzère [F] 68 F6
Donzy [F] 56 D3
Doohooma [IRL] 2 B3
Doonbeg [IRL] 2 B6
Doonloughan [IRL] 2 B4
Doorn [NL] 16 E5
Doornik (Tournai) [B] 28 G3
Dörarp [S] 162 C4
Dorchester [GB] 14 D3
Dorchester [GB] 12 F5
Dordives [F] 42 G5
Dordrecht [NL] 16 D5
Dores [GB] 6 D5
Dorfen [D] 60 F4
Dorfmark [D] 18 F6
Dorgali [I] 118 E4
Dório [GR] 136 D3
Dorking [GB] 14 E5
Dormagen [D] 30 G4
Dormánd [H] 64 E6
Dormans [F] 44 A3
Dornauberg [A] 72 E2
Dornbirn [A] 60 B6
Dornburg [D] 34 B6
Dorndorf [D] 46 F1
Dornes [F] 56 D5
Dornoch [GB] 6 E4
Dornstetten [D] 58 G2
Dornum [D] 18 C3
Dorog [H] 64 C6
Dorogobuž [RUS] 204 D5
Dorohoi [RO] 206 D4

Dorohucza [PL] 38 F6
Dorotea [S] 190 F5
Dörpen [D] 16 H3
Dörpstedt [D] 18 E2
Dorrington [GB] 10 D6
Dorsten [D] 30 H2
Dortan [F] 68 H1
Dortmund [D] 32 C4
Dorum [D] 18 D3
Dörverden [D] 18 E6
Dörzbach [D] 46 E5
Dosbarrios [E] 96 G2
Dos Hermanas [E] 94 G6
Dospat [BG] 130 D1
Douai [F] 28 F4
Douarnenez [F] 40 B3
Douchy [F] 42 G6
Doucier [F] 58 A6
Doudeville [F] 26 H2
Doué-la-Fontaine [F] 54 E2
Dougarie [GB] 8 C3
Douglas [GB] 8 D4
Douglas [GBM] 10 B2
Doulaincourt [F] 44 D6
Doulevant-le-Château [F] 44 C6
Doullens [F] 28 E4
Dounby [GB] 6 F2
Dourdan [F] 42 F4
Dourgne [F] 106 B4
Douvaine [F] 70 B2
Douzy [F] 44 D2
Dover [GB] 14 G5
Dovre [N] 180 G5
Dovsk [BY] 204 C6
Downham Market [GB] 14 F2
Downpatrick [GB] 2 G4
Dowra [IRL] 2 E3
Doxáto [GR] 130 D3
Dozulé [F] 26 G3
Drabov [UA] 206 F2
Dračevo [MK] 128 E1
Drachselsried [D] 48 D6
Drachten [NL] 16 F2
Dragalevci [BG] 150 F5
Drăgănești de Vede [RO] 148 B1
Drăgănești Olt [RO] 148 A1
Drăgănești Vlașca [RO] 148 C1
Dragaš [YU] 150 B6
Drăgășani [RO] 206 B6
Draginje [YU] 150 A1
Dragocvet [YU] 150 C2
Dragoman [BG] 150 F4
Dragomirovo [BG] 148 C3
Dragomirovo [BG] 148 B2
Dragør [DK] 156 H3
Dragovishtitsa [BG] 150 E5
Dragsfjärd [FIN] 176 E5
Dragsvik [N] 170 C1
Draguignan [F] 108 D5
Drahonice [CZ] 48 F6
Drahovce [SK] 62 H3
Dráma [GR] 130 D3
Drammen [N] 164 H1
Drangsness [IS] 194 C2
Dransfeld [D] 32 F4
Dranske [D] 20 D1
Draperstown [GB] 2 F3
Drasenhofen [A] 62 F3
Drávaszabolcs [H] 76 B6
Dravískos [GR] 130 C3
Dravograd [SLO] 74 C3
Drawno [PL] 20 H6
Drawsko Pomorski [PL] 20 H5
Drazdzewo [PL] 24 B6
Draženov [CZ] 48 D5
Drebkau [D] 34 F4
Dreilingen [D] 18 G6
Dren [YU] 150 B4
Drenchia [I] 72 H4
Drenovci [HR] 154 E2
Drenovets [BG] 150 F2
Drensteinfurt [D] 32 C3
Dresden [D] 34 E6
Dreux [F] 42 E3
Drevsjø [N] 182 D6
Drewitz [D] 34 C3
Drewitz [D] 34 E2
Drezdenko [PL] 36 B1

Dreznik–Grad [HR] 112 G2
Driebergen [NL] 16 E5
Driffield [GB] 10 G3
Drimnin [GB] 6 B6
Drimoleague [IRL] 4 B5
Drinjača [BIH] 154 E4
Drinovci [BIH] 152 B2
Drionville [F] 28 E2
Drivstua [N] 180 H4
Drlače [YU] 154 F4
Drnholec [CZ] 62 F2
Drniš [HR] 154 A5
Drøbak [N] 166 B2
Drobeta–Turnu Severin [RO] 206 B6
Drobin [PL] 36 H1
Drochtersen [D] 18 E3
Drogheda / Droichead Átha [IRL] 2 F5
Drohiczyn [PL] 38 E2
Drohobych [UA] 52 G5
Droichead Átha / Drogheda [IRL] 2 F5
Droichead Nua / Newbridge [IRL] 2 E6
Droitwich [GB] 12 G1
Dročłtowice [PL] 36 D5
Dromahair [IRL] 2 D3
Dromcolliher [IRL] 4 C4
Dromore [GB] 2 G4
Dromore [GB] 2 E3
Dromore West [IRL] 2 D3
Dronero [I] 108 F2
Dronfield [GB] 10 F5
Dronninglund [DK] 160 E3
Dronten [NL] 16 F4
Drosáto [GR] 128 H3
Drosendorf Stadt [A] 62 E2
Drosselbjerg [DK] 156 E3
Drossopigí [GR] 132 D3
Drumconrath [IRL] 2 F5
Drumevo [BG] 148 E3
Drumkeeran [IRL] 2 D3
Drumlish [IRL] 2 E4
Drummore [GB] 8 C5
Drumnadrochit [GB] 6 D5
Drumquin [GB] 2 E3
Drumshanbo [IRL] 2 D4
Drumsna [IRL] 2 D4
Drusenheim [F] 44 H5
Druskininkai [LT] 24 F3
Drusti [LV] 200 F4
Druten [NL] 16 E5
Druzhba [BG] 148 G3
Drvar [BIH] 154 A3
Drvenik [HR] 152 B3
Dryanovo [BG] 148 C4
Drymós [GR] 128 H4
Dryópi [GR] 136 F2
Dryopída [GR] 138 C2
Dryós [GR] 138 E3
Drzewica [PL] 38 B5
Duagh [IRL] 4 C3
Dub [YU] 150 A2
Dubá [CZ] 48 G2
Dubăsari [MD] 206 E4
Duben [D] 34 E4
Dubica [HR] 154 B2
Dublin / Baile Átha Cliath [IRL] 2 F6
Dubna [RUS] 204 F3
Dubnica nad Váhom [SK] 64 A2
Dŭbnitsa [BG] 130 C1
Dubno [UA] 206 C2
Dubrovica [UA] 204 A7
Dubrovnik [HR] 152 C4
Ducey [F] 26 D4
Duchally [GB] 6 D3
Duchcov [CZ] 48 E2
Ducherow [D] 20 E4
Duclair [F] 26 H3
Dudelange [L] 44 E3
Duderstadt [D] 32 G4
Düdingen [CH] 58 D6
Dudley [GB] 10 D6
Dueñas [E] 88 F1
Duesund [N] 170 B2
Dueville [I] 72 D6
Duffield [GB] 10 E5
Dufftown [GB] 6 F5
Duga Poljana [YU] 150 B4

Duga Resa [HR] 112 G1
Dugi Rat [HR] 152 A2
Dugła [TR] 144 C2
Dugo Selo [HR] 74 F6
Duhovščina [RUS] 204 D4
Duingt [F] 70 B3
Duino [I] 72 H5
Duisburg [D] 30 G3
Dukat [AL] 128 A6
Dukat [YU] 150 E5
Dukla [PL] 52 D5
Dŭkštas [LT] 202 H4
Dŭlbok Izvor [BG] 148 C6
Duleek [IRL] 2 F5
Dŭlgopol [BG] 148 F3
Dülken [D] 30 F3
Dülmen [D] 16 H6
Dulnain Bridge [GB] 6 E5
Dulovka [RUS] 200 G4
Dulovo [BG] 148 E1
Dumaca [YU] 154 F3
Dumbarton [GB] 8 D3
Dumbrăveni [RO] 148 F1
Dumfries [GB] 8 D5
Dumlupınar [TR] 144 H2
Dun [F] 44 D3
Dunaff [IRL] 2 F1
Dunafödvár [H] 76 C3
Dunaharaszti [H] 76 C1
Dunajevcy [UA] 206 D3
Dunajská Streda [SK] 62 H5
Dunakeszi [H] 64 C6
Dunany [IRL] 2 F5
Dunapataj [H] 76 C3
Dunaszekcső [H] 76 C5
Dunaújváros [H] 76 C2
Dunavecse [H] 76 C2
Dunavtsi [BG] 150 E2
Dunbar [GB] 8 F3
Dunbeath [GB] 6 F3
Dunblane [GB] 8 E2
Dunboyne [IRL] 2 F6
Duncormick [IRL] 4 F5
Dundaga [LV] 200 C4
Dundalk / Dún Dealgan [IRL] 2 F4
Dún Dealgan / Dundalk [IRL] 2 F4
Dundee [GB] 8 F2
Dundonnell [GB] 6 D4
Dundrennan [GB] 8 D5
Dunfanaghy [IRL] 2 E1
Dunfermline [GB] 8 E3
Dungannon [GB] 2 F3
Dungarvan [IRL] 4 E5
Dungavel [GB] 8 D4
Dungiven [GB] 2 F2
Dungloe [IRL] 2 E2
Dungourney [IRL] 4 D5
Dunje [MK] 128 E3
Dunkeld [GB] 8 E2
Dunkerque [F] 14 H6
Dunkerque Ouest [F] 14 H6
Dunkineely [IRL] 2 D2
Dun Laoghaire [IRL] 2 F6
Dunlavin [IRL] 4 F3
Dunleer [IRL] 2 F5
Dun-le-Palestel [F] 54 H5
Dunloy [GB] 2 G2
Dunmanway [IRL] 4 C5
Dunmore [IRL] 2 C4
Dunmore East [IRL] 4 E5
Dunmurry [GB] 2 G3
Dún na nGall / Donegal [IRL] 2 E2
Dunoon [GB] 8 C3
Duns [GB] 8 F4
Dunscore [GB] 8 D5
Dunshaughlin [IRL] 2 F5
Dunstable [GB] 14 E3
Dun-sur-Auron [F] 56 C4
Duntulm [GB] 6 B4
Dunure [GB] 8 C4
Dunvegan [GB] 6 B4
Dupnitsa [BG] 150 F6
Durach [BG] 148 E2
Duran [BG] 148 E2
Durango [E] 82 H4
Durankulak [BG] 148 G1
Duras [F] 66 E4

Durasıllı [TR] 144 E3
Durban–Corbières [F] 106 C5
Durbe [LV] 200 B6
Durbuy [B] 30 E5
Dúrcal [E] 102 E4
Düren [D] 30 G4
Durham [GB] 8 F6
Durness [GB] 6 D2
Dürnkrut [A] 62 G4
Dürnstein [A] 62 D4
Durón [E] 90 A5
Durrës [AL] 128 A3
Durrow [IRL] 4 E3
Durrus [IRL] 4 B5
Dursley [GB] 12 G3
Dursunbey [TR] 144 E1
Durtal [F] 42 A6
Duruelo de la Sierra [E] 90 A2
Dusetos [LT] 202 G4
Dúskotna [BG] 148 E3
Dusnok [H] 76 C4
Dusocin [PL] 22 E5
Düsseldorf [D] 30 G3
Duszniki–Zdrój [PL] 50 B3
Duved [S] 182 E1
Düvertepe [TR] 144 E2
Düzağac [TR] 144 H2
Dve Mogili [BG] 148 C2
Dverberg [N] 192 C3
Dvor [HR] 154 A2
Dvorce [CZ] 50 D4
Dvůr Králové nad Labem [CZ] 50 A3
Dwingeloo [NL] 16 G3
Dyce [GB] 6 F6
Dylewo [PL] 24 C5
Dymchurch [GB] 14 F5
Dynów [PL] 52 E4
Dyrnesvågen [N] 180 F1
Dyulino [BG] 148 F3
Dyuni [BG] 148 F4
Dzeržinsk [BY] 204 B5
Dzhankoy [UA] 206 G5
Dzhurovo [BG] 150 G4
Dziadkowice [PL] 38 E2
Działdowo [PL] 22 G5
Działoszyce [PL] 52 B3
Działoszyn [PL] 36 F6
Dziemiany [PL] 22 C3
Dzierzgoń [PL] 22 F4
Dzierżoniów [PL] 50 C2
Dzigolj [YU] 150 D3
Dzivin [BY] 38 H3
Dziwnów [PL] 20 F3
Džumajlija [MK] 128 F1
Džurin [UA] 206 D3
Dżwierzuty [PL] 22 H4
Dzyarechyn [BY] 24 H5

E

Ealing [GB] 14 E4
Earl's Colne [GB] 14 F3
Easdale [GB] 8 C2
Easingwold [GB] 10 F3
Easky [IRL] 2 D3
Eastbourne [GB] 14 E6
East Cowes [GB] 12 H5
East Dereham [GB] 14 G2
East Grinstead [GB] 14 E5
East Kilbride [GB] 8 D3
Eastleigh [GB] 12 H5
Eastoft [GB] 10 G4
Eastwood [GB] 10 F5
Eaux–Bonnes [F] 84 D4
Eaux–Chaudes [F] 84 D4
Eauze [F] 66 D6
Ebberston [GB] 10 G3
Ebbo / Epoo [FIN] 178 B4
Ebbw Vale [GB] 12 F2
Ebelsbach [D] 46 F3
Ebeltoft [DK] 156 E1
Ebenfurth [A] 62 F5
Eben im Pongau [A] 72 H1
Ebensee [A] 62 A5
Eberbach [D] 46 D5
Ebermannstadt [D] 46 G4
Ebern [D] 46 G3
Eberndorf [A] 74 C3

Ebersbach [D] 48 G1
Ebersberg [D] 60 E4
Eberschwang [A] 60 H4
Ebersdorf [D] 18 E4
Eberstein [A] 74 C3
Eberswalde [D] 34 F1
Ebingen [D] 58 G3
Éboli [I] 120 F4
Ebrach [D] 46 F4
Ebreichsdorf [A] 62 F5
Ebreuil [F] 56 C6
Ebstorf [D] 18 G6
Eccleshall [GB] 10 D5
Eceabat [TR] 130 H5
Echallens [CH] 70 C1
Echallon [F] 68 H2
Echarri / Etxarri [E] 84 A3
Échevennoz [I] 70 D3
Echínos [GR] 130 E2
Échourgnac [F] 66 E3
Echternach [L] 44 F2
Écija [E] 102 B2
Ečka [YU] 154 G1
Eckartsberga [D] 34 B6
Eckernförde [D] 18 F1
Eckerö [FIN] 176 A5
Ecommoy [F] 42 B5
Ecouis [F] 28 C6
Ecsegfalva [H] 76 F2
Ecthe [D] 32 G4
Ecueillé [F] 54 G3
Ecury [F] 44 B4
Ed [S] 166 C4
Eda glasbruk [S] 166 D1
Edam [NL] 16 E4
Edane [S] 166 E2
Edderton [GB] 6 E4
Eddleston [GB] 8 E4
Ede [NL] 16 E5
Edebäck [S] 172 F6
Edefors [S] 184 C1
Edefors [S] 198 A2
Edelény [H] 64 F4
Edenbridge [GB] 14 E5
Edenderry [IRL] 2 E6
Edenkoben [D] 46 B5
Edersee [D] 32 E5
Édessa [GR] 128 F4
Edewecht [D] 18 C5
Edgeworthstown [IRL] 2 E5
Edinburgh [GB] 8 E3
Edincik [TR] 146 D4
Ediniţa [MD] 206 D3
Edirne [TR] 146 A2
Edland [N] 164 D1
Édolo [I] 72 B4
Edremit [TR] 144 C1
Edsbro [S] 168 E1
Edsbruk [S] 162 G1
Edsbyn [S] 174 C2

Edsele [S] 184 D1
Edsleskog [S] 166 D4
Edsvalla [S] 166 E2
Eeklo [B] 28 G1
Efendiköprüsü [TR] 144 G2
Eferding [A] 62 B4
Efkarpia [GR] 128 H3
Eforie [RO] 206 E6
Efpálio [GR] 132 F5
Efýra [GR] 136 C2
Egebæk [DK] 156 B3
Egeln [D] 34 B3
Egense [DK] 160 E4
Eger [H] 64 E5
Egerlövö [H] 64 F5
Egernsund [DK] 156 C4
Egersund [N] 164 B4
Egervár [H] 74 G2
Egestorf [D] 18 F5
Egg [A] 60 B6
Eggedal [N] 170 G5
Eggenburg [A] 62 E3
Eggenfelden [D] 60 G3
Eggesin [D] 20 E4
Eggum [N] 192 B4
Eghezée [B] 30 D5
Egiertowo [PL] 22 D3
Egilsstaðir [IS] 194 G5
Egletons [F] 68 A3
Eglingham [GB] 8 G5
Eglinton [GB] 2 F2
Egmond aan Zee [NL] 16 D3
Egna / Neumarkt [I] 72 D4
Egremont [GB] 8 D6
Egtved [DK] 156 C2
Eguzon [F] 54 G5
Egyek [H] 64 F6
Ehingen [D] 60 B3
Ehnen [L] 44 F3
Ehra–Lessien [D] 32 H2
Ehrenburg [D] 18 D6
Ehrenhausen [A] 74 D3
Ehrwald [A] 60 D6
Eibar [E] 82 H4
Eibenstock [D] 48 C2
Eibergen [NL] 16 G5
Eibiswald [A] 74 D3
Eich [D] 46 C4
Eichendorf [D] 60 G3
Eichstätt [D] 60 D2
Eidanger [N] 164 G3
Eide [N] 164 C3
Eide [N] 164 B4
Eide [N] 180 E2
Eidfjord [N] 170 D4
Eiði [DK] 160 B1
Eidsbugarden [N] 170 F1
Eidsdal [N] 180 E4
Eidsfoss [N] 164 G2
Eidslandet [N] 170 B3

Eidsøra [N] 180 F3
Eidsvåg [N] 180 F3
Eidsvoll [N] 172 C5
Eidsvoll verk [N] 172 C5
Eigenrieden [D] 32 G5
Eikelandsosen [N] 170 B4
Eiken [N] 164 C4
Eikenes [N] 180 B6
Eiksund [N] 180 C4
Eilenburg [D] 34 D5
Eilsleben [D] 34 A3
Eina [N] 172 B4
Einavoll [N] 172 B4
Einbeck [D] 32 F3
Eindhoven [NL] 30 E2
Einsiedeln [CH] 58 G6
Eisenach [D] 32 G6
Eisenberg [D] 34 B6
Eisenerz [A] 62 C6
Eisenhüttenstadt [D] 34 G3
Eisenkappel [A] 74 C4
Eisenstadt [A] 62 F5
Eisfeld [D] 46 G2
Eišiškės [LT] 24 H2
Eislingen [D] 60 B2
Eitorf [D] 30 H5
Eivissa [E] 104 C5
Ejby [DK] 156 D3
Ejea de los Caballeros [E] 84 C6
Ejstrupholm [DK] 156 C1
Ejulve [E] 90 E6
Ekáli [GR] 134 C6
Ekedalen [S] 166 F6
Ekenäs [S] 166 E4
Ekenäs / Tammisaari [FIN] 176 E6
Ekenässjön [S] 162 E3
Ekerö [S] 168 D3
Ekinli [TR] 146 H3
Ekshärad [S] 172 F5
Eksjö [S] 162 E2
Ekträsk [S] 190 H5
Ekzarh Antimovo [BG] 148 E4
Elaiochoria [GR] 130 B5
Elaiónas [GR] 132 G5
El Alcornocal [E] 96 B5
El Aljunzarejo [E] 104 C2
Elämäjärvi [FIN] 198 D6
Elantxobe [E] 82 H3
Elassóna [GR] 132 F1
El Astillero [E] 82 F3
Eláti [GR] 132 E2
Elátia [GR] 132 H4
Elatoú [GR] 132 F5
El Barraco [E] 88 E5
Elbasan [AL] 128 B3
El Berrón [E] 78 H3
Elbeuf [F] 26 H4

Elbigenalp [A] 72 B1
Elbingerode [D] 32 H4
Elbląg [PL] 22 F3
El Bodón [E] 86 H2
El Bonillo [E] 96 H5
El Bosque [E] 100 H4
Elburg [NL] 16 F4
Elburgo / Burgelu [E] 102 B4
El Burgo de Ebro [E] 90 E4
El Burgo de Osma [E] 90 A3
El Cabaco [E] 88 B4
el Campello [E] 104 E2
El Canal [E] 104 C6
El Carpio de Tajo [E] 96 E1
El Castillo de las Guardas [E] 94 G5
Elche / Elx [E] 104 D2
Elche de la Sierra [E] 104 B1
Elçili [TR] 146 B2
El Coronil [E] 100 H3
El Cubo de Tierra del Vino [E] 80 H5
El Cuervo [E] 100 G3
Elda [E] 104 D2
Eldalsosen [N] 170 C1
Eldena [D] 20 A5
Elefsína [GR] 134 B6
Elefthéri [GR] 132 G2
Eleftherochóri [GR] 128 E6
Eleftheroúpoli [GR] 130 D3
Eleja [LV] 200 D6
El Ejido [E] 102 F5
Elek [H] 76 G3
Elena [BG] 148 C4
El Escorial [E] 88 F5
El Espinar [E] 88 E4
Elgå [N] 182 D5
El Gargantón [E] 96 E3
El Garrobo [E] 94 G5
Elgg [CH] 58 G5
Elgin [GB] 6 E5
Elgol [GB] 6 B5
El Grado [E] 90 G3
el Grau / Grao [E] 98 F6
El Guijo [E] 96 C5
Elimäki [FIN] 178 C3
Elin Pelin [BG] 150 G5
Elisenwaara [RUS] 188 G6
Eliseyna [BG] 150 G4
Elizondo [E] 84 C3
Elizondo / Baztan [E] 82 H4
Ełk [PL] 24 D4
Elkhovo [BG] 148 E5
Ellenberg [D] 46 E6
Ellesmere [GB] 10 D5
Elling [DK] 160 E2
Ellingen [D] 46 G6
Ellon [GB] 6 G6
Ellös [S] 166 C6
Ellrich [D] 32 H4
Ellwangen [D] 46 E6
Elm [CH] 58 G6
Elmalı [TR] 142 H2
El Masnou [E] 92 A4
El Médano [E] 100 C5
El Minguillo [E] 96 G4
El Molar [E] 88 G5
El Molinillo [E] 96 E2
El Moral [E] 102 H2
Elmpt [D] 30 F3
Elmshorn [D] 18 F3
Elne [F] 92 G1
Elnesvågen [N] 180 E2
Élos [GR] 140 B5
Előszállás [H] 76 C3
Eloúnta [GR] 140 F4
el Palmar [E] 98 F5
El Pardo [E] 88 F5
El Paular [E] 88 F4
El Pedroso [E] 94 H5
El Perelló [E] 98 F5
El Perelló [E] 92 B5
Elphin [IRL] 2 D4
El Piñero [E] 80 H5
el Pinós / Pinoso [E] 104 D2
El Pito [E] 78 G3
el Pla de Santa Maria [E] 92 C4
el Pont de Suert [E] 84 F6
el Port / Sóller [E] 104 E4

el Port de la Selva [E] 92 G2
El Portil [E] 94 E6
el Prat de Llobregat [E] 92 E5
El Puente del Arzobispo [E] 96 D1
El Puerto de Santa Maria [E] 100 F4
El Real [E] 78 C2
El Real de San Vicente [E] 88 D6
El Recuenco [E] 90 B6
El Rocío [E] 94 F6
El Ronquillo [E] 94 G5
El Rubio [E] 102 B2
El Sabinar [E] 102 H2
El Saler [E] 98 E5
El Salobral [E] 98 B5
El Saucejo [E] 102 B3
Elsdorf [D] 30 G4
El Serrat [AND] 84 H6
Elsfleth [D] 18 D5
Elst [NL] 16 E5
Elsten [D] 18 C6
Elster [D] 34 D4
Elsterberg [D] 48 C2
Elsterwerda [D] 34 E5
El Tejar [E] 102 C3
Elten [D] 16 F6
El Tiemblo [E] 88 E5
Eltmann [D] 46 F3
El Toboso [E] 96 G3
El Tormillo [E] 90 G3
El Tumbalejo [E] 94 F5
Eltville [D] 46 B3
Elva [EST] 200 F3
Elvas [P] 86 F6
Elvbrua [N] 182 D6
El Vendrell [E] 92 D5
Elverum [N] 172 C3
Elvestad [N] 166 B2
El Villar de Arnedo [E] 84 A5
El Viso [E] 96 C5
El Viso del Alcor [E] 94 H6
Elx / Elche [E] 104 D2
Ely [GB] 14 F2
Elzach [D] 58 F2
Elze [D] 32 F3
Emådalen [S] 172 G2
Embessós [GR] 132 E3
Embleton [GB] 8 G5
Emboriós [GR] 134 G5
Emboriós [GR] 142 B3
Embrun [F] 108 D2
Embute [LV] 200 C6
Emden [D] 16 H2
Emecik [TR] 142 D3
Emet [TR] 144 F1
Emiralem [TR] 144 C3
Emlichheim [D] 16 G4
Emmaboda [S] 162 F5
Emmaljunga [S] 162 C6
Emmeloord [NL] 16 F3
Emmen [NL] 16 G3
Emmendingen [D] 58 E3
Emmerich [D] 16 F6
Emőd [H] 64 F5
Emona [BG] 148 G4
Empoli [I] 110 E5
Empónas [GR] 142 D5
Emporeió [GR] 142 C4
Empuriabrava [E] 92 G2
Empúria–Brava [E] 102 B5
Emsdetten [D] 16 H5
Emsfors [S] 162 G4
Emskirchen [D] 46 F5
Emstek [D] 18 C6
Emyvale [IRL] 2 F4
Enånger [S] 174 E1
Encamp [AND] 84 H6
Encinas de Abajo [E] 88 C3
Encinasola [E] 94 F3
Encs [H] 64 F4
Endelave By [DK] 156 D2
Enden [N] 180 H6
Endingen [D] 58 E2
Endröd [H] 76 F2
Enebakk [N] 166 C1
Enese [H] 62 H6
Enez [TR] 130 H3

Enfesta / Pontecesures [E] 78 B3
Enfield [GB] 14 E4
Enfield [IRL] 2 E6
Engelberg [CH] 70 F1
Engelhartszell [A] 62 A3
Engelia [N] 170 H4
Engeln [D] 18 D6
Engelskirchen [D] 30 H4
Engelsviken [N] 166 B3
Engen [D] 58 G3
Enger [D] 32 D2
Engerdal [N] 182 D6
Engerneset [N] 172 D1
Engesvang [DK] 160 C6
Enghien [B] 28 H3
Engjane [N] 180 F2
Englefontaine [F] 28 G4
Engstingen [D] 58 H2
Énguera [E] 98 E6
Enguídanos [E] 98 C3
Engure [LV] 200 D5
Enkhuizen [NL] 16 E3
Enklinge [FIN] 176 B5
Enköping [S] 168 C2
Enna [I] 126 E3
Ennezat [F] 68 D2
Ennis / Inis [IRL] 2 C6
Enniscorthy [IRL] 4 F4
Enniscrone [IRL] 2 C3
Enniskean [IRL] 4 C5
Enniskillen [GB] 2 E3
Ennistymon [IRL] 2 B5
Enns [A] 62 C4
Eno [FIN] 188 G2
Enonkoski [FIN] 188 E4
Enontekiö [FIN] 192 G4
Enschede [NL] 16 G5
Ensisheim [F] 58 D3
Entlebuch [CH] 58 E6
Entraygues–sur–Truyère [F] 68 B5
Entre Ambos–os–Rios [P] 80 C4
Entrevaux [F] 108 E4
Entrèves [I] 70 C3
Entroncamento [P] 86 D4
Enviken [S] 174 C4
Enying [H] 76 B2
Epannes [F] 54 D4
Epanomí [GR] 128 H5
Epe [D] 16 G5
Epe [NL] 16 F4
Épernay [F] 44 B3
Épernon [F] 42 E4
Épila [E] 90 D4
Épinal [F] 58 C2
Episcopía [I] 120 H5
Episkopí [GR] 140 C4
Epitálio [GR] 136 C2
Epône [F] 42 E3
Epoo / Ebbo [FIN] 178 B4
Eppan / Appiano [I] 72 D3
Eppingen [D] 46 C5
Epsom [GB] 14 E4
Eptachóri [GR] 128 D6
Eraclea [I] 72 F6
Eraclea–Mare [I] 72 F6
Eräjärvi [FIN] 176 G1
Erateiní [GR] 132 G5
Eratirá [GR] 128 E5
Erba [I] 70 G4
Erbach [D] 46 D4
Erbalunga [F] 114 C2
Erbendorf [D] 48 B4
Ercolano [I] 120 E3
Ercsi [H] 76 C2
Érd [H] 76 C1
Erdek [TR] 146 D4
Erdevik [YU] 154 F2
Erding [D] 60 E4
Eresós [GR] 134 G2
Erétria [GR] 134 C5
Erfde [D] 18 E2
Erftstadt [D] 30 G5
Erfurt [D] 32 H6
Ergama [TR] 144 D1
Ergili [TR] 146 D5
Ērgļi [LV] 200 E5
Ergoldsbach [D] 60 F3
Erice [I] 126 B2
Ericeira [P] 86 A4

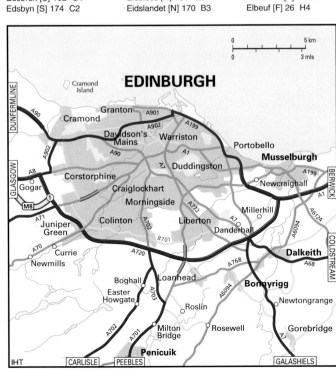

EDINBURGH

Cramond Island
DUNFERMLINE
A90
Granton
A901
Cramond
A902
Davidson's Mains
A199
Warriston
A90
A1
Portobello
Musselburgh
Duddingston
GLASGOW
A8
Gogar
A902
Corstorphine
M8
A71
A1
Craiglockhart
A199
Newcraighall
BERWICK
Juniper Green
Morningside
A772
Millerhill
A1
A6124
Colinton
Liberton
A702
A6094
Danderhall
COLDSTREAM
A68
Currie
B701
Newmills
A720
A768
Dalkeith
A68
Boghall
Loanhead
A703
A6094
Bonnyrigg
Easter Howgate
Newtongrange
Roslin
A702
Rosewell
A701
Gorebridge
Milton Bridge
A7
IHT
Penicuik
CARLISLE PEEBLES
GALASHIELS

Ericek [TR] 146 F4
Erikli [TR] 146 B4
Eriksberg [S] 190 F4
Erikslund [S] 184 D4
Eriksmåla [S] 162 E5
Eringsboda [S] 162 E6
Erkelenz [D] 30 F4
Erla [E] 84 C6
Erlangen [D] 46 G4
Erlenbach [D] 46 D4
Erlsbach [A] 72 E2
Ermelo [NL] 16 E4
Ermenonville [F] 42 G3
Ermidas–Aldeia [P] 94 C3
Ermióni [GR] 136 F3
Ermoúpolis [GR] 138 D2
Ermsleben [D] 34 B4
Erndtebrück [D] 32 D6
Ernée [F] 26 D6
Ernstbrunn [A] 62 F3
Erquy [F] 26 B4
Erratzu [E] 84 C3
Erro [E] 84 C3
Errogie [GB] 6 D5
Erronkari / Roncal [E] 84 C4
Ersekë [AL] 128 D5
Ersmark [S] 198 A6
Erstein [F] 44 H6
Eršy [RUS] 204 E5
Ertenvåg [N] 192 B6
Ertuğrul [TR] 144 D1
Ervenik [HR] 112 H5
Ervidel [P] 94 D3
Ervik [N] 180 B4
Ervy–le–Châtel [F] 44 A6
Erwitte [D] 32 D4
Erxleben [D] 34 B3
Erythrés [GR] 134 B6
Eržvilkas [LT] 202 E5
Esa / Yesa [E] 84 C4
Esbjerg [DK] 156 A2
Esbo / Espoo [FIN] 176 G5
Escalada [E] 82 E4
Escalaplano [I] 118 D6
Escalona [E] 88 E6
Escandón, Puerto de– [E]
    98 E2
Escároz / Ezkaroze [E] 84
    C4
Escatrón [E] 90 F5
Eschede [D] 32 G1
Eschenbach [D] 46 H4
Eschenburg–Eibelshausen
    [D] 32 D6
Eschenlohe [D] 60 D6
Eschershausen [D] 32 F3
Esch–sur–Alzette [L] 44 E3
Esch–sur–Sûre [L] 44 E2
Eschwege [D] 32 G5
Eschweiler [D] 30 F4
Escombreras [E] 104 C4
Escos [F] 84 D2
Es Cubells [E] 104 C5
Escúllar [E] 102 F4
Eşen [TR] 142 G4
Esence [TR] 146 E4
Esens [D] 18 C3
Esenyurt [TR] 146 E3
es Figueral [E] 104 C5
Esguevillas de Esgueva [E]
    88 F1
Esher [GB] 14 E4
Eskdalemuir [GB] 8 E5
Eskelhem [S] 168 F4
Eskiçine [TR] 142 D1
Eskifjörður [IS] 194 G5
Eskihisar [TR] 142 D2
Eskilstuna [S] 168 B3
Eskin [TR] 144 F3
Eskişehir [TR] 146 H5
Eslohe [D] 32 D5
Eslöv [S] 158 C2
Eşme [TR] 144 F4
Es Mercadal [E] 104 H4
Espa [N] 172 C4
Espalion [F] 68 B5
Esparreguera [E] 92 D4
Espedal [N] 170 G1
Espejo [E] 102 C2
Espeland [N] 170 B4
Espelette [F] 84 C2
Espeli [N] 164 D4

Espelkamp [D] 32 E2
Espera [E] 100 G3
Espiel [E] 96 C5
Espinama [E] 82 D3
Espinho [P] 80 B4
Espinosa de los Monteros
    [E] 82 E4
Espírito Santo [P] 94 D4
Esplantas [F] 68 D5
Espoo / Esbo [FIN] 176 G5
Es Port d'Alcúdia [E] 104
    F4
Esposende [P] 78 A6
Espot [E] 84 G6
Esposende [P] 78 A6
Esse / Ähtävä [FIN] 198 C6
Essen [D] 30 H3
Essen [D] 18 C6
Essenbach [D] 60 F3
Esslingen [D] 58 H1
Essunga [S] 166 D6
Estada [E] 90 G3
Estagel [F] 106 C6
Estaing [F] 68 B5
Estaires [F] 28 F3
Estanyol [E] 104 E5
Estarreja [P] 80 B5
Estavayer–le–Lac [CH] 58
    C6
Este [I] 110 G1
Estella / Lizarra [E] 84 A4
Estellenchs [E] 104 D5
Estepa [E] 102 B3
Estepona [E] 100 H5
Esternay [F] 42 H4
Esterri d'Àneu [E] 84 G5
Esterwegen [D] 18 C5
Estissac [F] 44 A6
Estói [P] 94 C6
Estoril [P] 86 A5
Estrées–St–Denis [F] 28 E6
Estremoz [P] 86 E6
Esztergom [H] 64 C5
Étables–sur–Mer [F] 26 B4
Etain [F] 44 E3
Etalle [B] 44 E2
Étampes [F] 42 F4
Étang–sur–Arroux [F] 56 F4
Etaples [F] 28 D3
Eteläinen [FIN] 176 G2
Etili [TR] 146 B5
Etne [N] 164 B1
Etrepagny [F] 28 C6
Etretat [F] 26 G2
Etropole [BG] 150 G4
Ettelbruck [L] 44 F2
Ettenheim [D] 58 E2
Ettlingen [D] 46 B6
Etxarri / Echarri [E] 84 A3
Eu [F] 28 C4
Eugénie–les–Bains [F] 66
    C6
Eupen [B] 30 F5
Eura [FIN] 176 D2
Eurajoki [FIN] 176 C2
Euratsfeld [A] 62 C5
Europoort [NL] 16 C5
Euskirchen [D] 30 G5
Eussenhausen [D] 46 F2
Eutin [D] 18 G3
Eutzsch [D] 34 D4
Evanger [N] 170 C3
Evaux–les–Bains [F] 56 B6
Évdilos [GR] 138 G1
Evendorf [D] 18 F5
Evenskjoer [N] 192 D4
Everöd [S] 158 D2
Evesham [GB] 12 H2
Evian–les–Bains [F] 70 C2
Evijärvi [FIN] 186 D1
Evinochóri [GR] 132 E5
Evisa [F] 114 A4
Evje [N] 164 D4
Evolène [CH] 70 D3
Évora [P] 94 D1
Évora Monte [P] 86 D6
Evran [F] 26 C5
Evreux [F] 42 D2
Evron [F] 26 E6
Evry [F] 42 F4
Évzonoi [GR] 128 G3
Ewelme [GB] 14 D3
Exaplátanos [GR] 128 F3

Éxarhos [GR] 132 H5
Excideuil [F] 66 G2
Exeter [GB] 12 E4
Exford [GB] 12 E3
Exmes [F] 26 G5
Exmouth [GB] 12 E5
Exochí [GR] 130 C2
Exohí [GR] 128 G5
Extertal [D] 32 E3
Eydehavn [N] 164 F5
Eyemouth [GB] 8 F4
Eyguières [F] 106 H4
Eygurande [F] 68 B2
Eylie [F] 84 G5
Eymet [F] 66 E4
Eymoutiers [F] 66 H2
Eynsford [GB] 14 E4
Eyrarbakki [IS] 194 B5
Eythorne [GB] 14 G5
Ezcaray [E] 82 F6
Ezere [LV] 200 C6
Ezermuiža [LV] 200 C4
Ezernieki [LV] 200 G6
Ezernijeki [LV] 200 D6
Ezine [TR] 130 H6
Ezkaroze / Escároz [E]
    84 C4

F

Faaborg [DK] 156 D4
Faak [A] 74 A3
Fåberg [N] 172 B2
Fabero [E] 78 F4
Fabriano [I] 116 B1
Facture [F] 66 C3
Faenza [I] 110 G4
Faeto [I] 120 F2
Fafe [P] 80 C3
Făgăraş [RO] 206 C5
Fågelfors [S] 162 F4
Fågelsjö [S] 182 G6
Fågelsundet [S] 174 F4
Fagerås [S] 166 E2
Fagerhult [S] 162 F4
Fagernes [N] 170 G3
Fagernes [N] 192 E2
Fagersanna [S] 166 F5
Fagersta [S] 168 A1
Fagerstrand [N] 166 B1
Fäggeby [S] 174 D5
Faglavik [S] 162 B1
Fagurhólsmyri [IS] 194 E6
Faial [P] 100 B3
Faido [CH] 70 F2
Fai della Paganella [I] 72
    C4
Fair Head [GB] 2 G2
Fakenham [GB] 14 G1
Fakse [DK] 156 G4
Fakse Ladeplads [DK] 156
    G4
Falaise [F] 26 F4
Falatádos [GR] 138 E2
Falcade [I] 72 E4
Falconara Marittima [I] 112
    C6
Falcone [I] 124 A7
Faldsled [DK] 156 D4
Falerna [I] 124 D5
Falerna Marina [I] 124 D5
Falerum [S] 162 G1
Faliráki [GR] 142 E4
Falkenberg [D] 34 E5
Falkenberg [S] 160 H4
Falkenstein [D] 48 C2
Falkenstein [D] 48 C6
Falkirk [GB] 8 E3
Falköping [S] 166 E6
Fallersleben [D] 32 H2
Fallet [N] 172 C5
Fällfors [S] 198 A4
Fallingbostel [D] 18 F6
Falmouth [GB] 12 C5
Falset [E] 90 H6
Falsterbo [S] 156 H3
Falstone [GB] 8 F5
Fălticeni [RO] 206 C4
Falun [S] 174 C4
Fámjin [DK] 160 A3

Fana [N] 170 B4
Fanári [GR] 132 F2
Fanári [GR] 130 F3
Fanjeaux [F] 106 B4
Fannrem [N] 180 H1
Fano [I] 112 C5
Fanós [GR] 128 G3
Fântânele [RO] 148 B2
Fara Novarese [I] 70 F4
Fårbo [S] 162 G3
Farébersviller [F] 44 G4
Fareham [GB] 12 H5
Färgelanda [S] 166 C5
Färila [S] 184 C6
Faringdon [GB] 12 H3
Farini [I] 110 C2
Färjestaden [S] 162 G5
Farkadhónas [GR] 132 F2
Farkasgyepü [H] 74 H2
Farkaždin [YU] 154 G1
Fârliug [RO] 76 H6
Färlöv [S] 158 D1
Färna [S] 168 B2
Färnäs [S] 172 G3
Farnborough [GB] 14 D4
Farnese [I] 114 G3
Farnham [GB] 14 D4
Faro [P] 94 D6
Fårösund [S] 168 H3
Farranfore [IRL] 4 B4
Fársala [GR] 132 G3
Farsø [DK] 160 D4
Farstad [N] 180 E2
Farsund [N] 164 C5
Farum [DK] 156 G2
Fårvang [DK] 160 D6
Fasano [I] 122 E3
Fasgar [E] 78 G5
Fáskruðsfjörður [IS] 194 G5
Fasso Umbertiano [I] 110
    G2
Faster [DK] 156 B1
Fasterholt [DK] 156 C1
Fatež [RUS] 204 E6
Fátima [P] 86 C3
Fättjaur [S] 190 E3
Faucogney–et–la–Mer [F]
    58 C3
Faulensee [CH] 70 E1
Faulquemont [F] 44 F4
Fauske [N] 192 C6
Fauville [F] 26 H2
Favara [E] 98 E5
Favara [I] 126 D4
Faverges [F] 70 B3
Faverney [F] 58 B3
Faversham [GB] 14 F5
Favone [F] 114 B5
Fawley [GB] 12 H5

Fayence [F] 108 D4
Fayet [F] 106 D3
Fayl–Billot [F] 58 A3
Feakle [IRL] 2 C6
Fearnan [GB] 8 E1
Fearnmore [GB] 6 C4
Fécamp [F] 26 G2
Feda [N] 164 C5
Fegen [S] 162 B4
Feggeklit [DK] 160 C4
Fegyvernek [H] 76 F1
Fehrbellin [D] 34 D1
Fehring [A] 74 E2
Feios [N] 170 D2
Feiring [N] 172 C4
Feketić [YU] 76 D6
Feld [A] 72 H3
Feldafing [D] 60 D5
Feldbach [A] 74 E2
Feldberg [D] 58 F3
Feldberg [D] 20 D5
Feldkirch [A] 58 H5
Feldkirchen [A] 74 B3
Feldkirchen [D] 60 E5
Feldsted [DK] 156 C4
Felechosa [E] 82 B3
Felguieras [P] 80 C3
Felixstowe [GB] 14 G3
Fellbach [D] 58 H1
Felletin [F] 68 B1
Fellingsbro [S] 168 A3
Felnac [RO] 76 G4
Felsőszentiván [H] 76 C4
Felsőtárkány [H] 64 E5
Feltre [I] 72 E5
Femundsenden [N] 182 D6
Fenagh [IRL] 2 E4
Fene [E] 78 D2
Fenékpuszta [H] 74 G3
Fener [I] 72 E5
Fenestrelle [I] 70 C5
Fénétrange [F] 44 G5
Feneu [F] 40 H6
Fénis [I] 70 D3
Fenit [IRL] 4 B3
Feochaig [GB] 2 H2
Feolin Ferry [GB] 8 B2
Feragen [N] 182 D4
Ferbane [IRL] 2 D5
Ferdinandshof [D] 20 E4
Fère–Champenoise [F] 44
    B4
Fère–en–Tardenois [F] 44
    A3
Ferentino [I] 116 B6
Féres [GR] 130 H3
Feria [E] 94 G3

Feričanci [HR] 154 D1
Ferla [I] 126 G5
Ferlach [A] 74 B3
Ferleiten [A] 72 G1
Fermignano [I] 110 H6
Fermo [I] 116 C2
Fermoselle [E] 80 G5
Fermoy [IRL] 4 D4
Fernancaballero [E] 96 E4
Fernán Núñez [E] 102 C2
Ferns [IRL] 4 F4
Ferovac [HR] 154 C1
Ferradina [I] 122 D4
Ferrara [I] 110 G2
Ferreira [E] 78 E2
Ferreira do Alentejo [P] 94
    D3
Ferreira do Zêzere [P] 86
    D3
Ferreries [E] 104 G4
Ferreruela de Huerva [E] 90
    D5
Ferrette [F] 58 D4
Ferriere [I] 110 C3
Ferrières [F] 42 G6
Ferrières–sur–Sichon [F] 68
    D2
Ferring [DK] 160 B5
Ferrol [E] 78 D1
Ferryhill [GB] 10 F2
Fertőd [H] 62 G6
Fertőrákos [H] 62 F6
Fertőszentmiklós [H] 62 G6
Festøy [N] 180 D4
Festvåg [N] 192 B6
Fethard [IRL] 4 E4
Fethard [IRL] 4 F5
Fethiye [TR] 142 G4
Fetsund [N] 166 C1
Fettercairn [GB] 8 F1
Feucht [D] 46 G5
Feuchtwangen [D] 46 F6
Feurs [F] 68 E2
Fevåg [N] 190 B6
Fevik [N] 164 E5
Fiamignano [I] 116 B4
Fibiş [RO] 76 G5
Ficulle [I] 114 H3
Fiddleton [GB] 8 E5
Fidenza [I] 110 D2
Fidje [N] 164 E4
Fieberbrunn [A] 60 F6
Fier [AL] 128 A4
Fiera di Primiero [I] 72 E4
Fiesch [CH] 70 E2
Fiésole [I] 110 F5
Figari [F] 114 B6
Figeac [F] 66 H5
Figeholm [S] 162 G3
Figgjo [N] 164 B3

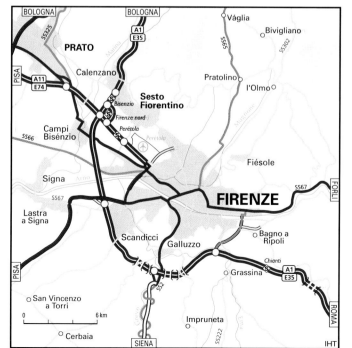

Figline Valdarno [I] 110 F6
Figueira da Foz [P] 80 A6
Figueira de Castelo Rodrigo [P] 80 E6
Figueiró dos Vinhos [P] 86 D3
Figueres [E] 92 G2
Filáki [GR] 132 G3
Fiľakovo [SK] 64 D4
Filevo [BG] 148 C6
Filey [GB] 10 G3
Filí [GR] 134 C6
Filia [GR] 134 G2
Filiaşi [RO] 206 B6
Filiátes [GR] 132 C2
Filiatrá [GR] 136 C3
Filippiáda [GR] 132 D3
Filipstad [S] 166 F2
Filiriá [GR] 128 G4
Fillan [N] 190 A6
Fillefjell Pass [N] 170 E2
Filótas [GR] 128 F4
Filóti [GR] 138 F3
Filottrano [I] 116 C1
Filskov [DK] 156 B2
Filzmoos [A] 72 H1
Finale Emília [I] 110 F2
Finale Ligure [I] 108 H3
Fiñana [E] 102 F4
Finby / Särkisalo [FIN] 176 E5
Finiq [AL] 132 B1
Finisterre / Fisterra [E] 78 A2
Finja [S] 158 C1
Finnbo [S] 174 C4
Finnbyen [N] 192 B4
Finnea [IRL] 2 E5
Finneid [N] 192 C6
Finneidfjord [N] 190 D2
Finnentrop [D] 32 C5
Finnsnes [N] 192 D3
Finow [D] 34 E1
Finsand [N] 170 H4
Finspång [S] 168 A5
Finsterwalde [D] 34 E5
Finstown [GB] 6 F2
Finström [FIN] 176 A5
Fintona [GB] 2 F3
Fionnphort [GB] 8 B1
Fiorenzuola d'Arda [I] 110 C2
Fira / Thíra [GR] 138 F5
Firenze [I] 110 F5
Firenzuola [I] 110 F4
Firkeel [IRL] 4 A5
Firlej [PL] 38 E4
Firminy [F] 68 E3
Fiscal [E] 84 E5
Fischamend [A] 62 F5
Fischbach [D] 46 H4
Fischbeck [D] 34 C2
Fischen [D] 60 B6
Fishbourne [GB] 12 H5
Fishguard [GB] 4 H6
Fiskárdo [GR] 132 C5
Fiskebäckskil [S] 166 C6
Fiskebøl [N] 192 C4
Fiskö [FIN] 176 C4
Fismes [F] 44 A3
Fissíni [GR] 130 F6
Fisterra / Finisterre [E] 78 A2
Fitero [E] 84 A6
Fíties [GR] 132 E4
Fitjar [N] 170 A5
Fiuggi [I] 116 B6
Fiumefreddo Bruzio [I] 124 D4
Fiumefreddo di Sicilia [I] 124 B8
Fiumicíno [I] 114 H6
Fivemiletown [GB] 2 F3
Fivizzano [I] 110 D4
Fjæra [N] 170 C5
Fjærland [N] 170 D1
Fjälkinge [S] 158 D2
Fjällasen [S] 192 F5
Fjällbacka [S] 166 C5
Fjällnäs [S] 182 D4
Fjaltring [DK] 160 B5
Fjand Gårde [DK] 160 B5

Fjäras [S] 160 H3
Fjellerup [DK] 160 E5
Fjellsrud [N] 166 C1
Fjelstrup [DK] 156 C3
Fjerritslev [DK] 160 D3
Fjone [N] 164 E3
Fjugesta [S] 166 G3
Flå [N] 170 G4
Fladdabister [GB] 6 G4
Fladungen [D] 46 F2
Flaine [F] 70 C3
Flakk [N] 182 B1
Flåm [N] 170 D3
Flamborough [GB] 10 H3
Flambourári [GR] 132 D1
Flärke [S] 184 G1
Flatabø [N] 170 C4
Flateby [N] 166 C1
Flåten [N] 192 F1
Flateyri [IS] 194 C1
Flatmark [N] 180 F4
Flatråker [N] 170 B5
Flattnitz [A] 74 B2
Flatval [N] 190 A6
Flavenskjold [DK] 160 E3
Flavigny-sur-Moselle [F] 44 E5
Fleet [GB] 14 D4
Fleetwood [GB] 10 D3
Flekke [N] 170 B1
Flekkefjord [N] 164 C5
Flen [S] 168 C4
Flensburg [D] 156 C5
Flers [F] 26 E4
Flesberg [N] 164 G1
Flesnes [N] 192 C3
Fleurance [F] 84 G2
Fleuré [F] 54 F4
Fleurier [CH] 58 C6
Fleurus [B] 30 C5
Fleury [F] 28 C6
Flims [CH] 70 G1
Flims Waldhaus [CH] 70 G1
Flins [F] 42 F3
Flint [GB] 10 D4
Flisa [N] 172 D4
Fliseryd [S] 162 G4
Flix [E] 90 H5
Flize [F] 44 C2
Floby [S] 162 C1
Floda [S] 160 H2
Flogned [S] 166 D1
Flogny-la-Chapelle [F] 56 F1
Flöha [D] 48 D1
Florac [F] 68 D6
Florange [F] 44 E3
Florennes [B] 30 C5
Florenville [B] 44 D2
Floreşti [MD] 206 D4
Florídia [I] 126 G5
Flórina [GR] 128 E4
Florø [N] 180 B5
Florstadt [D] 46 D2
Florvåg [N] 170 A3
Flötningen [S] 182 D6
Fluberg [N] 170 H3
Flüelen [CH] 58 F6
Flumeri [I] 120 F2
Flumet [F] 70 B3
Fluminimaggiore [I] 118 B6
Flums [CH] 58 H6
Foča [BIH] 152 D2
Foça [TR] 144 B4
Fockbek [D] 18 F2
Focşani [RO] 206 D5
Fódele [GR] 140 E4
Foggia [I] 120 G1
Föglö [FIN] 168 H1
Fohnsdorf [A] 74 C2
Foiano di Chiana [I] 114 G1
Foinikoús [GR] 136 D4
Foix [F] 84 H5
Fojnica [BIH] 152 D2
Földeák [H] 76 F4
Foldereid [N] 190 C4
Földes [H] 76 G1
Foldingbro [DK] 156 B3
Foleá [GR] 130 D4
Folégandros [GR] 138 E4

Folelli [F] 114 C3
Folgaria [I] 72 C5
Folgarida [I] 72 C4
Folgoso [E] 78 E4
Foligno [I] 116 A2
Folkärna [S] 174 D5
Folkestad [N] 180 C4
Folkestone [GB] 14 F5
Follafoss [N] 190 C5
Folldal [N] 180 H5
Föllinge [S] 190 E6
Follónica [I] 114 E2
Folmava [CZ] 48 D5
Fölsbyn [S] 166 D2
Fondamente [F] 106 D3
Fondi [I] 120 C1
Fondo [I] 72 C3
Fonfría [E] 80 G4
Fonfría [E] 90 D5
Fonni [I] 118 D5
Fontainebleau [F] 42 G5
Fontaine-de-Vaucluse [F] 106 H3
Fontaine-Française [F] 56 H3
Fontaine-le-Dun [F] 26 H2
Fontanellato [I] 110 D2
Fontanelle [I] 72 F5
Fontanosas [E] 96 D4
Fontecha [E] 82 G5
Fontenay-le-Comte [F] 54 C4
Fontenay-Trésigny [F] 42 G4
Fontevraud-l'Abbaye [F] 54 E2
Font-Romeu [F] 92 E1
Fontstown [IRL] 4 F3
Fontvieille [F] 106 G4
Fonyód [H] 74 H3
Fonzaso [I] 72 E5
Fóppolo [I] 70 H3
Föra [S] 162 G4
Forbach [D] 58 F1
Forbach [F] 44 G4
Forcalquier [F] 108 C3
Forcarei [E] 78 C4
Forchheim [D] 46 G4

Ford [GB] 8 C2
Førde [N] 164 B1
Førde [N] 180 C6
Fordingbridge [GB] 12 G4
Fordongianus [I] 118 C5
Forenza [I] 120 H3
Forfar [GB] 8 F2
Forges-les-Eaux [F] 28 C5
Forio [I] 120 D3
Førland [N] 164 C5
Forlì [I] 110 G4
Forlì del Sánnio [I] 116 D6
Forlimpopoli [I] 110 G4
Formazza [I] 70 F2
Formby [GB] 10 D3
Formerie [F] 28 D5
Formia [I] 120 C2
Formigine [I] 110 E3
Formiguères [F] 92 E1
Formofoss [N] 190 C5
Fornaci di Barga [I] 110 D4
Fornalutx [E] 104 E4
Fornells [E] 104 H4
Forni Avoltri [I] 72 F3
Forni di Sopra [I] 72 F4
Forni di Sotto [I] 72 F4
Forno Alpi Graie [I] 70 C5
Forno di Zoldo [I] 72 E4
Fornos de Algodres [P] 80 D6
Fornovo di Taro [I] 110 D3
Forøy [N] 190 D1
Forráskút [H] 76 E4
Forres [GB] 6 E5
Fors [S] 174 D5
Fors [S] 166 D6
Forsbacka [S] 174 E4
Forsby / Koskenkylä [FIN] 178 B4
Forserum [S] 162 D2
Forshaga [S] 166 F2
Forsheda [S] 162 C4
Forshem [S] 166 E5
Forsmark [S] 174 F5
Forsmark [S] 190 F3
Forsmo [S] 184 E2
Forsnäs [S] 190 G2
Forsnes [N] 180 F1

Forssa [FIN] 176 F3
Forst [D] 34 G4
Fort Augustus [GB] 6 D5
Forte dei Marmi [I] 110 D5
Forte di Bibbiona [I] 114 E1
Forth [D] 46 G5
Fort-Mahon-Plage [F] 28 D3
Fortrose [GB] 6 E4
Fortuna [E] 104 C2
Fortuneswell [GB] 12 F5
Fortun [N] 170 E1
Forvik [N] 190 D3
Fos [F] 84 F5
Fossano [I] 108 G2
Fossbakken [N] 192 D3
Fosses [B] 30 C5
Fossombrone [I] 112 B6
Fos-sur-Mer [F] 106 G5
Foucarmont [F] 28 C4
Fouesnant [F] 40 B3
Fougères [F] 26 D5
Fougerolles [F] 58 C3
Foulain [F] 56 H2
Fouras [F] 54 C5
Fourcès [F] 66 D6
Fourfourás [GR] 140 D5
Foúrka [GR] 128 D6
Fourmies [F] 28 G5
Fournels [F] 68 C5
Fournés [GR] 140 C4
Foúrnoi [GR] 138 H1
Fourquet [F] 66 F6
Fours [F] 56 E4
Foústani [GR] 128 G3
Fowey [GB] 12 C5
Fownhope [GB] 12 G2
Foxford [IRL] 2 C3
Foynes [IRL] 4 C3
Foz [E] 78 E2
Foz do Arelho [P] 86 B3
Foz Giraldo [P] 86 E3
Frabosa Soprana [I] 108 G3
Fraga [E] 90 G5
Fraize [F] 58 D2
Framley [DK] 156 D1

Framlingham [GB] 14 G3
Frammersbach [D] 46 D3
Frammestad [S] 166 D6
Frampol [PL] 52 F2
Francardo [F] 114 B3
Francavilla al Mare [I] 116 D4
Francavilla di Sicilia [I] 124 A8
Francavilla Fontana [I] 122 F4
Francelos [P] 80 B4
Francofonte [I] 126 G4
Frändefors [S] 166 D5
Franeker [NL] 16 F2
Frangísta [GR] 132 E4
Frangkokástelo [GR] 140 C5
Frangy [F] 70 A2
Frankenberg [D] 32 E5
Frankenberg [D] 48 D1
Frankenburg [A] 60 H4
Frankenmarkt [A] 60 H5
Frankenthal [D] 46 B4
Frankfurt (Oder) [D] 34 G3
Frankfurt am Main [D] 46 C3
Fränsta [S] 184 D4
Františkovy Lázné [CZ] 48 C3
Franzburg [D] 20 C3
Franz Josephs-Höhe [A] 72 F2
Frascati [I] 116 A6
Frasdorf [D] 60 F5
Fraserburgh [GB] 6 G5
Frashër [AL] 128 C5
Frasno, Puerto de– [E] 90 D4
Fratel [P] 86 E4
Fratte Polesine [I] 110 G2
Frauenau [D] 60 H2
Frauenfeld [CH] 58 G4
Frauenstein [D] 48 E1
Frayssinet [F] 66 G4
Frechen [D] 30 G4
Frechilla [E] 82 C6
Freckenhorst [D] 32 C3
Fredensborg [DK] 156 G2
Fredericia [DK] 156 C2

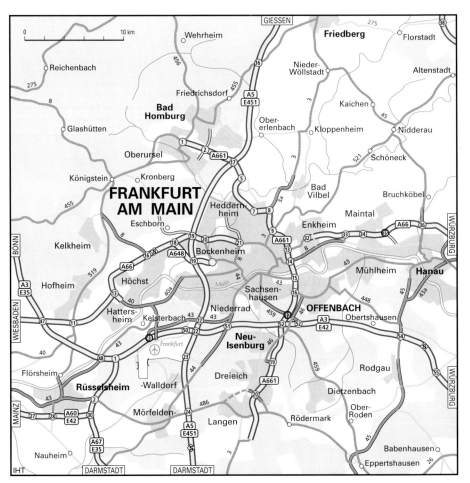

Frederiks [DK] 160 C5
Frederiksberg [DK] 156 F3
Frederikshavn [DK] 160 E3
Frederikssund [DK] 156 G2
Frederiksværk [DK] 156 G2
Fredrika [S] 190 G5
Fredriksberg [S] 172 G5
Fredrikstad [N] 166 B3
Fregenal de la Sierra [E] 94 G3
Fregene [I] 114 H5
Freiberg [D] 48 E1
Freiburg [D] 18 E3
Freiburg im Breisgau [D] 58 E3
Freiensteinau [D] 46 D2
Freihung [D] 48 B5
Freilassing [D] 60 G5
Freising [D] 60 E3
Freistadt [A] 62 C3
Freital [D] 48 E1
Freixedas [P] 80 E6
Freixianda [P] 86 D3
Freixo de Espada à Cinta [P] 80 F5
Frejev [DK] 160 D4
Fréjus [F] 108 D5
Frenchpark [IRL] 2 D4
Frenštát pod Radhoštěm [CZ] 50 E5
Freren [D] 32 C1
Freshford [IRL] 4 E4
Freshwater [GB] 12 H5
Fresnay-sur-Sarthe [F] 26 F6
Fresnes [F] 28 F4
Fresnes [F] 58 B3
Fresnes-en-Woëvre [F] 44 E4
Fresno Alhándiga [E] 88 C4
Fresno de la Ribera [E] 88 D1
Fréteval [F] 42 D6
Fretzdorf [D] 20 C6
Freudenberg [D] 46 D4
Freudenberg [D] 32 C6
Freudenstadt [D] 58 F2
Frévent [F] 28 E3
Freyenstein [D] 20 B5
Freyming Merlebach [F] 44 F4
Freystadt [D] 46 G6
Freyung [D] 60 H2
Fri [GR] 140 G3
Fribourg [CH] 58 D6
Frick [CH] 58 E4
Fridafors [S] 162 D6
Fridingen [D] 58 G3
Friedberg [A] 74 E1
Friedberg [D] 60 D3
Friedberg [D] 46 C2
Friedeburg [D] 18 C4
Friedersdorf [D] 34 F3
Friedewald [D] 32 F6
Friedland [D] 32 F5
Friedland [D] 20 D4
Friedland [D] 34 F3
Friedrichroda [D] 46 F1
Friedrichshafen [D] 58 H4
Friedrichskoog [D] 18 E3
Friedrichsort [D] 18 G2
Friedrichstadt [D] 18 E2
Friesach [A] 74 B2
Friesack [D] 34 D1
Friesoythe [D] 18 C5
Friggesund [S] 184 D6
Frihetsli [N] 192 E3
Frillesås [S] 160 H3
Frinton-on-Sea [GB] 14 G4
Friol [E] 78 D3
Fristad [S] 162 B2
Fritsla [S] 162 B2
Fritzlar [D] 32 E5
Frödinge [S] 162 F2
Frodsham [GB] 10 D4
Frohburg [D] 34 C6
Frohnleiten [A] 74 D1
Froissy [F] 28 D5
Frombork [PL] 22 F2

Frome [GB] 12 G4
Fromental [F] 26 F5
Frómista [E] 82 D5
Fronsac [F] 84 F4
Fronteira [P] 86 E5
Frontenhausen [D] 60 F3
Frontera [E] 100 A6
Frontignan [F] 106 E4
Fronton [F] 84 H2
Fröseke [S] 162 F4
Frosinone [I] 116 C6
Frosolone [I] 120 E1
Frøstrup [DK] 160 C3
Frøvik [S] 166 H2
Fruges [F] 28 E3
Frutigen [CH] 70 D1
Frýdek-Místek [CZ] 50 F5
Frýdlant [CZ] 48 G1
Frýdlant nad Ostravicí [CZ] 50 F5
Frygnowo [PL] 22 G5
Frymburk [CZ] 62 B3
Fryšták [CZ] 50 D6
Frysztak [PL] 52 D4
Frýýdlant [CZ] 48 G1
Ftéri [GR] 132 F6
Fubine [I] 70 E6
Fucécchio [I] 110 E5
Fuencaliente [E] 96 D5
Fuencarral [E] 88 F5
Fuendejalón [E] 90 D3
Fuendetodos [E] 90 E4
Fuengirola [E] 102 B5
Fuenlabrada de los Montes [E] 96 C3
Fuenmayor [E] 82 G6
Fuensalida [E] 96 E1
Fuente Álamo [E] 98 C6
Fuente Álamo de Murcia [E] 104 C4
Fuentecén [E] 88 G2
Fuente Dé [E] 82 D3
Fuente de Cantos [E] 94 G3
Fuente del Arco [E] 94 H4
Fuente del Maestre [E] 94 G3
Fuente de Santa Cruz [E] 88 E3
Fuente el Fresno [E] 96 F3
Fuente el Sauz [E] 88 G5
Fuente el Sol [E] 88 D3
Fuenteguinaldo [E] 86 H2
Fuentelcésped [E] 88 G2
Fuentelespino de Haro [E] 96 H3
Fuentelespino de Moya [E] 98 D3
Fuentemilanos [E] 88 F4
Fuente Obejuna [E] 96 B5
Fuente Palmera [E] 102 B1
Fuentepinilla [E] 90 B3
Fuenterrabía / Hondarribia [E] 84 B2
Fuentes [E] 98 C2
Fuentesaúco [E] 80 H6
Fuentes de Andalucia [E] 102 A2
Fuentes de Ayódar [E] 98 F3
Fuentes de Ebro [E] 90 E4
Fuentes de Jiloca [E] 90 D4
Fuentes de Oñoro [E] 86 H2
Fuentes de Ropel [E] 82 A5
Fuerte del Rey [E] 102 E2
Fügen [A] 72 E1
Fuglebjerg [DK] 156 F3
Fuhrberg [D] 32 G1
Fulda [D] 46 E2
Fulnek [CZ] 50 E5
Fülöpszállás [H] 76 C3
Fulpmes [A] 72 D1
Fulunäs [S] 172 E2
Fumay [F] 30 C6
Fumel [F] 66 F5
Funäsdalen [S] 182 E4
Funchal [P] 100 B3
Fundão [P] 86 F2
Fundres [I] 72 E2
Furadouro [P] 80 B4
Furculeşti [RO] 148 B2

Furnace [GB] 8 C2
Furnes (Veurne) [B] 28 F1
Fürstenau [D] 32 C1
Fürstenberg [D] 20 D5
Fürstenfeld [A] 74 E2
Fürstenfeldbruck [D] 60 D4
Fürstenwalde [D] 34 F2
Fürstenwerder [D] 20 D5
Fürstenzell [D] 60 H3
Furta [H] 76 G2
Fürth [D] 46 G5
Furth im Wald [D] 48 D6
Furtwangen [D] 58 F3
Furuby [S] 162 E4
Furudal [S] 172 H2
Furuflaten [N] 192 E2
Furusund [S] 168 F2
Furuvik [S] 174 E4
Fusa [N] 170 B4
Fuscaldo [I] 124 D4
Fusch [A] 72 G1
Fushë Arrëz [AL] 128 B1
Fushë-Krujë [AL] 128 B2
Fushë-Kuqe [AL] 128 B2
Fushë Muhurr [AL] 128 C2
Fusio [CH] 70 F2
Füssen [D] 60 C6
Futog [YU] 154 F1
Futrikelv [N] 192 E2
Füzesabony [H] 64 E5
Füzesgyarmat [H] 76 G2
Fuzeta [P] 94 D6
Fyláki [GR] 130 H1
Fynshav [DK] 156 D4
Fyresdal [N] 164 E3

G

Gabarret [F] 66 D6
Gabčíkovo [SK] 62 H5
Gabicce Mare [I] 112 B5
Gąbin [PL] 36 H2
Gabrovo [BG] 148 C4
Gacé [F] 26 G5
Gacko [BIH] 152 D3
Gäddede [S] 190 E5
Gadebusch [D] 18 H4
Gadjač [UA] 206 G2
Gadna [H] 64 F4
Gádor [E] 102 G5
Gadžin Han [YU] 150 D4
Gaël [F] 26 B5
Găeşti [RO] 206 C6
Gaeta [I] 120 C2
Gagarin [RUS] 204 E4
Gaggenau [D] 46 B6
Gagliano Castelferrato [I] 126 F3
Gagliano del Capo [I] 122 G6
Gagnef [S] 172 H4
Gaildorf [D] 46 E6
Gaillac [F] 106 B2
Gaillimh / Galway [IRL] 2 C5
Gaillon [F] 28 C6
Gainsborough [GB] 10 F5
Gáïo [GR] 132 B3
Gairloch [GB] 6 C4
Gaj [YU] 154 H2
Gajary [SK] 62 G4
Gakovo [HR] 74 G6
Galanádo [GR] 138 F3
Galanta [SK] 62 H4
Galapagar [E] 88 F5
Galashiels [GB] 8 E4
Galata [BG] 148 F3
Galatás [GR] 136 G2
Galaţi [RO] 206 D5
Galati Marina [I] 124 B7
Galatina [I] 122 G5
Galátista [GR] 130 B5
Galatone [I] 122 G5
Galaxídi [GR] 132 G5
Galbally [IRL] 4 D4
Gáldar [E] 100 C5
Galeata [I] 110 G5
Galera [E] 102 G3
Galéria [F] 114 A3
Galgaguta [H] 64 D5

Galgamácsa [H] 64 D6
Galicea Mare [RO] 150 F1
Galiny [PL] 22 H3
Galissás [GR] 138 D2
Galisteo [E] 86 H4
Galizano [E] 82 F3
Gallarate [I] 70 F4
Gallargues [F] 106 F4
Gallegos de Solmirón [E] 88 C4
Galliate [I] 70 F5
Gallípoli [I] 122 G5
Gällivare [S] 192 F6
Gällö [S] 182 H3
Gallur [E] 90 D3
Galovo [BG] 150 G2
Galston [GB] 8 D3
Galtelli [I] 118 E4
Galten [N] 182 D6
Galton [DK] 156 D1
Galtür [A] 72 B2
Galveias [E] 86 D5
Gálvez [E] 96 E2
Galway / Gallimh [IRL] 2 C5
Gamaches-en-Vexin [F] 28 C4
Gambara [I] 110 D1
Gambárie [I] 124 C7
Gaming [A] 62 D5
Gamla Uppsala [S] 168 D1
Gamleby [S] 162 G4
Gamlingay [GB] 14 E3
Gammel Skagen [DK] 160 E2
Gammelstaden [S] 198 B3
Gammertingen [D] 58 H3
Gams [CH] 58 H5
Gamvik [N] 196 D1
Gamzigrad [YU] 150 D2
Gan [F] 84 E3
Ganacker [D] 60 G3
Gand (Gent) [B] 28 G2
Gandal [N] 164 B3
Gândara [P] 86 E2
Ganderkesee [D] 18 D5
Gandesa [E] 90 G6
Gandia [E] 98 F6
Gandino [I] 70 H4
Gandria [CH] 70 G3
Gandrup [DK] 160 E4
Gandvik [N] 196 E2
Ganges [F] 106 E3
Gangi [I] 126 E3
Gangkofen [D] 60 G3
Gankovo [RUS] 204 D1
Gannat [F] 68 D1
Gänserndorf [A] 62 F4
Gap [F] 108 D2
Garaballa [E] 98 D3
Gara Khitrino [BG] 148 E2
Garbagna [I] 110 B2
Garbów [PL] 38 D5
Garching [D] 60 G4
Garciaz [F] 96 B2
Gârcov [RO] 148 A2
Garda [I] 72 C6
Gardanne [F] 108 B5
Gârdby [S] 162 G5
Gardelegen [D] 34 B2
Gardíki [GR] 132 F4
Garding [D] 18 E2
Gardone Riviera [I] 72 B5
Gardone Val Trompia [I] 72 B5
Gårdony [H] 76 B2
Gårdskär [S] 174 F4
Gårdslösa [S] 162 G5
Gardstad [N] 190 C4
Gårdstånga [S] 158 C2
Garein [F] 66 C5
Garelochead [GB] 8 D2
Garen [N] 170 D4
Garešnica [HR] 74 G6
Garéssio [I] 108 G3
Gargaliánoi [GR] 136 C4
Gargellen [A] 72 A2
Gargilesse-Dampierre [F] 54 H5
Gargnano [I] 72 C5

Gargnäs [S] 190 G3
Gargždai [LT] 202 D4
Garípa [GR] 140 E5
Garkalne [LV] 200 D5
Garlasco [I] 70 F5
Garlstorf [D] 18 F5
Garmisch Partenkirchen [D] 60 D6
Garoza [LV] 200 D5
Garpenberg [S] 174 D5
Garraf [E] 92 D5
Garrafe de Torío [E] 78 H5
Garray [E] 90 B2
Garrel [D] 18 C5
Garrison [GB] 2 E3
Garristown [IRL] 2 F5
Garrovillas [E] 86 G4
Garrucha [E] 102 H5
Gars am Kamp [A] 62 E3
Garsdale Head [GB] 10 E2
Garsnas [S] 158 D3
Garstang [GB] 10 D3
Gartow [D] 20 A6
Gartringen [D] 58 G1
Gartz [D] 20 E5
Garvagh [GB] 2 G2
Garvão [P] 94 C3
Garwolin [PL] 38 C4
Garz [D] 20 D2
Gåsborn [S] 166 G1
Gaschurn [A] 72 B2
Gascueña [E] 98 B1
Gasen [A] 74 D1
Gastoúni [GR] 136 B2
Gasztony [H] 74 F2
Gata [N] 172 C4
Gata de Gorgos [E] 104 F1
Gatchina [RUS] 178 H6
Gatehouse of Fleet [GB] 8 D5
Gáter [H] 76 E3
Gateshead [GB] 8 G6
Gátova [E] 98 E4
Gattinara [I] 70 E4
Gaucín [E] 100 H4
Gaulstad [N] 190 C5
Gaupne [N] 170 D1
Gautestad [N] 164 D4
Gavaloú [GR] 132 E5
Gavardo [I] 72 B6
Gavarnie [F] 84 E5
Gávavencsellő [H] 64 G4
Gaverina Terme [I] 72 A5
Gavi [I] 110 A2
Gavião [P] 86 E4
Gavirate [I] 70 F4
Gävle [S] 174 E4
Gavoi [I] 118 D4
Gavray [F] 26 D4
Gávrio [GR] 134 E6
Gávros [GR] 128 E5
Gavry [RUS] 200 G5
Gävunda [S] 172 G4
Gåxsjö [S] 190 E6
Gazoldo degli Ippoliti [I] 110 E1
Gázoros [GR] 130 C3
Gdańsk [PL] 22 E2
Gdov [RUS] 200 G2
Gdów [PL] 52 B4
Gdynia [PL] 22 E2
Geashill [IRL] 2 E6
Gebesee [D] 32 H6
Gebze [TR] 146 F3
Gedem [D] 46 D2
Gedinne [B] 44 D1
Gedney Drove End [GB] 10 G6
Gedser [DK] 20 B1
Gedsted [DK] 160 D4
Gedved [DK] 156 D1
Geel [B] 30 D3
Geertruidenberg [NL] 16 D6
Geesthacht [D] 18 G4
Gefell [D] 48 B2
Gefrees [D] 46 H3
Gefýra [GR] 132 G3
Gefyra [GR] 128 H4
Gehren [D] 46 G2

Geilenkirchen [D] 30 F4
Geilo [N] 170 E4
Geilo [N] 196 D2
Geiranger [N] 180 E4
Geisa [D] 46 E1
Geiselhöring [D] 60 F2
Geisenfeld [D] 60 E3
Geisenhausen [D] 60 F3
Geisingen [D] 58 G3
Geislingen [D] 60 B3
Geisnes [N] 190 C4
Geithain [D] 34 D6
Geithus [N] 170 G6
Geitvågen [N] 192 B6
Gela [I] 126 E5
Geldern [D] 30 G2
Geldrop [NL] 30 E2
Geleen [NL] 30 F4
Gelembe [TR] 144 D2
Gelgaudiškis [LT] 202 E5
Gelibolu [TR] 146 B5
Gelida [E] 92 D4
Gelnhausen [D] 46 D3
Gelsenkirchen [D] 30 H3
Gelting [D] 156 C5
Gembloux [B] 30 D5
Gémenos [F] 108 B5
Gemerská Poloma [SK] 64 E3
Gemert [NL] 30 F2
Gemlik [TR] 146 F4
Gemona del Friuli [I] 72 G4
Gémozac [F] 54 C6
Gemünd [D] 30 F5
Gemünden [D] 46 E3
Gemünden [D] 32 E6
Gemünden [D] 44 H2
Genappe [B] 30 C4
Gençay [F] 54 E4
Génelard [F] 56 F5
Generalski Stol [HR] 112 G1
General Toshevo [BG] 148 F1
Genève [CH] 70 B2
Gengenbach [D] 58 F2
Genillé [F] 54 G3
Genk [B] 30 E4
Genlis [F] 56 H4
Gennádio [GR] 142 D5
Gennep [NL] 16 F6
Gennes [F] 54 E2
Génolhac [F] 68 D6
Génova [I] 110 B3
Gent (Gand) [B] 28 G2
Genthin [D] 34 C2
Gentioux [F] 68 A2
Genzano di Lucánia [I] 120 H3
Genzano di Roma [I] 116 A6
Georgioúpoli [GR] 140 C4
Georgi Traykov [BG] 148 F3
Georgsheil [D] 18 B4
Gera [D] 48 C1
Geraardsbergen [B] 28 H3
Gerabronn [D] 46 E5
Gerace [I] 124 D7
Gérakas [GR] 136 F4
Geráki [GR] 136 E4
Gerakiní [GR] 130 B5
Gérardmer [F] 58 D2
Geras [A] 62 E3
Gerbéviller [F] 44 F6
Gerbstedt [D] 34 B4
Gerchsheim [D] 46 E4
Geremeas [I] 118 D7
Gerena [E] 94 G5
Gerês [P] 78 B6
Geretsried [D] 60 E5
Gérgal [E] 102 G5
Gerlos [A] 72 E1
Germay [F] 44 D6
Germencik [TR] 144 D5
Germersheim [D] 46 B5
Gernika-Lumo [E] 82 H4
Gernrode [D] 34 A4
Gernsbach [D] 58 F1
Gernsheim [D] 46 C4
Gerola Alta [I] 70 H3
Gerolimenas [GR] 136 E5

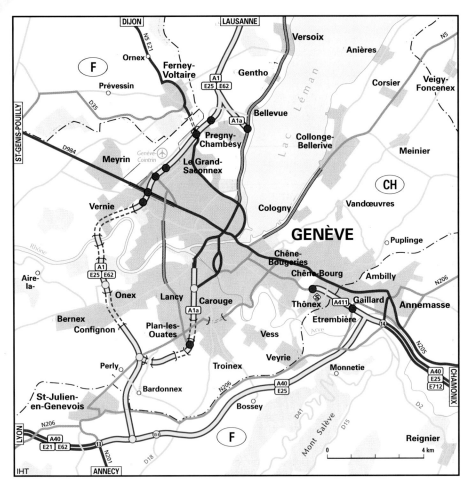

Gerolstein [D] 30 G6
Gerolzhofen [D] 46 F4
Gerona / Girona [E] 92 F3
Gerovo [HR] 112 F1
Gerrards Cross [GB] 14 E4
Gersfeld [D] 46 E2
Gershofen [D] 60 D3
Gesäter [S] 166 C4
Gescher [D] 16 G6
Geseke [D] 32 D4
Gesualdo [I] 120 F3
Gesunda [S] 172 G3
Geta [FIN] 176 A5
Getafe [E] 88 F6
Getaria [E] 84 A2
Gettorf [D] 18 F2
Getxo [E] 82 G3
Gevgelija [MK] 128 G3
Gevrey–Chambertin [F] 56 G4
Gex [F] 70 B2
Geyikli [TR] 130 H6
Geyre [TR] 144 F5
Geyve [TR] 146 G3
Gföhl [A] 62 D3
Ghalipsós [GR] 130 C4
Ghedi [I] 72 B6
Gheorghieni [RO] 206 C4
Ghilarza [I] 118 C4
Ghimpaţi [RO] 148 C1
Ghisonaccia [F] 114 C4
Ghisoni [F] 114 B4
Giannitsá [GR] 128 G4
Giardinetto [I] 120 G2
Giardini Naxos [I] 124 B8
Giarmata [RO] 76 G5
Giarratana [I] 126 F5
Giarre [I] 124 A8
Giba [I] 118 B7
Gibellina [I] 126 B2
Gibellina Vecchia [I] 126 C2
Gibostad [N] 192 D2
Gibraleón [E] 94 E5
Gibraltar [GBZ] 100 G5
Gic [H] 74 H1
Gidle [PL] 50 G1
Gieboldehausen [D] 32 G4
Giedraičiai [LT] 202 G5
Gielniów [PL] 38 A5

Gien [F] 56 C2
Giengen [D] 60 C3
Giens [F] 108 C6
Gieselwerder [D] 32 F4
Giessen [D] 46 C1
Gieten [NL] 16 G3
Giethoorn [NL] 16 F3
Gietrzwałd [PL] 22 G4
Gifhorn [D] 32 H2
Gigen [BG] 148 A2
Giglio Porto [I] 114 E4
Gignac [F] 106 E4
Gijón [E] 82 B1
Giksi [LV] 200 E4
Gilford [GB] 2 G4
Gilleleje [DK] 156 G1
Gillhov [S] 182 G4
Gillingham [GB] 14 F4
Gillingham [GB] 12 G4
Gimat [F] 84 G2
Gimel–les–Cascades [F] 66 H3
Gimnó [GR] 134 C5
Gimo [S] 174 F5
Gimont [F] 84 G3
Gîngiova [RO] 150 G2
Ginosa [I] 122 D4
Gióia del Colle [I] 122 E3
Gióia Táuro [I] 124 C6
Gioiosa Marea [I] 126 G1
Giornico [CH] 70 G2
Giovinazzo [I] 122 D2
Giraltovce [SK] 52 D6
Girifalco [I] 124 D5
Giromagny [F] 58 C3
Girona / Gerona [E] 92 F3
Gironella [E] 92 E2
Girvan [GB] 8 C4
Gisburn [GB] 10 E3
Gislaved [S] 162 C3
Gislev [DK] 156 E3
Gisors [F] 28 C6
Gissi [I] 116 E5
Gistaín [E] 84 F5
Gistel [B] 28 F1
Gistrup [DK] 160 E4
Gittun [S] 190 G2
Giuliana [I] 116 D3
Giurgiţa [RO] 150 G2

Giurgiu [RO] 148 C1
Give [DK] 156 C2
Givet [F] 30 D6
Givors [F] 68 F3
Givry [B] 28 H4
Givry [F] 56 G5
Givry–en–Argonne [F] 44 C4
Giżalki [PL] 36 E3
Gizeux [F] 54 F2
Giżycko [PL] 24 C3
Gjemnes [N] 180 F2
Gjerbës [AL] 128 C5
Gjerde [N] 180 D6
Gjermundshamn [N] 170 B5
Gjern [DK] 160 D6
Gjerrild [DK] 160 F5
Gjerstad [N] 164 F4
Gjersvik [N] 190 D4
Gjeving [N] 164 F4
Gjirokastër [AL] 128 C6
Gjølme [N] 180 H1
Gjøra [N] 180 G3
Gjóv [DK] 160 B1
Gjøvik [N] 172 B3
Gkoritsá [GR] 136 E4
Gkoúra [GR] 136 D1
Gladbeck [D] 30 H2
Gladenbach [D] 32 D6
Glamis [GB] 8 F2
Glamoč [BIH] 154 B4
Glåmos [N] 182 C3
Glamsbjerg [DK] 156 D3
Glandore [IRL] 4 B5
Glandorf [D] 32 D2
Glanmire [IRL] 4 C5
Glanworth [IRL] 4 D4
Glarus [CH] 58 G6
Glasgow [GB] 8 D3
Glashütte [D] 48 E1
Glashütten [A] 74 C3
Glastonbury [GB] 12 F4
Glauchau [D] 48 C1
Glava [S] 166 D2
Glavan [BG] 148 D5
Glavanovtsi [BG] 150 F2
Glavičice [BIH] 154 E3
Glavnik [YU] 150 C4

Gleann Cholm Cille / Glencolumbkille [IRL] 2 D2
Give [DK] 156 C2
Gleinalm Tunnel [A] 74 D1
Gleisdorf [A] 74 E2
Glenamaddy [IRL] 2 D4
Glenamoy [IRL] 2 C3
Glenarm [GB] 2 G3
Glenavy [GB] 2 G3
Glenbarr [GB] 2 H1
Glencoe [GB] 6 C6
Glencolumbkille / Gleann Cholm Cille [IRL] 2 D2
Glendaruel [GB] 8 C2
Glendoll [GB] 8 F1
Gleneagles [GB] 8 E2
Glenealy [IRL] 4 G4
Glenegedale [GB] 2 G1
Glenfinnan [GB] 6 C6
Glengarriff [IRL] 4 B5
Glenhull [GB] 2 F3
Glénic [F] 54 H5
Glenluce [GB] 8 C5
Glenmore [IRL] 4 E4
Glenrothes [GB] 8 E3
Glenties [IRL] 2 E2
Glenville [IRL] 4 D5
Gletsch [CH] 70 F2
Glewitz [D] 20 C3
Glifáda [GR] 132 F5
Glifádha [GR] 136 G1
Glimåkra [S] 158 D1
Glin [IRL] 4 C3
Glina [HR] 112 H1
Glinka [PL] 50 G5
Glinojeck [PL] 38 A1
Glinsce / Glinsk [IRL] 2 B4
Glinsk / Glinsce [IRL] 2 B4
Glissjöberg [S] 182 G5
Gliwice [PL] 50 F3
Gllavë [AL] 128 B5
Głodowa [PL] 22 B3
Gloggnitz [A] 62 E6
Głogów [PL] 36 B5
Głogówek [PL] 50 E3
Głogów Malopolski [PL] 52 E3

Glömminge [S] 162 G5
Glóssa [GR] 134 B3
Glossop [GB] 10 E4
Glostrup [DK] 156 G2
Gloucester [GB] 12 G2
Główczyce [PL] 22 C2
Glowe [D] 20 D2
Glöwen [D] 20 B6
Glowno [PL] 36 H4
Gložan [YU] 154 F1
Glozhene [BG] 150 G2
Glozhene [BG] 148 A4
Głubczyce [PL] 50 E3
Glubokoje [BY] 204 B4
Głuchołazy [PL] 50 D3
Glücksburg [D] 156 C4
Glückstadt [D] 18 E3
Gluda [LV] 200 D5
Gluhov [UA] 204 E7
Glumsø [DK] 156 F3
Glušci [YU] 154 F2
Głuszyca [PL] 50 B2
Glýfa [GR] 132 H3
Glykí [GR] 132 C3
Glynde [GB] 14 E5
Glyngøre [DK] 160 C4
Glyn Neath [GB] 12 E2
Gmünd [A] 72 H2
Gmünd [A] 62 C3
Gmund [D] 60 E5
Gmunden [A] 62 A5
Gnarp [S] 184 E5
Gnarrenburg [D] 18 E4
Gnesta [S] 168 D4
Gniechowice [PL] 50 C1
Gniew [PL] 22 E4
Gniewkowo [PL] 36 E1
Gniezno [PL] 36 D2
Gnisvärd [S] 168 F4
Gnjilane [YU] 150 D5
Gnocchetta [I] 110 H2
Gnoien [D] 20 C3
Gnosall [GB] 10 D5
Gnosjö [S] 162 C3
Göbel [TR] 146 D5
Gobowen [GB] 10 C5
Goch [D] 16 F6
Göd [H] 64 C6
Godalming [GB] 14 D5
Godby [FIN] 176 A5
Godech [BG] 150 F4
Godelheim [D] 32 F4
Godętowo [PL] 22 D2
Godkowo [PL] 22 G3
Godovič [SLO] 74 B5
Godowa [PL] 52 D4
Gödre [H] 76 A4
Godshill [GB] 12 H5
Goes [NL] 16 B6
Göhren [D] 20 E2
Goirle [NL] 30 E2
Góis [P] 86 E2
Góito [I] 110 E1
Gojani i Madh [AL] 128 B1
Gojsaliči [BIH] 154 E4
Gökçdağ [TR] 144 F1
Gökçen [TR] 144 D4
Gokels [D] 18 F2
Gol [N] 170 F3
Gola [HR] 74 G4
Golå [N] 170 H1
Gołąb [PL] 38 D5
Golaja Pristan [UA] 206 F5
Gołańcz [PL] 36 D1
Golchen [D] 20 D4
Gölcük [TR] 146 G3
Gölcük [TR] 144 E4
Golçük [TR] 142 E2
Golčův Jeníkov [CZ] 48 H4
Golczewo [PL] 20 F4
Gołdap [PL] 24 D2
Goldbach [D] 46 D3
Goldberg [D] 20 B4
Goldden [N] 192 G2
Goldelund [D] 156 B5
Golden [IRL] 4 D4
Goldenstedt [D] 18 D6
Goleen [IRL] 4 B5
Golegã [P] 86 D4

Golema Crcorija [MK] 150 E6
Golemo Selo [YU] 150 D5
Goleniów [PL] 20 F5
Goleniowy [PL] 50 H2
Golfe–Juan [F] 108 E5
Golfo Aranci [I] 118 E2
Golfo di Sogno [F] 114 B6
Gölhisar [TR] 142 G1
Golina [PL] 36 E3
Goliševa [LV] 200 G5
Gollhofen [D] 46 F4
Golling [A] 60 G6
Gölmarmara [TR] 144 D3
Golmayo [E] 90 B3
Goloby [UA] 204 A7
Gölpazarı [TR] 146 H4
Golpejas [E] 80 G6
Golspie [GB] 6 E4
Golssen [D] 34 E4
Golub Dobrzyń [PL] 22 E6
Golubovci [YU] 152 E4
Gołuchów [PL] 36 E4
Golyalo Krushevo [BG] 148 E5
Gölyazı [TR] 146 E5
Gołymin–Ošrodek [PL] 38 B1
Golzow [D] 34 D3
Gómara [E] 90 C3
Gombo [I] 110 D5
Gomel [BY] 204 C6
Gommern [D] 34 B3
Gönc [H] 64 G3
Goncelin [F] 70 A4
Gondomar [P] 80 C4
Gondrecourt [F] 44 D5
Gondrin [F] 66 D6
Gönen [TR] 146 D5
Góni [GR] 132 G1
Goniądz [PL] 24 E4
Gonnosfanádiga [I] 118 C6
Goole [GB] 10 F4
Goor [NL] 16 G5
Göpfritz [A] 62 D3
Goppenstein [CH] 70 E2
Göppingen [D] 60 B2
Góra [PL] 36 C5
Góra [PL] 36 H2
Góra Kalwaria [PL] 38 C3
Góra Puławska [PL] 38 D5
Góra Swiętej Anny [PL] 50 E3
Goražde [BIH] 152 E1
Gordaliza del Pino [E] 82 B5
Gordes [F] 106 H3
Gördes [TR] 144 E2
Gördes [TR] 144 E3
Gordon [GB] 8 F4
Gorebridge [GB] 8 E3
Goren Chiflik [BG] 148 F3
Gorenja Vas [SLO] 74 B5
Goresbridge [IRL] 4 F4
Gorey [IRL] 4 F4
Gorgonzola [I] 70 G5
Goričan [HR] 74 F4
Goricë [AL] 128 D4
Gorinchem [NL] 16 D5
Gorino Veneto [I] 110 H3
Göritz [D] 20 E5
Gorízia [I] 72 H5
Gorki [RUS] 178 G5
Gorki [BY] 204 C5
Gørlev [DK] 156 F3
Gorlice [PL] 52 C5
Görlitz [D] 34 G6
Gorna Kremena [BG] 150 G3
Gorna Oryakhovitsa [BG] 148 C3
Gorna Studena [BG] 148 C3
Gorni Tsibur [BG] 150 F2
Gornja Grabovica [BIH] 152 C2
Gornja Kamenica [YU] 150 E3
Gornja Klina [YU] 150 B5
Gornja Ploča [HR] 112 G4
Gornja Radgona [SLO] 74 E3
Gornja Sabanta [YU] 150 C2

Gornja Toponica [YU] 150 D3
Gornja Tuzla [BIH] 154 E3
Gornji Lapac [HR] 112 H4
Gornji Milanovac [YU] 150 B2
Gornji Podgradci [BIH] 154 B2
Gornji Ravno [BIH] 152 B1
Gornji Vakuf [BIH] 152 B1
Górno [PL] 52 C1
Gorodets [RUS] 200 H2
Gorodišče [UA] 206 F3
Gorodok [BY] 204 C4
Górowo [PL] 22 G2
Górowo Iławeckie [PL] 22 G2
Gorredijk [NL] 16 F2
Gorron [F] 26 E5
Gørslev [DK] 156 G3
Gort [IRL] 2 C5
Gortin [GB] 2 F3
Görükle [TR] 146 E4
Gorzanów [PL] 50 C3
Görzke [D] 34 C3
Gorzkowice [PL] 36 G6
Górzna [PL] 22 B5
Górzno [PL] 22 F6
Gorzów Śląski [PL] 50 F1
Gorzów Wielkopolski [PL] 34 H2
Górzyca [PL] 34 G2
Gorzyń [PL] 36 B2
Gosau [A] 60 H6
Gošča [UA] 206 D2
Göschenen [CH] 70 F1
Gościno [PL] 20 G3
Gosforth [GB] 10 D1
Goslar [D] 32 G3
Gospari [LV] 200 F6
Gospič [HR] 112 G4
Gosport [GB] 12 H5
Gossau [CH] 58 H5
Gosselies [B] 30 C5
Gossensass / Colle Isarco [I] 72 D2
Gössl [A] 62 B6
Gössweinstein [D] 46 G4
Gostilicy [RUS] 178 G5
Gostivar [MK] 128 D1
Gostkow [PL] 36 F4
Göstling [A] 62 C5
Gostomia [PL] 22 A6
Gostycyn [PL] 22 C5
Gostyń [PL] 36 C4
Gostynin [PL] 36 G2
Goszczanówko [PL] 36 A2
Göteborg [S] 160 G2
Götene [S] 166 E5

Gotha [D] 32 H6
Gothem [S] 168 G4
Gotse Delchev [BG] 130 C1
Gotthard Tunnel [CH] 70 F2
Göttingen [D] 32 F4
Götzis [A] 58 H5
Gouarec [F] 26 A5
Gouda [NL] 16 D5
Gouménissa [GR] 128 G3
Goumois [CH] 58 C5
Gouniá [GR] 132 B2
Gourdon [F] 66 G4
Gourin [F] 40 C3
Gournay-en-Bray [F] 28 C5
Goúrnes [GR] 140 E4
Gourniá [GR] 140 G5
Gourock [GB] 8 C3
Gouveia [P] 80 D6
Goúves [GR] 140 E5
Gouzon [F] 56 B6
Govedartsi [BG] 150 G6
Govedjari [HR] 152 B3
Gowran [IRL] 4 F4
Gózd [PL] 52 B1
Gozdnica [PL] 34 H5
Graal-Müritz [D] 20 B2
Grab [BIH] 152 D4
Gråbo [S] 160 H2
Grabow [D] 20 A5
Grabów [PL] 36 F3
Grabówka [PL] 24 F5
Grabownica Starzeńska [PL] 52 E1
Grabów n Prosną [PL] 36 E5
Gračac [HR] 112 H4
Gračanica [BIH] 154 D3
Gračanica [YU] 154 F4
Gračanica [YU] 150 C5
Graçay [F] 54 H3
Grächen [CH] 70 E2
Gračišče [HR] 112 D2
Gradac [BIH] 152 C3
Gradac [HR] 152 B3
Gradačac [BIH] 154 D2
Graddis [N] 190 F1
Gräddö [S] 168 F2
Gradec [BG] 150 E2
Gradefes [E] 82 C4
Gradets [BG] 148 D4
Gradina [YU] 150 E4
Gradisca d'Isonzo [I] 72 H5
Gradizsk [UA] 206 F3
Grado [E] 78 G3
Grado [I] 72 G6
Gradsko [MK] 128 F2
Græsted [DK] 156 G1
Grafenau [D] 60 H2

Gräfenberg [D] 46 G4
Gräfenhainichen [D] 34 C4
Grafenwöhr [D] 48 B4
Grafing [D] 60 E4
Grafrath [D] 60 D4
Gräfsnäs [S] 162 A1
Gragnano [I] 120 E3
Grahovo [YU] 152 D4
Graiguenamanagh [IRL] 4 F4
Grajewo [PL] 24 D4
Gralhos [P] 80 D3
Grallagh [IRL] 2 D4
Gram [DK] 156 B3
Gramada [BG] 150 E2
Gramat [F] 66 G4
Gramatikovo [BG] 148 F5
Graménó [GR] 132 C2
Gramkow [D] 20 A3
Gramméni Oxyá [GR] 132 F4
Grammichele [I] 126 F4
Gramsh [AL] 128 C4
Gramzda [LV] 200 B6
Gramzow [D] 20 E5
Gran [N] 172 B4
Granada [E] 102 E4
Granadilla de Abona [E] 100 C5
Granard [IRL] 2 E4
Granátula de Calatrava [E] 96 F4
Grancey [F] 56 G3
Grandas de Salime [E] 78 F3
Grandcamp-Maisy [F] 26 E2
Grand-Champ [F] 26 A6
Grande-Fougeray [F] 40 F5
Grandpré [F] 44 C3
Grandrieu [F] 68 D5
Grandson [CH] 58 C6
Grandvilliers [F] 28 D5
Grañén [E] 90 F3
Grängärde [S] 172 H5
Grange [IRL] 2 D3
Grangemouth [GB] 8 E3
Grange-over-Sands [GB] 10 D2
Grängesberg [S] 172 H6
Granges-sur-Vologne [F] 58 D2
Granítsa [GR] 132 E3
Granja [P] 80 B4
Granja de Moreruela [E] 82 A6
Granja de Torrehermosa [E] 96 B5

Grankulla / Kauniainen [FIN] 176 H5
Grankullavik [S] 162 H3
Granlunda [S] 168 C1
Gränna [S] 162 D1
Granollers [E] 92 E4
Granön [S] 190 H5
Gransee [D] 20 D6
Gransherad [N] 164 F1
Gran Tarajal [E] 100 E5
Grantham [GB] 10 F6
Grantown-on-Spey [GB] 6 E5
Grantshouse [GB] 8 F4
Granville [F] 26 D4
Granvin [S] 170 C3
Granvollen [N] 172 B4
Grao / el Grau [E] 98 F6
Grasmere [GB] 10 D2
Gräso [S] 174 F5
Grassano [I] 122 C4
Grassau [D] 60 F5
Grasse [F] 108 E4
Gråsten [DK] 156 C4
Grästorp [S] 166 D6
Gratkorn [A] 74 D2
Graulhet [F] 106 B3
Graus [E] 90 H3
Grava [S] 166 E2
Grávalos [E] 84 A5
Gravdal [N] 192 B4
Gravdal [N] 164 B4
Grave [NL] 16 E6
Gravedona [I] 70 G3
Gravelines [F] 14 H6
Gravellona-Toce [I] 70 F3
Gravesend [GB] 14 F4
Graviá [GR] 132 G4
Gravoúna [GR] 130 E3
Gray [F] 58 A4
Grays [GB] 14 F4
Graz [A] 74 D2
Grazalema [E] 100 H4
Grazzanise [I] 120 D2
Grazzano Visconti [I] 110 C2
Grčak [YU] 150 C3
Grdelica [YU] 150 D4
Greaca [RO] 148 D1
Great Ayton [GB] 10 F2
Great Dunmow [GB] 14 F3
Great Malvern [GB] 12 G2
Great Torrington [GB] 12 D3
Great Yarmouth [GB] 14 H2
Great Yeldham [GB] 14 F3
Grebbestad [S] 166 B4
Grebenstein [D] 32 F5
Greding [D] 46 G6
Greencastle [GB] 2 G5
Greenock [GB] 8 D3
Greenwich [GB] 14 E4
Greetsiel [D] 16 H1
Gregolímano [GR] 132 H4
Greifenburg [A] 72 G3
Greiffenberg [D] 20 E6
Greifswald [D] 20 D3
Grein [A] 62 C4
Greiz [D] 48 C2
Grenaa [DK] 160 F5
Grenade [F] 66 C6
Grenade [F] 84 H2
Grenchen [CH] 58 D5
Grenivík [IS] 194 E3
Grenoble [F] 68 H4
Grense-Jakobselv [N] 196 F3
Gréolières [F] 108 E4
Gréoux-les-Bains [F] 108 C4
Gressoney-la-Trinité [I] 70 E3
Gressoney-St-Jean [I] 70 E4
Gresten [A] 62 D5
Gretna Green [GB] 8 E5
Greussen [D] 32 H5
Greve in Chianti [I] 110 F6
Grevená [GR] 128 E6
Grevenbroich [D] 30 G4

Grevenbrück [D] 32 C5
Grevenmacher [L] 44 F2
Grevesmühlen [D] 18 H3
Greve Strand [DK] 156 G3
Greyabbey [GB] 2 H4
Greystones [IRL] 4 G3
Grez-en-Bouère [F] 40 H5
Gries-am-Brenner [A] 72 D2
Griesbach [D] 60 H3
Gries in Sellrain [A] 72 D1
Grieskirchen [A] 62 A4
Griffen [A] 74 C3
Grignan [F] 106 H2
Grignols [F] 66 D5
Grillby [S] 168 C2
Grimaldi [I] 124 D5
Grimaud [F] 108 D5
Grimma [D] 34 D6
Grimmen [D] 20 D3
Grimsbu [N] 180 H5
Grimsby [GB] 10 G4
Grímsstaðir [IS] 194 F4
Grimstad [N] 164 E5
Grindaheim [N] 170 F2
Grindavík [IS] 194 B4
Grinde [N] 164 A1
Grindelwald [CH] 70 E1
Grindjord [N] 192 D4
Grindsted [DK] 156 B2
Griñón [E] 88 F6
Gripenberg [S] 162 E1
Grisignano di Zocco [I] 72 D6
Grisolles [F] 84 H2
Grisslehamn [S] 174 G6
Grivitsa [BG] 148 B3
Grižkabūdis [LT] 202 E5
Gröbers [D] 34 C5
Grobina [LV] 200 B6
Gröbming [A] 74 B1
Grocka [YU] 154 H3
Gródek [PL] 38 G1
Gródek nad Dunajcem [PL] 52 C4
Gröditz [D] 34 E5
Grodków [PL] 50 D2
Grodzeń [PL] 36 G1
Grodziec [PL] 50 F4
Grodziec [PL] 36 A6
Grodzisk Mazowiecki [PL] 38 B3
Grodzisk Wielkoposki [PL] 36 B3
Groenlo [NL] 16 G5
Groix [F] 40 C4
Grojdibodu [RO] 148 A2
Grójec [PL] 38 B4
Grömitz [D] 18 H3
Gromnik [PL] 52 C4
Gromo [I] 72 A4
Gronau [D] 16 G5
Gronau [D] 32 F3
Grong [N] 190 C5
Grönhögen [S] 158 G1
Gröningen [D] 34 A3
Groningen [NL] 16 G2
Grønnes [N] 180 E3
Grönskåra [S] 162 F4
Grósio [I] 72 B4
Grossarl [A] 72 G1
Grossbeeren [D] 34 E2
Grossbreitenbach [D] 46 G2
Grossburgwedel [D] 32 G2
Grossenbrode [D] 18 H2
Grossenhain [D] 34 E5
Grossenkneten [D] 18 C5
Grossenzersdorf [A] 62 F4
Grosseto [I] 114 F3
Gross-Gerau [D] 46 C3
Gross-Gerungs [A] 62 C3
Grosshabersdorf [D] 46 F5
Grosshöchstetten [CH] 58 E6
Gross Mohrdorf [D] 20 C2
Gross Oesingen [D] 32 H1
Grosspetersdorf [A] 74 F2
Grossraming [A] 62 C5
Gross Räschen [D] 34 F5
Gross Schönebeck [D] 34 E1

Gross-Siegharts [A] 62 D3
Gross-Umstadt [D] 46 D3
Grostenquin [F] 44 F4
Grosuplje [SLO] 74 C5
Grotli [N] 180 E5
Grottaglie [I] 122 F4
Grottaminarda [I] 120 F2
Grottammare [I] 116 D2
Grotteria [I] 124 D7
Grouw [NL] 16 F2
Grovfjorden [N] 192 D3
Grovo [N] 164 F3
Grozd'ovo [BG] 148 F3
Grua [N] 172 B5
Grubišno Polje [HR] 74 G6
Gruda [HR] 152 D4
Grudusk [PL] 22 H6
Grudziądz [PL] 22 E5
Gruemirë [AL] 152 E5
Gruissan [F] 106 D5
Grums [S] 166 E3
Grünau [A] 62 B5
Grünberg [D] 46 D1
Grünburg [A] 62 B5
Grundarfjördur [IS] 194 B3
Grundfors [S] 190 E4
Grundforsen [S] 172 E2
Grundlsee [A] 62 A6
Grundsel [S] 190 H3
Grundsund [S] 166 C6
Grundtjärn [S] 184 E1
Grünenplan [D] 32 F3
Grünheide [D] 34 F2
Grünstadt [D] 46 B4
Grunwald [PL] 22 G5
Grupčin [MK] 128 D1
Grüsch [CH] 58 H6
Gruyères [CH] 70 C1
Gruža [YU] 150 B2
Gruzdžiai [LT] 202 E3
Grybów [PL] 52 C5
Grycksbo [S] 172 H4
Gryfice [PL] 20 G4
Gryfino [PL] 20 F5
Gryfów Śląski [PL] 48 H1
Grykë [AL] 128 A4
Gryllefjord [N] 192 D2
Gryt [S] 168 C6
Grytgöl [S] 166 H4
Grythyttan [S] 166 G2
Grzmiąca [PL] 22 A4
Grzybno [PL] 22 F5
Gschnitz [A] 72 D2
Gschwend [D] 46 E6
Gstaad [CH] 70 D2
Gstadt [D] 60 F5
Gsteig [CH] 70 D2
Guadahortuna [E] 102 E3
Guadalajara [E] 88 G5
Guadalcanal [E] 94 H4
Guadalest [E] 104 E2
Guadalmina [E] 102 A5
Guadalupe [E] 96 C2
Guadarrama [E] 88 F5
Guadix [E] 102 F4
Gualachulain [GB] 8 C1
Gualdo Tadino [I] 116 B2
Gualin House [GB] 6 D2
Guarcino [I] 116 C6
Guarda [P] 86 G2
Guardamar del Segura [E] 104 D3
Guárdia [I] 124 C4
Guardiagrele [I] 116 D5
Guardia Lombardi [I] 120 F3
Guardia Sanframondi [I] 120 E2
Guardo [E] 82 C4
Guareña [E] 94 H2
Guarromán [E] 96 E6
Guasila [I] 118 C6
Guastalla [I] 110 E2
Gúbbio [I] 116 A1
Guben [D] 34 G4
Guberevac [YU] 150 B2
Gubin [PL] 34 G4
Gubkin [RUS] 204 F7
Gudavac [BIH] 154 A2
Gudhjem [DK] 158 E4
Gudow [D] 18 G4

Gudvangen [N] 170 D2
Guebwiller [F] 58 D3
Güéjar Sierra [E] 102 E4
Guémené-Penfao [F] 40 F5
Guémené-sur-Scorff [F] 40 D3
Guenange [F] 44 F3
Guer [F] 26 B6
Guérande [F] 40 D6
Guéret [F] 54 H6
Guérigny [F] 56 D4
Guethary [F] 84 C2
Gueugnon [F] 56 E5
Güglingen [D] 46 C6
Guglionesi [I] 116 F5
Guía de Isora [E] 100 B5
Guichen [F] 26 C6
Guidonia [I] 116 A5
Guignes [F] 42 G4
Guijuelo [E] 88 C4
Guildford [GB] 14 D4
Guillaumes [F] 108 E3
Guillena [E] 94 G5
Guillestre [F] 108 E2
Guilvinec [F] 40 B3
Güímar [E] 100 C5
Guimarães [P] 80 C3
Guimiliau [F] 40 C2
Guînes [F] 14 G6
Guingamp [F] 26 A4
Guipry [F] 40 F4
Guísamo [E] 78 D2
Guisborough [GB] 10 G2
Guise [F] 28 G5
Guisnje [YU] 150 A5
Guitiriz [E] 78 D2
Guîtres [F] 66 D3
Gujan-Mestras [F] 66 B3
Gulbene [LV] 200 F4
Guldborg [DK] 156 F5
Gullabo [S] 162 F6
Gulladuff [GB] 2 G3
Gullaskruv [S] 162 F4
Gullhaug [N] 164 H2
Gullringen [S] 162 F2
Gullspång [S] 166 F4
Gullstein [N] 180 F1
Güllü [TR] 144 F4
Güllüce [TR] 146 E5
Güllük [TR] 142 C2
Gülpınar [TR] 134 G1
Gulsele [S] 190 F6
Gulsvik [N] 170 G4
Gülübintsi [BG] 148 D5
Gülübovo [BG] 148 D5
Gulyantsi [BG] 148 B2
Gumiel de Hizán [E] 88 G2
Gummersbach [D] 32 C5
Gumpoldskirchen [A] 62 F5
Gumtow [D] 20 B6
Gümüldür [TR] 144 C5
Gümüşpınar [TR] 146 D2
Gümüşsu [TR] 144 H4
Gümüşyeni [TR] 146 G5
Gümzovo [BG] 150 E2
Gundelfingen [D] 60 C3
Gundelsheim [D] 46 D5
Güney [TR] 144 G5
Güney [TR] 144 F4
Güngörmez [TR] 144 D1
Günlüce [TR] 144 F1
Gunnarn [S] 190 G4
Gunnarskog [S] 166 D1
Gunnebo [S] 162 G2
Gunten [CH] 70 E1
Güntersberge [D] 32 H4
Guntersblum [D] 46 C4
Guntersdorf [A] 62 E3
Guntín [E] 78 D3
Günzburg [D] 60 C3
Gunzenhausen [D] 46 F6
Güre [TR] 144 H3
Güre [TR] 144 F3
Güreci [TR] 146 B5
Gurgazu [F] 114 B6
Gurk [A] 74 B2
Gurkovo [BG] 148 C4
Gürpınar [TR] 146 E3
Gürsu [TR] 146 F4
Gurtnellen [CH] 70 F1
Gusev [RUS] 24 D1
Gusmar [AL] 128 B6

Gúspini [I] 118 C6
Güssing [A] 74 F2
Gustavsberg [S] 168 E3
Gustavsfors [S] 166 D3
Güstrow [D] 20 B4
Gusum [S] 168 B6
Gutcher [GB] 6 H3
Gutenstein [A] 62 E5
Gütersloh [D] 32 D3
Guttannen [CH] 70 F1
Gützkow [D] 20 D3
Güzelbahçe [TR] 144 C4
Guzet-Neige [F] 84 H5
Gvardeysk [RUS] 24 B1
Gvarv [N] 164 F2
Gvozd [YU] 152 E3
Gwatt [CH] 70 D1
Gwyddgrug [GB] 12 E1
Gy [F] 58 B4
Gya [N] 164 B4
Gylling [DK] 156 D2
Gyoma [H] 76 F2
Gyömrő [H] 76 D1
Gyöngyös [H] 64 E5
Gyöngyöspata [H] 64 D5
Győr [H] 62 H6
Gysinge [S] 174 E5
Gýtheio [GR] 136 E4
Gyttorp [S] 166 G2
Gyueshevo [BG] 150 E6
Gyula [H] 76 G3

H

Häädemeeste [EST] 200 D3
Haag [A] 62 C4
Haag [D] 60 F4
Haag am Hausruck [A] 62 A4
Haaksbergen [NL] 16 G5
Haapajärvi [FIN] 198 D6
Haapamäki [FIN] 186 E4
Haapamäki [FIN] 198 E6
Haapavesi [FIN] 198 D5
Haapsalu [EST] 200 D2
Haar [D] 60 E4
Haarby [DK] 156 D3
Haaren [D] 32 E4
Haarlem [NL] 16 D4
Habartice [CZ] 48 G1
Habay [B] 44 E2
Hablingbo [S] 168 F5
Habo [S] 162 D2
Hachenburg [D] 46 B1
Hachmühlen [D] 32 F2
Hackås [S] 182 G3
Hacketstown [IRL] 4 F4
Hackland [GB] 6 G2
Håcksvik [S] 162 B3
Hadamar [D] 46 B2
Haddington [GB] 8 F3
Haderslev [DK] 156 C3
Haderup [DK] 160 C5
Hadım [TR] 144 G4
Hadleigh [GB] 14 G3
Hadlow [GB] 14 F5
Hadmersleben [D] 34 B3
Hadsten [DK] 160 D6
Hadsund [DK] 160 E4
Hadžiči [BIH] 152 C1
Hægeland [N] 164 D5
Hafnarfjörður [IS] 194 B4
Hagafoss [N] 170 F3
Hagby [S] 162 F5
Hagebro [DK] 160 C5
Hagen [D] 32 C4
Hagen [D] 18 D4
Hagenow [D] 18 H5
Hagetmau [F] 84 E2
Hagfors [S] 172 F6
Häggenås [S] 182 H1
Häggsjömon [S] 190 G5
Haglebu [N] 170 G4
Hagondange [F] 44 E4
Haguenau [F] 44 H5
Hahn [D] 18 C4
Hahnbach [D] 46 H5
Hahót [H] 74 G3
Haigerloch [D] 58 G2

Hailsham [GB] 14 E6
Hailuoto [FIN] 198 D4
Hainburg [A] 62 G4
Hainfeld [A] 62 E5
Hainichen [D] 48 D1
Hajdúböszörmény [H] 64 G6
Hajdúdorog [H] 64 G5
Hajdúhadház [H] 64 H5
Hajdúnánás [H] 64 G5
Hajdúsámson [H] 64 H6
Hajdúszoboszló [H] 64 G6
Hajdúszovát [H] 76 G1
Hajnówka [PL] 38 F1
Hajós [H] 76 C4
Håkenby [N] 166 C3
Hakkas [S] 196 A7
Hakkenpää [FIN] 176 D4
Halámky [CZ] 62 C2
Halberstadt [D] 34 A3
Hald [DK] 160 E5
Halden [N] 166 C3
Haldensee [A] 60 C6
Haldensleben [D] 34 B2
Halesowen [GB] 10 D6
Halesworth [GB] 14 G3
Halhjem [N] 170 B4
Halifax [GB] 10 E4
Halikko [FIN] 176 E4
Halitpaşa [TR] 144 D3
Haljala [EST] 200 E1
Halk [DK] 156 C3
Halkirk [GB] 6 F3
Hallabro [S] 162 E6
Halle [B] 28 H3
Halle [D] 34 C5
Halle [D] 32 D3
Hällefors [S] 166 G2
Hälleforsnäs [S] 168 B3
Hallein [A] 60 G6
Hallen [S] 182 G2
Hallenberg [D] 32 D5
Hallerud [S] 166 G4
Hällestad [S] 166 H5
Hällevadsholm [S] 166 C5
Hälleviksstrand [S] 166 C6
Hallingby [N] 170 H5
Hall in Tirol [A] 72 D1
Hällnäs [S] 190 H5
Hallsberg [S] 166 H4
Hallshuk [S] 168 G3
Hallstahammar [S] 168 B2
Hallstatt [A] 62 A6
Hallstavik [S] 168 E1
Halltorp [S] 162 F6
Halluin [B] 28 F2
Halmstad [S] 162 B5
Hals [DK] 160 E4
Halsa [N] 180 F2
Hal'shany [BY] 202 H6
Halsskov [DK] 156 E3
Halstead [GB] 14 F3
Halsteren [NL] 16 C6
Halsua [FIN] 186 E1
Haltdalen [N] 182 C3
Haltern [D] 30 H2
Haltwhistle [GB] 8 F5
Haluna [FIN] 188 D1
Halver [D] 32 C5
Halwill [GB] 12 D4
Ham [F] 28 F5
Hamamköy [TR] 144 E5
Hamar [N] 172 C3
Hambergen [D] 18 D5
Hamburg [D] 18 F4
Hamburgsund [S] 166 B5
Hamdibey [TR] 146 C6
Hamdorf [D] 18 F2
Hämeenkyrö [FIN] 176 E1
Hämeenlinna [FIN] 176 G3
Hämeler Wald [D] 32 G2
Hameln [D] 32 F2
Hamersleben [D] 34 A3
Hamidiye [TR] 146 B3
Hamilton [GB] 8 D3
Hamina [FIN] 178 D3
Hamlagrøosen [N] 170 C3
Hamm [D] 32 C3
Hammar [S] 166 G4
Hammarland [FIN] 176 A5
Hammarstrand [S] 184 D2

Hammaslahti [FIN] 188 F3
Hammel [DK] 160 D6
Hammelburg [D] 46 E3
Hammer [N] 190 C5
Hammerdal [S] 182 H1
Hammerfest [N] 196 B2
Hamminkeln [D] 16 G6
Hamnbukt [N] 192 H1
Hamneidet [N] 192 F1
Hamningberg [N] 196 F1
Hamoir [B] 30 E5
Hamra [S] 172 H1
Hamrångefjärden [S] 174 E3
Hamre [N] 164 E5
Hamula [FIN] 186 G2
Hamzali [MK] 128 H2
Hamziči [BIH] 152 C2
Hån [S] 166 C2
Hanau [D] 46 D3
Hânceşti [MD] 206 D4
Handegg [CH] 70 F1
Handen [S] 168 E3
Handlová [SK] 64 B3
Handöl [S] 182 E2
Hanerau-Hademarschen [D] 18 E2
Hanestad [N] 182 C6
Hangö / Hanko [FIN] 176 E6
Han i Hotit [AL] 152 E4
Hankamäki [FIN] 198 F6
Hankasalmi [FIN] 186 H4
Hankensbüttel [D] 32 H1
Hanko / Hangö [FIN] 176 E6
Hann-Münden [D] 32 F5
Hannover [D] 32 F2
Hannut (Hannut) [B] 30 D4
Hannut (Hannuit) [B] 30 D4
Han Pijesak [BIH] 154 E4
Hansnes [N] 192 E1
Hanstedt [D] 18 F5
Hanstholm [DK] 160 C3
Han-sur-Lesse [B] 30 D6
Hantháza [H] 76 D2
Hanušovce [SK] 64 G2
Hanušovice [CZ] 50 C4
Hanya [TR] 144 E2
Haparanda [S] 198 C2
Häppälä [FIN] 186 H4
Hara [EST] 200 D2
Harads [S] 198 A2
Häradsbäck [S] 162 D5
Haraneset [N] 190 C4
Harboøre [DK] 160 B4
Harburg [D] 60 C2
Harburg [D] 18 F4
Hardegg [A] 62 E3
Hardegsen [D] 32 F4
Hardelot-Plage [F] 28 D2
Hardenberg [NL] 16 G4
Hardenberg [NL] 16 G4
Harderwijk [NL] 16 E4
Hardeshøj [DK] 156 C4
Hardheim [D] 46 D4
Hareid [N] 180 C3
Haren [D] 16 H3
Haren [NL] 16 G2
Harestua [N] 172 B5
Harewood [GB] 10 F3
Harfleur [F] 26 G3
Hargla [EST] 200 F4
Hargshamn [S] 174 G5
Haría [E] 100 E4
Harjavalta [FIN] 176 D2
Harjunmaa [FIN] 188 C5
Harjunsalmi [FIN] 186 F6
Harkány [H] 76 B5
Harlech [GB] 10 B5
Hårlev [DK] 156 G3
Harlingen [NL] 16 E2
Harlösa [S] 158 C2
Harlow [GB] 14 E4
Harmancık [TR] 146 F6
Harmånger [S] 184 E6
Härmänkylä [FIN] 198 F4
Härmänmäki [FIN] 198 F4
Harndrup [DK] 156 D3
Härnösand [S] 184 F4
Haro [E] 82 G5
Harodz'ki [BY] 202 H6

Haroldswick [GB] 6 H3
Haroué [F] 44 E6
Harpefoss [N] 170 H1
Harpenden [GB] 14 E3
Harplinge [S] 162 B5
Harpstedt [D] 18 D6
Harrachov [CZ] 48 H2
Harran [N] 190 D5
Harrogate [GB] 10 F3
Harrow [GB] 14 E4
Harsefeld [D] 18 E4
Harsewinkel [D] 32 D3
Harsprange [S] 190 H1
Harstad [N] 192 D3
Harstad [N] 166 D1
Harsum [D] 32 G2
Harsvik [N] 190 B5
Harta [H] 76 C3
Hartberg [A] 74 E1
Hartha [D] 34 D6
Hartland [GB] 12 D3
Hartlepool [GB] 10 G2
Hartley Wintney [GB] 14 D4
Hartmannshain [D] 46 D2
Hartola [FIN] 186 G6
Harwich [GB] 14 G3
Harzgerode [D] 34 A4
Hasanağa [TR] 146 E5
Hasanpaşa [TR] 146 G5
Haselund [D] 18 E1
Haselünne [D] 18 B6
Hasköy [TR] 146 B2
Hasköy [TR] 144 G3
Haslach [A] 62 B3
Haslach [D] 58 F2
Hasle [DK] 158 E4
Haslemere [GB] 14 D5
Haslev [DK] 156 G3
Hasparren [F] 84 C2
Hasseki [TR] 134 H4
Hassel [D] 18 E6
Hassela [S] 184 E5
Hasselfelde [D] 32 H4
Hasselfors [S] 166 G4
Hasselt [D] 30 E4
Hasselt [NL] 16 F4
Hassfurt [D] 46 F3
Hasslach [D] 46 H3
Hassle [S] 166 F4
Hassleben [D] 20 D5
Hässleholm [S] 158 D1
Hastersboda [FIN] 168 H1
Hastiere-Lavaux [B] 30 D6
Hastings [GB] 14 F6
Hästveda [S] 158 D1
Hasvik [N] 196 A2
Hatě [CZ] 62 E3
Haţeg [RO] 206 B5
Hatfield [GB] 14 E3
Hatfjelldal [N] 190 E3
Hatherleigh [GB] 12 D4
Hattem [NL] 16 F4
Hatten [D] 190 D2
Hattingen [D] 30 H3
Hattstedt [D] 18 E1
Hattula [FIN] 176 G2
Hattuvaara [FIN] 188 H1
Hattuvaara [FIN] 198 G6
Hatvan [H] 64 D6
Hatvik [N] 170 B4
Haugan [N] 190 B6
Haugastøl [N] 170 E4
Hauge [N] 164 B5
Haugesund [N] 164 A1
Hauggrend [N] 164 E2
Haughom [N] 164 C4
Haugsdorf [A] 62 E3
Haugsten [N] 170 G1
Hauho [FIN] 176 G2
Haukå [N] 180 B5
Haukeligrend [N] 164 D1
Haukeliseter [N] 170 D5
Haukipudas [FIN] 198 D3
Haukivuori [FIN] 188 C5
Haunersdorf [D] 60 G3
Hausach [D] 58 F2
Häusern [D] 58 F4
Hausham [D] 60 E5
Hausjärvi [FIN] 176 H3
Hautajärvi [FIN] 196 F7

Haut-Asco [F] 114 B3
Haute-Nendaz [CH] 70 D2
Hauteville-Lompnes [F] 68 H2
Hauteville Plage [F] 26 D3
Hautmont [F] 28 G4
Havant [GB] 14 D5
Havdhem [S] 168 G5
Håvedalen [S] 166 C4
Havelange [B] 30 D5
Havelberg [D] 34 C1
Haverdal [S] 162 B5
Haverfordwest [GB] 12 D1
Haverhill [GB] 14 F3
Håverud [S] 166 D4
Havířov [CZ] 50 F4
Hävla [S] 168 B4
Havlejčkův Brod [CZ] 48 D4
Havlíčkův Brod [CZ] 48 H5
Havneby [DK] 156 A4
Havnebyen [DK] 156 F1
Havnsø [DK] 156 F2
Havøysund [N] 196 B1
Havran [TR] 144 C1
Havsa [TR] 146 B2
Havstensund [S] 166 B4
Hawarden [GB] 10 D4
Hawes [GB] 10 E2
Hawick [GB] 8 E4
Hawkinge [GB] 14 F5
Hawkshead [GB] 10 D2
Hayange [F] 44 E3
Hayle [GB] 12 B5
Hay-on-Wye [GB] 12 F2
Hayrabolu [TR] 146 B3
Haywards Heath [GB] 14 E5
Hazebrouck [F] 28 E2
Hazel Grove [GB] 10 E4
Hazlov [CZ] 48 C3
Headcorn [GB] 14 F5
Headford [IRL] 2 C4
Heanor [GB] 10 F5
Heathfield [GB] 14 E5
Heby [S] 168 C1
Hechingen [D] 58 G2
Hechtel [B] 30 E3
Hed [S] 168 A2
Hedal [N] 170 G4
Heddal [N] 164 F2
Hédé [F] 26 C5
Hedehusene [DK] 156 G2
Hedemora [S] 174 D5
Heden [S] 172 E1
Hedenäset [S] 196 B8
Hedensted [DK] 156 C2
Hedesunda [S] 174 E5
Hedeviken [S] 182 F4
Hedon [GB] 10 G4
Hee [DK] 160 B6
Heek [D] 16 H5
Heemstede [NL] 16 D4
Heerde [NL] 16 F4
Heerenveen [NL] 16 F3
Heerlen [NL] 30 F4
Heeze [NL] 30 E3
Heggenes [N] 170 G2
Heglibister [GB] 6 G4
Hegra [N] 182 C1
Hegyeshalom [H] 62 G5
Hegyhátsál [H] 74 F2
Heia [N] 192 E3
Heide [D] 18 E2
Heidelberg [D] 46 C5
Heiden [D] 16 G6
Heidenau [D] 48 E1
Heidenheim [D] 60 C2
Heidenreichstein [A] 62 D2
Heikendorf [D] 18 G2
Heiland [N] 164 F3
Heilbronn [D] 46 D5
Heiligenberg [D] 58 H4
Heiligenblut [A] 72 G2
Heiligenhafen [D] 18 H2
Heiligenkreuz [A] 74 F2
Heiligenkreuz [A] 74 F2
Heiligenstadt [D] 32 G5
Heilsbronn [D] 46 F5
Heimaey [IS] 194 C6
Heimdal [N] 182 B1

Heimertingen [D] 60 B4
Heinävaara [FIN] 188 G2
Heinävesi [FIN] 188 E3
Heino [NL] 16 F4
Heinola [FIN] 178 B2
Heinsberg [D] 30 F4
Heiterwang [A] 60 C6
Heituinlahti [FIN] 178 D2
Hejde [S] 168 G5
Hejlsminde [DK] 156 C3
Hejnice [CZ] 48 H1
Hejnsvig [DK] 156 B2
Hel [PL] 22 E2
Heldrungen [D] 34 A5
Helechal [E] 96 B4
Helensburgh [GB] 8 D2
Helgum [S] 184 E2
Helissandur [IS] 194 B2
Hell [N] 182 C1
Hella [IS] 194 C5
Hella [N] 170 D1
Helle [N] 164 F4
Helleland [N] 164 B4
Hellendoorn [NL] 16 G4
Hellermaa [EST] 200 C2
Hellesøy [N] 170 A3
Hellesylt [N] 180 D4
Hellevad [DK] 156 B4
Hellevik [N] 170 B1
Hellevoetsluis [NL] 16 C5
Helligskogen [N] 192 F3
Hellín [E] 104 B1
Hellsö [FIN] 168 H1
Helmond [NL] 30 E2
Helmsdale [GB] 6 E3
Helmsley [GB] 10 F3
Helmstedt [D] 34 A3
Helnessund [N] 192 C5
Helsa [D] 32 F5
Helsby [GB] 10 D4
Helsingborg [S] 156 H1
Helsinge [DK] 156 G1
Helsingfors / Helsinki [FIN] 176 H5
Helsingør [DK] 156 H1
Helsinki / Helsingfors [FIN] 176 H5
Helston [GB] 12 B5
Hemau [D] 46 H6

Hemel Hempstead [GB] 14 E3
Hemer [D] 32 C4
Hëming [F] 44 G5
Hemling [S] 190 G6
Hemmet [DK] 156 A1
Hemmoor [D] 18 E3
Hemnes [N] 166 C2
Hemnesberget [N] 190 D2
Hemsby [GB] 14 H2
Hemse [S] 168 G5
Hemsedal [N] 170 F3
Hemslingen [D] 18 F5
Hen [N] 170 H5
Henán [S] 166 C6
Hendaye [F] 84 B2
Hendek [TR] 146 H3
Hengelo [NL] 16 G5
Hengersberg [D] 60 G2
Henichesk [UA] 206 G5
Hénin Beaumont [F] 28 F3
Henley-on-Thames [GB] 14 D4
Hennan [S] 184 D5
Henneberg [D] 46 F2
Hennebont [F] 40 C4
Hennef [D] 30 H5
Henne Strand [DK] 156 A2
Henningsvær [N] 192 B4
Henrichemont [F] 56 C3
Henriksfjäll [S] 190 E4
Henryków [PL] 50 C2
Henstedt-Ulzburg [D] 18 F3
Heppenheim [D] 46 C4
Heradsbygd [N] 172 C3
Herbault [F] 54 G1
Herbertingen [D] 58 H3
Herbertstown [IRL] 4 D4
Herbesthal [B] 30 F5
Herbeumont [B] 44 D2
Herbignac [F] 40 E5
Herborn [D] 46 C1
Herbrechtingen [D] 60 C3
Herby [PL] 50 F2
Herceg Novi [YU] 152 D4
Hercegovac [HR] 74 G6
Hercegovska Goleša [YU] 152 E2

Hercegszántó [H] 76 C5
Herdla [N] 170 A3
Hereford [GB] 12 G2
Héreg [H] 64 B6
Hereke [TR] 146 F3
Herencia [E] 96 G3
Herend [H] 74 H2
Herentals [B] 30 D3
Herfølge [DK] 156 G3
Herford [D] 32 E2
Hergiswil [CH] 58 F6
Héricourt [F] 58 C4
Heringsdorf [D] 20 E3
Herisau [CH] 58 H5
Hérisson [F] 56 C5
Herleshausen [D] 32 G6
Hermagor [A] 72 G3
Hermannsburg [D] 18 F6
Hermansverk [N] 170 D2
Heřmanův Městec [CZ] 50 A4
Herment [F] 68 B2
Hermeskeil [D] 44 G3
Hernani [E] 84 B2
Herne [D] 30 H3
Herne Bay [GB] 14 G5
Heroldsberg [D] 46 G5
Herøya [N] 164 G3
Herre [N] 164 G3
Herrenberg [D] 58 G1
Herrera [E] 102 B2
Herrera del Duque [E] 96 C3
Herrera de los Navarros [E] 90 D5
Herrera de Pisuerga [E] 82 D5
Herreruela [E] 86 G5
Herrljunga [S] 162 B1
Herrnburg [D] 18 G3
Herrnhut [D] 48 G1
Herröskkatan [FIN] 168 G1
Herrsching [D] 60 D4
Herrskog [S] 184 F3
Hersbruck [D] 46 H5
Herselt [B] 30 D3
Herstmonceux [GB] 14 E5
Hertford [GB] 14 E3

Hervás [E] 88 B5
Hervik [N] 164 B2
Herzberg [D] 32 G4
Herzberg [D] 34 E4
Herzberg [D] 34 D1
Herzfeld [D] 32 D4
Herzfelde [D] 34 F2
Herzlake [D] 18 B6
Herzogenaurach [D] 46 G5
Herzogenburg [A] 62 E4
Herzsprung [D] 20 C6
Hesdin [F] 28 D3
Hesel [D] 18 C4
Hesnæs [DK] 20 B1
Hessich-Lichtenau [D] 32 F5
Hess Oldendorf [D] 32 F2
Hessvik [N] 170 C4
Hestenesøyri [N] 180 C5
Hestra [S] 162 C3
Hestra [S] 162 E1
Heswall [GB] 10 D4
Hetin [YU] 76 F6
Hettange-Grande [F] 44 E3
Hettstedt [D] 34 B4
Hetvehely [H] 76 A5
Heustreu [D] 46 F2
Heves [H] 64 E6
Hévíz [H] 74 G3
Hevlin [CZ] 62 F3
Hexham [GB] 8 F6
Heyrieux [F] 68 G3
Heysham [GB] 10 D2
Hidasnémeti [H] 64 G3
Hıdırdıvani [TR] 144 F2
Hieflau [A] 62 C6
Hiersac [F] 54 D6
Hietanen [FIN] 188 C6
Hietaniemi [FIN] 196 E8
Hietaperä [FIN] 198 F5
Highclere [GB] 12 H4
Highworth [GB] 12 H3
High Wycombe [GB] 14 D4
Higuera de la Serena [E] 96 B4
Higuera la Real [E] 94 F3
Higueruela [E] 98 C5
Hiirola [FIN] 188 C5
Hiitinen / Hitis [FIN] 176 E6

Híjar [E] 90 F5
Hilchenbach [D] 32 C5
Hildal [N] 170 C5
Hildburghausen [D] 46 G2
Hilden [D] 30 G4
Hilders [D] 46 E2
Hildesheim [D] 32 G3
Hiliadoú [GR] 134 C4
Hillegom [NL] 16 D4
Hillerød [DK] 156 G2
Hillerstorp [S] 162 C3
Hillesøy [N] 192 D2
Hillsand [S] 190 E5
Hillsborough [GB] 2 G4
Hillswick [GB] 6 G3
Hilltown [GB] 2 G4
Hilmo [N] 182 C2
Hilpoltstein [D] 46 G6
Hilterfingen [CH] 70 E1
Hilvarenbeek [NL] 30 E2
Hilversum [NL] 16 E4
Himanka [FIN] 198 C5
Himarë [AL] 128 B6
Himmelpforten [D] 18 E4
Hinckley [GB] 10 E6
Hindås [S] 160 H2
Hindelang [D] 60 C6
Hindhead [GB] 14 D5
Hindsig [DK] 156 B2
Hinnerjoki [FIN] 176 D3
Hinnerup [DK] 160 D6
Hinojosa del Duque [E] 96 C4
Hinterrhein [CH] 70 G2
Hintersee [D] 20 E4
Hinterstoder [A] 62 B6
Hinterthal [A] 72 G1
Hintertux [A] 72 D1
Hinterweidenthal [D] 44 H4
Hinterzarten [D] 58 F3
Hirschaid [D] 46 G4
Hirschau [D] 48 B5
Hirschberg [D] 48 B2
Hirschegg [A] 60 B6
Hirschhorn [D] 46 C5
Hirsilä [FIN] 186 E6
Hirsingue [F] 58 D4
Hirson [F] 28 G5
Hîrşova [RO] 206 D6
Hirtshals [DK] 160 E2
Hirvaskoski [FIN] 198 E3
Hirvensalmi [FIN] 186 H6
Hirwaun [GB] 12 F2
Hisarcık [TR] 144 F2
Hita [E] 88 H5
Hitchin [GB] 14 E3
Hitiaş [RO] 76 H6
Hitis / Hiitinen [FIN] 176 E6
Hittarp [S] 156 H1
Hitterdal [N] 182 D4
Hitzacker [D] 18 H5
Hiukkajoki [FIN] 188 F5
Hjallerup [DK] 160 E3
Hjälmseryd [S] 162 D3
Hjärtum [S] 166 C6
Hjelle [N] 180 D5
Hjelle [N] 180 C5
Hjellestad [N] 170 A4
Hjelmeland [N] 164 B2
Hjerkinn [N] 180 G4
Hjerpsted [DK] 156 B4
Hjerting [DK] 156 A2
Hjo [S] 166 F6
Hjøllund [DK] 156 C1
Hjørring [DK] 160 E2
Hjorte [DK] 156 D3
Hjortkvarn [S] 166 H4
Hjortsberga [S] 158 F1
Hjulsbro [S] 168 A6
Hlinsko [CZ] 50 B4
Hlohovec [SK] 62 H4
Hluboká nad Vltavou [CZ] 62 C2
Hlučín [CZ] 50 E4
Hmelnicki [UA] 206 D3
Hniezdne [SK] 52 B6
Hnilec [SK] 64 E2
Hnúšťa–Likier [SK] 64 D3
Hobro [DK] 160 D5
Hocalar [TR] 144 H3
Höchberg [D] 46 E4

Hochburg [A] 60 G4
Hochdonn [D] 18 E3
Hochdorf [CH] 58 F5
Höchenschwand [D] 58 F4
Hochfelden [F] 44 H5
Hochspeyer [D] 46 B4
Höchst [D] 46 D4
Höchstädt [D] 60 C3
Höchstadt [D] 46 G4
Hockenheim [D] 46 C5
Hodalen [N] 182 C4
Hodenhagen [D] 18 E6
Hodkovice nad Mohelkou [CZ] 48 G2
Hódmezővásárhely [H] 76 E4
Hodonín [CZ] 62 G2
Hodoš [SLO] 74 F3
Hodošan [HR] 74 F4
Hoedekenskerke [NL] 28 H1
Hoek van Holland [NL] 16 C5
Hof [D] 48 B3
Hof [D] 58 F1
Hof [IS] 194 F6
Hofgeismar [D] 32 F4
Hofheim [D] 46 F3
Hofles [N] 190 C4
Höfn [IS] 194 F6
Hofors [S] 174 D4
Hofsós [IS] 194 E3
Hofstad [N] 190 B5
Höganäs [S] 156 H1
Högfors [S] 166 H1
Höghult [S] 162 F2
Högklint [S] 168 F4
Högsäter [S] 166 D5
Högsby [S] 162 F4
Høgset [N] 180 E2
Hogstorp [S] 166 C5
Hőgyész [H] 76 B4
Hohenau [A] 62 G3
Hohenberg [A] 62 E5
Hohenbrunn [D] 60 E4
Hohenems [A] 58 H5
Höhenkirchen [D] 60 E4
Hohenlimburg [D] 32 C4
Hohenlinden [D] 60 F4
Hohenlockstedt [D] 18 F3
Hohenpeissenberg [D] 60 D5
Hohenschwangau [D] 60 C6
Hohentauern [A] 74 C1
Hohenwestedt [D] 18 F2
Hohrodberg [F] 58 D3
Hohwacht [D] 18 G2
Hoisko [FIN] 186 D2
Højer [DK] 156 B4
Højerup [DK] 156 G4
Højslev Stby [DK] 160 C5
Hojsova Straž [CZ] 48 D6
Hok [S] 162 D3
Hökåsen [S] 168 B2
Hokksund [N] 164 G1
Holand [N] 190 D5
Holbæk [DK] 156 F2
Holbeach [GB] 10 G6
Holdorf [D] 32 D1
Holeby [DK] 20 A1
Holešov [CZ] 50 D6
Holič [SK] 62 G3
Holice [CZ] 50 B4
Höljes [S] 172 E3
Hollabrunn [A] 62 E3
Hollád [H] 74 G3
Hollandstoun [GB] 6 G1
Høllen [N] 164 D6
Hollenstedt [D] 18 F4
Hollfeld [D] 46 G4
Hollingsholm [N] 180 E2
Hollola [FIN] 188 H3
Hollum [NL] 16 F1
Höllviksnäs [S] 156 H3
Holm [DK] 156 C4
Holm [FIN] 198 B6
Holm [N] 166 B3
Holm [N] 190 C4
Holm [RUS] 204 C3
Hólmavík [IS] 194 C2

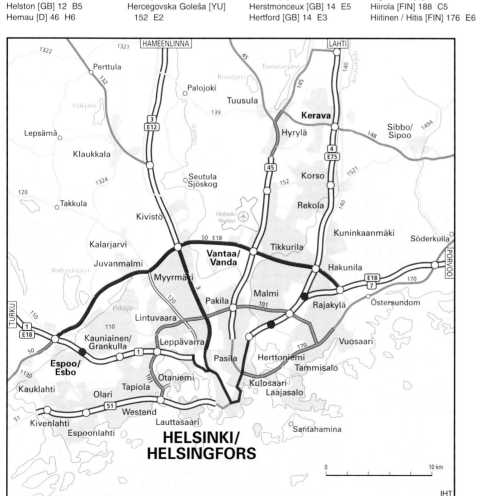

Holmec [SLO] 74 C3
Holmegil [N] 166 C3
Holmes Chapel [GB] 10 D4
Holmestrand [N] 164 H2
Holmfirth [GB] 10 E4
Holmsjö [S] 162 F6
Holmsund [S] 198 A6
Holmsveden [S] 174 E3
Holovne [UA] 38 G5
Holøydal [N] 182 C5
Holstebro [DK] 160 B5
Holsted [DK] 156 B2
Holsworthy [GB] 12 D4
Holt [GB] 14 G1
Holten [NL] 16 G5
Holtet [N] 166 C4
Holtet [N] 172 D4
Holwerd [NL] 16 F1
Holycross [IRL] 4 E4
Holyhead [GB] 10 B3
Holy Islands [GB] 8 G4
Holywell [GB] 12 F4
Holywell [GB] 10 C4
Holywood [GB] 2 G3
Holzdorf [D] 34 D4
Holzgau [A] 72 B1
Holzkirchen [D] 60 E5
Holzleitensattel [A] 72 C1
Holzminden [D] 32 F3
Homberg [D] 32 F6
Homberg [D] 46 D1
Homburg [D] 44 G4
Hommelstø [N] 190 D3
Hommelvik [N] 182 C1
Hommersåk [N] 164 B3
Homps [F] 106 C4
Hondarribia / Fuenterrabía [E] 84 B2
Hönebach [D] 32 F6
Hønefoss [N] 170 H5
Honfleur [F] 26 G3
Høng [DK] 156 F3
Honiton [GB] 12 F4
Honkajoki [FIN] 186 C5
Honkakoski [FIN] 186 B6
Honne [D] 32 G1
Hønning [DK] 156 B3
Honningsvåg [N] 180 B4
Honningsvåg [N] 196 C1
Honrubia [E] 98 B3
Hontalbilla [E] 88 F3
Hontianske–Nemce [SK] 64 C4
Hontoria del Pinar [E] 90 A2
Hoogerheide [NL] 30 C2
Hoogeveen [NL] 16 G3
Hoogezand [NL] 16 G2
Hoogkarspel [NL] 16 E3
Hoogstraten [B] 30 D2
Hooksiel [D] 18 C3
Höör [S] 158 C2
Hoorn [NL] 16 E3
Hopeman [GB] 6 E4
Hopfgarten [A] 60 F6
Hoplandsjøen [N] 170 A2
Hoppula [FIN] 196 E8
Hopseidet [N] 196 D1
Hopsten [D] 32 C2
Hopton–on–Sea [GB] 14 H2
Hoptrup [DK] 156 C3
Hora–Sv–Šebestiána [CZ] 48 D2
Horažďovice [CZ] 48 E6
Horb [D] 58 G2
Horbelev [DK] 20 B1
Hörby [S] 158 C2
Horcajo de Santiago [E] 96 H2
Horda [S] 162 D4
Hordain [F] 28 F4
Horgen [CH] 58 F5
Horgoš [YU] 76 E5
Horia [RO] 76 G4
Hořice [CZ] 50 A3
Horitschon [A] 62 F6
Horn [A] 62 E3
Horn [D] 32 E3
Horn [D] 58 G4
Horn [N] 170 H4
Horn [N] 190 D3

Horn [S] 162 F2
Hornachos [E] 94 H3
Hornachuelos [E] 96 B6
Hornbæk [DK] 156 G1
Hornberg [D] 58 F2
Hornburg [D] 152 H3
Horncastle [GB] 10 G5
Horndal [S] 174 D5
Horne de DK] 156 D4
Horne [DK] 156 D4
Horneburg [D] 18 F4
Hörnefors [S] 190 H6
Horní Benešov [CZ] 50 D4
Horní Cerekev [CZ] 48 H6
Horní Lideč [CZ] 50 E6
Hornindal [N] 180 D5
Hørning [DK] 156 D1
Horní Planá [CZ] 62 B3
Horní Vltavice [CZ] 62 A2
Hornnes [N] 164 D4
Hornos [E] 102 G1
Hornos de Peal [E] 102 F2
Hornoy [F] 28 D5
Hornsea [GB] 10 G4
Hornslet [DK] 160 E6
Hörnum [D] 156 A4
Hornum [DK] 160 D4
Horodok [UA] 52 G4
Horol [UA] 206 G2
Hořovice [CZ] 48 E4
Horred [S] 160 H3
Horsens [DK] 156 D2
Horsham [GB] 14 E5
Hørsholm [DK] 156 G2
Horslunde [DK] 156 E4
Horšovský Týn [CZ] 48 D5
Horst [D] 18 G5
Horst [NL] 30 F3
Hörstel [D] 32 C2
Horstmar [D] 16 H5
Horsunlu [TR] 144 F5
Hort [H] 64 D6
Horten [N] 164 H2
Hortezuela [E] 90 A3
Hortigüela [E] 88 H1
Hortobágy [H] 64 G6
Horton–in–Ribblesdale [GB] 10 E2
Hørve [DK] 156 F2
Horw [CH] 58 F6
Hosenfeld [D] 46 E2
Hospental [CH] 70 F1
Hospital [IRL] 4 D4
Hossa [FIN] 198 F3
Hossegor [F] 66 A6
Hostalric [E] 92 F4
Hostens [F] 66 C4
Hostinné [CZ] 50 A2
Hostomice [CZ] 48 F4
Hotagen [S] 190 E5
Hotin [UA] 206 D3
Hoting [S] 190 F5
Hotton [B] 30 E6
Hou [DK] 160 E4
Houdain [F] 28 E3
Houdan [F] 42 E3
Houdelaincourt [F] 44 D5
Houeillès [F] 66 D5
Houffalize [B] 30 E6
Houghton le Spring [GB] 8 G6
Houlgate [F] 26 F3
Hourtin [F] 66 C2
Hourtin–Plage [F] 66 C2
Houton [GB] 6 F2
Houtsala [FIN] 176 C5
Houtskär / Houtskari [FIN] 176 C5
Houtskari / Houtskär [FIN] 176 C5
Hov [DK] 156 D1
Hov [N] 170 H3
Hova [S] 166 F4
Hovda [N] 170 Q3
Hovden [N] 164 D1
Hovden [N] 192 B3
Hove [DK] 156 F2
Hove [DK] 160 B5
Hove [GB] 14 E5
Hövelhof [D] 32 E3
Hoven [DK] 156 B1
Hovet [N] 170 E3
Hovin [N] 164 F1

Hovland [N] 170 C4
Hovmantorp [S] 162 E5
Hovsta [S] 166 H3
Howth [IRL] 2 F6
Höxter [D] 32 F4
Hoya [D] 18 E6
Høyanger [N] 170 C1
Høydalen [N] 164 F3
Høydalsmo [N] 164 E2
Hoyerswerda [D] 34 F5
Hoylake [GB] 10 D4
Høylandet [N] 190 C4
Hoyos [E] 86 G3
Hoyos del Espino [E] 88 C5
Hradec Králové [CZ] 50 A3
Hradec nad Moravicí [CZ] 50 E4
Hrádek [CZ] 62 F3
Hrádek nad Nisou [CZ] 48 G1
Hrafnagill [IS] 194 E3
Hraivaron [RUS] 206 H1
Hranice [CZ] 50 E5
Hrebenne [PL] 52 G3
Hřensko [CZ] 48 F1
Hriňová [SK] 64 D3
Hríssafa [GR] 136 E4
Hristianó [GR] 136 C3
Hristós [GR] 138 G1
Hrob [CZ] 48 E2
Hrochův Týnec [CZ] 50 B4
Hrodno [BY] 24 F4
Hronov [CZ] 50 B2
Hrotovice [CZ] 62 E2
Hrtkovci [YU] 154 F2
Hrubieszów [PL] 52 G1
Hrušovany [CZ] 62 F3
Hrvace [HR] 152 A1
Huben [A] 72 F2
Hucknall [GB] 10 F5
Hucqueliers [F] 28 D3
Huddersfield [GB] 10 E4
Huddinge [S] 168 D3
Hudiksvall [S] 174 E1
Huedin [RO] 206 B4
Huelgoat [F] 40 C2
Huelma [E] 102 E3
Huelva [E] 94 E6
Huércal de Almería [E] 102 G5
Huércal–Overa [E] 102 H4
Huerta de Valdecarábanos [E] 96 G2
Huesca [E] 84 D6
Huéscar [E] 102 G3
Huete [E] 98 A1
Huétor Tájar [E] 102 D3
Hüfingen [D] 58 F3
Hufthamar [N] 170 A4
Hugh Town [GB] 12 A5
Huhdasjärvi [FIN] 178 C2
Huhus [FIN] 188 C4
Huittinen [FIN] 176 E2
Huizen [NL] 16 D3
Huizen [NL] 16 E4
Hulín [CZ] 50 D6
Hulk [CZ] 62 H2
Hull [GB] 10 G4
Hullsjön [S] 184 D4
Hulsing [DK] 160 E2
Hulst [NL] 28 H1
Hult [S] 162 E2
Hult [S] 166 F3
Hultanäs [S] 162 E4
Hultsfred [S] 162 F3
Humble [DK] 156 E5
Humenné [SK] 64 H2
Humlebæk [DK] 156 G2
Humlum [DK] 160 B5
Humpolec [CZ] 48 H5
Humppi [FIN] 186 F2
Humppila [FIN] 176 F3
Hundested [DK] 156 G2
Hundorp [N] 170 H1
Hunedoara [RO] 206 B5
Hünfeld [D] 46 E1
Hungen [D] 46 D2
Hungerford [GB] 12 H3

Hunnebostrand [S] 166 B5
Hunspach [F] 46 B6
Hunstanton [GB] 10 H6
Huntingdon [GB] 14 E2
Huntly [GB] 6 F5
Huopanankoski [FIN] 186 F2
Hurbanovo [SK] 64 B5
Hurdal [N] 172 B4
Huriel [F] 56 C5
Hurissalo [FIN] 188 D6
Hürsovo [BG] 148 E2
Hurstpierpoint [GB] 14 E5
Hurup [DK] 160 B4
Hurva [S] 158 C2
Husa [S] 190 D1
Húsavík [IS] 194 F3
Husby [DK] 160 B5
Husby Långhundra [S] 168 D2
Husby–Sjuhundra [S] 168 E2
Hushinish [GB] 6 B3
Huşi [RO] 206 D4
Husinec [CZ] 62 B2
Huskvarna [S] 162 D2
Husnes [N] 170 B5
Hust [UA] 206 B3
Hustopeče [CZ] 62 F2
Husum [D] 18 E1
Husum [S] 184 G2
Huta Zawadzka [PL] 38 A4
Hutovo [BIH] 152 C3
Hüttschlag [A] 72 G1
Huttwil [CH] 58 E5
Huy [B] 30 D5
Hvalba [DK] 160 A3
Hvalpsund [DK] 160 C4
Hvalvík [DK] 160 B1
Hvam [N] 172 B6
Hvammstangi [IS] 194 D3
Hvar [HR] 152 A2
Hveragerði [IS] 194 B5
Hvidbjerg [DK] 160 B4
Hvide Sande [DK] 156 A1
Hvittingfoss [N] 164 G2
Hvolsvöllur [IS] 194 C5
Hyde [GB] 10 E4
Hyen [N] 180 C5
Hyères [F] 108 C6
Hyggen [N] 164 H1
Hylestad [N] 164 D3
Hyllested Skovgårde [DK] 160 F6
Hyltebruk [S] 162 B4
Hynnekleiv [N] 164 E4
Hyrynsalmi [FIN] 198 F4
Hyssna [S] 160 H2
Hythe [GB] 14 F5
Hytti [FIN] 178 E2
Hyväniemi [FIN] 196 E8
Hyvinkää [FIN] 176 H4
Hyypiö [FIN] 196 D7

I

Ianca [RO] 148 A2
Iaşi [RO] 206 D4
Íasmos [GR] 130 F2
Ibañeta, Puerto de– [Eur.] 84 C3
Ibbenburen [D] 32 C2
Ibeas de Juarros [E] 82 E6
Ibestad [N] 192 D3
Ibi [E] 104 E1
Ibieca [E] 84 D6
Ibrány [H] 64 H4
İbrikbaba [TR] 146 B4
İbriktepe [TR] 130 H2
Ichenhausen [D] 60 C3
Idanha–a–Nova [P] 86 F3
Idar–Oberstein [D] 44 H3
Idjoš [YU] 76 E5
Idre [S] 182 E6
Idrija [SLO] 74 B5
Idritsa [RUS] 200 H5
Idro [I] 72 B5
Idstein [D] 46 C2
Iecava [LV] 200 D5
Ieper (Ypres) [B] 28 F2

Ierápetra [GR] 140 G5
Ierissós [GR] 130 C5
Ieropigí [GR] 128 D5
Ifjord [N] 196 D2
Igal [H] 76 A4
Igalo [YU] 152 D4
Igate [LV] 200 E4
Igea Marina [I] 110 H5
Igelfors [S] 168 A4
Iggesund [S] 174 E1
Iglesias [I] 118 B6
Igliauka [LT] 24 F1
Igls [A] 72 D1
Ignalina [LT] 202 H4
Ignatpol [UA] 204 B7
Iğneada [TR] 146 D1
Igołomia [PL] 52 B3
Igoumenítsa [GR] 132 C2
Igrane [HR] 152 B2
Igriés [E] 84 D6
Igualada [E] 92 D4
Iharosberény [H] 74 G4
Ii [FIN] 198 D3
Ilıca [TR] 146 D5
Iisaku [EST] 200 F1
Iisalmi [FIN] 198 E6
Iittin [FIN] 178 B2
IJmuiden [NL] 16 D4
Ikaalinen [FIN] 186 D6
Ikast [DK] 160 C6
Ikhtiman [BG] 150 G5
Iklad [FIN] 176 C5
Ilanz [CH] 70 G1
Iława [PL] 22 F4
Ilbla / Illby [FIN] 178 B4
Il Casalone [I] 114 G4
Ilchester [GB] 12 F4
Ildır [TR] 134 H4
İlhan [TR] 146 D4
Ílhavo [P] 80 B5
Ilia [RO] 206 B5
Iličevsk [UA] 206 E5
Ilidža [BIH] 152 D1
Ilirska Bistrica [SLO] 74 B6
Ilkeston [GB] 10 F5
Ilkley [GB] 10 E3
Illano [E] 78 F3
Illar [E] 102 F5
Illa Ravena [E] 104 F5
Illby / Ilbla [FIN] 178 B4
Illertissen [D] 60 B4
Illiers [F] 42 D5
Illiers–Combray [F] 42 D5
Illingen [D] 46 C6
Illmitz [A] 62 G6
Illo [FIN] 176 E2
Ilmajoki [FIN] 186 C3
Il'me [RUS] 178 F1
Ilmenau [D] 46 G1
Ilminster [GB] 12 F4
Ilok [HR] 154 F1
Ilomantsi [FIN] 188 G2
Iłowa [PL] 34 H5
Iłowiec [PL] 22 A5
Ilsenburg [D] 32 H3
Ilshofen [D] 46 E6
Ilskov [DK] 160 C6
Ilūkste [LV] 200 F6
Ilvesjoki [FIN] 186 C4
Iłża [PL] 38 C6
Imatra [FIN] 178 E1
Ímeros [GR] 130 F3
Immenhausen [D] 32 F5
Immenstaad [D] 58 H4
Immenstadt [D] 60 B5
Immingham [GB] 10 G4
Imola [I] 110 G4
Imotski [HR] 152 B2
Imperia [I] 108 G4
Imphy [F] 56 D4
Impilakhti [RUS] 188 H5
Impiö [FIN] 198 E2
İmroz [TR] 130 G5
Inari [FIN] 196 D4
Inca [E] 104 E5
Inch [IRL] 4 B4
Inch [IRL] 4 D5
Inchbae Lodge [GB] 6 D4
Inchigeelagh [IRL] 4 C5

Inchnadamph [GB] 6 D3
İnciraltı [TR] 144 C4
İncirköy [TR] 142 G3
İncirliova [TR] 144 D5
Incisa in Val d'Arno [I] 110 F6
Indal [S] 184 E4
Independenta [RO] 148 F1
Indjija [YU] 154 G2
Indre Brenna [N] 196 C2
Indura [BY] 24 F4
İnece [TR] 146 B2
Inecik [TR] 146 C3
İnegöl [TR] 146 F5
Ineu [RO] 76 H4
Infiesto [E] 82 C2
Ingå / Inkoo [FIN] 176 G5
Ingatestone [GB] 14 F4
Ingelheim [D] 46 B3
Ingelmunster [B] 28 G2
Ingelstad [S] 162 E5
Ingenio [E] 100 C6
Ingleton [GB] 10 E2
Ingoldmells [GB] 10 H5
Ingolsbenning [S] 174 D5
Ingolstadt [D] 60 E2
Ingram [GB] 8 F5
Ingwiller [F] 44 G5
İnhisar [TR] 146 H4
Iniesta [E] 98 C4
Iniö [FIN] 176 C5
Inis / Ennis [IRL] 2 C6
Inishannon [IRL] 4 C5
Inkee [FIN] 198 F2
Inkoo / Ingå [FIN] 176 G5
Innbygda [N] 172 D2
Inndyr [N] 192 B6
Innellan [GB] 8 C3
Innerleithen [GB] 8 E4
Innertkirchen [CH] 70 F1
Innfjorden [N] 180 E3
Innhavet [N] 192 C5
Innichen / San Candido [I] 72 E3
Inning [D] 60 D4
Innsbruck [A] 72 D1
Innset [N] 192 E3
İnönü [TR] 146 H5
Inowłódz [PL] 38 A5
Inowrocław [PL] 36 E1
Ins [CH] 58 D5
Insch [GB] 6 F6
Insjön [S] 172 H4
Insko [PL] 20 G5
Insurăţei [RO] 206 D6
Interlaken [CH] 70 E1
Intra [I] 70 F3
Inveraray [GB] 8 C2
Inverbervie [GB] 8 G1
Inverey [GB] 6 E6
Invergarry [GB] 6 D5
Invergordon [GB] 6 E4
Inverkeilor [GB] 8 F2
Invermoriston [GB] 6 D5
Inverness [GB] 6 D5
Inverurie [GB] 6 F6
Inzell [D] 60 G5
Ioánnina [GR] 132 D2
Iolanda di Savóia [I] 110 G2
Íos [GR] 138 E4
Ipéria [GR] 132 G2
Iphofen [D] 46 F4
İpsala [TR] 130 H3
Ipswich [GB] 14 G3
Irákleia [GR] 138 F4
Irákleia [GR] 130 B3
Irakleío [GR] 140 E4
Irdning [A] 62 B6
Iregszemcse [H] 76 B3
Iréo [GR] 142 B1
Irig [YU] 154 F2
Irsina [I] 122 C3
Irun [E] 84 B2
Irurita [E] 84 B3
Irurtzun [E] 84 B3
Irvine [GB] 8 C3
Irvinestown [GB] 2 E3
Isaba / Izaba [E] 84 C4
İsabey [TR] 144 G4
Isaccea [RO] 206 D6

Janovice nad Úhlavou [CZ]
48 D5
Janów [PL] 50 G2
Janów [PL] 24 E4
Janowiec [PL] 38 D5
Janowiec Wielkopolski [PL]
36 D1
Janów Lubelski [PL] 52 E2
Janowo [PL] 22 H5
Janów Podlaski [PL] 38 F3
Janské Lazně [CZ] 50 A2
Jänsmässholmen [S] 190
D6
Januszewice [PL] 38 A5
Janville [F] 42 E5
Janzé [F] 26 C6
Jäppilä [FIN] 188 C4
Jarafuel [E] 98 D5
Jaraicejo [E] 96 B1
Jaraíz de la Vera [E] 88 B5
Jarandilla de la Vera [E] 88
B5
Järbo [S] 174 D4
Jarcevo [RUS] 204 D4
Jarczew [PL] 38 D4
Jard–sur–Mer [F] 54 B3
Jaren [N] 172 B4
Jaren [S] 166 C3
Jargeau [F] 42 E6
Jarkovac [YU] 154 H1
Järkvissle [S] 184 E3
Järlåsa [S] 168 C1
Jarmen [D] 20 D3
Jarmolincy [UA] 206 D3
Järna [S] 168 D4
Jarnac [F] 54 D6
Jarnages [F] 54 H6
Järnforsen [S] 162 F3
Jarny [F] 44 E4
Jarocin [PL] 36 D4
Jaroměř [CZ] 50 B3
Jaroměřice nad Rokytnou
[CZ] 62 E2
Jarosław [PL] 52 F3
Jarosławiec [PL] 22 B2
Järpen [S] 182 F2
Järva–Jaani [EST] 200 E2
Järvakandi [EST] 200 E2
Järvelä [FIN] 176 H3
Järvenpää [FIN] 176 H4
Järvsö [S] 174 D1
Jaša Tomič [YU] 154 H1
Jasenak [HR] 112 F2
Jasenovac [HR] 154 B1
Jasenovets [BG] 148 D2
Jasenovo [YU] 152 E3
Jasenovo [YU] 150 A3
Jashchera [RUS] 200 H1
Jasień [PL] 34 G4
Jasienica [PL] 50 F4
Jasienica Rosielna [PL] 52
E4
Jasika [YU] 150 C3
Jasionówka [PL] 24 E5
Jašiūnai [LT] 202 G6
Jasło [PL] 52 D4
Jastrebarsko [HR] 74 D6
Jastrowie [PL] 22 B5
Jastrzębie–Zdrói [PL] 50 F4
Jászapáti [H] 64 E6
Jászárokszállás [H] 64 E6
Jászberény [H] 64 E6
Jászfelsószentgyörgy [H] 76
E1
Jászfényszaru [H] 64 D6
Jászkisér [H] 76 E1
Jászladány [H] 76 E1
Jät [S] 162 E5
Játar [E] 102 G3
Jauge [F] 66 C3
Jaun [CH] 70 D1
Jaungulbene [LV] 200 F4
Jauniniumuiža [LV] 200 C6
Jaunjelgava [LV] 200 E5
Jaunpils [LV] 200 C5
Jauranna [LV] 200 F4
Jaurplebalga [LV] 200 F4
Jausiers [F] 108 E2
Jävall [N] 166 C2
Javarus [FIN] 196 D7
Jávea / Xàbia [E] 104 F1
Jävenitz [D] 34 B2

Javier / Xabier [E] 84 C4
Javoříčko [CZ] 50 C5
Javorník [CZ] 50 C3
Jävre [S] 198 B4
Javron [F] 26 F5
Jawor [PL] 36 B6
Jaworzno [PL] 50 G3
Jayena [E] 102 D4
Jebel [RO] 76 G6
Jedburgh [GB] 8 F4
Jedlina–Zdrój [PL] 50 B2
Jedovnice [CZ] 50 C6
Jędrzejów [PL] 52 B2
Jedwabne [PL] 24 D5
Jedwabno [PL] 22 H5
Jeesiö [FIN] 196 D6
Jēkabpils [LV] 200 F5
Jektevik [N] 170 B5
Jektvik [N] 190 D1
Jelah [BIH] 154 D3
Jelcy [RUS] 204 D3
Jelcz–Laskowice [PL] 50
D1
Jelenia Góra [PL] 50 A1
Jelgava [LV] 200 D5
Jelizarovo [RUS] 200 G3
Jelling [DK] 156 C2
Jelnja [RUS] 204 D5
Jełowa [PL] 50 E2
Jels [DK] 156 C3
Jelsa [HR] 152 A3
Jelsa [N] 164 B2
Jelsi [I] 120 F1
Jemnice [CZ] 62 D2
Jena [D] 46 H1
Jenbach [A] 60 E6
Jeneč [CZ] 48 F3
Jennersdorf [A] 74 E2
Jeppo / Jepua [FIN] 186
C1
Jepua / Jeppo [FIN] 186
C1
Jerez de la Frontera [E] 100
F3
Jerez del Marquesado [E]
102 F4
Jerez de los Caballeros [E]
94 F3
Jerggul Holmestrand [N]
192 H2
Jergucati [AL] 132 B1
Jérica [E] 98 E3
Jerichow [D] 34 C2
Jerup [DK] 160 E2
Jerxheim [D] 34 A3
Jerzu [I] 118 E5
Jerzwałd [PL] 22 F4
Jesberg [D] 32 E6
Jesenice [A] 74 B4
Jesenice [CZ] 48 E3
Jeseník [CZ] 50 D3
Jesi [I] 116 C1
Jésolo [I] 72 F6
Jessen [D] 34 D4
Jessheim [N] 172 C5
Jeumont [F] 28 H4
Jevenstedt [D] 18 F2
Jever [D] 18 C4
Jevíčko [CZ] 50 C5
Jevišovice [CZ] 62 E2
Jevnaker [N] 170 H5
Jezerane [HR] 112 G2
Jezerišče [BY] 204 C4
Jezero [BIH] 154 B3
Jezersko [SLO] 74 B4
Ježewo [PL] 36 H1
Jeżewo [PL] 24 E5
Jeziorany [PL] 22 H3
Jeżów [PL] 36 H4
Jičín [CZ] 48 H3
Jieznas [LT] 24 G1
Jihlava [CZ] 48 H5
Jijona / Xixona [E] 104 E2
Jilava [RO] 140 D6
Jilemnice [CZ] 48 H2
Jílové u Prahy [CZ] 48 F4
Jiltjaur [S] 190 F3
Jimbolia [RO] 76 F5
Jimena [E] 102 E2
Jimena de la Frontera [E]
100 H5

Ísafjörður [IS] 194 C1
Ísane [N] 180 C5
Isbister [GB] 6 G3
Íscar [E] 88 E2
Ischgl [A] 72 B2
Ischia [I] 120 D3
Isdes [F] 56 C2
Ise [N] 166 C3
Iselle [I] 70 E2
Iselsberg [A] 72 G2
Iseo [I] 72 A5
Iserlohn [D] 32 C4
Isernia [I] 120 E1
Isfjorden [N] 180 E3
İshaklı [TR] 146 B4
Isigny-sur-Mer [F] 26 E3
Işıklı [TR] 144 H3
Ísili [I] 118 D6
İskele [TR] 142 E2
Iskra [RUS] 178 F3
Isla [E] 82 F3
Isla Cristina [E] 94 D5
Isle of Whithorn [GB] 8 C5
Isle Ornsay [GB] 6 C5
Islivig / Islibhig [GB] 6 B2
Ismaning [D] 60 E4
Isnäs [FIN] 178 B4
Isny [D] 60 B5
Iso–Äiniö [FIN] 176 H2
Iso–Evo [FIN] 176 H2
Isojoki [FIN] 186 B5
Isokylä [FIN] 196 E7
Isokyrö [FIN] 186 B2
Isola [F] 108 E3
Isola del Gran Sasso d'Italia
[I] 116 C4
Isola della Scala [I] 110 F1
Isola del Liri [I] 116 C6
Ísola di Capo Rizzuto [I] 124
F5
Isola 2000 [F] 108 E3
Isona [E] 92 C2
Isorella [I] 110 D1
Isperikh [BG] 148 E2
Íspica [I] 126 G5
Issa [RUS] 200 H5
Isselburg [D] 16 F6
Issogne [I] 70 D4
Issoire [F] 68 C3

Issoudun [F] 56 B4
Is-sur-Tille [F] 56 H3
İstanbul [TR] 146 E3
Istarske Toplice [HR] 112
D1
Istérnia [GR] 138 E1
Istha [D] 32 E5
Isthmía [GR] 136 F1
Istiaía [GR] 134 A3
Istibanja [MK] 128 G1
Istranca [TR] 146 D2
Istres [F] 106 C5
Istria [RO] 206 E6
Istunmäki [FIN] 186 H3
Isums [S] 168 G4
Itäkylä [FIN] 186 D2
Itéa [GR] 132 G5
Itéa [GR] 132 F2
Itéa [GR] 128 F6
Itháki [GR] 132 D5
Itri [I] 120 C2
Íttiri [I] 118 C3
Itxassou [F] 84 C2
Itzehoe [D] 18 F3
Ivalo [FIN] 196 D4
Ivančice [CZ] 62 F2
Ivančiči [BIH] 154 D4
Ivančna Gorica [SLO] 74
C5
Ivanec [HR] 74 E4
Ivangorod [RUS] 200 G1
Ivangrad [YU] 150 A5
Ivanič Grad [HR] 74 F6
Ivanjica [YU] 150 B3
Ivanjska [BIH] 154 B2
Ivankovo [HR] 154 E1
Ivano–Frankove [UA] 52
G4
Ivano–Frankovsk [UA] 206
C3
Ivanovo [BG] 148 E3
Ivanovo [BY] 204 A6
Ivanska [HR] 74 G6
Ivanski [BG] 148 E3
Ivaylovgrad [BG] 130 G1
Iveland [N] 164 D5
Ivréa [I] 70 E4
İvrindi [TR] 144 C1
Ivry-la-Bataille [F] 42 E3

Ivybridge [GB] 12 D5
Iwonicz–Zdrój [PL] 52 D5
Iwye [BY] 204 A5
Ixia [GR] 142 E4
Ixworth [GB] 14 G3
Izaba / Isaba [E] 84 C4
Izbica Kujawski [PL] 36 F2
Izbiceni [RO] 148 A2
Izbicko [PL] 50 E2
Izborsk [RUS] 200 G3
Izeda [P] 80 F4
Izegem [B] 28 G2
Izernore [F] 68 H2
Izgrev [BG] 148 G5
Izium [UA] 206 H2
Izmail [UA] 206 E5
İzmir [TR] 144 C4
İzmit [TR] 146 G3
Iznájar [E] 102 C3
Iznalloz [E] 102 E3
İznik [TR] 146 G4
Izola [SLO] 72 H6
Izsák [H] 76 D3
Izvor [BG] 150 F5
Izvor [MK] 128 D2
Izvor [MK] 128 E2
Izvor [YU] 150 D2

J

Jaakonvaara [FIN] 188 G1
Jaala [FIN] 178 C2
Jaalanka [FIN] 198 E4
Jaama [EST] 200 G1
Jablanac [HR] 112 F3
Jablanica [BIH] 152 C1
Jablonec nad Nisou [CZ] 48
H2
Jablonica [SK] 62 H3
Jablonicki, pereval– [UA]
206 C3
Jabłonka [PL] 50 H5
Jabłonna [PL] 36 B3
Jablonné v Podještědi [CZ]
48 G2
Jabłonowo Pomorskie [PL]
22 E5

Jablunkov [CZ] 50 F5
Jabugo [E] 94 F4
Jabuka [BIH] 152 E1
Jabuka [YU] 152 E2
Jabuka [YU] 154 G2
Jabukovik [YU] 150 E4
Jaca [E] 84 D5
Jáchymov [CZ] 48 D3
Jade [D] 18 C4
Jadraque [E] 88 H5
Jægerspris [DK] 156 G2
Jægervatn [N] 192 E2
Jaén [E] 102 E2
Jagel [D] 18 F1
Jagotin [UA] 206 F2
Jagsthausen [D] 46 D5
Jajce [BIH] 154 C4
Jakabszállás [H] 76 D3
Jäkkvik [S] 190 F2
Jakobstad / Pietarsaari [FIN]
198 B6
Jakokoski [FIN] 188 F2
Jakšič [HR] 154 C1
Jakubany [SK] 52 C6
Jakuszyce [PL] 48 H1
Jalasjärvi [FIN] 186 C4
Jaligny-sur-Besbre [F] 56
D6
Jałówka [PL] 24 G6
Jamaja [EST] 200 C3
Jämijärvi [FIN] 186 C6
Jäminkipohja [FIN] 186 E5
Jämjö [S] 158 G1
Jammerdal [N] 172 D5
Jamnička Kiselica [HR] 112
H1
Jampol [UA] 206 D3
Jampol [UA] 206 C2
Jämsä [FIN] 186 F5
Jämsänkoski [FIN] 186
F5
Jämshög [S] 158 E1
Janakkala [FIN] 176 G3
Jänese [EST] 200 F1
Janja [BIH] 154 F3
Janjina [BIH] 152 B3
Jánoshalma [H] 76 D4
Jánosháza [H] 74 G2
Jánossomorja [H] 62 G5

Jimramov [CZ] 50 B5
Jince [CZ] 48 F4
Jindřichův Hradec [CZ] 48 G6
Jirkov [CZ] 48 E2
Joachimsthal [D] 20 D6
Jobbágyi [H] 64 D5
Jock [S] 196 B8
Jódar [E] 102 F2
Jodoigne [B] 30 D4
Joensuu [FIN] 188 F2
Joesjö [S] 190 E3
Jõgeva [EST] 200 F2
Johanngeorgenstadt [D] 48 D2
Johansfors [S] 162 F5
John O'Groats [GB] 6 F3
Johnstone [GB] 8 D3
Johnstown [IRL] 4 E3
Jõhvi [EST] 200 F1
Joigny [F] 42 H6
Joinville [F] 44 C5
Jokijärvi [FIN] 186 H2
Jokikylä [FIN] 198 D5
Jokikyla [FIN] 198 D6
Jokikylä [FIN] 198 F4
Jokioinen [FIN] 176 F3
Jokiperä [FIN] 186 B3
Jokipii [FIN] 186 C4
Jokkmokk [S] 190 H1
Joloskylä [FIN] 198 D3
Jomala [FIN] 176 A5
Jönåker [S] 168 C5
Jonava [LT] 202 F5
Joncy [F] 56 F5
Jondal [N] 170 C4
Joniškis [LT] 200 D6
Jönköping [S] 162 D2
Jonzac [F] 66 D1
Jordanów [PL] 50 H5
Jordanów Śląski [PL] 50 C1
Jördenstorf [D] 20 C3
Jordet [N] 172 D2
Jörlanda [S] 160 G1
Jormvattnet [S] 190 E4
Jörn [S] 190 H4
Joroinen [FIN] 188 D4
Jørpeland [N] 164 B3
Jošanička Banja [YU] 150 B3
Joševka [BIH] 154 C3
Josipdol [HR] 112 G2
Josipovac [HR] 76 B6
Jössefors [S] 166 D2
Josselin [F] 26 B6
Jostedal [N] 180 D6
Jósvafő [H] 64 F3
Jouarre [F] 42 H4
Jougne [F] 58 B6
Joukokylä [FIN] 198 F3
Joure [NL] 16 F3
Journaankylä [FIN] 178 B4
Joutsa [FIN] 186 G6
Joutseno [FIN] 178 E2
Joutsijärvi [FIN] 196 E7
Joyeuse [F] 68 E6
Józefów [PL] 52 F2
Józefów [PL] 38 C3
Józsa [H] 64 G6
Juankoski [FIN] 188 D1
Juan-les-Pins [F] 108 E5
Judaberg [N] 164 B2
Judenburg [A] 74 C2
Judinsalo [FIN] 186 G6
Juelsminde [DK] 156 D2
Jugon-les-Lacs [F] 26 B5
Juhnov [RUS] 204 E5
Juillac [F] 66 G3
Juist [D] 16 H1
Jukkasjärvi [S] 192 F5
Jule [N] 190 D5
Jülich [D] 30 F4
Julierpass [CH] 70 H2
Jullouville [F] 26 D4
Jumeaux [F] 68 D3
Jumièges [F] 26 H3
Jumilla [E] 104 C1
Jumisko [FIN] 196 E8
Jumurda [LV] 200 E5
Jung [S] 166 E6
Juniville [F] 44 C3

Junkerdal [N] 190 F1
Junosuando [S] 192 G5
Junqueira [P] 80 E4
Junsele [S] 190 F6
Juntusranta [FIN] 198 F3
Juodupė [LT] 200 F6
Juojärvi [FIN] 188 E3
Juoksenki [FIN] 196 C8
Juokslahti [FIN] 186 F5
Juorkuna [FIN] 198 E4
Jupiter [RO] 148 G1
Jurbarkas [LT] 202 E5
Jurjevo [HR] 112 F2
Jurków [PL] 52 B4
Jūrmala [LV] 200 D5
Jurmo [FIN] 176 D6
Jurmo [FIN] 176 C4
Jurmu [FIN] 198 E3
Jurowce [PL] 24 E5
Jurva [FIN] 186 B3
Jurvala [FIN] 178 D2
Jussey [F] 58 B3
Jüterbog [D] 34 D3
Jutrosin [PL] 36 D5
Juuka [FIN] 188 E1
Juupajoki [FIN] 186 E6
Juva [FIN] 188 D5
Juvigny-le-Tertre [F] 26 E4
Juvola [FIN] 188 E4
Juvre [DK] 156 B3
Juzennecourt [F] 44 C6
Južnyj [RUS] 22 H2
Jyderup [DK] 156 F2
Jyllinge [DK] 156 G2
Jyllinkoski [FIN] 186 C5
Jyväskylä [FIN] 186 G4

K

Kaamanen [FIN] 196 D4
Kaamasmukka [FIN] 196 D4
Kaanaa [FIN] 186 E6
Kaaresuvanto [FIN] 192 G4
Kaarssen [D] 18 H5
Kaatsheuvel [NL] 16 D6
Kaavi [FIN] 188 D2
Kaba [H] 76 G1
Kabakca [TR] 146 D2
Kabalar [TR] 144 G4
Kabaltepe [TR] 130 H5
Kabböle [FIN] 178 B4
Kâbdalis [S] 190 H2
Kabelvåg [N] 192 B4
Kableshkovo [BG] 148 F4
Kač [YU] 154 F1
Kačanik [YU] 150 C6
Kachanovo [RUS] 200 G4
Kačikol [YU] 150 C5
Kácov [CZ] 48 G4
Kaczorów [PL] 50 B5
Kadaň [CZ] 48 E3
Kadarkút [H] 74 H4
Kadıköy [TR] 146 B4
Kadiköy [TR] 144 F4
Kadrifakovo [MK] 128 F1
Kadzidło [PL] 24 C5
Kåfjord [N] 196 C1
Kagarlyk [UA] 206 E2
Kåge [S] 198 A4
Kågeröd [S] 158 C2
Kahla [D] 46 H1
Kaiáfa [GR] 136 C2
Käina [EST] 200 C2
Kainach bei Voitsberg [A] 74 D2
Kaindorf [A] 74 E2
Kainasto [FIN] 186 B4
Kainu [FIN] 186 D1
Kainulasjärvi [S] 192 G6
Kainuunkylä [FIN] 196 B8
Kaipiainen [FIN] 178 C2
Kairala [FIN] 196 E7
Kaisersesch [D] 30 G6
Kaiserslautern [D] 44 H3
Kaisheim [D] 60 D2
Kaišiadorіs [LT] 202 F5
Kaivanto [FIN] 198 E4
Kajaani [FIN] 198 E5

Kakanj [BIH] 154 D4
Kakavi [AL] 132 C1
Kakhovka [UA] 206 G4
Käkilahti [FIN] 198 E5
Kaklik [TR] 144 G5
Kakóvatos [GR] 136 C3
Kakslauttanen [FIN] 196 D5
Kaktyni [LV] 200 E5
Kál [H] 64 E6
Kälä [FIN] 186 H5
Kalaja [FIN] 198 D6
Kalajoki [FIN] 198 C5
Kalak [N] 196 D2
Kalakoski [FIN] 186 D4
Kalamáki [GR] 132 H2
Kalamariá [GR] 128 H4
Kalamáta [GR] 136 D4
Kalámi [GR] 140 C4
Kalamítsi [GR] 130 D6
Kálamos [GR] 134 C5
Kalamotí [GR] 134 G5
Kalampáka [GR] 132 E2
Kalándra [GR] 130 B6
Kalá Nerá [GR] 132 H2
Kalanti [FIN] 176 C3
Kálathos [GR] 142 E5
Kalavárda [GR] 142 D4
Kalávryta [GR] 136 D1
Kalbe [D] 34 B1
Kale [TR] 142 F1
Kaleköy [TR] 130 G5
Kaléntzi [GR] 136 C1
Kaléntzi [GR] 132 D2
Kalérgo [GR] 134 D5
Kalesija [BIH] 154 E3
Kalety [PL] 50 F2
Kalevala [RUS] 198 G3
Kálfafell [IS] 194 D6
Kalí [GR] 128 G4
Kaliánoi [GR] 136 E1
Kalinkoviči [BY] 204 C7
Kalinovik [BIH] 152 D2
Kalinovka [UA] 206 D2
Kaliráhi [GR] 128 E6
Kalisz [PL] 36 E4
Kalisz Pomorski [PL] 20 H5
Kalivári [GR] 134 E6
Kalix [S] 198 C2
Kaljazin [RUS] 204 F3
Kalkan [TR] 142 G4
Kalkar [D] 16 F6
Kall [S] 182 F1
Kallaste [EST] 200 F2
Kållered [S] 160 H2
Kalli [EST] 200 D3
Kallimasiá [GR] 134 G5
Kallinge [S] 158 F1
Kallislahti [FIN] 188 E5
Kallithéa [GR] 136 D2
Kallithéa [GR] 128 G6
Kallithéa [GR] 130 C6
Kallithéas [GR] 142 E4
Kallmünz [D] 48 B6
Kallo [FIN] 192 H5
Kalloní [GR] 136 F2
Kalloní [GR] 134 G2
Kállósemjén [H] 64 H5
Kallsedet [S] 190 D6
Kallunki [FIN] 196 F7
Kalmar [S] 162 G5
Kalmari [FIN] 186 F3
Kalna [YU] 150 E3
Kalná nad Hronom [SK] 64 B4
Kalnciems [LV] 200 D5
Kalochóri [GR] 128 E5
Kaló Chorió [GR] 140 F5
Kalocsa [H] 76 C4
Kalofer [BG] 148 B5
Kalogriá [GR] 132 E6
Kaloí Liménes [GR] 140 E5
Kalonéri [GR] 128 E5
Kaló Nero [GR] 136 C3
Kaloskopí [GR] 132 G4
Kalotina [BG] 150 F4
Kaloyan [BG] 148 F2

Kaloyanovo [BG] 148 B5
Káloz [H] 76 B2
Kalpákio [GR] 132 C1
Kals [A] 72 F2
Kalsdorf [A] 74 D2
Kaltanenai [LT] 202 G4
Kaltenkirchen [D] 18 F3
Kaltennordheim [D] 46 F2
Kaltinėnai [LT] 202 E4
Kaluga [RUS] 204 F5
Kalugerovo [BG] 148 A5
Kalundborg [DK] 156 E2
Kalush [UA] 206 C3
Kałuszyn [PL] 38 C3
Kalvåg [N] 180 B5
Kalvarija [LT] 24 E2
Kalvatn [N] 180 D4
Kalvehave [DK] 156 G4
Kälviä [FIN] 198 C6
Kalvitsa [FIN] 188 C5
Kalvola [FIN] 176 G2
Kalwang [A] 74 C1
Kalwaria Zebrzydowska [PL] 50 H4
Kálymnos [GR] 142 B3
Kám [H] 74 G2
Kamáres [GR] 138 D3
Kamáres [GR] 138 E3
Kamarína [GR] 132 C3
Kamário [GR] 142 B3
Kamariótissa [GR] 130 F4
Kambánis [GR] 128 H4
Kámbos [GR] 140 B4
Kámbos [GR] 132 F5
Kamchiya [BG] 148 F3
Kámen [CZ] 48 G5
Kamen [D] 32 C4
Kamenari [YU] 152 D4
Kámena Voúrla [GR] 132 H4
Kamen Bryag [BG] 148 G2
Kamenec-Podolski [UA] 206 D3
Kamenica [MK] 150 E6
Kamenice nad Lipou [CZ] 48 G6
Kamenka [RUS] 178 F3
Kamenka [UA] 206 F3
Kamennogorsk [RUS] 178 F2
Kamenný Újezd [CZ] 62 C2
Kameno [BG] 148 F4
Kamensko [HR] 152 B2
Kamensko [HR] 154 C1
Kamenz [D] 34 F6
Kamëz [AL] 128 B2
Kamianka-Dniprovska [UA] 206 G4
Kamień [PL] 52 E3
Kamienica [PL] 52 B5
Kamieniec Ząbkowicki [PL] 50 C2
Kamień Krajenskie [PL] 22 C5
Kamienna Góra [PL] 50 B2
Kamień Pomorski [PL] 20 F3
Kamieńsk [PL] 36 G6
Kamnik [SLO] 74 C4
Kampen [D] 156 A4
Kampen [NL] 16 F4
Kamp Lintfort [D] 30 G3
Kampor [HR] 112 F3
Kámpos [GR] 136 D4
Kámpos [GR] 138 H2
Kamula [FIN] 198 E5
Kamyanets [BY] 38 G2
Kamyanyuki [BY] 38 G2
Kanala [FIN] 186 E1
Kanála [GR] 138 C2
Kanália [GR] 132 H2
Kańczuga [PL] 52 E3
Kandava [LV] 200 C5
Kandel [D] 46 B5
Kandern [D] 58 E4
Kandersteg [CH] 70 D2
Kandestederne [DK] 160 E2
Kándia [GR] 136 F2
Kandíla [GR] 136 E2
Kandira [TR] 146 G2

Kanestraum [N] 180 F2
Kanfanar [HR] 112 D2
Kangádio [GR] 136 C1
Kangasaho [FIN] 186 E3
Kangasala [FIN] 176 F1
Kangaskylä [FIN] 198 D6
Kangaslampi [FIN] 188 D4
Kangasniemi [FIN] 186 H5
Kangos [S] 192 G5
Kangosjärvi [FIN] 192 G5
Kanjiža [YU] 76 E5
Kankaanpää [FIN] 186 C6
Kannonkoski [FIN] 186 F2
Kannus [FIN] 198 C5
Kanpaneta / Campanas [E] 84 B4
Kansız [TR] 146 E5
Kantala [FIN] 188 C4
Kántanos [GR] 140 B5
Kantomaanpää [FIN] 196 C8
Kantorp [S] 168 B4
Kantti [FIN] 186 C5
Kanturk [IRL] 4 C4
Kányavár [H] 74 F3
Kaolinovo [BG] 148 E2
Kaonik [BIH] 154 D4
Kaonik [YU] 150 C3
Kapaklı [TR] 144 D3
Kapaklı [TR] 146 E4
Kapandríti [GR] 134 C5
Kāpas [LV] 200 C5
Kapčiamiestis [LT] 24 F3
Kapfenberg [A] 74 D1
Kapıkırı [TR] 142 C1
Kapinci [HR] 74 H6
Kapitan Andreevo [BG] 146 A2
Kaplice [CZ] 62 C3
Kapméni Chora [GR] 136 G2
Kápolna [H] 64 E5
Kaposvár [H] 76 A4
Kapp [N] 172 B4
Kappeln [D] 18 F1
Kappelshamn [S] 168 G3
Kappelskär [S] 168 F2
Kaprun [A] 72 F1
Kapsáli [GR] 136 F6
Kápsas [GR] 136 E2
Kapušany [SK] 64 G2
Kapuvar [H] 62 G6
Karabayır [TR] 142 G2
Karabeylı [TR] 144 G3
Karabiga [TR] 146 C4
Karabörtlen [TR] 142 E2
Karaburun [TR] 144 B4
Karaburun [TR] 146 E2
Karacabey [TR] 146 E5
Karacaköy [TR] 146 D2
Karacalar [TR] 144 D2
Karaçam [TR] 144 D2
Karacaoğlan [TR] 146 B2
Karacasu [TR] 144 F5
Karahallı [TR] 144 G4
Karaköy [TR] 144 F4
Karamanlı [TR] 144 H6
Karamürsel [TR] 146 F3
Karamyshevo [RUS] 200 H3
Karancslapujtő [H] 64 D4
Karaova [TR] 142 C2
Karapelit [BG] 148 F2
Karapürçek [TR] 146 H3
Karasjok [N] 192 G2
Karasu [TR] 146 H2
Karataş [TR] 144 E3
Karats [S] 190 G1
Karavás [GR] 136 F6
Karavostásis [GR] 138 E4
Karavukovo [YU] 154 E1
Karawanken Tunnel [Eur.] 74 D2
Karayakuplu [TR] 146 G3
Kårböle [S] 182 H6
Karby [DK] 160 C4
Karcag [H] 76 F1
Kardakáta [GR] 132 C6
Kardam [BG] 148 G1

Kardámaina [GR] 142 B3
Kardámyla [GR] 134 G4
Kardamýli [GR] 136 D4
Kardašova-Řečice [CZ] 48 G6
Kardeljevo [HR] 152 B3
Karditsa [GR] 132 F2
Kärdla [EST] 200 C2
Kardoskút [H] 76 F4
Kärevere [EST] 200 F2
Kargı [TR] 142 F3
Kargowa [PL] 36 B3
Karhujärvi [FIN] 196 E7
Karhukangas [FIN] 198 D5
Karhula [FIN] 178 C4
Kariá [GR] 136 E2
Kariá [GR] 128 G6
Karianí [GR] 130 C4
Kariés [GR] 136 E3
Karigasniemi [FIN] 196 C3
Karijoki [FIN] 186 B4
Karine [TR] 142 B1
Karinkanta [FIN] 198 D4
Karioúpoli [GR] 136 E5
Karis / Karjaa [FIN] 176 F5
Karise [DK] 156 G3
Karítaina [GR] 136 D2
Karjaa / Karis [FIN] 176 F5
Karjala [FIN] 176 D3
Karkaloú [GR] 136 D2
Kärki [LV] 200 E4
Karkkila [FIN] 176 G4
Karkku [FIN] 176 E1
Kärkölä [FIN] 176 H3
Karksi-Nuia [EST] 200 E3
Karlby [FIN] 168 H1
Karlebotn [N] 196 E2
Karleby / Kokkola [FIN] 198 C6
Karlholmsbruk [S] 174 F4
Karlino [PL] 20 H3
Karlivka [UA] 206 G2
Karlobag [HR] 112 F4
Karlovac [HR] 112 G1
Karlovási [GR] 144 C5
Karlova Studánka [CZ] 50 D4
Karlovo [BG] 148 B4
Karlovy Vary [CZ] 48 D3
Karlsborg [S] 166 G5
Karlsborg [S] 198 C3
Karlshafen [D] 32 F4
Karlshamn [S] 158 E1
Karlskoga [S] 166 G3
Karlskrona [S] 158 F1
Karlslunde Strand [DK] 156 G3
Karlsrud [N] 170 F5
Karlsruhe [D] 46 B6
Karlstad [S] 166 F3
Karlstadt [D] 46 E3
Karlstift [A] 62 C3
Karnobat [BG] 148 E4
Karousádes [GR] 132 A2
Karow [D] 20 B4
Karpacz [PL] 50 A2
Kárpathos [GR] 140 H3
Karpenísi [GR] 132 F4
Karpuzlu [TR] 142 D1
Karrebæksminde [DK] 156 F4
Kärsämä [FIN] 198 D4
Kärsämäki [FIN] 198 D5
Kārsava [LV] 200 G5
Karsikas [FIN] 198 D5
Karşıyaka [TR] 146 D4
Karstadt [D] 20 A5
Karstø [N] 164 A2
Karstula [FIN] 186 F3
Kartal [TR] 146 F3
Kartena [LT] 202 D4
Karttula [FIN] 186 H2
Karungi [S] 198 C2
Karunki [FIN] 198 C2
Karup [DK] 160 C5
Karuse [EST] 200 D2
Karvala [FIN] 186 D2

Kärväskylä [FIN] 186 G1
Karvia [FIN] 186 C5
Karvik [N] 192 F2
Karviná [CZ] 50 F4
Karvio [FIN] 188 E3
Karyá [GR] 132 C4
Karyés [GR] 130 D5
Karyótissa [GR] 128 G4
Kárystos [GR] 134 D6
Kås [DK] 160 D3
Kaş [TR] 142 H4
Kasaba [TR] 142 H4
Kašalj [YU] 150 B4
Kåseberga [S] 158 D3
Kasejovice [CZ] 48 E5
Kasfjord [N] 192 C3
Kashira [RUS] 204 F4
Kasimierz Biskupi [PL] 36
  E3
Kašin [RUS] 204 F3
Kaskii [FIN] 188 D5
Kaskinen / Kaskö [FIN] 186
  A4
Kaskö / Kaskinen [FIN] 186
  A4
Kaslania Pass [GR] 128 F5
Käsmu [EST] 200 E1
Kasnäs [FIN] 176 E6
Káspakos [GR] 130 F6
Kašperské Hory [CZ] 48 E6
Kaspichan [BG] 148 E3
Kassándreia [GR] 130 B6
Kassel [D] 32 F5
Kassiópi [GR] 132 B2
Kastanéa [GR] 136 E1
Kastaneá [GR] 128 G5
Kastaniá [GR] 132 F3
Kastaniá [GR] 136 E4
Kastaniá [GR] 136 F5
Kastaniá [GR] 132 E2
Kastaniés [GR] 146 A2
Kastellaun [D] 44 H2
Kastélli [GR] 140 B4
Kastélli [GR] 140 F5
Kaštel Stari [HR] 154 A5
Kaštel Žegarski [HR] 112
  H5
Kasterlee [B] 30 D3
Kastl [D] 46 H5
Kastlösa [S] 162 G6
Kastorf [D] 18 G4
Kastoría [GR] 128 E5
Kastráki [GR] 132 E4
Kástro [GR] 136 B1
Kástro [GR] 134 A5
Kastrosykiá [GR] 132 C3
Kastrup [DK] 156 H3
Kasvandu [EST] 200 E2
Kaszaper [H] 76 F4
Katáfito [GR] 130 C2
Katákolo [GR] 136 B2
Katápola [GR] 138 G4
Katará Pass [GR] 132 D1
Katastári [GR] 136 A2
Katerbow [D] 20 D4
Kateríni [GR] 128 G5
Kätkäsuvanto [FIN] 192 G4
Kätkasuvanto [FIN] 192 G4
Katlanovo [MK] 128 E1
Katlenburg–Duhm [D] 32
  G4
Káto Achaïa [GR] 132 E6
Kato Alepochóri [GR] 134
  B6
Káto Asséa [GR] 136 D3
Katóchi [GR] 132 E5
Kato Doliana [GR] 136 E3
Káto Kleitoría [GR] 136 D1
Káto Makrinoú [GR] 132 E5
Káto Nevrokópi [GR] 130
  C2
Káto Samikó [GR] 136 C2
Káto Tithoréa [GR] 132 H5
Katoúna [GR] 132 D4
Káto Velitsés [GR] 136 C1
Káto Vérmio [GR] 128 F5
Katovice [CZ] 48 E6
Káto Vlasiá [GR] 136 D1
Káto Vrondoú [GR] 130 C2
Katowice [PL] 50 G3
Káto Zákros [GR] 140 H5
Katrineholm [S] 168 B4

Katschberg Tunnel [A] 72
  H2
Kattavía [GR] 142 D5
Katthammarsvik [S] 168
  G5
Kattisavan [S] 190 G4
Katundi i Ri [AL] 128 A2
Katuntsi [BG] 130 B2
Katwijk aan Zee [NL] 16 C4
Katy Wrocławskie [PL] 50
  C1
Kaub [D] 46 B3
Kaufbeuren [D] 60 C5
Kaufering [D] 60 D4
Kaufungen [D] 32 F5
Kauhajärvi [FIN] 186 D2
Kauhajoki [FIN] 186 B4
Kauhava [FIN] 186 C2
Kaukalampi [FIN] 176 H3
Kaukonen [FIN] 192 H5
Kauksi [EST] 200 F2
Kaulinranta [FIN] 196 B8
Kaunas [LT] 202 F5
Kaunata [LV] 200 G5
Kauniainen / Grankulla [FIN]
  176 H5
Kaunisjoenssu [S] 192
  G5
Kaunispää [FIN] 196 D5
Kauns [A] 72 C1
Kaupanger [N] 170 D2
Kauša [LV] 200 F6
Kausala [FIN] 178 B3
Kaustinen [FIN] 198 C6
Kautokeino [N] 192 G3
Kauttua [FIN] 176 D3
Kavacık [TR] 144 E1
Kavacık [TR] 146 B3
Kavadarci [MK] 128 F2
Kavajë [AL] 128 A3
Kavak [TR] 146 B4
Kavaklıdere [TR] 142 E1
Kavála [GR] 130 D3
Kavarna [BG] 148 G2
Kävlinge [S] 158 C2
Kávos [GR] 132 B3
Kavoúsi [GR] 140 G5
Kaxholmen [S] 162 D2
Kayaköy [TR] 142 G3
Käylä [FIN] 196 F8
Kaymakçi [TR] 144 E4
Kaymaz [TR] 146 G2
Kaynarca [TR] 146 G2
Kayran [TR] 144 F5
Kaysersberg [F] 58 D2
Kazanci [BIH] 154 B4
Kažani [MK] 128 E3
Kazanlŭk [BG] 148 C4
Kaz'any [BY] 202 H4
Kazarmá [GR] 136 D4
Kazimierza Wielka [PL] 52
  B3
Kazimierz Dolny [PL] 38 D5
Kâzımpaşa [TR] 146 G3
Kazincbarcika [H] 64 F4
Kazlu–Rūda [LT] 24 F1
Kaznějov [CZ] 48 E4
Kcynia [PL] 22 C6
Kdyně [CZ] 48 D5
Kéa [GR] 138 C2
Keadue [IRL] 2 D4
Keady [GB] 2 F4
Kecel [H] 76 C4
Kecskemét [H] 76 D2
Kėdainiai [LT] 202 F5
Kédros [GR] 132 F3
Kędzierzyn–Koźle [PL] 50
  E3
Keel [IRL] 2 B3
Keelby [GB] 10 G4
Keenagh [IRL] 2 D5
Kefalári [GR] 136 E1
Kéfalos [GR] 142 B3
Kefermarkt [A] 62 C4
Kefken [TR] 146 G2
Keflavik [IS] 194 B4
Kehl [D] 44 H6
Kehra [RUS] 200 E1
Keighley [GB] 10 E3
Keikyä [FIN] 176 E2
Keila [EST] 200 D1
Keila–Joa [EST] 200 D1

Keipene [LV] 200 E5
Keitele [FIN] 186 G1
Keith [GB] 6 F5
Kekava [LV] 200 D5
Kelankyla [FIN] 198 E2
Kelberg [D] 30 G6
Kelbra [D] 32 H5
Keld [GB] 10 E2
Kelebia [H] 76 D4
Kelebija [YU] 76 D5
Keles [TR] 146 F5
Kélla [GR] 128 F4
Kellenhusen [D] 18 H2
Kellinghusen [D] 18 F3
Kello [FIN] 198 D3
Kelloselkä [FIN] 196 F7
Kells [GB] 2 G3
Kells [IRL] 2 F5
Kells [IRL] 4 B4
Kelmė [LT] 202 E4
Kelso [GB] 8 F4
Kelujärvi [FIN] 196 D6
Kemalive [TR] 144 E3
Kemalpaşa [TR] 144 D4
Kember [D] 34 D4
Kemer [TR] 142 G3
Kemer [TR] 144 F5
Kemer [TR] 146 C4
Kemerburgaz [TR] 146
  E2
Kemi [FIN] 198 C3
Kemijärvi [FIN] 196 E7
Kemiö / Kimito [FIN] 176
  E5
Kemnath [D] 48 B4
Kemnitz [D] 20 D3
Kempele [FIN] 198 D4
Kempen [D] 30 G3
Kempston [GB] 14 E3
Kempten [D] 60 C5
Kendal [GB] 10 E2
Kenderes [H] 76 F1
Kendice [SK] 64 G2
Kendro [GR] 136 C1
Kengyel [H] 76 E2
Kenilworth [GB] 12 H1
Kenmare [IRL] 4 B4
Kenmore [GB] 8 E1
Kennacraig [GB] 8 C3
Kenninghall [GB] 14 G2
Kentrikó [GR] 128 H3
Kenzingen [D] 58 E2
Kepez [TR] 146 B5
Kępice [PL] 22 B3
Kepno [PL] 36 E6
Kepsut [TR] 144 D1
Keradokampos [GR] 140
  F5
Keramidi [GR] 132 H2
Keramotí [GR] 130 E3
Kerasóna [GR] 132 D3
Keratéa [GR] 136 H1
Kerava [FIN] 176 H4
Kerch [UA] 206 H5
Kerdýlia [GR] 130 C4
Kerecsend [H] 64 E5
Kergu [EST] 200 E2
Kerí [GR] 136 A2
Kerimäki [FIN] 188 F5
Kerken [D] 30 G3
Kerkini [GR] 128 H3
Kerkrade [NL] 30 F4
Kérkyra [GR] 132 B2
Kerma [FIN] 188 E3
Kermen [BG] 148 D4
Kernascléden [F] 40 C3
Kernovo [RUS] 178 F5
Kerpen [D] 30 G4
Kerpiçlik [TR] 144 F2
Kërrabë [AL] 128 B3
Kerteminde [DK] 156 E3
Kerzers [CH] 58 D6
Kesälahti [FIN] 188 G5
Keşan [TR] 146 B3
Kesarevo [BG] 148 D3
Kesh [GB] 2 E3
Keskikylä [FIN] 198 D4
Kessingland [GB] 14 H3
Kesten'ga [RUS] 198 H2

Kestilä [FIN] 198 E5
Keswick [GB] 8 E6
Keszthely [H] 74 G3
Kétegyháza [H] 76 G3
Kętrzyn [PL] 24 C3
Kettering [GB] 14 E2
Kettlewell [GB] 10 E3
Kettwig [D] 30 G3
Ketzin [D] 34 D2
Keula [D] 32 G5
Keuruu [FIN] 186 F4
Kevelaer [D] 30 F2
Kevo [FIN] 196 D3
Keynsham [GB] 12 G3
Kežmarok [SK] 52 B6
Kharkiv [UA] 206 H2
Kharmanli [BG] 148 D6
Khaskovo [BG] 148 C6
Kherson [UA] 206 F4
Khisariya [BG] 148 B5
Khiytola [RUS] 178 G1
Khlebarovo [BG] 148 D2
Khodoriv [UA] 206 C2
Khyriv [UA] 52 F5
Kiáto [GR] 132 H6
Kibæk [DK] 156 B1
Kiberg [N] 196 F2
Kiburi [LV] 200 B6
Kičevo [MK] 128 D2
Kichenitsa [BG] 148 D2
Kichevo [BG] 148 F2
Kidałowice [PL] 52 F3
Kidderminster [GB] 12 G1
Kidlington [GB] 14 D3
Kidsgrove [GB] 10 E5
Kidwelly [GB] 12 E2
Kiefersfelden [D] 60 F6
Kiel [D] 18 G2
Kielce [PL] 52 B1
Kielder [GB] 8 F5
Kiental [CH] 70 E1
Kierinki [FIN] 196 C7
Kiernozia [PL] 36 H3
Kiesila [FIN] 178 D1
Kietrz [PL] 50 E4
Kifisiá [GR] 134 C6
Kifjord [N] 196 D1
Kihelkonna [EST] 200 C3
Kihlanki [FIN] 192 G6
Kihniö [FIN] 186 D5
Kiihtelysvaara [FIN] 188 G3
Kiikka [FIN] 176 E2
Kiikoinen [FIN] 176 E1
Kiilopää [FIN] 196 D5
Kiiminki [FIN] 198 D3
Kiiskilä [FIN] 198 D6
Kiistala [FIN] 196 C6
Kije [PL] 52 B2
Kijevo [GR] 154 A4
Kijevo [YU] 150 B5
Kikala [FIN] 176 F4
Kikerino [RUS] 178 G6
Kikinda [YU] 76 F5
Kikół [PL] 36 G1
Kil [N] 164 F4
Kil [S] 166 E2
Kiláda [GR] 136 F3
Kilafors [S] 174 D2
Kilbaha [IRL] 2 A6
Kilbeggan [IRL] 2 E5
Kilberry [GB] 8 B3
Kilberry [IRL] 2 F5
Kilbirnie [GB] 8 C3
Kilboghamn [N] 190 D2
Kilbotn [N] 192 D3
Kilcar / Cill Charthaigh [IRL]
  2 D2
Kilchattan [GB] 8 C3
Kilchoan [GB] 6 B6
Kilcock [IRL] 2 F6
Kilcoole [IRL] 4 G3
Kilconnell [IRL] 2 D5
Kilcormac [IRL] 2 D6
Kilcullen [IRL] 2 E6
Kilcurry [IRL] 2 F4
Kildare [IRL] 2 E6
Kildonan Lodge [GB] 6 E3
Kildorrery [IRL] 4 D4
Kildress [GB] 2 F3
Kilen [N] 164 F2
Kilfenora [IRL] 2 B5

Kilfinnane [IRL] 4 D4
Kilgarvan [IRL] 4 B4
Kilifarevo [BG] 148 C4
Kilija [UA] 206 E5
Kilingi–Nõmme [EST] 200
  E3
Kilitbahir [TR] 130 H5
Kilkee [IRL] 2 B6
Kilkeel [GB] 2 G4
Kilkenny / Cill Chainnigh
  [IRL] 4 E4
Kilkhampton [GB] 12 D4
Kilkieran / Cill Ciaráin [IRL]
  2 B4
Kilkinlea [IRL] 4 C3
Kilkís [GR] 128 H3
Killadysert [IRL] 2 B6
Killala [IRL] 2 C3
Killaloe [IRL] 2 C6
Killarney / Cill Airne [IRL] 4
  B4
Killashandra [IRL] 2 E4
Killashee [IRL] 2 D5
Killeigh [IRL] 2 E6
Killenaule [IRL] 4 E4
Killeter [GB] 2 E3
Killimer [IRL] 2 B6
Killimor [IRL] 2 D5
Killin [GB] 8 D2
Killinkoski [FIN] 186 D4
Killorglin [IRL] 4 B4
Killybegs [IRL] 2 D2
Killyleagh [GB] 2 G4
Kilmacolm [GB] 8 D3
Kilmacrenan [IRL] 2 E2
Kilmacthomas [IRL] 4 E5
Kilmaganny [IRL] 4 E4
Kilmaine [IRL] 2 C4
Kilmallock [IRL] 4 D4
Kilmanahan [IRL] 4 E4
Kilmarnock [GB] 8 D3
Kilmartin [GB] 8 C2
Kilmeaden [IRL] 4 E5
Kilmeage [IRL] 2 E6
Kilmeedy [IRL] 4 C4
Kilmelford [GB] 8 C2
Kilmichael [IRL] 4 C5
Kilmore Quay [IRL] 4 F5
Kilnaleck [IRL] 2 E4
Kilnsea [GB] 10 H4
Kiloran [GB] 8 B2
Kilpisjärvi [FIN] 192 F3
Kilpua [FIN] 198 D5
Kilrea [GB] 2 G2
Kilrush [IRL] 2 B6
Kilshannig [IRL] 4 B3
Kilsyth [GB] 8 D3
Kiltealy [IRL] 4 F4
Kiltimagh [IRL] 2 C4
Kilvakkala [FIN] 186 D6
Kilwinning [GB] 8 C3
Kiminki [FIN] 186 E2
Kimito / Kemiö [FIN] 176
  E5
Kimméria [GR] 130 E2
Kímolos [GR] 138 D4
Kimry [RUS] 204 F3
Kinbrace [GB] 6 E3
Kincardine [GB] 8 E3
Kincraig [GB] 6 D6
Kindberg [A] 62 D6
Kindelbrück [D] 32 H5
Kinding [D] 46 G6
Kinetá [GR] 134 B6
Kingisepp [RUS] 200 G1
Kingissepp [EST] 200 C3
Kingsbridge [GB] 12 D5
Kingsclere [GB] 12 H4
Kingscourt [IRL] 2 F5
Kingsdown [GB] 14 G5
King's Lynn [GB] 14 F1
Kingston [GB] 6 F5
Kington [GB] 12 F1
Kınık [TR] 142 G4
Kınık [TR] 142 G2
Kınık [TR] 144 C2
Kınık [TR] 146 F5
Kınıkyeri [TR] 142 F5
Kinloch [GB] 6 B5
Kinlochbervie [GB] 6 D2
Kinlochewe [GB] 6 C4

Kinloch Hourn [GB] 6 C5
Kinlochleven [GB] 6 C6
Kinloch Rannoch [GB] 8 E1
Kinna [S] 162 B3
Kinnadoohy [IRL] 2 B4
Kinnarp [S] 162 C1
Kinnegad [IRL] 2 E5
Kinnitty [IRL] 2 D6
Kinnula [FIN] 186 F1
Kinross [GB] 8 E2
Kinsale [IRL] 4 C5
Kinsarvik [N] 170 C4
Kintai [LT] 202 D4
Kintaus [FIN] 186 F4
Kinvarra [IRL] 2 C5
Kióni [GR] 132 D5
Kiónia [GR] 138 E2
Kipen' [RUS] 178 G5
Kipi [EST] 200 C3
Kipina [FIN] 198 E3
Kipinä [FIN] 198 E3
Kiraz [TR] 144 E4
Kirbla [EST] 200 D2
Kirby–in–Ashfield [GB] 10
  F5
Kircasalih [TR] 146 B2
Kirchbach [A] 74 E2
Kirchberg [A] 60 F6
Kirchberg [D] 44 H2
Kirchberg [D] 46 E5
Kirchberg an der Pielach [A]
  62 D5
Kirchdorf [D] 32 E1
Kirchdorf an der Krems [A]
  62 B5
Kirchenlamitz [D] 48 B3
Kirchenthumbach [D] 46 H4
Kirchhain [D] 32 E6
Kirchheim [D] 32 F6
Kirchheimbolanden [D] 46
  B4
Kirchheim unter Teck [D] 58
  H1
Kirchlinteln [D] 18 E6
Kirchschlag [A] 62 F6
Kirchundem [D] 32 C5
Kircubbin [GB] 2 H4
Kireç [TR] 144 E1
Kiriáki [GR] 132 H5
Kırkağaç [TR] 144 D2
Kirkbean [GB] 8 D5
Kirkburn [GB] 10 G3
Kirkby Lonsdale [GB] 10 E2
Kirkcaldy [GB] 8 E3
Kirkcolm [GB] 8 C5
Kirkcudbright [GB] 8 D5
Kirkehamn [N] 164 B5
Kirke Hvalsø [DK] 156 F3
Kirkenær [N] 172 D4
Kirkenes [N] 196 E3
Kirkham [GB] 10 D3
Kirkholt [DK] 160 E3
Kírki [GR] 130 G3
Kirkjubæjarklaustur [IS] 194
  D6
Kirkjubøur [DK] 160 B2
Kirkkonummi / Kyrkslätt
  [FIN] 176 G5
Kırklareli [TR] 146 B1
Kirkmuirhill [GB] 8 D3
Kirkwall [GB] 6 G2
Kirn [D] 44 H2
Kirov [RUS] 204 E5
Kirovohrad [UA] 206 F3
Kirovsk [RUS] 204 C1
Kirovsk [BY] 204 C6
Kirovskoye [RUS] 178 G3
Kirriemuir [GB] 8 F2
Kirtorf [D] 46 D1
Kiruna [S] 192 F5
Kisa [S] 162 F1
Kısacık [TR] 144 B1
Kişaköy [TR] 144 F3
Kisbér [A] 64 A6
Kiseljak [BIH] 152 C1
Kisielice [PL] 22 F4
Kisielnica [PL] 24 D5

Kisko [FIN] 176 F5
Kisköre [H] 64 F6
Kiskőrös [H] 76 D3
Kiskundorozsma [H] 76 E4
Kiskunfélegyháza [H] 76 E3
Kiskunhalas [H] 76 D4
Kiskunlacháza [H] 76 C2
Kiskunmajsa [H] 76 D4
Kisslegg [D] 60 B5
Kistanje [HR] 112 H5
Kistelek [H] 76 E4
Kisterenye [H] 64 D5
Kisújszállás [H] 76 F1
Kisvárda [H] 64 H4
Kiszkowo [PL] 36 D2
Kiszombor [H] 76 F4
Kíta [GR] 136 E5
Kitajaur [S] 190 H2
Kitee [FIN] 188 G4
Kiten [BG] 148 F5
Kitka [FIN] 196 F8
Kítros [GR] 128 G5
Kitsi [FIN] 198 H6
Kittelfjäll [S] 190 E4
Kittilä [FIN] 192 H5
Kittsee [A] 62 G5
Kitula [FIN] 176 F4
Kitzbühel [A] 60 F6
Kitzingen [D] 46 F4
Kiuruvesi [FIN] 198 E6
Kivadár [H] 74 H5
Kivéri [GR] 136 E2
Kivesjärvi [FIN] 198 E4
Kiviapaja [FIN] 188 E5
Kivijärvi [FIN] 186 F2
Kivik [S] 158 D3
Kivilahti [FIN] 188 G1
Kiviöli [EST] 200 F1
Kivitaipale [FIN] 196 D8
Kivi–Vigala [EST] 200 D2
Kivotós [GR] 128 E6
Kıyıkışlacık [TR] 142 C2
Kıyıköy [TR] 146 D1
Kızılcadağ [TR] 142 H2
Kizilkoltuk [TR] 144 F2
Kjækan [N] 192 F2
Kjellerup [DK] 160 D6
Kjerret [N] 172 D6
Kjerringøy [N] 192 B5
Kjerringvåg [N] 190 A6
Kjerringvik [N] 190 C6
Kjøllefjord [N] 196 D1
Kjölur [IS] 194 D4
Kjøpsvik [N] 192 C4
Kladanj [BIH] 154 E4
Kladnica [YU] 150 A3
Kladnice [HR] 154 A5
Kladno [CZ] 48 F3
Kladovo [YU] 206 B6
Kladruby [CZ] 48 D4
Klagenfurt [A] 74 B3
Klaipėda [LT] 202 D4
Klaksvík [DK] 160 B1
Klamila [FIN] 178 D3
Klanac [HR] 112 G3
Klanxbüll [D] 156 B4
Klarup [DK] 160 E4
Klašnice [BIH] 154 C2
Klässbol [S] 166 E2
Kláśterec nad Ohří [CZ] 48 D3
Kláśtor [SK] 64 C2
Klatovy [CZ] 48 D5
Klaukkala [FIN] 176 G4
Klaus an der Pyhrnbahn [A] 62 B5
Klausdorf [D] 34 E3
Klausen / Chiusa [I] 72 D3
Klazienaveen [NL] 16 H3
Kłecko [PL] 36 D2
Kleczew [PL] 36 D3
Kleinhaugsdorf [A] 62 E3
Kleisoúra [GR] 132 D3
Klemensker [DK] 158 E4
Klenčí [CZ] 48 D5
Klenike [YU] 150 D5
Klenjë [AL] 128 C2
Klepp [N] 164 A3
Kleppestø [N] 170 A3
Klešno [PL] 36 A1

Klevar [N] 164 F2
Kleve [D] 16 F6
Klevshult [S] 162 D3
Klezeno [RUS] 200 G4
Kliczków [PL] 34 H5
Klietz [D] 34 C1
Klimátia [GR] 132 C2
Kliment [BG] 148 E2
Klimontów [PL] 52 B3
Klimpfjäll [S] 190 E4
Klin [RUS] 204 F4
Klina [YU] 150 B5
Klinča Selo [HR] 74 E6
Klincy [RUS] 204 D6
Klingenbach [A] 62 F6
Klingenmunster [D] 46 B5
Klingenthal [D] 48 C3
Klink [D] 20 C5
Klintehamn [S] 168 F5
Klintholm [DK] 156 G4
Kliplev [DK] 156 C4
Klippan [S] 158 C1
Klippen [S] 190 E3
Klippinge [DK] 156 G3
Klis [HR] 152 A2
Klisino [PL] 50 E3
Klisura [BG] 148 A4
Klisura [YU] 150 E5
Klitmøller [DK] 160 C3
Klixbüll [D] 156 B4
Kljajičevo [YU] 76 D6
Kljuc [BIH] 154 B3
Kłobuck [PL] 50 F1
Kłobuczyn [PL] 36 B5
Kłodawa [PL] 34 H1
Kłodawa [PL] 36 F3
Kłodzko [PL] 50 C3
Kløfta [N] 172 B5
Klokkarvik [N] 170 A4
Klokočevac [YU] 150 D1
Klos [AL] 128 B2
Klos [AL] 128 B1
Kloštar [HR] 74 G5
Klösterle [A] 72 B1
Klosterneuburg [A] 62 F4
Klosters [CH] 72 A2
Kloten [S] 166 H1
Klötze [D] 34 A1
Klubbukt [N] 196 B2
Kl'ucovoje [RUS] 178 F3
Kluczbork [PL] 50 E1
Kluki [PL] 36 G5
Kluki [PL] 22 C1
Klukowa Huta [PL] 22 D3
Klupe [BIH] 154 C3
Klütz [D] 18 H3
Klyastsitsy [BY] 200 H6
Knaben [N] 164 C4
Knäred [S] 162 B5
Knaresborough [GB] 10 F3
Knarvik [N] 170 B3
Knebel [DK] 160 E6
Knezevi Vinogradi [HR] 76 C6
Kneževo [HR] 76 B5
Knezha [BG] 150 G3
Knežica [BIH] 154 B2
Knič [YU] 150 B2
Knidas [TR] 142 C4
Kniebis [D] 58 F2
Knighton [GB] 10 C6
Knights Town [IRL] 4 A4
Knin [HR] 154 A4
Knislinge [S] 158 D1
Knittelfeld [A] 74 C2
Knivsta [S] 168 D2
Knjaževac [YU] 150 E3
Knock [IRL] 2 C4
Knockan [GB] 6 D3
Knockcroghery [IRL] 2 D5
Knocknalina [IRL] 2 C2
Knocktopher [IRL] 4 E4
Knokke–Heist [B] 28 G1
Knottingley [GB] 10 F4
Knudshoved [DK] 156 E3
Knurów [PL] 50 F3
Knutby [S] 168 E1
Knutsford [GB] 10 D4

Kobarid [SLO] 72 H4
Kobbfoss [N] 196 E3
København [DK] 156 H2
Kobeřice [CZ] 50 E4
Kobilyane [BG] 130 F1
Kobišnica [YU] 150 E1
Koblenz [D] 30 H6
Kobryn [BY] 38 G2
Kobułty [PL] 24 B4
Kobylany [PL] 38 F3
Kobylin [PL] 36 D4
Kobyłka [PL] 38 C2
Kobyl'nik [BY] 202 H5
Kocaali [TR] 146 H2
Kocaçeşme [TR] 146 B4
Kocakaymaz [TR] 146 G2
Kočani [MK] 128 G1
Koçarlı [TR] 144 D5
Koceljevo [YU] 150 A1
Kočerin [BIH] 152 B2
Kočevje [SLO] 74 C6
Kochel [D] 60 D5
Kocherinovo [BG] 150 F6
Kochmar [BG] 148 F2
Kock [PL] 38 E4
Kodeń [PL] 38 F3
Kofçaz [TR] 146 B1
Køge [DK] 156 G3
Kohila [EST] 200 D2
Kohtla–Järve [EST] 200 F1
Koigi [EST] 200 E2
Koilovtsi [BG] 148 B3
Koirakoski [FIN] 198 F6
Koivu [FIN] 196 C8
Koivulahti / Kvevlax [FIN] 186 B2
Koivumäki [FIN] 188 E3
Kojetín [CZ] 50 D6
Kokála [GR] 136 E5
Kökar [FIN] 168 H1
Kokava nad Rimavicou [SK] 64 D3
Kokemäki [FIN] 176 D2
Kokin Brod [YU] 150 A3
Kókino Neró [GR] 132 H1
Kokkário [GR] 144 C5

Kokkokylä [FIN] 198 E2
Kokkola / Karleby [FIN] 198 C6
Koklë [AL] 128 C4
Koknese [LV] 200 E5
Kokonvaara [FIN] 188 E2
Kokořín [CZ] 48 G3
Koksijde–Bad [B] 28 F1
Kolacze [PL] 38 F5
Kolari [FIN] 192 H5
Kolari [YU] 154 H3
Kolárovo [SK] 64 A5
Koláry [SK] 64 C5
Kolasen [S] 190 D6
Kolašin [YU] 152 E3
Kolbäck [S] 168 B2
Kołbacz [PL] 20 F5
Kolbermoor [D] 60 F5
Kolbiel [PL] 38 C3
Kolbotn [N] 166 B1
Kolbuszowa [PL] 52 D3
Kolby [DK] 156 E2
Kolby Kås [DK] 156 E2
Kołczewo [PL] 20 F3
Kołczygłowy [PL] 22 C3
Koldby [DK] 160 B4
Kolding [DK] 156 C3
Koleczkowo [PL] 22 D2
Kolho [FIN] 186 E5
Koli [FIN] 188 F1
Kolín [CZ] 48 H4
Kolind [DK] 160 E6
Kolindró [GR] 128 G5
Kolínes [GR] 136 E3
Köljala [EST] 200 C3
Kolka [LV] 200 C4
Kölleda [D] 34 A5
Kollund [DK] 156 C4
Kolmården [S] 168 B5
Köln [D] 30 G4
Kolno [PL] 24 C5
Koło [PL] 36 F3
Kołobrzeg [PL] 20 G3
Kolokolovo [RUS] 200 G2
Kolomyja [UA] 206 C3
Kolonia Korytnica [PL] 38 D4
Kolonjë [AL] 128 B4

Kolonowskie [PL] 50 F2
Koloveč [CZ] 48 D5
Kolpino [RUS] 204 C1
Kölsillre [S] 182 H4
Kolsva [S] 168 B2
Koluszki [PL] 36 H4
Kolvereid [N] 190 C4
Kolymvári [GR] 140 B4
Komádi [H] 76 G2
Koman [AL] 128 B1
Komańcza [PL] 52 E5
Kómara [GR] 130 H1
Komárno [SK] 64 B5
Komarno [UA] 52 G4
Komárom [H] 64 A6
Komar Prolaz [BIH] 154 C4
Koméno [GR] 132 D3
Kómi [GR] 138 E1
Kómi [GR] 134 G5
Komiža [HR] 116 H2
Komjáti [H] 64 F3
Komló [H] 76 B4
Komniná [GR] 130 E2
Kómninádes [GR] 128 D5
Komorane [YU] 150 C5
Komotiní [GR] 130 E2
Kömpöc [H] 76 E4
Kompóti [GR] 132 D3
Konak [YU] 154 H1
Končanica [HR] 74 G6
Konče [MK] 128 G2
Kondolovo [BG] 148 F5
Kondoros [H] 76 F3
Kondrič [HR] 154 D1
Kong [DK] 156 F4
Konga [S] 162 E6
Köngäs [FIN] 192 H5
Kongerslev [DK] 160 E4
Konginkangas [FIN] 186 G3
Kongsberg [N] 164 G1
Kongsfjord [N] 196 E1
Kongshavn [N] 164 F5
Kongsnes [N] 170 C2
Kongsvinger [N] 172 D5
Konice [CZ] 50 C5
Koniecpol [PL] 50 H2
Königsbrück [D] 34 F6
Königsbrunn [D] 60 D4

Königsee [D] 46 G2
Königsfeld [D] 58 F3
Königshofen [D] 46 E4
Königslutter [D] 32 H2
Königssee [D] 60 G6
Königstein [D] 46 C2
Königstein [D] 48 F1
Königswiesen [A] 62 C4
Königswinter [D] 30 H5
Königs–Wusterhausen [D] 34 E3
Konin [PL] 36 E3
Koniskós [GR] 132 F1
Konispol [AL] 132 B2
Kónitsa [GR] 128 D6
Köniz [CH] 58 D6
Konjic [BIH] 152 C1
Könnern [D] 34 B4
Konnerud [N] 164 H1
Konnevesi [FIN] 186 G3
Könnu [EST] 200 E1
Konopište [CZ] 48 G4
Konotop [PL] 36 B4
Konotop [PL] 20 H5
Konotop [UA] 204 D7
Końskie [PL] 38 A6
Konsko [MK] 128 G3
Konsmo [N] 164 D5
Konstancin–Jeziorna [PL] 38 B3
Konstantynów [PL] 38 E3
Konstantynów Łodzki [PL] 36 G4
Konstanz [D] 58 G4
Konteenperä [FIN] 196 E8
Kontiás [GR] 130 F6
Kontinjoki [FIN] 198 F5
Kontiolahti [FIN] 188 F2
Kontiomäki [FIN] 198 F4
Kontokali [GR] 132 B2
Kontopoúli [GR] 130 F6
Konttajärvi [FIN] 192 H6
Konush [BG] 148 C6
Konz [D] 44 F2
Köörtilä [FIN] 186 B6
Koosa [EST] 200 F2
Koparnes [N] 180 C4

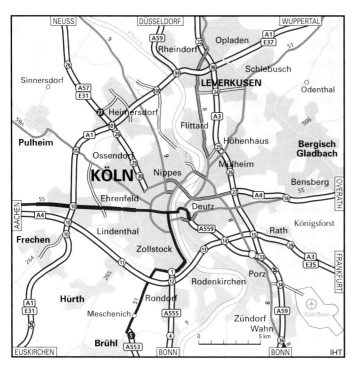

Kópasker [IS] 194 F3
Kópavogur [IS] 194 B4
Köpenick [D] 34 E2
Koper [SLO] 72 H6
Köpernitz [D] 20 C6
Kopervik [N] 164 A2
Kópháza [H] 62 F6
Kopidlno [CZ] 48 H3
Köping [S] 168 B2
Köpingsvik [S] 162 G4
Koplik [AL] 152 E5
Köpmanholmen [S] 184 G2
Köpmannebro [S] 166 D4
Kopor'ye [RUS] 178 F5
Koppang [N] 172 C1
Kopparberg [S] 166 H1
Kopperå [N] 182 D1
Kopperby [D] 18 F1
Koppom [S] 166 D2
Koprivets [BG] 148 C3
Koprivnica [HR] 74 G5
Koprivshtitsa [BG] 148 A5
Köprübaşı [TR] 144 F5
Köprübaşı [TR] 144 E3
Köprühisar [TR] 146 G4
Köprüören [TR] 144 G1
Koprzywnica [PL] 52 D2
Köpu [EST] 200 D1
Korbach [D] 32 E5
Korbevac [YU] 150 D5
Korbielów [PL] 50 G5
Korcë [AL] 128 D5
Korcula [HR] 152 B3
Korczyców [PL] 34 G3
Korczyna [PL] 52 D4
Korentovaara [FIN] 188 H1
Korfantów [PL] 50 D2
Körfez [TR] 146 G3
Kórfos [GR] 136 F2
Korgen [N] 190 D2
Koria [FIN] 178 C3
Korinós [GR] 128 G5
Korinth [DK] 156 D4
Kórinthos [GR] 136 F1
Korisós [GR] 128 E5
Korissía [GR] 138 C2
Korita [BIH] 152 D3
Korita [HR] 152 C4
Koríthi [GR] 136 A1
Körmend [H] 74 F2
Korneuburg [A] 62 F4
Kórnik [PL] 36 C3
Kornsjø [N] 166 C4
Kornwestheim [D] 58 H1
Kőrnye [H] 64 B6
Koromacno [HR] 112 E2
Koróni [GR] 136 D4
Koronós [GR] 138 F3
Koronoúda [GR] 128 H3
Koronowo [PL] 22 D5

Koropí [GR] 136 H1
Körösladány [H] 76 G2
Köröstarcsa [H] 76 G2
Korosten [UA] 206 E1
Korostyšev [UA] 206 E2
Korpavár [H] 74 G4
Korpilahti [FIN] 186 G5
Korpilombolo [S] 196 B7
Korpo / Korppoo [FIN] 176 C5
Korpoström [FIN] 176 C5
Korppoo / Korpo [FIN] 176 C5
Korsberga [S] 162 E3
Korsholm [S] 158 C2
Korskrogen [S] 184 C6
Korsmo [N] 172 C5
Korsnäs [FIN] 186 A3
Korsø [DK] 160 C3
Korsør [DK] 156 E3
Korsun–Ševčenkovski [UA] 206 F2
Korsveien [N] 182 B2
Korsze [PL] 24 B3
Korten [BG] 148 D4
Kortesjärvi [FIN] 186 C1
Korthí [GR] 138 D1
Kortrijk (Courtrai) [B] 28 G2
Korucu [TR] 144 C2
Korup [DK] 156 D3
Korušce [HR] 154 A5
Korvala [FIN] 196 D7
Korvaluoma [FIN] 186 C5
Koryčany [CZ] 62 G2
Korycin [PL] 24 E4
Korydallós [GR] 132 E1
Koryfási [GR] 136 C4
Kos [GR] 142 C3
Kosanica [YU] 152 E2
Koščian [PL] 36 C3
Kościelec [PL] 36 F5
Kościerzyna [PL] 22 D3
Kose [EST] 200 E1
Kösedere [TR] 134 G1
Kosel [MK] 128 D3
Koserow [D] 20 E3
Košetice [CZ] 48 G5
Košice [SK] 64 G3
Kosjerič [YU] 150 A2
Kösk [TR] 144 E5
Koška [YU] 154 D1
Koskenkorva [FIN] 186 C3
Koskenkylä / Forsby [FIN] 178 B4
Koskenpää [FIN] 186 F5
Koski [FIN] 176 E4
Koski [FIN] 176 H2
Koskimäki [FIN] 186 B3
Koskolovo [RUS] 178 F6
Koškovce [SK] 52 E6

Koskue [FIN] 186 C4
Kosmás [GR] 136 E3
Kosmonosy [CZ] 48 G3
Kosovo Polje [YU] 150 C5
Kosovska Mitrovica [YU] 150 C4
Kosów Lacki [PL] 38 D2
Kóssen [A] 60 F5
Kósta [GR] 136 F3
Kosta [S] 162 E5
Kostajnica [HR] 154 B2
Kostanjevac [HR] 74 D6
Kostelec nad Černými [CZ] 48 G4
Kostelec nad Labem [CZ] 48 G3
Kostelec nad Orlicí [CZ] 50 B3
Kostenets [BG] 150 G5
Kostiantynivka [UA] 206 H3
Kostinbrod [BG] 150 F4
Kostomłoty [PL] 36 C6
Kostomuksha [RUS] 198 G4
Kostopol [UA] 206 D1
Kóstos [GR] 138 E3
Kostrzyn [PL] 36 D2
Kostrzyn [PL] 34 G2
Kosturino [MK] 128 G2
Koszalin [PL] 20 H3
Koszęcin [PL] 50 F2
Kosztowo [PL] 22 C6
Koszuty [PL] 36 D3
Koszyce [PL] 52 B3
Kotala [FIN] 186 E4
Kotala [FIN] 196 F7
Kotë [AL] 128 B5
Kotel [BG] 148 D4
Kőtelec [H] 76 E1
Köthen [D] 34 C4
Kotka [FIN] 178 C4
Kotlarnia [PL] 50 F3
Kotly [RUS] 178 F6
Kotola [FIN] 196 F7
Kotor [YU] 152 D4
Kotorsko [BIH] 154 D2
Kotor Varoš [BIH] 154 C3
Kotovsk [UA] 206 E4
Kotowice [PL] 50 G2
Kótronas [GR] 136 E4
Kötschach–Mauthen [A] 72 G3
Kotten [NL] 16 G6
Kötzting [D] 48 D6
Koufália [GR] 128 G4
Koufós [GR] 130 C6
Kouklií [GR] 132 C1
Koukounariés [GR] 134 B3
Koúmani [GR] 136 C2

Koúndouros [GR] 138 C2
Kourenda [GR] 132 C2
Kournás [GR] 140 C5
Kouroúta [GR] 136 B2
Koutsóchero [GR] 132 G2
Koutsourás [GR] 140 G5
Kouvola [FIN] 178 C3
Kovachevica [BG] 130 C1
Kovachevtsi [BG] 150 F5
Kovačica [YU] 154 G2
Kovarskas [LT] 202 G4
Kovero [FIN] 188 G2
Kovin [YU] 154 H2
Kovland [S] 184 E4
Kowal [PL] 36 G2
Kowale Oleckie [PL] 24 D3
Kowalewo Pomorskie [PL] 22 E6
Kowary [PL] 50 A2
Köyceğiz [TR] 142 F2
Köyliö [FIN] 176 D2
Koyunhis [TR] 146 F4
Kozak [TR] 144 C2
Kozáni [GR] 128 F5
Kozarac [BIH] 154 B2
Kozar Belene [BG] 148 B3
Kozica [HR] 152 B2
Koziegłowy [PL] 50 G2
Kozienice [PL] 38 C4
Kozina [SLO] 74 A6
Kozlodui [BG] 150 G2
Kozłowo [PL] 22 G5
Kozluk [BIH] 154 E3
Kožmin [PL] 36 D4
Kozolupy [CZ] 48 D4
Kozpınar [TR] 146 G5
Kožuchów [PL] 36 A4
Kozyürük [TR] 146 B3
Kräckelbäcken [S] 172 G2
Kragenæs [DK] 156 F4
Kragerø [N] 164 F4
Kragujevac [YU] 150 C2
Krahës [AL] 128 B5
Krajenka [PL] 22 B5
Krajn [AL] 128 B1
Krajnik Dolny [PL] 20 E6
Kråkberget [N] 192 C3
Krakhella [N] 170 B1
Krakovets' [UA] 52 F3
Kraków [PL] 52 A4
Krakow am See [D] 20 B4
Králíky [CZ] 50 C4
Kraljevica [HR] 112 E2
Kraljevo [YU] 150 B3
Kralovany [SK] 50 G6
Královec [CZ] 50 B2
Kralovice [CZ] 48 E4
Kralovsky Chlmec [SLO] 64 H3
Kralupy nad Vltavou [CZ] 48 F3
Kramatorsk [UA] 206 H3
Kramfors [S] 184 F3
Kranenburg [D] 16 F6
Kranevo [BG] 148 G2
Krani [MK] 128 D4
Kraniá Elassónas [GR] 132 F1
Kranichfeld [D] 46 G1
Kranídi [GR] 136 F3
Kranj [SLO] 74 B4
Kranjá [GR] 132 E1
Kranjska Gora [SLO] 72 H3
Krapanj [HR] 112 H6
Krapina [HR] 74 E4
Krapinske Toplice [HR] 74 E5
Krapkowice [PL] 50 E2
Krasen [BG] 148 F1
Krasiczyn [PL] 52 F4
Krasna [YU] 154 G2
Kraślava [LV] 200 G6
Kraslice [CZ] 48 C3
Krásná [CZ] 48 G1
Krásná Lípa [CZ] 48 G1
Krasne Folwarczne [PL] 24 E5
Krašnik [PL] 52 E1
Krasnogorodskoye [RUS] 200 G5
Krasnohrad [UA] 206 G2
Krásno nad Kysucou [SK] 50 F5

Krasnoperekopsk [UA] 206 G5
Krasnosielec [PL] 24 B6
Krasnovo [BG] 148 A5
Krasnoye Selo [RUS] 178 H5
Krasnoznamensk [RUS] 202 E5
Krasny Holm [RUS] 204 F2
Krasnyje Gory [RUS] 200 H1
Krasnystaw [PL] 38 F6
Krastë [AL] 128 C2
Krasznokvajda [H] 64 F3
Krátigos [GR] 134 H2
Kratovo [MK] 150 E6
Kratovska Stena [YU] 150 A2
Krauchenwies [D] 58 H3
Kravarsko [HR] 74 E6
Kraymorie [BG] 148 F4
Krefeld [D] 30 G3
Kremastí [GR] 142 E4
Kremenchuk [UA] 206 G3
Kremenec [UA] 206 C2
Kremmen [D] 34 D1
Kremna [YU] 152 E1
Kremnica [SK] 64 C3
Krems [A] 62 E4
Kremsmünster [A] 62 B5
Krepoljin [YU] 150 D1
Kresna [BG] 130 B1
Krestcy [RUS] 204 D2
Kréstena [GR] 136 C2
Kreuth [D] 60 E6
Kreuzlingen [CH] 58 G4
Kreuztal [D] 32 C6
Kreva [BY] 202 H6
Kriakénava [LT] 202 F4
Krichim [BG] 148 B6
Krieglach [A] 62 D6
Kriezá [GR] 134 C5
Krikkovo [RUS] 178 F6
Krimml [A] 72 E1
Krimpen aan de IJssel [NL] 16 D5
Krinídes [GR] 130 D3
Kristdala [S] 162 G3
Kristianopel [S] 158 G1
Kristiansand [N] 164 D5
Kristianstad [S] 158 D2
Kristiansund [N] 180 F2
Kristiinankaupunki / Kristinestad [FIN] 186 A5
Kristineberg [S] 190 G4
Kristinehamn [S] 166 F3
Kristinehov [S] 158 D2
Kristinestad / Kristiinankaupunki [FIN] 186 A5
Kristóni [GR] 128 H3
Kritiniá [GR] 142 D5
Kritsá [GR] 140 F5
Kriva Feja [YU] 150 E5
Kriváň [SK] 64 D3
Kriva Palanka [MK] 150 E6
Krivelj [YU] 150 D2
Krivodol [BG] 150 F3
Krivogaštani [MK] 128 E3
Krivoje Ozero [UA] 206 E4
Křivoklát [CZ] 48 E4
Křižanov [CZ] 50 B6
Križevci [HR] 74 F5
Krk [HR] 112 E2
Krka [SLO] 74 C5
Krnjača [YU] 154 G2
Krnjeuša [BIH] 154 A3
Krnov [CZ] 50 D4
Krobia [PL] 36 C4
Kroczyce [PL] 50 G2
Krøderen [N] 170 G5
Krokebol [N] 166 C1
Krokeés [GR] 136 E4
Kroken [N] 190 E3
Krokom [S] 182 G2
Krokowa [PL] 22 D1
Krokstad [S] 166 C5
Krokstadøra [N] 180 H1
Krokstrand [N] 190 E2

Królowy Most [PL] 24 F5
Kroměříž [CZ] 50 D6
Krompachy [SK] 64 F2
Kronach [D] 46 H3
Kronoby / Kruunupyy [FIN] 198 C6
Kronshtadt [RUS] 178 G4
Kröpelin [D] 20 B3
Kropp [D] 18 F2
Kroppenstedt [D] 34 B3
Kropstädt [D] 34 D3
Krościenko nad Dunajcem [PL] 52 B5
Krosna [LT] 24 F2
Krośniewice [PL] 36 G3
Krosno [PL] 52 D4
Krosno [PL] 22 F3
Krosno Odrzanskie [PL] 34 H3
Krossbu [N] 180 E6
Krotoszyn [PL] 36 D4
Krouna [CZ] 50 B4
Kruiningen [NL] 28 H1
Krujë [AL] 128 B2
Krumbach [D] 60 C4
Krumë [AL] 150 B6
Krumovgrad [BG] 130 F1
Krumpendorf [A] 74 B3
Krün [D] 60 D6
Krupá [CZ] 48 E3
Krupac [BIH] 152 D1
Krupac [BIH] 152 C2
Krupaja [YU] 150 C1
Krupa na Vrbasu [BIH] 154 B3
Krupanj [YU] 154 F3
Krupe [PL] 38 F6
Krupina [SK] 64 C4
Krupište [MK] 128 F1
Krusá [DK] 156 C4
Kruševac [YU] 150 C3
Kruševo [MK] 128 E2
Krushari [BG] 148 F1
Krushevets [BG] 148 F5
Krushovene [BG] 148 A2
Krute [YU] 152 E5
Krutvatn [N] 190 E3
Kruunupyy / Kronoby [FIN] 198 C6
Kryekuq [AL] 128 A4
Kryksæterøra [N] 180 G1
Krylbo [S] 174 D6
Krylovo [RUS] 24 C2
Krymne [UA] 38 H4
Krynica [PL] 52 C5
Krynica Morska [PL] 22 F2
Krynki [PL] 24 F5
Kryspinów [PL] 50 H4
Kryvyi Rih [UA] 206 G3
Krzęcin [PL] 20 G6
Krzeczów [PL] 36 F6
Krzepice [PL] 50 F1
Krzeszów [PL] 52 E2
Krzeszów [PL] 50 B2
Krzeszowice [PL] 50 H3
Krzeszyce [PL] 34 G2
Krzynowłoga Mała [PL] 22 H6
Krzywiń [PL] 36 C4
Krzyż [PL] 36 B1
Ksar es–Seghir [Eur.] 100 G6
Książ Wielki [PL] 52 A2
Ktísmata [GR] 132 C1
Kubbe [S] 184 F1
Küblis [CH] 72 A2
Kubrat [BG] 148 D2
Kuç [AL] 128 B6
Kučevo [YU] 150 D1
Kuchl [A] 60 G6
Kučište [YU] 150 A5
Kucovë [AL] 128 B4
Küçükbahçe [TR] 134 H4
Küçükçekmece [TR] 146 E3
Küçükkuyu [TR] 134 H1
Kudever' [RUS] 200 H5
Kudirkos Naumiestis [LT] 24 E1
Kudowa–Zdrój [PL] 50 B3

Kufstein [A] 60 F6
Kuggerud [N] 172 C5
Kuha [FIN] 198 E2
Kühlungsborn [D] 20 B3
Kuhmalahti [FIN] 176 G1
Kuhmo [FIN] 198 G5
Kuhmoinen [FIN] 176 H1
Kuhstedt [D] 18 E4
Kühtai [A] 72 C1
Kuivajärvi [FIN] 198 G4
Kuivaniemi [FIN] 198 D3
Kuivasjärvi [FIN] 186 C5
Kukës [AL] 128 C1
Kukko [FIN] 186 E3
Kuklin [PL] 22 H5
Kuks [CZ] 50 B3
Kukuj [RUS] 204 D2
Kukujevci [YU] 154 F2
Kukurečani [MK] 128 E3
Kula [BG] 150 E2
Kula [TR] 144 F3
Kula [YU] 76 D6
Kulalar [TR] 144 E2
Kulata [BG] 130 B2
Kuldīga [LV] 200 C5
Kuleli [TR] 146 B2
Kulennoinen [FIN] 188 F5
Kulhuse [DK] 156 G2
Kuliai [LT] 202 D4
Kullaa [FIN] 176 D1
Kulmbach [D] 46 H3
Kuloharju [FIN] 198 E2
Kulykiv [UA] 52 H3
Kumafşarı [TR] 142 G1
Kumane [YU] 76 E6
Kumanovo [MK] 150 D6
Kumarlar [TR] 146 B5
Kumbağ [TR] 146 C3
Kümbet [TR] 146 H5
Kumkale [TR] 130 H5
Kumköy [TR] 146 E2
Kumla [S] 166 H3
Kumlinge [FIN] 176 B5
Kumola [RUS] 188 G6
Kumrovec [HR] 74 E5
Kumuu [FIN] 198 G4
Kunda [EST] 200 F1
Kunes [N] 196 C2
Kungälv [S] 160 G1
Kungsängen [S] 168 D2
Kungsbacka [S] 160 H3
Kungshamn [S] 166 B5
Kungsör [S] 168 B3
Kunhegyes [H] 76 F1
Kunmadaras [H] 76 F1
Kunovice [CZ] 62 H2
Kunowo [PL] 36 C4
Kunpeszér [H] 76 C2
Kunrau [D] 34 A2
Kunštát [CZ] 50 C5
Kunszentmárton [H] 76 E3
Kunszentmiklós [H] 76 C2
Kunžak [CZ] 48 H6
Künzelsau [D] 46 E5
Kuolio [FIN] 198 F2
Kuoloyarvi [RUS] 196 F7
Kuona [FIN] 198 D6
Kuopio [FIN] 188 D2
Kuortane [FIN] 186 D3
Kuosku [FIN] 196 E6
Kupferberg [D] 46 H3
Kupferzell [D] 46 E5
Kupiansk [UA] 206 H2
Kupiškis [LT] 202 G4
Kupkovo [RUS] 200 G2
Kupli [LV] 200 D5
Küplü [TR] 130 H2
Küplü [TR] 146 G4
Kuprava [LV] 200 G4
Kupres [BIH] 154 C4
Kurbnesh [AL] 128 B1
Kurčatov [RUS] 204 E7
Kurd [H] 76 B4
Kŭrdzhali [BG] 130 F1
Kurejoki [FIN] 186 D2
Kuremäe [EST] 200 F1
Kurevere [EST] 200 C3
Kurgolovo [RUS] 178 E5
Kurikka [FIN] 186 C4
Kurilo [BG] 150 F4
Kuřim [CZ] 50 B6

Kurkiyeki [RUS] 188 G6
Kürnare [BG] 148 B4
Kurów [PL] 38 D5
Kurowice [PL] 36 H4
Kurozweki [PL] 52 C2
Kuršėnai [LT] 202 E4
Kuršiši [LV] 200 C6
Kursk [RUS] 204 F7
Kursu [FIN] 196 E7
Kuršumlija [YU] 150 C4
Kuršumlijska Banja [YU] 150 C4
Kurşunlu [TR] 146 F4
Kurşunlu [TR] 146 D4
Kurtakko [FIN] 192 H5
Kurtköy [TR] 146 G3
Kuru [FIN] 186 D6
Kurvinen [FIN] 198 F2
Kurzętnik [PL] 22 F5
Kuşadasi [TR] 144 D5
Kusel [D] 44 H3
Küssnacht [CH] 58 F6
Kustavi [FIN] 176 C4
Kuşuköy [TR] 144 F2
Kuta [YU] 152 E3
Kütahya [TR] 144 G1
Kutemajärvi [FIN] 186 H5
Kutina [HR] 154 B1
Kutná Hora [CZ] 48 H4
Kutno [PL] 36 G3
Kuttanen [FIN] 192 G4
Kuttura [FIN] 196 D5
Kúty [SK] 62 G3
Kuusaa [FIN] 186 G4
Kuusaa [FIN] 198 D5
Kuusajoki [FIN] 196 C6
Kuusalu [EST] 200 E1
Kuusamo [FIN] 196 F8
Kuusankoski [FIN] 178 C3
Kuusjärvi [FIN] 188 E2
Kuvšinovo [RUS] 204 E3
Kuyucak [TR] 144 E5
Kuzmin [YU] 154 F2
Kuzmina [PL] 52 E5
Kužnica [PL] 24 F4
Kuzuluk [TR] 146 H3
Kvænangsbotn [N] 192 F2
Kværndrup [DK] 156 D4
Kvaløyseter [N] 190 B5
Kvalsund [N] 196 B2
Kvalvåg [N] 180 F2
Kvalvåg [N] 170 A5
Kvam [N] 180 H6
Kvam [N] 190 C5
Kvanndal [N] 170 C4
Kvanne [N] 180 F2
Kvarnberg [S] 172 G2
Kvås [N] 164 C5
Kvėdarna [LT] 202 D4
Kvelde [N] 164 G3
Kvenvær [N] 190 A6
Kvevlax / Koivulahti [FIN] 186 B2
Kvicksund [S] 168 B2
Kvikkjokk [S] 190 G1
Kvikne [N] 182 B4
Kvillsfors [S] 162 F3
Kvinesdal [N] 164 C5
Kvinlog [N] 164 C4
Kvissleby [S] 184 E5
Kvisvik [N] 180 F2
Kvitnes [N] 180 F2
Kwidzyn [PL] 22 E4
Kwilcz [PL] 36 B2
Kybartai [LT] 24 E1
Kyïv [UA] 206 E2
Kyjov [CZ] 62 G2
Kyläinpää [FIN] 186 B3
Kyleakin [GB] 6 C5
Kyle of Lochalsh [GB] 6 C5
Kyllaj [S] 168 G4
Kyllburg [D] 44 F1
Kyllíni [GR] 136 B1
Kylmäkoski [FIN] 176 F2
Kými [GR] 134 C4
Kymönkoski [FIN] 186 G2
Kyparissía [GR] 136 C3
Kyritz [D] 20 B6
Kyrkhult [S] 162 D6
Kyrkslätt / Kirkkonummi [FIN] 176 G5

Kyrö [FIN] 176 E4
Kyrönlahti [FIN] 186 D6
Kyröskoski [FIN] 176 E1
Kyrping [N] 170 B6
Kyšice [CZ] 48 F3
Kysucké Nové Mesto [SK] 50 F6
Kýthira [GR] 136 F6
Kýthnos [GR] 138 C2
Kytömäki [FIN] 198 F4
Kyustendil [BG] 150 E6
Kyyjärvi [FIN] 186 E2

L

Laa an der Thaya [A] 62 F3
Laage [D] 20 B3
Laajoki [FIN] 176 D3
Laakajärvi [FIN] 198 F5
Laakirchen [A] 62 A5
La Alameda [E] 96 E5
La Alamedilla [E] 88 E4
La Alberca [E] 88 B4
La Alberca de Záncara [E] 98 A3
La Albuera [E] 94 G2
La Algaba [E] 94 G6
La Almarcha [E] 98 B3
La Almolda [E] 90 F4
La Almudena [E] 104 B2
La Almunia de Doña Godina [E] 90 D4
Laanila [FIN] 196 D5
La Antilla [E] 94 E6
La Azohía [E] 104 C4
Labajos [E] 88 E4
la Balme [F] 68 G5
La Baña [E] 78 F6
La Bañeza [E] 78 G6
La Barrela [E] 78 D4
La Bassée [F] 28 F3
Labastide-d'Armagnac [F] 66 D6
La Bastide de-Sérou [F] 84 H5
Labastide-Murat [F] 66 G4
La Bastide-Puylaurent [F] 68 D6
Labastide-Rouairoux [F] 106 C4
La Bâtie-Neuve [F] 108 D2
La Baule [F] 40 E6
La Bazoche-Gouet [F] 42 D5
Łabędzie [PL] 20 H4
la Bégude-de-Mazenc [F] 68 F6
La Belle Etoile [F] 44 A5
Labenne [F] 66 A6
La Bérarde [F] 70 A5
L'Aber-Wrac'h [F] 40 B1
Labin [HR] 112 E2
Labinot Fushë [AL] 128 C3
Łabiszyn [PL] 36 E1
Lábod [H] 74 H4
Laboe [D] 18 G2
Labouheyre [F] 66 B5
La Bourboule [F] 68 C2
La Bóveda de Toro [E] 88 D2
Labrags [LV] 200 B5
Labrède [F] 66 C3
La Bresse [F] 58 D3
La Brillanne [F] 108 C3
Labrit [F] 66 C5
Łabunie [PL] 52 G1
Laç [AL] 128 B2
La Cabrera [E] 88 G4
La Caillere-St-Hilaire [F] 54 C3
La Calahorra [E] 102 F4
La Calera [E] 100 B5
La Caletta [I] 118 E3
Lacalm [F] 68 C5
La Calzada de Calatrava [E] 96 E5
La Calzada de Oropesa [E] 88 C6
La Campana [E] 102 A2

La Cañada de Cañepla [E] 102 H3
Lacanau [F] 66 C2
Lacanau-Océan [F] 66 B2
La Canourgue [F] 68 C6
La Capelle [F] 28 G5
Lacapelle-Marival [F] 66 H4
La Capte [F] 108 C6
Lačarak [YU] 154 F2
La Carlota [E] 102 B2
La Carolina [E] 96 E6
Lacaune [F] 106 C3
La Cavalerie [F] 106 D3
Lacave [F] 66 G4
Lacco Ameno [I] 120 D3
Lacedonia [I] 120 G2
La Celle-Dunoise [F] 54 H5
Lăceni [RO] 148 B1
La Chaise-Dieu [F] 68 D3
La Chambre [F] 70 B4
Lachanás [GR] 130 B3
Lachaniá [GR] 142 D5
La Chapelle [F] 68 F1
La Chapelle-d'Angillon [F] 56 C3
la Chapelle-en-Valgaudemar [F] 70 A6
La Chapelle-en-Vercors [F] 68 G5
La Chapelle-Glain [F] 40 G5
La Charité-sur-Loire [F] 56 D3
La Chartre [F] 42 C6
La Châtaigneraie [F] 54 D3
La Châtre [F] 54 H5
La Chaux-de-Fonds [CH] 58 C5
La Ciotat [F] 108 B5
La Clayette [F] 56 F6
La Clusaz [F] 70 B3
La Cluse [F] 68 H2
La Cluse-et-Mijoux [F] 58 B6
Lacock [GB] 12 G3
La Codosera [E] 86 F5
Lacona [I] 114 D3
Láconi [I] 118 D5
La Coquille [F] 66 G2
La Coronada [E] 96 B3
La Coruña / A Coruña [E] 78 C2
La Côte-St-André [F] 68 G4
Lacourt [F] 84 G5
La Courtine [F] 68 B2
la Couvertoirade [F] 106 E3
Lacq [F] 84 D3
La Croisière [F] 54 G5
La Croixille [F] 26 D6
La Croix-Valmer [F] 108 D6
La Cumbre [F] 96 B1
La Cure [F] 70 B1
Łąd [PL] 36 E3
Ladbergen [D] 32 C2
Ladby [DK] 156 E3
Lądek-Zdrój [PL] 50 C3
Ládi [GR] 130 H1
Ladíspoli [I] 114 H5
Ladoeiro [P] 86 F3
Ladon [F] 42 H6
La Encinilla y El Rubio [E] 100 G3
La Espina [E] 78 G3
La Estrella [E] 96 D1
La Fère [F] 28 F6
La Ferrière-en-Parthenay [F] 54 E3
Laferté [F] 58 B3
La Ferté-Bernard [F] 42 C5
La Ferté-Gaucher [F] 42 H4
La Ferté-Macé [F] 26 F5
La Ferté-Milon [F] 42 H3
La Ferté-sous-Jouarre [F] 42 H3
La Ferté-St-Aubin [F] 56 B1
La Ferté-Vidame [F] 26 H5

Laffrey [F] 68 H5
Láfka [GR] 136 E1
La Flèche [F] 42 B6
La Flotte [F] 54 B4
La Font de la Figuera [E] 98 D6
Lafortunada [E] 84 E5
La Fregeneda [E] 80 E5
La Frua [I] 70 F2
La Fuente de San Esteban [E] 80 F6
La Gacilly [F] 40 E5
Lagan [S] 162 C4
Laganás [GR] 136 B2
La Garde-Freinet [F] 108 D5
La Garriga [E] 92 E4
La Garrovilla [E] 94 G1
Lage [D] 32 E3
Lagg [GB] 8 B2
La Gineta [E] 98 B5
Lagkáda [GR] 136 E4
Lagkáda [GR] 134 G4
Lagkadás [GR] 130 B4
Lagkádia [GR] 136 D2
Lagkadíkia [GR] 130 B4
Lagnieu [F] 68 G2
Lagny [F] 42 G3
Lagoa [P] 94 B5
Lagonegro [I] 120 G5
Lagonísi [GR] 136 H1
Lágos [GR] 130 F3
Lagos [P] 94 B5
Łagów [PL] 52 C1
Łagów [PL] 34 H3
la Granadella [E] 90 H5
La Grand-Combe [F] 106 F2
La Grande-Motte [F] 106 F4
La Granja [E] 88 F4
La Granjuela [E] 96 B5
Lagrasse [F] 106 C5
La Grave [F] 70 B5
La Guardia / A Guarda [E] 96 G2
La Guardia / A Guarda [E] 78 A5
Laguardia / Biasteri [E] 82 G6
La Guardia de Jaén [E] 102 E2
Laguarta [E] 84 E5
Laguépie [F] 66 H6
La Guerche [F] 56 D4
La Guerche-de-Bretagne [F] 40 G4
Laguiole [F] 68 B5
Laguna de Duero [E] 88 E2
Laguna del Marquesado [E] 98 C2
Laguna de Santiago [E] 100 B5
Lahane [F] 66 B5
La Haye-du-Puits [F] 26 D2
Lahemaa [EST] 200 D1
La Hermida [E] 82 D3
Lahinch [IRL] 2 B5
Lahnstein [D] 30 H6
Laholm [S] 162 B5
Lahr [D] 58 E2
Lahti [FIN] 178 B2
La Hutte [F] 26 F6
Laichingen [D] 60 B3
Laide [GB] 6 C3
L'Aigle [F] 26 G5
La Iglesuela del Cid [E] 98 F2
Laignes [F] 56 F2
Laiguéglia [I] 108 G4
L'Aiguillon [F] 54 B4
Laihia [FIN] 186 B3
Laikko [FIN] 188 F6
Lailiás [GR] 130 C2
Laimbach [A] 62 D4
Lainate [I] 70 G4
Lairg [GB] 6 E3
La Isla [E] 82 C2
Laissac [F] 68 B6

Laísta [GR] 132 D1
Laisvall [S] 190 F2
Laitikkala [FIN] 176 G2
Laitila [FIN] 176 D3
La Javie [F] 108 D3
Lajkovac [YU] 150 A1
la Jonquera [E] 92 G2
Lajoskomárom [H] 76 B3
Lajosmizse [H] 76 D2
Łąka Prudnicka [PL] 50 D3
Lakatnik [BG] 150 F4
Lakaträsk [S] 196 A8
Lakavica [MK] 128 G2
Lakhdenpokh'ya [RUS] 188 G6
Lakitelek [H] 76 E3
Lákka [GR] 132 B3
Lakkí [GR] 142 B2
Lákkoi [GR] 140 C4
Lákkoma [GR] 130 G4
Lakolk [DK] 156 A3
Lakópetra [GR] 132 E6
Lakselv [N] 192 H1
Laktasi [BIH] 154 C2
Lála [GR] 136 C2
La Lantejuela [E] 102 B2
Lalapaşa [TR] 146 B1
l'Albagés [E] 90 H5
L'Albi [E] 92 B4
L'Alcúdia [E] 88 E5
l'Alcora / Alcora [E] 98 F3
L'Alcúdia de Crespins [E] 98 E6
L'Aldea [E] 92 B5
La Lima [I] 110 E4
Lalín [E] 78 C4
Lalinde [F] 66 F4
La Línea de la Concepción [E] 100 H5
Lalm [N] 180 G6
La Loupe [F] 26 H6
Lalouvesc [F] 68 F4
La Louvière [B] 28 H4
L'Alpe-d'Huez [F] 70 A5
La Luisiana [E] 102 B2
Lam [D] 48 D6
La Machine [F] 56 D4
La Maddalena [I] 118 E2
Lama dei Peligni [I] 116 D5
La Magdalena [E] 78 G5
La Malène [F] 68 C6
Lamalou-les-Bains [F] 106 D4
La Manga del Mar Menor [E] 104 D4
Lamarche [F] 58 B2
Lamarque [F] 66 C2
Lamas do Vouga [P] 80 B5
Lamastre [F] 68 F5
La Matanza [E] 82 B5
La Maucarrière [F] 54 E3
Lambach [A] 62 B4
Lamballe [F] 26 B4
Lamberhurst [GB] 14 F5
Lambesc [F] 106 H4
Lambley [GB] 8 E6
Lambourn [GB] 12 H3
Lambrecht [D] 46 B5
Lamego [P] 80 D4
L'Ametlla de Mar [E] 92 B5
Lamezia Terme [I] 124 D5
Lamía [GR] 132 G4
Lammhult [S] 162 D4
Lammi [FIN] 176 H2
La Molina [E] 92 E2
La Mongie [F] 84 F4
La Mothe-Achard [F] 54 B3
Lamotte-Beuvron [F] 56 B2
La Motte-Chalancon [F] 108 B2
la Motte-du-Caire [F] 108 C2
Lampaanjärvi [FIN] 186 H1
Lampaul [F] 40 A1
Lampaul-Plouarzel [F] 40 A1
Lámpeia [GR] 136 C1
Lampeland [N] 164 G1
Lampeter [GB] 10 B6
L'Ampolla [E] 92 B5

Lamprechtshausen [A] 60 G5
Lämsänkylä [FIN] 198 F2
Lamsfeld [D] 34 F4
Lamstedt [D] 18 E4
La Mudarra [E] 88 E1
La Muela [E] 90 F4
La Mure [F] 68 H5
Lamure-sur-Azergues [F] 68 F2
Lana [I] 72 C3
Lanaja [E] 90 F4
La Napoule-Plage [F] 108 E5
Lanark [GB] 8 D4
La Nava de Ricomalillo [E] 96 D1
Lancaster [GB] 10 D2
Lanchester [GB] 8 F6
Lanciano [I] 116 E5
Lancing [GB] 14 E5
Łańcut [PL] 52 E3
Landau [D] 60 G3
Landau [D] 46 B5
Landeck [A] 72 C1
Landerneau [F] 40 B2
Landeryd [S] 162 B4
Landesbergen [D] 32 E1
Landete [E] 98 D3
Landévennec [F] 40 B2
Landivisiau [F] 40 C2
Landivy [F] 26 D5
Landkirchen [D] 18 H2
Landmannalaugur [IS] 194 D5
Landön [S] 182 G1
Landquart [CH] 58 H6
Landrecies [F] 28 G4
Landsberg [D] 60 D4
Landsberg [D] 34 C5
Landsbro [S] 162 E3
Landshut [D] 60 F3
Landskrona [S] 156 H2
Landstuhl [D] 44 H3
Landvetter [S] 160 H2
Lanesborough [IRL] 2 D5
La Neuve-Lyre [F] 26 H5
La Neuveville [CH] 58 D5
Langa [DK] 160 D5
Långå [S] 182 F4
Langa de Duero [E] 88 H2
Långåminne [FIN] 186 B3
Langangen [N] 164 G3
Langballig [D] 156 C5
Långban [S] 166 G1
Langeac [F] 68 D4
Langeais [F] 54 F2
Längelmäki [FIN] 186 F6
Langelsheim [D] 32 G3
Langen [A] 72 B1
Langen [D] 46 C3
Langen [D] 18 D4
Langenargen [D] 58 H4
Langenau [D] 60 B3
Langenburg [D] 46 E5
Längenfeld [A] 72 C2
Langenfeld [D] 30 G4
Langenhahn [D] 46 B1
Langenhorn [D] 156 B5
Langenisarhofen [D] 60 G3
Langenlois [A] 62 E4
Langennaundorf [D] 34 E5
Langenselbold [D] 46 D3
Langenthal [CH] 58 E5
Langenwang [A] 62 E6
Langenzenn [D] 46 F5
Langeoog [D] 18 B3
Langeskov [DK] 156 E3
Langesund [N] 164 G3
Langevåg [N] 164 A1
Langevåg [N] 180 C3
Langewiese [D] 32 D5
Langfjord [N] 192 F1
Långflon [S] 172 E3
Langhirano [I] 110 D3
Langholm [GB] 8 E5
Långlöt [S] 162 G5
Långnäs [FIN] 176 B5
Langnau im Emmental [CH] 58 E6
Langø [DK] 156 E5

Langogne [F] 68 D5
Langoiran [F] 66 D3
Langon [F] 66 D4
Langport [GB] 12 F4
Langquaid [D] 60 F2
Langres [F] 56 H2
Långsele [S] 184 E2
Långserud [S] 166 D3
Långshyttan [S] 174 D5
Langula [D] 32 G5
Langwarden [D] 18 D4
Langwedel [D] 18 E6
Langweid [D] 60 D3
Lanhelas [P] 78 A5
Lanjarón [E] 102 E5
Lankas [LV] 200 B5
Länkipohja [FIN] 186 F6
Lanmeur [F] 40 C1
Lannabruk [S] 166 G3
Lannemezan [F] 84 F4
Lannevesi [FIN] 186 F3
Lannilis [F] 40 B1
Lannion [F] 40 D1
Lanobre [F] 68 B3
La Noguera [E] 98 D1
Lanouaille [F] 66 G2
Lansjärv [S] 196 A8
Lanškroun [CZ] 50 C4
Lanslebourg-Mont-Cenis [F] 70 C5
Lantosque [F] 108 F4
Lanusei [I] 118 E5
Lanvollon [F] 26 A4
Lanzá [E] 78 C2
Lanžhot [CZ] 62 G3
Lanzo d'Intelvi [I] 70 G3
Lanzo Torinese [I] 70 D5
La Oliva [E] 100 E5
Laon [F] 28 G6
La Orotava [E] 100 C5
La Paca [E] 104 B3
La Pacaudière [F] 68 E1
Lapalisse [F] 56 D6
La Pallice [F] 54 B4
La Palma del Condado [E] 94 F6
La Palmyre [F] 54 B6
La Palud-sur-Verdon [F] 108 D4
Lápas [GR] 132 E6
La Pelechaneta / Pelejaneta [E] 98 F3
la Péruse [F] 54 E6
La Petite-Pierre [F] 44 G5
Lapeyrade [F] 66 D5
Lapinjärvi / Lappträsk [FIN] 178 B3
Lapinlahti [FIN] 188 C1
La Plagne [F] 70 B4
La Plaza / Teverga [E] 78 G4
Laplume [F] 66 E5
la Pobla de Lillet [E] 92 E2
la Pobla de Segur [E] 92 C1
la Pobla de Vallbona [E] 98 E4
la Pobla Tornesa [E] 98 G3
La Pola de Gordón [E] 78 H5
La Portera [E] 98 D4
Lapoutroie [F] 58 D2
Lapovo [YU] 150 C2
Lappago / Lappach [I] 72 E2
Lappäjärvi [FIN] 192 G4
Lappajärvi [FIN] 186 D2
Läppe [S] 168 B3
Lappeenranta [FIN] 178 E2
Lappfjärd / Lapväärtti [FIN] 186 B5
Lappfors [FIN] 186 C1
Lappi [FIN] 176 D3
Lappo [FIN] 176 C5
Lappohja / Lappvik [FIN] 176 F6
Lappoluobbal [N] 192 G2
Lappträsk [S] 198 C2
Lappträsk / Lapinjärvi [FIN] 178 B3
Lappvattnet [S] 198 A5

Lappvik / Lappohja [FIN] 176 F6
Lapseki [TR] 146 B5
Laptevo [RUS] 200 H5
Lapua [FIN] 186 C2
La Puebla de Almoradiel [E] 96 G3
La Puebla de Cazalla [E] 102 A3
La Puebla de los Infantes [E] 96 B6
La Puebla del Río [E] 94 G6
La Puebla de Montalbán [E] 96 E1
La Puebla de Valdavia [E] 82 D4
La Puebla de Valverde [E] 98 E2
La Punt [CH] 72 A3
Lapväärtti / Lappfjärd [FIN] 186 B5
Łapy [PL] 24 E6
Laqueuille [F] 68 C2
L'Aquila [I] 116 C4
La Rábita [E] 102 E5
Laracha [E] 78 C2
Laragh [IRL] 4 G3
Laragne-Montéglin [F] 108 C2
La Rambla [E] 102 C2
L'Arbresle [F] 68 F2
Lärbro [S] 168 G4
Larche [F] 66 G3
Larche [F] 108 E2
Lårdal [N] 164 E2
Lardaro [I] 72 C4
Larderello [I] 114 F1
Lárdos [GR] 142 E5
Lardosa [P] 86 F3
Laredo [E] 82 F3
La Réole [F] 66 D4
La Restinga [E] 100 A6
Largentière [F] 68 E6
L'Argentiére-la-Bessée [F] 70 B6
Largo [GB] 8 F3
Largs [GB] 8 C3
Lari [F] 114 C2
La Rinconada [E] 94 G6
Larino [I] 116 F6
Lárisa [GR] 132 G2
Larkollen [N] 166 B3
Larmor [F] 40 C4
Larne [GB] 2 G3
La Robla [E] 78 H5
La Roca de la Sierra [E] 86 G6
la Roca del Vallès [E] 92 E4
La Roche-Bernard [F] 40 E5
La Roche-Chalais [F] 66 E2
La Roche-en-Ardenne [B] 30 E6
La Rochefoucauld [F] 54 E6
La Rochelle [F] 54 C4
La Roche-Posay [F] 54 F3
La Roche-sur-Foron [F] 70 B2
La Roche-sur-Yon [F] 54 B3
La Rochette [F] 70 A4
Larochette [L] 44 F2
La Roda [E] 98 B4
La Roda de Andalucía [E] 102 B3
Laroquebrou [F] 68 A4
La Roquebrussanne [F] 108 C5
Laroque-des-Arcs [F] 66 G5
Laroque-d'Olmes [F] 106 A5
La Roque-Gageac [F] 66 G4
Larrau [F] 84 D3
Larseng [N] 192 E2
Larsmo / Luoto [FIN] 198 C6

Larsnes [N] 180 C4
l'Artigue [F] 84 H5
La Rubia [E] 90 B2
Laruns [F] 84 D4
Larvik [N] 164 G3
Lárymna [GR] 134 B5
La Salvetat [F] 66 H6
La Salvetat-sur-Agout [F] 106 C3
Läsänkoski [FIN] 188 C5
Lasarte-Oria [E] 84 B2
La Sauceda [E] 100 G4
Låsby [DK] 160 D6
Las Cabezas de San Juan [E] 100 G3
Las Casas de Besaya [E] 82 E3
la Sénia [E] 92 A6
la Seu d'Urgell [E] 92 D1
La Seyne [F] 108 C6
Łasin [PL] 22 E5
Łask [PL] 36 G5
Łaskarzew [PL] 38 C4
Laško [SLO] 74 D5
Laskowice [PL] 50 D3
Las Navas de la Concepción [E] 96 B6
Las Navas del Marqués [E] 88 E5
Las Negras [E] 102 H5
La Solana [E] 96 G4
La Souterraine [F] 54 G5
Lasovo [YU] 150 D2
Las Palmas de Gran Canaria [E] 100 D5
Las Pedroñeras [E] 96 H3
La Spézia [I] 110 C4
Las Rozas [E] 88 F5
Lassan [D] 20 E3
Lassay [F] 26 E5
Lassigny [F] 28 E6
Las Torres de Cotillas [E] 104 C3
Lastovo [HR] 152 A3
Lastra a Signa [I] 110 E5
Lastres [E] 82 C2
Lastrup [D] 18 C6
Lastva [BIH] 152 D4
Lašva [BIH] 154 D4
Las Ventas con Peña Aguilera [E] 96 E2
Łaszczów [PL] 52 G2
Laterza [I] 122 D4
Lathen [D] 16 H3
Latheron [GB] 6 F3
La Thuile [I] 70 C4
Latiano [I] 122 F4
Latikberg [S] 190 F5
Latina [I] 120 B1
Latisana [I] 72 G5
la Torre [E] 98 D4
la Torre Baixa [E] 98 D2
La Torresaviñán [E] 90 A5
La Tour-du-Pin [F] 68 G3
La Tranche-sur-Mer [F] 54 B4
La Tremblade [F] 54 B5
La Trimouille [F] 54 G4
La Trinité [F] 40 D5
La Trinité-Porhoët [F] 26 B5
Latronico [I] 120 H5
Latronquière [F] 66 H4
La Turbie [F] 108 F4
Laubrières [F] 40 G5
La Wantzenau [F] 44 H6
Laucha [D] 34 B5
Lauchhammer [D] 34 E5
Laudal [N] 164 D5
Lauder [GB] 8 F4
Laudio / Llodio [E] 82 G6
Laudona [LV] 200 F5
Lauenau [D] 32 F2
Lauenburg [D] 18 G5
Lauenstein [D] 48 E2
Läyliäinen [FIN] 176 G4
Laza [E] 78 D6
Lazarevac [YU] 150 B1
Lazarovo [YU] 154 G1

Laufenburg [CH] 58 F4
Laufenburg [D] 58 F4
Lauffen [D] 46 D6
Laugar [IS] 194 F3
Laugarbakki [IS] 194 C3
Laugarvatn [IS] 194 C4
Laugharne [GB] 12 D2
Lauingen [D] 60 C3
Laujar de Andarax [E] 102 F5
Laukaa [FIN] 186 G4
Laukka [FIN] 198 D4
Lauksundskaret [N] 192 F1
Laukuva [LT] 202 E4
Laukvik [N] 192 C5
Laukvik [N] 192 B4
Laukvik [N] 192 D2
Launceston [GB] 12 D4
Laupen [CH] 58 D6
Laupheim [D] 60 B4
Lauragh [IRL] 4 B5
Laurencetown [IRL] 2 D5
Laurenzana [I] 120 H4
Lauria [I] 120 H5
Laurière [F] 54 G6
Lausanne [CH] 70 C1
Lauter [S] 168 H3
Lauterbach [D] 46 E1
Lauterbourg [F] 46 B6
Lauterbrunnen [CH] 70 E1
Lautere [LV] 200 F5
Lauterecken [D] 44 H3
Lauterhofen [D] 46 H5
Lautiosaari [FIN] 198 C2
Lautrec [F] 106 B3
Lauvsnes [N] 190 C5
Lauvstad [N] 180 C4
Lauvuskylä [FIN] 198 G5
Lauvvik [N] 164 B3
Lauwersoog [NL] 16 G1
Lauzerte [F] 66 F5
Lauzun [F] 66 E4
Lavagna [I] 110 B3
Laval [F] 26 E6
la Vall d'Uixó [E] 98 F4
Lavamünd [A] 74 C3
Låvang [N] 190 D2
Lávara [GR] 130 H2
Lavardac [F] 66 E5
Lavardin [F] 42 C6
Lavarone [I] 72 D5
Lavaur [F] 106 B3
La Vecilla [E] 82 B3
Lavelanet [F] 106 A5
Lavello [I] 120 H3
Lavelsloh [D] 32 E2
Lavenham [GB] 14 F3
La Venta [E] 102 F4
la Veurdre [F] 56 D4
Lavia [FIN] 176 E1
Lavik [N] 170 B2
la Villa [I] 72 E3
Lavinio-Lido di Enea [I] 120 A1
La Virgen del Camino [E] 78 H5
Lavìs [I] 72 C4
Lavit [F] 66 F6
Lavong [N] 190 D2
La Voulte-sur-Rhône [F] 68 F5
Lavoûte-Chilhac [F] 68 D4
Lavoûte-sur-Loire [F] 68 D4
Lavre [P] 86 C6
Lávrion [GR] 136 H1
Lavry [RUS] 200 G4
Laxå [S] 166 G4
Laxe [E] 78 B2
Laxey [GBM] 10 C2
Laxo [GB] 6 G3
Laxsjö [S] 190 E6
Laxtjärn [S] 172 G5
Laxviken [S] 190 E6
Layer Marney [GB] 14 F4
La Yesa [E] 98 E3

Lazdijai [LT] 24 F2
Laži [LV] 200 C4
Lazise [I] 72 C6
Łaziska Górne [PL] 50 F3
Lazkao [E] 84 A3
Làzne Kynžvart [CZ] 48 C4
La Zubia [E] 102 E4
Łazy [PL] 22 A2
Leadenham [GB] 10 F5
Leaden Roding [GB] 14 F4
Leadhills [GB] 8 D4
Leamington Spa [GB] 14 D2
Leap [IRL] 4 B5
Leatherhead [GB] 14 E4
Łeba [PL] 22 C1
Lebach [D] 44 G3
Lebane [YU] 150 D4
Le Bar [F] 108 E4
Le Barp [F] 66 C4
Le Beausset [F] 108 C5
Lebesby [N] 196 D2
Le Blanc [F] 54 G4
Łebno [PL] 22 D2
Le Boréon [F] 108 F3
Łebork [PL] 22 C2
Le Boulou [F] 92 G1
Le Bourg d'Oisans [F] 68 H5
Le Bourget [F] 68 H3
le Bousquet-d'Orb [F] 106 D3
Lebrija [E] 100 G3
Le Bugue [F] 66 F3
Lebus [D] 34 G2
Le Calanche [F] 114 A4
le Caloy [F] 66 C6
Le Cap-d'Agde [F] 106 E5
Le Cateau-Cambrésis [F] 28 G4
Le Catelet [F] 28 F5
Le Caylar [F] 106 E3
Lecce [I] 122 G4
Lecco [I] 70 G4
Lécera [E] 90 E5
Lech [A] 72 B1
Lechainá [GR] 136 B1
L'Echalp [F] 70 C6
le Chambon-sur-Lignon [F] 68 E4
Le Chateau-d'Oléron [F] 54 B5
Le Châtelard [F] 70 A3
Le Châtelet [F] 56 B4
Le Chesne [F] 44 C2
Le Cheylard [F] 68 E5
Lechlade [GB] 12 H3
Lechovice [CZ] 62 F2
Léchovo [GR] 128 E5
Leci [LV] 200 B5
Leciñena [E] 90 F3
Leck [D] 156 B4
Le Conquet [F] 40 A2
Le Creusot [F] 56 F5
Le Croisic [F] 40 D6
Le Crotoy [F] 28 D3
Lectoure [F] 66 E6
Łęczna [UA] 38 E5
Łęczyca [PL] 20 G5
Łęczyca [PL] 36 G3
Ledaña [E] 98 C4
Ledbury [GB] 12 G2
Ledeč nad Sázavou [CZ] 48 H5
Ledesma [E] 80 G6
Lédignan [F] 106 F3
Ledigos [E] 82 C5
Ledmore [GB] 6 D3
Lednice [CZ] 62 G2
Lednogora [PL] 36 D2
Le Donjon [F] 56 E6
Le Dorat [F] 54 F5
Lędyczek [PL] 22 B5
Leeds [GB] 10 F3
Leek [GB] 10 E5
Leek [NL] 16 G2
Leenane [IRL] 2 B4
Leer [D] 18 B4
Leerdam [NL] 16 D5
Leese [D] 32 E1
Leesi [EST] 200 E1
Leeuwarden [NL] 16 F2

Le Faou [F] 40 B2
Le Faouët [F] 40 C3
le Fayet [F] 70 C3
Lefka [BG] 146 A1
Lefkáda [GR] 132 D4
Lefkáda [GR] 128 G4
Lefkadíti [GR] 132 G5
Léfkes [GR] 138 E3
Lefkímmi [GR] 132 B3
Lefkógia [GR] 130 C2
Léfktra [GR] 134 A5
le Folgoet [F] 40 B1
Le Fossat [F] 84 H4
Legbąd [PL] 22 D4
Legden [D] 16 H5
Legé [F] 54 B2
Legionowo [PL] 38 B2
Legnago [I] 110 F1
Legnano [I] 70 F4
Legnica [PL] 36 B6
Legrad [HR] 74 G4
Le Grand-Bourg [F] 54 G6
Le Grand-Lucé [F] 42 C5
Le Grand-Pressigny [F] 54 F3
Le Grau-du-Roi [F] 106 F4
Legrená [GR] 136 H2
le Gressier [F] 66 B3
Leguatiano [E] 82 G4
Léguevin [F] 84 H3
Le Havre [F] 26 G3
Lehnice [SK] 62 H5
Lehnin [D] 34 D3
Le Hohwald [F] 44 G6
Lehrberg [D] 46 F5
Lehre [D] 32 H2
Lehrte [D] 32 G2
Lehtimäki [FIN] 186 D3
Lehtiniemi [FIN] 196 E8
Leibnitz [A] 74 D3
Leicester [GB] 10 F6
Leiden [NL] 16 D4
Leie [EST] 200 E3
Leighlinbridge [IRL] 4 F4
Leighton Buzzard [GB] 14 E3
Leikanger [N] 180 B4
Leikanger [N] 170 D2
Leinefelde [D] 32 G5
Leinesodden [N] 190 D2
Leini [I] 70 D5
Leipheim [D] 60 C3
Leipojärvi [S] 192 F6
Leipsoí [GR] 142 B2
Leipzig [D] 34 C5
Leira [N] 170 G3
Leirbotn [N] 192 G1
Leirbotnvatn [N] 192 G1
Leirgulen [N] 180 B5
Leiria [P] 86 C3
Leiro [E] 78 C4
Leirosa [P] 86 C2
Leirosen [N] 190 D2
Leirpollskogen [N] 196 D2
Leirvik [DK] 160 B1
Leirvik [N] 170 B1
Leirvik [N] 170 B5
Leirvika [N] 190 D2
Leisi [EST] 200 C3
Leisnig [D] 34 D6
Leissigen [CH] 70 E1
Leiston [GB] 14 G3
Leitzkau [D] 34 C3
Leivádia [GR] 132 H5
Leivonmäki [FIN] 186 G5
Lejasciems [LV] 200 F4
Lekáni [GR] 130 D2
Lekeitio [E] 82 H4
Lekenik [HR] 74 E6
Lekhchevo [BG] 150 F3
Leki Górne [PL] 52 C4
Leknes [N] 192 B4
Leknes [N] 180 D4
Leknica [PL] 34 G5
Leksand [S] 172 H4
Leksberg [S] 166 F5
Leksvik [N] 190 D1
Lekunberri [E] 84 B3
Lekvattnet [S] 172 E5
Le Lauzet-Ubaye [F] 108 D2

Le Lavandou [F] 108 D6
Lelice [PL] 36 H1
Le Lion-d'Angers [F] 40 H6
Lelkowo [PL] 22 G2
Lelle [EST] 200 E2
Le Locle [CH] 58 C5
Le Logis-du-Pin [F] 108 D4
Le Loroux-Bottereau [F] 54 C1
Le Louroux [F] 40 G6
Lelów [PL] 50 H2
Le Luc [F] 108 D5
Le Ludd [F] 42 B6
Lelystad [NL] 16 E4
Lem [DK] 156 B1
Le Mans [F] 42 B5
Le Markstein [F] 58 D3
Le Mas-d'Azil [F] 84 H4
Le Mayet [F] 68 D1
Lembach [F] 44 H5
Lembeye [F] 84 E3
Le Merlerault [F] 26 G5
Lemförde [D] 32 D1
Lemgo [D] 32 E3
Lemke [D] 32 F1
Lemland [FIN] 176 B6
Lemmenjoki [FIN] 196 D4
Lemmer [NL] 16 F3
Le Monastier [F] 68 E5
Le Monêtier-les-Bains [F] 70 B5
Le Mont-Dore [F] 68 C2
Le Montet [F] 56 D5
Le Mont-St-Michel [F] 26 D4
Lempäälä [FIN] 176 F2
Lempdes [F] 68 C3
Lempdes [F] 68 C3
Lemreway / Leumrabhagh [GB] 6 B3
Le Muret [F] 66 C4
Le Muy [F] 108 D5
Lemvig [DK] 160 B5
Lena [N] 172 B4
Lenart [SLO] 74 E3
Lencloître [F] 54 E3
Lend [A] 72 G1
Lendava [SLO] 74 F3
Lendery [RUS] 198 H6
Lendinara [I] 110 G2
Le Neubourg [F] 26 H4
Lengerich [D] 32 C2
Lenggries [D] 60 E5
Lengyeltóti [H] 74 H3
Lenham [GB] 14 F5
Lenhovda [S] 162 E4
Lenin [BY] 204 B6
Lenk [CH] 70 D2
Lennartsfors [S] 166 C3
Lenningen [N] 170 G2
Lenno [I] 70 G3
Lennoxtown [GB] 8 D3
Leno [I] 72 B6
Lenora [CZ] 62 B2
Le Nouvion-en-Thiérache [F] 28 G5
Lens [F] 28 F3
Lensahn [D] 18 H2
Lensvik [N] 180 H1
Léntas [GR] 140 E5
Lentföhrden [D] 18 F3
Lenti [H] 74 F3
Lentiira [FIN] 198 G4
Lenting [D] 60 E2
Lentini [I] 126 G4
Lentvaris [LT] 24 H1
Lenzburg [CH] 58 F5
Lenzen [D] 20 A6
Lenzerheide [CH] 70 H1
Lenzkirch [D] 58 F3
Leoben [A] 74 D1
Leogang [A] 60 G6
Leominster [GB] 12 G1
León [E] 78 H5
Léon [F] 66 B5
Leonberg [D] 58 G1
Leóndio [GR] 136 E2
Leonessa [I] 116 B3
Leonforte [I] 126 F3
Leonídio [GR] 136 F3

Leontário [GR] 136 D3
Leopoldsburg [B] 30 E3
Leopoldsdorf [A] 62 F4
Le Palais [F] 40 C5
Lepe [E] 94 E5
Le-Péage-de-Roussillon [F] 68 F4
Lepel [BY] 204 B5
Lepenoú [GR] 132 E4
Le Perthus [F] 92 G2
Lepetane [YU] 152 D4
Le Pin-au-Haras [F] 26 G5
l'Epine [F] 44 C4
Lepoglava [HR] 74 E4
Le Poiré-sur-Vie [F] 54 B3
Le Pont-de-Beauvoisin [F] 68 H4
Le Pont-de-Claix [F] 68 H5
le Pont-de-Montvert [F] 68 D6
Le Pontet [F] 66 D2
Le Portel [F] 28 D2
Leposavič [YU] 150 C4
Le Pouldu [F] 40 C4
Le Pouzin [F] 68 F5
Lépoura [GR] 134 C5
Leppäjärvi [FIN] 192 G4
Leppälahti [FIN] 188 F3
Leppävesi [FIN] 186 G4
Leppävirta [FIN] 188 D3
Leppiniemi [FIN] 198 D4
Lépreo [GR] 136 C3
Lepsény [H] 76 B2
Leptokaryá [GR] 128 G6
Le Puy [F] 68 D4
Le Puy-en-Velay [F] 68 D4
Le Quesnoy [F] 28 G4
Le Rabot [F] 56 B2
Lerbäck [S] 166 H4
Lercara Friddi [I] 126 D3
Lerga [E] 84 B4
Lerici [I] 110 C4
Lérida / Lleida [E] 90 H4
Lerín [E] 84 A4
Lerma [E] 88 G1
Lermoos [A] 60 D6
Le Rozier [F] 106 E2
Lerresfjord [N] 196 B2
Lerum [S] 160 H2

Le Russey [F] 58 C5
Lerwick [GB] 6 G4
Lés [E] 84 F5
Les [RO] 76 H2
Lesa [I] 70 F4
Les Abrets [F] 68 H3
Les Adrets [F] 108 E5
Les Aix-d'Angillon [F] 56 C3
Lešak [YU] 150 B4
Lesaka [E] 84 B3
les Aldudes [F] 84 C3
Les Andelys [F] 28 C6
Les Arcs [F] 70 C4
Les Arcs [F] 108 D5
les Avants [CH] 70 C1
les Avellanes [E] 92 B2
Les Baux-de-Provence [F] 106 G4
les Borges Blanques [E] 92 B3
Les Cabannes [F] 106 A5
L'Escala [E] 92 G3
Lescar [F] 84 E3
L'Escarène [F] 108 F4
Les Contamines-Montjoie [F] 70 C3
les Coves de Vinromà [E] 98 G2
Les Deux-Alpes [F] 70 A5
Les Diablerets [CH] 70 D2
Les Echarmeaux [F] 68 F1
Les Echelles [F] 68 H4
Les Epesses [F] 54 C2
Les Escaldes [AND] 84 H6
Les Essarts [F] 54 C3
Les Eyzies-de-Tayac [F] 66 F3
Les Gets [F] 70 C2
Les Halles [F] 68 F3
Les Haudères [CH] 70 D3
Les Hayons [F] 28 C5
Les Herbiers [F] 54 C2
Les Houches [F] 70 C3
Les Issambres [F] 108 D5
Lesja [N] 180 G5
Lesjaskog [N] 180 F4
Lesjaverk [N] 180 F4

Lesjöfors [S] 166 F1
Leskelä [FIN] 198 D5
Lesko [PL] 52 E5
Leskovac [YU] 150 D4
Leskovik [AL] 128 D6
Leskovo [BG] 148 F1
Les Laumes [F] 56 F3
Les Lecques [F] 108 B5
Les Menuires [F] 70 B4
Lesmont [F] 44 B5
Lésna [H] 48 H1
Lesneven [F] 40 B1
Lešnica [PL] 50 E3
Lešnica [YU] 154 F3
Lésniów Wielki [PL] 34 H4
Lesogorskiy [RUS] 178 F2
Lesparre-Médoc [F] 66 C2
Les Pieux [F] 26 D2
Les Planches-en-Montagne [F] 58 B6
les Planes d'Hostoles [E] 92 F3
l'Espluga de Francolí [E] 92 C4
Les Ponts-de-Cé [F] 40 H6
Les Riceys [F] 56 F1
Les Rosiers [F] 54 E1
les Rotes [E] 104 F1
Les Rousses [F] 70 B1
Les Sables-d'Olonne [F] 54 B3
Lessay [F] 26 D3
Lessebo [S] 162 E5
Lessines [B] 28 G3
l'Estartit [E] 92 G3
Lestelle Bétharram [F] 84 E4
Lestijärvi [FIN] 198 D6
Les Trois-Epis [F] 58 D2
Les Trois-Moutiers [F] 54 E2
Lesum [D] 18 D5
Les Vans [F] 68 E6
Leszczyny [PL] 50 F3
Leszno [PL] 36 C4
Leszno [PL] 38 B3
Letchworth [GB] 14 E3
Le Teil [F] 68 F6

Le Teilleul [F] 26 E5
le Temple [F] 66 C3
Letenye [H] 74 F4
Le Thillot [F] 58 C3
Letičev [UA] 206 D3
Letkés [H] 64 C5
Letmathe [D] 32 C4
Letnitsa [BG] 148 B3
Le Touquet-Paris-Plage [F] 28 D3
Le Touvet [F] 68 H4
Letovice [CZ] 50 C5
Le Trayas [F] 108 E5
Le Tréport [F] 28 C4
Letschin [D] 34 G2
Letterfrack [IRL] 2 B4
Letterkenny [IRL] 2 E2
Lettermore [GB] 6 E3
Lettermullan [IRL] 2 B5
Leu [RO] 150 G1
Leucate [F] 106 D6
Leuchars [GB] 8 F2
Leuglay [F] 56 G2
Leuk [CH] 70 D2
Leukerbad [CH] 70 D2
Leumrabhagh / Lemreway [GB] 6 B3
Leuna [D] 34 C5
Leutasch [A] 60 D6
Leutenberg [D] 46 H2
Leutkirch [D] 60 B5
Leutschach [A] 74 D3
Leuven (Louvain) [B] 30 D4
Leuze [B] 28 G3
Levajok [N] 196 C3
Le Val-André [F] 26 B4
Levan [AL] 128 A4
Levanger [N] 190 C6
Levanto [FIN] 176 H3
Lévanto [I] 110 C4
Le Vaudreuil [F] 28 B6
Leven [GB] 8 F3
Levens [F] 108 E4
Le Verdon [F] 54 B6
Leverkusen [D] 30 G4
Le Vernet [F] 108 D3
Levet [F] 56 C4
Levice [SK] 64 B4
Levico Terme [I] 72 D5

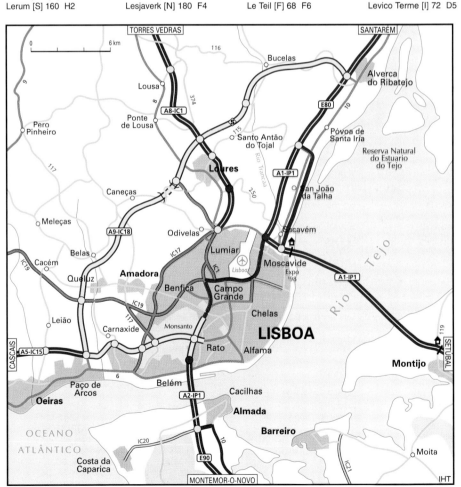

Levidi [GR] 136 D2
Levie [F] 114 B5
Levier [F] 58 B5
Le Vigan [F] 106 E3
Levoča [SK] 64 E2
Levroux [F] 54 H3
Levski [BG] 148 B3
Lewes [GB] 14 E5
Lewin Brzeski [PL] 50 D2
Leyburn [GB] 10 F2
Leysdown [GB] 14 F5
Leysin [CH] 70 C2
Leżajsk [PL] 52 E3
Lézardrieux [F] 26 A3
Lezay [F] 54 E5
Lezhë [AL] 128 B1
Lézignan–Corbières [F] 106 C5
Lezoux [F] 68 D2
Lezuza [E] 98 A5
Lgov [RUS] 204 E7
L'Hospitalet de l'Infant [E] 92 B5
l'Hospitalet de Llobregat [E] 92 E4
l'Hospitalet–l'Andorre [F] 92 E1
Lianokládi [GR] 132 G4
Liapádes [GR] 132 B2
Libáň [CZ] 48 H3
Liběohov [CZ] 48 F3
Liberec [CZ] 48 G2
Libiąż [PL] 50 G3
Libochovice [CZ] 48 F3
Libohovë [AL] 132 C1
Libourne [F] 66 D3
Libramont [B] 44 D1
Librazhd [AL] 128 C3
Licata [I] 126 E4
Lich [D] 46 C2
Lichfield [GB] 10 E6
Lichtenau [D] 32 E4
Lichtenberg [D] 46 H2
Lichtenfels [D] 46 G3
Lichtenstein [D] 48 C2
Lichtenvoorde [NL] 16 G5
Lickershamn [S] 168 G4
Lički Osik [HR] 112 G3
Licko Lešče [HR] 112 G3

Licques [F] 14 G6
Lida [BY] 204 A5
Liden [S] 162 E2
Liden [S] 184 E4
Lidhult [S] 162 C5
Lidingö [S] 168 E3
Lidköping [S] 166 E5
Lido degli Estensi [I] 110 H3
Lido di Camaiore [I] 110 D5
Lido di Castel Fusano [I] 114 H6
Lido di Fermo [I] 116 D2
Lido di Jésolo [I] 72 F6
Lido di Latina [I] 120 B1
Lido di Metaponto [I] 122 D4
Lido di Nazioni [I] 110 H3
Lido di Óstia [I] 114 H6
Lido di Pomposa [I] 110 H3
Lido di Scanzano [I] 122 D5
Lido di Spina [I] 110 H3
Lido di Torre Mileto [I] 116 G5
Lido di Venézia [I] 110 H1
Lidoríki [GR] 132 G5
Lido Silvana [I] 122 F4
Lidsjöberg [S] 190 E5
Lidzbark [PL] 22 G5
Lidzbark Warminski [PL] 22 H3
Liebenau [D] 32 E1
Liebenwalde [D] 34 E1
Lieberose [D] 34 F4
Liebling [RO] 76 G6
Liedenpohja [FIN] 186 D4
Liège (Luik) [B] 30 E5
Lieksa [FIN] 198 G6
Lielvärde [LV] 200 E5
Lienz [A] 72 F2
Liepāja [LV] 200 B6
Liepna [LV] 200 G4
Lier [B] 30 D3
Lierbyen [N] 164 H1
Liérganes [E] 82 F3
Liernais [F] 56 F4
Liesa [E] 84 D6
Liesjärvi [FIN] 186 E4
Liestal [CH] 58 E4

Lieto [FIN] 176 E4
Liétor [E] 98 B6
Lieurey [F] 26 G4
Lievestuore [FIN] 186 G4
Lievikoski [FIN] 176 D2
Liezen [A] 62 B6
Liezere [LV] 200 F5
Lifford [IRL] 2 F2
Liffré [F] 26 C6
Ligieri [LV] 200 E5
Lignano Pineta [I] 72 G6
Lignano Sabbiadoro [I] 72 G6
Ligneuville [B] 30 F6
Lignières [F] 56 B4
Ligny–en–Barrois [F] 44 D5
Ligueil [F] 54 F3
Liháda [GR] 132 H4
Lihme [DK] 160 C5
Lihula [EST] 200 D2
Liiva [EST] 200 C2
Lijeva Rijeka [YU] 152 E4
Likenäs [S] 172 E4
Likófos [GR] 130 H2
Likórahi [GR] 128 D6
Lilaste [LV] 200 D5
Lild Strand [DK] 160 C3
Lilienfeld [A] 62 D5
Liljendal [FIN] 178 B4
Lilla Edet [S] 166 D6
Lillafüred [H] 64 F4
Lille [DK] 156 G3
Lille [F] 28 F3
Lillebonne [F] 26 H3
Lillehammer [N] 172 B2
Lillerød [DK] 156 G2
Lillers [F] 28 E3
Lillesand [N] 164 E5
Lillestrøm [N] 166 C1
Lille Værløse [DK] 156 G2
Lillhärdal [S] 182 G6
Lillholmsjö [S] 182 G1
Lillo [E] 96 G2
Lillögda [S] 190 G5
Limanowa [PL] 52 B5
Limavady [GB] 2 F2
Limbaži [LV] 200 E4
Limbourg [B] 30 F5
Limburg [D] 46 B2

Limedsforsen [S] 172 F3
Limenária [GR] 130 E4
Liménas [GR] 134 C4
Liméni [GR] 136 E5
Limerick / Luimneach [IRL] 4 D3
Limhamn [S] 156 H3
Limín Chersonísou [GR] 140 F4
Liminka [FIN] 198 D4
Limín Litochórou [GR] 128 G6
Liminpuro [FIN] 198 E4
Limmared [S] 162 C2
Límnes [GR] 136 F2
Límni [GR] 134 B4
Limniá [GR] 130 D3
Límnos [GR] 134 G4
Limoges [F] 66 G1
Limogne–en–Quercy [F] 66 F2
Limone Piemonte [I] 108 F3
Limonest [F] 68 F2
Limone sul Garda [I] 72 C5
Limours [F] 42 F4
Limoux [F] 106 B5
Lin [AL] 128 D3
Linachamari [RUS] 196 F3
Linares [E] 102 E1
Linares de Mora [E] 98 F2
Linares de Riofrío [E] 88 B4
Linariá [GR] 134 D3
Lincoln [GB] 10 G5
Lind [DK] 156 B1
Lindås [S] 162 F5
Lindau [D] 60 B5
Lindau [D] 34 C3
Lindaunis [D] 18 F1
Linde [DK] 160 B5
Lindenberg [D] 60 B5
Lindenfels [D] 46 C4
Linderhof [D] 60 D6
Lindern [D] 18 C6
Lindesberg [S] 166 H2
Lindesnäs [S] 172 G5
Lindholm [DK] 160 D3
Lindlia [N] 170 G4
Lindome [S] 160 H2
Líndos [GR] 142 E5

Limedsforsen [S] 172 F3
Lindow [D] 20 C6
Linge [N] 180 E4
Lingbo [S] 174 E3
Lingen [D] 16 H4
Linghed [S] 174 D4
Linghem [S] 168 A5
Linguaglossa [I] 124 A8
Linköping [S] 168 A5
Linlithgow [GB] 8 E3
Linneryd [S] 162 E5
Linova [BY] 38 H2
Linovo [RUS] 200 G4
Linsdal [S] 162 G5
Linsell [S] 182 F5
Linthal [CH] 58 G6
Linton [GB] 14 F3
Lintula [RUS] 178 G4
Lintzel [D] 18 F6
Linz [A] 62 B4
Linz [D] 30 H5
Lioni [I] 120 F3
Liozno [BY] 204 C4
Lipa [BIH] 152 B1
Lípa [CZ] 48 G1
Lipany [SK] 52 C6
Lipar [YU] 76 D6
Lipcani [UA] 206 D3
Liperi [FIN] 188 F3
Liphook [GB] 14 D5
Lipiany [PL] 20 F6
Lipica [SLO] 72 H6
Lipik [HR] 154 B1
Lipinki Łużyckie [PL] 34 G5
Lipka [PL] 22 C5
Lipljan [YU] 150 C5
Lipnica [PL] 22 C3
Lipnice nad Sázavou [CZ] 48 H5
Lipnik [PL] 52 D2
Lipník nad Bečvou [CZ] 50 D5
Lipno [CZ] 62 B3
Lipno [PL] 36 G1
Lipova [RO] 76 H4
Lipovljani [HR] 154 B1
Lipovo Polie [HR] 112 G3
Lipowo [PL] 22 G4
Lippborg [D] 32 D4

Lippstadt [D] 32 D4
Lipsk [PL] 24 F4
Lipsko [PL] 38 C6
Liptovská Osada [SK] 64 C2
Liptovská Teplička [SK] 64 E2
Liptovský–Mikuláš [SK] 64 D2
Lisbellaw [GB] 2 E3
Lisboa [P] 86 B5
Lisburn [GB] 2 G4
Liscarroll [IRL] 4 C4
Lisdoonvarna [IRL] 2 B5
Liseleje [DK] 156 G1
Liselund [DK] 156 G4
Lisia Góra [PL] 52 C3
Lisieux [F] 26 G4
Liskeard [GB] 12 D4
Lisle [F] 106 B2
L'Isle–Adam [F] 42 F3
L'Isle–de–Noé [F] 84 F3
L'Isle–en–Dodon [F] 84 G3
L'Isle–Jourdain [F] 84 H3
L'Isle–Jourdain [F] 54 F5
L'Isle–sur–la–Sorgue [F] 106 H3
L'Isle–sur–le–Doubs [F] 58 C4
Lisle–sur–Tarn [F] 106 B2
Lismore [IRL] 4 D5
Lisnaskea [GB] 2 E4
Lišnja [BIH] 154 C2
Lišov [CZ] 62 C2
Lisse [NL] 16 D4
Lisskogsbrändan [S] 172 F4
List [D] 156 A4
Lişteava [RO] 150 G2
Listeid [N] 164 C5
Lištica [BIH] 152 C2
Listowel [IRL] 4 C3
Lit [S] 182 H2
Litene [LV] 200 F4
Lit–et–Mixe [F] 66 B5
Lithakiá [GR] 136 A2
Lithínes [GR] 140 G5
Lití [GR] 128 H4
Litija [SLO] 74 C5

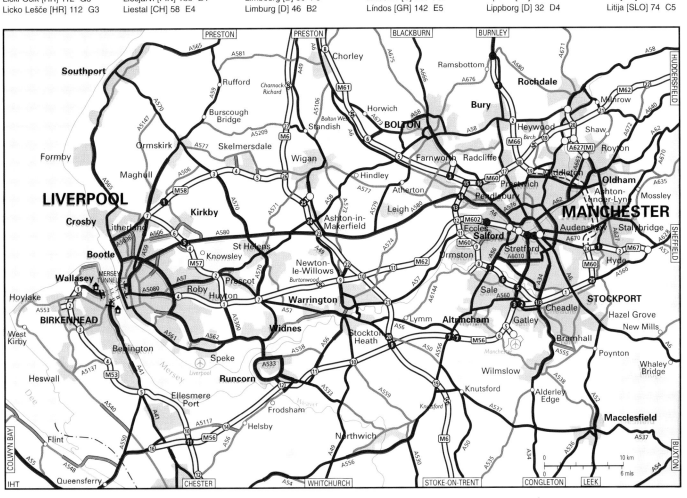

Litke [H] 64 D4
Litóchoro [GR] 128 G6
Litoměřice [CZ] 48 F2
Litomyšl [CZ] 50 B4
Litovel [CZ] 50 C5
Litslena [S] 168 C2
Littlehampton [GB] 14 D5
Littlemill [GB] 6 E5
Littleport [GB] 14 F2
Littleton Panell [GB] 12 G4
Little Walsingham [GB] 10 H6
Litvínov [CZ] 48 E2
Liuboml' [UA] 38 G5
Livade [HR] 112 D1
Livaderó [GR] 130 D2
Livadhja [AL] 132 B1
Livádi [GR] 130 B5
Livádi [GR] 128 G6
Livádi [GR] 138 D3
Livádia [GR] 142 C4
Livaditis [GR] 130 E2
Līvāni [LV] 200 F6
Livarot [F] 26 G4
Livernon [F] 66 H5
Liverpool [GB] 10 D4
Livigno [I] 72 B3
Livingston [GB] 8 E3

Livmy [RUS] 204 F6
Livno [BIH] 152 B1
Livorno [I] 110 D6
Livorno Ferraris [I] 70 E5
Livreá [GR] 128 F5
Livron [F] 68 F5
Livron–Sur–Drôme [F] 68 F5
Liw [PL] 38 D2
Lixoúri [GR] 132 C6
Lizard [GB] 12 B5
Lizarra / Estella [E] 84 A4
Lizy [F] 42 G3
Ljig [YU] 150 B1
Ljørdalen [S] 172 E2
Ljosland [N] 164 D4
Ljubaništa [MK] 128 D4
Ljubar [UA] 206 D2
Ljubelj [SLO] 74 B4
Ljubercy [RUS] 204 F4
Ljubinje [BIH] 152 C3
Ljubljana [SLO] 74 B5
Ljubno [SLO] 74 C4
Ljubovija [YU] 154 F4
Ljubovo [HR] 112 G3
Ljubuški [BIH] 152 B2
Ljubytino [RUS] 204 D2
Ljudinovo [RUS] 204 E5

Ljugarn [S] 168 G5
Ljungby [S] 162 C5
Ljungbyhed [S] 158 C1
Ljungbyholm [S] 162 F5
Ljungdalen [S] 182 E3
Ljungsbro [S] 166 H5
Ljungskile [S] 166 C6
Ljusdal [S] 184 D6
Ljusfallshammar [S] 166 H4
Ljusne [S] 174 F2
Ljutiči [YU] 152 E2
Ljutomer [SLO] 74 E4
Llafranc [E] 92 G3
Llagostera [E] 92 F3
Llanberis [GB] 10 B4
Llanbister [GB] 10 C6
Llançà [E] 92 G2
Llandeilo [GB] 12 E2
Llandiloes [GB] 10 C6
Llandissilio [GB] 12 D1
Llandovery [GB] 12 E1
Llandrillo [GB] 10 C5
Llandrindod Wells [GB] 10 C6
Llandudno [GB] 10 C4
Llanelli [GB] 12 E2
Llanengan [GB] 10 B5
Llanerchymedd [GB] 10 B3

Llanes [E] 82 D2
Llanfair Caereinion [GB] 10 C5
Llanfairfechan [GB] 10 C4
Llanfyllin [GB] 10 C5
Llangefni [GB] 10 B4
Llangollen [GB] 10 C5
Llangurig [GB] 10 C6
Llanrwst [GB] 10 C4
Llanstephan [GB] 12 E2
Llantrisant [GB] 12 F3
Llantwit Major [GB] 12 E3
Llanuwchllyn [GB] 10 C5
Llavorsí [E] 84 G6
Lleida / Lérida [E] 90 H4
Llerena [E] 94 H4
Lles de Cerdanya [E] 92 D1
Llíria [E] 98 E4
L'Ile-Bouchard [F] 54 F2
L'Ile-Rousse [F] 114 B3
Llodio / Laudio [E] 82 G4
Lloret de Mar [E] 92 F4
Llucmajor [E] 104 E5
Lnáře [CZ] 48 E5
Loano [I] 108 G3
Löbau [D] 34 G6
Lobenstein [D] 46 H2
Łobez [PL] 20 G4

Lobios [E] 78 C6
Löbnitz [D] 20 C2
Lobón [E] 94 G2
Loburg [D] 34 C3
Łobżenica [PL] 22 C5
Locana [I] 70 D4
Locarno [CH] 70 F3
Loccum [D] 32 E2
Lochailort [GB] 6 C5
Lochaline [GB] 6 C6
Locharbriggs [GB] 8 D5
Loch Baghasdail / Lochboisdale [GB] 6 A4
Lochboisdale / Loch Baghasdail [GB] 6 A4
Lochcarron [GB] 6 C4
Lochearnhead [GB] 8 D2
Lochem [NL] 16 F5
Loches [F] 54 G3
Loch Garman / Wexford [IRL] 4 F5
Lochgilphead [GB] 8 C2
Lochgoilhead [GB] 8 D2
Lochinver [GB] 6 D3
Loch nam Madadh / Lochmaddy [GB] 6 A3
Loch nam Madadh / Lochmaddy [GB] 6 A3

Łochocin [PL] 36 G1
Łochów [PL] 38 C2
Lochranza [GB] 8 C3
Lockenhaus [A] 74 F1
Lockerbie [GB] 8 E5
Löcknitz [D] 20 E5
Locmaria [F] 40 C5
Locmariaquer [F] 40 D5
Locminé [F] 26 A6
Locorotondo [I] 122 E3
Locquirec [F] 40 C1
Locri [I] 124 D7
Locronan [F] 40 B3
Loctudy [F] 40 B3
Loddon [GB] 14 G2
Lodè [I] 118 E3
Lode [LV] 200 E4
Lodejnoje Pole [RUS] 204 D1
Löderup [S] 158 D3
Lodève [F] 106 D3
Lodi [I] 70 G5
Løding [N] 192 B6
Lødingen [N] 192 C4
Lodosa [E] 84 A5
Lödöse [S] 160 H1
Łódź [PL] 36 G4
Loeches [E] 88 G6

Loen [N] 180 D5
Løfallstrand [N] 170 B5
Lofer [A] 60 G6
Lofsdal [FIN] 176 D5
Lofsdalen [S] 182 F5
Loftahammar [S] 162 G2
Lofthouse [GB] 10 F3
Lofthus [N] 170 C4
Loftus [GB] 10 G2
Loga [D] 18 B4
Loga [N] 164 C5
Logatec [SLO] 74 B5
Lögdeå [S] 184 H1
Logi [RUS] 178 F5
Logojsk [BY] 204 B5
Logosanto [I] 110 H3
Logroño [E] 82 G6
Logrosán [E] 96 C2
Logstein [N] 190 B6
Løgstør [DK] 160 D4
Løgumkloster [DK] 156 B4
Lohals [DK] 156 E4
Lohberg [D] 48 D6
Lohéac [F] 26 C6
Lohikoski [FIN] 188 E6
Lohiniva [FIN] 192 H6
Lohja [FIN] 176 G5
Löhne [D] 32 E2
Lohne [D] 18 C6
Lohnsfeld [D] 46 B4
Lohr [D] 46 E3
Lohtaja [FIN] 198 C5
Lohvica [UA] 206 F2
Loiano [I] 110 F4
Loimaa [FIN] 176 E3
Lóiri [I] 118 E3
Loitz [D] 20 D3
Loja [E] 102 D3
Lojanice [YU] 154 F3
Lojsta [S] 168 G5
Lojt Kirkeby [DK] 156 C4
Lokakylä [FIN] 186 F2
Lokalahti [FIN] 176 C4
Lokča [SK] 50 G5
Løken [N] 166 C1
Lokeren [B] 28 H2
Loket [CZ] 48 D3
Lokka [FIN] 196 E6
Løkken [DK] 160 D3
Løkken Verk [N] 180 H2
Loknja [RUS] 204 C3
Lökösháza [H] 76 G4
Lokot [RUS] 204 E6
Loksa [EST] 200 E1
Lokve [N] 166 C1
Lokve [SLO] 72 H5
Lokve [YU] 154 H2
l'Olleria [E] 98 E6
Lölling [A] 74 C2
Lom [BG] 150 F2
Lom [N] 180 F5
Lombez [F] 84 G3
Lomello [I] 70 F6
Lomen [N] 170 F2
Lomma [S] 156 H2
Lomme [F] 28 F3
Lommel [B] 30 E3
Lomnice nad Lužnicí [CZ] 62 C2
Lomonosov [RUS] 178 G5
Lompolo [FIN] 192 H4
Łomża [PL] 24 D5
Lonato [I] 72 B6
Loncari [BIH] 154 E2
Lončarica [HR] 74 G6
Londinières [F] 28 C4
London [GB] 14 E4
Londonderry [GB] 2 F2
Lonevåg [N] 170 B3
Longá [GR] 132 F1
Longaníkos [GR] 136 D3
Longarone [I] 72 E4
Long Eaton [GB] 10 F6
Longeau [F] 56 H2
Longford [IRL] 2 E4
Longhoughton [GB] 8 G5
Long Melford [GB] 14 F3
Longny-au-Perche [F] 26 G6
Longobucco [I] 124 E4
Longpont [F] 42 H3
Long Preston [GB] 10 E3

Longridge [GB] 10 D3
Longroiva [P] 80 E5
Long Stratton [GB] 14 G2
Long Sutton [GB] 10 G6
Longtown [GB] 8 E5
Longué [F] 54 E1
Longueau [F] 28 E5
Longuyon [F] 44 E3
Longwy [F] 44 E3
Lonigo [I] 110 F1
Löningen [D] 18 C6
Łoniów [PL] 52 D2
Lono [N] 164 C1
Lönsboda [S] 162 D6
Lønsdal [N] 190 E1
Lønset [N] 180 E3
Lønset [N] 180 G3
Lons-le-Saunier [F] 56 H5
Lønstrup [DK] 160 D2
Looberghe [F] 14 H6
Looe [GB] 12 D5
Loosdorf [A] 62 D4
Lopar [HR] 112 F3
Lopare [BIH] 154 E3
Lopatica [MK] 128 E3
Lopatovo [RUS] 200 H3
Lopera [E] 102 D1
Loppi [FIN] 176 G3
Lopud [HR] 152 C4
Łopuszna [PL] 52 B5
Łopuszno [PL] 52 B1
Lora del Río [E] 102 A1
Lorca [E] 104 B3
Lorcé [B] 30 E5
Lorch [D] 60 B2
Lorch [D] 46 B3
Lordosa [P] 80 C5
Lørenskog [N] 166 B1
Lorentzen [F] 44 G5
Loreo [I] 110 H2
Loreto [I] 116 C1
Loreto Aprutino [I] 116 D4
Lorgues [F] 108 D5
Lorica [I] 124 E4
Lorient [F] 40 C4
Lőrinci [H] 64 D6
Loriol-sur-Drôme [F] 68 F5
Lormes [F] 56 E3
Lormont [F] 66 D3
Loro Ciuffenna [I] 110 F6
Lörrach [D] 58 E4
Lorris [F] 42 F6
Lorup [D] 18 B5
Los [S] 172 H1
Los Alcázares [E] 104 C4
Los Arcos [E] 82 H6
Losar de la Vera [E] 88 B5
Los Arenales del Sol / Arenals del Sol [E] 104 D3
Los Barrios [E] 100 G5
Los Canarios [E] 100 A5
Los Caños de Meca [E] 100 F5
Los Corrales de Buelna [E] 82 E3
Los Cristianos [E] 100 C5
Losenstein [A] 62 C5
Los Escullos [E] 102 H6
Losheim [A] 44 G3
Losheim [D] 30 F6
Łosice [PL] 38 E3
Los Isidros [E] 98 D4
Los Llanos de Aridane [E] 100 A5
Los Navalmorales [E] 96 D2
Los Navalucillos [E] 96 D2
Los Olmos [E] 90 E6
Łososina Dolna [PL] 52 B4
Los Palacios y Villafranca [E] 100 G2
l'Ospedale [F] 114 B5
Los Santos de Maimona [E] 94 G3
Los Sauces [E] 100 A5
Lossburg [D] 58 F2
Lossiemouth [GB] 6 F4
Lostwithiel [GB] 12 C4
Los Urrutias [E] 104 C4
Los Villares [E] 102 E2
Los Yébenes [E] 96 F2
Lote [N] 180 C5

Loten [N] 172 C3
Lotorp [S] 168 B5
Lötschberg Tunnel [CH] 70 E2
Lotte [D] 32 D2
Löttorp [S] 162 H4
Löttorp-Högby [S] 162 H4
Lotzorai [I] 118 E5
Loudéac [F] 26 A5
Loudes [F] 68 D4
Loudun [F] 54 E3
Loué [F] 42 B5
Loue [FIN] 196 C8
Loughborough [GB] 10 F6
Loughbrickland [GB] 2 G4
Loughgall [GB] 2 F4
Loughglinn [IRL] 2 D4
Loughrea [IRL] 2 C5
Louhans [F] 56 G5
Louisburgh [IRL] 2 B4
Loukás [GR] 136 E2
Loukhi [RUS] 198 H1
Loukíssia [GR] 134 B5
Loukusa [FIN] 198 E2
Loulay [F] 54 D5
Loulé [P] 94 C5
Louny [CZ] 48 E3
Lourdes [E] 78 D2
Lourdes [F] 84 E4
Louredo [P] 80 D3
Lourenzá [E] 78 E2
Lourinhã [P] 86 B4
Loúros [GR] 132 D3
Lousã [P] 86 E2
Lousada [P] 80 C4
Louth [GB] 10 G5
Loutrá [GR] 138 C2
Loutrá [GR] 134 H2
Loutrá [GR] 136 D2
Loutrá Aidipsoú [GR] 134 A4
Loutrá Aridéas [GR] 128 F3
Loutrá Eleftherón [GR] 130 D4
Loutrá Kaïtsas [GR] 132 F3
Loutráki [GR] 136 F1
Loutráki [GR] 132 D4
Loutrá Kounoupélli [GR] 132 E6
Loutrá Kyllínis [GR] 136 B2
Loutrá Lagkadá [GR] 130 B4
Loutrá Smokóvou [GR] 132 F3
Loutrá Vólvis [GR] 130 B4
Loutrá Ypátis [GR] 132 G4
Loutró Elénis [GR] 136 F1
Loutrós [GR] 130 G3
Loútsa [GR] 134 C6
Louvain (Leuven) [B] 30 D4
Louviers [F] 28 B6
Lövånger [S] 198 B5
Lovasberény [H] 76 B1
Lövberga [S] 190 F6
Lovech [BG] 148 B3
Lovére [I] 72 A5
Loviisa / Lovisa [FIN] 178 B4
Lovisa / Loviisa [FIN] 178 B4
Lövnäs [S] 190 G2
Lövő [H] 62 G6
Lovosice [CZ] 48 F2
Lovran [HR] 112 E1
Lovrenc na Pohorju [SLO] 74 D3
Lovrin [RO] 76 F5
Lövstabruk [S] 174 F5
Low Brunton [GB] 8 F5
Löwenberg [D] 34 E1
Lower Killeyan [GB] 2 G1
Lowestoft [GB] 14 H2
Lowick [GB] 8 F4
Łowicz [PL] 36 H3
Lož [SLO] 74 B6
Lozarevo [BG] 148 E4
Lozari [F] 114 B3
Lozen [BG] 148 A6
Lozenets [BG] 148 G5
Loznica [BG] 148 D3
Loznica [YU] 154 F3
Lozovac [HR] 112 H6

Lozoya [E] 88 G4
Lozoyuela [E] 88 G4
Lozzo di Cadore [I] 72 F3
Luanco [E] 78 H3
Luarca [E] 78 G2
Lubaczów [PL] 52 F3
Lubań [PL] 36 H6
Lubāna [LV] 200 F5
Lubarda [BIH] 112 H2
Lubartów [PL] 38 E5
Lubasz [PL] 36 C1
Lubawa [PL] 22 F5
Lubawka [PL] 50 B2
Lübbecke [D] 32 E2
Lübben [D] 34 F4
Lübbenau [D] 34 F4
Lübbow [D] 18 H6
Lübeck [D] 18 G3
Lubenec [CZ] 48 E3
Lubersac [F] 66 G2
Lubia [E] 90 B3
Lubiąż [PL] 36 B6
Lubichowo [PL] 22 D4
Lubień [PL] 50 H5
Lubień Kujawski [PL] 36 G2
Lubieszyn [PL] 20 F5
Lubin [PL] 36 B5
Lubiń [PL] 36 C4
Lublin [PL] 38 E5
Lubliniec [PL] 50 F2
Lubniewice [PL] 34 H2
Lubny [UA] 206 F2
Lubomino [PL] 22 G3
Luboń [PL] 36 C3
Luboniek [PL] 36 F3
Luboradz [PL] 36 B6
Lubowidz [PL] 22 G6
Łubowo [PL] 36 D2
Lubraniec [PL] 36 F2
Lubrín [E] 102 H5
Lubsko [PL] 34 G4
Lübtheen [D] 18 H5
Lucan [IRL] 2 F6
Lucca [I] 110 D5
Lucena del Cid [E] 98 F3
Lucena del Cid / Llucena [E] 102 C3
Lucenay [F] 56 F4
Luc-en-Diois [F] 68 G6
Lučenec [SK] 64 D4
Lucera [I] 120 G1
Lüchow [D] 18 H6
Luciana [E] 96 E4
Lucignano [I] 114 G1
Lucito [I] 116 E6
Luck [UA] 206 C1
Luckau [D] 34 F4
Luckenwalde [D] 34 E3
Lückstedt [D] 34 B1

Luco dei Marsi [I] 116 C5
Luçon [F] 54 C3
Luc-sur-Mer [F] 26 F3
Ludbreg [HR] 74 F4
Lüdenscheid [D] 32 C5
Lüderitz [D] 34 B2
Ludgershall [GB] 12 H4
Ludinghausen [D] 16 H6
Ludlow [GB] 10 D6
Ludvika [S] 172 H5
Ludwigsburg [D] 46 D6
Ludwigshafen [D] 46 C4
Ludwigshafen [D] 58 G4
Ludwigslust [D] 20 A5
Ludwigsstadt [D] 46 H2
Ludza [LV] 200 G5
Luga [RUS] 200 H2
Lugagnano Val d'Arda [I] 110 C2
Lugano [CH] 70 G3
Lügde [D] 32 E3
Lugnås [S] 166 F5
Lugo [E] 78 E3
Lugo [I] 110 G4
Lugoj [RO] 206 A5
Lugones [E] 78 H3
Luhačovice [CZ] 62 H2
Luhalahti [FIN] 186 D6
Luhanka [FIN] 186 G6
Luhtapohja [FIN] 188 G2
Luhtikylä [FIN] 178 A3
Luib [GB] 8 C2
Luidja [EST] 200 C2
Luigny [F] 42 D5
Luik (Liège) [B] 30 E5
Luikonlahti [FIN] 188 E2
Luimneach / Limerick [IRL] 4 D3
Luino [I] 70 F3
Luka [YU] 150 D1
Lukanja [SLO] 74 D4
Lukavac [BIH] 154 D3
Lŭki [BG] 148 B6
Lukovë [AL] 132 B1
Lukovica [SLO] 74 C4
Lukovit [BG] 148 A3
Lukovo [MK] 128 C3
Lukovo [YU] 150 D2
Luľovo Šugarje [HR] 112 G4
Łuków [PL] 38 D3
Lukšič [HR] 154 A5
Lukta [PL] 22 G4
Luleå [S] 198 B3
Lüleburgaz [TR] 146 C2
Lumbarda [HR] 152 B3
Lumbier / Irunberri [E] 84 C4
Lumbrales [E] 80 F6
Lumbres [F] 28 E2

Lumezzane [I] 72 B5
Lumijoki [FIN] 198 D4
Lummen [B] 30 E4
Lumparland [FIN] 176 B5
Lumsås [DK] 156 F2
Lun [HR] 112 F3
Lunas [F] 106 D3
Lund [S] 158 C2
Lunda [S] 168 D2
Lundamo [N] 182 B2
Lunde [N] 164 F2
Lunde [N] 180 D6
Lunde [S] 184 F3
Lundeborg [DK] 156 E4
Lunden [D] 18 E2
Lunderseter [N] 172 D5
Lunderskov [DK] 156 C3
Lüneburg [D] 18 G5
Lunel [F] 106 F4
Lünen [D] 32 C4
Lunéville [F] 44 F5
Lungern [CH] 70 E1
Lungro [I] 120 H6
Lungvik [S] 184 F3
Luninec [BY] 204 A6
Lunna [BY] 24 G4
Lünne [D] 16 H4
Lunz [A] 62 D5
Luogosanto [I] 118 D2
Luopioinen [FIN] 176 G1
Luostari [RUS] 196 F3
Luoto / Larsmo [FIN] 198 C6
Lupeni [RO] 206 B5
Lupiac [F] 84 F2
Lupoglav [HR] 74 F6
Luque [E] 102 C2
Lurcy-Lévis [F] 56 D4
Lure [F] 58 C3
Lureuil [F] 54 G4
Lurgan [GB] 2 G4
Lušci Palanka [BIH] 154 A3
Lüsens [A] 72 D1
Lushnjë [AL] 128 B4
Lusi [FIN] 178 B2
Lusignan [F] 54 E4
Lusigny [F] 44 B6
Lusk [IRL] 2 F6
Lus-la-Croix-Haute [F] 68 G6
Luso [P] 80 B6
Luss [GB] 8 D2
Lussac-les-Châteaux [F] 54 F4
Lussac-les-Églises [F] 54 G5
Lussan [F] 106 G3
Lustenau [A] 58 H5
Luster [N] 170 E1
Lutago / Luttach [I] 72 E2

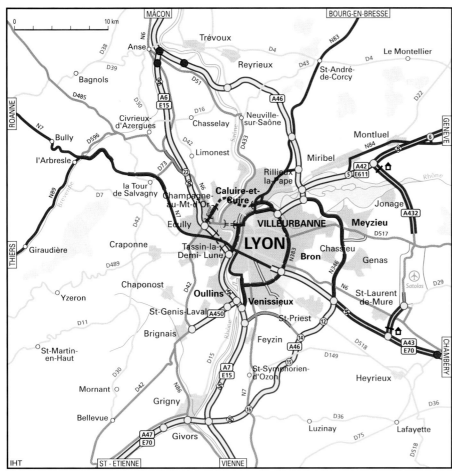

Lutcza [PL] 52 D4
Lutherstadt Eisleben [D] 34 B5
Lutherstadt Wittenberg [D] 34 D4
Lütjenburg [D] 18 G2
Lutnes [N] 172 E3
Lutol Suchy [PL] 36 A3
Lutomiersk [PL] 36 G4
Luton [GB] 14 E3
Lutrá [GR] 132 E4
Lutrini [LV] 200 C5
Lutry [PL] 22 H3
Lutterworth [GB] 14 D2
Lututów [PL] 36 F5
Lützen [D] 34 C4
Lutzmannsburg [A] 74 F1
Lützow [D] 18 H4
Luumäki [FIN] 178 D2
Luusua [FIN] 196 E8
Luvia [FIN] 176 C2
Luvozero [RUS] 198 G4
Luxembourg [L] 44 F3
Luxeuil–les–Bains [F] 58 C3
Luxey [F] 66 C5
Luzaide / Valcarlos [E] 84 C3
Lužani [HR] 154 C2
Luzarches [F] 42 F3
Luzern [CH] 58 F6
Luz–St–Sauveur [F] 84 E4
Luzy [F] 56 E5
Luzzara [I] 110 E2
Luzzi [I] 124 D4
L'viv [UA] 52 H4
Lwówek [PL] 36 B2
Lwówek Śląski [PL] 36 A6
Lyady [RUS] 200 G2
Lyaskelya [RUS] 188 H5
Lyaskovets [BG] 148 C3
Lybster [GB] 6 F3
Lychen [D] 20 D5
Lyckeby [S] 158 F1
Lycksele [S] 190 G5
Lydd [GB] 14 F6
Lydiard Tregoze [GB] 12 H3
Lydney [GB] 12 G2
Lye [S] 168 G5

Lygoúrio [GR] 136 F2
Lygre [N] 170 B5
Lyme Regis [GB] 12 F4
Lymington [GB] 12 H5
Lympne [GB] 14 F5
Lyndhurst [GB] 12 H5
Lyness [GB] 6 F2
Lyngby [DK] 156 G2
Lyngdal [N] 164 C5
Lyngør [N] 164 F4
Lyngså [DK] 160 E3
Lyngseidet [N] 192 E2
Lynmouth [GB] 12 E3
Lynton [GB] 12 E3
Lyon [F] 68 F3
Lyons–la–Forêt [F] 28 C6
Lysá nad Labem [CZ] 48 G3
Lysebotn [N] 164 C3
Lysekil [S] 166 C6
Lysøysund [N] 190 B5
Lyss [CH] 58 D5
Lysvik [S] 166 E1
Lytham St Annes [GB] 10 D3
Lyuben [BG] 148 B5
Lyubimets [BG] 148 D6

M

Maalahti / Malax [FIN] 186 B3
Maaninka [FIN] 188 C1
Maaninkavaara [FIN] 196 E8
Maanselkä [FIN] 198 F5
Maardu [EST] 200 E1
Maarianhamina / Mariehamn [FIN] 176 A5
Maarianvaara [FIN] 188 E2
Maarja [EST] 200 F2
Maaseik [B] 30 F3
Maasmechelen [B] 30 E4
Maassluis [NL] 16 C5
Maastricht [NL] 30 E4

Mablethorpe [GB] 10 H5
Macael [E] 102 G4
Maçanet de la Selva [E] 92 F4
Mação [P] 86 E4
Maccagno [I] 70 F3
Macclesfield [GB] 10 E4
Macduff [GB] 6 F5
Maceda [E] 78 D5
Macedo de Cavaleiros [P] 80 F4
Macerata [I] 116 C1
Macerata Féltria [I] 110 H5
Măceşu de Jos [RO] 150 G2
Machault [F] 44 C3
Mâchecourt [F] 54 B2
Machico [P] 100 B3
Machliny [PL] 22 A5
Machrihanish [GB] 2 H2
Machynlleth [GB] 10 B5
Maciejowice [PL] 38 C4
Mackenrode [D] 32 G4
Mâcon [F] 68 G1
Macotera [E] 88 D3
Macroom [IRL] 4 C5
Macugnaga [I] 70 E3
Mád [H] 64 G4
Madan [BG] 130 E1
Madängsholm [S] 162 C1
Madara [BG] 148 E3
Maddaloni [I] 120 E2
Made [NL] 16 D6
Madekoski [FIN] 198 D4
Maderuelo [E] 88 G3
Madésimo [I] 70 G2
Madliena [LV] 200 E5
Madona [LV] 200 F5
Madonna del Ponte [I] 112 C5
Madonna di Campíglio [I] 72 C4
Madonna di Senales / Unserfrau [I] 72 C2
Madonna di Tirano [I] 72 B4
Madrid [E] 88 F5
Madridejos [E] 96 F3

Madrigal de las Altas Torres [E] 88 D3
Madrigal de la Vera [E] 88 C5
Madrigalejo [E] 96 B2
Madroñera [E] 96 B2
Mæbo [N] 164 D6
Maella [E] 90 G6
Mære [N] 190 C5
Mafra [P] 86 B4
Magallón [E] 90 D3
Magalluf [E] 104 D5
Magaña [E] 90 C2
Magaz de Pisuerga [E] 88 F1
Magdeburg [D] 34 B3
Magellarë [AL] 128 C2
Magenta [I] 70 F5
Magerholm [N] 180 D3
Magescq [F] 66 B6
Maghera [GB] 2 G3
Magherafelt [GB] 2 G3
Magierowa Wola [PL] 38 C4
Magione [I] 114 H2
Maglaj [BIH] 154 D3
Maglavit [RO] 150 F2
Maglehem [S] 158 D2
Maglehøj Strand [DK] 18 H1
Magliano dei Marsi [I] 116 C5
Magliano in Toscana [I] 114 F3
Magliano Sabina [I] 116 A4
Maglič [YU] 150 B3
Máglie [I] 122 G5
Magnac–Laval [F] 54 G5
Magnor [N] 166 D1
Magny–Cours [F] 56 D4
Magny–en–Vexin [F] 42 E2
Magueulone [F] 106 E4
Maguiresbridge [GB] 2 E3
Maherádo [GR] 136 A2
Maheriv [UA] 52 G3
Mahide [E] 80 G3
Mahlu [FIN] 186 F3
Mahmutlar [TR] 144 D4
Mahmutsevketpaşa [TR] 146 F2

Mahora [E] 98 C4
Mahovo [HR] 74 F6
Maia [P] 80 B3
Maials [E] 90 H5
Maîche [F] 58 C5
Máida [I] 124 D5
Maidenhead [GB] 14 D4
Maidstone [GB] 14 F5
Maienfeld [CH] 58 H6
Maijanen [FIN] 196 C7
Maillezais [F] 54 C4
Mailly–le–Camp [F] 44 B5
Maintenon [F] 42 E4
Mainua [FIN] 198 E5
Mainz [D] 46 C3
Maiori [I] 120 E4
Mairena del Alcor [E] 94 H6
Maisach [D] 60 D4
Maišiogala [LT] 202 G5
Maissau [A] 62 E3
Maja [HR] 154 A1
Majadahonda [E] 88 F5
Majaelrayo [E] 88 H4
Majavatn [N] 190 D4
Majdanek [PL] 38 E5
Majdanpek [YU] 150 D1
Makarska [HR] 152 B2
Makedonski Brod [MK] 128 E2
Makhnovka [RUS] 200 H4
Makkola [FIN] 188 E4
Makó [H] 76 F4
Makov [SK] 50 F6
Makovo [MK] 128 E3
Maków [PL] 50 H3
Mąkowarsko [PL] 22 C5
Maków Mazowiecki [PL] 38 B1
Makrakómi [GR] 132 F4
Mákri [GR] 136 E2
Mákri [GR] 130 G3
Makrinítsa [GR] 132 H2
Makriplágio [GR] 130 D2
Makrohóri [GR] 128 G5
Makrýammos [GR] 130 E4
Makrýgialos [GR] 140 G5
Maksamaa / Maxmo [FIN] 186 B2
Malá [S] 190 G4
Mala Bosna [YU] 76 D5
Malacky [SK] 62 G4
Maladzyechna [BY] 204 B5
Málaga [E] 102 C4
Malagón [E] 96 F3
Malahide [IRL] 2 F6
Malaja Višera [RUS] 204 D2
Mala Krsna [YU] 154 H3
Malalbergo [I] 110 F3
Malaryta [BY] 38 G4
Malaucène [F] 106 H3
Malax / Maalahti [FIN] 186 B3
Malbork [PL] 22 E3
Malbuisson [F] 58 B6
Malcésine [I] 72 C5
Malchin [D] 20 C4
Malchow [D] 20 C5
Maldegem [B] 28 G1
Maldon [GB] 14 F4
Malé [I] 72 C4
Malechowo [PL] 22 B3
Máleme [GR] 140 B4
Malente–Gremsmühlen [D] 18 G2
Máles [GR] 140 F5
Malesco [I] 70 F3
Malesherbes [F] 42 F5
Malesína [GR] 134 B4
Malestroit [F] 26 B6
Malhadas [P] 80 G4
Mália [E] 140 F4
Malicorne [F] 42 B5
Mali Idjos [YU] 76 D6
Malin [IRL] 2 F1
Malines (Mechelen) [B] 30 C3
Malingsbo [S] 166 H1

Malin More [IRL] 2 D2
Malinska [HR] 112 E2
Maliq [AL] 128 D4
Mališevo [YU] 150 B5
Maliskylä [FIN] 198 D5
Maljovica [BG] 150 G6
Malkara [TR] 146 B3
Małkinia Górna [PL] 38 D1
Malko Gradishte [BG] 148 D6
Malko Tŭrnovo [BG] 146 C1
Mallaig [GB] 6 B5
Mallersdorf [D] 60 F2
Málles Venosta / Mals im Vinschgau [I] 72 B2
Malling [DK] 156 D1
Mallnitz [A] 72 G2
Mallow [IRL] 4 C4
Malm [N] 190 C5
Malmbäck [S] 162 D2
Malmberget [S] 192 F6
Malmédy [B] 30 F5
Malmesbury [GB] 12 G3
Malmköping [S] 168 C3
Malmö [S] 156 H3
Malmslätt [S] 166 H5
Malo [I] 72 D5
Maloja [CH] 70 H2
Malo–les–Bains [F] 14 H6
Malón [GR] 142 E5
Malonno [I] 72 B4
Małopolski [PL] 52 D3
Måloy [N] 180 B5
Malpartida de Cáceres [E] 86 G5
Malpartida de Plasencia [E] 88 B5
Malpica de Bergantiños [E] 78 C1
Mälpils [LV] 200 E5
Malšice [CZ] 48 G6
Mals im Vinschgau / Málles Venosta [I] 72 B2
Målsnes [N] 192 E2
Malta [A] 72 H2
Malta [LV] 200 G6
Maltat [F] 56 E5
Maltby [GB] 10 F4
Maltepe [TR] 146 F3
Maltepe [TR] 146 C5
Malton [GB] 10 G3
Malu [RO] 150 G1
Malung [S] 172 F4
Malungen [N] 172 C4
Maluszyn [PL] 50 H1
Malveira [P] 86 B4
Malvik [N] 182 C1
Mały Płock [PL] 24 D5
Mamaia [RO] 206 D6
Mamarrosa [P] 80 B6
Mamers [F] 26 G6
Mammola [I] 124 D7
Mamonovo [RUS] 22 G2
Mána [GR] 136 E1
Manacor [E] 104 E5
Manamansalo [FIN] 198 E4
Manasija [YU] 150 C2
Mancha Real [E] 102 E2
Manchester [GB] 10 E4
Manching [D] 60 E2
Manciano [I] 114 G3
Mancier [F] 66 D6
Mandal [N] 164 D6
Mándalen [N] 180 E3
Mándas [I] 118 D6
Mandelieu [F] 108 E5
Mandello del Lario [I] 70 G3
Mandelos [YU] 154 F2
Manderscheid [D] 44 G1
Mándra [GR] 134 B6
Mándra [GR] 130 H2
Mandráki [GR] 142 C4
Manduria [I] 122 F4
Manerba del Garda [I] 72 B6
Manérbio [I] 72 A6
Manětín [CZ] 48 D4
Mánfa [H] 76 B5
Manfredónia [I] 120 H1
Mangalia [RO] 148 G1
Manganári [GR] 138 F4
Mangen [N] 166 C1

Manger [N] 170 A3
Mängsbodarna [S] 172 F3
Mangualde [P] 80 C6
Maniago [I] 72 F4
Manisa [TR] 144 D3
Mank [A] 62 D5
Månkarbo [S] 174 E5
Mańki [PL] 22 G4
Manlleu [E] 92 E3
Mannheim [D] 46 C4
Mano [F] 66 C4
Manolas [GR] 136 B1
Manorbier [GB] 12 D2
Manorhamilton [IRL] 2 D3
Manosque [F] 108 C4
Manresa [E] 92 D3
Månsarp [S] 162 D2
Manschnow [D] 34 G2
Mansfeld [D] 34 B4
Mansfield [GB] 10 F5
Mansilla de las Mulas [E] 78 H6
Mansle [F] 54 E6
Mansoniemi [FIN] 186 C6
Mantamádos [GR] 134 H2
Manteigas [P] 86 F2
Mantes [F] 42 E3
Mantorp [S] 166 H6
Mantoudi [GR] 134 B4
Mantova [I] 110 E1
Mäntsälä [FIN] 178 A3
Mänttä [FIN] 186 F5
Mäntyharju [FIN] 178 C1
Mäntyjärvi [FIN] 196 E8
Mäntylahti [FIN] 188 C1
Mäntyluoto [FIN] 176 C1
Manyas [TR] 146 D5
Manzanares [E] 96 F4
Manzanares el Real [E] 88 F5
Manzanera [E] 98 E3
Manzanilla [E] 94 F6
Manzat [F] 68 C1
Maó / Mahón [E] 104 H5
Maqueda [E] 88 E6
Maranchón [E] 90 B5
Maranello [I] 110 E3
Marano di Napoli [I] 120 D3
Marano Lagunare [I] 72 G5
Marans [F] 54 C4
Maratea [I] 120 G5
Marateca [P] 86 B6
Marathiás [GR] 132 F5
Marathókampos [GR] 144 C6
Marathónas [GR] 134 C6
Marathópoli [GR] 136 C4
Márathos [GR] 140 E4
Marazion [GB] 12 B5
Marbach [D] 46 D6
Marbäck [S] 162 C2
Marbella [E] 102 B5
Marboz [F] 68 G1
Marburg [D] 32 D6
Marcali [H] 74 H3
Marčana [HR] 112 D2
March [GB] 14 F2
Marchaux [F] 58 B4
Marche-en-Famenne [B] 30 D6
Marchegg [A] 62 G4
Marchena [E] 102 A2
Marcheprime [F] 66 C3
Marciac [F] 84 E2
Marciana Marina [I] 114 D2
Marcianise [I] 120 E3
Marcigny [F] 56 E6
Marcilla [E] 84 B5
Marcillac-Vallon [F] 68 B5
Marcillat [F] 56 C6
Marcilly-le-Hayer [F] 42 H5
Marcinowice [PL] 50 C1
Marckolsheim [F] 58 E2
Marebbe / St Vigil [I] 72 E3
Marennes [F] 54 B5
Mareuil [F] 66 F2
Mareuil [F] 54 C3
Margam [GB] 12 E2
Marganec [UA] 206 G4
Margarítes [GR] 140 D4

Margaríti [GR] 132 C3
Margate [GB] 14 G5
Margherita di Savoia [I] 120 H2
Margonin [PL] 22 B6
Marhaň [SK] 52 D6
Mariager [DK] 160 D5
Maria Laach [D] 30 H6
Mariannelund [S] 162 F2
Mariánské Lázně [CZ] 48 D4
Maria Saal [A] 74 B3
Maria Taferl [A] 62 D4
Maria Wörth [A] 74 B3
Mariazell [A] 62 D5
Maribo [DK] 20 A1
Maribor [SLO] 74 E3
Mariedamm [S] 166 H4
Mariefred [S] 168 C3
Mariehamn / Maarianhamina [FIN] 176 A5
Marieholm [S] 158 C2
Marieholm [S] 162 C3
Marielyst [DK] 20 B1
Marienberg [D] 48 D2
Marienborn [D] 34 A3
Mariestad [S] 166 F5
Marifjøra [N] 170 D1
Marignane [F] 106 H5
Marigny-le-Châtel [F] 44 A5
Marijampolė [LT] 24 E1
Marikostinovo [BG] 130 B2
Marín [E] 78 B4
Marina [EST] 200 E3
Marina [GR] 128 E4
Marina [HR] 116 H1
Marina di Alberese [I] 114 F3
Marina di Árbus [I] 118 B6
Marina di Camerota [I] 120 G5
Marina di Campo [I] 114 D3
Marina di Caronía [I] 126 F2
Marina di Carrara [I] 110 D4
Marina di Castagneto-Donorático [I] 114 E1
Marina di Chiéuti [I] 116 F5
Marina di Gáiro [I] 118 E6
Marina di Ginosa [I] 122 E4
Marina di Gioiosa Jónica [I] 124 D7
Marina di Grosseto [I] 114 F3
Marina di Léuca [I] 122 G6
Marina di Massa [I] 110 D4
Marina di Pietrasanta [I] 110 D5
Marina di Pisa [I] 110 D5
Marina di Ragusa [I] 126 F5
Marina di Ravenna [I] 110 H3
Marina di San Vito [I] 116 E4
Marina di Torre Grande [I] 118 B5
Marina di Vasto [I] 116 E5
Marina Gorka [BY] 204 B5
Marina Palmense [I] 116 D2
Marina Romea [I] 110 H3
Marine de Sisco [F] 114 C2
Marinella [I] 126 B3
Marineo [I] 126 D2
Marines [F] 42 F2
Maringues [F] 68 D2
Marinha Grande [P] 86 C3
Marinkainen [FIN] 198 C5
Mar'insko [RUS] 200 G2
Maristella [I] 118 B3
Märjamaa [EST] 200 D2
Marjaniemi [FIN] 198 C4
Marjovaara [FIN] 188 G2
Markaryd [S] 162 C6
Markdorf [D] 58 H4
Market Deeping [GB] 14 E1
Market Drayton [GB] 10 D5
Market Harborough [GB] 14 E2

Markethill [GB] 2 F4
Market Rasen [GB] 10 G5
Market Weighton [GB] 10 G4
Markhina [FIN] 192 G4
Marki [PL] 38 B3
Markina-Xemein [E] 82 H4
Märkisch Buchholz [D] 34 E3
Markleugast [D] 46 H3
Markneukirchen [D] 48 C3
Markópoulo [GR] 136 H1
Markópoulo [GR] 136 A1
Markovac [YU] 150 C1
Markova Sušica [MK] 128 E1
Markranstädt [D] 34 C5
Markt Bibart [D] 46 F4
Marktbreit [D] 46 E4
Markt Erlbach [D] 46 F5
Marktheidenfeld [D] 46 E4
Markt-Indersdorf [D] 60 E3
Marktl [D] 60 G4
Marktoberdorf [D] 60 C5
Marktredwitz [D] 48 C4
Markt St Florian [A] 62 B4
Markt St Martin [A] 62 F6
Marktzeuln [D] 46 G3
Markušica [HR] 154 E1
Marl [D] 30 H2
Marlborough [GB] 12 H3
Marle [F] 28 G5
Marlenheim [F] 44 G6
Marlow [D] 20 C3
Marlow [GB] 14 D4
Marma [S] 174 E4
Marmande [F] 66 E4
Marmara [TR] 146 C4
Marmaraereğlisi [TR] 146 D3
Marmári [GR] 134 D6
Marmaris [TR] 142 E3
Mármaro [GR] 134 G4
Marmelete [P] 94 B4
Marmolejo [E] 102 D1
Marmoutier [F] 44 G5
Marnay [F] 58 A4
Marne [D] 18 E3
Marnitz [D] 20 B5

Maróneia [GR] 130 F3
Maróstica [I] 72 D5
Marotta [I] 112 C6
Marpíssa [GR] 138 E3
Marquartstein [D] 60 F5
Marquion [F] 28 F4
Marquise [F] 14 G6
Marradi [I] 110 F5
Marrasjärvi [FIN] 196 C7
Marrebæk [DK] 20 B1
Marsala [I] 126 B2
Marsberg [D] 32 E4
Marsciano [I] 116 A2
Marseillan [F] 106 E4
Marseillan-Plage [F] 106 E5
Marseille [F] 106 H5
Marseille-en-Beauvaisis [F] 28 D5
Marshavitsy [RUS] 200 H4
Marshaw [GB] 10 E3
Marshfield [GB] 12 G3
Marsico Nuovo [I] 120 G4
Marsiliana [I] 114 F3
Märsta [S] 168 D2
Marstal [DK] 156 D4
Marstrand [S] 160 G1
Marta [I] 114 G3
Martano [I] 122 G5
Martel [F] 66 H3
Martelange [B] 44 E2
Marten [BG] 148 D1
Martfü [H] 76 E2
Marthon [F] 66 F1
Martigné-Ferchaud [F] 40 G5
Martigny [CH] 70 C2
Martigues [F] 106 H5
Martim Longo [P] 94 D4
Martin [SK] 64 C2
Martina / Martinsbruck [CH] 72 B2
Martina Franca [I] 122 E3
Martín de Yeltes [E] 88 B3
Martinniemi [FIN] 198 D3
Martíno [GR] 134 B5
Martinsbruck / Martina [CH] 72 B2
Martinsicuro [I] 116 D3

Mártis [I] 118 C3
Martna [EST] 200 D2
Martock [GB] 12 F4
Martofte [DK] 156 E3
Martonvaara [FIN] 188 F1
Martonvásár [H] 76 C1
Martorell [E] 92 D4
Martos [E] 102 D2
Martti [FIN] 196 E6
Marttila [FIN] 176 E4
Marvão [P] 86 F5
Marvejols [F] 68 C5
Marwałd [PL] 22 G5
Marxwalde [D] 34 F2
Marxzell [D] 46 B6
Marynin [PL] 38 F5
Maryport [GB] 8 D6
Marzabotto [I] 110 F4
Marzahna [D] 34 D3
Marzahne [D] 34 D2
Marzocca [I] 112 C6
Maschen [D] 18 F5
Mas de las Matas [E] 90 F6
Masegoso de Tajuña [E] 90 A5
Maser [I] 72 E5
Masevaux [F] 58 D3
Masi [N] 192 G2
Masku [FIN] 176 D4
Maslenica [HR] 112 G4
Maslovare [BIH] 154 C3
Massa [I] 110 D4
Massafra [I] 122 E4
Massa Lubrense [I] 120 E4
Massa Marittima [I] 114 F2
Massat [F] 84 H5
Massay [F] 56 B3
Masseret [F] 66 G2
Masseube [F] 84 G3
Massiac [F] 68 C3
Mastergeehy [IRL] 4 A4
Mas Thibert [F] 106 G4
Mastichári [GR] 142 B3
Mästocka [S] 162 B5
Masty [BY] 24 G3
Maszecwo [PL] 34 G3
Maszewo [PL] 20 G5
Matabuena [E] 88 G4
Mátala [GR] 140 D5

Matalebreras [E] 84 A6
Matallana de Torío [E] 82 B5
Mataró [E] 92 E4
Mataruška Banja [YU] 150 B3
Matelica [I] 116 B2
Matera [I] 122 D4
Mateševo [YU] 152 E3
Mátészalka [H] 206 B3
Matfors [S] 184 E5
Matha [F] 54 D5
Mathay [F] 58 C4
Matignon [F] 26 B4
Matiši [LV] 200 E4
Matka [MK] 128 E1
Matlock [GB] 10 E5
Matos [P] 94 D3
Matosinhos [P] 80 B4
Matour [F] 56 F6
Mátrafüred [H] 64 E5
Mátraháza [H] 64 E5
Matrei am Brenner [A] 72 D1
Matrei in Osttirol [A] 72 F2
Mattersburg [A] 62 F6
Mattighofen [A] 60 G4
Mattinata [I] 116 H6
Mattsee [A] 60 G5
Matulji [HR] 112 E1
Matyli [BY] 24 G3
Maubeuge [F] 28 G4
Maubourguet [F] 84 F3
Mauchline [GB] 8 D4
Mauerkirchen [A] 60 H4
Maula [FIN] 198 C2
Maulbronn [D] 46 C6
Mauléon [F] 54 D2
Mauléon-Licharre [F] 84 D3
Maulévrier [F] 54 D2
Maumtrasna [IRL] 2 B4
Maupertus-sur-Mer [F] 26 D2
Maura [N] 172 B5
Maure [F] 26 B6
Mauriac [F] 68 B3
Maurnes [N] 192 C3

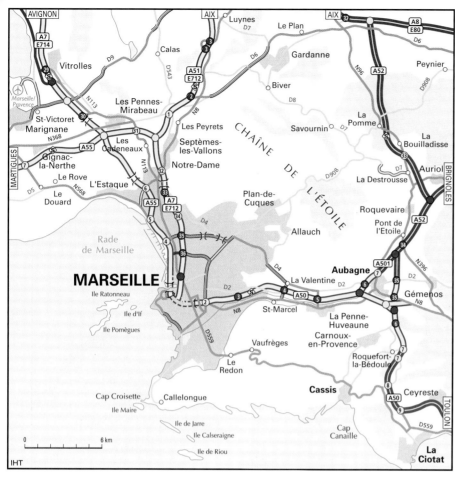

Mauron [F] 26 B6
Maurs [F] 66 H5
Maurstad [N] 180 B5
Maury [F] 106 C6
Mautern [A] 74 C1
Mauterndorf [A] 72 H2
Mauth [D] 62 A2
Mauthausen [A] 62 C4
Mauvezin [F] 84 G2
Mauvoisin [CH] 70 D3
Mauzé–sur–le–Mignon [F] 54 C4
Mavréli [GR] 132 F1
Mavrhóri [GR] 128 E5
Mavroklíssio [GR] 130 H2
Mavromáta [GR] 132 F3
Mavrommáti [GR] 136 D3
Mavrothálassa [GR] 130 C3
Mavrovi Hanovi [MK] 128 D2
Mavrovo [MK] 128 D2
Mavrovoúni [GR] 136 E5
Mavrovoúni [GR] 132 G2
Maxmo / Maksamaa [FIN] 186 B2
Maybole [GB] 8 C4
Mayen [D] 30 H6
Mayenne [F] 26 E6
Mayet [F] 42 B6
Mayfield [GB] 14 E5
Maynooth [IRL] 2 F6
Mayorga [E] 82 B5
Mayrhofen [A] 72 E1
Mäyry [FIN] 186 D3
Mazagón [E] 94 E6
Mazamet [F] 106 C4
Mazara del Vallo [I] 126 B3
Mazarrón [E] 104 B4
Mažeikiai [LT] 200 C6
Mazères [F] 106 A4
Mazetown [GB] 2 G4
Mázia [GR] 132 D2
Mazıköy [TR] 142 D2
Mazilmaja [LV] 200 B6
Mazirbe [LV] 200 C4
Mazsalaca [LV] 200 E3
Mazurki [PL] 38 C4
Mazzalve [LV] 200 E6
Mazzarino [I] 126 E4

Mazzaró [I] 124 B8
Mazzarone [I] 126 F5
Mcensk [RUS] 204 F6
Mdzewo [PL] 22 G6
Mealhada [P] 80 B6
Meare [GB] 12 F4
Meaux [F] 42 G3
Mechelen (Malines) [B] 30 C3
Mechernich [D] 30 G5
Meckenbeuren [D] 58 H4
Medak [HR] 112 C4
Medby [N] 192 C6
Mede [I] 70 F6
Medebach [D] 32 D5
Medellín [E] 96 A3
Medemblik [NL] 16 E3
Medena Selišta [BIH] 154 B4
Meden Rudnik [BG] 148 F4
Medenychi [UA] 52 H5
Medevi [S] 166 G3
Medgidia [RO] 206 D6
Medgyesegyháza [H] 76 G3
Mediaş [RO] 206 C5
Medicina [I] 110 G3
Medinaceli [E] 90 B4
Medina del Campo [E] 88 E2
Medina de Pomar [E] 82 F4
Medina de Rioseco [E] 82 B6
Medina–Sidonia [E] 100 G4
Medininkai [LT] 202 G5
Medjumajdan [HR] 154 A2
Medle [S] 198 A4
Médoussa [GR] 130 E2
Medskogen [S] 172 D4
Medstugan [S] 182 E1
Medulin [HR] 112 D3
Medvedja [YU] 150 D4
Medveď'ov [SK] 62 H5
Medvida [HR] 112 H5
Medvode [SLO] 74 B5
Medzilaborce [SK] 52 E6
Medžitlija [MK] 128 E4
Meerane [D] 48 C1
Meersburg [D] 58 H4
Mefjordvaer [N] 192 D2

Méga Dério [GR] 130 G2
Megáli Vólvi [GR] 130 B4
Megalochóri [GR] 132 F2
Megálo Livádi [GR] 138 C3
Megálon Chorió [GR] 142 C4
Megalópoli [GR] 136 D3
Mégara [GR] 134 B6
Megève [F] 70 B3
Meg Horió [GR] 132 F4
Megísti [TR] 142 H4
Megyaszó [H] 64 F2
Mehadia [RO] 206 A6
Mehamn [N] 196 D1
Mehun–sur–Yèvre [F] 56 B3
Meijel [NL] 30 F3
Meilen [CH] 58 F5
Meina [I] 70 F4
Meine [D] 32 H2
Meinerzhagen [D] 32 C5
Meiningen [D] 46 F2
Meira [F] 78 E3
Meiräni [LV] 200 F5
Meiringen [CH] 70 E1
Meisenheim [D] 44 H3
Meissen [D] 34 E6
Meitingen [D] 60 D3
Męka [PL] 36 F5
Mel [I] 72 E4
Mélampes [GR] 140 D5
Melaniós [GR] 134 G4
Melbeck [D] 18 G5
Melbourn [GB] 14 E3
Melbu [N] 192 C4
Meldal [N] 180 H2
Meldola [I] 110 G4
Meldorf [D] 18 E2
Melegnano [I] 70 G5
Melenci [YU] 76 E6
Melfi [I] 120 G3
Melgaço [P] 78 C5
Melgar de Fernamental [E] 82 D5
Melhus [N] 182 B1
Melide [E] 78 D3

Melides [P] 94 B2
Meligalás [GR] 136 D3
Melíki [GR] 128 G5
Melilli [I] 126 G4
Mélisey [F] 58 C3
Melíssi [GR] 132 E1
Melissópetra [GR] 128 D6
Melito di Porto Salvo [I] 124 C8
Melitopol' [UA] 206 H4
Melk [A] 62 D4
Melksham [GB] 12 G3
Mellakoski [FIN] 196 C8
Mellansel [S] 184 F1
Mellbystrand [S] 162 B5
Melle [D] 32 D2
Melle [F] 54 D5
Mellendorf [D] 32 F1
Mellerud [S] 166 D5
Mellieha [M] 126 C6
Mellilä [FIN] 176 E3
Mellin [D] 34 A1
Mellrichstadt [D] 46 F2
Melmerby [GB] 8 E6
Melnica [YU] 150 C1
Melnik [BG] 130 B2
Mělník [CZ] 48 F3
Mel'nikovo [RUS] 178 G2
Melrose [GB] 8 F4
Melsetter [GB] 6 F2
Melsomvik [N] 164 H3
Melsungen [D] 32 F5
Meltaus [FIN] 196 C7
Melton Constable [GB] 14 G1
Melton Mowbray [GB] 10 F6
Meltosjärvi [FIN] 196 C8
Melun [F] 42 G4
Melvaig [GB] 6 C3
Melvich [GB] 6 E2
Mélykút [H] 76 D4
Melzo [I] 70 G5
Membrío [E] 86 F4
Memmingen [D] 60 B4
Mena [UA] 204 D7
Menággio [I] 70 G3
Menai Bridge [GB] 10 B4
Menasalbas [E] 96 E2

Menat [F] 56 C6
Mendavia [E] 82 H6
Mende [F] 68 C6
Menden [D] 32 C4
Menderes [TR] 144 C4
Menemen [TR] 144 C4
Menen [B] 28 F2
Menesjärvi [FIN] 196 D4
Menetés [GR] 140 H3
Menfi [I] 126 C3
Ménfőcsanak [H] 62 H6
Mengamuñoz [E] 88 D4
Mengen [D] 58 H3
Mengeš [SLO] 74 C4
Mengíbar [E] 102 E1
Mengishevo [BG] 148 E3
Menídi [GR] 132 D3
Ménina [GR] 132 C2
Mens [F] 68 H6
Menstrup [DK] 156 F4
Menthon [F] 70 B3
Menton [F] 108 F4
Meppel [NL] 16 F3
Meppen [D] 16 H4
Mequinenza [E] 90 G5
Mer [F] 54 H1
Mera de Boixo [E] 78 D1
Meráker [N] 182 D1
Meran / Merano [I] 72 D3
Merano / Meran [I] 72 D3
Merate [I] 70 G4
Mercatale [I] 114 H1
Mercatino Conca [I] 110 H5
Mercato San Severino [I] 120 F3
Mercato Saraceno [I] 110 G5
Merčez [YU] 150 C4
Merdrignac [F] 26 B5
Méréville [F] 42 F5
Mergozzo [I] 70 F3
Méribel [F] 70 B4
Méribel–les–Allues [F] 70 B4
Meriç [TR] 130 H2
Mérichas [GR] 138 C2
Merichleri [BG] 148 C5
Mérida [E] 94 H2
Merijärvi [FIN] 198 C5
Merikarvia [FIN] 186 B6
Merimasku [FIN] 176 D4
Měřín [CZ] 50 A5
Mering [D] 60 D4
Merkendorf [D] 46 F6
Merkine [LT] 24 G2
Merklingen [D] 60 B3
Merlara [I] 110 F1
Merligen [CH] 70 E1
Mern [DK] 156 G4
Mernye [H] 76 A4
Mersch [D] 30 F4
Mersch [L] 44 F2
Merseburg [D] 34 C5
Mersinbeleni [TR] 144 D6
Mērsrags [LV] 200 C4
Merthyr Tydfil [GB] 12 F2
Mértola [P] 94 D4
Méru [F] 42 F2
Mervans [F] 56 G5
Merville [F] 28 E3
Méry [F] 44 A5
Merzig [D] 44 F3
Mesagne [I] 122 F4
Mesão Frio [P] 80 D4
Meschede [D] 32 D5
Meschers–sur–Gironde [F] 54 C6
Mešeišta [MK] 128 D3
Mesenikólas [GR] 132 F3
Meshaw [GB] 12 E4
Mesinge [DK] 156 E3
Meskiá [GR] 140 C4
Meslay [F] 40 H5
Mesnalien [N] 172 B2
Mesnil–Val [F] 28 C4
Mesocco [CH] 70 G2
Mesochóra [GR] 132 E2
Mésola [I] 110 H2
Mesolóngi [GR] 132 E5
Mesón do Vento [E] 78 C2
Mesopótamo [GR] 132 C3

Mespelbrunn [D] 46 D3
Messariá [GR] 138 D1
Messdorf [D] 34 B1
Messimvría [GR] 130 G3
Messina [I] 124 B7
Messines de Baixo [P] 94 C5
Messíni [GR] 136 D4
Messkirch [D] 58 G3
Messlingen [S] 182 E3
Messohóri [GR] 132 F1
Messohóri [GR] 130 G3
Messtetten [D] 58 G3
Mestá [GR] 134 G5
Mestanza [E] 96 E5
Mestervik [N] 192 E2
Mésti [GR] 130 G3
Mestlin [D] 20 B4
Město Albrechtice [CZ] 50 D3
Město Libavá [CZ] 50 D5
Mestre [I] 72 E6
Mesvres [F] 56 F5
Metabief [F] 58 B6
Metaljka [BIH] 152 E2
Metamórfosi [GR] 130 C5
Metaxás [GR] 128 F6
Méteren [F] 28 F2
Méthanon [GR] 136 G2
Methlick [GB] 6 F5
Methóni [GR] 136 C4
Methóni [GR] 128 G5
Metkovič [HR] 152 C3
Metlika [SLO] 74 D6
Metnitz [A] 74 B2
Metóchi [GR] 132 E6
Metsäkylä [FIN] 178 C3
Metsäkylä [FIN] 198 F3
Metsälä / Ömossa [FIN] 186 B5
Metsküla [EST] 200 C3
Métsovon [GR] 132 D1
Metten [D] 60 G2
Mettet [B] 30 C5
Mettingen [D] 32 C2
Mettlach [D] 44 F3
Mettmann [D] 30 G3
Metz [F] 44 E4
Metzervisse [F] 44 F3
Metzingen [D] 58 H2
Meulan [F] 42 F3
Meung–sur–Loire [F] 42 E6
Meuselwitz [D] 34 C6
Mevagissey [GB] 12 C5
Mevik [N] 190 D1
Mexilhoeira Grande [P] 94 B5
Meximieux [F] 68 G2
Meyenburg [D] 20 B5
Meymac [F] 68 B2
Meyrargues [F] 108 B4
Meyrueis [F] 106 E2
Meyzieu [F] 68 G3
Mézapos [GR] 136 E5
Mezdra [BG] 150 G4
Mèze [F] 106 E4
Mézel [F] 108 D3
Mężenin [PL] 24 D6
Mežgorje [UA] 206 B3
Mézières [F] 54 F5
Mézières–en–Brenne [F] 54 G4
Mézilhac [F] 68 E5
Mézin [F] 66 D6
Mezőberény [H] 76 G3
Mezőcsát [H] 64 F5
Mezőhegyes [H] 76 F4
Mezőkeresztes [H] 64 F5
Mezőkovácsháza [H] 76 F4
Mezőnyárád [H] 64 F5
Mezőörs [H] 64 A6
Mezőszilas [H] 76 B3
Mezőtúr [H] 76 F2
Mezquita de Jarque [E] 90 E6
Mezzolombardo [I] 72 C4
Mgarr [M] 126 C5
Miabhig / Miavag [GB] 6 B2
Miączyn [PL] 52 G1
Miajadas [E] 86 H6
Miami Platja [E] 90 H6
Mianowice [PL] 22 C2

Miasteczko Śląskie [PL] 50 F2
Miastko [PL] 22 B3
Miavag / Miabhig [GB] 6 B2
Michalove [SK] 64 H2
Michałów [PL] 38 C6
Michałówek [PL] 38 B3
Michałowo [PL] 24 F6
Micheldorf [A] 62 B5
Michelstadt [D] 46 D4
Michów [PL] 38 D5
Mickleby [GB] 10 G2
Middelburg [NL] 16 B6
Middelfart [DK] 156 C3
Middelharnis [NL] 16 C5
Middelkerke–Bad [B] 28 F1
Middlesbrough [GB] 10 F2
Middleton [GB] 14 D5
Middleton in Teesdale [GB] 10 E1
Middlewich [GB] 10 D4
Midhurst [GB] 14 D5
Midleton [IRL] 4 D5
Midlum [D] 18 D3
Midsland [NL] 16 E1
Midstkogberget [N] 172 D2
Midtgulen [N] 180 B5
Mid Yell [GB] 6 H3
Miechów [PL] 50 H3
Mieders [A] 72 D1
Międzdroje [PL] 20 F3
Międzybórz [PL] 36 D5
Międzybrodzie Bialskie [PL] 50 G4
Międzychod [PL] 36 B2
Międzygórze [PL] 50 C3
Międzylesie [PL] 50 C3
Międzyrzec Podlaski [PL] 38 E3
Międzyrzecz [PL] 36 A2
Miedzywodzie [PL] 20 F3
Miehikkälä [FIN] 178 D3
Miejsce Piastowe [PL] 52 D5
Miejska Górka [PL] 36 C5
Miélan [F] 84 F3
Mielec [PL] 52 D3
Mielno [PL] 20 H3
Mieluskylä [FIN] 198 D5
Mierasjärvi [FIN] 196 D3
Mieraslompolo [FIN] 196 D3
Miercurea Ciuc [RO] 206 C5
Mieres [E] 78 H4
Mieron [N] 192 G3
Mieroszów [PL] 50 B2
Miersig [RO] 76 H2
Mierzyno [PL] 22 D1
Miesbach [D] 60 E5
Mieścisko [PL] 36 D2
Mieste [D] 34 B2
Miesterhorst [D] 34 A2
Mieszkowice [PL] 34 G1
Mietoinen [FIN] 176 D4
Mifol [AL] 128 A5
Migennes [F] 42 H6
Migliarino [I] 110 G3
Migliónico [I] 122 D4
Mignano Monte Lungo [I] 120 D1
Mihăeşti [RO] 148 B1
Mihajlovac [YU] 150 E1
Mihalgazi [TR] 146 H4
Mihla [D] 32 G6
Mijas [E] 102 B5
Mijoux [F] 70 A1
Mikhaylovo [BG] 150 G3
Mikkeli [FIN] 188 C6
Mikołajki [PL] 24 C4
Mikołajki Pomorskie [PL] 22 F4
Mikolin [PL] 50 D2
Mikołów [PL] 50 F3
Mikre [BG] 148 A4
Mikró Dérieio [GR] 130 G2
Mikró Horió [GR] 132 F4
Mikrókambos [GR] 128 H4
Mikrópoli [GR] 130 C3
Mikrothíves [GR] 132 H3
Mikstat [PL] 36 E5
Mikulčice [CZ] 62 G3
Mikulov [CZ] 62 F3

Mikulovice [CZ] 50 D3
Miland [N] 170 F5
Milano [I] 70 G5
Milano Marittima [I] 110 H4
Milanovac [HR] 76 A6
Milanówek [PL] 38 B3
Milâs [TR] 142 D2
Mílatos [GR] 140 F4
Milazzo [I] 124 B7
Mildenhall [GB] 14 F2
Milejczyce [PL] 38 F2
Milejewo [PL] 22 F3
Milena [I] 126 D3
Mileševo [YU] 150 A3
Mileševo [YU] 76 E6
Miletiči [HR] 112 G4
Mileto [I] 124 D6
Milevsko [CZ] 48 F5
Milford [GB] 14 D5
Milford [IRL] 2 F2
Milford Haven [GB] 12 D2
Milford–on–Sea [GB] 12 G5
Mili̇ći [BIH] 154 E4
Milicz [PL] 36 D5
Milies [GR] 134 A2
Milín [CZ] 48 F5
Milína [GR] 134 A3
Milintello in Val di Catania [I] 126 F4
Millares [E] 98 E5
Millas [F] 92 F1
Millau [F] 106 D2
Millbay [GB] 2 H3
Millesimo [I] 108 G3
Millom [GB] 10 D2
Millport [GB] 8 C3
Millstatt [A] 72 H3
Millstreet [IRL] 4 C4
Milltown [IRL] 4 B4
Milltown Malbay [IRL] 2 B6
Milmarcos [E] 90 C5
Milmersdorf [D] 20 D6
Milna [HR] 152 A2
Miločer [YU] 152 D4
Milocin [RO] 38 D5
Milos [GR] 138 D4
Milosavci [BIH] 154 C2
Miloševa Kula [YU] 150 D1
Miłosław [PL] 36 D3
Milovaig [GB] 6 B4
Milow [D] 20 A5
Milówka [PL] 50 G5
Miltach [D] 48 D6
Miltenberg [D] 46 D4
Milton Keynes [GB] 14 E3
Milyutino [RUS] 200 H2
Mimizan [F] 66 B4
Mimizan–Plage [F] 66 B4
Mimoň [CZ] 48 G2
Mina de Sâo Domingos [P] 94 D4
Minas de Riotinto [E] 94 F5
Minateda–Horca [E] 104 B1
Minaya [E] 98 B4
Mindelheim [D] 60 C4
Minden [D] 32 E2
Mindin [F] 40 E6
Mindszent [H] 76 E3
Minehead [GB] 12 E3
Minerbio [I] 110 F3
Minervino Murge [I] 120 H2
Minervio [F] 114 C2
Minglanilla [E] 98 C4
Miničevo [YU] 150 E3
Minnesund [N] 172 C4
Minsen [D] 18 C3
Minsk [BY] 204 B5
Mińsk Mazowiecki [PL] 38 C3
Minster [GB] 14 F4
Mintlaw [GB] 6 G5
Minturno [I] 120 D1
Miočič [HR] 154 A5
Miokovičevo [HR] 74 H6
Mionica [YU] 150 A1
Mira [E] 110 H1
Mira [E] 98 D3
Mira [I] 72 E6
Mira [P] 80 B6
Miraflores de la Sierra [E] 88 F4

Miramar [F] 108 E5
Miramare [I] 112 B5
Miramas [F] 106 G4
Mirambeau [F] 66 D2
Miramont–de–Guyenne [F] 66 E4
Miranda de Ebro [E] 82 G5
Miranda do Corvo [P] 86 D2
Miranda do Douro [P] 80 G4
Mirande [F] 84 F3
Mirandela [P] 80 E4
Mirándola [I] 110 F2
Mirano [I] 72 E6
Mirantes [E] 78 G5
Miravet [E] 90 H6
Mirebeau [F] 54 E3
Mirebeau [F] 56 H3
Mirecourt [F] 44 E6
Mirepoix [F] 106 B5
Mironovka [UA] 206 F2
Mirosławiec [PL] 20 H5
Mirošov [CZ] 48 E5
Mirovice [CZ] 48 F5
Mirovo [BG] 150 G5
Mirow [D] 20 C5
Mirow [PL] 50 G2
Mirsk [PL] 48 H1
Misilmeri [I] 126 D2
Miskolc [H] 64 F4
Miskolctapolca [H] 64 F5
Missanello [I] 120 H5
Misso [EST] 200 F4
Mistegná [GR] 134 H2
Mistelbach [A] 62 F3
Misten [N] 192 B5
Misterbianco [I] 126 G3
Misterhult [S] 162 G3
Mistrás [GR] 136 E4
Mistretta [I] 126 F2
Misurina [I] 72 E3
Mišurin Rog [UA] 206 G3
Misvær [N] 192 C6
Miszewo [PL] 22 D2
Mitchelstown [IRL] 4 D4
Míthymna [GR] 134 G2
Mitrašinci [MK] 128 G1

Mitrópoli [GR] 132 F3
Mittådalen [S] 182 E3
Mittelberg [A] 72 C2
Mittelberg [A] 60 B6
Mittelberg [D] 60 C5
Mittenwald [D] 60 D6
Mittenwalde [D] 20 D5
Mittenwalde [D] 34 E3
Mittersill [A] 72 F1
Mitterteich [D] 48 C4
Mittewald [A] 72 F3
Mittweida [D] 48 D1
Mitwitz [D] 46 G3
Mizil [RO] 206 C6
Miziya [BG] 150 G2
Mjåland [N] 164 E4
Mjällby [S] 158 E2
Mjölby [S] 166 H6
Mjøndalen [N] 164 G1
Mjørlund [N] 172 B4
M. Kalívia [GR] 132 F2
Mladá Boleslav [CZ] 48 G3
Mladá Vožice [CZ] 48 G5
Mladé Buky [CZ] 50 A2
Mladenovac [YU] 150 B1
Mlado Nagoričane [MK] 150 D6
Mława [PL] 22 G6
Mlekarevo [BG] 148 D5
Mlini [HR] 152 C4
Mliniště [BIH] 154 B4
Młynary [PL] 22 F3
Młynarze [PL] 24 C6
Mnich [CZ] 48 G6
Mnichovo Hradiště [CZ] 48 G2
Mnichow [PL] 52 B2
Mniów [PL] 52 B1
Mníšek pod Brdy [CZ] 48 F4
Mniszek [PL] 38 B5
Mo [N] 172 C4
Mo [S] 166 G3
Moaña [E] 78 B4
Moate [IRL] 2 E5
Moča [SK] 64 B5
Mocejón [E] 96 F1
Móchlos [GR] 140 G4
Mochowo [PL] 36 G1

Mochy [PL] 36 B4
Mittådalen [S] 182 E3
Möckern [D] 34 C3
Mockfjärd [S] 172 H4
Möckmühl [D] 46 D5
Moclín [E] 102 D3
Modane [F] 70 B5
Modave [B] 30 D5
Módena [I] 110 E3
Módica [I] 126 F5
Modigliana [I] 110 G4
Modliborzyce [PL] 52 E1
Modliszewko [PL] 36 D2
Modra [SK] 62 G4
Modrica [BIH] 154 D2
Modrište [MK] 128 E2
Modugno [I] 122 D2
Moelv [N] 172 B3
Moen [N] 190 C6
Moen [N] 192 E3
Moena [I] 72 D4
Moers [D] 30 G3
Moesgård [DK] 156 D1
Moffat [GB] 8 E4
Mogadouro [P] 80 F5
Mogán [E] 100 C6
Mogielnica [PL] 38 B4
Mogilev–Podolski [UA] 206 D3
Mogilno [PL] 36 E2
Mogil'ov [BY] 204 C5
Móglia [I] 110 E2
Mogliano Veneto [I] 72 E6
Moglicë [AL] 128 C4
Mogón [E] 102 F2
Mogorella [I] 118 C5
Moguer [E] 94 E6
Mohács [H] 76 B5
Mohärad [S] 162 D4
Moheda [S] 162 D4
Mohelnice [CZ] 50 C4
Mohill [IRL] 2 E4
Möhkö [FIN] 188 H2
Moholm [S] 166 F5
Mohora [H] 64 D5
Mohos [GR] 140 F4
Moi [N] 164 C4
Moià [E] 92 E3

Moikipää / Molpe [FIN] 186 A3
Moimenta da Beira [P] 80 D5
Mo–i–Rana [N] 190 E2
Moirans [F] 68 G4
Moirans–en–Montagne [F] 56 H6
Moíres [GR] 140 E5
Mõisaküla [EST] 200 E3
Moissac [F] 66 F6
Moita [P] 86 B5
Mojácar [E] 102 H5
Mojkovac [YU] 152 E3
Mojstrana [SLO] 74 B4
Mokobody [PL] 38 D3
Mokra Gora [YU] 152 E1
Mokresh [BG] 150 F2
Mokrin [YU] 76 F5
Mokronog [SLO] 74 D5
Möksy [FIN] 186 E2
Mol [B] 30 D3
Mol [YU] 76 E6
Mola di Bari [I] 122 E3
Moláoi [GR] 136 F4
Molare [I] 108 H2
Mold [GB] 10 C4
Molde [N] 180 E3
Moldjord [N] 192 B6
Moldova Nouă [RO] 206 A6
Møldrup [DK] 160 D5
Moledo [P] 78 A5
Molėtai [LT] 202 G4
Molfetta [I] 122 D2
Moliden [S] 184 G2
Molières [F] 66 F6
Molina de Aragón [E] 90 C5
Molina de Segura [E] 104 C3
Molinella [I] 110 G3
Molinos [E] 90 E6
Molins de Rei [E] 92 E4
Moliterno [I] 120 H5
Molkom [S] 166 F2
Mollas [AL] 128 D5
Möllbrücke [A] 72 G2
Mölle [S] 160 H6
Möllenbeck [D] 20 D5
Mollerussa [E] 92 C3

Mollet del Vallès [E] 92 E4
Molliens [F] 28 D4
Mollina [E] 102 C3
Mölln [D] 18 G4
Mollösund [S] 160 G1
Mölltorp [S] 166 G5
Mølnarodden [N] 192 B5
Mölndal [S] 160 G2
Mölnlycke [S] 160 H2
Mólos [GR] 132 G4
Moloskovitsy [RUS] 178 F6
Moloy [F] 56 G3
Molpe / Moikipää [FIN] 186 A3
Molsheim [F] 44 G6
Molveno [I] 72 C4
Mombeltrán [E] 88 D5
Momchilgrad [BG] 130 F1
Momin Prohod [BG] 150 G5
Mommark [DK] 156 D4
Momo [I] 70 F4
Monachil [E] 102 E4
Monaco [MC] 108 F4
Monaghan [IRL] 2 F4
Monasterace Marina [I] 124 E6
Monasterevin [IRL] 2 E6
Monasterio de Leyre [E] 84 C4
Monastir [I] 118 C6
Monastiráki [GR] 130 G3
Monastiráki [GR] 132 D4
Monbaroccio [I] 112 B5
Moncalieri [I] 70 D6
Moncalvo [I] 70 E6
Monção [P] 78 B5
Mönchdorf [A] 62 C4
Mönchengladbach [D] 30 G3
Mönchhof [A] 62 G5
Monchique [P] 94 B4
Moncofa [E] 98 F4
Moncontour [F] 26 B5
Moncoutant [F] 54 D3
Mondariz [E] 78 B5
Mondariz–Balneario [E] 78 B5
Mondéjar [E] 88 G6
Mondello [I] 126 C1
Mondim de Basto [P] 80 D4
Mondolfo [I] 112 C6
Mondoñedo [E] 78 E2
Mondorf–les–Bains [L] 44 F3
Mondoubleau [F] 42 C5
Mondoví [I] 108 G3
Mondragone [I] 120 D2
Mondsee [A] 60 H5
Monéglia [I] 110 C4
Monegrillo [E] 90 F4
Monemvasía [GR] 136 F5
Monesi [I] 108 F3
Monesterio [E] 94 G4
Monestier–de–Clermont [F] 68 G5
Monêtier–Allemont [F] 108 C2
Moneygall [IRL] 2 D6
Moneymore [GB] 2 F3
Monfalcone [I] 72 H5
Monfero [E] 78 D2
Monflanquin [F] 66 F5
Monforte [P] 86 E5
Monforte da Beira [P] 86 F4
Monforte de Lemos [E] 78 D4
Mongstad [N] 170 A2
Monguelfo / Welsberg [I] 72 E3
Monheim [D] 60 D2
Moniaive [GB] 8 D5
Mönichkirchen [A] 62 E6
Möniste [EST] 200 F4
Monistrol–d'Allier [F] 68 D4
Monistrol de Montserrat [E] 92 D4
Monistrol–sur–Loire [F] 68 E4
Monivea [IRL] 2 C5
Mónki [PL] 24 E5

Monmouth [GB] 12 G2
Monnickendam [NL] 16 D4
Monninkylä [FIN] 178 A4
Monodéndri [GR] 132 C1
Monólithos [GR] 142 D5
Monopoli [I] 122 E3
Monor [H] 76 D1
Monóvar / Monòver [E] 104 D2
Monòver / Monóvar [E] 104 D2
Monpazier [F] 66 F4
Monplaisir [F] 42 C5
Monreal / Elo [E] 84 B4
Monreal del Campo [E] 90 D6
Monreale [I] 126 C2
Monroy [E] 86 H5
Monroyo [E] 98 G1
Mons (Bergen) [B] 28 G4
Monsanto [P] 86 G3
Monsaraz [P] 94 E2
Monschau [D] 30 F5
Monségur [F] 66 D4
Monsélice [I] 110 G1
Monsheim [D] 46 B4
Mønsted [DK] 160 C5
Mönsterås [S] 162 G4
Monsummano Terme [I] 110 E5
Montabaur [D] 46 B2
Montacute [GB] 12 F4
Montagnac [F] 106 E4
Montagnana [I] 110 F1
Montaigu [F] 54 C2
Montaigu–de–Quercy [F] 66 F5
Montaigut [F] 56 C6
Montaione [I] 110 E6
Montalbán [E] 90 E6
Montalbano Elicona [I] 124 A7
Montalbano Jonico [I] 122 D5
Montalbo [E] 98 A2
Montalcino [I] 114 G2
Montaldo di Cosola [I] 110 B2
Montalieu [F] 68 G3
Montalivet–les–Bains [F] 66 C1
Montalto delle Marche [I] 116 C2
Montalto di Castro [I] 114 G4
Montalto Ligure [I] 108 G4
Montalto Uffugo [I] 124 D4
Montalvão [P] 86 E4
Montamarta [E] 80 H4
Montana [BG] 150 F3
Montana [CH] 70 D2
Montañana [E] 90 E4
Montánchez [E] 86 H6
Montanejos [E] 98 E3
Montaren [F] 106 G3
Montargil [P] 86 D5
Montargis [F] 42 F6
Montargull / Artesa de Segre [E] 92 C2
Montastruc la–Conseillère [F] 106 A3
Montauban [F] 66 F6
Montauban [F] 26 C5
Montbard [F] 56 F2
Montbazens [F] 66 H5
Montbazon [F] 54 F2
Montbéliard [F] 58 C4
Montbenoît [F] 58 C5
Montblanc [E] 92 C4
Montbonnot [F] 68 H4
Montbrison [F] 68 E3
Montbron [F] 66 F1
Montbrun–les–Bains [F] 108 B3
Montceau–les–Mines [F] 56 F5
Montchanin [F] 56 F5
Montcornet [F] 28 G6
Montcuq [F] 66 F5
Mont–de–Marsan [F] 66 C6
Montdidier [F] 28 E5
Monte [P] 100 B3

Montealegre del Castillo [E] 98 C6
Monte Redondo [P] 86 C2
Montebelluna [I] 72 E5
Montebourg [F] 26 D2
Montebruno [I] 110 B3
Monte–Carlo [MC] 108 F4
Montecatini–Terme [I] 110 E5
Montécchio [I] 112 B5
Montecchio Emilia [I] 110 D3
Montécchio Maggiore [I] 72 D6
Montech [F] 66 F6
Montecorvino Rovella [I] 120 F4
Monte da Pedra [P] 86 E4
Montefalco [I] 116 A2
Montefalcone nel Sannio [I] 116 E6
Montefiascone [I] 114 H3
Montefiorino [I] 110 E4
Montefrío [E] 102 D3
Montegiordano Marina [I] 122 D5
Monte Gordo [P] 94 D5
Montegrotto Terme [I] 110 G1
Montehermoso [E] 86 H3
Monte Isola [I] 72 A5
Montejícar [E] 102 E3
Montel–de–Gelat [F] 68 C1
Montélimar [F] 68 F6
Montella [I] 120 F3
Montellano [E] 100 H3
Montemor–o–Novo [P] 86 C6
Montemor–o–Velho [P] 86 D2
Montemurlo [I] 110 E5
Montendre [F] 66 D2
Montenegro de Cameros [E] 90 B2
Montenero di Bisáccia [I] 116 E5
Montepulciano [I] 114 G2
Montereale [I] 116 B4
Montereale Valcellina [I] 72 F4

Montereau [F] 42 G5
Monte Redondo [P] 86 C2
Monteriggioni [I] 114 F1
Monteroni d'Arbia [I] 114 G1
Monteroni di Lecce [I] 122 G5
Monterosso al Mare [I] 110 C4
Monterotondo [I] 116 A5
Monterroso [E] 78 D4
Monterrubio de la Serena [E] 96 B4
Monte San Biagio [I] 120 C1
Montesano sulla Marcellana [I] 120 G5
Monte San Savino [I] 114 G1
Monte Sant' Angelo [I] 116 H6
Montesarchio [I] 120 E2
Montescaglioso [I] 122 D4
Montesilvano Marina [I] 116 D4
Montesquieu–Volvestre [F] 84 H4
Montesquiou [F] 84 F3
Montevarchi [I] 110 F6
Monteverde [I] 120 G3
Montfaucon–en–Velay [F] 68 E4
Montferrat [F] 108 D4
Montfort [F] 66 B6
Montfort [F] 26 C6
Montfort [F] 42 E5
Montgat [E] 92 E4
Montgenèvre [F] 70 B6
Montgiscard [F] 106 A3
Montgomery [GB] 10 C6
Montguyon [F] 66 D2
Monthermé [F] 44 C1
Monthey [CH] 70 C2
Monthois [F] 44 C3
Monthureaux–sur–Saône [F] 58 B2
Monti [I] 118 D3
Monticelli Terme [I] 110 D3
Montichiari [I] 72 B6

Monticiano [I] 114 F2
Montiel [E] 96 G5
Montier–en–Der [F] 44 C5
Montignac [F] 66 G3
Montigny–le–Roi [F] 58 A2
Montigny–sur–Aube [F] 56 G2
Montijo [E] 94 G1
Montijo [P] 86 B5
Montilla [E] 102 C2
Montivilliers [F] 26 G3
Montlieu–la–Garde [F] 66 D2
Mont–Louis [F] 92 E1
Montluçon [F] 56 C5
Montluel [F] 68 G2
Montmarault [F] 56 C6
Montmédy [F] 44 D3
Montmélian [F] 70 A4
Montmeyan [F] 108 C4
Montmirail [F] 42 C5
Montmirail [F] 42 H4
Montmirey [F] 56 H4
Montmoreau–St–Cybard [F] 66 E2
Montmorillon [F] 54 F4
Montmort [F] 44 A4
Montoire–sur–le–Loir [F] 42 C6
Montoito [P] 94 E2
Montório [E] 82 E5
Montorio al Vomano [I] 116 C3
Montoro [E] 102 D1
Montpellier [F] 106 E4
Montpezat [F] 42 G6
Montpon–Ménestérol [F] 66 E3
Montpont–en–Bresse [F] 56 G6
Montréal [F] 66 D6
Montréal [F] 106 B4
Montréal [F] 56 F3
Montredon–Labessonnie [F] 106 C3
Montréjeau [F] 84 F4
Montrésor [F] 54 G3
Montret [F] 56 G5
Montreuil [F] 28 D3

Montreuil–aux–Lions [F] 42 H3
Montreuil–Bellay [F] 54 E2
Montreux [CH] 70 C1
Montrevault [F] 54 C1
Montrevel [F] 68 G1
Montrichard [F] 54 G2
Montroi / Montroy [E] 98 E5
Mont–roig del Camp [E] 90 H6
Montrond–les–Bains [F] 68 E3
Montrose [GB] 8 F2
Montroy / Montroi [E] 98 E5
Montsalvy [F] 68 B5
Montsauche–les–Settons [F] 56 F3
Montségur [F] 106 A5
Montseny [E] 92 E3
Montsoreau [F] 54 E2
Mont–sous–Vaudrey [F] 56 H5
Monts–s–Guesnes [F] 54 E3
Montsûrs [F] 26 E6
Monza [I] 70 G4
Monze [F] 106 C5
Monzón [E] 90 G3
Monzón de Campos [E] 82 D6
Monzuno [I] 110 F4
Moordorf [D] 18 B4
Moosburg [D] 60 F3
Moosinning [D] 60 E4
Mór [H] 76 B1
Mora [E] 96 F2
Mora [P] 86 D5
Mora [S] 172 G3
Mora [S] 174 C5
Mora, Puerto de la– [E] 102 E4
Morača [YU] 152 E3
Móra d'Ebre [E] 90 H6
Mora de Rubielos [E] 98 E2
Moradillo de Roa [E] 88 G2
Morąg [PL] 22 G3
Mórahalom [H] 76 E4
Moraitika [GR] 132 B2
Móra la Nova [E] 90 H6

N

Náfpaktos [GR] 132 F5
Náfplio [GR] 136 F2
Naglarby [S] 174 C5
Nagłowice [PL] 52 A2
Nagold [D] 58 G2
Nagu / Nauvo [FIN] 176 D5
Nagyatád [H] 74 H4
Nagybajom [H] 74 H4
Nagybaracska [H] 76 C5
Nagycenk [H] 62 F6
Nagycserkesz [H] 64 G5
Nagydorog [H] 76 B3
Nagygyimót [H] 74 H1
Nagyhalász [H] 64 H4
Nagyigmánd [H] 64 A6
Nagyiván [H] 64 F6
Nagykálló [H] 64 H5
Nagykanizsa [H] 74 G4
Nagykáta [H] 76 D1
Nagykónyi [H] 76 B3
Nagykőrös [H] 76 D2
Nagylak [H] 76 F4
Nagylóc [H] 64 D5
Nagymágocs [H] 76 F3
Nagymaros [H] 64 C5
Nagyoroszi [H] 64 C5
Nagyszénás [H] 76 F3
Nagyvázsony [H] 74 H2
Naharros [E] 98 B2
Nahe [D] 18 F3
Naila [D] 46 H3
Nailloux [F] 106 A4
Nailsea [GB] 12 F3
Nailsworth [GB] 12 G3
Naipu [RO] 148 C1
Nairn [GB] 6 E5
Najac [F] 66 H6
Nájera [E] 82 G6
Nakkila [FIN] 176 D2
Nakło nad Notecią [PL] 22 C6
Nakovo [YU] 76 F5
Nakskov [DK] 156 E5
Nälden [S] 182 G2
Nałęczów [PL] 38 D5
Nálepkovo [SK] 64 F2
Näljänkä [FIN] 198 F3
Nalzen [F] 106 A5
Namdalseid [N] 190 C5
Náměšť nad Oslavou [CZ] 50 B6
Námestovo [SK] 50 G5
Namsos [N] 190 C5
Namsskogan [N] 190 D4
Namur [B] 30 D5
Namysłów [PL] 36 D6
Nanclares de la Oca / Langraiz Oka [E] 82 G5
Nancy [F] 44 E5
Nangis [F] 42 G4
Nannestad [N] 172 B5
Nans–les–Pins [F] 108 C5
Nant [F] 106 E3
Nantes [F] 40 F6
Nanteuil–le–Haudouin [F] 42 G3
Nantiat [F] 54 G6
Nantua [F] 68 H2
Nantwich [GB] 10 D5
Náousa [GR] 138 E3
Náoussa [GR] 128 F4
Nápoli [I] 120 E3
Napp [N] 192 B4
Narach [BY] 202 H5
Narberth [GB] 12 D1
Narbolía [I] 118 C5
Narbonne [F] 106 D5
Narbonne–Plage [F] 106 D5
Narbuvollen [N] 182 C4
Narcao [I] 118 B7
Nardo [I] 122 G5
Narechenski Bani [BG] 148 B6
Narew [PL] 24 F6
Narila [FIN] 188 D5
Narkaus [FIN] 196 D8
Narlıca [TR] 146 F4
Narni [I] 116 A4
Naro [I] 126 D4
Naro–Fominsk [RUS] 204 F4

Narol [PL] 52 G2
Narón [E] 78 D4
Närpes / Närpiö [FIN] 186 A4
Närpiö / Närpes [FIN] 186 A4
Narta [HR] 74 G6
Narva [EST] 200 G1
Narva–Jõesuu [EST] 200 G1
Narvik [N] 192 D4
Nås [S] 172 G5
Näsåker [S] 184 E1
Näsäud [RO] 206 C4
Nasbinals [F] 68 C5
Našice [HR] 154 D1
Nasielsk [PL] 38 B2
Näsinge [S] 166 C4
Naso [I] 124 B6
Nassau [D] 46 B2
Nassereith [A] 72 C1
Nässjö [S] 162 D2
Nästansjö [S] 190 F4
Nastola [FIN] 178 B3
Näsviken [S] 174 E1
Natalinci [YU] 150 B1
Nattavaara [S] 198 A1
Nättraby [S] 158 F1
Naturno / Naturns [I] 72 C3
Naturns / Naturno [I] 72 C3
Nauders [A] 72 B2
Nauen [D] 34 D2
Naujoji Akmenė [LT] 200 C6
Naul [IRL] 2 F5
Naumburg [D] 34 B6
Naunhof [D] 34 D5
Naustbukta [N] 190 C4
Naustdal [N] 180 C6
Nauste [N] 180 F3
Nautsi [RUS] 196 E4
Nauvo / Nagu [FIN] 176 D5
Nava [E] 82 C2
Navacerrada [E] 88 F4
Nava de la Asunción [E] 88 E3
Nava del Rey [E] 88 D2
Navahermosa [E] 96 E2
Navalcarnero [E] 88 F6
Navaleno [E] 90 A2
Navalguijo [E] 88 C5
Navalmanzano [E] 88 F3
Navalmoral [E] 88 D5
Navalmoral de la Mata [E] 88 B6
Navalón [E] 98 D6
Navalperal de Pinares [E] 88 E5
Navalvillar de Pela [E] 96 B3
Navan / An Uaimh [IRL] 2 F5
Navarredonda de Gredos [E] 88 C5
Navarrenx [F] 84 D3
Navarrés [E] 98 E5
Navarrete [E] 82 G6
Navàs [E] 92 E3
Navascués / Nabaskoze [E] 84 C4
Navas del Madroño [E] 86 G4
Navas del Rey [E] 88 E5
Navas de San Juan [E] 102 F1
Navatalgordo [E] 88 D5
Navekvaren [S] 168 C5
Navelli [I] 116 C4
Nave Redonda [P] 94 B4
Naverstad [S] 166 C4
Navia [E] 78 F2
Navilly [F] 56 G5
Navlja [RUS] 204 E6
Náxos [GR] 138 E3
Nazaré [P] 86 C3
Nazilli [TR] 144 E5
Ndroq [AL] 128 B3
Nea Anchiálos [GR] 132 H3
Néa Artáki [GR] 134 B5
Néa Epídavros [GR] 136 F2
Néa Fókaia [GR] 130 B6
Néa Kallikráteia [GR] 130 B5

Néa Karváli [GR] 130 D3
Néa Koróni [GR] 136 D4
Neale [IRL] 2 C4
Néa Mádytos [GR] 130 C4
Néa Mákri [GR] 134 C6
Néa Michanióna [GR] 128 H5
Néa Moudanía [GR] 130 B5
Néa Moudaniá [GR] 130 B5
Néa Péramos [GR] 130 D3
Néa Plágia [GR] 130 B5
Neapoli [GR] 136 F5
Neápoli [GR] 140 F4
Neápoli [GR] 128 E5
Néa Poteídaia [GR] 130 B5
Néa Róda [GR] 130 C5
Néa Roúmata [GR] 140 B4
Néa Sánda [GR] 130 G2
Néa Skióni [GR] 130 C6
Néa Stýra [GR] 134 D5
Neath [GB] 12 E2
Néa Tríglia [GR] 130 B5
Neauvic [F] 66 E3
Néa Vissa [GR] 130 H1
Néa Zichni [GR] 130 C3
Nebiler [TR] 144 C2
Nebra [D] 34 B5
Neckarelz [D] 46 D5
Neckargemünd [D] 46 C5
Neckargerach [D] 46 D5
Neckarsteinach [D] 46 C5
Neckarsulm [D] 46 D5
Neda [E] 78 D1
Nedelišče [HR] 74 F4
Nedervetil / Alaveteli [FIN] 198 C1
Neder Vindinge [DK] 156 F4
Nedre Soppero [S] 192 F4
Nedstrand [N] 164 B2
Nędza [PL] 50 E3
Neede [NL] 16 G5
Needham Market [GB] 14 G3
Neermoor [D] 18 B4
Negorci [MK] 128 G3
Negotin [YU] 150 E1
Negotino [MK] 128 F2
Negovanovci [BG] 150 E2
Negrar [I] 72 C6
Negreira [E] 78 B3
Negru Vodă [RO] 148 G1
Neheim–Hüsten [D] 32 C4
Nehoiu [RO] 206 C5
Neiden [N] 196 E3
Nejdek [CZ] 48 D3
Neksø [DK] 158 E4
Nelas [P] 80 C6
Nelidovo [RUS] 204 D4
Nellim [FIN] 196 E4
Nellimö [FIN] 196 E4
Nelson [GB] 10 E3
Neman [RUS] 202 D5
Nembro [I] 70 H4
Neméa [GR] 136 E1
Nemenčinė [LT] 202 G5
Németkér [H] 76 C3
Nemirov [UA] 206 E3
Nemours [F] 42 G5
Nemšová [SK] 64 A2
Nemyriv [UA] 52 G3
Nenagh [IRL] 2 D6
Nendeln [FL] 58 H5
Neochóri [GR] 136 B1
Neochori [GR] 132 E5
Neochóri [GR] 132 E3
Neohóri [GR] 134 C5
Neohóri [GR] 132 F2
Néon Monastíri [GR] 132 G3
Néon Petrítsi [GR] 130 B2
Néos Marmarás [GR] 130 C6
Nepi [I] 114 H4
Nepomuk [CZ] 48 E5
Neptun [RO] 148 G1
Nérac [F] 66 E5
Neratovice [CZ] 48 G3
Neresheim [D] 60 C2
Nereta [LV] 200 E6
Nereto [I] 116 D3

Nerežišča [HR] 152 A2
Neringa [LT] 202 D5
Néris–les–Bains [F] 56 C6
Nerja [E] 102 D5
Nérondes [F] 56 C4
Nerpio [E] 102 H2
Nersingen [D] 60 B3
Nerskogen [N] 180 H3
Nerva [E] 94 F5
Nervesa della Battaglia [I] 72 E5
Nervi [I] 110 B3
Nerviano [I] 70 G4
Nes [N] 170 H4
Nes [N] 170 D1
Nes [NL] 16 F1
Nesbyen [N] 170 G4
Nesebür [BG] 148 F4
Nesflaten [N] 164 C1
Neskaupstaður [IS] 194 G5
Nesle [F] 28 F5
Nesna [N] 190 D2
Nesoddtangen [N] 166 B1
Nespereira [P] 80 C3
Nesseby [N] 196 E2
Nesselwang [D] 60 C5
Nestáni [GR] 136 E2
Nesterov [RUS] 204 D1
Nestório [GR] 128 D5
Nesttun [N] 170 B4
Nesvik [N] 164 A6
Nesviž [BY] 204 A4
Netherwitton [GB] 8 F5
Netolice [CZ] 62 B2
Netretič [HR] 112 G1
Netta [PL] 24 E4
Nettancourt [F] 44 C4
Nettetal [D] 30 F3
Nettuno [I] 120 B1
Neubeckum [D] 32 D3
Neuberg an der Mürz [A] 62 D6
Neubrandenburg [D] 20 D4
Neubukow [D] 20 A3
Neubulach [D] 58 G1
Neuburg [D] 60 H3
Neuburg [D] 50 D2
Neuchâtel [CH] 58 C5
Neu Darchau [D] 18 G5
Neudorf [D] 46 C5
Neudorf–Platendorf [D] 32 H2
Neuenburg [D] 58 E3
Neuenbürg [D] 46 C6
Neuenburg [D] 18 C4
Neuenhaus [D] 16 G4
Neuenkirchen [D] 18 F5
Neuenwalde [D] 18 D4
Neufahrn [D] 60 F3
Neuf–Brisach [F] 58 E3

Neufchâteau [B] 44 D2
Neufchâteau [F] 44 D6
Neufchâtel [F] 44 B2
Neufchâtel–en–Bray [F] 28 C5
Neufelden [A] 62 B3
Neuffen [D] 58 H2
Neugersdorf [D] 48 G1
Neuhaus [D] 46 H4
Neuhaus [D] 46 G2
Neuhaus [D] 60 H3
Neuhaus [D] 18 E3
Neuhaus [D] 32 F4
Neuhaus [D] 18 H5
Neuhausen am Rheinfall [CH] 58 F4
Neuhof [D] 34 E3
Neuhofen an der Krems [A] 62 B4
Neuillé Port–Pierre [F] 54 F1
Neuilly–l'Évêque [F] 58 A3
Neuilly–St–Front [F] 42 H3
Neu–Isenburg [D] 46 C3
Neukalen [D] 20 C4
Neukirch [D] 34 F6
Neukirchen [A] 72 F1
Neukirchen [D] 156 B4
Neukloster [D] 20 A3
Neulengbach [A] 62 E4
Neum [BIH] 152 C3
Neumarkt [A] 74 B2
Neumarkt [A] 60 H5
Neumarkt [D] 46 H5
Neumarkt–St Veit [D] 60 F4
Neu–Moresnet [B] 30 F5
Neumorschen [D] 32 F6
Neu Mukran [D] 20 D2
Neumünster [D] 18 F3
Neunagelberg [A] 62 C3
Neunburg [D] 48 C5
Neung–sur–Beuvron [F] 56 B2
Neunkirchen [A] 62 E6
Neunkirchen [D] 44 G3
Neuötting [D] 60 G4
Neupölla [A] 62 D3
Neuruppin [D] 20 C6
Neusiedl am See [A] 62 G5
Neuss [D] 30 G3
Neustadt [D] 32 E6
Neustadt [D] 60 E2
Neustadt [D] 46 G2
Neustadt [D] 48 B1
Neustadt [D] 58 F3
Neustadt [D] 18 H3
Neustadt [D] 34 C1
Neustadt [D] 34 F6
Neustadt am Rübenberge [D] 32 F2

Neustadt an der Aisch [D] 46 F5
Neustadt an der Waldnaab [D] 48 C4
Neustadt an der Weinstrasse [D] 46 B5
Neustadt–Glewe [D] 20 A5
Neustift [A] 72 D1
Neustrelitz [D] 20 C5
Neuves–Maisons [F] 44 E5
Neuvic [F] 68 B3
Neuville [F] 68 F2
Neuville [F] 54 E3
Neuville–aux–Bois [F] 42 E5
Neuvy [F] 54 H4
Neuvy–sur–Barangeon [F] 56 C3
Neuwied [D] 30 H6
Nevel [RUS] 204 C4
Nevers [F] 56 D4
Nevesinje [BIH] 152 C2
Nevlunghavn [N] 164 G3
Newark–on–Trent [GB] 10 F5
Newbiggin–by–the–Sea [GB] 8 G5
Newbliss [IRL] 2 F4
Newborough [GB] 10 B4
Newbridge / Droichead Nua [IRL] 2 E6
Newburgh [GB] 6 G6
Newburgh [GB] 8 E2
Newbury [GB] 12 H4
Newby Bridge [GB] 10 D2
Newcastle [GB] 2 G4
Newcastle Emlyn [GB] 10 A6
Newcastleton [GB] 8 E5
Newcastle–under–Lyme [GB] 10 E5
Newcastle upon Tyne [GB] 8 G6
Newcastle West [IRL] 4 C3
New Cumnock [GB] 8 D4
Newent [GB] 12 G3
New Galloway [GB] 8 D5
Newhaven [GB] 14 E6
Newinn [IRL] 4 D4
Newmarket [GB] 14 F3
Newmarket [IRL] 4 C4
Newmarket–on–Fergus [IRL] 2 C6
New Pitsligo [GB] 6 G5
Newport [GB] 4 H6
Newport [GB] 14 E5
Newport [GB] 10 D5
Newport [GB] 12 F3
Newport [IRL] 2 C3

Newport [IRL] 4 D3
Newport-on-Tay [GB] 8 F2
Newport Pagnell [GB] 14 E3
Newquay [GB] 12 C4
New Quay [GB] 10 B6
New Romney [GB] 14 F5
New Ross [IRL] 4 F4
Newry [GB] 2 F4
Newton Abbot [GB] 12 E5
Newtonferry / Port nan Long [GB] 6 A3
Newtonmore [GB] 6 D6
Newton Stewart [GB] 8 C5
Newtown [GB] 10 C6
Newtownabbey [GB] 2 G3
Newtownards [GB] 2 G3
Newtown Butler [GB] 2 E4
Newtownhamilton [GB] 2 F4
Newtownmountkennedy [IRL] 4 G3
Newtownstewart [GB] 2 F3
Nexon [F] 66 G2
Neyland [GB] 12 D2
Nežilovo [MK] 128 E2
Nežin [UA] 204 D7
Nibe [DK] 160 D4
Nicaj-Shalë [AL] 150 A6
Nicastro [I] 124 D5
Nice [F] 108 E4
Nickelsdorf [A] 62 G5
Nicolosi [I] 126 G3
Nicosia [I] 126 F3
Nicotera [I] 124 C6
Nidderau [D] 46 D2
Nidzica [PL] 22 G5
Niebla [E] 94 F5
Nieborow [PL] 36 H3
Niebüll [D] 156 B4
Nieby [D] 156 C5
Niechorze [PL] 20 G3
Niedalino [PL] 20 H3
Niederalteich [D] 60 G3
Niederau [A] 60 F6
Niederaula [D] 46 E1
Niederbronn-les-Bains [F] 44 H5
Niederkrüchten [D] 30 F3
Nieder Stotzingen [D] 60 C3
Niederwinkling [D] 60 G2
Nieder-Wöllstadt [D] 46 C2
Niedrzwica Duża [PL] 38 E6
Niemcza [PL] 50 C2
Niemegk [D] 34 D3
Niemisel [S] 198 B2
Niemisjärvi [FIN] 186 H4
Niemodlin [PL] 50 D2
Nienburg [D] 32 F1
Nienhagen [D] 20 B3
Niepołomice [PL] 52 B4
Nieppe [F] 28 F3
Nierstein [D] 46 C3
Niesky [D] 34 G5
Nieszawa [PL] 36 F1
Nieuil [F] 54 E6
Nieuweschans [NL] 16 H2
Nieuwpoort [B] 28 F1
Nigrán [E] 78 B5
Nigríta [GR] 130 B3
Niinimäki [FIN] 188 D3
Niinisalo [FIN] 186 C6
Niinivesi [FIN] 186 C6
Níjar [E] 102 G5
Nijkerk [NL] 16 E5
Nijmegen [NL] 16 E6
Nijverdal [NL] 16 G4
Níkaia [GR] 132 G2
Nikel' [RUS] 196 F3
Níki [GR] 128 E4
Nikiá [GR] 142 C4
Nikifóros [GR] 130 D3
Nikíssiani [GR] 130 D3
Nikitas [GR] 130 C5
Nikkaluokta [S] 192 E5
Nikkaroinen [FIN] 178 A1
Nikkeby [N] 192 F1
Nikola Kozlevo [BG] 148 E2
Nikolayevo [RUS] 200 H2

Nikopol [BG] 148 B2
Nikopol' [UA] 206 G4
Nikšić [YU] 152 E3
Nilsiä [FIN] 188 D1
Nîmes [F] 106 F3
Niméfea [GR] 130 F2
Nin [HR] 112 G4
Ninove [B] 28 H3
Niort [F] 54 D4
Nirou Khani [GR] 140 E4
Niš [YU] 150 D3
Nisa [P] 86 E4
Nisákio [GR] 132 B2
Niscemi [I] 126 F4
Niška Banja [YU] 150 D3
Niskakoski [RUS] 196 E4
Nisko [PL] 52 E2
Nissi [EST] 200 D2
Nissilä [FIN] 198 E5
Nitaure [LV] 200 E5
Nitlax [FIN] 176 F6
Nitra [SK] 64 A4
Nitrianske Pravno [SK] 64 B2
Nitrianske Rudno [SK] 64 B3
Nitry [F] 56 F2
Nittedal [N] 172 B5
Nittenau [D] 48 C6
Nittendorf [D] 60 F2
Nittkvarn [S] 166 G1
Nivá [DK] 156 G2
Nivala [FIN] 198 D5
Nivelles [B] 28 H3
Niversac [F] 66 F3
Nižná [SK] 50 H6
Nižná Boca [SK] 64 D2
Nizza Monferrato [I] 108 H2
Njegoševo [YU] 76 D6
Njurunda [S] 184 E5
Noailles [F] 28 D6
Noain (Elorz) [E] 84 B4
Noale [I] 72 E6
Noceda [E] 78 F5
Nocera [I] 120 E3
Nocera Umbra [I] 116 B2
Noceto [I] 110 D2
Noci [I] 122 E3
Nocito [E] 84 D6
Nodeland [N] 164 D5
Nods [F] 58 B5
Noé [F] 84 H4
Noépoli [I] 122 C5
Noeux [F] 28 E3
Nogales [E] 94 G2
Nogara [I] 110 F1
Nogaro [F] 84 F2
Nogent [F] 56 H2
Nogent-le-Roi [F] 42 E4
Nogent-le-Rotrou [F] 26 G6
Nogent-sur-Seine [F] 42 H5
Nogersund [S] 158 E2
Noginsk [RUS] 204 F4
Nohfelden [D] 44 G3
Noia [E] 78 B3
Noirétable [F] 68 E2
Noirmoutier-en-l'Ile [F] 54 A2
Noja [E] 82 F3
Nokia [FIN] 176 F1
Nol [S] 160 H1
Nola [I] 120 E3
Nol Alafors [S] 160 H1
Nolay [F] 56 F4
Noli [I] 108 H3
Nomeny [F] 44 E5
Nomexy [F] 44 E6
Nömme [EST] 200 E2
Nonancourt [F] 26 H5
Nonant-le-Pin [F] 26 G5
Nonantola [I] 110 F3
Nonnenhorn [D] 58 H4
Nontron [F] 66 F2
Nonza [F] 114 C2
Noordwijk aan Zee [NL] 16 C4
Noormarkku [FIN] 176 D1
Nora [S] 166 H2
Nora [S] 168 B6
Nørager [DK] 160 D4

Norberg [S] 168 B1
Norcia [I] 116 B3
Nordausques [F] 14 H6
Nordberg [N] 180 F5
Nordborg [DK] 156 C4
Nordby [DK] 156 E1
Nordby [DK] 156 A3
Norddeich [D] 16 H1
Nordeide [N] 170 C1
Norden [D] 16 H1
Nordenham [D] 18 D4
Norderney [D] 18 B3
Norderstedt [D] 18 F4
Nordfjordeid [N] 180 C5
Nordfold [N] 192 C5
Nordhalben [D] 46 H2
Nordhausen [D] 32 H5
Nordhorn [D] 16 H4
Nordkapp [N] 196 C1
Nordkirchen [D] 32 C3
Nordkisa [N] 172 C5
Nordkjosbotn [N] 192 E3
Nordli [N] 190 D5
Nordmaling [S] 184 H1
Nordmark [S] 166 F1
Nordmela [N] 192 C3
Nordre Osen [N] 172 D2
Nordskot [N] 192 C5
Nordskov [DK] 156 E2
Nordwalde [D] 16 H5
Noresund [N] 170 G4
Norg [NL] 16 G2
Norheimsund [N] 170 C4
Norrahammar [S] 162 D2
Norraker [S] 190 E5
Norra Mellby [S] 158 C1
Norra Tresund [S] 190 F4
Norrboda [S] 174 G5
Norrboda [S] 172 H3
Norrby [S] 190 G4
Nørre Åby [DK] 156 D3
Nørre Alslev [DK] 156 F5
Norre Bergnäss [S] 190 G2
Nørre Broby [DK] 156 D3
Nørre Lyndelse [DK] 156 D3
Nørre Nebel [DK] 156 A2
Nørre Snede [DK] 156 C1
Nørresundby [DK] 160 D3
Nørre Vejrup [DK] 156 B2
Nørre Vorupør [DK] 160 B4
Norr Hede [S] 182 F4
Norrhult [S] 162 E4
Norrköping [S] 168 B5
Norrnäs [FIN] 186 A4
Norrskedika [S] 174 G5
Norrsundet [S] 174 E3
Norrtälje [S] 168 E2
Norsholm [S] 168 B5
Norsjö [S] 190 H4
Norsjövallen [S] 190 H4
Nort [F] 40 F6
Nörten-Hardenberg [D] 32 G4
Northallerton [GB] 10 F2
Northam [GB] 12 D3
Northampton [GB] 14 D2
North Berwick [GB] 8 F3
Northeim [D] 32 G4
Northiam [GB] 14 F5
Northleach [GB] 12 H2
Northwall [GB] 6 G1
North Walsham [GB] 14 G2
Northwich [GB] 10 D4
Norton [GB] 10 G3
Nortorf [D] 18 F2
Norwich [GB] 14 G2
Nosovka [UA] 206 F1
Nossebro [S] 166 D6
Nössemark [S] 166 C3
Nossen [D] 34 E6
Nötö [FIN] 176 D6
Noto [I] 126 G5
Notodden [N] 164 F2
Nøtterøy [N] 164 H3
Nottingham [GB] 10 F5
Nottuln [D] 16 H6
Nouan-le-Fuzelier [F] 56 B2

Nouans-les-Fontaines [F] 54 A3
Nouvion [F] 28 D4
Nova [EST] 200 D2
Nova [H] 74 F3
Nová Baňa [SK] 64 B4
Nová Bystřice [CZ] 62 D2
Novachene [BG] 150 G4
Novaci [MK] 128 E3
Nova Crnja [YU] 76 F6
Novaféltria [I] 110 H5
Nova Gorica [SLO] 72 H5
Nova Gradiska [HR] 154 C1
Nova Kahovka [UA] 206 G4
Novaja Kahovka [UA] 206 G4
Novaja Ladoga [RUS] 204 D1
Novajidrány [H] 64 G4
Nováky [SK] 64 B3
Nova Levante / Welschnofen [I] 72 D3
Novalja [HR] 112 F4
Nová Paka [CZ] 48 H2
Nova Pazova [YU] 154 G2
Novara [I] 70 F5
Novara di Sicilia [I] 124 A7
Novasil' [RUS] 204 F6
Novate Mezzola [I] 70 H3
Nova Topola [BIH] 154 C2
Nova Varoš [YU] 150 A3
Nova Zagora [BG] 148 D5
Nové Hrady [CZ] 62 C3
Novelda [I] 104 D2
Novellara [I] 110 E2
Nové Město nad Metují [CZ] 50 B3
Nové Mesto nad Váhom [SK] 64 A3
Nové Město na Moravě [CZ] 50 B5
Noventa Vicentina [I] 110 G1
Noves [F] 106 G3
Nové Sady [SK] 64 A4
Nové Strašecí [CZ] 48 E3
Nové Zámky [SK] 64 B5
Novgorod [RUS] 204 C2
Novgorodka [RUS] 200 H4
Novgorod-Severski [UA] 204 D6
Novi Bečej [YU] 76 E6
Novi di Módena [I] 110 E2
Novi Dojran [MK] 128 H3
Novigrad [HR] 112 G5
Novigrad [HR] 112 D1
Novigrad Podravski [HR] 74 G5
Novi Han [BG] 150 G5
Novi Kazarci [YU] 76 F5
Novi Kneževac [YU] 76 E5
Novi Krichim [BG] 148 B6
Novi Ligure [I] 110 A2
Novi Marof [HR] 74 F5
Novion-Porcien [F] 28 H6
Novi Pazar [BG] 148 E2
Novi Pazar [YU] 150 B4
Novi Sad [YU] 154 F1
Novi Travnik [BIH] 154 C4
Novi Vinodolski [HR] 112 F2
Novoarhangelsk [UA] 206 E3
Novo Brdo [YU] 150 C5
Novograd-Volynski [UA] 206 D2
Novogrudok [BY] 204 A5
Novo Mesto [SLO] 74 D6
Novo Miloševo [YU] 76 E6
Novomoskovsk [RUS] 204 F5
Novomoskovsk [UA] 206 G3
Novorzhev [RUS] 200 H4
Novoselë [AL] 128 A5
Novoselets [BG] 148 D5
Novo Selo [BG] 150 D1
Novo Selo [BG] 148 D2
Novo Selo [MK] 128 H2
Novosel'ye [RUS] 200 H3

Novosokolniki [RUS] 204 C4
Novoukrainka [UA] 206 F3
Novoukraïnka [UA] 52 H2
Novovolyns'k [UA] 52 H1
Novovoroncovka [UA] 206 G4
Novozybkov [RUS] 204 D6
Novska [HR] 154 B1
Nový Bohumín [CZ] 50 F4
Nový Bor [CZ] 48 G2
Novy Bug [UA] 206 F4
Nový Bydžov [CZ] 48 H3
Novy Bykov [UA] 206 F2
Nový Jičín [CZ] 50 E5
Nový Knín [CZ] 48 F4
Nowa Brzeźnica [PL] 36 G6
Nowa Cerekwia [PL] 50 E4
Nowa Dęba [PL] 52 D2
Nowa Karczma [PL] 22 D3
Nowa Karczma [PL] 22 F2
Nowa Ruda [PL] 50 C2
Nowa Sarzyna [PL] 52 E3
Nowa Słupia [PL] 52 C1
Nowa Sól [PL] 36 A4
Nowe [PL] 22 E4
Nowe Brzesko [PL] 52 B3
Nowe Miasteczko [PL] 36 A4
Nowe Miasto [PL] 36 D3
Nowe Miasto Lubawskie [PL] 22 F5
Nowe Miasto nad Pilicą [PL] 38 B5
Nowe Skalmierzyce [PL] 36 E4
Nowe Warpno [PL] 20 E4
Nowogard [PL] 20 G4
Nowogród [PL] 24 C5
Nowogród Bobrzański [PL] 34 H4
Nowogrodziec [PL] 34 H6
Nowosielec [PL] 52 E2
Nowowola [PL] 24 F4
Nowy Duninów [PL] 36 G2
Nowy Dwór [PL] 24 F4
Nowy Dwór Gdański [PL] 22 E3
Nowy Dwór Mazowiecki [PL] 38 B2
Nowy Korczyn [PL] 52 C3
Nowy Majdan [PL] 52 F2
Nowy Sącz [PL] 52 C5
Nowy Staw [PL] 22 E3
Nowy Targ [PL] 52 A5
Nowy Tomyśl [PL] 36 B3
Nowy Wiśnicz [PL] 52 B4
Nowy Zmigród [PL] 52 D5
Noyant [F] 42 B6
Noyers [F] 56 F2
Noyers-sur-Jabron [F] 108 C3
Noyon [F] 28 F6
Nozay [F] 40 F5
Nozeroy [F] 58 B6
Nubledo [E] 78 H3
Nueva-Carteya [E] 102 C2
Nuévalos [E] 90 C4
Nuevo Baztán [E] 88 G6
Nuijamaa [FIN] 178 E2
Nuits-St-Georges [F] 56 G4
Nules [E] 98 F4
Nulvi [I] 118 C3
Numana [I] 116 C1
Numancia [E] 90 B3
Nummela [FIN] 176 G4
Nummi [FIN] 176 F4
Nummijärvi [FIN] 186 C4
Nummikoski [FIN] 186 C5
Nunnanen [FIN] 192 H4
Nunnanlahti [FIN] 188 E1
Nuneaton [GB] 14 D1
Nuño Gómez [E] 88 D6
Nunspeet [NL] 16 F4
Nuorgam [FIN] 196 D2
Nuoro [I] 118 D4
Nur [PL] 38 D1
Nurallao [I] 118 D5
Nuraminis [I] 118 C6

Nürburg [D] 30 G6
Nurmaa [FIN] 178 C1
Nurmes [FIN] 198 G6
Nurmijärvi [FIN] 176 H4
Nurmijärvi [FIN] 198 G6
Nurmo [FIN] 186 C3
Nurmulža [LV] 200 C5
Nürnberg [D] 46 G5
Nürtingen [D] 58 H1
Nusret [TR] 144 D1
Nuštar [HR] 154 E1
Nutheim [N] 164 F2
Nuttlar [D] 32 D5
Nuupas [FIN] 198 D2
N. Vi [S] 162 E2
Nyåker [S] 190 H6
Nybergsund [N] 172 D2
Nyborg [DK] 156 E3
Nybro [S] 162 F5
Nyby [DK] 156 G4
Nydrí [GR] 132 D4
Nye [S] 162 E3
Nyékládháza [H] 64 F5
Nyhammar [S] 172 H5
Nyhem [S] 184 C3
Nyírábrány [H] 64 H6
Nyíracsád [H] 64 H6
Nyíradony [H] 64 H5
Nyírbátor [H] 206 B3
Nyírbogát [H] 64 H5
Nyíregyháza [H] 64 H5
Nyírtelek [H] 64 G5
Nyírtura [H] 64 H5
Nykarleby / Uusikaarlepyy [FIN] 186 C1
Nykøbing [DK] 20 B1
Nykøbing [DK] 156 F2
Nykøbing [DK] 160 C4
Nyköping [S] 168 C5
Nykrogen [S] 168 B1
Nykroppa [S] 166 G2
Nykvarn [S] 168 D3
Nyland [S] 184 F3
Nymburk [CZ] 48 G3
Nymindegab [DK] 156 A1
Nynäshamn [S] 168 D4
Nyon [CH] 70 B1
Nyons [F] 106 H2
Nýrsko [CZ] 48 D6
Nyrud [N] 196 E4
Nysa [PL] 50 D2
Nysäter [S] 166 E3
Nyskoga [S] 172 E4
Nyskolla [N] 172 B2
Nysted [DK] 20 B1
Nystova [N] 170 E2
Nytrøa [N] 182 B4

O

Oakham [GB] 10 F6
Oandu [EST] 200 F1
Oanes [N] 164 B3
Oban [GB] 8 C1
O Barco de Valdeorras [E] 78 E5
Obbola [S] 198 A6
Obejo [E] 96 C6
Obeliai [LT] 202 G3
Oberammergau [D] 60 D6
Oberau [D] 60 D6
Oberaudorf [D] 60 F6
Oberdrauburg [A] 72 G3
Obergrafendorf [A] 62 D4
Obergünzburg [D] 60 C5
Obergurgl [A] 72 C2
Oberhausen [D] 30 G3
Oberhof [D] 46 G1
Oberhofen [CH] 70 E1
Oberjoch [D] 60 C6
Oberkirch [D] 58 F1
Oberkochen [D] 60 B2
Obernai [F] 44 G4
Obernberg [A] 60 H4
Obernburg [D] 46 D4
Oberndorf [A] 60 G5
Oberndorf [D] 58 G2
Obernzell [D] 62 A3
Oberpullendorf [A] 74 F1
Oberriet [CH] 58 H5

Ober-Roden [D] 46 C3
Obersickte [D] 32 H3
Obersontheim [D] 46 E6
Oberstaufen [D] 60 B6
Oberstdorf [D] 60 B6
Obersuhl [D] 32 F6
Obertauern [A] 72 H1
Obertraubling [D] 60 F2
Obertraun [A] 62 A6
Obervellach [A] 72 G2
Oberviechtach [D] 48 C5
Oberwald [CH] 70 F2
Oberwart [A] 74 F1
Oberwesel [D] 46 B3
Oberwiesenthal [D] 48 D2
Oberwölz [A] 74 B2
Oberzeiring [A] 74 C1
Óbidos [P] 86 B3
Obing [D] 60 F5
Objat [F] 66 G3
Objazda [PL] 22 B2
Öblarn [A] 62 B6
Oblęcin [PL] 52 E1
Obninsk [RUS] 204 F4
Obnova [BG] 148 B3
Ö. Bodane [S] 166 D4
O Bolo [E] 78 E5
Oborishte [BG] 148 A5
Oborniki [PL] 36 C2
Oborniki Śląskie [PL] 36 C6
Obory [CZ] 48 F5
Oboyan' [RUS] 204 F7
Obrenovac [YU] 154 G3
Obrochishte [BG] 148 G2
Obrovac [HR] 152 A1
Obrovac [HR] 112 G5
Obsteig [A] 72 C1
Obzor [BG] 148 F3
Ocaklı [TR] 146 B4
Očakov [UA] 206 F4
Ocaña [E] 96 G1
O Carballiño [E] 78 C4
Occhiobello [I] 110 G2
Ochagavía / Otsagi [E] 84 C4
Ochojec [PL] 50 F3
Ochsenfurt [D] 46 E4
Ochsenhausen [D] 60 B4
Ochthoniá [GR] 134 C4
Ochtrup [D] 16 H5
Ockelbo [S] 174 E3
Ocrkavlje [BIH] 152 D2
Ócsa [H] 76 C1
Öcsöd [H] 76 E2
Odda [N] 170 C5
Odder [DK] 156 D1
Oddesund [DK] 160 B5
Ödeby [S] 166 H3
Odeceixe [P] 94 B4
Odeleite [P] 94 D5
Odelzhausen [D] 60 D4
Odemira [P] 94 B3
Ödemiş [TR] 144 E4
Odensbacken [S] 166 H3
Odense [DK] 156 D3
Odensvi [S] 162 F2
Oderberg [D] 34 F1
Oderljunga [S] 158 C1
Oderzo [I] 72 F5
Ödeshög [S] 166 G6
Odessa [UA] 206 E5
Odiham [GB] 14 D4
Odivelas [P] 86 B5
Odojev [RUS] 204 F5
Odolanów [PL] 36 D5
Odorheiu Secuiesc [RO] 206 C5
Odry [CZ] 50 E5
Odrzywół [PL] 38 B5
Ødsted [DK] 156 C2
Odum [DK] 160 E6
Odžaci [YU] 154 E1
Odžak [BIH] 154 D2
Odžak [YU] 152 E2
Odziena [LV] 200 E5
Oebisfelde [D] 34 A2
Oederan [D] 48 D1
Oeding [D] 16 G6
Oelde [D] 32 D3
Oelsnitz [D] 48 C2
Oettingen [D] 46 F6
Oetz [A] 72 C1

Ófehértó [H] 64 H5
Offenbach [D] 46 C3
Offenburg [D] 44 H6
Offida [I] 116 C2
Ofir [P] 80 B3
Ofte [N] 164 E2
Ogenbargen [D] 18 C4
Ogliastro Cilento [I] 120 F4
Ogre [LV] 200 E5
Ogrodzieniec [PL] 50 G2
O Grove [E] 78 B4
Ogulin [HR] 112 G2
Ohlava [FIN] 198 D3
Ohrdruf [D] 46 G1
Ohrid [MK] 128 D3
Öhringen [D] 46 D5
Ohs [S] 162 D4
Oía [GR] 138 F5
Oijärvi [FIN] 198 D3
Oikarainen [FIN] 196 D8
Oinói [GR] 134 B6
Oiron [F] 54 E3
Oirschot [NL] 30 E2
Oisemont [F] 28 D4
Oissel [F] 28 B6
Oisterwijk [NL] 16 D6
Oítilon [GR] 136 E5
Oitti [FIN] 176 H3
Oituz, Pasul- [RO] 206 C5
Öjaby [S] 162 D4
Ojakylä [FIN] 198 E4
Ojcowo [PL] 50 H3
Öjebyn [S] 198 B3
Ojén [E] 102 B5
Okalewo [PL] 22 F6
Okehampton [GB] 12 D4
Oker [D] 32 G3
Oklaj [HR] 112 H5
Okol [AL] 150 A6
Okonek [PL] 22 B5
Okonin [PL] 22 E5
Okopy Nowe [PL] 38 G5
Oksakoski [FIN] 186 E1
Oksböl [DK] 156 A2
Oksdøl [N] 190 C5
Øksendrup [DK] 156 E4
Øksfjord [N] 192 F1
Okučani [HR] 154 C1
Okuninka [PL] 38 F4
Ólafsfjörður [IS] 194 E2
Ólafsvík [IS] 194 B3
Ö. Lagnö [S] 168 E2
Olaine [LV] 200 D5
Olargues [F] 106 D4
Oława [PL] 50 D1
Olazagutia / Olazti [E] 82 H5
Olazti / Olazagutia [E] 82 H5
Olbernhau [D] 48 E2
Ólbia [I] 118 E3
Oldcastle [IRL] 2 E5
Oldeide [N] 180 B5
Olden [N] 180 D5
Oldenburg [D] 18 C5
Oldenburg [D] 18 H2
Oldenzaal [NL] 16 G5
Olderdalen [N] 192 F2
Olderfjord [N] 196 C2
Oldham [GB] 10 E4
Oldmeldrum [GB] 6 F6
Old Warden [GB] 14 E3
Oleby [S] 172 E5
Olecko [PL] 24 D3
Oléggio [I] 70 F4
Oleiros [E] 78 B3
Oleiros [P] 86 E3
Ølen [N] 164 B1
Olesa de Montserrat [E] 92 D4
Oleśnica [PL] 36 D6
Olesno [PL] 50 F1
Oleszyce [PL] 52 F3
Oletta [F] 114 C3
Olette [F] 92 F1
Olevsk [UA] 204 B7
Ølgod [DK] 156 B2
Olhão [P] 94 C6
Olhava [FIN] 198 D3
Oliana [E] 92 D2
Olíena [I] 118 D4
Ólimbos [GR] 140 H2

Olite [E] 84 B5
Oliva [E] 98 F6
Oliva de la Frontera [E] 94 F3
Oliva de Mérida [E] 94 H2
Olivares de Júcar [E] 98 B3
Oliveira de Azeméis [P] 80 B5
Oliveira de Frades [P] 80 C5
Oliveira do Bairro [P] 80 B5
Oliveira do Hospital [P] 86 E2
Olivenza [E] 94 F2
Olivet [F] 42 E6
Olivone [CH] 70 G2
Olkusz [PL] 50 G3
Ollaberry [GB] 6 G3
Ollerton [GB] 10 F5
Ollerup [DK] 156 D4
Olliergues [F] 68 D2
Öllölä [FIN] 188 G3
Ölmbrotorp [S] 166 H3
Olmedilla de Alarcón [E] 98 B3
Olmedillo de Roa [E] 88 G2
Olmedo [E] 88 E3
Olmedo [I] 118 B3
Olmeto [F] 114 B5
Olmillos de Sasamón [E] 82 E5
Olney [GB] 14 E2
Olofström [S] 158 E1
Olomouc [CZ] 50 D5
Olonzac [F] 106 C4
Oloron-Ste-Marie [F] 84 D3
Olot [E] 92 F2
Olovo [BIH] 154 E4
Olpe [D] 32 C5
Øls [DK] 160 D5
Olsätter [S] 166 F2
Olsberg [D] 32 D5
Ölserud [S] 166 E4
Olshammar [S] 166 G4
Olst [NL] 16 F4
Olsztyn [PL] 22 H4
Olsztyn [PL] 50 G2
Olsztynek [PL] 22 G4
Olszyna [PL] 34 G4
Olszyna [PL] 34 H6
Oltedal [N] 164 B3
Olten [CH] 58 E5
Olteni [RO] 148 B1
Oltenita [RO] 148 D1
Olteren [N] 192 E3
Oltre il Colle [I] 70 H4
Olula del Río [E] 102 H4
Ólvega [E] 90 C3
Olvera [E] 102 A3
Olympía [GR] 136 C2
Olympías [GR] 130 C4
Olýmpoi [GR] 134 G5
Omagh [GB] 2 F3
Omalós [GR] 140 C5
Omegna [I] 70 F3
Ömerköy [TR] 146 D5
Omiš [HR] 152 A2
Omišalj [HR] 112 E2
Ommen [NL] 16 G4
Omoljica [YU] 154 H2
Ömossa / Metsälä [FIN] 186 B5
Omurtag [BG] 148 D3
Oña [E] 82 F5
Oñati [E] 82 H4
Onchan [GBM] 10 C2
Onda [E] 98 F3
Ondara [E] 104 F1
Ondarroa [E] 82 H4
Oneşti [RO] 206 D5
Onguera [E] 82 D2
Onkamo [FIN] 188 G3
Onkamo [FIN] 196 F7
Onkiniemi [FIN] 178 B1
Onnaing [F] 28 G4
Onsaker [N] 170 H4
Onsala [S] 160 G3
Onsevig [DK] 156 E4
Ontinyent [E] 98 E6
Ontojoki [FIN] 198 F5

Ontur [E] 98 C6
Oola [IRL] 4 D4
Oostburg [NL] 28 G1
Oosterbeek [NL] 16 F5
Oosterend [NL] 16 E1
Oosterhout [NL] 16 D6
Oosterwolde [NL] 16 G3
Oostmalle [B] 30 D3
Ootmarsum [NL] 16 G4
Opaka [BG] 148 D2
Opalenica [PL] 36 B3
Opařany [CZ] 48 F5
Opatija [HR] 112 E1
Opatów [PL] 36 E6
Opatów [PL] 52 D1
Opatówek [PL] 36 E4
Opatowiec [PL] 52 B3
Opava [CZ] 50 E4
Opinan [GB] 6 C3
Opladen [D] 30 G4
Opočno [CZ] 50 B3
Opoczno [PL] 38 A5
Opole [PL] 50 E2
Opole Lubelskie [PL] 38 D6
Oporów [PL] 36 G3
O Porriño [E] 78 B5
Opovo [YU] 154 G2
Oppach [D] 34 G6
Oppaker [N] 172 C5
Oppdal [N] 170 B2
Oppdal [N] 180 H3
Oppegård [N] 166 B1
Oppenau [D] 58 F2
Oppenheim [D] 46 C3
Opphaug [N] 190 B6
Oppheid [N] 192 C4
Oppheim [N] 170 C3
Óppido Lucano [I] 120 H3
Óppido Mamertina [I] 124 C7
Oppola [RUS] 188 G5
Opuzen [HR] 152 B3
Ora / Auer [I] 72 D4
Oradea [RO] 76 H2
Orahovac [YU] 150 B6
Orahovica [HR] 154 D1
Oraison [F] 108 C3
Orajärvi [FIN] 192 H6
Orange [F] 106 G3
Orani [I] 118 D4
Oranienbaum [D] 34 C4
Oranienburg [D] 34 E1
Oranmore [IRL] 2 C5
Oraovica [YU] 150 D4
Orašac [MK] 150 D4
Orasi [F] 114 B6
Orašje [BIH] 154 E2
Orăştie [RO] 206 B5
Oravainen / Oravais [FIN] 186 C2
Oravais / Oravainen [FIN] 186 C2
Oravi [FIN] 188 E4
Oravikoski [FIN] 188 D3
Oravisalo [FIN] 188 F3
Oravița [RO] 206 A6
Oravská Polhora [SK] 50 G5
Oravský Podzámok [SK] 50 G6
Ørbæk [DK] 156 E3
Orbassano [I] 70 D6
Orbe [CH] 58 C6
Orbec [F] 26 G4
Orbetello [I] 114 F4
Orbey [F] 58 D2
Ørby [DK] 156 E1
Ørbyhus [S] 174 F5
Orcera [E] 102 G1
Orches [F] 54 F3
Orchies [F] 28 F3
Orchómenos [GR] 132 H5
Orciéres [F] 70 A6
Ordes [E] 78 C2
Ordino [AND] 84 H6
Orduña [E] 82 G4

Örebro [S] 166 H3
Orechovno [RUS] 200 H2
Öregcsertő [H] 76 C4
Öregrund [S] 174 G5
Orehoved [DK] 156 F4
Orel [RUS] 204 F6
Ören [TR] 144 G2
Ören [TR] 142 D2
Ören [TR] 144 C2
Örencik [TR] 144 G1
Orense / Ourense [E] 78 C5
Oreoí [GR] 134 A3
Oresak [BG] 148 B4
Orestiáda [GR] 130 H1
Orford [GB] 14 G3
Orgáni [GR] 130 G2
Orgaz [E] 96 F2
Orgelet [F] 56 H6
Orgenvika [N] 170 G5
Orgeval [F] 42 F3
Orgon [F] 106 H4
Orgosolo [I] 118 D4
Orgovány [H] 76 D3
Orhaneli [TR] 146 F5
Orhangazi [TR] 146 F4
Orhaniye [TR] 130 H3
Orhanlar [TR] 146 D5
Orhei [MD] 206 E4
Ør. Hvidbjerg [DK] 160 C4
Oria [E] 102 H4
Oria [I] 122 F4
Orihuela [E] 104 D3
Orihuela del Tremedal [E] 98 D1
Orikum [AL] 128 A6
Orimattila [FIN] 178 B3
Oriní [GR] 130 C3
Orio [E] 84 B2
Oriolo [I] 122 D5
Oripää [FIN] 176 E3
Orissaare [EST] 200 C3
Oristano [I] 118 C5
Orivesi [FIN] 186 E6
Orizare [BG] 148 F4
Ørjarvik [N] 180 E2
Ørje [N] 166 C2
Órjiva [E] 102 E5
Orkanger [N] 180 H1
Örkelljunga [S] 158 C1
Örkény [H] 76 D2
Orléans [F] 42 E6
Orlik nad Vltavou [CZ] 48 F5
Orlovat [YU] 154 G1
Orly [F] 42 F4
Orlyak [BG] 148 F2
Ormanlı [TR] 146 D2
Ormea [I] 108 G3
Ormemyr [N] 164 F1
Órmos [GR] 138 D1
Órmos [GR] 128 H5
Órmos Panagías [GR] 130 C5
Ormož [SLO] 74 E4
Ormsjö [S] 190 F5
Ormskirk [GB] 10 D4
Ornans [F] 58 B5
Ornavasso [I] 70 F3
Ørnes [N] 190 D4
Ørnes [N] 190 D1
Orneta [PL] 22 G3
Ørnhøj [DK] 160 B6
Örnsköldsvik [S] 184 G2
Orolik [HR] 154 E1
Oron-la-Ville [CH] 70 C1
Oropesa [E] 88 C6
Oropesa del Mar / Orpesa [E] 98 G3
Orosei [I] 118 E4
Orosháza [H] 76 F3
Oroszlány [H] 64 B6
Oroszló [H] 76 B4
Orpesa / Oropesa del Mar [E] 98 G3
Orpington [GB] 14 E4
Orrefors [S] 162 F5
Orroli [I] 118 D6

Orsa [S] 172 G3
Orša [BY] 204 C5
Orsara di Puglia [I] 120 G2
Orscholz [D] 44 F3
Orsebo [S] 162 E1
Orsières [CH] 70 C3
Örsjö [S] 162 F5
Ørslev [DK] 156 G4
Örslösa [S] 166 E5
Orsogna [I] 116 D5
Orşova [RO] 206 A6
Orsoya [BG] 150 F2
Ørsta [N] 180 C4
Ørsted [DK] 160 E5
Örsundsbro [S] 168 D2
Ort [A] 60 H4
Ortaca [TR] 142 F3
Ortaca [TR] 146 B5
Ortakent [TR] 142 C2
Ortaklar [TR] 144 D5
Orta Nova [I] 120 G2
Ortaoba [TR] 146 C5
Orta S Giúlio [I] 70 F4
Orte [I] 116 A4
Ortenberg [D] 46 D2
Ortenburg [D] 60 H3
Orth [A] 62 F4
Orthez [F] 84 D2
Orthovoúni [GR] 132 E1
Ortigueira [E] 78 E1
Ortisei / St Ulrich [I] 72 D3
Ortona [I] 116 E4
Ortrand [D] 34 E6
Örträsk [S] 190 H5
Ortueri [I] 118 C5
Ørum [DK] 160 E5
Ørum [DK] 160 D5
Orume [I] 118 D4
Ørvella [N] 164 F2
Orvieto [I] 114 H3
Orvinio [I] 116 B5
Oryakhovo [BG] 150 G2
Orzesze [PL] 50 F3
Orzinuovi [I] 70 H5
Orzola [E] 100 E4
Orzysz [PL] 24 C4
Os [N] 182 C4
Osby [S] 162 C6
Oschatz [D] 34 D5
Oschersleben [D] 34 B3
Óschiri [I] 118 D3
Ose [N] 164 D3
Osečina [YU] 154 F3
Oseja de Sajambre [E] 82 C3
Osen [N] 190 B5
Osenets [BG] 148 D2
Osera de Ebro [E] 90 F4
Osie [PL] 22 D4
Osieczna [PL] 36 C4
Osiek [PL] 22 E4
Osijek [HR] 76 C6
Osikovitsa [BG] 150 G4
Ósilo [I] 118 C3
Osimo [I] 116 C1
Osinja [BIH] 154 C2
Ósios Loukás [GR] 132 H5
Osipaonica [YU] 154 H3
Osipoviči [BY] 204 B6
Osječenica [YU] 152 D4
Oskar [S] 162 F5
Oskarshamn [S] 162 G3
Oskarström [S] 162 B5
Øskendalsøra [N] 180 F3
Oskowo [PL] 22 C2
Osl'any [SK] 64 B3
Oslo [N] 166 B1
Øsløs [DK] 160 C3
Osmaneli [TR] 146 G4
Os'mino [RUS] 200 H1
Ösmo [S] 168 D4
Osnabrück [D] 32 D2
Ošno [PL] 34 G2
Osoblaha [CZ] 50 D3
Osor [HR] 112 E3
Osorno la Mayor [E] 82 D5
Osowo Leśne [PL] 22 D4
Osøyro [N] 170 B4
Ospedaletti [I] 108 F4

Oss [NL] 16 E6
Óssa [GR] 130 B4
Ossa de Montiel [E] 96 H5
Ossiach [A] 74 B3
Östansjö [S] 190 G3
Östansjö [S] 166 G4
Östanvik [S] 172 H3
Ostaškov [RUS] 204 D3
Östavall [S] 184 C4
Ostbevern [D] 32 C3
Østbirk [DK] 156 C1
Østby [N] 172 E2
Osted [DK] 156 G3
Ostellato [I] 110 G3
Østenå [N] 164 F2
Østerbø [N] 170 E3
Osterburg [D] 34 B1
Osterburken [D] 46 D5
Österbybruk [S] 174 F5
Østerby Havn [DK] 160 F3
Osterbymo [S] 162 E2
Österfärnebo [S] 174 E5
Osterhofen [D] 60 G3
Osterholz–Scharmbeck [D] 18 D5
Øster Hurup [DK] 160 E4
Østerild [DK] 160 C3
Østerlars [DK] 158 E4
Østermarie [DK] 158 E4
Osterode [D] 32 G4
Östersund [S] 182 G2
Östersundom [FIN] 176 H5
Øster Ulslev [DK] 20 B1
Östervåla [S] 174 E5
Ostervallskog [S] 166 C2
Østhammar [S] 174 G5
Ostheim [D] 46 F2
Osthofen [D] 46 B4
Ostiglia [I] 110 F2
Oštinski Pogost [RUS] 204 E1
Ostiz [E] 84 B3
Ostra [I] 112 C6
Östraby [S] 158 C2
Ostrach [D] 58 H3
Östra Ed [S] 162 G1
Östra Frölunda [S] 162 B3
Östra Kärne [S] 166 G2

Ostrava [CZ] 50 E4
Oštrelj [BIH] 154 A3
Ostritz [D] 48 G1
Ostróda [PL] 22 G4
Ostrołęka [PL] 24 C6
Ostroróg [PL] 36 B2
Ostros [YU] 128 A1
Ostrov [CZ] 48 D3
Ostrov [RUS] 200 G4
Ostrowice [PL] 20 H4
Ostrowiec [PL] 22 B3
Ostrowiec Świętokrzyski [PL] 52 C1
Ostrowite [PL] 22 D5
Ostrów Mazowieka [PL] 38 D1
Ostrów Wielkopolski [PL] 36 E5
Ostrožac [BIH] 112 H3
Ostrožac [BIH] 152 C1
Ost Ryd [S] 168 B5
Ostrzeszów [PL] 36 E5
Ostuni [I] 122 F3
Osuna [E] 102 B3
Oswestry [GB] 10 C5
Oświecim [PL] 50 G4
Osztopán [H] 74 H4
Otalampi [FIN] 176 G4
Otanmäki [FIN] 198 E5
Otava [FIN] 188 C6
Otepää [EST] 200 F3
Oterma [FIN] 198 E4
Otero de Bodas [E] 80 H3
Oteševo [MK] 128 D4
Othery [GB] 12 F4
Otley [GB] 10 F3
Otmuchów [PL] 50 D3
Otnes [N] 182 C6
Otocac [HR] 112 G3
Otočec [SLO] 74 D5
Otok [HR] 154 E2
Otoka [BIH] 154 A2
Otorowo [PL] 36 C2
Otranto [I] 122 H5
Otrokovice [CZ] 50 D6
Otsagi / Ochagavía [E] 84 C4
Otta [N] 180 G6
Ottana [I] 118 D4

Ottaviano [I] 120 E3
Ottenby [S] 158 G1
Ottenschlag [A] 62 D4
Ottensheim [A] 62 B4
Otterbach [D] 44 H3
Otterburn [GB] 8 F5
Otter Ferry [GB] 8 C2
Otterlo [NL] 16 E5
Otterndorf [D] 18 E3
Ottersberg [D] 18 E5
Ottersøy [N] 190 C4
Otterup [DK] 156 D3
Ottery St Mary [GB] 12 E4
Öttevény [H] 62 H6
Ottobeuren [D] 60 C4
Ottone [I] 110 B3
Ottsjö [S] 182 E2
Ottweiler [D] 44 G3
Otwock [PL] 38 C3
Oucques [F] 42 D6
Oud Beijerland [NL] 16 C5
Ouddorp [NL] 16 B5
Oudenaarde [B] 28 G2
Oude–Pekela [NL] 16 H2
Oudewater [NL] 16 D5
Oughterard [IRL] 2 C4
Ouistreham [F] 26 F3
Oulainen [FIN] 198 D5
Oullins [F] 68 F3
Oulu [FIN] 198 D4
Oulujoki [FIN] 198 D4
Oulunsalo [FIN] 198 D4
Oulx [I] 70 B5
Oundle [GB] 14 E2
Ouranópoli [GR] 130 D5
Ourense / Orense [E] 78 C5
Ourique [P] 94 C4
Ourol [E] 78 E2
Oust [F] 84 G5
Outokumpu [FIN] 188 E2
Ouzouer–le–Marché [F] 42 D6
Ovada [I] 108 H2
Ovakent [TR] 144 E4
Ovar [P] 80 B4
Ovčar Banja [YU] 150 B2
Ovelgönne [D] 18 F4
Ovenstädt [D] 32 E2

Ottaviano [I] 120 E3
Overåneset [N] 180 E4
Overath [D] 30 H4
Överbyn [S] 172 E5
Overgård [N] 192 E3
Overhalla [N] 190 C5
Over Jerstal [DK] 156 C3
Överkalix [S] 196 B8
Överlida [S] 162 B3
Övermark / Ylimarkku [FIN] 186 B4
Överö [FIN] 176 B5
Overscaig [GB] 6 D3
Övertänger [S] 174 C3
Overton [GB] 12 H4
Övertorneå [S] 196 B8
Överturingen [S] 182 H4
Överum [S] 162 G1
Oviedo [E] 78 H3
Ovindoli [I] 116 C5
Øvre Årdal [N] 170 E1
Øvre Moen [N] 164 C2
Øvre Rendal [N] 182 C6
Övre Soppero [S] 192 F4
Øvrestøl [N] 180 E4
Ovruč [UA] 204 B7
Ovtrup [DK] 156 A2
Owschlag [D] 18 F2
Oxberg [S] 172 G3
Oxborough [GB] 14 F2
Oxelösund [S] 168 C5
Oxford [GB] 14 D3
Oxie [S] 156 H3
Oxília [GR] 132 E1
Oxwich [GB] 12 E2
Øy [N] 164 E4
Øyenkilen [N] 166 B3
Øyer [N] 172 B2
Øyermoen [N] 172 D5
Øyestad [N] 164 E5
Oyntdartfjørður [DK] 160 B1
Oyonnax [F] 68 H2
Øyslebø [N] 164 D5
Øystese [N] 170 C4
Oyten [D] 18 E5
Ozalj [HR] 74 D6
Ozarów [PL] 52 D1
Ożarów Mazowieki [PL] 38 B3

Ožbalt [SLO] 74 D3
Ózd [H] 64 E4
Ožďany [SK] 64 D4
Ozerki [RUS] 178 F4
Ozersk [RUS] 24 C2
Ozieri [I] 118 D3
Ozimek [PL] 50 E2
Ozorkow [PL] 36 G4

P

Pääjärvi [FIN] 186 F3
Paakkila [FIN] 188 E2
Paatinen [FIN] 176 D4
Paavola [FIN] 198 D4
Pabianice [PL] 36 G4
Pabradė [LT] 202 G5
Paceco [I] 126 B2
Pachino [I] 126 G6
Pacov [CZ] 48 G5
Pacsa [H] 74 G3
Pacyna [PL] 36 H3
Pacy–sur–Eure [F] 42 E3
Paczków [PL] 50 D3
Padarosk [BY] 24 H6
Padasjoki [FIN] 176 H1
Padborg [DK] 156 C4
Padej [YU] 76 E5
Paderborn [D] 32 E4
Paderne [P] 94 C5
Padiham [GB] 10 E3
Padina [YU] 154 H2
Padjene [HR] 112 H5
Padova [I] 110 G1
Padrenda [E] 78 C5
Padrógão Grande [P] 86 E3
Padrón [E] 78 B3
Padru [I] 118 E3
Padstow [GB] 12 C4
Padul [E] 102 E4
Paesana [I] 108 F2
Paestum [I] 120 F4
Pag [HR] 112 F4
Pagani [I] 120 E3
Pagégiai [LT] 202 D5
Pagny [F] 44 E4
Páhi [H] 76 D3
Pahiá [GR] 138 G5
Pahiá Ámos [GR] 140 G5
Pahranichny [BY] 24 G5
Paianía [GR] 134 C6
Paide [EST] 200 E2
Paijärvi [FIN] 178 D3
Pailhès [F] 84 H4
Paimboeuf [F] 40 E6
Paimio [FIN] 176 E4
Paimpol [F] 26 A3
Paisley [GB] 8 D3
Pajala [S] 192 G6
Pájara [E] 100 E5
Pajares, Puerto de– [E] 78 H4
Pajęczno [PL] 36 F6
Pakošč [PL] 36 E1
Pakoštane [HR] 112 G5
Pakosze [PL] 22 G3
Pakrac [HR] 154 B1
Pakruojis [LT] 202 F3
Paks [H] 76 C3
Palacios del Sil [E] 78 F4
Palacios de Sanabria [E] 80 G3
Paladru [F] 68 H4
Palafrugell [E] 92 G3
Palagianello [I] 122 E4
Palagiano [I] 122 E4
Palagonia [I] 126 F4
Palaiá Epídavros [GR] 136 F2
Palaikastro [GR] 140 H4
Palaiochóra [GR] 140 B5
Palaiochóri [GR] 130 C5
Palaiokastrítsa [GR] 132 A2
Palaiópoli [GR] 138 D1
Palaiópoli [GR] 130 G4
Pálairos [GR] 132 D4
Palaiseau [F] 42 F4
Palamás [GR] 132 F2
Palamós [E] 92 G3

Palamut [TR] 144 D3
Palanga [LT] 202 D4
Palas de Rei [E] 78 D3
Palasi [EST] 200 F1
Palatítsia [GR] 128 G5
Palatna [YU] 150 C4
Palau [I] 118 E2
Palavas–les–Flots [F] 106 F4
Palazzolo [I] 70 H4
Palazzolo Acréide [I] 126 G5
Palazzo San Gervasio [I] 120 H3
Paldiski [EST] 200 D1
Pale [BIH] 152 D1
Pāle [LV] 200 E4
Palena [I] 116 D5
Palencia [E] 82 C6
Paleohori [GR] 132 D3
Paleohóri [GR] 136 E3
Paleópirgos [GR] 132 F5
Palermo [AL] 128 B6
Palermo [I] 126 C2
Palestrina [I] 116 B5
Palič [YU] 76 D5
Palinuro [I] 120 G5
Paliomonastiri [GR] 132 E2
Paliópirgos [GR] 132 F2
Paliouriá [GR] 132 E1
Palioúrion [GR] 130 C6
Paliseul [B] 44 D1
Pälkäne [FIN] 176 G2
Palkino [RUS] 200 G4
Pallarés [E] 94 G4
Pallaruelo de Monegros [E] 90 F4
Pallasgreen [IRL] 4 D3
Pallastunturi [FIN] 192 H4
Pallíni [GR] 134 C6
Palma del Río [E] 102 B1
Palma de Mallorca [E] 104 E5
Palma di Montechiaro [I] 126 D4
Palmadula [I] 118 B3
Palma Nova [E] 104 D5
Palmanova [I] 72 G5
Palmela [P] 86 B6
Palmi [I] 124 C7
Palo del Colle [I] 122 D2
Páloi [GR] 142 C4
Palojärvi [FIN] 192 G4
Palojärvi [FIN] 196 C8
Palojoensuu [FIN] 192 G4
Palokastër [AL] 128 C6
Palokki [FIN] 188 E3
Palomaa [FIN] 196 D4
Palomäki [FIN] 198 F6
Palomares [E] 104 A5
Palomas [E] 94 H2
Palombara Sabina [I] 116 B5
Palos de la Frontera [E] 94 E6
Palota [SK] 52 E6
Pålsboda [S] 166 H4
Paltamo [FIN] 198 F4
Paltaniemi [FIN] 198 E5
Paluzza [I] 72 G3
Pamhagen [A] 62 G6
Pamiątkowo [PL] 36 C2
Pamiers [F] 106 A4
Pampilhosa da Serra [P] 86 E3
Pamplona / Iruña [E] 84 B4
Pamporovo [BG] 130 E1
Pamucak [TR] 144 D5
Pamukçu [TR] 144 D1
Pamukkale [TR] 144 G5
Pamukova [TR] 146 G3
Pamukyazı [TR] 144 D5
Panagía [GR] 134 C5
Panagía [GR] 140 F5
Panagía [GR] 130 E4
Panagyurishte [BG] 148 A5
Panajë [AL] 128 A5
Panassac [F] 84 G3
Panayır [TR] 144 E2
Pančevo [YU] 154 H2
Pancharevo [BG] 150 F5
Pancorvo [E] 82 F5

Pandėlys [LT] 200 E6
Pandino [I] 70 G5
Pandrup [DK] 160 D3
Panes [E] 82 D3
Panetólio [GR] 132 E5
Panevėžys [LT] 202 F4
Pangbourne [GB] 14 D4
Paniza [E] 90 D4
Paniza, Puerto de– [E] 90 D5
Pankakoski [FIN] 198 G6
Panki [PL] 50 F1
Pannonhalma [H] 62 H6
Panormítis [GR] 142 D4
Pánormos [GR] 138 E1
Pánormos [GR] 140 D4
Pantánassa [GR] 136 F5
Pãntäne [FIN] 186 B4
Pantelej [MK] 128 G1
Pantelleria [I] 126 A4
Pantón [E] 78 D4
Pantymenyn [GB] 12 D1
Panxón [E] 78 B5
Páola [I] 124 D4
Pápa [H] 74 H1
Papadiánika [GR] 136 F5
Papasidero [I] 120 H6

Papenburg [D] 18 B5
Papile [LT] 200 C6
Papilys [LT] 200 E6
Papowo Biskupie [PL] 22 E5
Pappenheim [D] 60 D2
Parábita [I] 122 G5
Paraćin [YU] 150 C2
Parád [H] 64 E5
Paradas [E] 100 H2
Paradeísi [GR] 142 E4
Paradeísia [GR] 136 D3
Paradyż [PL] 38 A5
Parainen / Pargas [FIN] 176 D5
Parakilá [GR] 134 G2
Paralía [GR] 136 F4
Paralía [GR] 132 F6
Paralía [GR] 128 G5
Paralía Akrátas [GR] 132 G6
Paralía Ástrous [GR] 136 E3
Paralía Iríon [GR] 136 F2
Paralía Kýmis [GR] 134 C4
Paralía Platanoú [GR] 132 G6
Paralía Skotínas [GR] 128 H6

Páramo del Sil [E] 78 F4
Paramythí [GR] 132 C2
Paranéstio [GR] 130 D2
Parantala [FIN] 186 F3
Parapótamos [GR] 132 C2
Parassapuszta [H] 64 C5
Paravóla [GR] 132 E5
Paray–le–Monial [F] 56 E6
Parcent [E] 104 F1
Parchim [D] 20 B5
Parczew [PL] 38 E4
Pardubice [CZ] 50 A4
Paredes [P] 80 C4
Paredes de Coura [P] 78 B5
Paredes de Nava [E] 82 C6
Paredes de Sigüenza [E] 90 A4
Parentis–en–Born [F] 66 B4
Parey [D] 34 C2
Párga [GR] 132 C3
Pargas / Parainen [FIN] 176 D5
Pargny–sur–Saulx [F] 44 C4
Pargolovo [RUS] 178 H4

Parikkala [FIN] 188 F5
Paris [F] 42 F3
Parkalompolo [S] 192 G5
Parkano [FIN] 186 D5
Parkeston Quay [GB] 14 G3
Parkkila [FIN] 198 D5
Parkkima [FIN] 198 D6
Parknasilla [IRL] 4 B4
Parkumäki [FIN] 188 E5
Parłówko [PL] 20 F4
Parma [I] 110 D2
Pärnu [EST] 200 D3
Pärnu–Jaagupi [EST] 200 D2
Páros [GR] 138 E3
Parpan [CH] 70 H1
Parsberg [D] 46 H6
Partakko [FIN] 196 D4
Partakoski [FIN] 178 D1
Partanna [I] 126 B3
Partenen [A] 72 B2
Parthenay [F] 54 D3
Parthéni [GR] 136 E2
Parthéni [GR] 142 B2
Partille [S] 160 H2

Partinello [F] 114 A3
Partinico [I] 126 C2
Partizani [YU] 150 B1
Partizánske [SK] 64 B3
Partizanske Vode [YU] 150 A3
Partry [IRL] 2 C4
Pâryd [S] 162 F5
Pasaia [E] 84 B2
Paşayiğit [TR] 146 B3
Paşcani [RO] 206 D4
Pas de la Casa [AND] 84 H6
Pas–en–Artois [F] 28 E4
Pasewalk [D] 20 E5
Pasiecznik [PL] 50 A1
Pasiene [LV] 200 G5
Påskallavik [S] 162 G4
Pasłęk [PL] 22 F3
Pašman [HR] 112 G5
Passage East [IRL] 4 E5
Passage West [IRL] 4 D5
Passá Limáni [GR] 134 G5
Passau [D] 60 H3
Passignano sul Trasimeno [I] 114 H2

Pastavy [BY] 202 H4
Pastor [E] 78 C3
Pastrana [E] 88 H6
Pasvalys [LT] 200 E6
Pasym [PL] 22 H4
Pásztó [H] 64 D5
Patay [F] 42 E5
Pateley Bridge [GB] 10 F3
Patergassen [A] 74 A3
Paterna [E] 98 E4
Paterna de Rivera [E] 100 G4
Paternion [A] 72 H3
Paternò [I] 126 G3
Paternopoli [I] 120 F3
Patersdorf [D] 60 G2
Patitíri [GR] 134 C3
Pátmos [GR] 138 H2
Patoniemi [FIN] 196 F8
Patoniva [FIN] 196 D3
Patos [AL] 128 B4
Pátra [GR] 132 F6
Patreksfjörður [IS] 194 B2
Patrickswell [IRL] 4 D3
Patrington [GB] 10 G4
Patsch [A] 72 D1

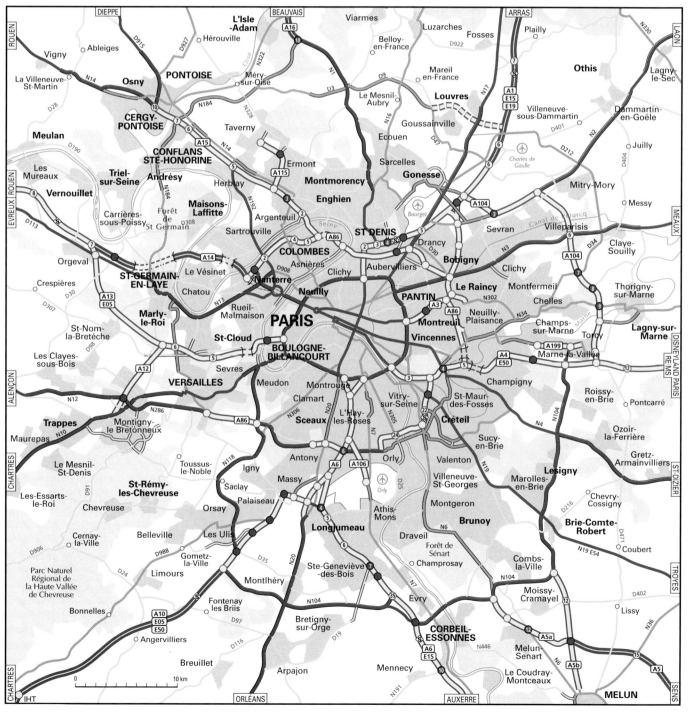

Pattada [I] 118 D3
Pattensen [D] 32 F2
Patterdale [GB] 10 D1
Pattijoki [FIN] 198 D4
Pau [F] 84 E3
Pauillac [F] 66 C2
Paulhaguet [F] 68 D4
Păuliş [RO] 76 H4
Pauliström [S] 162 F3
Paulstown [IRL] 4 F4
Pavel Banya [BG] 148 C5
Pavia [I] 70 G6
Pavia [P] 86 D5
Pavilly [F] 28 B5
Pavilosta [LV] 200 B5
Pávliani [GR] 132 G4
Pavlikeni [BG] 148 C3
Pávlos [GR] 134 A5
Pavlovsk [RUS] 178 H5
Pavullo nel Frignano [I] 110 E4
Pavy [RUS] 200 H3
Paxoí [GR] 132 C3
Payerne [CH] 58 C6
Paymogo [E] 94 E4
Payrac [F] 66 G4
Pazardzhik [BG] 148 A6
Pazarköy [TR] 146 C6
Pazaryeri [TR] 146 G5
Pazin [HR] 112 D2
Pchelino [RUS] 178 F3
Peal de Becerro [E] 102 F2
Péaule [F] 40 E5
Peč [YU] 150 B5
Peccioli [I] 110 E6
Pechenga [RUS] 196 F3
Pechina [E] 102 G5
Pecica [RO] 76 G4
Pecineaga [RO] 148 G1
Pecka [YU] 154 F4
Peckelsheim [D] 32 E4
Pečory [RUS] 200 G3
Pec pod Sněžkou [CZ] 50 A2
Pécs [H] 76 B5
Pécsvárad [H] 76 B5
Pedaso [I] 116 D2
Pédio [GR] 142 D4
Pedráces / Pedratsches [I] 72 E3
Pedrafita do Cebreiro, Puerto– [E] 78 E4
Pedralba [E] 98 E4
Pedratsches / Pedráces [I] 72 E3
Pedraza [E] 88 G3
Pedreguer [E] 104 F1
Pedreira [E] 78 D2
Pedrera [E] 96 F3
Pedrizas, Puerto de las– [E] 102 C4
Pedro Abad [E] 102 D1
Pedro Andrés [E] 102 H2
Pedro Bernardo [E] 88 D5
Pedrógão [P] 94 E3
Pedrógão [P] 86 C2
Pedro Martínez [E] 102 F3
Pedro Muñoz [E] 96 G3
Pedrosillo el Ralo [E] 88 C3
Peebles [GB] 8 E4
Peel [GBM] 10 B1
Peenemünde [D] 20 E3
Peera [FIN] 192 F3
Péfkos [GR] 140 F5
Péfkos [GR] 128 D5
Pega [P] 86 G2
Pegau [D] 34 C6
Peggau [A] 74 D2
Pegli [I] 110 A3
Pegnitz [D] 46 H4
Pego [E] 104 F1
Pegões [P] 86 C6
Peguera [E] 104 D5
Pehčevo [MK] 128 H1
Pehlivanköy [TR] 146 B2
Peine [D] 32 G2
Peïra–Cava [F] 108 F4
Peiraías [GR] 134 C6
Peiss [D] 60 E5
Peissenberg [D] 60 D5
Peiting [D] 60 D5
Peitz [D] 34 F4

Pejo [I] 72 C3
Pekkala [FIN] 196 D8
Pelasgía [GR] 132 H4
Pełczyce [PL] 20 G6
Pelejaneta / La Pelechaneta [E] 98 F3
Pélekas [GR] 132 B2
Peletá [GR] 136 F4
Pelhřimov [CZ] 48 H5
Pelkosenniemi [FIN] 196 E7
Pélla [GR] 128 G4
Pellegrino Parmense [I] 110 C2
Pellegrue [F] 66 E4
Pellesmäki [FIN] 188 C2
Pellinge / Pellinki [FIN] 178 B5
Pellinki / Pellinge [FIN] 178 B5
Pello [FIN] 196 C7
Pello [S] 196 C7
Pellosniemi [FIN] 178 C1
Pelovo [BG] 148 A3
Pelplin [PL] 22 E4
Peltosalmi [FIN] 198 E6
Peltovuoma [FIN] 192 H4
Pélussin [F] 68 F3
Pembroke [GB] 12 D2
Peñacerrada [E] 82 G5
Penacova [P] 86 E2
Peñafiel [E] 88 F2
Penafiel [P] 80 C4
Peñaflor [E] 102 B1
Penamacor [P] 86 G3
Peñaranda de Bracamonte [E] 88 D3
Peñaranda de Duero [E] 88 H2
Peñarroya–Pueblonuevo [E] 96 B5
Penarth [GB] 12 F3
Peñascosa [E] 96 H6
Peñas de San Pedro [E] 98 B6
Peñausende [E] 80 H5
Pendik [TR] 146 F3
Pendine [GB] 12 D2
Penela [P] 86 D2
Penestin [F] 40 E5
Peniche [P] 86 B3
Penicuik [GB] 8 E3
Peñíscola / Peníscola [E] 98 G2
Peníscola / Peñíscola [E] 98 G2
Penkridge [GB] 10 D6
Penkum [D] 20 E5
Pennabilli [I] 110 H5
Penne [I] 116 D4
Penrith [GB] 8 E6
Penryn [GB] 12 C5
Pentálofos [GR] 128 E6
Pentrez–Plage [F] 40 B2
Penzance [GB] 12 B5
Penzberg [D] 60 D5
Penzlin [D] 20 D5
Pępowo [PL] 36 C4
Peqin [AL] 128 B3
Perachóra [GR] 134 A6
Peraía [GR] 128 H5
Perälä [FIN] 186 B4
Peraleda del Zaucejo [E] 96 B4
Peralejos de las Truchas [E] 90 C6
Perales del Alfambra [E] 98 E1
Peralta [E] 84 B5
Pérama [GR] 140 D4
Pérama [GR] 132 D2
Peranka [FIN] 198 F3
Perä–Posio [FIN] 196 E8
Peräseinäjoki [FIN] 186 C4
Perast [YU] 152 D4
Perchauer Sattel [A] 74 B2
Perchtoldsdorf [A] 62 F5
Percy [F] 26 D3
Perdasdefogu [I] 118 D6
Perdigão [P] 86 E4
Pérdika [GR] 136 G2
Pérdika [GR] 132 C3

Pereda de Ancares [E] 78 F4
Peredo [P] 80 F4
Pereiro [P] 94 D5
Perejaslav–Hmelnicki [UA] 206 F2
Pereščepino [UA] 206 H3
Pereslavl–Zalesski [RUS] 204 F3
Peretu [RO] 148 B1
Pereval Uzhots'kyi [UA] 52 F6
Perfugas [I] 118 C3
Perg [A] 62 C4
Pérgine Valsugana [I] 72 D4
Pergola [I] 112 B6
Perho [FIN] 186 E2
Periam [RO] 76 F5
Periana [E] 102 C4
Périers [F] 26 D3
Périgueux [F] 66 F3
Periš [YU] 150 E3
Perişoru [RO] 150 F1
Perissa [GR] 138 F5
Perivóli [GR] 132 G2
Perjen Tunnel [A] 72 C1
Perkáta [H] 76 C2
Perkpolder [NL] 28 H1
Perleberg [D] 20 B6
Perlez [YU] 154 G1
Perly [PL] 24 C2
Përmet [AL] 128 C6
Pernå [FIN] 178 B4
Pernat [HR] 112 E2
Pernes [F] 106 H3
Pernes–les–Fontaines [F] 106 H3
Pernik [BG] 150 F5
Perniö [FIN] 176 F5
Pernitz [A] 62 E5
Pernu [FIN] 196 E8
Péronne [F] 28 F5
Perosa Argentina [I] 70 C6
Pérouges [F] 68 G2
Perpignan [F] 92 G1
Perranporth [GB] 12 C4
Perros–Guirec [F] 40 D1
Persberg [S] 166 G2
Persenbeug [A] 62 D4
Pershagen [S] 168 D3
Pershore [GB] 12 H2
Perstorp [S] 158 C1
Perth [GB] 8 E2
Pertisau [A] 60 E6
Pertoča [SLO] 74 E3
Pertoúli [GR] 132 E2
Pertteli [FIN] 176 F4
Pertuis [F] 108 B4
Pertunmaa [FIN] 178 B1
Perúgia [I] 116 A2
Perushtica [BG] 148 B6
Perušič [HR] 112 G3
Péruwelz [B] 28 G3
Pervomajsk [UA] 206 E3
Pervomajskoje [RUS] 178 G3
Pésaro [I] 112 B5
Pescaglia [I] 110 D5
Pescara [I] 116 D4
Pescasseroli [I] 116 C6
Péschici [I] 116 H5
Peschiera del Garda [I] 72 B6
Pescia [I] 110 E5
Pescina [I] 116 C5
Pescocostanzo [I] 116 D5
Pescolanciano [I] 116 D6
Pescopagano [I] 120 G3
Peshkëpija [AL] 128 B5
Peshkopi [AL] 128 C2
Peshtera [BG] 148 A6
Pesiökylä [FIN] 198 F3
Pesmes [F] 58 H4
Pesocani [MK] 128 D3
Pesochnyj [RUS] 178 H4
Peso da Régua [P] 80 D4
Pessalompolo [FIN] 196 C8
Pessáni [GR] 130 G2
Pessin [D] 34 D2
Peštani [MK] 128 D4
Pestovo [RUS] 204 E2
Pešurići [BIH] 152 E1

Peta [P] 86 C5
Petäiskylä [FIN] 198 G5
Petäjävesi [FIN] 186 F4
Petalídi [GR] 136 D4
Pétange [L] 44 E3
Peterborough [GB] 14 E2
Peterchurch [GB] 12 F2
Peterculter [GB] 6 F6
Peterhead [GB] 6 G5
Peterlee [GB] 10 F1
Petersdorf [D] 18 H2
Petersdorf [D] 20 B3
Petersfield [GB] 14 D5
Petershagen [D] 32 E2
Pétervására [H] 64 E5
Petilia Policastro [I] 124 E5
Petkula [FIN] 196 D6
Petkus [D] 34 E3
Petlovača [YU] 154 F3
Petoússi [GR] 132 C2
Petra [E] 104 E5
Pétra [GR] 128 G6
Pétra [GR] 134 G2
Petralia Soprana [I] 126 E3
Petrálona [GR] 130 B5
Petraná [GR] 128 F5
Petrelë [AL] 128 B3
Petrella Tifernina [I] 116 E6
Petrer [E] 104 D2
Petreto–Bicchisano [F] 114 B5
Petrich [BG] 130 B2
Petrila [RO] 206 B5
Petrinja [HR] 154 A1
Petrodvorets [RUS] 178 G5
Pétrola [E] 98 C6
Petronell–Carnuntum [A] 62 G5
Petroşani [RO] 206 B5
Petrosino [I] 126 B3
Petrotá [GR] 146 A2
Petroússa [GR] 130 C2
Petrovac [YU] 152 E5
Petrovac [YU] 150 C1
Petrovaradin [YU] 154 F1
Petrovice [CZ] 48 F5
Petroviči [BIH] 152 B2
Petrovka [RUS] 178 F2
Petřvald [CZ] 50 E5
Petsákoi [GR] 132 F6
Petsikko [FIN] 196 D3
Pettenbach [A] 62 B5
Petworth [GB] 14 D5
Pettigo [GB] 2 E3
Peuerbach [A] 62 A4
Peura [FIN] 196 C8
Peurasuvanto [FIN] 196 D6
Pevensey [GB] 14 E6
Pewsey [GB] 12 H4
Peyrat–le–Chateaux [F] 66 H1
Peyrehorade [F] 84 D2
Peyrolles [F] 108 B4
Peyruis [F] 108 C3
Pézenas [F] 106 E4
Pezinok [SK] 62 G4
Pezoùla [GR] 130 E3
Pfaffendorf [D] 46 G3
Pfaffenhausen [D] 60 C4
Pfaffenhofen [D] 60 E3
Pfäffikon [CH] 58 G5
Pfäffikon [CH] 58 G5
Pfafflar [A] 72 C1
Pfänder Tunnel [CH] 60 B6
Pfarrkirchen [D] 60 G3
Pfatter [D] 60 F2
Pfeffenhausen [D] 60 F3
Pforzheim [D] 46 C6
Pfreimd [D] 48 C5
Pfronten [D] 60 C6
Pfullendorf [D] 58 H3
Pfullingen [D] 58 H2
Pfunds [A] 72 C2
Pfungstadt [D] 46 C4
Phalsbourg [F] 44 G5
Philippeville [B] 30 C6
Philippsreut [D] 62 A2
Philippsthal [D] 32 F6
Piacenza [I] 70 H6
Piádena [I] 110 D1
Piana [F] 114 A4
Piana Crixia [I] 108 H2

Piana degli Albanesi [I] 126 C2
Pian Castagna [I] 108 H2
Pianella [I] 114 G1
Piani Resinelli [I] 70 G4
Pianoro [I] 110 F4
Pias [P] 94 E3
Pias [P] 94 E2
Piaseczno [PL] 38 B3
Piaski [PL] 36 C4
Piaski [PL] 38 E6
Piastów [PL] 38 B3
Piaszczyna [PL] 22 C3
Piątek [PL] 36 G3
Piatra [RO] 148 B2
Piatra Neamţ [RO] 206 C4
Piatra Olt [RO] 150 G1
Piazza al Serchio [I] 110 D4
Piazza Armerina [I] 126 E4
Piazza Brembana [I] 70 H4
Piazzatorre [I] 70 H3
Piazzola sul Brenta [I] 72 D6
Pičan [HR] 112 E2
Picassent [E] 98 E5
Picerno [I] 120 G4
Pickering [GB] 10 G3
Pico [I] 120 C1
Picquigny [F] 28 D4
Piechowice [PL] 48 H1
Piecki [PL] 24 C4
Piedicavallo [I] 70 E4
Piedicroce [F] 114 C3
Piediluco [I] 116 B4
Piedimonte Matese [I] 120 E2
Piedimulera [I] 70 E3
Piedrabuena [E] 96 E4
Piedrafita de Babia [E] 78 G4
Piedrahita [E] 88 C4
Piedralaves [E] 88 D5
Piekary Śląskie [PL] 50 F3
Pieksämäki [FIN] 188 C4
Pielavesi [FIN] 186 H1
Pieniężno [PL] 22 G3
Piennes [F] 44 E3
Pieńsk [PL] 34 G6
Pienza [I] 114 G2
Pierowall [GB] 6 G1
Pierre–Buffière [F] 66 G2
Pierre–de–Bresse [F] 56 H5
Pierrefitte [F] 44 D4
Pierrefitte–Nestalas [F] 84 E4
Pierrefonds [F] 42 G2
Pierrefort [F] 68 B4
Pierrelatte [F] 106 G2
Pierroton [F] 66 C3
Pieski [PL] 34 H2
Pieskowa Skala [PL] 50 H3
Piešťany [SK] 62 H3
Pietarsaari / Jakobstad [FIN] 198 B6
Pietragalla [I] 120 H3
Pietralba [I] 114 B3
Pietra Ligure [I] 108 G3
Pietralunga [I] 116 A1
Pietramelara [I] 120 D2
Pietraperzia [I] 126 E4
Pietrasanta [I] 110 D5
Pietrowice [PL] 50 D3
Pietrzwałd [PL] 22 G4
Pieve di Cadore [I] 72 F3
Pieve di Teco [I] 108 G4
Pievepelago [I] 110 E4
Pieve Santo Stéfano [I] 110 G6
Pigés [GR] 132 E3
Pigna [I] 108 F4
Pihkala [FIN] 198 D5
Pihlajalahti [FIN] 188 E5
Pihlajavaara [FIN] 188 H1
Pihlava [FIN] 176 C1
Pihtipudas [FIN] 186 F1
Piikkiö [FIN] 176 E4
Piipola [FIN] 198 D5
Piispajärvi [FIN] 198 F3
Piittisjärvi [FIN] 196 D8
Pikalevo [RUS] 204 E1

Pila [I] 110 H2
Pila [I] 70 D4
Piła [PL] 22 B6
Pilar de la Mola [E] 104 C6
Pilastri [I] 110 F2
Pilat–Plage [F] 66 B3
Pilés [E] 140 H3
Pilgrimstad [S] 182 H3
Píli [GR] 134 B6
Pilica [PL] 50 H2
Pílio [GR] 134 B4
Pilis [H] 76 D1
Pilisvörösvár [H] 64 C6
Pilviškiai [LT] 24 E1
Pilzno [PL] 52 C4
Pina de Ebro [E] 90 F4
Piñar [E] 102 E3
Pinarejos [E] 88 F3
Pinarellu [F] 114 B5
Pınarhisar [TR] 146 C2
Pınarköy [TR] 142 D2
Pınarlar [TR] 144 G6
Pincehely [H] 76 B3
Pińczów [PL] 52 B2
Pineda de Mar [E] 92 F4
Pinerolo [I] 70 C6
Pineto [I] 116 D3
Piney [F] 44 B5
Pinhal Novo [P] 86 B5
Pinhel [P] 80 E6
Pinkafeld [A] 74 E1
Pino [F] 114 C2
Pino do Val [E] 78 B2
Pinols [F] 68 D4
Pinoso / el Pinós [E] 104 D2
Pinos Puente [E] 102 D3
Pinsk [BY] 204 A6
Pintamo [FIN] 198 E3
Pinto [E] 88 F6
Pinwherry [GB] 8 C4
Pinzolo [I] 72 C4
Pióbbico [I] 110 H6
Piombino [I] 114 E2
Pionerskiy [RUS] 202 C5
Pionki [PL] 38 C5
Pionsat [F] 56 C6
Piossasco [I] 70 D6
Piotrkowice [PL] 52 B2
Piotrków Trybunalski [PL] 36 H5
Piotrów [PL] 38 E6
Piotrowice [PL] 38 C3
Piotta [CH] 70 F2
Piove di Sacco [I] 110 G1
Piovene–Rocchette [I] 72 D5
Pipriac [F] 40 F4
Piqeras [AL] 132 B1
Piqueras, Puerto de– [E] 90 B2
Piran [SLO] 72 H6
Piras [I] 118 E3
Pirdop [BG] 148 A4
Pirgadíkia [GR] 130 C5
Pirgí [GR] 134 G5
Piriac–sur–Mer [F] 40 D5
Pirin [BG] 130 B2
Pirjatin [UA] 206 F2
Pirkkala [FIN] 176 F1
Pirmasens [D] 44 H4
Pirna [D] 48 F1
Pirnmill [GB] 8 C3
Pirok [MK] 128 D1
Pirot [YU] 150 E4
Pirou–Plage [F] 26 D3
Pirovac [HR] 112 G6
Pirttikoski [FIN] 196 E8
Pirttikylä / Pörtom [FIN] 186 B3
Pisa [I] 110 D5
Pisanets [BG] 148 D2
Pişchia [RO] 76 G5
Pisciotta [I] 120 F5
Písek [CZ] 48 F6
Pishcha [UA] 38 G4
Pisodéri [GR] 128 E4
Pisogne [I] 72 B5
Pisses [GR] 138 C2
Pissos [F] 66 C4
Pistianá [GR] 132 D3
Pisticci [I] 122 D4
Pistóia [I] 110 E5

Pisz [PL] 24 C4
Piteå [S] 198 B3
Piteşti [RO] 206 C6
Pithiviers [F] 42 F5
Pitigliano [I] 114 G3
Pitkäjärvi [FIN] 176 F4
Pitkälahti [FIN] 188 C2
Pitlochry [GB] 8 E1
Pitomača [HR] 74 G5
Pitvaros [H] 76 F4
Pivka [SLO] 74 B6
Pivnica [HR] 74 H6
Piwniczna [PL] 52 C5
Pizarra [E] 102 B4
Pizzighettone [I] 70 H6
Pizzo [I] 124 D6
Pizzoli [I] 116 C4
Pjatihatki [UA] 206 G3
Pjätteryd [S] 162 C5
Plabennec [F] 40 B1
Plage de Pineto [F] 114 C3
Plagiá [GR] 130 G2
Plaisance [F] 84 F2
Pláka [GR] 130 F6
Plakiás [GR] 140 D5
Plana [BIH] 152 D3
Planá [CZ] 48 D4
Planá nad Lužnicí [CZ] 48 G6
Plancios [I] 72 E3
Plancoët [F] 26 B4
Plandište [YU] 154 H1
Plan-du-Lac [F] 70 C2
Plánice [CZ] 48 E5
Planina [SLO] 74 B5
Planina [SLO] 74 D5
Planjane [HR] 154 A5
Plansee [A] 60 C6
Plasencia [E] 88 B5
Plasencia del Monte [E] 84 D6
Plaški [HR] 112 G2
Plasy [CZ] 48 E4
Plataés [GR] 134 B6
Platamona Lido [I] 118 C3
Platamónas [GR] 128 H6
Platamónas [GR] 130 D3
Platanés [GR] 140 D4
Platánia [GR] 136 C3
Plataniá [GR] 134 B3
Plataniás [GR] 140 C4
Platanistós [GR] 134 D6
Plátanos [GR] 136 E3
Plátanos [GR] 140 B4
Plátanos [GR] 136 C2
Platariá [GR] 132 C2
Platerów [PL] 38 E2
Plati [I] 124 C7
Platiána [GR] 136 C2
Platígiali [GR] 132 D5
Platís [GR] 138 E2
Platja d'Aro [E] 92 G4
platja des Canar [E] 104 C5
Plátsa [GR] 136 E4
Plattling [D] 60 G3
Platýkampos [GR] 132 G2
Platýs Gialós [GR] 138 D3
Platystomo [GR] 132 F4
Plau [D] 20 B5
Plaue [D] 34 C2
Plauen [D] 48 C2
Plav [YU] 150 A5
Plavinas [LV] 200 F5
Plavna [YU] 150 E1
Plavsk [RUS] 204 F5
Playa Blanca [E] 100 E5
Playa de San Juán [E] 104 E2
Pleaux [F] 68 A3
Plech [D] 46 H4
Pleinfeld [D] 46 G6
Plélan-le-Grand [F] 26 B6
Pleniţa [RO] 150 F1
Plentzia [E] 82 G3
Plépi [GR] 136 G2
Plešivec [SK] 64 E3
Plesse [F] 40 F5
Plestin-les-Grèves [F] 40 C1
Pleszew [PL] 36 E4
Pleternica [HR] 154 C1
Plettenberg [D] 32 C5

Pleumartin [F] 54 F4
Pleven [BG] 148 A3
Pleyben [F] 40 C2
Pliego [E] 104 B3
Plikáti [GR] 128 D6
Pliska [BG] 148 E2
Plitvice [HR] 112 G3
Plitvički Ljeskovac [HR] 112 G3
Pljevlja [YU] 152 E2
Ploaghe [I] 118 C3
Ploče [HR] 152 B3
Plochingen [D] 58 H1
Płock [PL] 36 H2
Ploërmel [F] 26 B6
Ploieşti [RO] 206 C6
Plomári [GR] 134 H3
Plombières-les-Bains [F] 58 C3
Plomin [HR] 112 E2
Plön [D] 18 G2
Plonéour Lanvern [F] 40 B3
Płońsk [PL] 38 A2
Plopii Slăviteşti [RO] 148 B2
Płoskinia [PL] 22 G2
Płoty [PL] 20 G4
Plouaret [F] 40 D2
Plouay [F] 40 C4
Ploubalay [F] 26 C4
Ploudalmézeau [F] 40 B1
Plouescat [F] 40 B1
Plougasnou [F] 40 C1
Plougastel-Daoulas [F] 40 B2
Plouguenast [F] 26 B5
Plouha [F] 26 A4
Plouigneau [F] 40 C2
Ploumanac'h [F] 40 D1
Plouray [F] 40 C3
Plovdiv [BG] 148 B6
Plozévet [F] 40 B3
Plumbridge [GB] 2 F2
Plunge [LT] 202 D4
Pluty [PL] 22 G2
Pluvigner [F] 40 D4
Plužine [YU] 152 D2
Płużnica [PL] 22 E5
Plymouth [GB] 12 D5
Plympton [GB] 12 D5
Plýtra [GR] 136 F5
Plyussa [RUS] 200 H2
Plzeň [CZ] 48 E4
Pniewo [PL] 38 C2
Pniewy [PL] 36 B2
Poarta de Fier a Transilvaniei [RO] 206 B5
Pobedino [RUS] 202 E5
Pobes [E] 82 G5
Pobiedziska [PL] 36 D2
Pobierowo [PL] 20 F3
Pobikry [PL] 38 E1
Pobra de Brollón, A- / Puebla del Brollón [E] 78 D4
Pobra do Caramiñal / Puebla del Caramiñal [E] 78 B3
Počátky [CZ] 48 H6
Počep [RUS] 204 D6
Pöchlarn [A] 62 D4
Počitelj [BIH] 152 C3
Pocking [D] 60 H4
Pocklington [GB] 10 G3
Počuta [YU] 150 A2
Podari [RO] 150 G1
Podbořany [CZ] 48 E3
Podborovje [RUS] 200 G3
Poddębice [PL] 36 F4
Poděbrady [CZ] 48 H3
Podence [P] 80 F4
Podensac [F] 66 D2
Podersdorf am See [A] 62 G5
Podgaje [PL] 22 B5
Podgarič [HR] 74 F6
Podgora [HR] 152 B2
Podgorač [HR] 154 D1
Podgorac [YU] 150 D2
Podgorica [YU] 152 E4
Podgorie [AL] 128 D4

Podgrad [SLO] 112 E1
Podgradec [AL] 128 D4
Podhalański [PL] 50 H4
Podivín [CZ] 62 G3
Podklasztorze [PL] 36 H5
Podkoren [SLO] 72 H3
Podkova [BG] 130 F2
Podkrepa [BG] 148 C6
Podkrivań [SK] 64 D3
Podnovlje [BIH] 154 D2
Podochóri [GR] 130 C4
Podolsk [RUS] 204 F4
Podravska Slatina [HR] 74 H6
Podromanija [BIH] 152 D1
Podslon [BG] 148 D5
Podujevo [YU] 150 C4
Podunavci [YU] 150 B3
Poeldijk [NL] 16 C5
Poetto [I] 118 D7
Poggendorf [D] 20 D3
Poggibonsi [I] 110 E6
Póggio Rusco [I] 110 F2
Pogoniani [GR] 132 C1
Pogoritsa [BG] 148 D3
Pogórze [PL] 50 D3
Pogrodzie [PL] 22 F2
Pohja [FIN] 176 G1
Pohja / Pojo [FIN] 176 F5
Pohja-Lankila [FIN] 188 F6
Pohjaslahti [FIN] 196 D8
Pohjaslahti [FIN] 186 E5
Pohjoislahti [FIN] 186 F4
Pohořelice [CZ] 62 F2
Poian Braşov [RO] 206 C5
Poiana Mare [RO] 150 F2
Poibrene [BG] 148 A5
Pointe des Poulains [F] 40 C5
Poirino [I] 70 D6
Poissons [F] 44 D6
Poitiers [F] 54 E4
Poix [F] 28 D5
Poix-Terron [F] 44 C2
Pojate [YU] 150 C2
Pojo / Pohja [FIN] 176 F5
Pokka [FIN] 196 C5
Pokój [PL] 50 E1
Pokrovske [UA] 206 H3
Pokupsko [HR] 112 H1
Pola de Allande [E] 78 F3
Pola de Laviana [E] 82 B2
Pola de Lena [E] 78 H4
Pola de Siero [E] 78 H3
Pola de Somiedo [E] 78 G4
Połajewo [PL] 36 C1
Polán [E] 96 E2
Polanica-Zdrój [PL] 50 C3
Połaniec [PL] 52 C2
Polanów [PL] 22 B3
Polcenigo [I] 72 F5
Połczyn [PL] 22 C3
Połczyn-Zdrój [PL] 20 H4
Pölde [EST] 200 C3
Polegate [GB] 14 E6
Polesella [I] 110 G2
Polessk [RUS] 202 D5
Polgár [H] 64 G5
Polgárdi [H] 76 B2
Poliani [GR] 136 D3
Poliçan [AL] 128 C6
Poliçan [AL] 128 C5
Policastro Bussentino [I] 120 G5
Police [PL] 20 F5
Police nad Metují [CZ] 50 B2
Políchnitos [GR] 134 G2
Polička [CZ] 50 B5
Policoro [I] 122 D5
Polignano a Mare [I] 122 E3
Poligny [F] 58 A6
Polikástano [GR] 128 E5
Polikrayshte [BG] 148 C3
Polipótamo [GR] 128 E4
Polistena [I] 124 D7
Politiká [GR] 134 B4
Poljana [HR] 154 B1
Polkowice [PL] 36 B5

Pöllau [A] 74 E1
Polle [D] 32 F3
Pollença [E] 104 E4
Pollfoss [N] 180 E5
Polloch [GB] 6 B6
Polmak [N] 196 D2
Polock [BY] 204 B4
Polohy [UA] 206 H4
Polomka [SK] 64 D2
Polop [E] 104 E2
Polperro [GB] 12 D5
Polski Gradets [BG] 148 D5
Polski Trŭmbesh [BG] 148 C3
Polsko Kosovo [BG] 148 C3
Poltava [UA] 206 G2
Põltsamaa [EST] 200 E2
Põlva [EST] 200 F3
Polvela [FIN] 188 E1
Polvijärvi [FIN] 188 F2
Polyany [RUS] 178 F4
Polýgyros [GR] 130 B5
Polýkastro [GR] 128 G3
Pomarance [I] 114 F1
Pomarico [I] 122 D4
Pomarkku [FIN] 176 D1
Pombal [P] 86 D2
Pomellen [D] 20 E5
Pomeroy [GB] 2 F3
Pomézia [I] 116 A6
Pomezí nad Ohří [CZ] 48 C3
Pomigliano d'Arco [I] 120 E3
Pomorie [BG] 148 F4
Pompaples [CH] 70 B1
Pompei [I] 120 E3
Pompey [F] 44 E5
Pómpia [GR] 140 E5
Pomysk Maly [PL] 22 C3
Poncin [F] 68 H2
Ponferrada [E] 78 F5
Poniatowa [PL] 38 D6
Poniky [SK] 64 C3
Ponoarele [RO] 206 B6
Pons [F] 54 C6
Ponsa [FIN] 176 G1
Ponsacco [I] 110 E6
Pont [I] 70 C4
Pontacq [F] 84 E3
Ponta do Sol [P] 100 A3
Pontailler-sur-Saône [F] 56 H4
Pont-à-Mousson [F] 44 E4
Pontarion [F] 54 H6
Pontarlier [F] 58 B6
Pontassieve [I] 110 F5
Pontaubault [F] 26 D4

Pont-Audemer [F] 26 G3
Pontaumur [F] 68 C2
Pont-Aven [F] 40 C3
Pont Canavese [I] 70 D4
Pont Cellier [F] 56 D5
Pontcharra [F] 70 A4
Pontchartrain [F] 42 E3
Pontchâteau [F] 40 E5
Pont-Croix [F] 40 B3
Pont-d'Ain [F] 68 G2
Pont-de-Briques [F] 28 D2
Pont-de-Dore [F] 68 D2
Pont-de-l'Arche [F] 28 B6
Pont-de-Roide [F] 58 C4
Pont-de-Salars [F] 68 B6
Pont-d'Espagne [F] 84 E4
Pont-de-Vaux [F] 56 G6
Ponte Arche [I] 72 C4
Ponteareas [E] 78 B5
Pontebba [I] 72 G3
Ponte-Caldelas [E] 78 B4
Ponteceso [E] 78 B2
Pontecesures [E] 78 B3
Pontechianale [I] 108 E2
Pontecorvo [I] 120 C1
Ponte da Barca [P] 78 B6
Pontedecimo [I] 110 B3
Ponte de Lima [P] 78 B6
Ponte della Venturina [I] 110 E4
Ponte dell'Oglio [I] 110 C2
Pontedera [I] 110 E6
Ponte de Sôr [P] 86 D5
Pontedeume [E] 78 D2
Ponte di Legno [I] 72 B4
Ponte di Piave [I] 72 F5
Pontefract [GB] 10 F4
Ponteland [GB] 8 F6
Pontelandolfo [I] 120 E2
Ponte-Leccia [F] 114 B3
Pontelongo [I] 110 G1
Ponte nelle Alpi [I] 72 E4
Pont-en-Royans [F] 68 G5
Ponte Nuovo [F] 114 B3
Ponterwyd [GB] 10 B6
Ponte San Pietro [I] 70 H4
Pontes de García Rodríguez, As- / Puentes de García Rodríguez [E] 78 D2
Ponte Tresa [CH] 70 F3
Ponte Ulla [E] 78 C3
Pontevedra [E] 78 B4
Pontevico [I] 110 D1
Pontgibaud [F] 68 C2
Pontigny [F] 56 E1
Pontinia [I] 120 B1
Pontinvrea [I] 108 H3
Pontisméno [GR] 130 B3
Pontivy [F] 26 A5

Pont-l'Abbé [F] 40 B3
Pont-l'Evêque [F] 26 G3
Pontlevoy [F] 54 G2
Pontllanfraith [GB] 12 F2
Pontoise [F] 42 F3
Pontokómi [GR] 128 F5
Pontoon [IRL] 2 C3
Pontorson [F] 26 D4
Pont-Réan [F] 26 C6
Pontremoli [I] 110 C3
Pontresina [CH] 72 A3
Pontrieux [F] 26 A3
Pontrilas [GB] 12 F1
Ponts [E] 92 C3
Pont-Scorff [F] 40 C4
Pont-St-Esprit [F] 106 G2
Pont-St-Martin [I] 70 D4
Pont-St-Vincent [F] 44 E5
Pont-sur-Yonne [F] 42 G5
Pontvallain [F] 42 B6
Pontypool [GB] 12 F2
Pontypridd [GB] 12 F2
Poole [GB] 12 G5
Poperinge [B] 28 F2
Poppenhausen [D] 46 F3
Poppi [I] 110 G6
Poprad [SK] 64 E2
Popsko [BG] 130 G1
Populónia [I] 114 G2
Porazava [BY] 24 G6
Porcuna [E] 102 D1
Porczyny [PL] 36 F4
Pordenone [I] 72 F5
Pordim [BG] 148 B3
Pordoi, Passo- [I] 72 E3
Poręba [PL] 50 G2
Poreč [HR] 112 D2
Porech'ye [BY] 24 G3
Pori [FIN] 176 D1
Porjus [S] 190 H1
Porkhov [RUS] 200 H3
Porlock [GB] 12 E3
Pörnbach [D] 60 E3
Pornic [F] 54 B1
Pornichet [F] 40 E6
Porokylä [FIN] 198 F6
Poronin [PL] 52 A6
Póros [GR] 132 D5
Póros [GR] 136 G2
Póros [GR] 132 D6
Poroszló [H] 64 F6
Porozina [HR] 112 E2
Pórpi [GR] 130 F3
Porquerolles [F] 108 C6

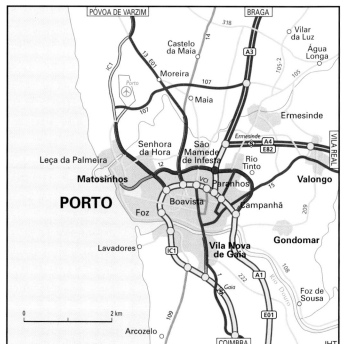

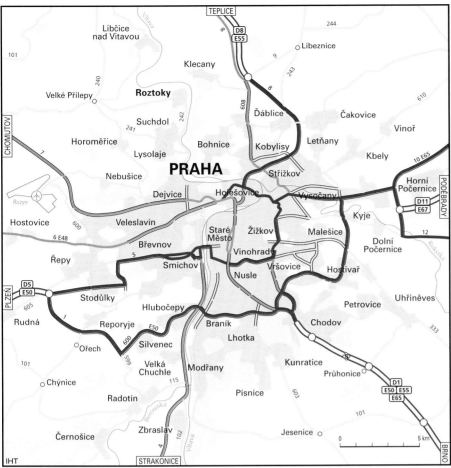

Porrentruy [CH] 58 D4
Porretta Terme [I] 110 E4
Porsgrunn [N] 164 G3
Portacloy [IRL] 2 C2
Portadown [GB] 2 G4
Portaferry [GB] 2 H4
Portalegre [P] 86 E5
Portalrubio [E] 90 D6
Portardawe [GB] 12 E2
Portariá [GR] 132 H2
Portarlington [IRL] 2 E6
Port Askaig [GB] 8 B2
Portavogie [GB] 2 H4
Portbail [F] 26 D2
Port–Barcarès [F] 92 G1
Portbou [E] 92 G2
Port–Camargue [F] 106 F4
Port Charlotte [GB] 8 B2
Portchester [GB] 12 H5
Port–Cros [F] 108 D6
Port d'Adaia [E] 104 H4
Port–de–Bouc [F] 106 G5
Port de Pollença [E] 104 F4
Portel [P] 94 E2
Portela do Home [E] 78 B6
Port Ellen [GB] 2 H1
Portelo [P] 80 F3
Port–en–Bessin [F] 26 E3
Port Erin [GBM] 2 H5
Pôrtes [GR] 136 G2
Port Eynon [GB] 12 E2
Portglenone [GB] 2 G3
Port–Grimaud [F] 108 D5
Porth [GB] 12 F2
Porthcawl [GB] 12 E3
Port Henderson [GB] 6 C4
Porthmadog [GB] 10 B4
Porticcio [F] 114 A5
Portile de Fier [Eur.] 206 B6
Portilla de la Reina [E] 82 D3
Portillo [E] 88 E2
Portimão [P] 94 B5
Portimo [FIN] 196 D8
Portinatx [E] 104 C5
Portinho da Arrábida [P] 86 B6
Portishead [GB] 12 F3
Port–Joinville [F] 54 A2

Portlairge / Waterford [IRL] 4 E5
Port–la–Nouvelle [F] 106 D5
Port Laoise [IRL] 2 E6
Port–Leucate [F] 106 D6
Portloe [GB] 12 C5
Port–Louis [F] 40 C4
Portmahomack [GB] 6 E4
Portman [E] 104 C4
Port–Manech [F] 40 C4
Portmarnock [IRL] 2 F6
Port Mór [GB] 6 B5
Portnacroish [GB] 8 C1
Portnahaven [GB] 2 G1
Port nan Long / Newtonferry [GB] 6 A3
Port–Navalo [F] 40 D5
Port Nis / Port of Ness [GB] 6 C2
Porto [F] 114 A4
Porto [P] 80 B4
Porto Alto [P] 86 B5
Porto Azzurro [I] 114 E3
Pórto Cárras [GR] 130 C6
Portocelo [P] 78 E1
Porto Ceresio [I] 70 F3
Porto Cervo [I] 118 E2
Porto Cesareo [I] 122 G5
Portochéli [GR] 136 F3
Porto Colom [E] 104 F5
Porto Corsini [I] 110 H3
Porto Covo [P] 94 B3
Porto Cristo [E] 104 F5
Porto da Cruz [P] 100 B3
Porto d'Áscoli [I] 116 D3
Porto de Mós [P] 86 C3
Porto do Son [E] 78 B3
Porto Empedocle [I] 126 D4
Porto Ércole [I] 114 F4
Portoferráio [I] 114 D2
Portofino [I] 110 B3
Port of Ness / Port Nis [GB] 6 C2
Porto Garibaldi [I] 110 H3
Pórto Germenó [GR] 134 B6
Pórto Kágio [GR] 136 E5
Porto Levante [I] 110 H2
Pörtom / Pirttikylä [FIN] 186 B3

Portomaggiore [I] 110 G3
Portomarín [E] 78 D4
Porto Moniz [P] 100 A3
Portomouro [E] 78 C3
Porto Novo [P] 86 B4
Porto–Pollo [F] 114 A5
Porto Potenza Picena [I] 116 C1
Portør [N] 164 F4
Pórto Ráfti [GR] 136 H1
Porto Recanati [I] 116 C1
Porto Rotondo [I] 118 E2
Portorož [SLO] 72 H6
Porto San Giorgio [I] 116 D2
Porto Sant'Elpidio [I] 116 C1
Porto Santo Stéfano [I] 114 F4
Portoscuso [I] 118 B7
Porto Tolle [I] 110 H2
Porto Tórres [I] 118 B3
Porto–Vecchio [F] 114 B6
Portovenere [I] 110 C4
Portpatrick [GB] 8 B5
Portreath [GB] 12 C5
Portree [GB] 6 B4
Portroe [IRL] 2 C6
Portrush [GB] 2 G2
Portsmouth [GB] 12 H5
Port–Ste–Marie [F] 66 E5
Portstewart [GB] 2 G2
Port–St–Louis–du–Rhône [F] 106 G5
Port St. Mary [GB] 10 B2
Port–sur–Saône [F] 58 B3
Port Talbot [GB] 12 E2
Portuairk [GB] 6 B6
Portumna [IRL] 2 D6
Port–Vendres [F] 92 G2
Port William [GB] 8 C5
Porvoo / Borgå [FIN] 178 B4
Porządzie [PL] 38 C1
Porzuna [E] 96 E3
Posada [E] 78 H3

Portomaggiore [I] 110 G3
Posada [E] 82 D2
Posada [I] 118 E3
Posadas [E] 102 B1
Poschiavo [CH] 72 B3
Posedarje [HR] 112 G5
Poseidonía [GR] 138 D2
Poshnjë [AL] 128 B4
Posio [FIN] 196 E8
Positano [I] 120 E4
Possagno [I] 72 E5
Pössneck [D] 46 H2
Posta [I] 116 B4
Postbridge [GB] 12 D4
Postojna [SLO] 74 B6
Postoloprty [CZ] 48 E3
Postomino [PL] 22 B2
Posušje [BIH] 152 B2
Potamiá [GR] 130 E4
Potamiés [GR] 140 F4
Potamoí [GR] 130 D2
Potamós [GR] 136 F6
Potamós [GR] 140 A3
Potamoúla [GR] 132 E4
Potenza [I] 120 H4
Potenza Picena [I] 116 C1
Potes [E] 82 D3
Potoci [BIH] 152 C2
Potok [HR] 154 B1
Potok [PL] 52 D4
Potrogruaro [I] 72 F5
Potsdam [D] 34 D2
Pottenstein [A] 62 E5
Pottenstein [D] 46 H4
Potters Bar [GB] 14 E4
Pöttmes [D] 60 D3
Pouancé [F] 40 G5
Pougues–les–Eaux [F] 56 D4
Pouilly [F] 56 D3
Pouilly–en–Auxois [F] 56 F3
Pouilly–sous–Charlieu [F] 68 E1
Poulton–le–Fylde [GB] 10 D3
Poúnda [GR] 138 E3
Poussu [FIN] 198 F2
Pouyastruc [F] 84 F3
Pouzauges [F] 54 C3
Považská Bystrica [SK] 64 B2

Poviglio [I] 110 E2
Povlja [HR] 152 A2
Póvoa [P] 94 E3
Póvoa de Lanhoso [P] 80 C3
Póvoa de Varzim [P] 80 B3
Powburn [GB] 8 F5
Powidz [PL] 36 E2
Powodow [PL] 36 G4
Poyatos [E] 98 C1
Poyntzpass [GB] 2 G4
Poyra [TR] 146 H5
Poyralı [TR] 146 C2
Poyrazdamları [TR] 144 E3
Poysdorf [A] 62 F3
Pöytyä [FIN] 176 E3
Poza de la Sal [E] 82 F5
Požarevac [YU] 206 A6
Pozazal, Puerto– [E] 82 E4
Požega [YU] 150 A2
Požeranje [YU] 150 C6
Poznań [PL] 36 C2
Pozo Alcón [E] 102 F3
Pozoblanco [E] 96 C5
Pozo–Cañada [E] 98 B6
Pozohondo [E] 98 B6
Požrzadło [PL] 34 H3
Pozuel de Ariza [E] 90 C4
Pozuelo de Zarzón [E] 86 H3
Pozzallo [I] 126 F6
Pozzomaggiore [I] 118 C4
Pozzuoli [I] 120 D3
Prabuty [PL] 22 F4
Prača [BIH] 152 D1
Prachatice [CZ] 62 B2
Pradelle [F] 68 G6
Pradelles [F] 68 D5
Prades [F] 92 F1
Pradillo [E] 90 B1
Pradła [PL] 50 H2
Prado del Rey [E] 100 H4
Pradoluengo [E] 82 F6
Præstø [DK] 156 G4
Prägraten [A] 72 F2
Praha [CZ] 48 F3
Prahecq [F] 54 D4
Prahovo [YU] 150 E1
Praia a Mare [I] 120 G6
Praia da Barra [P] 80 B5
Praia da Vieira [P] 86 C2
Praia de Mira [P] 80 A5
Praia Grande [P] 86 A5
Praiano [I] 120 E4
Praias–Sado [P] 86 B6
Praisós [GR] 140 G5
Prakovce [SK] 64 F2
Pralognan–la–Vanoise [F] 70 B4
Prali [I] 70 C6
Pralormo [I] 70 C6
Prámanta [GR] 132 D2
Pranjani [YU] 150 B2
Prapatnica [HR] 116 H1
Prassiá [GR] 132 E3
Prassies [GR] 140 D4
Praszka [PL] 36 F6
Pratella [I] 120 D1
Prati di Tivo [I] 116 C4
Prato [I] 110 E5
Prats de Lluçanès [E] 92 E3
Prats–de–Mollo–la–Preste [F] 92 F2
Prauthoy [F] 56 H3
Pravdinsk [RUS] 22 H2
Pravets [BG] 150 G4
Pravia [E] 78 G3
Pravlov [CZ] 62 F3
Prečno [HR] 74 F6
Précy–sous–Thil [F] 56 F3
Predappio [I] 110 G4
Predazzo [I] 72 D4
Preddvor [SLO] 74 B4
Predeal [RO] 206 C5
Predejane [YU] 150 E4
Predel [SLO] 72 H4
Predeşti [RO] 150 F1
Predlitz [A] 74 B2
Predoi / Prettau [I] 72 E2
Pré–en–Pail [F] 26 F5
Preesall [GB] 10 D3
Preetz [D] 18 G2

Pregarten [A] 62 C4
Preili [LV] 200 F6
Prekal [AL] 150 A6
Preko [HR] 112 G5
Prelog [HR] 74 F4
Přelouč [CZ] 48 H4
Prémery [F] 56 D3
Premià de Mar [E] 92 E4
Premnitz [D] 34 C2
Prenjas [AL] 128 C3
Prenzlau [D] 20 E5
Přerov [CZ] 50 D5
Prerow [D] 20 C2
Preselentsi [BG] 148 G2
Preševo [YU] 150 D6
Prešov [SK] 64 G2
Pressac [F] 54 F5
Pressath [D] 48 B4
Pressbaum [A] 62 E4
Prestatyn [GB] 10 C4
Pré St–Didier [I] 70 C3
Presteigne [GB] 12 F1
Prestestranda [N] 164 F3
Prestfoss [N] 170 G5
Přeštice [CZ] 48 D5
Preston [GB] 10 D3
Prestwick [GB] 8 C4
Prettau / Predoi [I] 72 E2
Prettin [D] 34 D4
Pretzsch [D] 34 D4
Preuilly–sur–Claise [F] 54 G3
Préveranges [F] 56 B5
Préveza [GR] 132 D4
Pribeta [SK] 64 B5
Priboj [BIH] 154 E3
Priboj [YU] 152 E2
Příbor [CZ] 50 E5
Pribovce [SK] 64 C2
Přibram [CZ] 48 F5
Přibyslav [CZ] 50 A4
Prichsenstadt [D] 46 F4
Pridvorci [BIH] 152 C2
Pridvorica [YU] 150 B3
Priego [E] 90 B6
Priego de Córdoba [E] 102 C3
Priekule [LV] 200 B6
Priekuli [LV] 200 E4
Prien [D] 60 F5
Prienai [LT] 24 F1
Prievidza [SK] 64 B3
Prigrevica [YU] 76 C6
Prijeboj [HR] 112 G3
Prijedor [BIH] 154 B2
Prijepolje [YU] 150 A3
Prilep [MK] 128 E2
Prilike [YU] 150 A3
Priluka [BIH] 152 B1
Priluki [UA] 206 F2
Primda [CZ] 48 C4
Primel–Trégastel [F] 40 C1
Primolano [I] 72 D5
Primorsk [RUS] 22 G1
Primorsk [RUS] 178 F4
Primorsko [BG] 148 F5
Primor'ye [RUS] 202 C5
Primošten [HR] 116 H1
Primstal [D] 44 G3
Princes Risborough [GB] 14 D3
Princetown [GB] 12 D4
Prínos [GR] 130 E4
Priolo Gargallo [I] 126 G4
Priozersk [RUS] 178 G1
Prirečnyj [RUS] 196 F4
Priseltsi [BG] 148 F3
Prislop, Pasul– [RO] 206 C4
Prisoje [BIH] 152 B1
Prissac [F] 54 G4
Priština [YU] 150 C5
Pritzerbe [D] 34 C2
Pritzier [D] 18 H5
Pritzwalk [D] 20 B5
Privas [F] 68 F5
Priverno [I] 120 C1
Privlaka [HR] 112 F4
Prizna [HR] 112 F3
Prizren [YU] 150 B6

Prizzi [I] 126 D3
Prnalija [MK] 128 G1
Prnjavor [BIH] 154 C2
Prnjavor [YU] 154 F3
Probištip [MK] 128 F1
Probstzella [D] 46 H2
Prochowice [PL] 36 B6
Prodromós [GR] 132 H5
Proença-a-Nova [P] 86 E3
Profítis [GR] 130 B4
Profondeville [B] 30 D5
Progled [BG] 130 E1
Prohor Pčinjski [YU] 150 D6
Prókhoma [GR] 128 H4
Prokópi [GR] 134 B4
Prokuplje [YU] 150 D4
Prolaz [BG] 148 D3
Promachónas [GR] 130 B2
Prómahi [GR] 128 F3
Promna [PL] 38 B4
Pronsfeld [D] 30 F6
Propriano [F] 114 A5
Prosotsáni [GR] 130 C3
Prostějov [CZ] 50 C5
Prószków [PL] 50 E2
Proszowice [PL] 52 B3
Protiči [BIH] 154 B4
Protivín [CZ] 48 F6
Prötzel [D] 34 F2
Prousós [GR] 132 E4
Provadiya [BG] 148 F3
Provins [F] 42 H5
Prozor [BIH] 152 C1
Pruchnik [PL] 52 F4
Prudhoe [GB] 8 F6
Prudnik [PL] 50 D3
Prüm [D] 30 F6
Pruna [E] 102 A3
Prundu [RO] 148 D1
Prunete [F] 114 C4
Prunetta [I] 110 E5
Prunn [D] 60 E2
Prusice [PL] 36 C5
Pruszcz [PL] 22 D5
Pruszcz Gdański [PL] 22 E3
Pruszków [PL] 38 B3
Pruzhany [BY] 38 H1
Pruzhicy [RUS] 178 F6
Przasnysz [PL] 24 B6
Przechlewo [PL] 22 C4
Przedbórz [PL] 36 H6
Przedecz [PL] 36 F3
Przemków [PL] 36 A5
Przemyśl [PL] 52 F4
Przewale [PL] 52 G2
Przeworsk [PL] 52 E3
Przezmark [PL] 22 F4
Przybiernów [PL] 20 F4
Przybychowo [PL] 36 C1
Przylesie [PL] 50 D2
Przysucha [PL] 38 B5
Przyszowa [PL] 52 B5
Przytoczna [PL] 36 A2
Przytoczno [PL] 38 D4
Przytyk [PL] 38 B5
Pšaca [MK] 150 E6
Psachná [GR] 134 B4
Psará [GR] 134 F4
Psarshai [BY] 202 H6
Psáthi [GR] 138 D4
Psathópyrgos [GR] 132 F5
Psihikó [GR] 132 G2
Psihró [GR] 140 F5
Pskov [RUS] 200 G3
Pszczew [PL] 36 A2
Pszczyna [PL] 50 G4
Ptolemáida [GR] 128 F5
Ptuj [SLO] 74 E4
Ptujska Gora [SLO] 74 E4
Puchberg [A] 62 E5
Púchov [SK] 50 F6
Pučišća [HR] 152 A2
Puck [PL] 22 D1
Puçol [E] 98 F4
Pudasjärvi [FIN] 198 E3
Puddletown [GB] 12 F5
Puebla de Alcocer [E] 96 C3
Puebla de Don Fadrique [E] 102 H2

Puebla de Don Rodrigo [E] 96 D3
Puebla de Guzmán [E] 94 E4
Puebla de la Calzada [E] 94 G1
Puebla del Brollón / Pobra de Brollón, A- [E] 78 D4
Puebla del Caramiñal / Pobra do Caramiñal [E] 78 B3
Puebla de Lillo [E] 82 C3
Puebla de Obando [E] 86 G6
Puebla de Sanabria [E] 80 G3
Puebla de Vallés [E] 88 G4
Puente Almuhey [E] 82 C4
Puente de Domingo Flórez [E] 78 E5
Puente de Génave [E] 96 G6
Puente de Montañana [E] 92 B2
Puente Genil [E] 102 C2
Puente la Reina / Gares [E] 84 B4
Puente la Reina de Jaca [E] 84 D5
Puentelarra [E] 82 G5
Puentes de García Rodríguez / Pontes de García Rodríguez, As- [E] 78 D2
Puente Viesgo [E] 82 E3
Puerto Banús [E] 102 A5
Puerto Castilla [E] 88 C5
Puerto de Itziar [E] 82 H4
Puerto de la Cruz [E] 100 C5
Puerto del Rosario [E] 100 E5
Puerto de Mazarrón [E] 104 C4
Puerto de San Vicente [E] 96 C2
Puerto Lápice [E] 96 F3
Puertollano [E] 96 E5
Puerto Lumbreras [E] 104 A4
Puerto Real [E] 100 F4
Puerto Rey [E] 104 A5
Puffendorf [D] 30 F4
Puget-sur-Argens [F] 108 D5
Puget-Théniers [F] 108 E4
Puget-Ville [F] 108 C5
Pugnochiuso [I] 116 H6
Puhos [FIN] 188 F4
Puhos [FIN] 198 E3
Puig [E] 98 F4
Puigcerdà [E] 92 E1
Puig-reig [E] 92 E3
Puiseaux [F] 42 F5
Puivert [F] 106 B5
Pukavik [S] 158 E1
Pukë [AL] 128 B1
Pukiš [BIH] 154 E3
Pula [HR] 112 D3
Pula [I] 118 C7
Puławy [PL] 38 D5
Pulborough [GB] 14 D5
Pulju [FIN] 192 H4
Pulkau [A] 62 E3
Pulkkila [FIN] 198 D5
Pulkovo [RUS] 178 H5
Pulpí [E] 104 B4
Pulsnitz [D] 34 F6
Pułtusk [PL] 38 B1
Pumpėnai [LT] 202 F4
Punkalaidun [FIN] 176 E2
Punta Ala [I] 114 E2
Punta de Moraira [E] 104 F2
Puntagorda [E] 100 A5
Punta Križa [HR] 112 E3
Punta Marina [I] 110 H4

Punta Prima [E] 104 H5
Punta Umbría [E] 94 E6
Puokio [FIN] 198 E4
Puolanka [FIN] 198 E4
Purbach [A] 62 F5
Purchena [E] 102 G4
Purgstall [A] 62 D5
Purkersdorf [A] 62 E4
Purmerend [NL] 16 D4
Purullena [E] 102 F4
Pürvomay [BG] 148
Puša [LV] 200 G6
Pushkinskiye Gory [RUS] 200 H4
Puškin [RUS] 178 H5
Puškino [RUS] 204 F4
Püspökladány [H] 76 G1
Pustevny [CZ] 50 E5
Pustków [PL] 52 D3
Pustoška [RUS] 204 C4
Pusula [FIN] 176 G4
Puszczykowo [PL] 36 C3
Pusztamonostor [H] 64 D6
Pusztaszemes [H] 76 A3
Putaja [FIN] 176 E1
Putanges-Pont-Ecrepin [F] 26 F5
Putbus [D] 20 D2
Putignano [I] 122 E3
Putikko [FIN] 188 F5
Putim [CZ] 48 F6
Putinci [YU] 154 G2
Putineiu [RO] 148 C1
Putineiu [RO] 148 B2
Putivl [UA] 204 E7
Putlitz [D] 20 B5
Putnok [H] 64 E4
Puttelange [F] 44 G4
Putten [NL] 16 E4
Puttgarden [D] 20 A2
Puumala [FIN] 188 E6
Puurmani [EST] 200 F2
Puy de Dôme [F] 68 C2
Puy-Guillaume [F] 68 D2
Puylaurens [F] 106 B3
Puy-l'Evêque [F] 66 F5
Pwllheli [GB] 10 B4
Pyhäjärvi [FIN] 198 E6
Pyhäjärvi [FIN] 196 D7
Pyhäjoki [FIN] 198 C5
Pyhäkylä [FIN] 198 F3
Pyhältö [FIN] 178 D3
Pyhämaa [FIN] 176 C3
Pyhäntä [FIN] 198 E5
Pyhäntaka [FIN] 178 B2
Pyhäranta [FIN] 176 C3
Pyhäsalmi [FIN] 198 E6
Pyhäselkä [FIN] 188 F3
Pyhtää / Pyttis [FIN] 178 C4
Pyla-sur-Mer [F] 66 B3
Pylí [GR] 142 B3
Pýli [GR] 132 E2
Pylkönmäki [FIN] 186 F3
Pýlos [GR] 136 C4
Pyntäinen [FIN] 186 B6
Pyrgakia [GR] 138 F3
Pýrgoi [GR] 128 F4
Pýrgos [GR] 136 C2
Pýrgos [GR] 140 E5
Pýrgos [GR] 144 C5
Pýrgos Diroú [GR] 136 E5
Pyrsógianni [GR] 128 D6
Pyrzyce [PL] 20 F6
Pyšely [CZ] 48 G4

Pyskowice [PL] 50 F3
Pytalovo [RUS] 200 G4
Pythagóreon [GR] 142 B1
Pyttis / Pyhtää [FIN] 178 C4
Pyzdry [PL] 36 D3

Q

Quakenbrück [D] 18 C6
Quarré-les-Tombes [F] 56 F3
Quarteira [P] 94 C5
Quartu S Elena [I] 118 D7
Quebradas [P] 86 C4
Quedlinburg [D] 34 A4
Queluz [P] 86 B5
Quercamps [F] 28 E2
Quercianella [I] 110 D6
Querfurt [D] 34 B5
Quesada [E] 102 F2
Questembert [F] 40 E5
Quettehou [F] 26 D2
Quiberon [F] 40 C5
Quickborn [D] 18 F4
Quillan [F] 106 B5
Quimper [F] 40 B3
Quimperlé [F] 40 C4
Quinéville [F] 26 E2
Quingey [F] 58 B5
Quintana de la Serena [E] 96 B3
Quintana del Puente [E] 82 D6
Quintanaortuño [E] 82 E5
Quintanar de la Orden [E] 96 G3
Quintanar de la Sierra [E] 90 A2
Quintanar del Rey [E] 98 B4
Quintanilha [P] 80 G4
Quintanilla de las Viñas [E] 88 H1
Quintanilla de Onésimo [E] 88 F2
Quintanilla-Sobresierra [E] 82 E5
Quintin [F] 26 A4
Quinto [E] 90 F4
Quiroga [E] 78 E5
Quissac [F] 106 F3
Qyteti Stalin [AL] 128 B4

R

Råå [S] 156 H2
Raab [A] 62 A4
Raabs an der Thaya [A] 62 D2
Raahe [FIN] 198 C4
Rääkkylä [FIN] 188 F3
Raalte [NL] 16 F4
Raanujärvi [FIN] 196 C7
Raattama [FIN] 192 H4
Rab [HR] 112 F3
Rabac [HR] 112 E2
Rábade [E] 78 D3
Rábafüzes [H] 74 F2
Rabastens [F] 106 B2
Rabastens-de-Bigorre [F] 84 F3
Rabat [M] 126 C6
Rábatamasi [H] 62 G6
Rabbalshede [S] 166 C5
Rabí [CZ] 48 E6
Rabisha [BG] 150 E2
Rabka [PL] 50 H5
Rabsztyn [PL] 50 H3
Rača [SK] 62 G4
Rača [YU] 150 C1
Rača [YU] 150 C4
Racalmuto [I] 126 D4
Racconigi [I] 108 G2
Ráches [GR] 132 H4
Raciąż [PL] 36 H1
Raciążek [PL] 36 F1
Racibórz [PL] 50 E4

Ráckeve [H] 76 C2
Rackwick [GB] 6 F2
Rączki [PL] 22 G5
Raczki [PL] 24 E3
Råda [S] 166 F1
Radalj [YU] 154 E3
Rădăuţi [RO] 206 C4
Radawnica [PL] 22 B5
Radcliffe-on-Trent [GB] 10 F5
Raddusa [I] 126 F3
Rade [D] 18 F4
Råde [N] 166 B3
Radeberg [D] 34 F6
Radebeul [D] 34 E6
Radeburg [D] 34 E6
Radeče [SLO] 74 D5
Radegast [D] 34 C4
Radenci [SLO] 74 E3
Radenthein [A] 72 H3
Radevormwald [D] 30 H4
Radkersburg [A] 74 E3
Radko Dimitrievo [BG] 148 E3
Radków [PL] 50 B2
Radlje ob Dràvi [SLO] 74 D3
Radmirje [SLO] 74 C4
Radna [RO] 76 H4
Radnevo [BG] 148 D5
Radnica [PL] 34 H3
Radnice [CZ] 48 E4
Radolfzell [D] 58 G4
Radom [PL] 38 C5
Radomin [PL] 22 F6
Radomir [BG] 150 F5
Radomiru [RO] 150 G1
Radomsko [PL] 36 G6
Radomyśśl Wielki [PL] 52 C3
Radošina [SK] 64 A3
Radoškoviči [BY] 204 B5
Radošovce [SK] 62 G3
Radostowo [PL] 22 H3
Radotín [CZ] 48 F4
Radovanu [RO] 150 F1
Radovets [BG] 146 A1
Radoviš [MK] 128 G2
Radovljica [SLO] 74 B4
Radowo Wielkie [PL] 20 G4
Radstadt [A] 72 H1
Radstock [GB] 12 G3
Radujevac [YU] 150 E1
Radun' [BY] 24 H3
Radviliškis [LT] 202 F4
Radymno [PL] 52 F4
Radzanów [PL] 22 G6
Radziądz [PL] 36 C5
Radziejów [PL] 36 F2
Radziwie [PL] 36 G2
Radzymin [PL] 38 B2
Radzyn Chełmiński [PL] 22 E5
Radzyń Podlaski [PL] 38 E4
Raesfeld [D] 16 G6
Raffadali [I] 126 D4
Rafína [GR] 134 C6
Rafsbotn [N] 192 G1
Ragaciems [LV] 200 D5
Ragana [LV] 200 E5
Ragaška Slatina [SLO] 74 D4
Rågeleje [DK] 156 G1
Raglan [GB] 12 F2
Ragusa [I] 126 F5
Raguva [LT] 202 F4
Raharney [IRL] 2 E5
Rahden [D] 32 E2
Råholt [N] 172 C5
Rahov [UA] 206 C3
Räisälä [FIN] 196 E7
Raisio [FIN] 176 D4
Raistakka [FIN] 196 E8
Raivala [FIN] 186 C5
Raja-Jooseppi [FIN] 196 E5

Rajamäki [FIN] 176 G4
Rajë [AL] 150 A6
Rajec [SK] 64 B2
Rajecké Teplice [SK] 64 B2
Rajgród [PL] 24 E4
Rajka [H] 62 G5
Raka [SLO] 74 D5
Rakamaz [H] 64 G4
Rakitovo [BG] 148 A6
Rakkestad [N] 166 C2
Rákóczifalva [H] 76 E2
Rákos [H] 76 F4
Rakoszyce [PL] 36 C6
Rakovica [HR] 112 G2
Rakovitsa [BG] 150 E2
Rakovník [CZ] 48 E3
Rakovski [BG] 148 B5
Raków [PL] 52 C2
Rakvere [EST] 200 F1
Ralja [YU] 154 G3
Ramacastañas [E] 88 D5
Ramacca [I] 126 F4
Ramales de la Victoria [E] 82 F3
Ramallosa [E] 78 B5
Ramberg [N] 192 B4
Rambervillers [F] 44 F6
Rambin [D] 20 D2
Rambouillet [F] 42 E4
Ramkvilla [S] 162 E4
Rammen [S] 166 F1
Ramnäs [S] 168 B2
Ramsau [A] 72 H1
Ramsberg [S] 166 H2
Ramsele [S] 184 D1
Ramsey [GB] 14 F2
Ramsey [GBM] 8 C6
Ramsgate [GB] 14 G5
Rämshyttan [S] 172 H5
Ramsjö [S] 184 C5
Ramstein [D] 44 H3
Ramsund [N] 192 D4
Ramvik [S] 184 F3
Ramygala [LT] 202 F4
Råna [N] 164 C5
Ranalt [A] 72 D2
Randaberg [N] 164 A3
Randalstown [GB] 2 G3
Randan [F] 68 D1
Randazzo [I] 124 A8
Randen [N] 180 G5
Randers [DK] 160 D5
Randín [E] 78 C6
Randsverk [N] 180 G6
Råneå [S] 198 B2
Rânes [F] 26 F5
Rangstrup [DK] 156 C3
Rankweil [A] 58 H5
Rannoch Station [GB] 8 D1
Rantasalmi [FIN] 188 E4
Rantsila [FIN] 198 D4
Ranua [FIN] 198 D2
Ranum [DK] 160 D4
Raon-l'Etape [F] 44 F6
Rapallo [I] 110 B3
Räpina [EST] 200 G3
Rapla [EST] 200 D2
Rapness [GB] 6 G1
Rapolla [I] 120 G3
Raposa [P] 86 C5
Rapperswil [CH] 58 G5
Rappottenstein [A] 62 D3
Rapsáni [GR] 132 G1
Raron [CH] 70 E2
Raša [HR] 112 E2
Rascafría [E] 88 F4
Raseiniai [LT] 202 E4
Rasharkin [GB] 2 G2
Rasivaara [FIN] 188 F3
Raška [YU] 150 B4
Rasktinkylä [FIN] 198 G5
Rasná [CZ] 48 H6
Rasovo [BG] 150 F2
Rast [RO] 150 F2
Rastatt [D] 46 B6
Råsted [DK] 160 D5
Rastede [D] 18 C5
Rastenfeld [A] 62 D3
Rasteš [MK] 128 D1

Rasti [FIN] 196 C6
Rastošnica [BIH] 154 E3
Rätansbyn [S] 182 G4
Rateče [SLO] 72 H3
Ratekau [D] 18 G3
Rathangen [IRL] 2 E6
Rathcoole [IRL] 2 F6
Rathcormack [IRL] 4 D5
Rathdrum [IRL] 4 G4
Rathenow [D] 34 C2
Rathfriland [GB] 2 G4
Rathkeale [IRL] 4 C3
Rath Luirc / Charleville [IRL] 4 C4
Rathmelton [IRL] 2 F2
Rathmolyon [IRL] 2 F5
Rathmullan / Rathmullen [IRL] 2 F2
Rathmullen / Rathmullan [IRL] 2 F2
Rathnew [IRL] 4 G4
Rathvilty [IRL] 4 F4
Ratingen [D] 30 G3
Ratne [UA] 38 H4
Ratten [A] 74 E1
Rattenberg [A] 60 E6
Rattersdorf [A] 74 F1
Rattosjärvi [FIN] 192 H6
Rättvik [S] 172 H3
Ratzeburg [D] 18 G4
Raubling [D] 60 F5
Raudaskylä [FIN] 198 D5
Raudeberg [N] 180 B4
Raufa [IS] 194 G3
Raufoss [N] 172 B3
Rauhala [FIN] 192 H5
Rauhaniemi [FIN] 188 E5
Rauland Høyfjellshotell [N] 164 E1
Rauma [FIN] 176 C2
Raumünzach [D] 58 F1
Rauna [LV] 200 E4
Rauris [A] 72 G1
Rautajärvi [FIN] 176 G1
Rautalampi [FIN] 186 H3
Rautas [S] 192 E5
Rautavaara [FIN] 198 F6
Rautila [FIN] 176 D4
Rautio [FIN] 198 C5
Rautjärvi [FIN] 178 F1
Rauvatn [N] 190 E2
Ravanusa [I] 126 E4
Rava–Rus'ka [UA] 52 G3
Ravatn [N] 190 D3
Ravda [BG] 148 F4
Ravello [I] 120 E4
Rävemåla [S] 162 E5
Ravenglass [GB] 10 D2
Ravenna [I] 110 H4
Ravensbrück [D] 20 D5
Ravensburg [D] 60 A5
Raversijde [B] 28 F1
Rävmarken [S] 166 C4
Ravna Dubrava [YU] 150 E4
Ravna Reka [YU] 150 D2
Ravno [BIH] 152 C3
Rawa Mazowiecka [PL] 38 A4
Rawicz [PL] 36 C5
Rawtenstall [GB] 10 E3
Rayleigh [GB] 14 F4
Rayol [F] 108 D6
Räyrinki [FIN] 186 D1
Razboj [BIH] 154 C2
Razbojna [YU] 150 C3
Razdrto [SLO] 74 B6
Razgrad [BG] 148 D2
Reading [GB] 14 D4
Réalmont [F] 106 B3
Realp [CH] 70 F1
Reanacloogheen [IRL] 4 D5
Reay [GB] 6 E2
Rebais [F] 42 H4
Reboly [RUS] 198 G5
Rebordelo [P] 80 E3
Rebŭrkovo [BG] 150 G4
Recanati [I] 116 C1
Recaş [RO] 76 H5
Recea [RO] 150 E1
Recey–sur–Ource [F] 56 G2

Rechnitz [A] 74 F1
Rečica [BY] 204 C6
Recke [D] 32 C2
Recklinghausen [D] 30 H2
Recoaro Terme [I] 72 C5
Recologne [F] 58 B4
Recsk [H] 64 G5
Recz [PL] 20 G5
Ręczno [PL] 36 H6
Reda [PL] 22 D2
Redalen [N] 172 B3
Redcar [GB] 10 G2
Redditch [GB] 12 H1
Redea [RO] 148 A1
Redefin [D] 18 H5
Rédics [H] 74 F3
Redon [F] 40 E5
Redondela [E] 78 B4
Redondo [P] 94 E1
Redruth [GB] 12 C5
Rees [D] 16 F6
Reeth [GB] 10 F2
Refnes [N] 192 C4
Refsnes [N] 192 C3
Reftele [S] 162 C4
Regalbuto [I] 126 F3
Regéc [H] 64 G4
Regen [D] 60 H2
Regensburg [D] 48 B6
Regenstauf [D] 48 B6
Reggello [I] 110 F6
Réggio di Calábria [I] 124 C7
Reggiolo [I] 110 E2
Réggio nell 'Emilia [I] 110 E3
Reghin [RO] 206 C4
Reguengos de Monsaraz [P] 94 E2
Rehau [D] 48 B3
Rehden [D] 32 E1
Rehna [D] 18 H4
Reichenau [D] 58 G4
Reichenau an der Rax [A] 62 E4
Reichenbach [D] 48 C2
Reichenbach [D] 34 G6
Reichenberg [D] 34 F2
Reichertshausen [D] 60 E3
Reichertshofen [D] 60 E3
Reiff [GB] 6 C3
Reigate [GB] 14 E5
Reignier [F] 70 B2
Reila [FIN] 176 C3
Reims [F] 44 B3
Reinach [CH] 58 E4
Reinach [CH] 58 F5
Reinberg [D] 20 D3
Reine [N] 192 B5
Reinfeld [D] 18 G3
Reinhardshagen [D] 32 F4
Reinheim [D] 46 C3
Reinosa [E] 82 E4
Reinsfeld [D] 44 G2
Reinsvoll [N] 172 B4
Reisbach [D] 60 G3
Reischach [D] 60 G4
Reischenhart [D] 60 F5
Reisjärvi [FIN] 198 D6
Reit im Winkl [D] 60 F5
Reitzehain [D] 48 D2
Rejmyre [S] 168 B4
Rejowiec Fabryczny [PL] 38 F6
Rejštejn [CZ] 48 E6
Reken [D] 16 G6
Remagen [D] 30 H5
Rémalard [F] 26 G6
Remels [D] 18 C4
Remeskylä [FIN] 198 E5
Remetea Mare [RO] 76 G5
Remich [L] 44 F3
Remiremont [F] 58 C3
Remnes [N] 190 D2
Remolinos [E] 90 E3
Remouchamps [B] 30 E5
Remoulins [F] 106 G3
Remscheid [D] 30 H4
Rémuzat [F] 108 B2
Rena [N] 172 C2
Renaison [F] 68 E2
Renaix (Ronse) [B] 28 G3

Rencēni [LV] 200 E4
Renchen [D] 58 F1
Renda [LV] 200 C5
Rendal [N] 180 G2
Rende [I] 124 D4
Rendsburg [D] 18 F2
Rengínio [GR] 132 H4
Reni [UA] 206 D5
Renko [FIN] 176 G3
Renkum [NL] 16 E5
Rennebu [N] 180 H3
Rennerod [D] 46 B1
Rennes [F] 26 C6
Rennweg [A] 72 H2
Renon / Ritten [I] 72 D3
Rens [DK] 156 B4
Rensjön [S] 192 E4
Rentería / Errenteria [E] 84 B2
Rentína [GR] 132 F3
Rentína [GR] 130 C4
Répáshuta [H] 64 F5
Répcelak [H] 74 G1
Repino [RUS] 178 G4
Repki [UA] 204 C7
Replot / Raippaluoto [FIN] 186 A2
Repojoki [FIN] 196 C5
Reposaari [FIN] 176 C1
Reppen [N] 190 D1
Repvåg [N] 196 C2
Requena [E] 98 D4
Rerik [D] 20 A3
Res [AL] 128 C1
Reşadiye [TR] 142 D3
Resana [I] 72 E6
Resen [MK] 128 D3
Rešetilovka [UA] 206 G2
Reshety [RUS] 200 H4
Reşiţa [RO] 206 A5
Resko [PL] 20 G4
Resmo [S] 162 G5
Ressons [F] 28 E6
Reszel [PL] 24 B3
Retamar [E] 102 G5
Retamosa [E] 96 C1
Retford [GB] 10 F5
Rethel [F] 44 C2

Rethem [D] 18 E6
Réthymno [GR] 140 D4
Retiers [F] 40 G4
Retortillo de Soria [E] 90 A3
Retournac [F] 68 E4
Rétság [H] 64 C5
Retuerta del Bullaque [E] 96 E2
Retz [A] 62 E3
Reuilly [F] 56 B3
Rennebu [N]
Rennerod [D] 46 B1
Reusel [NL] 30 E3
Reuterstadt Stavenhagen [D] 20 C4
Reutlingen [D] 58 H2
Reutte [A] 60 C6
Revel [F] 106 B4
Revfülöp [H] 74 H3
Révigny [F] 44 C4
Révigny–sur–Ornain [F] 44 C4
Revin [F] 44 C1
 Řevničov [CZ] 48 E3
Revonlahti [FIN] 198 D4
Revsnes [N] 170 D2
Revsnes [N] 190 B5
Revúca [SK] 64 E3
Rewal [PL] 20 F3
Reyðarfjörður [IS] 194 G5
Reykhólar [IS] 194 C2
Reykholt [IS] 194 B3
Reykjahlíð [IS] 194 F4
Reykjavík [IS] 194 B4
Rēzekne [LV] 200 G5
Rezovo [BG] 148 G5
Rgotina [YU] 150 E2
Rhayader [GB] 10 C6
Rheda [D] 32 D3
Rhede [D] 16 G6
Rheinau [D] 44 H6
Rheinbach [D] 30 G5
Rheinberg [D] 30 G2
Rheinböllen [D] 44 H2
Rheindahlen [D] 30 F3
Rheine [D] 16 H5
Rheinfelden [CH] 58 E4
Rheinfelden [D] 58 E4
Rheinsberg [D] 20 C6
Rheinzabern [D] 46 B5

Rhenen [NL] 16 E5
Rhens [D] 30 H6
Rheydt [D] 30 G3
Rhinau [F] 58 E2
Rhinow [D] 34 C1
Rho [I] 70 G5
Rhosneigr [GB] 10 B4
Rhuddlan [GB] 10 C4
Rhyl [GB] 10 C4
Rhymney [GB] 12 F2
Rhynern [D] 32 C4
Rhynie [GB] 6 F2
Riaillé [F] 40 G6
Riákia [GR] 128 G5
Riaño [E] 82 C3
Rians [F] 108 C4
Riaza [E] 88 G3
Ribadavia [E] 78 C5
Ribadelago [E] 78 E6
Ribadeo [E] 78 F2
Ribadesella [E] 82 C2
Ribaforada [E] 84 B6
Ribarci [YU] 150 E5
Ribariče [YU] 150 B4
Ribaritsa [BG] 148 A4
Riba–roja de Túria [E] 98 E4
Ribe [DK] 156 B3
Ribeauville [F] 58 D2
Ribécourt [F] 28 E6
Ribeira Brava [P] 100 A3
Ribeira de Pena [P] 80 D3
Ribemont [F] 28 F5
Ribera [I] 126 C3
Ribérac [F] 66 E2
Ribera de Cardós [E] 84 G6
Ribera del Fresno [E] 94 H3
Ribes de Freser [E] 92 E2
Ribnica [BIH] 154 D3
Ribnica [SLO] 74 C6
Ribniţa [MD] 206 E4
Ribnitz–Damgarten [D] 20 C2
Ribolla [I] 114 F2
Ricadi [I] 124 C6
Říčany [CZ] 48 G4
Riccarton [GB] 8 E5

Riccia [I] 120 F1
Riccione [I] 112 B5
Richelieu [F] 54 F3
Richmond [GB] 10 F2
Richmond [GB] 14 E4
Richtenberg [D] 20 C3
Rickling [D] 18 G3
Ricla [E] 90 D4
Riddarhyttan [S] 166 H2
Ridjica [YU] 76 C5
Ried [A] 72 C2
Riedenburg [D] 60 E2
Riedern [D] 58 F4
Ried im Innkreis [A] 60 H4
Riedlingen [D] 58 H3
Riegel [D] 58 E2
Riegersburg [A] 74 E2
Riello [E] 78 G5
Rieneck [D] 46 E3
Riesa [D] 34 E5
Riesi [I] 126 E4
Riestedt [D] 34 B5
Rietavas [LT] 202 D4
Rietberg [D] 32 D3
Rieti [I] 116 B4
Rieumes [F] 84 H3
Rieupeyroux [F] 66 H6
Rieux [F] 84 H4
Riez [F] 108 C4
Riezlern [A] 60 B6
Riga [LV] 200 D5
Rigáni [GR] 132 F5
Rignac [F] 68 A5
Rihéa [GR] 136 F4
Riihimäki [FIN] 176 G3
Riihivaara [FIN] 198 G5
Riihivalkama [FIN] 176 F3
Riistavesi [FIN] 188 D2
Rijeka [HR] 112 E1
Rijeka Crnojevića [YU] 152 E4
Rijssen [NL] 16 G5
Riksgränsen [S] 192 D4
Rila [BG] 150 F6
Rillé [F] 54 F1
Rillo [E] 90 D6
Rima [I] 70 E3
Rimavská Sobota [SK] 64 E4

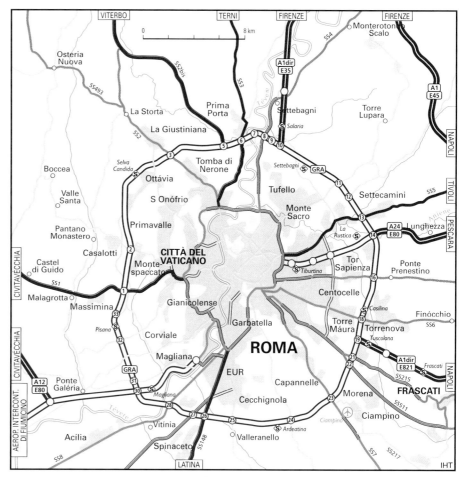

Rimbo [S] 168 E2
Rimella [I] 70 E3
Rimforsa [S] 162 F1
Rímini [I] 110 H5
Rîmnicu Sărat [RO] 206 D5
Rîmnicu Vîlcea [RO] 206 B6
Rimske Toplice [SLO] 74 D5
Rincón de la Victoria [E] 102 C5
Rincón de Soto [E] 84 A5
Rindal [N] 180 G2
Ring / An Rinn [IRL] 4 E5
Ringarum [S] 168 B6
Ringaskiddy [IRL] 4 D5
Ringe [DK] 156 D3
Ringebu [N] 170 H1
Ringkøbing [DK] 160 B6
Ringsted [DK] 156 F3
Ringwood [GB] 12 G5
Rinteln [D] 32 E2
Río [GR] 132 F5
Riobianco [I] 72 D2
Riolo Terme [I] 110 G4
Riom [F] 68 C2
Riomaggiore [I] 110 C4
Rio Maior [P] 86 C4
Riomar [E] 92 B6
Riom–ès–Montagnes [F] 68 B3
Rion–des–Landes [F] 66 B5
Rionegro del Puente [E] 80 G3
Rionero in Vúlture [I] 120 G3
Riópar [E] 96 H6
Rio Saliceto [I] 110 E2
Rio Torto [P] 80 D6
Rioz [F] 58 B4
Ripač [BIH] 112 H3
Ripanj [YU] 154 G3
Riparbella [I] 114 E1
Ripatransone [I] 116 C2
Ripley [GB] 10 E5
Ripon [GB] 10 F3
Riposto [I] 124 B8
Ripponden [GB] 10 E4
Riquewihr [F] 58 D2
Risan [YU] 152 D4
Risbäck [S] 190 E4
Riscle [F] 84 E2
Rish [BG] 148 E3
Risnes [N] 164 C4
Risnes [N] 170 B2
Risnovce [SK] 64 A4
Risør [N] 164 F4
Risøyhamn [N] 192 C3
Rissa [N] 190 B6
Risti [EST] 200 D2
Ristiina [FIN] 188 C6
Ristijärvi [FIN] 198 F4
Ristinge [DK] 156 E5
Ristna [EST] 200 C2
Ristovac [YU] 150 D5
Risum–Lindholm [D] 156 B5
Ritíni [GR] 128 G5
Rittmanshausen [D] 32 G6
Riva–Bella [F] 26 F3
Riva del Garda [I] 72 C5
Rivarolo Canavese [I] 70 D5
Rive–de–Gier [F] 68 F3
Rivesaltes [F] 92 G1
Rivoli [I] 70 D5
Rizári [GR] 128 F4
Rízoma [GR] 132 E2
Rizómata [GR] 128 G5
Rizómylos [GR] 136 D4
Rizómylos [GR] 132 H2
Rjánes [N] 180 C4
Rjukan [N] 170 F6
Roa [E] 88 G2
Roa [N] 172 B5
Roanne [F] 68 E2
Roavvegiedde [N] 196 D3
Robbio [I] 70 F4
Röbel [D] 20 C5
Robertsfors [S] 198 A5

Robleda [E] 86 H2
Robledillo de Gata [E] 86 H3
Robledo [E] 96 H5
Robledo de Chavela [E] 88 E5
Robledo del Buey [E] 96 D2
Robliza de Cojos [E] 88 B3
Rocamadour [F] 66 G4
Roccabianca [I] 110 D2
Roccadáspide [I] 120 F4
Rocca di Cambio [I] 116 C4
Rocca di Mezzo [I] 116 C4
Rocca di Neto [I] 124 F5
Rocca Imperiale [I] 122 D5
Roccalbegna [I] 114 G3
Roccalumera [I] 124 B8
Roccamonfina [I] 120 D2
Roccapalumba [I] 126 D2
Roccaraso [I] 116 D6
Rocca San Casciano [I] 110 G5
Rocca Sinibalda [I] 116 B4
Roccastrada [I] 114 F2
Roccaverano [I] 108 H2
Roccella Jónica [I] 124 D7
Rochdale [GB] 10 E4
Roche [E] 100 F4
Rochechouart [F] 54 F6
Rochefort [B] 30 D6
Rochefort [F] 54 C5
Rochefort–en–Terre [F] 40 E5
Rochefort–s–Nenon [F] 56 H4
Rochehaut [B] 44 D2
Rochemaure [F] 68 F6
Rocheservière [F] 54 B2
Rochester [GB] 14 F4
Rochlitz [D] 34 D6
Rockcorry [IRL] 2 F4
Rockenhausen [D] 46 B4
Rockneby [S] 162 G5
Rocroi [F] 28 H5
Róda [GR] 132 B1
Rodach [D] 46 G2
Roda de Isábena [E] 84 F6
Rødberg [N] 170 F5
Rødby [DK] 20 A1
Rødbyhavn [DK] 20 A1
Rødding [DK] 156 B3
Rødding [DK] 160 C5
Rödeby [S] 158 F1
Rodeiro [E] 78 C4
Rødekro [DK] 156 C4
Rodel / Roghadal [GB] 6 B3
Roden [NL] 16 G2
Rodenkirchen [D] 18 D4
Rodewald [D] 32 F1
Rodewisch [D] 48 C2
Rodez [F] 68 B6
Rødhus Klit [DK] 160 D3
Rodiá [GR] 132 G1
Rodi Gargánico [I] 116 G5
Roding [D] 48 C6
Rødkærsbro [DK] 160 D5
Rodolívos [GR] 130 C3
Rodópoli [GR] 128 H2
Ródos [GR] 142 E4
Rodrigatos de la Obispalía [E] 78 G4
Rødvig [DK] 156 G4
Roela [EST] 200 F1
Roermond [NL] 30 F3
Roeselare (Roulers) [B] 28 F2
Rogačev [BY] 204 C6
Rogačica [YU] 154 F4
Rogalin [PL] 36 C3
Rogatec [SLO] 74 E4
Rogatica [BIH] 152 E1
Rogatin [UA] 206 C2
Rogätz [D] 34 B2
Roghadal / Rodel [GB] 6 B3
Rogil [P] 94 B4
Rogliano [F] 114 C2
Rogliano [I] 124 D5

Rognac [F] 106 H5
Rognan [N] 192 C6
Rognes [N] 182 B2
Rogovo [RUS] 200 G4
Rogowo [PL] 36 D2
Rogozhinë [AL] 128 B3
Rogoznica [HR] 116 H1
Rogožno [PL] 36 C2
Rohan [F] 26 A5
Rohrbach [A] 62 B3
Rohrbach–lès–Bitche [F] 44 G4
Rohrberg [D] 34 A1
Rohr i. Niederb. [D] 60 F2
Roisel [F] 28 F5
Roja [LV] 200 C4
Rojão Grande [P] 80 C6
Röjdåfors [S] 172 E5
Rojişţea [RO] 150 G1
Rök [S] 166 G2
Rokietnica [PL] 52 F4
Rokiškis [LT] 202 G3
Rökkum [N] 180 F2
Røkland [N] 192 C6
Roknäs [S] 198 A3
Rokua [FIN] 198 E4
Rokycany [CZ] 48 E4
Røldal [N] 170 C5
Rolle [CH] 70 B1
Rolvsøy [N] 166 B3
Roma [I] 116 A5
Roma [S] 168 G4
Romagnano Sésia [I] 70 E4
Roman [BG] 150 G3
Roman [RO] 206 D4
Romangordo [E] 88 B6
Romanija [BIH] 152 D1
Romanshorn [CH] 58 H4
Romans–sur–Isère [F] 68 F5
Rombas [F] 44 E4
Rom By [DK] 160 B5
Romford [GB] 14 E4
Romilly–sur–Seine [F] 44 A5
Romny [UA] 206 G1

Romont [CH] 70 C1
Romorantin–Lanthenay [F] 54 H2
Romppala [FIN] 188 F1
Romsey [GB] 12 H4
Roncade [I] 72 E6
Roncal / Erronkari [E] 84 C4
Roncegno [I] 72 D4
Roncesvalles [E] 84 C3
Ronchamp [F] 58 C3
Ronchi dei Legionari [I] 72 H5
Ronciflione [I] 114 H4
Ronco Canavese [I] 70 D4
Roncofreddo [I] 110 H5
Ronco Scrivia [I] 110 B3
Ronda [E] 102 A4
Rønde [DK] 160 E6
Ronehamn [S] 168 G5
Rong [N] 170 C3
Rõngu [EST] 200 F3
Rönnäng [S] 160 G1
Rønne [DK] 158 E4
Ronneburg [D] 48 C1
Ronneby [S] 158 F1
Rønnede [DK] 156 G4
Rönnöfors [S] 190 D6
Rönö [S] 168 C5
Ronse (Renaix) [B] 28 G3
Roodeschool [NL] 16 G1
Roonah Quay [IRL] 2 B3
Roosendaal [NL] 16 C6
Roosky [IRL] 2 D4
Ropaži [LV] 200 E5
Ropczyce [PL] 52 D3
Ropeid [N] 164 B1
Ropinsalmi [FIN] 192 F3
Ropotovo [MK] 128 E2
Ropsha [RUS] 178 E6
Roquebillière [F] 108 F4
Roquebrune–Cap–Martin [F] 108 F4
Roquefort [F] 66 C5
Roquefort–sur–Soulzon [F] 106 D3
Roquemaure [F] 106 G3
Roquetas de Mar [E] 102 F5

Roquetes [E] 92 A5
Rörbäcksnäs [S] 172 E3
Rore [BIH] 154 B4
Røros [N] 182 C4
Rorschach [CH] 58 H5
Rørvig [DK] 156 F2
Rørvik [N] 190 C4
Rørvik [N] 164 C5
Ros' [BY] 24 G5
Rosala [FIN] 176 E6
Rosal de la Frontera [E] 94 E3
Rosans [F] 108 B2
Rosapenna [IRL] 2 E1
Rosarno [I] 124 C6
Rosche [D] 18 G6
Rošciszewo [PL] 36 H1
Roscoff [F] 40 C1
Roscommon [IRL] 2 D5
Roscrea [IRL] 2 D6
Rosegg [A] 74 B3
Rosen [BG] 148 F4
Rosendal [N] 170 B5
Rosenheim [D] 60 F5
Roses [E] 92 G2
Roseto degli Abruzzi [I] 116 D3
Roshchine [RUS] 178 G4
Rosice [CZ] 50 B6
Rosignano–Marittimo [I] 110 D6
Rosignano Solvay [I] 114 E1
Rosino [BG] 148 B4
Roskilde [DK] 156 G2
Rosko [PL] 36 B1
Roslags–Bro [S] 168 E1
Roslags kulla [S] 168 E2
Roslavl [RUS] 204 D5
Roslev [DK] 160 C4
Roslin [GB] 8 E3
Rosmaninhal [P] 86 F4
Rosolina Mare [I] 110 H2
Rosolini [I] 126 G5
Rosoman [MK] 128 F2

Rosporden [F] 40 C3
Rossano [I] 124 E4
Rossas [P] 80 C5
Ross Carberry [IRL] 4 C5
Rosscor [GB] 2 E3
Rosses Point [IRL] 2 D3
Rosshaupten [D] 60 C5
Rossiglione [I] 108 H2
Rossla [D] 34 A5
Rosslare Harbour [IRL] 4 F5
Rosslau [D] 34 C4
Rosslea [GB] 2 F4
Rossnes [N] 170 A3
Rossön [S] 190 F6
Ross–on–Wye [GB] 12 G2
Rossosz [PL] 38 F4
Røssvassbukt [N] 190 E3
Röstånga [S] 158 C2
Rostassac [F] 66 F5
Rostock [D] 20 B3
Rostrenen [F] 40 D3
Rostrevor [GB] 2 G4
Røsvik [N] 192 C5
Rosvik [S] 198 B3
Röszke [H] 76 E4
Roszki–Wodżki [PL] 24 E6
Rot [S] 172 F2
Rota [E] 100 F3
Rotemo [N] 164 D2
Rotenburg [D] 32 F6
Rotenburg [D] 18 E5
Rotgülden [A] 72 H2
Roth [D] 46 G5
Rötha [D] 34 C6
Rothbury [GB] 8 F5
Rothenburg [D] 34 G5
Rothenburg ob der Tauber [D] 46 E5
Rothéneuf [F] 26 C4
Rotherham [GB] 10 F4
Rothes [GB] 6 E5
Rothesay [GB] 8 C3
Rothwell [GB] 10 F4
Rotondella [I] 122 D5
Rotsund [N] 192 F2
Rott [D] 60 D5
Rott [D] 60 F5

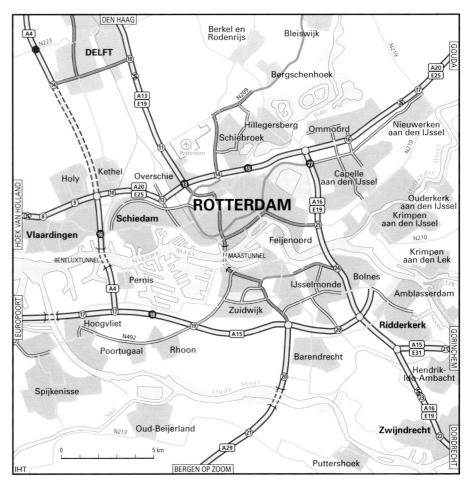

Rottach [D] 60 E5
Rottenbach [D] 46 G2
Rottenbuch [D] 60 D5
Rottenburg [D] 60 F3
Rottenburg [D] 58 G2
Rottenmann [A] 62 B6
Rotterdam [NL] 16 C5
Rotthalmünster [D] 60 H4
Rottingdean [GB] 14 E6
Röttingen [D] 46 E5
Rottne [S] 162 E4
Rottneros [S] 166 E1
Rottweil [D] 58 G3
Rötz [D] 48 C5
Roubaix [F] 28 F3
Roudnice nad Labem [CZ] 48 F3
Rouen [F] 28 B5
Rouffach [F] 58 D3
Rougé [F] 40 F5
Rougemont [F] 58 C4
Rougemont [F] 58 D3
Rouillac [F] 54 D6
Roujan [F] 106 D4
Roulers (Roeselare) [B] 28 F2
Roundstone [IRL] 2 B4
Roundwood [IRL] 4 G3
Roússa [GR] 130 G2
Roussillon [F] 106 H4
Rouvres–en–Xaintois [F] 44 E6
Rovaniemi [FIN] 196 D8
Rovato [I] 72 A6
Roverbella [I] 110 E1
Rovereto [I] 72 C5
Rövershagen [D] 20 B3
Roverud [N] 172 D5
Roviés [GR] 134 B4
Rovigo [I] 110 G2
Rovinj [HR] 112 D2
Rovišče [HR] 74 F5
Rovno [UA] 206 D2
Rów [PL] 20 F6
Rowy [PL] 22 B1
Royan [F] 54 B6
Royat [F] 68 C2
Roybon [F] 68 G4
Roye [F] 28 E5
Royère–de–Vassivière [F] 68 A1
Royken [N] 164 H1
Røyrvik [N] 190 D4
Røysheim [N] 180 F6
Royston [GB] 14 E3
Röyttä [FIN] 198 C3
Roza [BG] 148 D5
Rožaj [YU] 150 B5
Różan [PL] 24 C6
Różanki [PL] 34 H1
Rožanstvo [YU] 150 A3
Rozay–en–Brie [F] 42 G4
Rožmitál pod Třemšínen [CZ] 48 E5
Rožňava [SK] 64 E3
Rožnov pod Radhoštěm [CZ] 50 E5
Rożnów [PL] 52 B4
Rozogi [PL] 24 C5
Rozoy [F] 28 G6
Rozprza [PL] 36 H5
Rozvadov [CZ] 48 C4
Rozzano [I] 70 G5
Rrëshen [AL] 128 B1
Rtanj [YU] 150 D2
Ru [E] 78 D3
Ruabon [GB] 10 D5
Rubbestadneset [N] 170 A5
Rubena [E] 82 E6
Rubeži [YU] 152 E3
Rubielos de Mora [E] 98 E2
Rubiera [I] 110 E3
Rucava [LV] 202 D3
Ruciane–Nida [PL] 24 C4
Ruda [S] 162 F4
Ruda Maleniecka [PL] 38 A6
Rudare [YU] 150 C4
Rudawica [PL] 34 H5
Rüdesheim [D] 46 B3
Rūdiškés [LT] 24 H1
Rudka [PL] 38 E1

Rudkøbing [DK] 156 E4
Rudna [PL] 36 B5
Rudna [PL] 22 C5
Rudna Glava [YU] 150 D1
Rudnica [YU] 152 E2
Rudnica [YU] 150 B4
Rudnik [BG] 148 F3
Rudnik [PL] 52 E2
Rudnik [PL] 50 E3
Rudnik [YU] 150 B5
Rudnik [YU] 150 B2
Rudniki [PL] 50 F1
Rudnja [RUS] 204 C5
Rudno [PL] 22 E4
Rudolphstein [D] 46 H2
Rudolstadt [D] 46 H1
Rudozem [BG] 130 E1
Ruds–Vedby [DK] 156 F3
Rudzāti [LV] 200 F5
Rue [F] 28 D3
Rueda [E] 88 E2
Ruelle–sur–Touvre [F] 66 E1
Ruffano [I] 122 G6
Ruffec [F] 54 E5
Ruffieux [F] 70 A3
Rugāji [LV] 200 G5
Rugby [GB] 14 D2
Rugeley [GB] 10 E6
Rugles [F] 26 H5
Ruhällen [S] 168 C1
Rühen [D] 32 H2
Ruhland [D] 34 F5
Ruhmannsfelden [D] 60 G2
Ruhpolding [D] 60 G5
Ruidera [E] 96 G4
Rūjiena [LV] 200 E3
Ruka [FIN] 196 F8
Rukajärvi [FIN] 196 F8
Rülzheim [D] 46 B5
Rum [H] 74 G2
Ruma [YU] 154 F2
Rumburk [CZ] 48 G1
Rumia [PL] 22 D2
Rumigny [F] 28 H5
Rumilly [F] 70 A3
Rumo [FIN] 198 F5
Rumpani [LV] 200 F4
Runcorn [GB] 10 D4
Rundfloen [N] 172 E3
Rundhaug [N] 192 E3
Rundvik [S] 184 H1
Runni [FIN] 198 E6
Ruokojärvi [FIN] 192 H6
Ruokolahti [FIN] 178 E1
Ruona [FIN] 186 D3
Ruorasmäki [FIN] 186 H6
Ruovesi [FIN] 186 E5
Rupa [HR] 112 E1
Rupea [RO] 206 C5
Rupt [F] 58 C3
Rus [E] 102 F1
Rusalka [BG] 148 G2
Ruse [BG] 148 C2
Ruševo [HR] 154 D1
Rusdal [N] 164 B4
Ruse [EST] 200 F2
Rusfors [S] 190 G4
Rush [IRL] 2 F6
Rushden [GB] 14 E2
Rusiec [PL] 36 F5
Rusinowo [PL] 22 A6
Ruskeala [RUS] 188 G4
Ruski Krstur [YU] 76 D2
Ruskila [FIN] 188 D2
Ruskele [S] 190 G4
Rusne [LT] 202 D5
Rusokastro [BG] 148 F4
Rüsselsheim [D] 46 C3
Russenes [N] 196 C2
Russi [I] 110 G4
Rust [A] 62 F5
Rust [D] 58 E2
Rustad [N] 172 B5
Rustefjelbma [N] 196 D2
Ruswil [CH] 58 E6
Rutalahti [FIN] 186 G5
Rute [E] 102 C3
Rutenbrock [D] 16 H3
Rüthen [D] 32 D4
Ruthin [GB] 10 C4

Rüti [CH] 58 G5
Rutigliano [I] 122 E3
Rutledal [N] 170 B2
Ruukki [FIN] 198 D4
Ruurlo [NL] 16 F5
Ruutana [FIN] 176 F1
Ruvo di Puglia [I] 122 D2
Ruwer [D] 44 G2
Ruzhany [BY] 24 H6
Ruzhintsi [BG] 150 E3
Ružomberok [SK] 64 C2
Ry [DK] 156 D1
Ryakhovo [BG] 148 D1
Rybinsk [RUS] 204 F2
Rybnik [PL] 50 F4
Rychnov nad Kněžnou [CZ] 50 B3
Rychnowo [PL] 22 G4
Rychwał [PL] 36 E3
Ryd [S] 162 D6
Rydaholm [S] 162 D4
Ryde [GB] 12 H5
Rydzyna [PL] 36 C4
Rye [GB] 14 F5
Ryen [N] 164 E5
Rygge [N] 166 B2
Ryhälä [FIN] 188 E5
Ryki [PL] 38 D4
Rylsk [RUS] 204 E7
Rymań [PL] 20 G3
Rymanów [PL] 52 D5
Rýmařov [CZ] 50 D4
Rymättylä [FIN] 176 D5
Ryn [PL] 24 C3
Rynarzewo [PL] 22 D6
Ryomgård [DK] 160 E5
Rypefjord [N] 196 B2
Rypin [PL] 22 F6
Ryslinge [DK] 156 D3
Rysum [D] 16 H2
Rytel [PL] 22 C4
Rytro [PL] 52 B5
Ryuttyu [RUS] 188 H4
Rzeczenica [PL] 22 B4
Rzemień [PL] 52 D3
Rzepin [PL] 34 G3
Rzeszów [PL] 52 E3
Ržev [RUS] 204 E4
Rzgów [PL] 36 G4

S

Sääksjärvi [FIN] 186 D2
Sääksmäki [FIN] 176 F2
Saal [D] 60 F2
Saalbach [A] 72 F1
Saales [F] 44 G6
Saalfeld [D] 46 H2
Saalfelden [A] 60 G6
Saanen [CH] 70 D1
Saarbrücken [D] 44 G4
Saarburg [D] 44 F3
Saare [EST] 200 F2
Saarenkylä [FIN] 196 D8
Saarijärvi [FIN] 186 F3
Saarikoski [FIN] 192 F3
Saariväara [FIN] 198 G4
Saarlouis [D] 44 F3
Saas Almagell [CH] 70 E3
Saas–Fee [CH] 70 E3
Saas Grund [CH] 70 E3
Šabac [YU] 154 F2
Sabadell [E] 92 E4
Sabáudia [I] 120 B2
Sabbioneta [I] 110 E2
Sabile [LV] 200 C5
Sabiñánigo [E] 84 D5
Sabinosa [E] 100 A6
Sabinov [SK] 52 C6
Sabiote [E] 102 F2
Sables–d'Or–les–Pins [F] 26 B4
Sablé–sur–Sarthe [F] 42 A5
Sabres [F] 66 C5
Sabrosa [P] 80 D4
Sabugal [P] 86 G2
Săcălaz [RO] 76 G5
Sacavém [P] 86 B5
Sacecorbo [E] 90 B5
Sacedón [E] 88 H6

Saceruela [E] 96 D4
Sacile [I] 72 F5
Sádaba [E] 84 B5
Sadala [EST] 200 F2
Sadikov Bunar [YU] 150 E4
Sadki [PL] 22 C6
Sadova [RO] 150 G2
Sadovets [BG] 148 A3
Sadovo [BG] 148 B6
Sądów [PL] 34 G3
Sadská [CZ] 48 G3
Sädvaluspen [S] 190 F2
Sæbo [N] 170 D4
Sæbø [N] 180 D4
Sæbøvik [N] 170 B5
Sæby [DK] 160 E3
Sæd [DK] 156 B4
Saelices [E] 96 H2
Sælvig [DK] 156 E2
Saerbeck [D] 32 C2
Sætre [N] 164 H2
Sævareid [N] 170 B4
Sævråsvåg [N] 170 B3
Safa [TR] 146 G5
Safara [P] 94 E3
Säffle [S] 166 E3
Saffron Walden [GB] 14 F3
Safonovo [RUS] 204 D4
Sagard [D] 20 D2
Sagiáda [GR] 132 B2
Sagone [F] 114 A4
Sagres [P] 94 A5
Şagu [RO] 76 G5
Sagunt / Sagunto [E] 98 F4
Sagunto / Sagunt [E] 98 F4
Sagvåg [N] 170 A5
Ságvár [H] 76 A3
Sahagún [E] 82 C5
Sahalahti [FIN] 176 G1
Sahilköy [TR] 146 F2
Şahin [TR] 146 B3
Sahrajärvi [FIN] 186 F4
Saignelégier [CH] 58 D5
Saija [FIN] 196 E7
Saillagouse [F] 92 E1
Saillans [F] 68 G6
Sains [F] 28 G5
Sainte–Lucie–de–Tallano [F] 114 B5
Sainte–Marie–Sicché [F] 114 B5
Saintes [F] 54 C6
Saintfield [GB] 2 G4
Saint-Jacques [I] 70 D3
Saissac [F] 106 B4
Saivomuotka [S] 192 G4
Šajkaš [YU] 154 G1

Sajószentpéter [H] 64 F4
Saki [UA] 206 G5
Šakiai [LT] 202 E5
Sakskøbing [DK] 20 B1
Säkylä [FIN] 176 D3
Sala [S] 168 C1
Šaľa [SK] 64 A4
Salacgrīva [LV] 200 D4
Sala Consilina [I] 120 G4
Salahmi [FIN] 198 E5
Sálakos [GR] 142 D4
Salamanca [E] 80 H6
Salamína [GR] 134 B6
Salantai [LT] 202 D4
Salaóra [GR] 132 D4
Salar [E] 102 D4
Sälard [RO] 76 H1
Salardú [E] 84 G5
Salas [E] 78 G3
Salas de los Infantes [E] 88 H1
Salaspils [LV] 200 E5
Salau [F] 84 G5
Salaüš [YU] 150 E2
Salbohed [S] 168 B1
Salbris [F] 56 B2
Šalčininkai [LT] 202 G6
Salcombe [GB] 12 D5
Sălcuţa [RO] 150 F1
Saldaña [E] 82 C5
Saldus [LV] 200 C5
Sale [I] 70 F6
Saleby [S] 166 E5
Salem [D] 58 H4
Salema [P] 94 A5
Salemi [I] 126 B2
Salen [GB] 6 B6
Sälen [S] 172 E2
Salernes [F] 108 D4
Salerno [I] 120 F4
Salers [F] 68 B4
Salgótarján [H] 64 D4
Salhus [N] 170 B3
Sali [HR] 112 F5
Salice Terme [I] 70 F6
Salies–de–Béarn [F] 84 D2
Salies–du–Salat [F] 84 G4
Salignac–Eyvigues [F] 66 G4
Salihli [TR] 144 E4
Salinas [E] 78 H3
Salinas de Pinilla [E] 96 H5
Saline di Volterra [I] 114 F1
Sälinkää [FIN] 176 H3
Salins [F] 58 B5
Salins–les–Bains [F] 58 A5
Salir [P] 94 C5
Salisbury [GB] 12 G4
Salkoluokta [S] 192 E6

Salla [FIN] 196 E7
Sallanches [F] 70 B3
Sallent de Gállego [E] 84 D4
Salles [F] 66 C4
Salles [F] 106 A4
Salles–Curan [F] 106 D2
Sallmunds [S] 168 G6
Salme [EST] 200 C3
Salmivaara [FIN] 196 E7
Salo [FIN] 176 E4
Salò [I] 72 B6
Salobreña [E] 102 D5
Saloinen [FIN] 198 C4
Salon [F] 44 B5
Salon–de–Provence [F] 106 H4
Salonta [RO] 76 H3
Salou [E] 92 C5
Salsbruket [N] 190 C4
Salses–le–Château [F] 106 C6
Salsomaggiore Terme [I] 110 D2
Salt [E] 92 F3
Saltash [GB] 12 D5
Saltbæk [DK] 156 E2
Saltburn [GB] 10 G2
Saltcoats [GB] 8 C3
Saltergate [GB] 10 G3
Saltsjöbaden [S] 168 E3
Saltum [DK] 160 D3
Saltvik [FIN] 176 B5
Saluzzo [I] 108 F2
Salvacañete [E] 98 D2
Salvaterra de Magos [P] 86 C5
Salvaterra de Miño [E] 78 B5
Salvatierra / Agurain [E] 82 H5
Salvatierra de los Barros [E] 94 G2
Salviac [F] 66 G4
Salzburg [A] 60 G5
Salzgitter–Bad [D] 32 G3
Salzgitter–Lebenstedt [D] 32 G3
Salzhausen [D] 18 F5
Salzkotten [D] 32 D4
Salzwedel [D] 18 H6
Salzweg [D] 60 H3
Sama de Grado [E] 78 H4
Samadet [F] 66 C6
Samailli [TR] 144 E5
Samandıra [TR] 146 F3
Samarína [GR] 128 D6
Samassi [I] 118 C6
Samatan [F] 84 G3
Samate [LV] 200 B5

Sambiase [I] 124 D5
Sambir [UA] 52 G5
Sambuca di Sicilia [I] 126 C3
Sambucheto [I] 116 B3
Samedan [CH] 72 A3
Samer [F] 28 D2
Sámi [GR] 132 C6
Samitier [E] 84 E6
Şamlı [TR] 146 D6
Samobor [HR] 74 E6
Samoëns [F] 70 C2
Samoëns [F] 70 C3
Samokov [BG] 150 G5
Šamorín [SK] 62 G5
Samos [E] 78 E4
Sámos [GR] 144 C5
Samoš [YU] 154 H1
Samothráki [GR] 130 F4
Samovodene [BG] 148 C3
Sampéyre [F] 108 F2
Samtens [D] 20 D2
Samugheo [I] 118 C5
San Adrián [E] 84 A5
Sanaigmore [GB] 8 B2
San Anton Leitza [E] 84 B3
Sanary–sur–Mer [F] 108 C6
San Bartolomé [E] 100 E4
San Bartolomé de la Torre [E] 94 E5
San Bartolomeo in Galdo [I] 120 F1
San Benedetto dei Marsi [I] 116 C5
San Benedetto del Tronto [I] 116 D2
San Benedetto in Alpe [I] 110 G5
San Benedetto Po [I] 110 E2
San Bernardino [CH] 70 G2
San Bernardino, Tunnel del– [Eur.] 70 G2
San Biagio di Callalta [I] 72 F6
San Biágio Plátani [I] 126 D3
San Bonifácio [I] 110 F1
San Candido / Innichen [I] 72 E3
San Carlos del Valle [E] 96 G5
San Casciano dei Bagni [I] 114 G2
San Casciano in Val di Pesa [I] 110 F6
San Cataldo [I] 126 E3
San Cataldo [I] 122 G4
Sancergues [F] 56 D3
Sancerre [F] 56 D3
Sancey–le–Grand [F] 58 C5
Sanchidrián [E] 88 E4
San Cipirello [I] 126 C2
San Clemente [E] 98 A4
Sancoins [F] 56 D4
San Cosme (Barreiros) [E] 78 E2
San Cristóbal de la Laguna [E] 100 C5
San Cristóbal de la Vega [E] 88 E3
Sancti–Spiritus [E] 96 C3
Sancti Spiritus [E] 88 A3
Sand [N] 164 B1
Sand [N] 172 C4
Sanda [N] 164 F2
San Damiano d'Asti [I] 70 E6
Sandane [N] 180 C5
San Daniele del Friuli [I] 72 G4
San Daniele Po [I] 110 D2
Sandanski [BG] 130 B2
Sandared [S] 162 B2
Sandarne [S] 174 E2
Sandau [D] 34 C1
Sandbach [GB] 10 D5
Sandbanks [GB] 12 G5
Sandbukt [N] 192 F1
Sande [D] 18 C4
Sande [N] 164 H2

Sande [N] 170 C1
Sandefjord [N] 164 H3
Sandeid [N] 164 B1
San Demetrio Corone [I] 124 D4
Sanden [N] 164 F2
Sandgate [GB] 14 F5
Sandhem [S] 162 C1
Sandıklı [TR] 144 H3
Sand in Taufers / Campo Tures [I] 72 E2
Sandl [A] 62 C3
Sandnäset [S] 184 D4
Sandnes [N] 164 B3
Sandnes [N] 164 F3
Sandness [GB] 6 G3
Sandnessjøen [N] 190 D2
Sandoméri [GR] 136 C1
Sandomierz [PL] 52 D2
San Dónaci [I] 122 G4
San Doná di Piave [I] 72 F6
San Donato Milanese [I] 70 G5
Sándorfalva [H] 76 E4
Sandown [GB] 12 H5
Sandrigo [I] 72 D6
Sandset [N] 192 C3
Sandstad [N] 190 A6
Sandstad [N] 172 D4
Sandstedt [D] 18 D4
Sandur [DK] 160 A2
Sandvatn [N] 164 C4
Sandvig [DK] 158 E4
Sandvik [S] 162 G4
Sandvika [N] 164 H1
Sandvika [N] 190 C6
Sandviken [S] 174 E4
Sandvikvåg [N] 170 A5
Sandwich [GB] 14 G5
Sandwick [GB] 6 G4
Sandy [GB] 14 E3
San Emiliano [E] 78 G4
San Esteban [E] 84 B3
San Esteban de Gormaz [E] 88 H3
San Fele [I] 120 G3
San Felice Circeo [I] 120 B2
San Felice sul Panaro [I] 110 F2
San Ferdinando di Puglia [I] 120 H2
San Fernando [E] 100 F4
San Fratello [I] 126 F2
San Fruttuoso [I] 110 B3
Sangarcía [E] 88 E4
San Gavino Monreale [I] 118 C6
Sangazi [TR] 146 F3
Sangerhausen [D] 34 B5
San Germano [I] 70 E5
San Gimignano [I] 110 E6
San Ginesio [I] 116 C2
Sanginkylä [FIN] 198 E4
San Giorgio di Livenza [I] 72 F6
San Giórgio di Nogaro [I] 72 G5
San Giorgio Iónico [I] 122 F4
San Giovanni a Piro [I] 120 G5
San Giovanni di Sínis [I] 118 B5
San Giovanni in Croce [I] 110 D2
San Giovanni in Fiore [I] 124 E4
San Giovanni in Persiceto [I] 110 F3
San Giovanni Lupatoto [I] 110 F1
San Giovanni Rotondo [I] 116 G6
San Giovanni Suergiu [I] 118 B7
San Giovanni Valdarno [I] 110 F6
Sangis [S] 198 C2
San Giuliano Terme [I] 110 D5

San Giustino [I] 110 G6
Sangla [EST] 200 F3
Sangüesa / Zangoza [E] 84 C5
Sanguinet [F] 66 B4
Sáni [GR] 130 B6
Sanitz [D] 20 C3
San Javier [E] 104 D4
San José [E] 102 G6
San José / Sant Josep [E] 104 C5
San Juan de Alicante / Sant Joan d'Alacant [E] 104 E2
San Juan del Puerto [E] 94 E6
San Juan de Muskiz [E] 82 G3
Sankt–Michaelisdonn [D] 18 E3
Sankt–Peterburg [RUS] 178 H4
San Lazzaro di Savena [I] 110 F3
San Leonardo de Yagüe [E] 90 A2
San Leonardo in Passiria [I] 72 D2
San Lorenzo de Calatrava [E] 96 E5
San Lorenzo de El Escorial [E] 88 F5
San Lorenzo de la Parrilla [E] 98 B2
San Lorenzo in Campo [I] 112 B6
San Lorenzo Nuovo [I] 114 G3
San Luca [I] 124 C7
Sanlúcar de Barrameda [E] 100 F3
Sanlúcar la Mayor [E] 94 G6
San Lúcido [I] 124 D4
Sanluri [I] 118 C6
San Marcello Pistoiese [I] 110 E4
San Marco Argentano [I] 124 D4
San Marco dei Cavoti [I] 120 F2
San Marco in Lamis [I] 116 G6
San Marino [RSM] 110 H5
Sânmartin [RO] 76 H2
San Martín de la Vega [E] 88 F6
San Martín del Pedroso [E] 80 G4
San Martín de Pusa [E] 96 E1
San Martín de Unx [E] 84 B5
San Martín de Valdeiglesias [E] 88 E5
San Martino Buon Albergo [I] 72 C6
San Martino della Battaglia [I] 72 C6
San Martino di Castrozza [I] 72 E4
San Martino di Lupari [I] 72 E6
San Mateo de Gállego [E] 98 G2
San Mauro Castelverde [I] 126 E2
San Michele all'Ádige [I] 72 C4
San Michele Salentino [I] 122 F4
San Miguel de Bernúy [E] 88 G3
San Miguel de las Dueñas [E] 78 F5
San Miguel de Salinas [E] 104 D3
San Millán de la Cogolla [E] 82 G6
San Miniato [I] 110 E6
S. Anna [S] 168 C6
Sannazzaro de'Burgondi [I] 70 F6

Sannenmöser [CH] 70 D1
Sannicandro di Bari [I] 122 D3
Sannicandro Gargánico [I] 116 G6
San Nicolás de Tolentino [E] 100 C5
San Nicolò [I] 110 G3
San Nicolò Gerrei [I] 118 D6
Sanniki [PL] 36 H3
Sanok [PL] 52 E5
San Pancrazio Salentino [I] 122 F4
San Paolo di Civitate [I] 116 F6
San Paolo di Peltuino [I] 116 C4
San Pedro [E] 98 A5
San Pedro de Alcántara [E] 102 A5
San Pedro del Arroyo [E] 88 D4
San Pedro del Pinatar [E] 104 D4
San Pellegrino Terme [I] 70 H4
San Piero a Sieve [I] 110 F5
San Pietro in Casale [I] 110 F3
San Pietro Vernotico [I] 122 G4
San Polo d'Enza [I] 110 D3
San Prospero [I] 110 F2
San Priamo [I] 118 D7
San Quírico d'Orcia [I] 114 G2
San Rafael [E] 88 F4
San Remo [I] 108 F4
San Roque [E] 100 G5
San Roque [E] 78 C2
San Rufo [I] 120 G4
San Sadurniño [E] 78 D1
San Salvatore Monferrato [I] 110 A1
San Salvo [I] 116 E5
San Sebastián de la Gomera [E] 100 B5
San Sebastián–Donostia [E] 84 B2
San Sebastiano Curone [I] 110 B2
Sansepolcro [I] 110 G6
San Severino Marche [I] 116 B2
San Severo [I] 116 F6
Sanski Most [BIH] 154 B3
San Sosti [I] 124 D3
Santa Amalia [E] 96 A2
Santa Bárbara [E] 94 E4
Santa Caterina di Pittinuri [I] 118 B5
Santa Caterina Valfurva [I] 72 B3
Santa Caterina Villarmosa [I] 126 E3
Santa Cesarea Terme [I] 122 H5
Santa Clara–a–Velha [P] 94 B4
Santa Coloma de Farners [E] 92 F3
Santa Coloma de Queralt [E] 92 C4
Santa Colomba de Somoza [E] 78 F5
Santa Comba [E] 78 B2
Santa Comba de Rossas [P] 80 F4
Santa Cristina / St Christina [I] 72 D3
Santa Cristina d'Aro [E] 92 G3
Santa Croce di Magliano [I] 116 F6
Santa Croce sull'Arno [I] 110 E5
Santa Cruz [P] 100 B3

Sannenmöser [CH] 70 D1

Santa Cruz de Campezo / Santi Kurutze Kanpezu [E] 82 H6
Santa Cruz de la Palma [E] 100 A5
Santa Cruz de la Serós [E] 84 D5
Santa Cruz de la Zarza [E] 96 G2
Santa Cruz del Retamar [E] 88 E6
Santa Cruz de Moya [E] 98 D3
Santa Cruz de Mudela [E] 96 F5
Santa Cruz de Tenerife [E] 100 C5
Santadi [I] 118 C7
Santa Elena [E] 96 F6
Santaella [E] 102 B2
Santa Eufemia [E] 96 C4
Santa Eugènia [E] 78 B3
Santa Eulalia [E] 98 D1
Santa Eulalia [E] 78 H3
Santa Eulália [P] 86 F6
Santa Eulália del Río / Santa Eulària des Riu [E] 104 C5
Santa Eulària des Riu / Santa Eulalia del Río [E] 104 C5
Santa Fé [E] 102 E4
Sant'Agata dè Goti [I] 120 E2
Sant'Ágata di Militello [I] 126 F2
Sant'Agostino [I] 110 F3
Santa Luce [I] 110 D6
Santa Lucía [E] 100 C6
Santa Lucia del Mela [I] 124 B7
Santa Luzia [P] 94 C3
Santa Maddalena Vallalta [I] 72 E2
Santa Margalida [E] 104 E5
Santa Margarida de Montbui [E] 92 D4
Santa Margarida do Sado [P] 94 C2
Santa Margherita [I] 118 C7
Santa Margherita di Bélice [I] 126 C3
Santa Margherita Ligure [I] 110 B3
Santa María [E] 104 E5
Santa Maria a Piè di Chienti [I] 116 C2
Santa Maria Cápua Vetere [I] 120 E2
Santa Maria da Feira [P] 80 B4
Santa María de Cayón [E] 82 F3
Santa María de Huerta [E] 90 B4
Santa María de las Hoyas [E] 90 A2
Santa María del Campo [E] 82 E6
Santa María del Páramo [E] 78 G6
Santa María de Nieva [E] 102 H4
Santa Maria di Portonovo [I] 112 D6
Santa María la Real de Nieva [E] 88 E3
Santa Maria Maggiore [I] 70 F3
Santa Maria Navarrese [I] 118 E5
Santa Maria Nuova [I] 116 C1
Santa Marinella [I] 114 G5
Santa Marta [E] 94 G2
Santa Marta [E] 98 B4
Santa Marta de Tormes [E] 88 D3
Santana [P] 100 B3
Santana da Serra [P] 94 C4

Santana do Mato [P] 86 C5
Santander [E] 82 F3
Sant'Andrea Bagni [I] 110 D2
Sant' Andrea di Conza [I] 120 G3
Sant' Andrea Fríus [I] 118 D6
Sant' Ángelo in Vado [I] 110 H6
Sant' Angelo Lodigiano [I] 70 G5
Santa Ninfa [I] 126 B2
Sant' Antíoco [I] 118 B7
Sant Antoni de Portmany [E] 104 C5
Sant'Antonio di Gallura [I] 118 D2
Santanyí [E] 104 E6
Santa Olalla [E] 88 E6
Santa Olalla del Cala [E] 94 G4
Santa Pola [E] 104 D3
Santa Ponça [E] 104 D5
Sant'Arcangelo [I] 122 C5
Santarcángelo di Romagna [I] 110 H5
Santarém [P] 86 C4
Santa Severa [F] 114 C2
Santa Severa [I] 114 G5
Santas Martas [E] 78 H6
Santa Sofia [I] 110 G5
Santa Susanna [E] 92 F4
Santa Teresa di Riva [I] 124 B8
Santa Teresa Gallura [I] 118 D2
Sant Boi de Llobregat [E] 92 D4
Sant Carles de la Ràpita [E] 92 A6
Sant Celoni [E] 92 F4
Santed [E] 90 D5
Sant' Elia a Pianisi [I] 120 F1
Sant'Elia Fiumerapido [I] 120 D1
San Telmo [E] 94 F4
Santena [I] 70 D6
San Teodoro [I] 118 E3
Santéramo in Colle [I] 122 D3
Sant' Eufémia Lamézia [I] 124 D5
Sant Feliu de Codines [E] 92 E4
Sant Feliu de Guíxols [E] 92 G4
Sant Feliu de Llobregat [E] 92 F4
Sant Ferran de Ses Roquetes [E] 104 C6
Sant Francesc de Formentera [E] 104 C6
Santhià [I] 70 E5
Sant Hilari Sacalm [E] 92 F3
Sant Hipòlit de Voltregà [E] 92 E3
Santiago [P] 80 F5
Santiago de Alcántara [E] 86 F4
Santiago de Compostela [E] 78 C3
Santiago de la Espada [E] 102 G2
Santiago de la Ribera [E] 104 D4
Santiago do Cacém [P] 94 B2
Santiago do Escoural [P] 94 D1
Santibáñez de la Sierra [E] 88 B4
Santi Kurutze Kanpezu / Santa Cruz de Campezo [E] 82 H6
Santillana del Mar [E] 82 E3
Santisteban del Puerto [E] 102 F1
Sant Jaume d'Enveja [E] 92 B6

Sant Joan d'Alacant / San Juan de Alicante [E] 104 E2
Sant Joan de les Abadesses [E] 92 E2
Sant Joan de Llabritja [E] 104 C5
Sant Joan de Vilatorrada [E] 92 D3
Sant Josep / San José [E] 104 C5
Sant Juliá de Lória [AND] 84 H6
Sant Llorenç de Morunys [E] 92 D2
Sant Lluís [E] 104 H5
Sant Martí Sarroca [E] 92 D4
Sant Miquel de Balansat [E] 104 C5
Santo André [P] 94 B2
Santo Domingo de la Calzada [E] 82 G6
Santo Domingo de Silos [E] 88 H1
Santok [PL] 34 H2
Santoña [E] 82 F3
Santo Stefano Belbo [I] 108 H2
Santo Stefano di Cadore [I] 72 F3
Santo Stefano di Camastra [I] 126 F2
Santo Stefano Quisquina [I] 126 D3
Santo Stino di Livenza [I] 72 F5
Santo Tirso [P] 80 C3
Santo Tomé [E] 102 F2
Santo Tomé del Puerto [E] 88 G3
Sant Pere Pescador [E] 92 G3
Sant Pol de Mar [E] 92 F4
Sant Quirze de Besora [E] 92 E2
Sant Rafel [E] 104 C5
Sant Sadurní d'Anoia [E] 92 D4
Sant Tomàs [E] 104 G4
Santuário di Oropa [I] 70 E4
Santu Lussúrgiu [I] 118 C4
Santurtzi / Santurce [E] 82 G3
Sant Vicenç de Castellet [E] 92 D3
Sant Vicent del Raspeig / San Vicente del Raspeig [E] 104 E2
Sant Vicent de sa Cala [E] 104 C5
San Valentino alla Muta [I] 72 B2
San Venanzo [I] 114 H3
San Vicente de Alcántara [E] 86 F5
San Vicente de la Barquera [E] 82 E3
San Vicente del Raspeig / Sant Vicent del Raspeig [E] 104 E2
San Vincenzo [I] 114 E2
San Vito [I] 118 D6
San Vito al Tagliamento [I] 72 F5
San Vito dei Normanni [I] 122 F4
San Vito di Cadore [I] 72 E3
San Vito lo Capo [I] 126 B1
San Vito Romano [I] 116 B5
San Vittore delle Chiuse [I] 116 B1
Sanxay [F] 54 E4
Sanxenxo [E] 78 B4
Sanza [I] 120 G5
São Barnabé [P] 94 C4
São Bartolomeu de Messines [P] 94 C5
São Brás de Alportel [P] 94 C5

São Cristóvão [P] 94 D1
São Domingos [P] 94 C3
São Gregório [P] 78 C5
São Jacinto [P] 80 B5
São João da Madeira [P] 80 B4
São João da Pesqueira [P] 80 E5
São João da Serra [P] 80 C5
São João dos Caldeireiros [P] 94 D4
São Luis [P] 94 B3
São Manços [P] 94 E2
São Marcos da Ataboeira [P] 94 D4
São Marcos da Serra [P] 94 C4
São Martinho [P] 86 E2
São Martinho das Amoreiras [P] 94 C4
São Martinho do Porto [P] 86 B3
São Miguel de Acha [P] 86 F3
São Miguel de Machede [P] 94 E1
São Pedro de Muel [P] 86 C2
São Pedro de Solis [P] 94 D4
São Pedro do Sul [P] 80 C5
Saorge [F] 108 F4
São Romão [P] 94 C2
São Teotónio [P] 94 B4
Saou [F] 68 F6
São Vicente [P] 100 A3
São Vicente da Beira [P] 86 F3
Sapakpınar [TR] 146 G3
Sapanca [TR] 146 G3
Sapareva Banya [BG] 150 F5
Sapernoye [RUS] 178 G2
Sápes [GR] 130 G3
Şaphane [TR] 144 F2
sa Pobla [E] 104 E4
Sapotskin [BY] 24 F3
Sappada [I] 72 F3
Sappee [FIN] 176 H1
Sappemeer [NL] 16 G2
Sapri [I] 120 G5
Saqués [E] 84 D5
Sarafovo [BG] 148 F4
Sarajevo [BIH] 152 D1
Sarakíniko [GR] 134 B4
Saramon [F] 84 G3
Sáránd [H] 76 H1
Saranda [AL] 132 B1
Saránti [GR] 132 H6
Sarantsi [BG] 150 G4
Sarata [UA] 206 E5
Saray [TR] 146 D2
Saraycık [TR] 144 E3
Sarayköy [TR] 144 F5
Šarbanovac [YU] 150 D2
Sarbinowo [PL] 20 H3
Sarbinowo [PL] 34 G2
Sárbogárd [H] 76 B3
Sárdara [I] 118 C6
Šarengrad [HR] 154 E1
Sarentino / Sarntal [I] 72 D3
Sargans [CH] 58 H6
Sári [H] 76 C2
Sarıcakaya [TR] 146 H4
Sarıgöl [TR] 144 F4
Sarıkaya [TR] 144 E4
Sariñena [E] 90 G4
Sarısu [TR] 146 G3
Sariyer [TR] 146 E2
Sarkad [H] 76 G3
Sarkadkeresztúr [H] 76 G3
Sárkeresztúr [H] 76 B2
Särkijärvi [FIN] 198 E4
Särkijärvi [FIN] 192 H5
Särkilahti [FIN] 186 G6
Särkilahti [FIN] 188 F6
Särkisalmi [FIN] 188 F5
Särkisalo / Finby [FIN] 176 E5

Şarköy [TR] 146 C4
Sarlat-la-Canéda [F] 66 G4
Sarmizegetuza [RO] 206 B5
Särna [S] 172 E1
Sarnaki [PL] 38 E2
Sarnano [I] 116 C2
Sarnen [CH] 58 F6
Sárnico [I] 72 A5
Sarno [I] 120 E3
Sarnowa [PL] 36 C5
Sarnówek [PL] 38 C6
Sarntal / Sarentino [I] 72 D3
Sarny [UA] 204 A7
Särö [S] 160 G3
Saronída [GR] 136 H1
Saronno [I] 70 G4
Sárospatak [H] 64 G4
Šarovce [SK] 64 B5
Sarpsborg [N] 166 B3
Sarracín [E] 82 E6
Sarral [E] 92 C4
Sarralbe [F] 44 G4
Sarrebourg [F] 44 G5
Sarreguemines [F] 44 G4
Sárrétudvari [H] 76 G1
Sarre-Union [F] 44 G5
Sarria [E] 78 E4
Sarrión [E] 98 E2
Sarroch [I] 118 C7
Sarron [F] 84 E2
Sarsıla İskele [TR] 142 F3
Sársina [I] 110 G5
Sarstedt [D] 32 G2
Sart [TR] 144 E4
Sarteano [I] 114 G2
Sartène [F] 114 B5
Sárti [GR] 130 D6
Sartilly [F] 26 D4
Saruhanlı [TR] 144 D3
Sárvár [H] 74 G2
Sarvijoki [FIN] 186 B3
Sarvikumpu [FIN] 188 E3
Sarzana [I] 110 C4
Sarzeau [F] 40 D5
Sarzedas [P] 86 E3
Sasa [MK] 150 E6
Sa Savina [I] 104 C6
Sásd [H] 76 A4
Sassari [I] 118 C3
Sassello [I] 108 H3
Sassenage [F] 68 H4
Sassenberg [D] 32 D3
Sassenheim [NL] 16 D4
Sassnitz [D] 20 D2
Sassocorvaro [I] 110 H5
Sassoferrato [I] 116 B1
Sasso Marconi [I] 110 F4
Sassuolo [I] 110 E3
Šaštín-Stráže [SK] 62 G3
Šatalovo [RUS] 204 D5
Sátão [P] 80 D5
Sätenäs [S] 166 D5
Säter [S] 174 C5
Satırlar [TR] 144 D3
Sátoraljaújhely [H] 64 G3
Satovcha [BG] 130 C1
Satow [D] 20 B3
Satra brunn [S] 168 B1
Sátres [GR] 130 E2
Satrup [D] 18 F1
Sattanen [FIN] 196 D6
Satu Mare [RO] 206 B4
Saturn [RO] 148 G1
Saturnia [I] 114 G3
Saucats [F] 66 C4
Sauda [N] 164 C1
Sauðárkrókur [IS] 194 D3
Saudasjøen [N] 164 C1
Saue [EST] 200 D1
Sauerlach [D] 60 E5
Saugues [F] 68 D4
Saujon [F] 54 C6
Saukkola [FIN] 176 G4
Saukonkyla [FIN] 186 D2
Sauland [N] 164 F1
Saulgau [D] 58 H3
Saulieu [F] 56 F3
Saulkrasti [LV] 200 D4
Sault [F] 108 B3
Saulx [F] 58 B3

Saulxures [F] 58 C3
Saumur [F] 54 E2
Saundersfoot [GB] 12 D2
Sauvagnat [F] 68 B2
Sauve [F] 106 F3
Sauveterre-de-Béarn [F] 84 D2
Sauveterre-de-Guyenne [F] 66 D4
Sauvo [FIN] 176 E5
Sauxillanges [F] 68 D3
Sauze d'Oulx [I] 70 C5
Sauzé-Vaussais [F] 54 E5
Sauzon [F] 40 C5
Sava [I] 122 F4
Sävar [S] 198 A6
Savaştepe [TR] 144 D2
Save [S] 160 G2
Savelletri [I] 122 F3
Savelli [I] 124 E4
Savenay [F] 40 E6
Saverdun [F] 84 H4
Saverne [F] 44 G5
Savigliano [I] 108 F2
Savignac-les-Eglises [F] 66 F3
Savignano Irpino [I] 120 F2
Savignano sul Rubicone [I] 110 H5
Savigny-sur-Braye [F] 42 C5
Savijärvi [FIN] 198 G5
Savikylä [FIN] 198 F6
Savines-le-Lac [F] 108 D2
Savino Selo [YU] 154 F1
Saviore dell'Adamello [I] 72 B4
Savitaipale [FIN] 178 D2
Savnik [YU] 152 E3
Savognin [CH] 70 H2
Savona [I] 108 H3
Savonlinna [FIN] 188 E5
Savonranta [FIN] 188 F4
Sävsjö [S] 162 D3
Sävsjön [S] 166 G1
Savudrija [HR] 72 H6
Savukoski [FIN] 196 E6
Sävya [S] 168 D2
Sawston [GB] 14 F3
Sawtry [GB] 14 E2
Sax [E] 104 D2
Saxnäs [S] 190 E4
Säynätsalo [FIN] 186 G5
Säyneinen [FIN] 188 D1
Sázava [CZ] 48 G4
Sazonovo [RUS] 204 E2
Scaër [F] 40 C3
Scafa [I] 116 D4
Scalasaig [GB] 8 B2
Scalby [GB] 10 G3
Scalea [I] 120 H6
Scalloway [GB] 6 G4
Scandiano [I] 110 E3
Scanno [I] 116 D5
Scansano [I] 114 F3
Scanzano Jónico [I] 122 D5
Scarborough [GB] 10 G3
Scardovari [I] 110 H2
Scarinish [GB] 6 A6
Scarriff [IRL] 2 C6
Ščekino [RUS] 204 F5
Ščepan Polje [YU] 152 D2
Schaan [FL] 58 H6
Schachendorf [A] 74 F1
Schaffhausen [CH] 58 G4
Schafstädt [D] 34 B5
Schäftlam [D] 60 E5
Schagen [NL] 16 D3
Scharbeutz [D] 18 G3
Schärding [A] 60 H3
Scharnitz [A] 60 D6
Scharnstein [A] 62 B5
Scheer [D] 58 H3
Schéggia [I] 116 A1
Scheibbs [A] 62 D5
Scheifling [A] 74 B2
Scheinfeld [D] 46 F4
Schenefeld [D] 18 F3
Scherfede [D] 32 E4
Schermbeck [D] 30 G2
Schesslitz [D] 46 G3

Scheveningen [NL] 16 C5
Scheyern [D] 60 E3
Schieder [D] 32 E3
Schierling [D] 60 F2
Schiermonnikoog [NL] 16 G1
Schifferstadt [D] 46 B5
Schilde [B] 30 D3
Schilpário [I] 72 B4
Schiltach [D] 58 F2
Schio [I] 72 D5
Schirmeck [F] 44 G6
Schirnding [D] 48 C3
Schkeuditz [D] 34 C5
Schladen [D] 32 H3
Schladming [A] 72 H1
Schlanders / Silandro [I] 72 C3
Schlangenbad [D] 46 B3
Schleching [D] 60 F5
Schleiden [D] 30 F5
Schleiz [D] 48 B2
Schleswig [D] 18 F1
Schleusingen [D] 46 G2
Schlieben [D] 34 E4
Schlierbach [A] 62 B5
Schliersee [D] 60 E5
Schlitz [D] 46 E1
Schlotheim [D] 32 H5
Schluchsee [D] 58 F3
Schlüchtern [D] 46 E2
Schluderns / Sluderno [I] 72 C3
Schludersbach / Carbonin [I] 72 E3
Schlüsselfeld [D] 46 F4
Schlutup [D] 18 H3
Schmalkalden [D] 46 F1
Schmallenberg [D] 32 D5
Schmidmühlen [D] 48 B6
Schmilka [D] 48 F1
Schmöllin [D] 48 C1
Schmölln [D] 20 E5
Schnackenburg [D] 20 A6
Schnaittenbach [D] 48 B5
Schneeberg [D] 48 D2
Schneverdingen [D] 18 F5
Schober Pass [A] 74 C1
Schöder [A] 74 B2
Schöllkrippen [D] 46 D3
Schönau [D] 58 E3
Schönbeck [D] 20 D4
Schönberg [A] 72 D1
Schönberg [D] 48 C3
Schönberg [D] 60 H2
Schönberg [D] 18 G2
Schönberg [D] 18 H3
Schönbergerstrand [D] 18 G2
Schönebeck [D] 20 B6
Schönebeck [D] 34 B3
Schönecken [D] 44 F1
Schongau [D] 60 D5
Schönhagen [D] 18 G1
Schöningen [D] 32 H3
Schönmünzach [D] 58 F1
Schönthal [D] 48 C5
Schönwald [D] 58 F3
Schönwalde [D] 18 H2
Schönwalde [D] 34 E2
Schoondijke [NL] 28 G1
Schoonebeek [NL] 16 G4
Schoonhoven [NL] 16 D5
Schoonoord [NL] 16 G3
Schopfheim [D] 58 E4
Schöppenstedt [D] 32 H3
Schoppernau [A] 60 B6
Schöppingen [D] 16 H5
Schorndorf [D] 60 B2
Schotten [D] 46 D2
Schramberg [D] 58 F2
Schrems [A] 62 D3
Schriesheim [D] 46 C4
Schrobenhausen [D] 60 D3
Schröcken [A] 72 B1
Schruns [A] 72 A1
Schull [IRL] 4 B5
Schüpfheim [CH] 58 E6
Schuttertal [D] 58 E2
Schüttorf [D] 16 H5
Schwaan [D] 20 B3

Schwabach [D] 46 G5
Schwabhausen [D] 60 D4
Schwäbisch Gmünd [D] 60 B2
Schwäbisch Hall [D] 46 E6
Schwabmünchen [D] 60 C4
Schwaigern [D] 46 D5
Schwalenberg [D] 32 E3
Schwalmstadt-Treysa [D] 32 E6
Schwalmstadt-Ziegenhain [D] 32 E6
Schwanden [CH] 58 G6
Schwandorf [D] 48 B5
Schwanebeck [D] 34 A3
Schwanenstadt [A] 62 A5
Schwanewede [D] 18 D5
Schwaney [D] 32 E4
Schwarmstedt [D] 32 F1
Schwarzach [A] 72 G1
Schwarzburg [D] 46 G2
Schwarzenbach [D] 48 B3
Schwarzenbek [D] 18 G4
Schwarzenberg [D] 48 D2
Schwarzenfeld [D] 48 B5
Schwarzsee [CH] 70 D1
Schwaz [A] 72 E1
Schwechat [A] 62 F4
Schwedt [D] 20 E6
Schweich [D] 44 G2
Schweinfurt [D] 46 F3
Schwelm [D] 30 H3
Schwenningen [D] 58 F3
Schwerin [D] 20 A4
Schwerte [D] 32 C4
Schwetzingen [D] 46 C5
Schwyz [CH] 58 F6
Sciacca [I] 126 C3
Scicli [I] 126 F5
Scilla [I] 124 C7
Ščinawa [PL] 36 B5
Scole [GB] 14 G3
S. Colombano al Lambro [I] 70 G6
Sconser [GB] 6 B4
Scopello [I] 70 E4
Ščors [UA] 204 D7
Scorzè [I] 72 E6
Scotch Corner [GB] 10 F2
Scourie [GB] 6 D2
Scrabster [GB] 6 F2
Screeb [IRL] 2 B4
Scritto [I] 116 A1
Scunthorpe [GB] 10 G4
Scuol [CH] 72 B2
Seaford [GB] 14 E6
Seaham [GB] 8 G6
Seatoller [GB] 10 D1
Seaton [GB] 12 F4
Sebbersund [DK] 160 D4
Sebečevo [YU] 150 B4
Sebeş [RO] 206 B5
Sebezh [RUS] 200 H5
Sebnitz [D] 48 F1
Sebrenica [BIH] 154 F4
Seč [CZ] 48 E5
Seč [CZ] 50 A4
Sečanj [YU] 154 H1
Secemin [PL] 50 H2
Séchault [F] 44 C3
Seckau [A] 74 C1
Seclin [F] 28 F3
Secondigny [F] 54 D3
Sečovce [SK] 64 G3
Sedan [F] 44 D2
Sedbergh [GB] 10 E2
Séderon [F] 108 B2
Sedgefield [GB] 10 F2
Sédico [I] 72 E4
Sédilo [I] 118 C4
Sédini [I] 118 C3
Sedlčany [CZ] 48 F5
Sedlice [CZ] 48 F5
Sedrun [CH] 70 F1
Šeduva [LT] 202 F4
Sędziszów [PL] 52 D3
Sędziszów [PL] 52 A2
Seeboden [A] 72 H2
Seebruck [D] 60 F5
Seefeld in Tyrol [A] 72 D1
Seehausen [D] 34 B3
Seehausen [D] 20 A6

Seehausen [D] 34 D4
Seelbach [D] 58 E2
Seelisberg Tunnel [CH] 58 F6
Seelow [D] 34 F2
Seeon [D] 60 F5
Sées [F] 26 F5
Seesen [D] 32 G3
Seeshaupt [D] 60 D5
Seewalchen [A] 60 H5
Seewiesen [A] 62 D6
Seferihisar [TR] 144 C5
Segalstad bru [N] 172 B2
Segarcea [RO] 150 G1
Segerstad [S] 162 G6
Segesd [H] 74 G4
Seglinge [FIN] 176 B5
Segmon [S] 166 E3
Segonzac [F] 54 D6
Segorbe [E] 98 E3
Segovia [E] 88 F4
Segré [F] 40 G5
Segura [E] 102 G1
Segura [P] 86 G4
Segura de León [E] 94 G4
Segura de los Baños [E] 90 E6
Şehirlioğlu [TR] 144 F3
Sehnde [D] 32 G2
Seia [P] 86 F2
Seiches-sur-le-Loir [F] 40 H6
Seifhannersdorf [D] 48 G1
Seilhac [F] 66 H3
Seinäjoki [FIN] 186 C3
Seira [E] 84 F6
Seitenstetten [A] 62 C5
Seixal [P] 86 B5
Seixo [P] 80 C6
Sejerby [DK] 156 E2
Sejny [PL] 24 E3
Sejs [DK] 156 C1
Šeksna [RUS] 204 F1
Selanovtsi [BG] 150 G2
Selargius [I] 118 D7
Selaste [EST] 200 E1
Selb [D] 48 C3
Selbu [N] 182 C2
Selby [GB] 10 F4
Selce [HR] 112 F2
Selçuk [TR] 144 D5
Selde [DK] 160 C4
Selendi [TR] 144 F3
Selenicë [AL] 128 B5
Selent [D] 18 G2
Sélestat [F] 58 E2
Seleuş [RO] 76 H4
Selevac [YU] 150 B1
Selfoss [IS] 194 B5
Séli [GR] 128 F5
Selianítika [GR] 132 F6
Seligenstadt [D] 46 D3
Selimiye [TR] 142 C1
Selínia [GR] 136 G1
Selishtë [AL] 128 C2
Selište [YU] 150 D2
Seližarovo [RUS] 204 D3
Selje [N] 180 B4
Seljestad [N] 170 C5
Seljord [N] 164 F2
Selkirk [GB] 8 E4
Sella [E] 104 E2
Sellasía [GR] 136 E3
Selles [F] 54 H2
Sellía [GR] 140 D5
Sellières [F] 56 H5
Sellin [D] 20 E2
Sellye [H] 76 A5
Selm [D] 32 C3
Selmsdorf [D] 18 H3
Selnes [N] 190 B5
Selongey [F] 56 H3
Selsey [GB] 14 D5
Selsingen [D] 18 E4
Seltz [F] 46 B6
Selva di Cadore [I] 72 E3
Selva di Val Gardena / Wolkenstein in Gardena [I] 72 E3
Selvik [N] 180 B6
Selvino [I] 70 H4
Sem [N] 164 H3

Semblana [P] 94 C4
Semily [CZ] 48 H2
Semizovac [BIH] 152 D1
Semmering [A] 62 E6
Semmering Pass [A] 62 E6
Semur-en-Auxois [F] 56 F3
Seña [SK] 64 G3
Sena de Luna [E] 78 G4
Sénas [P] 106 H4
Senden [D] 16 H6
Sendenhorst [D] 32 C3
Senec [SK] 62 H4
Senftenberg [D] 34 F5
Senica [SK] 62 G3
Senigállia [I] 112 C6
Senise [I] 122 C5
Senj [HR] 112 F2
Senjehopen [N] 192 D2
Senlis [F] 42 G3
Sennecey-le-Grand [F] 56 G5
Sennelager [D] 32 E3
Sennen [GB] 12 B5
Sennestadt [D] 32 D3
Sennik [BG] 148 B4
Sénnori [I] 118 C3
Sennybridge [GB] 12 F2
Senohrad [SK] 64 C4
Senokos [BG] 148 G2
Senonches [F] 26 H6
Senones [F] 44 G6
Senorbì [I] 118 D6
Senovo [SLO] 74 D5
Senožeče [SLO] 74 B6
Sens [F] 42 G6
Sens-de-Bretagne [F] 26 D5
Senta [YU] 76 E5
Senterada [E] 92 C1
Sentilj [SLO] 74 D3
Šentjur [SLO] 74 D4
Šentvid pri Zavodnju [SLO] 74 C4
Šepetovka [UA] 206 D2
Sępólno Krajenskie [PL] 22 C5
Sępopol [PL] 22 H2
Septemvri [BG] 148 A6
Sept-Saulx [F] 44 B3
Sepúlveda [E] 88 G3
Sequeros [E] 88 B4
Seraincourt [F] 28 H6
Seraing [B] 30 E5
Seravezza [I] 110 D5
Sered' [SK] 62 H4
Seredka [RUS] 200 G3
Seregélyes [H] 76 B2
Seregno [I] 70 G4
Sérent [F] 26 B6
Serfaus [A] 72 C2
Sergiev Posad (Zagorsk) [RUS] 204 F3
Serhat [TR] 144 B1
Seriaji [LT] 24 F2
Seriate [I] 70 H4
Sérifos [GR] 138 D3
Serinhisar [TR] 144 G5
Sermaize-les-Bains [F] 44 C4
Sermide [I] 110 F2
Serock [PL] 38 B2
Serón [E] 102 G4
Serón de Nágima [E] 90 C3
Seròs [E] 90 G5
Serpa [P] 94 E3
Serpins [P] 86 E2
Serpuhov [RUS] 204 F4
Serracapriola [I] 116 F6
Serra de Agua [P] 100 B3
Serra dé Conti [I] 112 C6
Serradifalco [I] 126 D3
Serradilla [E] 88 A6
Serramazzoni [I] 110 E3
Serra Nova [E] 104 F5
Serra San Bruno [I] 124 D6
Serra San Quirico [I] 116 B1
Serrenti [I] 118 C6
Serres [F] 108 C2
Sérres [GR] 130 C3

Serri [I] 118 D6
Serrières [F] 68 F4
Sersale [I] 124 E5
Sertã [P] 86 E3
Sérvia [GR] 128 F6
Serviana [GR] 132 D2
Servigliano [I] 116 C2
Sesa [E] 90 F3
Seseña Nuevo [E] 96 G1
Sesimbra [P] 86 B6
Seskinore [GB] 2 F3
Sésklo [GR] 132 H2
Sesma [E] 82 H6
Sessa Aurunca [I] 120 D2
Šestanovac [HR] 152 B2
Sestao [E] 82 G3
Sesto / Sexten [I] 72 F3
Sesto al Reghena [I] 72 F5
Sesto Calende [I] 70 F4
Sesto Fiorentino [I] 110 F5
Sestola [I] 110 E4
Sesto S. Giovanni [I] 70 G5
Sestriere [I] 70 C5
Sestri Levante [I] 110 B4
Sestroretsk [RUS] 178 G4
Sestu [I] 118 C7
Sesvete [HR] 74 E5
Séta [GR] 134 C4
Šėta [LT] 202 F4
Setcases [E] 92 F2
Sète [F] 106 E4
Seter [N] 182 D5
Setermoen [N] 192 D3
Setihovo [BIH] 152 E1
Settebagni [I] 116 A5
Settimo Torinese [I] 70 D5
Settle [GB] 10 E3
Setúbal [P] 86 B6
Seui [I] 118 D5
Seulo [I] 118 D5
Seurre [F] 56 G4
Sevaster [AL] 128 B5
Sevastopol' [UA] 206 G6
Sevel [DK] 160 C5
Sevenoaks [GB] 14 E5
Sever [P] 80 C5
Sévérac-le-Château [F] 68 C6
Severin [D] 20 B4
Severin [HR] 74 G5
Ševětín [CZ] 62 C2
Sevettijärvi [FIN] 196 E3
Sevilla [E] 94 G6
Sevilleja de la Jara [E] 96 D2
Şevketiye [TR] 146 B5
Şevketiye [TR] 146 D5
Sevlievo [BG] 148 B4
Sevnica [SLO] 74 D5
Sevojno [YU] 150 A2
Sevrier [F] 70 B3
Sexten / Sesto [I] 72 F3
Seyches [F] 66 E4
Seyda [D] 34 D4
Seydiköy [TR] 144 C4
Seyðisfjörður [IS] 194 G5
Seyitömer [TR] 146 G6
Seymen [TR] 146 D3
Seyne [F] 108 D2
Seyssel [F] 68 H2
Seysses [F] 84 H3
Sezana [SLO] 72 H6
Sézanne [F] 44 A4
Sezimovo Ústí [CZ] 48 G5
Sezze [I] 120 B1
Sfáka [GR] 140 G5
Sfákia [GR] 140 C5
Sfintu Gheorghe [RO] 206 C5
Sforzacosta [I] 116 C2
S. Giovanni Bianco [I] 70 H4
Shabla [BG] 148 G2
Shaftesbury [GB] 12 G4
Shanagolden [IRL] 4 C3
Shanklin [GB] 12 H5
Shannonbridge [IRL] 2 D5
Sharnevo [BG] 148 D5
Shats'k [UA] 38 G4
Shawbury [GB] 10 D5
Shchuchin [BY] 24 H4
's Heerenberg [NL] 16 F6

Sheerness [GB] 14 F4
Sheffield [GB] 10 F4
Shefford [GB] 14 E3
Shëngjergj [AL] 128 B3
Shëngjin [AL] 128 A1
Shënmëri [AL] 150 B6
Shenval [GB] 6 E5
Shepshed [GB] 10 E6
Shepton Mallet [GB] 12 F4
Sherborne [GB] 12 F4
Shercock [IRL] 2 F4
Sheringham [GB] 14 G1
's-Hertogen-Bosch [NL] 16 E6
Shetaj [AL] 128 A2
Shiel Bridge [GB] 6 C5
Shieldaig [GB] 6 C4
Shifnal [GB] 10 D6
Shijak [AL] 128 A3
Shillelagh [IRL] 4 F4
Shinrone [IRL] 2 D6
Shipchenski Prokhad [BG] 148 C4
Shipka [BG] 148 C4
Shipkovo [BG] 148 B4
Shipley [GB] 10 E3
Shipston-on-Stour [GB] 12 H2
Shiroka Lŭka [BG] 130 D1
Shirokë [AL] 128 A1
Shivatsevo [BG] 148 D4
Shkodër [AL] 128 A1
Shkorpilovtsi [BG] 148 F3
Shmoylovo [RUS] 200 H3
Shoeburyness [GB] 14 F4
Shoreham-by-Sea [GB] 14 E5
Shotts [GB] 8 E3
Shranamanragh Bridge [IRL] 2 B3
Shrewsbury [GB] 10 D5
Shrewton [GB] 12 G4
Shrule [IRL] 2 C4
Shtërmen [AL] 128 B4
Shumen [BG] 148 E3
Siána [GR] 142 D5
Sianów [PL] 22 A3
Siare [EST] 200 D3
Siátista [GR] 128 E6
Šiauliai [LT] 202 E4
Sibari [I] 122 D6
Sibbo / Sippo [FIN] 176 H4
Šibenik [HR] 112 H6
Sibiu [RO] 206 B5
Sibnica [SLO] 148 G2
Sicignano degli Alburni [I] 120 G4
Šid [YU] 154 E2
Sidári [GR] 132 A2
Siddeburen [NL] 16 H2
Sideby / Siipyy [FIN] 186 A5
Sidensjö [S] 184 F2
Siderno [I] 124 D7
Sidiró [GR] 130 G2
Sidirókastro [GR] 130 B3
Sidmouth [GB] 12 E4
Sidra [PL] 24 F4
Sidzina [PL] 50 D2
Siecq [F] 54 D6
Siedlce [PL] 38 D3
Siedlinghausen [D] 32 D5
Siegburg [D] 30 H5
Siegen [D] 32 C6
Siegenburg [D] 60 E2
Sieggraben [A] 62 F6
Siegsdorf [D] 60 G5
Siekierki [PL] 34 F1
Siemiany [PL] 22 F4
Siemiatycze [PL] 38 E2
Siena [I] 114 F1
Sieniawa [PL] 52 F3
Sieniawka [PL] 48 G1
Sienno [PL] 38 C6
Sieppijärvi [FIN] 192 H6
Sieradz [PL] 36 F5
Sieraków [PL] 50 F2
Sieraków [PL] 36 B2
Sierakowice [PL] 22 D2
Sierck-les-Bains [F] 44 F3
Sierentz [F] 58 D4
Sierning [A] 62 B5
Sierpc [PL] 36 G1
Sierra de Luna [E] 84 C6
Sierra de Yeguas [E] 102 B3
Sierra Nevada [E] 102 E4
Sierre [CH] 70 D2
Siete Aguas [E] 98 D4
Sievi [FIN] 198 D5
Siewierz [PL] 50 G2
Sifjord [N] 192 D3
Siğacik [TR] 144 C5
Sigean [F] 106 D5
Sigerfjord [N] 192 C4
Siggjarvåg [N] 170 A5
Sighetu Marmaţiei [RO] 206 B3
Sighişoara [RO] 206 C5
Siglufjörður [IS] 194 E2
Sigmaringen [D] 58 H3
Signes [F] 108 C5
Signy-l'Abbaye [F] 28 H6
Sígri [GR] 134 G2
Sigtuna [S] 168 D2
Sigüeiro [E] 78 C3
Sigüenza [E] 90 A4
Sigulda [LV] 200 E5
Sihtuuna [FIN] 196 C8

Siikainen [FIN] 186 B6
Siikajoki [FIN] 198 D4
Siilinjärvi [FIN] 188 C2
Siipyy / Sideby [FIN] 186 A5
Siivikko [FIN] 198 E3
Sijarinska Banja [YU] 150 D5
Sikea [GR] 140 G5
Sikeå [S] 198 A5
Sikiá [GR] 132 F1
Sikinos [GR] 138 E4
Siklós [H] 76 B5
Sikovuono [FIN] 196 D4
Šilale [LT] 202 D4
Silandro / Schlanders [I] 72 C3
Silánus [I] 118 C4
Silbaš [YU] 154 F1
Silberstedt [D] 18 F1
Şile [TR] 146 F2
Sílíqua [I] 118 C7
Silistra [BG] 148 E1
Silivri [TR] 146 D3
Siljan [N] 164 G3
Siljansnäs [S] 172 G4
Silkås [S] 182 H1
Silkeborg [DK] 160 D6
Silla [E] 98 E5
Sillamäe [EST] 200 F1
Silleda [E] 78 C3
Sillé-le-Guillaume [F] 26 F6
Sillerud [S] 166 D3
Sillian [A] 72 F3
Silloth [GB] 8 D5
Silno [PL] 22 C4
Šilo [HR] 112 F2
Sils [E] 92 F3
Sils-Maria [CH] 70 H2
Šilutė [LT] 202 D5
Silva [E] 78 C2
Silvaplana [CH] 70 H2
Silvares [P] 86 F2
Silverdalen [S] 162 F3
Silvermines [IRL] 4 D3
Silves [P] 94 B5
Silvi Marina [I] 116 D4
Silz [A] 72 C1
Simancas [E] 88 E2
Simaság [H] 74 G1
Simat [RO] 76 G1
Simav [TR] 144 F2
Simaxis [I] 118 C5
Simbach [D] 60 G3
Simbach [D] 60 G4
Simeonovgrad [BG] 148 D6
Simferopol' [UA] 206 G6
Simitli [BG] 130 A1

Šimkaičiai [LT] 202 E5
Simlångsdalen [S] 162 B5
Şimleu Silvaniei [RO] 206 B4
Simmerath [D] 30 F5
Simmerberg [D] 60 B5
Simmern [D] 44 H2
Simo [FIN] 198 D3
Simonsbath [GB] 12 E3
Simonstorp [S] 168 B4
Simontornya [H] 76 B3
Simorre [F] 84 G3
Simpele [FIN] 188 F6
Simplon Dorf [CH] 70 E2
Simplonpass [CH] 70 E2
Simrishamn [S] 158 D3
Simuna [EST] 200 F2
Sinaia [RO] 206 C5
Sinalunga [I] 114 G2
Sinanaj [AL] 128 B5
Sinarcas [E] 98 D3
Sıncansarnıç [TR] 146 E5
Sindal [DK] 160 E2
Sindelfingen [D] 58 G1
Sindi [EST] 200 D3
Sındırgı [TR] 144 E2
Sinekçi [TR] 146 C5
Sinekli [TR] 146 D2
Sinemorets [BG] 148 G5
Sines [P] 94 B2
Sinettä [FIN] 196 C7
Sineu [E] 104 E5
Sinevo [RUS] 178 G2
Singen [D] 58 G4
Singleton [GB] 14 D5
Singsås [N] 182 B2
Singusdal [N] 164 F3
Siniscola [I] 118 E4
Sinj [HR] 152 A1
Sinnai [I] 118 D7
Sinnes [N] 164 C3
Sinópoli [I] 124 C7
Sinsheim [D] 46 C5
Sintra [P] 86 A5
Sinzig [D] 30 H5
Siófok [H] 76 A2
Sion [CH] 70 D2
Sion Mills [GB] 2 F2
Siorac–en–Périgord [F] 66 F4
Šipovo [BIH] 154 B4
Sippo / Sibbo [FIN] 176 H4
Sippola [FIN] 178 C3
Sira [N] 164 C4
Siracusa [I] 126 G5
Siret [RO] 206 C4
Sirevåg [N] 164 B4
Şiria [RO] 76 H4
Sirig [YU] 154 F1
Sirkka [FIN] 192 H5
Sirma [N] 196 D2
Sirmione [I] 72 B6
Sirnach [CH] 58 G5
Sirok [H] 64 E5
Široké [SK] 64 F2
Sirolo [I] 116 C1
Siruela [E] 96 C3
Širvintos [LT] 202 G5
Sisak [HR] 154 A1
Sisamón [E] 90 C4
Sisante [E] 98 B4
Šiščicy [BY] 204 B6
Sissa [I] 110 D2
Sissach [CH] 58 E4
Sissonne [F] 28 G6
Şiştarovät [RO] 76 H5
Sisteron [F] 108 C3
Sistiana [I] 72 H5
Siteía [GR] 140 G4
Sitges [E] 92 D5
Sitrama de Tera [E] 80 H3
Sittard [NL] 30 F4
Sittensen [D] 18 E5
Sittersdorf [A] 74 C3
Sittingbourne [GB] 14 F5
Siurua [FIN] 198 E3
Siusi [I] 72 D3
Sivac [YU] 76 D6
Sivakka [FIN] 198 G5
Sivakkavaara [FIN] 188 E2
Sivaslı [TR] 144 G3
Siverskiy [RUS] 178 H6

Síviri [GR] 130 B6
Sivota [GR] 132 C2
Six–Fours–les–Plages [F] 108 C6
Sixmilebridge [IRL] 2 C6
Sixpenny Handley [GB] 12 G4
Sizun [F] 40 B2
Sjasstroj [RUS] 204 D1
Sjenica [YU] 150 A4
Sjoa [N] 180 G6
Sjøåsen [N] 190 C5
Sjöbo [S] 158 C3
Sjøholt [N] 180 D3
Sjørup [DK] 160 C5
Sjötorp [S] 166 F4
Sjoutnäset [N] 190 E5
Sjøvegan [N] 192 D3
Sjövik [S] 160 H1
Sjuntorp [S] 166 D6
Sjusjøen [N] 172 B2
Skåbu [N] 170 G1
Skadovsk [UA] 206 F5
Skælskør [DK] 156 F3
Skærbæk [DK] 156 B3
Skafídia [GR] 136 B2
Skaftafell [IS] 194 E6
Skaftung [FIN] 186 A5
Skagaströnd [IS] 194 D2
Skagen [DK] 160 F2
Skaidi [N] 196 B2
Skaistkalne [LV] 200 E6
Skála [GR] 136 E4
Skála [GR] 132 D6
Skála [GR] 138 H2
Skála [GR] 134 A4
Skála [GR] 134 G2
Skała [PL] 50 H3
Skála Eresoú [GR] 134 G2
Skålan [S] 182 G4
Skaland [N] 192 D2
Skála Oropoú [GR] 134 C5
Skálavík [DK] 160 B2
Skalbmierz [PL] 52 B3
Skåldö [FIN] 176 F6
Skalica [SK] 62 G3
Skalitsa [BG] 148 D5
Skallelv [N] 196 F2
Skallerup Kit [DK] 160 E2
Skallskog [S] 172 G4
Skalmoldal [S] 190 E3
Skalotí [GR] 140 C5
Skalotí [GR] 130 D2
Skals [DK] 160 D5
Skålsjön [S] 174 D3
Skalstugan [S] 182 E1
Skandáli [GR] 130 F6
Skanderborg [DK] 156 D1
Skanes Fagerhult [S] 162 C6
Skånevik [N] 170 B6
Skänninge [S] 166 H6
Skanör [S] 156 H3
Skansen [N] 190 C6
Skansholm [S] 190 F4
Skåpafors [S] 166 D4
Skąpe [PL] 34 H3
Skara [S] 166 E5
Skarberget [N] 192 C4
Skärblacka [S] 168 A5
Skarð [IS] 194 C5
Skåre [S] 166 E2
Skärhamn [S] 160 G1
Skarnes [N] 172 C5
Skarpengland [N] 164 D5
Skärplinge [S] 174 F4
Skarsvåg [N] 196 C1
Skarszewy [PL] 22 D3
Skårup [DK] 156 E4
Skarvsjö [S] 190 F4
Skaryszew [PL] 38 C5
Skarżysko–Kamienna [PL] 38 B6
Skata [FIN] 176 E6
Skattungbyn [S] 172 G2
Skaudvilė [LT] 202 E4
Skaulo [S] 192 F5
Skave [DK] 160 C5
Skavik [N] 196 B2
Skawina [PL] 50 H4

Skee [S] 166 C4
Skegness [GB] 10 H5
Skei [N] 180 D6
Skei [N] 180 G2
Skei [N] 190 C4
Skeiðflötur [IS] 194 C6
Skeie [N] 164 C5
Skela [YU] 154 G3
Skelde [DK] 156 C4
Skellefteå [S] 198 A4
Skellefteham [S] 198 A4
Skelleftehamn [S] 198 A4
Skellefteestrand [S] 198 A4
Skelmersdale [GB] 10 D4
Skelmorlie [GB] 8 C3
Skender Vakuf [BIH] 154 C3
Skene [S] 162 B3
Skępe [PL] 36 G1
Skeppshult [S] 162 C4
Skerries [IRL] 2 F6
Ski [N] 166 B1
Skíathos [GR] 134 B3
Skibbereen [IRL] 4 B5
Skibby [DK] 156 G2
Skibniew–Podawce [PL] 38 D2
Skibotn [N] 192 E2
Skidal' [BY] 24 G4
Skien [N] 164 G3
Skierniewice [PL] 36 H4
Skiippagurra [N] 196 D2
Skillingaryd [S] 162 D3
Skillinge [S] 158 D3
Skiniás [GR] 140 F5
Skinnastaðir [IS] 194 F3
Skinnerup [DK] 160 C3
Skinnskatteberg [S] 168 A1
Skipness [GB] 8 C3
Skipton [GB] 10 E3
Skiptvet [N] 166 B2
Skive [DK] 160 C5
Skiveren [DK] 160 E2
Skivjane [YU] 150 B5
Skjærhalden [N] 166 B3
Skjeberg [N] 166 B3
Skjeggedal [N] 164 E4
Skjelten [N] 180 D3
Skjern [DK] 156 B1
Skjerstad [N] 192 C6
Skjervøy [N] 192 F1
Skjold [N] 164 B1
Skjold [N] 192 E3
Skjoldastraumen [N] 164 B1
Skjolden [N] 170 E1
Skjønhaug [N] 166 C2
Skoby [S] 168 D1
Skoczów [PL] 50 F4
Skodje [N] 180 D3
Skødstrup [DK] 160 E6
Škofja Loka [SLO] 74 B4
Škofljica [SLO] 74 C5
Skog [S] 174 E3
Skoganvarre [N] 192 H1
Skoger [N] 164 H2
Skogly [N] 196 E3
Skogn [N] 190 C6
Skogsby [S] 162 G5
Skogstorp [S] 168 B3
Skoki [PL] 36 D2
Skokloster [S] 168 D2
Sköldinge [S] 168 B4
Skole [UA] 52 G6
Skollenberg [N] 164 G2
Sköllersta [S] 166 H3
Skomdal [N] 164 E3
Skópelos [GR] 134 H2
Skópelos [GR] 134 B3
Skopí [GR] 140 G4
Skopiá [GR] 132 G3
Skopje [MK] 128 E1
Skopós [GR] 128 E4
Skopun [DK] 160 A2
Skórcz [PL] 22 E4
Skoroszów [PL] 36 D5
Skorovatn [N] 190 D4
Skørping [DK] 160 D4
Skórzec [PL] 38 D3
Skotoússa [GR] 130 B3
Skotselv [N] 164 G1
Skotterud [N] 166 D1

Skoulikariá [GR] 132 E3
Skoúra [GR] 136 E4
Skoútari [GR] 130 B3
Skovballe [DK] 156 D4
Skovby [DK] 156 D4
Skövde [S] 166 F6
Skrá [GR] 128 G3
Skrad [HR] 112 F1
Skradin [HR] 112 H6
Skråmestø [N] 170 A3
Skrea [S] 160 H4
Skreia [N] 172 B4
Skrīveri [LV] 200 E5
Skrunda [LV] 200 C5
Skudeneshavn [N] 164 A2
Skulgam [N] 192 E2
Skulsk [PL] 36 E2
Skulte [LV] 200 D4
Skultorp [S] 166 F6
Skultuna [S] 168 B2
Skuodas [LT] 200 B6
Skurup [S] 158 C3
Škušava [LV] 200 G5
Skuteč [CZ] 50 B4
Skutskär [S] 174 E4
Skutvik [N] 192 C6
Skvira [UA] 206 E2
Skwierzyna [PL] 34 H2
Skýdra [GR] 128 G4
Skýros [GR] 134 D3
Skyttmon [S] 184 C1
Skyttorp [S] 168 D1
Sládkovičovo [SK] 62 H4
Slagelse [DK] 156 F3
Slagnäs [S] 190 G3
Slaidburn [GB] 10 E3
Slane [IRL] 2 F5
Slangerup [DK] 156 G2
Slănic Moldova [RO] 206 C5
Slano [HR] 152 C3
Slantsy [RUS] 200 G1
Slaný [CZ] 48 F3
Slatina [HR] 74 E5
Slatina [RO] 206 B6
Slatina [YU] 150 B2
Slatiňany [CZ] 50 A4
Slatino [MK] 150 C6
Slåttevik [N] 164 A2
Slåtthog [S] 162 D4
Slattum [N] 172 B6
Slavgorod [BY] 204 C6
Slavkovichi [RUS] 200 H3
Slavkov u Brna (Austerlitz) [CZ] 50 C6
Slavonice [CZ] 62 D2
Slavonska Požega [HR] 154 C1
Slavonski Brod [HR] 154 D2
Slavyanovo [BG] 148 B3
Sława [PL] 36 B4
Sławatycze [PL] 38 F4
Sławków [PL] 50 G3
Sławno [PL] 22 B2
Sławoborze [PL] 20 H4
Sleaford [GB] 10 G6
Sledmere [GB] 10 G3
Slemmestad [N] 164 H1
Ślesin [PL] 22 C6
Ślesin [PL] 36 E3
Sletta [N] 190 D2
Slettestrand [DK] 160 D3
Sliedrecht [NL] 16 D5
Sliema [M] 126 C6
Sligachan [GB] 6 B4
Sligeach / Sligo [IRL] 2 D3
Sligo / Sligeach [IRL] 2 D3
Slite [S] 168 G4
Sliven [BG] 148 D4
Slivnitsa [BG] 150 F4
Slivo Pole [BG] 148 D1
Śliwice [PL] 22 D4
Slobozia [RO] 148 C2
Slobozia [RO] 206 D6
Slobozia Mândra [RO] 148 B2
Słomniki [PL] 52 A3
Slonim [BY] 204 A6

Słońsk [PL] 34 G2
Sloten [NL] 16 F3
Slough [GB] 14 E4
Slovac [YU] 150 A1
Slovenj Gradec [SLO] 74 D4
Slovenska Bistrica [SLO] 74 D4
Slovenská L'upča [SK] 64 C3
Slovenske Konjice [SLO] 74 D4
Slovenské Nové Mesto [SK] 64 G3
Sloviansk [UA] 206 H3
Słubice [PL] 34 G3
Sluck [BY] 204 B6
Sluderno / Schluderns [I] 72 C3
Sluis [NL] 28 G1
Sluis [NL] 16 C6
Slŭnchev Bryag [BG] 148 F4
Slunj [HR] 112 G2
Słupca [PL] 36 E3
Słupia [PL] 52 C3
Słupiec [PL] 50 C2
Słupno [PL] 36 H2
Słupsk [PL] 22 B2
Smålandsstenar [S] 162 C4
Smålasen [N] 190 D4
Smalfjord [N] 196 D2
Smalininkai [LT] 202 E5
Smârdioasa [RO] 148 C2
Smarhon' [BY] 202 H5
S. Maria della Versa [I] 70 G6
Smědeč [CZ] 62 B2
Smederevo [YU] 154 H3
Smederevska–Palanka [YU] 150 C1
Smedjebacken [S] 172 H5
Smela [UA] 206 F3
Smeland [N] 164 E3
Smelror [N] 196 F2
Smidary [CZ] 48 H3
Śmigiel [PL] 36 C4
Smilde [NL] 16 G3
Smiltene [LV] 200 F4
Smínthi [GR] 130 E2
Smögen [S] 166 B5
Smołdzino [PL] 22 C1
Smolen [PL] 50 H3
Smolensk [RUS] 204 D5
Smolyan [BG] 130 E1
Smolyanovtsi [BG] 150 F3
Smørfjord [N] 196 C2
Smørhamn [N] 180 B5
Smorten [N] 192 B4
Smyadovo [BG] 148 E3
Smyga [UA] 206 C2
Smygehamn [S] 158 C3
Snaptun [DK] 156 D2
Snarup [DK] 156 D4
Snåsa [N] 190 C5
Snedsted [DK] 160 C4
Sneek [NL] 16 F2
Sneem [IRL] 4 B4
Snigirevka [UA] 206 F4
Snina [SK] 64 H2
Snjatyn [UA] 206 C3
Šnjegotina Gornja [BIH] 154 C3
Snøde [DK] 156 E4
Snøfjord [N] 196 B2
Snogebaek [DK] 158 E4
Snössvallen [S] 182 F6
Snöstorp [S] 162 B5
Soave [I] 72 C6
Söbbön [S] 166 C4
Soběslav [CZ] 48 G6
Sobibór [PL] 38 G5
Sobieszów [PL] 50 A1
Sobkow [PL] 52 B2
Sobotište [SK] 62 H3
Sobotka [CZ] 48 H2
Sobótka [PL] 50 C1
Sobowidz [PL] 22 E3
Sobra [HR] 152 C3
Sobrado [E] 78 D3
Sobral de Monte Agraço [P] 86 B4
Sobran [TR] 146 H5

Sobreira Formosa [P] 86 E3
Søby [DK] 156 D4
Sočanica [YU] 150 C4
Sochaczew [PL] 38 A3
Sochaux [F] 58 C4
Sochocin [PL] 38 A2
Sochós [GR] 130 B4
Socodor [RO] 76 G3
Socovos [E] 104 B2
Socuéllamos [E] 96 H4
Sodankylä [FIN] 196 D6
Sodderby Karl [S] 168 E1
Söderåkra [S] 162 F6
Söderbärke [S] 168 A1
Söderfors [S] 174 E5
Söderhamn [S] 174 E2
Söderköping [S] 168 B5
Södertälje [S] 168 D3
Södra Vi [S] 162 F2
Sodražica [SLO] 74 C6
Sødring [DK] 160 E5
Soest [D] 32 D4
Soest [NL] 16 E5
Soestdijk [NL] 16 E5
Sofádes [GR] 132 F3
Sofikó [GR] 136 F1
Sofiya [BG] 150 F5
Sögel [D] 18 B6
Sogge bru [N] 180 E3
Sogndal [N] 170 D1
Sogndalstrand [N] 164 B5
Søgne [N] 164 D6
Söğüt [TR] 142 H2
Söğüt [TR] 146 H4
Söğütalan [TR] 146 E5
Soidinvaara [FIN] 198 F5
Soignies [B] 28 H3
Soini [FIN] 186 E3
Soinlahti [FIN] 198 E6
Soissons [F] 42 H2
Sokal' [UA] 52 H2
Söke [TR] 144 D5
Sokna [N] 170 H5
Soko Banja [YU] 150 D3
Sokolac [BIH] 154 E4
Sokółka [PL] 24 F5
Sokolniki [PL] 36 E5
Sokolov [CZ] 48 C3
Sokolovo [BG] 148 G2
Sokołów Małopolski [PL] 52 E3
Sokołów Podlaski [PL] 38 D2
Sola [N] 164 A3
Solana de los Barros [E] 94 G2
Solánas [I] 118 D7
Solares [E] 82 F3
Solberg [S] 190 G6
Solberg [S] 162 E2
Solberga [S] 162 E2
Solbjerg [DK] 160 C4
Solčava [SLO] 74 C4
Solcy [RUS] 204 C2
Solda / Sulden [I] 72 C3
Sölden [A] 72 C2
Soldeu [AND] 84 H6
Solec–Zdrój [PL] 52 C3
Solenzara [F] 114 B5
Solesmes [F] 28 G4
Solevåg [N] 180 D3
Solf / Sulva [FIN] 186 B2
Solfonn [N] 170 C5
Solheim [N] 170 B2
Solignac [F] 66 G1
Soligorsk [BY] 204 B6
Solihull [GB] 12 H1
Solin [HR] 152 A2
Solingen [D] 30 H4
Söll [A] 60 F6
Sollebrun [S] 162 B1
Sollefteå [S] 184 E2
Sollenau [A] 62 F5
Sollentuna [S] 168 D3
Söller [E] 104 E4
Søllerød [DK] 156 G2
Sollerön [S] 172 G3
Sollested [DK] 156 E5
Solliès–Pont [F] 108 C5
Solmaz [TR] 144 F6
Solnechnogorsk [RUS] 204 F4

Solnhofen [D] 60 D2
Solosancho [E] 88 D4
Sološnica [SK] 62 G4
Solothurn [CH] 58 D5
Solovi [RUS] 200 G3
Sölöz [TR] 146 F4
Solrød Strand [DK] 156 G3
Sølsnes [N] 180 E3
Solsona [E] 92 D2
Solt [H] 76 C3
Soltau [D] 18 F6
Soltvadkert [H] 76 D3
Solund [N] 170 A2
Sölvesborg [S] 158 E1
Solvorn [N] 170 D1
Soma [TR] 144 D2
Sombernon [F] 56 G3
Sombor [YU] 76 C6
Somerniemi [FIN] 176 F4
Somero [FIN] 176 F4
Somersham [GB] 14 F2
Somerton [GB] 12 F4
Somino [RUS] 204 E1
Sommariva del Bosco [I] 108 G2
Sommarset [N] 192 C5
Sommatino [I] 126 E4
Sommen [S] 162 E1
Sömmerda [D] 34 A6
Sommersted [DK] 156 C3
Sommesous [F] 44 B4
Sommières [F] 106 F3
Somogyszob [H] 74 G4
Somosierra [E] 88 G4
Somosierra, Puerto de– [E] 88 G4
Somovit [BG] 148 B2
Sompolno [PL] 36 F2
Son [N] 166 B2
Son Bou [E] 104 H4
Sonceboz [CH] 58 D5
Soncillo [E] 82 E4
Soncino [I] 70 H5
Sóndalo [I] 72 B3
Søndeled [N] 164 F4
Sønder Balling [DK] 160 C5
Sønderborg [DK] 156 C4
Sønderby [DK] 156 C4
Sønderby [DK] 160 B6
Sønderby [DK] 156 F4
Sønder Dråby [DK] 160 C4
Sønder Felding [DK] 156 B1
Sønderho [DK] 156 A3
Sønder Omme [DK] 156 B1
Sondershausen [D] 32 H5
Søndersø [DK] 156 D3

Søndervig [DK] 160 B6
Søndervika [N] 182 D4
Sondrio [I] 70 H3
Söndrum [S] 162 B5
Songesand [N] 164 B3
Sonka [FIN] 196 C8
Sonkajärvi [FIN] 198 E6
Sonneberg [D] 46 G2
Sonogno [CH] 70 F2
Sonsbeck [D] 30 G2
Sonseca [E] 96 F2
Sonta [YU] 76 C6
Sonthofen [D] 60 B6
Sontra [D] 32 F6
Son Xoriguer [E] 104 G4
Sopeira [E] 84 F6
Sopočani [YU] 150 B4
Sopot [BG] 148 B4
Sopot [PL] 22 E2
Sopot [YU] 150 B1
Sopron [H] 62 F6
Sora [I] 116 C6
Soragna [I] 110 D2
Söråker [S] 184 F4
Sorano [I] 114 G3
Sorbas [E] 102 H5
Sorbie [GB] 8 C5
Sørbø [N] 164 B2
Sore [F] 66 C4
Söréd [H] 76 B1
Søre Herefoss [N] 164 E5
Soresina [I] 70 H5
Sør–Flatanger [N] 190 B5
Sórgono [I] 118 D5
Sorgues [F] 106 G3
Sörgutvik [N] 190 C4
Soria [E] 90 B3
Soriano Calabro [I] 124 D6
Soriano nel Cimino [I] 114 H4
Sorica [SLO] 74 B4
Sorihuela del Guadalimar [E] 102 G1
Sorisdale [GB] 6 A6
Sorita [E] 98 G1
Sørli [N] 190 D5
Sorø [DK] 156 F3
Sørreisa [N] 192 D3
Sorrento [I] 120 E4
Sørrollnes [N] 192 D3
Sorsele [S] 190 G3
Sörsjön [S] 172 E2
Sorso [I] 118 C3
Sort [E] 84 G6
Sortavala [RUS] 188 H5
Sortino [I] 126 G4
Sortland [N] 192 C3

Sørumsand [N] 166 C1
Sorunda [S] 168 D4
Sörup [D] 156 C5
Sørup [DK] 160 D4
Sørvær [N] 196 A2
Sørvågen [N] 192 B5
Sørvágur [DK] 160 A1
Sörvattnet [S] 182 E5
Sõrve [EST] 200 C4
Sørvik [N] 192 D3
Sösdala [S] 158 C2
Sos del Rey Católico [E] 84 C5
Soses [E] 90 H5
Sošice [HR] 74 D6
Sošnica [PL] 50 G2
Sośnicowice [PL] 50 F3
Sosnovo [RUS] 178 G3
Sosnovyy Bar [RUS] 178 F5
Sosnowica [PL] 38 F5
Sosnowiec [PL] 50 G3
Sospel [F] 108 F4
Šostka [UA] 204 D7
Sotaseter [N] 180 E5
Søtholmen [N] 166 C4
Sotillo de la Adrada [E] 88 E5
Sotillo de las Palomas [E] 88 D6
Sotin [HR] 154 E1
Sotkamo [FIN] 198 F5
Sotkuma [FIN] 188 F2
Sotobañado y Priorato [E] 82 D5
Soto del Barco [E] 78 H3
Soto del Real [E] 88 F5
Sotresgudo [E] 82 D5
Sotrondio / San Martín del Rey Aurelio [E] 78 H4
Sotta [F] 114 B6
Sottomarina [I] 110 H1
Sottrum [D] 18 E5
Sottunga [FIN] 176 B5
Sotuélamos [E] 96 H4
Soúda [GR] 140 C4
Souesmes [F] 56 C2
Soufflenheim [F] 46 B6
Souflí [GR] 130 H2
Soúgia [GR] 140 B5
Souillac [F] 66 G4
Souilly [F] 44 D4
Soulac–sur–Mer [F] 54 B6
Soulaines-Dhuys [F] 44 C6
Soulópoulo [GR] 132 C4
Soultz [F] 58 D3
Soultz [F] 44 H5
Soumoulou [F] 84 E3
Soúnio [GR] 136 H2

Souppes–sur–Loing [F] 42 G5
Sourdeval [F] 26 E4
Soure [P] 86 D2
Sournia [F] 92 F1
Soúrpi [GR] 132 H3
Sousceyrac [F] 66 H4
Sousel [P] 86 E6
Soustons [F] 66 A6
Soutelo [E] 78 C4
Southam [GB] 14 D2
Southampton [GB] 12 H5
South Balloch [GB] 8 C4
Southborough [GB] 14 E5
Southend [GB] 2 H2
Southend-on-Sea [GB] 14 F4
Southminster [GB] 14 F4
South Molton [GB] 12 E4
Southport [GB] 10 D3
South Queensferry [GB] 8 E3
Southsea [GB] 12 H5
South Shields [GB] 8 G6
Southwell [GB] 10 F6
Southwold [GB] 14 H3
Souvála [GR] 136 G1
Souvigny [F] 56 D5
Søvassli [N] 180 H1
Sovata [RO] 206 C5
Soverato [I] 124 E6
Soveria Mannelli [I] 124 D5
Sövestad [S] 158 D3
Sovetsk [RUS] 202 D5
Sovetskiy [RUS] 178 F3
Søvik [N] 180 D3
Søyland [N] 164 A4
Spa [B] 30 E5
Spaichingen [D] 58 G3
Spakenburg [NL] 16 E4
Spalding [GB] 10 G6
Spálené Poříčí [CZ] 48 E5
Spalt [D] 46 G6
Spandau [D] 34 E2
Spangenberg [D] 32 F5
Spangereid [N] 164 C6
Sparanise [I] 120 D2
Spare [LV] 200 C5
Sparreholm [S] 168 C4
Spárta [GR] 134 B6
Spartà [I] 124 B7
Spárti [GR] 136 E4
Spárto [GR] 132 D4
Spasovo [BG] 148 G1
Spáta [GR] 134 C6
Spatharé [GR] 138 H1
Spean Bridge [GB] 6 C6
Spello [I] 116 A2
Spennymoor [GB] 10 F1
Spentrup [DK] 160 E5
Spercheiáda [GR] 132 F4
Sperlonga [I] 120 C2
Spétses [GR] 136 F3
Speyer [D] 46 C5
Spezzano Albanese [I] 124 D3
Spicino [RUS] 200 G2
Spiddal / An Spidéal [IRL] 2 B5
Spiegelau [D] 60 H2
Spiekeroog [D] 18 C3
Spielfeld [A] 74 D3
Spiez [CH] 70 E1
Spijkenisse [NL] 16 C5
Spíli [GR] 140 C4
Spilimbergo [I] 72 F4
Spinazzola [I] 120 H3
Spincourt [F] 44 E3
Špindlerův–Mlýn [CZ] 50 A2
Spionica Donja [BIH] 154 D3
Špišič Bukovica [HR] 74 G5
Spišská Belá [SK] 52 B6
Spišská Nová Ves [SK] 64 E2
Spišské Podhradie [SK] 64 F2

Spišský Štvrtok [SK] 64 E2
Spital am Pyhrn [A] 62 B6
Spittal an der Drau [A] 72 H3
Spittal of Glenshee [GB] 8 E1
Spitz [A] 62 D4
Spjald [DK] 160 B6
Spjelkavik [N] 180 D3
Spjutsund [FIN] 178 B4
Split [HR] 152 A2
Splügen [CH] 70 G2
Spodsbjerg [DK] 156 E4
Spoleto [I] 116 B3
Spoltore [I] 116 D4
Spotorno [I] 108 H3
Sprakensehl [D] 32 H1
Sprȩcowo [PL] 22 G4
Spremberg [D] 34 F5
Spresiano [I] 72 E5
Springe [D] 32 F2
Sproge [S] 168 F5
Squinzano [I] 122 G4
Srahmore [IRL] 2 C3
Srbac [BIH] 154 C2
Srbica [YU] 150 C5
Srbobran [YU] 76 E6
Srbovan [BG] 148 E1
Srdeviči [BIH] 152 B1
Srebârna [RO] 148 G1
Srebnoje [UA] 206 F1
Sredets [BG] 148 C5
Sredets [BG] 148 F5
Sredishte [BG] 148 F1
Sredni Verets'kyi Pereval– [UA] 206 B3
Srednogortsi [BG] 130 E1
Sredska [YU] 150 C6
Šrem [PL] 36 C3
Sremska Kamenica [YU] 154 F1
Sremska Mitrovica [YU] 154 F2
Sremska Rača [YU] 154 F2
Sremski Karlovci [YU] 154 F2
Srokowo [PL] 24 C3
Srpska Crnja [YU] 76 F6
Srpski Miletič [YU] 76 C6
S. Stefano d'Aveto [I] 110 C3
Staaken [D] 34 E2
Stabbestad [N] 164 F4
Stabbursnes [N] 192 H1
Stachy [CZ] 48 E6
Sta Comba Dão [P] 80 C6
Stade [D] 18 E4
Stadhampton [GB] 14 D3
Stadhlaigearraidh / Stilligarry [GB] 6 A4
Stadskanaal [NL] 16 H3
Stadt Allendorf [D] 32 E6
Stadthagen [D] 32 F2
Stadtilm [D] 46 G1
Stadtkyll [D] 30 F6
Stadtlauringen [D] 46 F3
Stadtlohn [D] 16 G5
Stadtoldendorf [D] 32 F3
Stadtroda [D] 48 B1
Stadtsteinach [D] 46 H3
St Aegyd [A] 62 D5
Staffelstein [D] 46 G3
Staffin [GB] 6 B4
Stafford [GB] 10 E5
St–Affrique [F] 106 D3
Stágira [GR] 130 C4
St–Agnant [F] 54 C5
St–Agrève [F] 68 E5
Stahle [D] 32 F3
St–Aignan [F] 40 G5
St–Aignan [F] 54 H2
Stainach [A] 62 B6
Staindrop [GB] 10 F2
Staines [GB] 14 E4
Stainville [F] 44 D5
Stainz [A] 74 D2
Stalač [YU] 150 C3

St–Alban [F] 68 C5
St Albans [GB] 14 E3
Stalden [CH] 70 E2
Stalheim [N] 170 D3
Stalída [GR] 140 F4
Stall [A] 72 G2
Stallarholmen [S] 168 C3
Ställdalen [S] 166 G1
Stalon [S] 190 F4
Stalowa Wola [PL] 52 E2
St–Amand–en–Puisaye [F] 56 D2
St–Amand–les–Eaux [F] 28 G3
St–Amand–Longpré [F] 42 C6
St–Amand–Montrond [F] 56 C4
St–Amans [F] 68 C5
St–Amant–Roche–Savine [F] 68 D3
St–Ambroix [F] 106 F2
St–Amé [F] 58 C3
Stamford [GB] 14 E1
Stamná [GR] 132 E5
St–Amour [F] 56 H6
Stams [A] 72 C1
Stamsund [N] 192 B4
St Andrä [A] 74 C3
St–André [F] 42 D3
St Andreasberg [D] 32 G4
St–André–de–Cubzac [F] 66 D3
St–André–les–Alpes [F] 108 D3
St Andrews [GB] 8 F2
Stange [N] 172 C4
Stangerum [DK] 160 E5
Stanghelle [N] 170 B3
Stanhope [GB] 8 F6
Stanišič [YU] 76 C5
Staňkov [CZ] 48 D5
Stanley [GB] 8 F6
St Annaparochie [NL] 16 F2
Stans [CH] 58 F6
Stansstad [CH] 58 F6
St–Anthème [F] 68 E3
St–Antoine [F] 68 G4
St Anton [A] 72 B1
St–Antonin–Noble–Val [F] 66 G6
Stany [PL] 52 D2
St–Août [F] 54 H4
Stapar [YU] 76 C6
Stapleford [GB] 10 F5
Staplehurst [GB] 14 F5
Stapnes [N] 164 B4
Stąporków [PL] 38 B6
Starachowice [PL] 38 B6
Staraja Russa [RUS] 204 C2
Stará L'ubovňa [SK] 52 C6
Stara Moravica [YU] 76 D5
Stara Novalja [HR] 112 F3
Stara Pazova [YU] 154 G2
Stara Reka [BG] 148 D4
Stara Wrona [PL] 38 B2
Stara Zagora [BG] 148 C5
Stare [PL] 24 E5
Stare Czarnowo [PL] 20 F5
Staré Město [CZ] 50 C3
Staré Město [CZ] 62 H2
Stargard–Szczeciński [PL] 20 F5
Stårheim [N] 180 C5
Starica [RUS] 204 E3
Starigrad [HR] 112 F3
Starigrad [HR] 152 A2
Stari Gradac [HR] 74 G5
Starigrad Paklenica [HR] 112 G4
Stari Mikanovci [HR] 154 D1
Stari Slankamen [YU] 154 G2
Starjak [HR] 74 E6
Starnberg [D] 60 D4
Starogard [PL] 20 G4
Starogard Gdański [PL] 22 E3

Starokonstantinov [UA] 206 D2
Staromieście [PL] 50 H2
Staro Nagoričane [MK] 150 D6
Staro Oryakhovo [BG] 148 F3
Staropol'ye [RUS] 200 G1
Staro Selo [BG] 148 D1
Starožreby [PL] 36 H2
Starup [DK] 156 B2
Starup [DK] 156 C3
Stary Dzierzgoń [PL] 22 F4
Stary Gózd [PL] 38 B5
Starý Hrozenkov [CZ] 64 A2
Staryi Sambir [UA] 52 F5
Staryje Dorogi [BY] 204 B6
Stary Plzenec [CZ] 48 E5
Stary Sącz [PL] 52 B5
Starý Smokovec [SK] 52 B6
Staryy Oskol [RUS] 204 F7
St Asaph [GB] 10 C4
St-Astier [F] 66 F3
Staszów [PL] 52 C2
Stathelle [N] 164 G3
Statland [N] 190 C5
St-Auban-sur-l'Ouvèze [F] 108 B2
St-Aubin-d'Aubigné [F] 26 C5
St-Aubin-du-Cormier [F] 26 D5
St-Aubin-sur-Mer [F] 26 F3
St-Aulaye [F] 66 E2
St Austell [GB] 12 C5
Stavang [N] 180 B6
Stavanger [N] 164 B3
Staveley [GB] 10 F5
Stavelot [B] 30 E5
Stavenisse [NL] 16 C6
Staveren [NL] 16 E3
Stavern [N] 164 G3
Stavertsi [BG] 148 A3
St-Avold [F] 44 F4
Stavrodrómi [GR] 136 D2
Stavrohóri [GR] 140 G5
Stavrós [GR] 140 C4
Stavrós [GR] 134 C6
Stavrós [GR] 132 C5
Stavrós [GR] 130 C4
Stavroúpoli [GR] 130 E2
Stavsjø [N] 172 B3
Stawiguda [PL] 22 G4
Stawiski [PL] 24 D5
Stawiszyn [PL] 36 E4
St-Aygulf [F] 108 D5
St-Bard [F] 68 B1
St-Béat [F] 84 F5
St-Beauzély [F] 106 D2
St-Benin [F] 56 D4
St-Benoît [F] 54 G5
St-Benoît-sur-Loire [F] 56 C1
St-Benoît-sur-Loire [F] 42 F6
St-Bertrand-de-Comminges [F] 84 F4
St Blasien [D] 58 F4
St-Blin [F] 44 D6
St-Bonnet [F] 68 H6
St-Bonnet-de-Joux [F] 56 F6
St-Bonnet-en-Champsaur [F] 70 A6
St-Bonnet-le-Château [F] 68 E3
St Boswells [GB] 8 F4
St-Brevin-les-Pins [F] 40 E6
St-Brice-en-Coglès [F] 26 D5
St-Brieuc [F] 26 B4
St-Calais [F] 42 C5
St-Cast-le-Guildo [F] 26 B4
St-Céré [F] 66 H4
St-Cergue [CH] 70 B1
St-Cernin [F] 68 B4
St-Chamas [F] 106 H4

St-Chamond [F] 68 F3
St-Chély-d'Apcher [F] 68 C5
St-Chély-d'Aubrac [F] 68 B5
St-Chinian [F] 106 D4
St Christina / Santa Cristina [I] 72 D3
St Christoph [A] 72 B1
St-Ciers [F] 66 D2
St-Cirq-Lapopie [F] 66 G5
St-Clar [F] 66 E6
St-Claud [F] 54 E6
St-Claude [F] 70 A1
St Clears [GB] 12 D2
St-Clément-sur-Durance [F] 108 E2
St-Côme-d'Olt [F] 68 B5
St-Cyprien [F] 66 F4
St-Cyprien-Plage [F] 92 G1
St David's [GB] 12 D1
St-Denis [F] 42 F3
St-Denis-d'Oléron [F] 54 B5
St-Denis d'Orques [F] 42 A5
St-Didier-en-Velay [F] 68 E4
St-Dié [F] 58 D2
St-Dizier [F] 44 C5
St-Donat-sur-l'Herbasse [F] 68 F4
Steane [N] 164 E2
Ste-Anne-d'Auray [F] 26 A6
Ste-Anne-la-Palud [F] 40 B2
Stechelberg [CH] 70 E2
Štěchovice [CZ] 48 F4
Steckborn [CH] 58 G4
Ste-Croix [CH] 58 C6
Ste-Croix-Volvestre [F] 84 G4
Steeg [A] 72 B1
Steenbergen [NL] 16 C6
Ste-Enimie [F] 68 C6
Steenvoorde [F] 28 E2
Steenwijk [NL] 16 F3
Stefáni [GR] 132 D3
Stefaniná [GR] 130 C4
Ste-Foy-la-Grande [F] 66 E3
Stegaros [N] 170 E5
Ste-Gauburge-Ste-Colombe [F] 26 G5
Stege [DK] 156 G4
Stegersbach [A] 74 E2
St-Egrève [F] 68 H4
Ste-Hélène [F] 66 C3
Ste-Hermine [F] 54 C3
Steigen [N] 192 C5
Stein [GB] 6 B4
Steinaberg bru [N] 170 C5
Steinach [A] 72 D2
Stein am Rhein [CH] 58 G4
Steinau [D] 46 E2
Steinberg [D] 156 C5
Steinestø [N] 170 B3
Steinfeld [A] 72 G3
Steinfeld [D] 32 D1
Steinfurt [D] 16 H5
Steingaden [D] 60 D5
Steinhausen [D] 60 B4
Steinheim [D] 32 E3
Steinhorst [D] 32 G1
Steinkjer [N] 190 C5
Steinløysa [N] 180 E2
Stein Pass [Eur.] 60 G6
Steinsholt [N] 164 G2
Ste-Livrade-sur-Lot [F] 66 E5
Stellendam [NL] 16 C5
St-Eloy-les-Mines [F] 56 C6
Ste-Marie-aux-Mines [F] 58 D2
Ste-Marie-de-Campan [F] 84 F4
Ste-Maure-de-Touraine [F] 54 F3
Ste-Maxime [F] 108 D5

Ste-Menehould [F] 44 C4
Ste-Mère-Eglise [F] 26 E2
St-Emilion [F] 66 D3
Stemó [GR] 136 E2
Sten [S] 162 D1
Stenay [F] 44 D3
Stenbjerg [DK] 160 B4
Stendal [D] 34 C2
Stende [LV] 200 C5
Steneby [S] 166 D4
St Englmar [D] 60 G2
Stení [GR] 134 C4
Stenlille [DK] 156 F3
Stenløse [DK] 156 G2
Stenness [GB] 6 F2
Stènoma [GR] 132 F4
Stensele [S] 190 F4
Stensjön [S] 162 E2
Stenstorp [S] 166 F6
Stenstrup [DK] 156 D4
Stenudden [S] 190 G2
Stenungsund [S] 160 G1
Steornabhagh / Stornoway [GB] 6 C2
Stepanci [MK] 128 E2
Stepnica [PL] 20 F4
Stepojevac [YU] 150 B1
Sterdyń-Osada [PL] 38 D2
Sternberg [D] 20 B4
Šternberk [CZ] 50 D5
Stérnes [GR] 140 C4
Sterzing / Vipiteno [I] 72 D2
Ste-Sévère [F] 56 B5
Stes-Maries-de-la-Mer [F] 106 F5
Ste-Suzanne [F] 42 A4
Stęszew [PL] 36 C3
Štětí [CZ] 48 F2
St-Étienne [F] 108 C3
St-Étienne [F] 68 E3
St-Étienne-de-Baïgorry [F] 84 C3
St-Étienne-de-St-Geoirs [F] 68 G4
St-Étienne-de-Tinée [F] 108 E3
St-Etienne-les-Orgues [F] 108 C3
Ste-Tulle [F] 108 C4
Stevenage [GB] 14 E3
Stewarton [GB] 8 D3
Stewartstown [GB] 2 F3
Steyerberg [D] 32 E1
Steyning [GB] 14 E5
Steyr [A] 62 B5
Stezherovo [BG] 148 B2
St-Fargeau [F] 56 D2
St-Firmin [F] 68 H6
St-Florent [F] 114 C3
St-Florent [F] 40 G6
St-Florent [F] 56 B3
St-Florentin [F] 56 E1
St. Florian [A] 60 H4
St-Flour [F] 68 C4
St-Fort-sur-Gironde [F] 66 D1
St-Fulgent [F] 54 C2
St Gallen [A] 62 C6
St Gallen [CH] 58 H5
St Gallenkirch [A] 72 B1
St-Galmier [F] 68 E3
St-Gaudens [F] 84 G4
St-Gaultier [F] 54 G4
St-Geniez-d'Olt [F] 68 B6
St-Genis-de-Saintonge [F] 66 D1
St-Genix-sur-Guiers [F] 68 H3
St Georgen [A] 74 C2
St Georgen [A] 60 H5
St Georgen [D] 58 F3
St-Georges [F] 40 G6
St-Georges-de-Didonne [F] 54 C6
St-Geours-de-Maremne [F] 66 B6
St-Germain [F] 66 G2
St-Germain [F] 42 F3
St-Germain-de-Joux [F] 68 H2

St-Germain-des-Fossés [F] 56 D6
St-Germain-des-Vaux [F] 26 D1
St-Germain-du-Bois [F] 56 G5
St-Germain-du-Plain [F] 56 G5
St-Germain-Laval [F] 68 E2
St-Germain-Lembron [F] 68 C3
St-Germain-l'Herm [F] 68 D3
St-Germain-Plage [F] 26 D3
St-Germer-de-Fly [F] 28 D6
St-Gervais [F] 106 D3
St-Gervais-d'Auvergne [F] 68 C1
St-Gervais-les-Bains [F] 70 C3
St-Géry [F] 66 G5
St-Gildas-des-Bois [F] 40 E5
St Gilgen [A] 60 H5
St-Gilles [F] 106 G4
St-Gilles-Croix-de-Vie [F] 54 B2
St Gingolph [CH] 70 C2
St-Girons [F] 84 G5
St-Girons-en-Marensin [F] 66 B5
St-Girons-Plage [F] 66 A5
St Goar [D] 46 B2
St Goarshausen [D] 46 B2
St-Gobain [F] 28 F6
St-Gorgon-Main [F] 58 B5
St-Guénolé [F] 40 B3
St-Guilhem-le-Desert [F] 106 E3
St Helens [GB] 10 D4
St-Helier [GBJ] 26 C3
St-Hilaire-de-Villefranche [F] 54 C5
St-Hilaire-du-Harcouët [F] 26 D5
St-Hippolyte [F] 58 C5
St-Hippolyte-du-Fort [F] 106 F2
St. Hoga [S] 160 G1
St-Honoré [F] 56 E4
St-Hubert [B] 44 D1
Stia [I] 110 G5
Stickney [GB] 10 G5
Stiens [NL] 16 F2
Stigen [S] 166 D5
Stigliano [I] 122 C4
Stigtomta [S] 168 C4
Stiklestad [N] 190 C6
Stilligarry / Stadhlaigearraidh [GB] 6 A4
Stillington [GB] 10 F3
Stilo [I] 124 D6
St-Imier [CH] 58 D5
Stimlje [YU] 150 C5
St Ingbert [D] 44 G4
Stintino [I] 118 B2
Stirling [GB] 8 E3
Štítary [CZ] 62 E2
Štíty [CZ] 50 C4
St Ives [GB] 12 B5
St Ives [GB] 14 F2
St-Jacut [F] 26 C4
St Jakob im Rosental [A] 74 B3
St-James [F] 26 D5
Stjärnsund [S] 174 D5
St-Jean-Brévelay [F] 26 A6
St-Jean-Cap-Ferrat [F] 108 F4
St-Jean-d'Angély [F] 54 D5
St-Jean-de-Bournay [F] 68 G3
St-Jean-de-Losne [F] 56 H4
St-Jean-de-Luz [F] 84 B2

St-Jean-de-Maurienne [F] 70 B5
St-Jean-de-Monts [F] 54 A2
St-Jean-du-Bruel [F] 106 E3
St-Jean-du-Gard [F] 106 F2
St-Jean-en-Royans [F] 68 G5
St-Jean-le-Thomas [F] 26 D4
St-Jean-Pied-de-Port [F] 84 C3
St-Jeoire [F] 70 B2
St Johann am Tauern [A] 74 C1
St Johann im Pongau [A] 72 G1
St Johann in Tirol [A] 60 F6
St Johnstown [IRL] 2 F2
St. John's Town of Dalry [GB] 8 D5
Stjørdal [N] 182 C1
St-Jorioz [F] 70 B3
St-Jory [F] 84 H3
St-Jouan-de-l'Isle [F] 26 B5
St-Jouin-de-Marnes [F] 54 E3
St-Juéry [F] 106 C2
St-Julien [F] 56 H6
St-Julien [F] 84 G4
St-Julien-Chapteuil [F] 68 E4
St-Julien-de-Vouvantes [F] 40 G5
St-Julien-en-Beauchêne [F] 68 G6
St-Julien-en-Genevois [F] 70 B2
St-Julien-l'Ars [F] 54 F4
St-Junien [F] 54 F6
St Just [GB] 12 B5
St-Just-en-Chaussée [F] 28 E6
St-Just-en-Chevalet [F] 68 E2
St-Justin [F] 66 D5
St Keverne [GB] 12 C5
St Lambrecht [A] 74 B2
St-Lary-Soulan [F] 84 F5
St-Laurent [F] 66 G1
St-Laurent [F] 26 E3
St-Laurent-en-Grandvaux [F] 70 B1
St-Laurent-Médoc [F] 66 C2
St-Leger [F] 56 F4
St-Léonard-de-Noblat [F] 66 H1
St Leonards-on-Sea [GB] 14 F6
St Leonhard [A] 62 D4
St-Leu-d'Esserent [F] 42 F2
St-Lizier [F] 84 G4
St-Lô [F] 26 E3
St Lorenzen [A] 72 F3
St-Louis [F] 58 E4
St-Loup-sur-Semouse [F] 58 C3
St-Luc [CH] 70 D2
St-Lunaire [F] 26 C4
St-Lys [F] 84 H3
St-Macaire [F] 66 D4
St-Maclou [F] 26 G3
St-Maixent-l'Ecole [F] 54 D4
St-Malo [F] 26 C4
St-Mamest [F] 66 F3
St-Marcellin [F] 68 G4
St Margaret's Hope [GB] 6 F2
St Märgen [D] 58 F3
St Mark's [GBM] 10 B2
St-Mars-la-Jaille [F] 40 G6
St-Martin-d'Auxigny [F] 56 C3
St-Martin-de-Londres [F] 106 E3

St-Martin-de-Ré [F] 54 B4
St-Martin-Vésubie [F] 108 F3
St-Martory [F] 84 G4
St Marys [GB] 6 G2
St-Mathieu [F] 66 F1
St-Mathieu-de-Tréviers [F] 106 E3
St-Maurice [CH] 70 C2
St-Maurice-Navacelles [F] 106 E2
St Maurice-sur-Moselle [F] 58 C3
St Mawes [GB] 12 C5
St-Maximin-la-Ste-Baume [F] 108 C5
St-Méen [F] 26 B5
St Michael [A] 72 H2
St Michael [A] 74 C1
St Michael [A] 74 F2
St-Michel-de-Maurienne [F] 70 B5
St-Michel-en-Grève [F] 40 D1
St-Michel-en-l'Herm [F] 54 C4
St-Michel-Mont-Mercure [F] 54 C3
St-Mihiel [F] 44 D4
St Moritz [CH] 70 H2
St-Nazaire [F] 40 E6
St-Nectaire [F] 68 C4
St Neots [GB] 14 E2
St-Nicolas [F] 40 E5
St Nicolas-de-Port [F] 44 E5
St-Nicolas-du-Pélem [F] 26 A4
St-Niklaas [B] 28 H2
St Niklaus [CH] 70 E2
St Nikolai [A] 74 B1
Støa [N] 172 E2
Stobi [MK] 128 F2
Stocka [S] 184 E6
Stockach [D] 58 G4
Stockaryd [S] 162 D3
Stockbridge [GB] 12 H4
Stockelsdorf [D] 18 G3
Stockerau [A] 62 F4
Stockheim [D] 46 G3
Stockholm [S] 168 D3
Stockport [GB] 10 E4
Stockton on Tees [GB] 10 F2
Stoczek Łukowski [PL] 38 D3
Stod [CZ] 48 D5
Stöde [S] 184 D4
Stødi [N] 190 E1
Stoðvarfjörður [IS] 194 G6
St Oedenrode [NL] 30 E2
Stoer [GB] 6 D3
Stojan Mikhaylovski [BG] 148 E2
Stoke Gabriel [GB] 12 E5
Stoke-on-Trent [GB] 10 E5
Stokesley [GB] 10 F2
Stoke sub Hamdon [GB] 12 F4
Stokke [N] 164 H3
Stokkemarke [DK] 156 F5
Stokkland [N] 164 F2
Stokkvågen [N] 190 D2
Stokmarknes [N] 192 C4
Štoky [CZ] 48 H5
Stolac [BIH] 152 C3
Stolberg [D] 30 F4
Stolin [BY] 204 A7
Stollberg [D] 48 D2
Stóllet [S] 172 E5
St Olof [S] 158 D3
Stolpe [D] 34 G2
Stołpie [PL] 38 F5
Stolzenau [D] 32 E1
St-Omer [F] 28 E2
Stómio [GR] 132 G1
Ston [HR] 152 C3
Stonařov [CZ] 48 H6
Stone [GB] 10 E5
Stonehaven [GB] 8 G1
Stoneleigh [GB] 14 D2

Stongfjorden [N] 180 B6
Stonglandseidet [N] 192 D3
Stopanja [YU] 150 C3
Stopnica [PL] 52 C2
Storå [S] 166 H2
Stora Blåsjön [S] 190 E4
Storås [N] 180 H2
Storbergvika [N] 190 D5
Storby [FIN] 174 H5
Stord [N] 170 B5
Stordal [N] 180 D4
Storebro [S] 162 F2
Storebru [N] 180 B6
Store Darum [DK] 156 B3
Store Heddinge [DK] 156 G3
Storekorsnes [N] 192 G1
Store Merløse [DK] 156 F3
Store Molvik [N] 196 E1
Støren [N] 182 B2
Storestølen [N] 170 E3
Storfjellseter [N] 182 B6
Storfjord [N] 192 E3
Storfors [S] 166 G2
Storforshei [N] 190 E2
Storfossen [N] 192 D4
Storjord [N] 190 E1
Storjord [N] 192 B6
Storkow [D] 34 F3
Storli [N] 180 G3
Storlien [S] 182 D2
Stormi [FIN] 176 E2
Stormyren [S] 190 G3
Stornoway / Steornabhagh [GB] 6 C2
Storo [I] 72 B5
Storoddan [N] 180 G1
Storsätern [S] 182 D5
Storsjö [S] 182 E3
Storslett [N] 192 F2
Storsteinnes [N] 192 E3
Storuman [S] 190 F4
Storvik [N] 192 F1
Storvik [S] 174 D4
Storvorde [DK] 160 E4
Storvreta [S] 168 D1
St Oswald [A] 62 C3
Stotel [D] 18 D4
Stotternheim [D] 32 H6

Stouby [DK] 156 C2
Stourbridge [GB] 10 D6
Stourport-on-Severn [GB] 12 G1
Stourton [GB] 12 G4
Støvring [DK] 160 D4
Stow [GB] 8 E4
Stowmarket [GB] 14 G3
Stow-on-the-Wold [GB] 12 H2
Stozher [BG] 148 F2
St-Palais [F] 84 D3
St-Palais-sur-Mer [F] 54 B6
St-Pardoux-la-Rivière [F] 66 F2
St Paul [A] 74 C3
St-Paul [F] 108 E4
St-Paul [F] 108 E2
St-Paul-Cap-de-Joux [F] 106 B3
St-Paul-de-Fenouillet [F] 106 C6
St-Pauliene [F] 68 D4
St-Paul-lès-Dax [F] 66 B6
St-Pé [F] 84 E4
St-Péray [F] 68 F5
St-Pere [F] 56 E3
St-Père-en-Retz [F] 40 E6
St. Peter [A] 74 B3
St Peter-Ording [D] 18 D2
St-Peter Port [GBG] 26 C2
St-Philbert [F] 54 B2
St-Pierre-d'Albigny [F] 70 A4
St-Pierre-de-Chartreuse [F] 68 H4
St-Pierre-de-Chignac [F] 66 F3
St-Pierre-d'Oléron [F] 54 B5
St-Pierre-Église [F] 26 E2
St-Pierre-le-Moûtier [F] 56 D4
St-Pierre-Quiberon [F] 40 C5
St-Pierre-sur-Dives [F] 26 F4

St-Pois [F] 26 E4
St-Pol-de-Léon [F] 40 C1
St-Pol-sur-Ternoise [F] 28 E3
St-Raphaël [F] 108 D5
St Pölten [A] 62 E4
St-Pons [F] 106 C4
St-Pons-de-Thomieres [F] 106 C4
St-Porchaire [F] 54 C5
St-Pourçain [F] 56 D6
St-Privat [F] 68 A3
St-Quay-Portrieux [F] 26 B4
St-Quentin [F] 28 F5
Strà [I] 110 G1
Straach [D] 34 D3
Strabane [GB] 2 F2
Strachan [GB] 8 G1
Strachur [GB] 8 C2
Stracin [MK] 150 D6
Stradbally [IRL] 4 F3
Stradbally [IRL] 4 B3
Stradbroke [GB] 14 G3
Stradella [I] 70 G6
Stradishall [GB] 14 F3
Stradone [IRL] 2 E4
Straduny [PL] 24 D3
Straelen [D] 30 F3
Straiton [GB] 8 C4
Strakonice [CZ] 48 E6
Straldzha [BG] 148 E4
Stralki [BY] 200 G6
Strålsnäs [S] 166 H6
Stralsund [D] 20 D2
St-Rambert [F] 68 E3
St-Rambert-d'Albon [F] 68 F4
St-Rambert-en-Bugey [F] 68 G2
Stranda [N] 180 D4
Strandby [DK] 160 E2
Strandby [DK] 160 C4
Strande [D] 18 G2
Strandebarm [N] 170 B4
Strandhill [IRL] 2 D3
Strangford [GB] 2 G4
Strängnäs [S] 168 C3
Strångsjö [S] 168 B4
Stráni [CZ] 62 H2

Stranice [SLO] 74 D4
Stranorlar [IRL] 2 E2
Stranraer [GB] 8 C5
St-Raphaël [F] 108 D5
Strasbourg [F] 44 H6
Strasburg [D] 20 E5
Strassburg [A] 74 B2
Strassfurt [D] 34 B4
Strasswalchen [A] 60 H5
Stratford-upon-Avon [GB] 12 H2
Strathaven [GB] 8 D3
Strathdon [GB] 6 E6
Stratóni [GR] 130 C4
Stratoníki [GR] 130 C4
Strátos [GR] 132 E5
Straubing [D] 60 G2
Straume [N] 170 B3
Straume [N] 192 B3
Straume [N] 164 E1
Straume [N] 164 F3
Straumen [N] 192 B6
Straumen [N] 180 F1
Straumen [N] 192 C6
Straumsnes [N] 192 D2
Straumsnes [N] 192 C4
Straupe [LV] 200 E4
Straupitz [D] 34 F4
Strausberg [D] 34 F2
Straussfurt [D] 32 H5
Stravaj [AL] 128 C4
Stravrós [GR] 134 B4
Straža [YU] 150 D2
Strážnice [CZ] 62 G2
Strážný [CZ] 62 A2
Strážske [SK] 64 H2
Štrba [SK] 64 E2
Štrbské Pleso [SK] 52 A6
Street [GB] 12 F4
Strehaia [RO] 206 B6
Strehla [D] 34 E5
Strelcha [BG] 148 A5
Strel'na [RUS] 178 H5
St-Rémy-de-Provence [F] 106 G4
St-Renan [F] 40 B2

Strenči [LV] 200 E4
Strengberg [A] 62 C4
Stresa [I] 70 F3
Strezimirovci [YU] 150 E4
Strib [DK] 156 C2
Stříbro [CZ] 48 D4
Strimasund [S] 190 E2
Strimonikó [GR] 130 B3
St-Riquier [F] 28 D4
Strmica [HR] 154 A4
Strmilov [CZ] 48 H6
Strobl [A] 60 H5
Strøby Egede [DK] 156 G3
Strofyliá [GR] 134 B4
Strokestown [IRL] 2 D4
Stromberg [D] 46 B3
St-Rome-de-Tarn [F] 106 D2
Strömfors [S] 198 A4
Strommen [N] 166 B1
Strømmen [N] 190 C6
Strömnäs [S] 190 F4
Stromness [GB] 6 F2
Strömsbruk [S] 184 E6
Stromsfors [S] 168 B5
Strömsnäsbruk [S] 162 C5
Strömstad [S] 166 B4
Strömsund [S] 190 E6
Stronachlacher [GB] 8 D2
Strongoli [I] 124 F4
Stronie Śląskie [PL] 50 C3
Strontian [GB] 6 B6
Stroove [IRL] 2 F2
Stropkov [SK] 52 D6
Stroud [GB] 12 G3
Strovlés [GR] 140 B5
Strub Pass [A] 60 G6
Strücklingen [D] 18 C5
Struer [DK] 160 B5
Struga [MK] 128 D3
Strugi-Krasnyye [RUS] 200 H2
Strumica [MK] 128 G2
Strumien [PL] 50 F4
Stryama [BG] 148 B5
Stryj [UA] 52 H5
Stryjów [PL] 52 F1
Stryków [PL] 36 G4
Stryn [N] 180 D5
Strzegocin [PL] 38 B2
Strzegom [PL] 50 B1
Strzelce [PL] 36 G3
Strzelce Krajeńskie [PL] 36 A1
Strzelce Małe [PL] 36 H6
Strzelce Opolskie [PL] 50 E2
Strzelin [PL] 50 C2
Strzelno [PL] 36 E2
Strzyżów [PL] 52 D4
Strzyżów [PL] 38 G6
St-Saëns [F] 28 C5
St-Satur [F] 56 D3
St-Saturnin-lès-Apt [F] 108 B3
St-Saulge [F] 56 E4
St-Sauvant [F] 54 E4
St-Sauveur-en-Puisaye [F] 56 D2
St-Sauveur-le-Vicomte [F] 26 D2
St-Sauveur-sur-Tinée [F] 108 E3
St-Savin [F] 66 D2
St-Savin [F] 54 F4
St-Seine-l'Abbaye [F] 56 G3
St-Sernin-sur-Rance [F] 106 C3
St-Sever [F] 66 C6
St-Sever [F] 26 E4
St-Sulpice [F] 106 B3
St-Symphorien [F] 66 C4
St-Symphorien-de-Lay [F] 68 E2
St-Symphorien-d'Ozon [F] 68 F3
St-Symphorien-sur-Coise [F] 68 F3
St-Thégonnec [F] 40 C2
St-Thiébault [F] 58 A2

St-Trivier-de-Courtes [F] 56 G6
St-Tropez [F] 108 D5
St-Truiden [B] 30 D4
Stubbekøbing [DK] 156 G5
Stuben [A] 72 B1
Štubik [YU] 150 E1
Studánky [CZ] 62 B3
Studena [BG] 150 F5
Studená [CZ] 48 H6
Studenica [YU] 150 B3
Studland [GB] 12 G5
Studley [GB] 12 H1
Stugudal [N] 182 D3
Stuguflåten [N] 180 F4
Stugun [S] 184 C2
Stühlingen [D] 58 F4
Stukenbrock [D] 32 E3
Stülpe [D] 34 E3
St Ulrich / Ortisei [I] 72 D3
Stupava [SK] 62 G4
Stupinigi [I] 70 D6
Stupino [RUS] 204 F4
Stupnik [HR] 74 E6
Sturminster Newton [GB] 12 G4
Šturovo [SK] 64 B5
Sturry [GB] 14 G5
St.-Ursanne [CH] 58 D4
Stuttgart [D] 58 H1
St-Vaast-la-Hougue [F] 26 E2
St Valentin [A] 62 C4
St-Valery-en-Caux [F] 26 H2
St-Valery-sur-Somme [F] 28 D4
St-Vallier-de-Thiey [F] 108 E4
St-Vallier-sur-Rhône [F] 68 F4
St-Vaury [F] 54 H5
St Veit [A] 74 B3
St-Véran [F] 108 E1
St-Vestec [CZ] 48 G3
St Vigil / San Vigilio [I] 72 E3
St Vincent [I] 70 D4
St-Vincent-de-Tyrosse [F] 66 A6
St-Vincent-les-Forts [F] 108 D2
St Vith [B] 30 F6
St-Vivien-de-Médoc [F] 66 C1
St-Wandrille [F] 26 H3
St Wendel [D] 44 G3
St Wolfgang [A] 60 H5
St-Yan [F] 56 E6
Stykkishólmur [IS] 194 B3
Stylída [GR] 132 G4
St-Yorre [F] 68 D1
St-Yrieix-la-Perche [F] 66 G2
Styrsö [S] 160 G2
Suadiye [TR] 146 G3
Suances [E] 82 E3
Suaredda [I] 118 E3
Subačius [LT] 202 F4
Subate [LV] 200 F6
Subbiano [I] 110 G6
Subiaco [I] 116 B5
Subotica [YU] 76 D5
Subotište [YU] 154 G2
Suceava [RO] 206 C4
Sučevici [HR] 112 H4
Sucha Beskidzka [PL] 50 H4
Suchań [PL] 20 G5
Suchdol nad Lužnicí [CZ] 62 C2
Suchedniów [PL] 38 B6
Suchorze [PL] 22 B3
Suchowola [PL] 24 E4
Suchożebry [PL] 38 D3
Süchteln [D] 30 G3
Sucina [E] 104 C3
Sućuraj [HR] 152 B3
Suda [RUS] 204 F2

Sudak [UA] 206 H6
Sudbø [N] 164 E1
Sudbury [GB] 14 F3
Süden [D] 18 E1
Süderbrarup [D] 18 F1
Süderende [D] 156 A4
Süderlugum [D] 156 B4
Sudova Vyshnia [UA] 52
 G4
Suðureyri [IS] 194 C1
Sueca [E] 98 E5
Sugères [F] 68 D3
Süğütlü [TR] 146 H2
Suhl [D] 46 G2
Suho Polje [BIH] 154 E3
Suhopolje [HR] 74 H6
Šuica [BIH] 152 B1
Suippes [F] 44 C3
Sukeva [FIN] 198 E5
Sukoły [PL] 24 E6
Sukošan [HR] 112 G5
Sükösd [H] 76 C4
Sul [N] 190 C6
Suldalsosen [N] 164 C1
Sulden / Solda [I] 72 C3
Suldrup [DK] 160 D4
Sulechow [PL] 36 A3
Sulęczyno [PL] 22 C3
Sulęin [PL] 34 H2
Sulejów [PL] 36 H5
Sulejówek [PL] 38 C3
Sulesund [N] 180 C3
Sulina [RO] 206 E6
Sulingen [D] 32 E1
Sulitjelma [N] 192 C6
Sulkava [FIN] 188 E5
Sulkavanjärvi [FIN] 186 G1
Sułkowice [PL] 50 H4
Süller [TR] 144 G4
Sully [F] 56 F4
Sully-sur-Loire [F] 56 C1
Sulmierzyce [PL] 36 G6
Sulmierzyce [PL] 36 D5
Sulmona [I] 116 D5
Süloğlu [TR] 146 B1
Sulów [PL] 36 D5
Sultanhisar [TR] 144 E5
Sultanköy [TR] 146 D3
Sulva / Solf [FIN] 186 B2
Sülysáp [H] 76 D1
Sulz [D] 58 G2
Sulzbach [D] 46 D6
Sulzbach–Rosenberg [D] 46
 H5
Sumartin [HR] 152 A2
Sumba [DK] 160 A3
Sümeg [H] 74 G2
Sumiswald [CH] 58 E6
Summa [FIN] 178 D3
Šumperk [CZ] 50 C4

Sumsa [FIN] 198 G4
Šumvald [CZ] 50 D4
Sumy [UA] 206 G1
Sund [FIN] 176 B5
Sund [N] 192 B6
Sund [S] 166 C3
Sundborn [S] 174 C4
Sundbron [S] 184 F3
Sundbyberg [S] 168 D3
Sunde [N] 190 A6
Sunderland [GB] 8 G6
Sundern [D] 32 C5
Sundhultsbrunn [S] 162
 E1
Sundre [S] 168 F6
Sunds [DK] 160 C6
Sundsfjord [N] 190 E1
Sundsøre [DK] 160 C4
Sundsvall [S] 184 E4
Sundvollen [N] 170 H5
Sungurlare [BG] 148 E4
Suni [I] 118 C4
Sunion [GR] 130 E2
Sunja [HR] 154 B1
Sunnansjö [S] 172 G5
Sunndalsøra [N] 180 F3
Sunne [S] 166 E1
Sunnemo [S] 166 F1
Sunnersta [S] 168 D2
Suntaži [LV] 200 E5
Suodenniemi [FIN] 176 E1
Suolahti [FIN] 186 G3
Suolovuobme [N] 192 G2
Suomenniemi [FIN] 178 D1
Suomijärvi [FIN] 186 C5
Suomusjärvi [FIN] 176 F4
Suomussalmi [FIN] 198 F3
Suonenjoki [FIN] 188 C3
Suopelto [FIN] 176 H1
Suorva [N] 192 D5
Suosjavrre [N] 192 H2
Suovanlahti [FIN] 186 G2
Superespot [E] 92 E2
Supetar [HR] 152 A2
Supino [I] 116 B6
Šuplja Stijena [YU] 152 E2
Supraśl [PL] 24 F5
Supru [FIN] 196 E3
Surahammar [S] 168 B2
Šurany [SK] 64 B5
Suraż [BY] 204 C4
Surčin [YU] 154 G2
Surduk [YU] 154 G2
Surdulica [YU] 150 E5
Surgères [F] 54 C5
Súria [E] 92 D3
Surju [EST] 200 E3
Surnadalsøra [N] 180 G2
šurŇenovac [HR] 154 D1
šurŇevik [BIH] 154 E3

Sürnitsa [BG] 130 C1
Sursee [CH] 58 E5
Surte [S] 160 H2
Survilliers [F] 42 G3
Susa [I] 70 C5
Susch [CH] 72 B2
Susek [YU] 154 F1
Sushitsa [BG] 148 C3
Sušice [CZ] 48 E6
Süssen [D] 60 B2
Susurluk [TR] 146 D5
Susz [PL] 22 F4
Sutivan [HR] 152 A2
Sutjeska [YU] 154 H1
Sutomore [YU] 152 E5
Sutri [I] 114 H4
Sutton Coldfield [GB] 10
 E6
Suure–Jaani [EST] 200
 E2
Suuremõisa [EST] 200 C2
Suva Reka [YU] 150 C6
Suvereto [I] 114 E2
Suvorovo [BG] 148 F2
Suwałki [PL] 24 E3
Suystamo [RUS] 188 H4
Suzzara [I] 110 E2
Svalöv [S] 158 C2
Svaneke [DK] 158 E4
Svanesund [S] 166 C6
Svängsta [S] 158 E1
Svanskog [S] 166 D3
Svanstein [S] 196 B8
Svanvik [N] 196 F3
Svappavaara [S] 192 F5
Svärdsjo [S] 174 D4
Svarstad [N] 164 G2
Svartå [S] 166 G3
Svärtinge [S] 168 B5
Svartisdalen [N] 190 E2
Svartlå [S] 198 A2
Svartnäs [S] 174 D3
Svartnes [N] 196 F2
Sväty Jur [SK] 62 G4
Svedala [S] 158 C3
Svedasai [LT] 202 G4
Sveg [S] 182 G5
Sveindal [N] 164 D4
Švėkšna [LT] 202 D4
Svelgen [N] 180 B5
Svellingen [N] 190 A6
Svelvik [N] 164 H2
Švenčionėliaj [LT] 202 H4
Švenčionys [LT] 202 H5
Svendborg [DK] 156 E4
Svenes [N] 164 E4
Svenljunga [S] 162 B3
Svensby [N] 192 E2
Svenstavik [S] 182 G3
Svenstrup [DK] 160 D4

Švermov [CZ] 48 F3
Sveti Naum [MK] 128 D4
Sveti Nikole [MK] 128 F1
Sveti Rok [HR] 112 G4
Sveti Stefan [YU] 152 E5
Světlá nad Sázavou [CZ] 48
 H5
Svetlogorsk [RUS] 202 C5
Svetlovodsk [UA] 206 G3
Svetogorsk [RUS] 178 F2
Svetozarevo [YU] 150 C2
Svetozar Miletic [YU] 76
 C5
Svetvinčenat [HR] 112 D2
Svidnik [SK] 52 D5
Švihov [CZ] 48 D5
Svilajnac [YU] 150 C1
Svilengrad [BG] 146 A2
Svinesund [S] 166 C3
Svingstad [N] 170 H3
Svingvoll [N] 170 H2
Svinhult [S] 162 E2
Svinninge [DK] 156 F2
Svir [BY] 202 H5
Svishtov [BG] 148 C2
Svislach [BY] 24 G5
Svitavy [CZ] 50 B4
Svodje [YU] 150 E4
Svoge [BG] 150 F4
Svolvær [N] 192 B4
Svorkmo [N] 180 H2
Svrčinovec [SK] 50 F5
Svrljig [YU] 150 D3
Svullrya [N] 172 D5
Swaffham [GB] 14 G2
Swalmen [NL] 30 F3
Swanage [GB] 12 G5
Swanlinbar [IRL] 2 E4
Swansea [GB] 12 E2
Swarożyn [PL] 22 E3
Swarzędz [PL] 36 C2
Swarzewo [PL] 22 D1
Swatragh [GB] 2 G2
Świdnica [PL] 50 B1
Świdnica [PL] 34 H4
Swidnik [PL] 38 E5
Świdwin [PL] 20 H4
Świebodzice [PL] 50 B1
Świebodzin [PL] 36 A3
Świecie [PL] 22 D5
Świecko [PL] 34 G3
Świeradów–Zdrój [PL] 48
 H1
Świerczów [PL] 50 E1
Świerzawa [PL] 50 B1
Świerzno [PL] 20 F3
Święta Anna [PL] 50 G1
Swieta Lipka [PL] 24 B3
Świętno [PL] 36 B2
Swindon [GB] 12 H3
Swinford [IRL] 2 C4
Świnoujście [PL] 20 E3
Swinton [GB] 8 F4
Swords [IRL] 2 F6
Syčevka [RUS] 204 E4
Syców [PL] 36 D6
Sykäräinen [FIN] 198 D6
Syke [D] 18 D6
Sykéa [GR] 136 F4
Sykeá [GR] 130 D6
Sykkylven [N] 180 D4
Sylling [N] 164 H1
Syltefjordfjellet [N] 196 E1
Symbister [GB] 6 H4
Sými [GR] 142 D4
Syötekylä [FIN] 198 E2
Syre [GB] 6 E3
Sysmä [FIN] 178 A1
Sysslebäck [S] 172 E4
Syston [GB] 10 F6
Syväjärvi [FIN] 196 D7
Syvänniemi [FIN] 188 C2
Syvde [N] 180 C4
Sysvten [DK] 160 E3
Syyspohja [FIN] 188 E6
Szabadszállás [H] 76 C3
Szabolcsbáka [H] 64 H4
Szadek [PL] 36 F4
Szakály [H] 76 B4
Szalkszentmárton [H] 76
 C2

Szalonna [H] 64 F3
Szamocin [PL] 22 B6
Szamotuły [PL] 36 C2
Szany [H] 74 G1
Szarvas [H] 76 F2
Szarvaskő [H] 64 E5
Szczawnica [PL] 52 B5
Szczebrzeszyn [PL] 52 F1
Szczecin [PL] 20 F5
Szczecinek [PL] 22 B4
Szczekociny [PL] 50 H2
Szczerców [PL] 36 G5
Szczucin [PL] 52 C3
Szczuczyn [PL] 24 D4
Szczyrk [PL] 50 G5
Szczytna [PL] 50 B3
Szczytno [PL] 24 B4
Szécsény [H] 64 D5
Szederkény [H] 76 B5
Szeged [H] 76 E4
Szeghalom [H] 76 G2
Szegvár [H] 76 E3
Székely [H] 64 H4
Székesfehérvár [H] 76
 B2
Székkutas [H] 76 F3
Szekszárd [H] 76 C4
Szendrő [H] 64 F4
Szentendre [H] 64 C6
Szentes [H] 76 E3
Szentlászló [H] 76 A5
Szentliszló [H] 74 G3
Szentlőrinc [H] 76 A5
Szerencs [H] 64 G4
Szerkutas [H] 76 F3
Szestno [PL] 24 B3
Szetlew [PL] 36 E3
Szgliget [H] 74 H3
Szigetvár [H] 76 A5
Szikszó [H] 64 F4
Szil [H] 62 G6
Szilvásvárad [H] 64 E4
Szklarska Poreba [PL] 48
 H1
Szklary [PL] 52 E4
Szklary Górne [PL] 36 B5
Szlichtyngowa [PL] 36 B4
Szob [H] 64 C5
Szolnok [H] 76 E2
Szombathely [H] 74 F2
Szonowice [PL] 50 E3
Szőny [H] 64 B6
Szprotawa [PL] 34 H5
Szreńsk [PL] 22 G6
Sztum [PL] 22 E4
Szubin [PL] 22 C6
Szumirad [PL] 50 E1
Szydłów [PL] 52 C2
Szydłów [PL] 36 G5
Szydłowiec [PL] 38 B6
Szymbark [PL] 22 F4
Szyplíski [PL] 24 E2

T

Taalintehdas / Dalsbruk
 [FIN] 176 E6
Taapajärvi [FIN] 192 H6
Taavetti [FIN] 178 D2
Tab [H] 76 A3
Tabaja [BIH] 152 C3
Tábara [E] 80 H4
Tabernas [E] 102 G5
Tabiano Bagni [I] 110
 D2
Taboada [E] 78 D4
Tábor [CZ] 48 G5
Tábua [P] 86 E2
Tabuaço [P] 80 D5
Tabuenca [E] 90 D3
Täby [S] 168 D2
Tachov [CZ] 48 C4
Tadcaster [GB] 10 F3
Tafalla [E] 84 B4
Tagaranna [EST] 200 C3
Taggia [I] 108 G4
Taghmon [IRL] 4 F5
Tagliacozzo [I] 116 B5
Táglio di Po [I] 110 H2
Tahal [E] 102 G4
Tahtaköprü [TR] 146 G5

Tai di Cadore [I] 72 F4
Tailfingen [D] 58 G2
Tain [GB] 6 E4
Tain–l'Hermitage [F] 68 F4
Taipadas [P] 86 C5
Taipaleenkyla [FIN] 186 D4
Taipalsaari [FIN] 178 D2
Tairbeart / Tarbert [GB] 6
 B3
Taivalkoski [FIN] 198 F3
Taivassalo [FIN] 176 C4
Taizé [F] 56 F6
Tajcy [RUS] 178 H5
Takácsi [H] 74 H1
Talamone [I] 114 F3
Talarrubias [E] 96 C3
Talaván [E] 86 H4
Talavera de la Reina [E] 88
 D6
Talavera la Real [E] 94 G1
Talayuelas [E] 98 D3
Tálkafjörður [IS] 194 B1
Talladale [GB] 6 C4
Tallaght [IRL] 2 F6
Tallard [F] 108 D2
Tällberg [S] 172 H3
Tallinn [EST] 200 D1
Talloires [F] 70 B3
Tallow [IRL] 4 D5
Talmont [F] 54 C6
Talmont–St–Hilaire [F] 54
 B3
Talsi [LV] 200 C5
Talvik [N] 192 G1
Tamajón [E] 88 H4
Tamames [E] 88 B3
Tamarë [AL] 152 F4
Tamarino [BG] 148 E5
Tamarite de Litera [E] 90
 H4
Tamási [H] 76 B3
Tambohuse [DK] 160 C4
Tammela [FIN] 176 F3
Tammensiel [D] 18 E1
Tammijärvi [FIN] 186 G5
Tammisaari / Ekenäs [FIN]
 176 F6
Tamnič [YU] 150 E2
Tampere [FIN] 176 F1
Tamsalu [EST] 200 E1
Tamsweg [A] 72 H2
Tamworth [GB] 10 E6
Tana bru [N] 196 D2
Tanágra [GR] 134 B5
Tancarville [F] 26 G3
Tandragee [GB] 2 G4
Tandsjöborg [S] 172 G1
Tångaberg [S] 160 H3
Tangen [N] 166 B3
Tangen [N] 166 C1
Tangen [N] 172 G3
Tanger [Eur.] 100 F6
Tangerhütte [D] 34 B2
Tangermünde [D] 34 C2
Tanhua [FIN] 196 E6
Taninges [F] 70 B2
Tankavaara [FIN] 196
 D5
Tanlay [F] 56 F2
Tann [D] 46 F1
Tannadice [GB] 8 F2
Tännäs [S] 182 E4
Tanne [D] 32 H4
Tannheim [A] 60 C6
Tannila [FIN] 198 D3
Tanum [S] 166 C4
Tanumshede [S] 166 C4
Tanvald [CZ] 48 H2
Taormina [I] 124 B8
Tapa [EST] 200 E1
Tapia de Casariego [E] 78
 F2
Tapionkylä [FIN] 196 C7
Tapionniemi [FIN] 196 E7
Tápiószecső [H] 76 D1
Tápiószele [H] 76 D1
Tapolca [H] 74 H3
Tapolcafő [H] 74 H1
Taps [DK] 156 C3
Taraklı [TR] 146 H4
Tarancón [E] 96 H2
Táranto [I] 122 E4

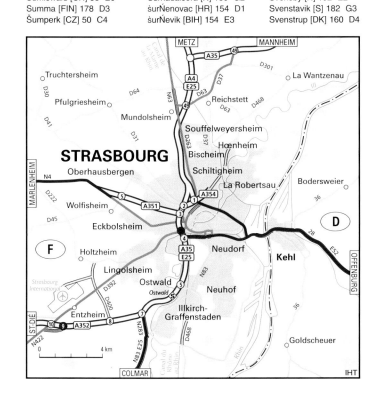

Tarare [F] 68 F2
Tarascon [F] 106 G4
Tarascon–sur–Ariège [F] 84 H5
Tarasp [CH] 72 B2
Tarazona [E] 84 A6
Tarazona de la Mancha [E] 98 B4
Tårbæk [DK] 156 H2
Tarbert [GB] 8 C3
Tarbert [IRL] 2 B6
Tarbert / Tairbeart [GB] 6 B3
Tarbes [F] 84 F3
Tarbet [GB] 8 D2
Tarcento [I] 72 G4
Tarčin [BIH] 152 C1
Tardets–Sorholus [F] 84 D3
Tärendö [S] 192 G6
Tarhos [H] 76 G3
Tarifa [E] 100 G6
Tarleton [GB] 10 D3
Tarm [DK] 156 B1
Tarmstedt [D] 18 E5
Tärnaby [S] 190 E3
Tarnaméra [H] 64 E6
Tarnawałka [PL] 52 G2
Tarnobrzeg [PL] 52 D2
Tarnogród [PL] 52 F2
Tarnos [F] 66 A6
Tarnów [PL] 52 C4
Tarnów [PL] 38 C4
Tarnowo Podgórne [PL] 36 C2
Tarnowskie Góry [PL] 50 F3
Tärnsjö [S] 174 E5
Tarouca [P] 80 D5
Tarp [D] 18 F1
Tarquínia [I] 114 G4
Tarquinia Lido [I] 114 G4
Tarragona [E] 92 C5
Tàrrega [E] 92 C3
Tårs [DK] 156 E4
Tårs [DK] 160 E3
Tarsia [I] 124 D3
Tarskavaig [GB] 6 B5
Tartas [F] 66 B6
Tartu [EST] 200 F3
Tårup [DK] 156 E3
Tarutino [MD] 206 E5
Tarvasjoki [FIN] 176 E4
Tarvisio [I] 72 H3
Taşbüku [TR] 142 E2
Täsch [CH] 70 E3
Taşköy [TR] 144 F3
Taşlıca [TR] 142 D3
Tassjö [S] 162 B6
Tåstrup [DK] 156 G2
Tata [H] 64 B6
Tatabánya [H] 64 B6
Tataháza [H] 76 D4
Tatarbunary [UA] 206 E5
Tatárszentgyörgy [H] 76 D2
Tatranská Kotlina [SK] 52 B6
Tau [N] 164 B3
Tauberbischofsheim [D] 46 E4
Taucha [D] 34 C5
Tauerntunnel [A] 72 G2
Tauern Tunnel [A] 72 H1
Taufers / Tubre [I] 72 B3
Taufkirchen [A] 60 H4
Taufkirchen [D] 60 F4
Taujėnai [LT] 202 G4
Taüll [E] 84 G6
Taunton [GB] 12 F4
Taunusstein [D] 46 B3
Tauplitz [A] 62 B6
Taurage [LT] 202 E5
Taurasi [I] 120 E3
Taurianova [I] 124 C7
Taurisano [I] 122 G6
Taurkains [LV] 200 E5
Tauste [E] 90 E3
Tauves [F] 68 B2
Tavannes [CH] 58 D5
Tavarnelle Val di Pesa [I] 110 F6
Tavas [TR] 144 G5
Tavastkenka [FIN] 198 E5
Tavaux [F] 56 H4
Taverna [I] 124 E5

Tavernelle [I] 114 H2
Tavernes [F] 108 C4
Tavernes de la Valldigna [E] 98 E6
Taviano [I] 122 G6
Tavira [P] 94 D5
Tavistock [GB] 12 D4
Tavşancıl [TR] 146 F3
Tavşanlı [TR] 144 G1
Taxenbach [A] 72 G1
Tayfur [TR] 146 B5
Tayinloan [GB] 2 H1
Tayport [GB] 8 F2
Tayvallich [GB] 8 C2
Tázlár [H] 76 D3
Tazones [E] 82 C1
Tczew [PL] 22 E3
Teano [I] 120 D2
Teascu [RO] 150 G1
Techendorf [A] 72 G3
Tecklenburg [D] 32 C2
Tecuci [RO] 206 D5
Teféli [GR] 140 E5
Tefenni [TR] 142 H1
Tegelen [NL] 30 F3
Tegernsee [D] 60 E5
Téglás [H] 64 H5
Teglio [I] 72 A4
Teguise [E] 100 E4
Teichel [D] 46 H1
Teignmouth [GB] 12 E5
Teillet [F] 106 C3
Teisendorf [D] 60 G5
Teisko [FIN] 186 E6
Tejn [DK] 158 E4
Teke [TR] 146 F2
Tekeriš [YU] 154 F3
Tekirdağ [TR] 146 C3
Telavåg [N] 170 A4
Telč [CZ] 48 H6
Telde [E] 100 D5
Telese Terme [I] 120 E2
Telford [GB] 10 D6
Telfs [A] 72 C1
Telgte [D] 32 C3
Telheiro [P] 94 B3
Telish [BG] 148 A3
Tellingstedt [D] 18 E2
Telšiai [LT] 202 E4
Telti [I] 118 D3
Tembleque [E] 96 G2
Temerin [YU] 154 F1
Temmes [FIN] 198 D4
Témpio Pausánia [I] 118 D3
Temple Bar [GB] 10 B6
Templemore [IRL] 4 E3
Templepatrick [GB] 2 G3
Templetouhy [IRL] 4 E3
Templin [D] 20 D6
Temse [B] 28 I I2
Temska [YU] 150 E3
Tenala / Tenhola [FIN] 176 F5
Tenbury Wells [GB] 12 G1
Tenby [GB] 12 D2
Tence [F] 68 E4
Tende [F] 108 F3
Tendilla [E] 88 H6
Tenebrón [E] 88 A3
Tenevo [BG] 148 E5
Tenhola / Tenala [FIN] 176 F5
Tenhult [S] 162 D2
Tenja [HR] 154 E1
Tennevik [N] 192 D4
Tennevoll [N] 192 D3
Tenterden [GB] 14 F5
Teolo [I] 110 G1
Tepasto [FIN] 192 H4
Tepecik [TR] 144 G1
Tepecik [TR] 146 F3
Tepeköy [TR] 144 E4
Tepelenë [AL] 128 B6
Teplá [CZ] 48 D4
Teplice [CZ] 48 E2
Teplice nad Metují [CZ] 50 B2
Teploye [RUS] 204 F5
Tepsa [FIN] 196 C6
Téramo [I] 116 C3
Ter Apel [NL] 16 H3
Teratyn [PL] 38 G6

Terebiń [PL] 52 G1
Terebishche [RUS] 200 G3
Terebovlja [UA] 206 C2
Terespol [PL] 38 F3
Terezín [CZ] 48 F2
Terezino Polje [HR] 74 H5
Tergnier [F] 28 F6
Terkoz [TR] 146 E2
Termal [TR] 146 F3
Termas de Monfortinho [P] 86 G3
Terme di Lurisia [I] 108 F3
Terme di Miradolo [I] 70 G6
Terme di Valdieri [I] 108 F3
Terme Luigiane [I] 124 C4
Terme S. Lucia [I] 116 C2
Términi Imerese [I] 126 D2
Terminillo [I] 116 B4
Terminón [E] 82 E5
Termís [GR] 134 H2
Térmoli [I] 116 F5
Termonfeckin [IRL] 2 F5
Terndrup [DK] 160 E4
Terneuzen [NL] 28 H1
Terni [I] 116 B4
Ternitz [A] 62 E6
Ternopol [UA] 206 C2
Térovo [GR] 132 D2
Terpan [AL] 128 B5
Terracina [I] 120 C2
Terradillos de los Templarios [E] 82 C5
Terråk [N] 190 D4
Terralba [I] 118 C5
Terranova di Pollino [I] 122 C6
Terrassa [E] 92 E4
Terrasson–la–Villedieu [F] 66 G3
Terrateig [E] 98 E6
Terriente [E] 98 D2
Tertenía [I] 118 E6
Teruel [E] 98 E2
Tervakoski [FIN] 176 G3
Tervel [BG] 148 F1
Tervo [FIN] 186 H2
Tervola [FIN] 198 C2
Tervuren [B] 30 C4
Terz [A] 62 D5
Terzaga [E] 90 C6
Tesegerague [E] 100 E5
Teslič [BIH] 154 C3
Teslui [RO] 150 G1
Tessin [D] 20 C3
Tessy sur–Vire [F] 26 E4
Tét [H] 62 H6
Tetbury [GB] 12 G3
Teterow [D] 20 C4
Teteven [BG] 148 A4
Tctovo [BG] 148 D2
Tetovo [MK] 128 D1
Tetrálofo [GR] 128 F5
Tettnang [D] 58 H4
Teufen [CH] 58 H5
Teulada [E] 104 F2
Teulada [I] 118 C7
Teupitz [D] 34 E3
Teuro [FIN] 176 F3
Teuva [FIN] 186 B4
Tevaniemi [FIN] 186 D6
Tevfikiye [TR] 130 H5
Teviothead [GB] 8 E5
Tewkesbury [GB] 12 G2
Tewli [BY] 38 G2
Thale [D] 34 A4
Thalfang [D] 44 G2
Thalheim [D] 48 D2
Thalmässing [D] 46 G6
Thalwil [CH] 58 F5
Thame [GB] 14 D3
Thann [F] 58 D3
Thannhausen [D] 60 C3
Tharandt [D] 48 E1
Thásos [GR] 130 E4
Thatcham [GB] 12 H4
Thaumiers [F] 56 C4
Thaxted [GB] 14 F3
Them [DK] 156 C1
Themar [D] 46 F2
Thénezay [F] 54 E3
Thenon [F] 66 F3
Theodosia [UA] 206 H6

Theológos [GR] 130 E4
Théoule [F] 108 E5
Thérma [GR] 138 G1
Thermá [GR] 130 G4
Thérmi [GR] 130 B4
Thermísia [GR] 136 G2
Thérmo [GR] 132 F5
Thérouanne [F] 28 E2
Thespies [GR] 134 A5
Thessaloníki [GR] 130 A4
Thetford [GB] 14 G2
Theux [B] 30 E5
Thevet–St–Julien [F] 56 B4
Theze [F] 84 E3
Thiaucourt–Regniéville [F] 44 C4
Thiberville [F] 26 G4
Thiélbemont–Farémont [F] 44 C5
Thiendorf [D] 34 E5
Thiene [I] 72 D5
Thiers [F] 68 D2
Thiersee [A] 60 F6
Thiesi [I] 118 C3
Thiessow [D] 20 E2
Thimariá [GR] 130 H3
Thimianá [GR] 134 G5
Thingeyri [IS] 194 C1
Thingvellir [IS] 194 C4
Thionville [F] 44 E3
Thíra / Fira [GR] 138 F5
Thirette [F] 68 H1
Thirsk [GB] 10 F3
Thisted [DK] 160 C4
Thísvi [GR] 132 H5
Thivars [F] 42 D4
Thiviers [F] 66 F2
Thizy [F] 68 F2
Thoissey [F] 68 G1
Tholey [D] 44 G3
Tholó [GR] 136 C3
Thomas Street [IRL] 2 D5
Thomastown [IRL] 4 E4
Thônes [F] 70 B3
Thonon [F] 70 B2
Thonon–les–Bains [F] 70 B2
Thorikó [GR] 136 H1
Thorlákshöfn [IS] 194 B5
Thornbury [GB] 12 G3
Thorney [GB] 14 F2
Thornhill [GB] 8 D4
Thórshöfn [IS] 194 G3
Thouarcé [F] 54 D2
Thouars [F] 54 E2
Thouría [GR] 136 D4
Thourio [GR] 130 H1
Threshfield [GB] 10 E3
Thueyts [F] 68 E5
Thuin [B] 28 H4
Thuir [F] 92 G1
Thum [D] 48 D2
Thun [CH] 70 D1
Thürkow [D] 20 C4
Thurles / Durlas Eile [IRL] 4 E3
Thurnau [D] 46 H3
Thurn Pass [A] 72 F1
Thurso [GB] 6 F2
Thury–Harcourt [F] 26 F4
Thusis [CH] 70 H1
Thyborøn [DK] 160 B4
Thyregod [DK] 156 C1
Tiana [I] 118 D5
Tibava [SK] 64 H2
Tibro [S] 166 F5
Ticha [BG] 148 D3
Tidaholm [S] 166 F6
Tidan [S] 166 F5
Tiefenbronn [D] 58 G1
Tiefencastel [CH] 70 H2
Tiefensee [D] 34 F2
Tiel [NL] 16 E5
Tielt [B] 28 G2
Tiemassaari [FIN] 188 D4
Tienen [B] 30 D4
Tiengen [D] 58 F4
Tiercé [F] 40 H6
Tiermas [E] 88 H3
Tierp [S] 174 F5
Tigharry / Tigh Ghearraidh [GB] 6 A3

Tigh Ghearraidh / Tigharry [GB] 6 A3
Tighina [MD] 206 E4
Tighnabruaich [GB] 8 C2
Tigkáki [GR] 142 C3
Tignes [F] 70 C4
Tihany [H] 76 A2
Tihuţa, Pasul– [RO] 206 C4
Tihvin [RUS] 204 D1
Tiistenjoki [FIN] 186 D3
Tikkaksoki [FIN] 186 G4
Tikkala [FIN] 186 F5
Tilburg [NL] 30 E2
Tilbury [GB] 14 F4
Til–Châtel [F] 56 H3
Tílisos [GR] 140 E4
Tillicoultry [GB] 8 E2
Tiltagals [LV] 200 F5
Tiltrem [N] 190 B5
Tilži [LV] 200 G5
Timahoe [IRL] 4 F3
Timişoara [RO] 76 G5
Timmel [D] 18 B4
Timmele [S] 162 C2
Timmendorfer Strand [D] 18 H3
Timmernabben [S] 162 G4
Timmersdala [S] 166 F5
Timrå [S] 184 E4
Tinahely [IRL] 4 F4
Tinajo [E] 100 E4
Tinca [RO] 76 H3
Tinchebray [F] 26 E4
Tineo [E] 78 G3
Tingelstad [N] 170 H4
Tinglev [DK] 156 B4
Tingsryd [S] 162 E5
Tingstäde [S] 168 G4
Tingvoll [N] 180 F2
Tínos [GR] 138 E2
Tintagel [GB] 12 C4
Tintinge [F] 56 B3
Tiobraid Arann / Tipperary [IRL] 4 D4
Tione di Trento [I] 72 C4
Tipperary / Tiobraid Arann [IRL] 4 D4
Tiranë [AL] 128 B3
Tirano [I] 72 B4
Tiraspol [MD] 206 E4
Tire [TR] 144 D5
Tirgo [E] 82 G6
Tîrgovişte [RO] 206 C6
Tîrgu Frumos [RO] 206 D4
Tîrgu Jiu [RO] 206 B6
Tîrgu Lăpuş [RO] 206 B4
Tîrgu Mureş [RO] 206 C5
Tîrgu Neamţ [RO] 206 C4
Tîrgu Secuiesc [RO] 206 C5
Tiriolo [I] 124 E5
Tirmo [FIN] 178 B4
Tîrnăveni [RO] 206 B5
Tírnavos [GR] 132 G1
Tirol / Tirolo [I] 72 C3
Tirolo / Tirol [I] 72 C3
Tirós [GR] 136 F3
Tirrénia [I] 110 D6
Tirschenreuth [D] 48 C4
Tirstrup [DK] 160 E6
Tiscar–Don Pedro [E] 102 F2
Tisno [HR] 112 G6
Tistrup [DK] 156 B2
Tisvilde [DK] 156 G1
Tiszaalpár [H] 76 E3
Tiszabábolna [H] 64 F6
Tiszacsege [H] 64 F6
Tiszaföldvár [H] 76 E2
Tiszafüred [H] 64 F6
Tiszakécske [H] 76 E2
Tiszalök [H] 64 G5
Tiszalúc [H] 64 F5
Tiszaörs [H] 64 F6
Tiszaroff [H] 76 E1
Tiszaszőlős [H] 64 F6
Tiszaújváros [H] 64 F5
Tiszavasvári [H] 64 G5
Titel [YU] 154 G1

Titisee [D] 58 F3
Titova Korenica [HR] 112 H3
Titov Veles [MK] 128 F1
Titran [N] 190 A6
Tittling [D] 60 H3
Tittmoning [D] 60 G4
Titz [D] 30 F4
Tiuccia [F] 114 A4
Tiukka / Tjöck [FIN] 186 B4
Tivat [YU] 152 D4
Tived [S] 166 G4
Tiverton [GB] 12 E4
Tivoli [I] 116 B5
Tizzano [F] 114 A6
Tjæreborg [DK] 156 B2
Tjällmo [S] 166 H5
Tjele [DK] 160 D5
Tjentište [BIH] 152 D2
Tjöck / Tiukka [FIN] 186 B4
Tjolmen [N] 190 E3
Tjøme [N] 164 H3
Tjong [N] 190 D1
Tjønnefoss [N] 164 E3
Tjørhom [N] 164 C3
Tjørnhom [N] 164 C5
Tjørnuvik [DK] 160 A1
Tjøtta [N] 190 D3
Tkon [HR] 112 G5
Tleń [PL] 22 D4
Tłuchowo [PL] 36 G1
Tłuszcz [PL] 38 C2
Tobarra [E] 98 B6
Tobercurry [IRL] 2 D3
Tobermore [GB] 2 F3
Tobermory [GB] 6 B6
Toblach / Dobbiaco [I] 72 E3
Tocha [P] 80 A6
Tocina [E] 94 H5
Töcksfors [S] 166 C2
Todi [I] 116 A3
Todoriči [BIH] 154 B4
Todtmoos [D] 58 E4
Todtnau [D] 58 E3
Tofte [N] 164 H2
Toftir [DK] 160 B2
Toftlund [DK] 156 B3
Togher [IRL] 2 D5
Tohmajärvi [FIN] 188 G3
Toholampi [FIN] 198 C6
Tohvri [EST] 200 E3
Toijala [FIN] 176 F2
Toivakka [FIN] 186 G5
Toivola [FIN] 178 C1
Töjby [FIN] 186 A4
Tojšići [BIH] 154 E3
Tokaj [H] 64 G4
Tokarnia [PL] 52 B2
Tokmak [UA] 206 H4
Toksovo [RUS] 178 H4
Tolastadh / Tolsta [GB] 6 C2
Tolcsva [H] 64 G4
Toledo [E] 96 F1
Tolentino [I] 116 C2
Tolfa [I] 114 G4
Tolg [S] 162 E4
Tolga [N] 182 C4
Tolkis / Tolkkinen [FIN] 178 B4
Tolkkinen / Tolkis [FIN] 178 B4
Tolkmicko [PL] 22 F2
Tollarp [S] 158 D2
Tølløse [DK] 156 F3
Tolmachevo [RUS] 200 H1
Tolmezzo [I] 72 G4
Tolmin [SLO] 72 H4
Tolna [H] 76 C4
Tolne [DK] 160 E2
Toló [GR] 136 F2
Tolob [GB] 6 G4
Toločin [BY] 204 C5
Tolosa [E] 84 B3
Tolox [E] 102 B4
Tolsta / Tolastadh [GB] 6 C2
Tolstoje [UA] 206 C3
Tolva [FIN] 196 F8

Tolve [I] 120 H4
Tomar [P] 86 D3
Tomaševo [YU] 150 A4
Tomaszów Lubelski [PL] 52 G2
Tomaszów Mazowiecki [PL] 36 H5
Tomatin [GB] 6 E5
TombebÅuf [F] 66 E4
Tomdoun [GB] 6 C5
Tomelilla [S] 158 D3
Tomelloso [E] 96 G4
Tomintoul [GB] 6 E5
Tomislavgrad [BIH] 152 B1
Tømmernes [N] 192 C5
Tommerup [DK] 156 D3
Tømmervåg [N] 180 F2
Tompa [H] 76 D4
Tomra [N] 180 D3
Tomter [N] 166 B2
Tona [E] 92 E3
Tonara [I] 118 D5
Tonbridge [GB] 14 E5
Tondela [P] 80 C6
Tønder [DK] 156 B4
Tongeren (Tongres) [B] 30 E4
Tongres (Tongeren) [B] 30 E4
Tongue [GB] 6 E2
Tonnay-Boutonne [F] 54 C5
Tonnay-Charente [F] 54 C5
Tonneins [F] 66 E5
Tonnerre [F] 56 F2
Tönning [D] 18 E2
Tønsberg [N] 164 H3
Tonstad [N] 164 C4
Tonypandy [GB] 12 F2
Toomyvara [IRL] 2 D6
Toourmakeady [IRL] 2 C4
Topchii [BG] 148 D2
Töpchin [D] 34 E3
Topliţa [RO] 206 C4
Toplou [GR] 140 G4
Topola [YU] 150 B1
Topolcani [MK] 128 E3
Topol'čany [SK] 64 B3
Topólia [GR] 140 B4
Topolovăţu [RO] 90 H5
Topolovgrad [BG] 146 A1
Topolovo [BG] 148 B6
Toporu [RO] 148 C1
Torà [E] 92 D3
Toral de los Vados [E] 78 F5
Torbalı [TR] 144 D4
Torbole [I] 72 C5
Torcello [I] 72 F6
Torcross [GB] 12 E5
Tordera [E] 92 F4
Tordesillas [E] 88 E2
Tordesilos [E] 90 C6
Töre [S] 198 B2
Töreboda [S] 166 F5
Torekov [S] 160 H6
Torelló [E] 92 E3
Toreno [E] 78 F5
Torfyanovka [RUS] 178 E3
Torgau [D] 34 D5
Torgelow [D] 20 E4
Torgiano [I] 116 A2
Torhamn [S] 158 G1
Torhout [B] 28 F2
Tori [EST] 200 E3
Torigni-sur-Vire [F] 26 E3
Torija [E] 88 H5
Torino [I] 70 D5
Torino di Sangro [I] 116 E5
Torino di Sangro Marina [I] 116 E5
Torla [E] 84 E5
Torma [EST] 200 F2
Tormac [RO] 76 H6
Törmänen [FIN] 196 D5
Törmänmäki [FIN] 198 E4
Törmäsjärvi [FIN] 196 C8
Tornal'a [SK] 64 E4
Torneträsk [S] 192 E4
Tornio [FIN] 198 C2
Tornjoš [YU] 76 E5
Toro [E] 88 D1

Törökszentmiklós [H] 76 E2
Toróni [GR] 130 C6
Torony [H] 74 F2
Torpa [S] 162 C5
Torpo [N] 170 F3
Torpoint [GB] 12 D5
Torpsbruk [S] 162 D4
Torquay [GB] 12 E5
Torralba [E] 96 F4
Torralba [E] 90 B4
Torrão [P] 94 D2
Torre [E] 102 D5
Torre Annunziata [I] 120 E3
Torre Beretti [I] 70 F6
Torreblanca [E] 98 G3
Torrecampo [E] 96 D5
Torre Canne [I] 122 F3
Torrecilla [E] 98 C1
Torre de Juan Abad [E] 96 G5
Torre de la Higuera [E] 100 F2
Torre del Bierzo [E] 78 F5
Torre del Compte [E] 102 E2
Torre del Greco [I] 120 E3
Torre del Lago Puccini [I] 110 D5
Torre del Mar [E] 102 C5
Torredembarra [E] 92 C5
Torre de Moncorvo [P] 80 E5
Torre de' Pásseri [I] 116 D4
Torre de Santa María [E] 86 H6
Torredonjimeno [E] 102 D2
Torre Faro [I] 124 C7
Torrefarrera [E] 90 H4
Torregamones [E] 80 G4
Torreguadiaro [E] 100 H5
Torreira [P] 80 B5
Torrejoncillo [E] 86 H4
Torrejón de Ardoz [E] 88 G6
Torrejón de la Calzada [E] 88 F4
Torrejón del Rey [E] 88 G5
Torrejón el Rubio [E] 88 A6
Torrelaguna [E] 88 G4
Torrelapaja [E] 90 C3
Torrelavega [E] 82 E3
Torrelobatón [E] 88 E1
Torrelodones [E] 88 F5
Torremaggiore [I] 116 F6
Torremolinos [E] 102 B5
Torremormojón [E] 82 C6
Torrenostra [E] 98 G3
Torrent [E] 98 E5
Torrente de Cinca [E] 90 G5
Torrenueva [E] 102 E5
Torre Orsaia [I] 120 G5
Torre-Pacheco [E] 104 C4
Torre Pellice [I] 70 C6
Torreperogil [E] 102 F2
Torre Santa Susanna [I] 122 F4
Torres Novas [P] 86 C4
Torres Vedras [P] 86 B4
Torrette di Fano [I] 112 C6
Torre Vã [P] 94 C3
Torrevieja [E] 104 D3
Torricella [I] 122 F5
Torri del Benaco [I] 72 C6
Torríglia [I] 110 B3
Torrijos [E] 96 E1
Tørring [DK] 156 C2
Torrita di Siena [I] 114 G2
Torroella de Montgrí [E] 92 G3
Torrox [E] 102 D5
Torsåker [S] 174 D4
Torsås [S] 162 F6
Torsborg [S] 182 F3
Torsby [S] 172 E5
Torshälla [S] 168 B3
Tórshavn [DK] 160 B2
Torsken [N] 192 D2
Torslanda [S] 160 G2
Torsminde [DK] 160 B5
Tortinmäki [FIN] 176 E4

Tórtoles de Esgueva [E] 88 G2
Tortolì [I] 118 E5
Tortona [I] 110 B2
Tortoreto Lido [I] 116 D3
Tortorici [I] 126 F2
Tortosa [E] 92 A5
Toruń [PL] 22 E6
Torup [S] 162 B4
Torup Strand [DK] 160 C3
Tõrva [EST] 200 E3
Tor Vaiánica [I] 116 A6
Torvikbukt [N] 180 F2
Tørvikbygd [N] 170 C4
Torvinen [FIN] 196 D7
Torvsjö [S] 190 F5
Toržok [RUS] 204 E3
Torzym [PL] 34 H3
Tosbotn [N] 190 D3
Toscaig [GB] 6 C4
Toscolano Maderno [I] 72 B5
Tosno [RUS] 204 C1
Tossa de Mar [S] 92 F4
Tösse [S] 166 D4
Tostedt [D] 18 F5
Tószeg [H] 76 E2
Toszek [PL] 50 F3
Totana [E] 104 B3
Totebo [S] 162 F2
Tôtes [F] 28 B5
Tótkomlós [H] 76 F4
Tøtlandsvik [N] 164 C2
Totnes [GB] 12 E5
Tottijärvi [FIN] 176 F2
Totton [GB] 12 H5
Toucy [F] 56 E2
Toul [F] 44 E5
Toulon [F] 108 C6
Toulon-sur-Arroux [F] 56 F5
Toulouse [F] 84 H3
Tourcoing [F] 28 F3
Tournai (Doornik) [B] 28 G3
Tournan [F] 42 G4
Tournay [F] 84 F4
Tournon [F] 68 F5
Tournon-d'Agenais [F] 66 F5
Tournon-St-Martin [F] 54 G4
Tournus [F] 56 G6
Tours [F] 54 F2
Tourves [F] 108 C5
Toury [F] 42 E5
Toužim [CZ] 48 D3
Tovarnik [HR] 154 E2
Tøvik [N] 180 E2
Towcester [GB] 14 D2
Töysä [FIN] 186 D3
Trabadelo [E] 78 E5
Trabanca [E] 80 G5
Traben-Trarbach [D] 44 G2
Trabía [I] 126 D2
Trabotivište [MK] 128 H1
Tracheiá [GR] 136 F2
Trädet [S] 162 C1
Trafoi [I] 72 B3
Tragacete [E] 98 C1
Trahíli [GR] 134 C5
Traian [RO] 148 B2
Traiguera [E] 92 A6
Traiskirchen [A] 62 F5
Traismauer [A] 62 E4
Trakai [LT] 24 H1
Trakoščan [HR] 74 E4
Tralee / Trá Lí [IRL] 4 B3
Trá Lí / Tralee [IRL] 4 B3
Tramaríglio [I] 118 B3
Tramatza [I] 118 C5
Tramelan [CH] 58 D5
Tramonti di Sopra [I] 72 F4
Tramore [IRL] 4 E5
Tranås [S] 158 D3
Tranås [S] 162 E1
Tranby [N] 164 H1
Trancoso [P] 80 D6
Tranderup [DK] 156 D4
Tranekær [DK] 156 E4
Tranemo [S] 162 C3
Tranent [GB] 8 F3
Trångsviken [S] 182 G2

Tranhult [S] 162 C3
Trani [I] 122 D2
Transtrand [S] 172 F3
Tranum Strand [DK] 160 D3
Tranvik [S] 168 E3
Trápani [I] 126 B2
Trapishte [BG] 148 D3
Trappes [F] 42 F4
Traryd [S] 162 C5
Träskvik [FIN] 186 B5
Träslövsläge [S] 160 H4
Trassem [D] 44 F3
Trăstenik [BG] 148 A3
Traun [A] 62 B4
Traunkirchen [A] 62 A5
Traunreut [D] 60 G5
Traunstein [D] 60 G5
Travemünde [D] 18 H3
Travers [CH] 58 C6
Travnik [BIH] 154 C4
Travo [F] 114 B5
Trbovlje [SLO] 74 C5
Trbatsch [D] 34 F3
Trebbin [D] 34 E3
Třebechovice pod Orebem [CZ] 50 B3
Třebenice [CZ] 48 F2
Trébeurden [F] 40 D1
Třebíč [CZ] 50 A6
Trebinje [BIH] 152 D3
Trebisacce [I] 122 D6
Trebišov [SK] 64 G3
Trebnje [SLO] 74 C5
Třeboň [CZ] 62 C2
Tréboul [F] 40 B3
Třebovice [CZ] 50 B4
Trebujena [E] 100 F3
Trecastagni [I] 126 G3
Trecate [I] 70 F5
Trecenta [I] 110 F2
Treffurt [D] 32 G5
Tregaron [GB] 10 B6
Trégastel [F] 40 D1
Tréguier [F] 26 A3
Treherbert [GB] 12 F2
Treia [D] 18 E1
Treignac [F] 66 H2
Treis [D] 44 H1
Trekanten [S] 162 F5
Trelleborg [S] 158 C3
Tremestieri [I] 124 B7
Tremezzo [I] 70 G3
Třemošná [CZ] 48 E4
Tremp [E] 92 C2
Trenčianska Turná [SK] 64 A2
Trenčín [SK] 64 A2
Trend [DK] 160 C4
Trendelburg [D] 32 F4
Trengereid [N] 170 B4
Trent [CH] 70 C3
Trento [I] 72 C4
Treppeln [D] 34 G3
Trescore Balneario [I] 70 H4
Tresenda [I] 72 B4
Tresfjord [N] 180 E3
Tresigallo [I] 110 G2
Treski [EST] 200 G3
Tresta [GB] 6 H3
Třeštice [CZ] 48 H6
Trets [F] 108 B5
Tretten [N] 170 H2
Treuchtlingen [D] 60 D2
Treuenbrietzen [D] 34 D3
Trevi [I] 116 B3
Trevíglio [I] 70 H5
Trevignano Romano [I] 114 H4
Treviso [I] 72 E6
Trévoux [F] 68 F2
Trezzo sull'Adda [I] 70 G4
Trgovište [YU] 150 E5
Trhové Sviny [CZ] 62 C2
Triaize [F] 54 C4
Triánta [GR] 142 E4
Triaucourt-en-Argonne [F] 44 D4
Tribanj Krušcica [HR] 112 G4
Triberg [D] 58 F3

Tribsees [D] 20 C3
Tricárico [I] 120 H4
Tricesimo [I] 72 G4
Trichiana [I] 72 E4
Trie [F] 84 F3
Trieben [A] 62 C6
Trier [D] 44 F2
Trieste [I] 72 H6
Trígono [GR] 128 E4
Trikala [GR] 132 F2
Trikalón [GR] 136 E1
Trikeri [GR] 134 A3
Trilj [HR] 152 A1
Trim [IRL] 2 F5
Trindade [P] 80 E4
Trindade [P] 94 D3
Třinec [CZ] 50 F5
Trinita d'Agultu [I] 118 D2
Trinitápoli [I] 120 H2
Trino [I] 70 E5
Triollo [E] 82 D4
Trípoli [GR] 136 E2
Triponzo [I] 116 B3
Tripótama [GR] 136 D1
Trittau [D] 18 G4
Trittenheim [D] 44 G2
Trivento [I] 116 E6
Trnava [SK] 62 H4
Trnovo [BIH] 152 D1
Troarn [F] 26 F3
Trocnov [CZ] 62 C2
Troense [DK] 156 E4
Trofaiach [A] 74 C1
Trofors [N] 190 D3
Trogir [HR] 116 H1
Troia [I] 120 G2
Tróia [P] 86 B6
Troickoje [UA] 206 E4
Troina [I] 126 F3
Trois-Ponts [B] 30 E5
Trojane [SLO] 74 C4
Trollhattan [S] 166 D6
Tromello [I] 70 F5
Tromsø [N] 192 E2
Trondheim [N] 182 B1
Trönninge [S] 162 B5
Trôo [F] 42 C6
Troon [GB] 8 C3
Tropea [I] 124 C6
Tropojë [AL] 150 B5
Trosa [S] 168 D4
Troškūnai [LT] 202 G4
Trossachs [GB] 8 D2
Trossingen [D] 58 G3
Tröstau [D] 48 B3
Trostberg [D] 60 F4
Trosterud [N] 166 C2
Trostjanec [UA] 206 G2
Trouville [F] 26 G3
Trowbridge [GB] 12 G3
Troyan [BG] 148 B4
Troyanovo [BG] 148 E4
Troyanski Pateka [BG] 148 B4
Troyes [F] 44 B6
Trpanj [HR] 152 B3
Trstená [SK] 50 H6
Trstenik [YU] 150 C3
Trsteno [HR] 152 C3
Trstín [SK] 62 H3
Truchtersheim [F] 44 H5
Trud [BG] 148 B5
Trujillo [E] 96 B1
Trün [BG] 150 E4
Trun [F] 26 F4
Truro [GB] 12 C5
Truskavets' [UA] 52 G5
Trustrup [DK] 160 F6
Trutnov [CZ] 50 B2
Trutnowy [PL] 22 E3
Tryavna [BG] 148 C4
Tryggelev [DK] 156 E5
Tryńcza [PL] 52 E3
Trýpi [GR] 136 E4
Trypití [GR] 130 C5
Trzcianka [PL] 22 A6
Trzciel [PL] 36 B3
Trzcinno [PL] 34 H1
Trzcińsko Zdrój [PL] 20 F6
Trzebiatów [PL] 20 G3

Trzebiel [PL] 34 G5
Trzebież [PL] 20 F4
Trzebinia [PL] 50 G3
Trzebnica [PL] 36 C6
Trzemeszno [PL] 36 E2
Trzepowo [PL] 22 D3
Tržič [SLO] 74 B4
Tsagkaráda [GR] 134 A2
Tsamandás [GR] 132 C1
Tsangário [GR] 132 C3
Tsapel'ka [RUS] 200 H3
Tsarevets [BG] 148 C2
Tsarevo [BG] 148 G5
Tsarítsani [GR] 132 G1
Tschernitz [D] 34 G5
Tsenovo [BG] 148 C2
Tsotili [GR] 128 E6
Tsoútsouros [GR] 140 F5
Tua [P] 80 E4
Tuaim / Tuam [IRL] 2 C4
Tuam / Tuaim [IRL] 2 C4
Tubilla del Agua [E] 82 E5
Tübingen [D] 58 G2
Tubre / Taufers [I] 72 B3
Tučepi [HR] 152 B2
Tuchan [F] 106 C5
Tüchen [D] 20 B6
Tuchola [PL] 22 D4
Tuchomie [PL] 22 C3
Tuchów [PL] 52 C4
Tuczno [PL] 20 H6
Tuddal [N] 164 F1
Tudela [E] 84 B6
Tudela de Duero [E] 88 E2
Tudulinna [EST] 200 F2
Tuffé [F] 42 C5
Tuhkakylä [FIN] 198 F5
Tui [E] 78 B5
Tuin [MK] 128 D2
Tuixén [E] 92 D2
Tüja [LV] 200 D4
Tukums [LV] 200 D5
Tula [RUS] 204 F5
Tulare [YU] 150 D5
Tuławki [PL] 22 H3
Tulca [RO] 76 H3
Tulcea [RO] 206 E6
Tulla [IRL] 2 C6
Tullamore [IRL] 2 E6
Tulle [F] 66 H3
Tullebolle [DK] 156 E4
Tullinge [S] 168 D3
Tullins [F] 68 G4
Tulln [A] 62 E4
Tullow [IRL] 4 F4
Tulppio [FIN] 196 F6
Tulsk [IRL] 2 D4
Tulžin [UA] 206 E3
Tum [PL] 36 G3
Tumba [S] 168 D3
Tummel Bridge [GB] 8 E1
Tun [S] 166 D5
Tuna [S] 162 F3
Tuna Hästberg [S] 172 H5
Tunbridge Wells [GB] 14 E5
Tunçbilek [TR] 146 G6
Tune [DK] 156 G3
Túnel del Cadí [E] 92 E2
Túnel de Viella [E] 84 F5
Tungelsta [S] 168 E4
Tungozero [RUS] 198 G2
Tunhovd [N] 170 F4
Tunnel de Bielsa [Eur.] 84 E5
Tunnel de Fréjus [Eur.] 70 B5
Tunnel du Mont-Blanc [Eur.] 70 C3
Tunnerstad [S] 162 D1
Tuohikotti [FIN] 178 C2
Tuolluvaara [S] 192 F5
Tuorila [FIN] 186 B6
Tupadly [PL] 36 E2
Tuplice [PL] 34 G4
Tura [H] 64 D6
Turaliči [BIH] 154 E4
Turan [TR] 146 F4
Turanli [TR] 144 C4
Turany [SK] 50 G6
Türas [TR] 146 G2
Turbe [BIH] 154 C4

Turčianske Teplice [SK] 64 C2
Turckheim [F] 58 D3
Turda [RO] 206 B4
Turégano [E] 88 F3
Turek [PL] 36 F4
Turenki [FIN] 176 G3
Turenne [F] 66 G3
Turgeliai [LT] 202 G6
Tŭrgovishte [BG] 148 D3
Turgut [TR] 142 D1
Turgutbey [TR] 146 C2
Turgutlu [TR] 144 D4
Turgutreis [TR] 142 C3
Türi [EST] 200 E2
Turi [I] 122 E3
Turiis'k [UA] 38 H5
Turís / Torís [E] 98 E5
Turka [UA] 52 F6
Türkeli [TR] 146 C4
Túrkeve [H] 76 F2
Türkheim [D] 60 C4
Türkmen [TR] 144 C3
Turku / Åbo [FIN] 176 D4
Turlough [IRL] 2 C4
Turmantas [LT] 202 H4
Turňa nad Bodvou [SK] 64 F3
Turnberry [GB] 8 C4
Turnhout [B] 30 D3
Türnitz [A] 62 D5
Turnov [CZ] 48 H2
Turnu Măgurele [RO] 148 B2
Turnu Roşu, Pasul– [RO] 206 H5
Turobin [PL] 52 F1
Túrony [H] 76 B5
Turów [PL] 38 E4
Turrach [A] 74 A2
Turre [E] 102 H5
Turriff [GB] 6 F5
Turtagrø [N] 170 E1
Turtola [FIN] 196 C8
Turunç [TR] 142 E3
Turzovka [PL] 50 F5
Tuscánia [I] 114 G4
Tushielaw Inn [GB] 8 E4
Tušilovic [HR] 112 G1
Tuszyn [PL] 36 G5
Tutin [YU] 150 B4
Tutjunniemi [FIN] 188 F3
Tutrakan [BG] 148 D1
Tutrakan [BG] 206 D6
Tuttlingen [D] 58 G3
Tutzing [D] 60 D5
Tuukkala [FIN] 186 H6
Tuulos [FIN] 176 G2
Tuupovaara [FIN] 188 G3
Tuusjärvi [FIN] 188 D2
Tuusniemi [FIN] 188 E2
Tuusula [FIN] 176 H4
Tuv [N] 170 F3
Tuzi [YU] 152 E4
Tuzla [BIH] 154 E3
Tuzla [TR] 146 F3
Tuzla [TR] 134 G1
Tuzlata [BG] 148 G2
Tvååker [S] 160 H4
Tvärålund [S] 190 H5
Tvedestrand [N] 164 F4
Tveita [N] 170 B4
Tveitsund [N] 164 E3
Tver (Kalinin) [RUS] 204 E3
Tverai [LT] 202 D4
Tversted [DK] 160 E2
Tvis [DK] 160 C5
Tvøroyri [DK] 160 A3
Tvorozhkovo [RUS] 200 G2
Tvrdošovce [SK] 64 A5
Tvŭrditsa [BG] 148 D4
Twardogóra [PL] 50 D1
Tweedsmuir [GB] 8 E4
Twimberg [A] 74 C2
Twist [D] 16 H4
Twistringen [D] 18 D6
Tworków [PL] 50 E4
Tworóg [PL] 50 F2
Twyford [GB] 14 D4
Tychowo [PL] 22 A4

Tychy [PL] 50 G3
Tyczyn [PL] 52 E4
Tyfors [S] 172 G5
Tyholland [GB] 2 F4
Tyin [N] 170 F2
Tykocin [PL] 24 E5
Tylawa [PL] 52 D5
Tylldal [N] 182 B5
Tylstrup [DK] 160 E3
Tymfristós [GR] 132 F4
Tympáki [GR] 140 D5
Tynemouth [GB] 8 G6
Tyniec [PL] 50 H4
Týniště nad Orlicí [CZ] 50 B3
Tynkä [FIN] 198 C5
Týn nad Vltavou [CZ] 48 F6
Tynset [N] 182 B4
Tyrävaara [FIN] 198 F3
Tyresö [S] 168 E3
Tyringe [S] 158 C1
Tyrislöt [S] 168 C6
Tyristrand [N] 170 H5
Tyrjänsaari [FIN] 188 G1
Tyrnävä [FIN] 198 D4
Tyrrellspass [IRL] 2 E5
Tysse [N] 170 B4
Tyssedal [N] 170 C5
Tystberga [S] 168 C4
Tyszki–Nadbory [PL] 24 D6
Tytuvėnai [LT] 202 E4
Tyulenovo [BG] 148 G2
Tyvsen [DK] 156 B4
Tywyn [GB] 10 B5
Tzermiádo [GR] 140 F5
Tzummarum [NL] 16 F2

U

Ub [YU] 150 A1
Úbeda [E] 102 F2
Ubergsmoen [N] 164 F4
Überlingen [D] 58 G4
Ubrique [E] 100 H4
Uchte [D] 32 E1
Uckange [F] 44 E3
Uckfield [GB] 14 E5
Ucria [I] 124 A7
Udbina [HR] 112 H4
Udbyhøj [DK] 160 E5
Udbyhøj Vasehuse [DK] 160 E5
Udden [S] 166 D5
Uddevalla [S] 166 C5
Uddheden [S] 166 E1
Uden [NL] 16 E6
Udine [I] 72 G5
Udovo [MK] 128 G2
Üdrupij [LV] 200 F4
Udvar [H] 76 B5
Ueckermünde [D] 20 E4
Uelsen [D] 16 G4
Uelzen [D] 18 G6
Uetersen [D] 18 F4
Uetze [D] 32 G2
Uffenheim [D] 46 F5
Ugăle [LV] 200 C5
Ugao [YU] 150 A4
Ugao–Miraballes [E] 82 G4
Ugento [I] 122 G6
Ugerløse [DK] 156 F3
Ugíjar [E] 102 F5
Ugine [F] 70 B3
Uglič [RUS] 204 F3
Ugljan [HR] 112 F5
Ugljane [HR] 152 A2
Ugrinovci [YU] 150 B2
Ugürchin [BG] 148 A4
Uğurlutepe [TR] 130 G5
Uherske Mineralne [PL] 52 E5
Uherské Hradiště [CZ] 62 H2
Uherský Brod [CZ] 62 H2
Uhlířské Janovice [CZ] 48 G4
Uhříněves [CZ] 48 G4
Uig [GB] 6 B4

Uimaharju [FIN] 188 G1
Uithoorn [NL] 16 D4
Uithuizen [NL] 16 G1
Ujazd [PL] 50 E3
Ujazd [PL] 36 H5
Ujazd [PL] 52 C2
Újfehértó [H] 64 H5
Ujście [PL] 22 B6
Újszász [H] 76 E1
Ukkola [FIN] 188 F1
Ukmerge [LT] 202 G5
Ukonjärvi [FIN] 196 D4
Ula [TR] 142 E2
Ul'anka [SK] 64 C3
Ulan Majorat [PL] 38 E4
Ulanów [PL] 52 E2
Ulbjerg [DK] 160 D5
Ulceby Cross [GB] 10 G5
Ulcinj [YU] 152 E5
Uldum [DK] 156 C2
Ulefoss [N] 164 F2
Ulëzë [AL] 128 B2
Ulfborg [DK] 160 B5
Ulinia [PL] 22 C1
Uljma [YU] 154 H2
Ulla [BY] 204 C4
Ullapool [GB] 6 D3
Ullared [S] 162 B4
Ullatti [S] 192 F6
Ulldecona [E] 92 A6
Ulldemolins [E] 90 H5
Ullerslev [DK] 156 E3
Üllés [H] 76 E4
Üllő [H] 76 D1
Ullock [GB] 8 D6
Ulm [D] 60 B3
Ulme [P] 86 D4
Ulmen [D] 44 G1
Ulmeni [RO] 148 D1
Ulnes [N] 170 G2
Ulog [BIH] 152 D2
Ulricehamn [S] 162 C2
Ulrika [S] 162 E1
Ulriksfors [S] 190 E6
Ulsberg [N] 180 H3
Ulsta [GB] 6 H3
Ulsted [DK] 160 E4
Ulsteinvik [N] 180 C4
Ulstrup [DK] 156 E2
Ulstrup [DK] 160 D5
Uluabat [TR] 146 E5
Ulubey [TR] 144 G3
Uludağ [TR] 146 F5
Ulvália [N] 172 D3
Ulverston [GB] 10 D2
Ulvestad [N] 170 D1
Ulvik [N] 170 D3
Ulvila [FIN] 176 D2
Ulvsjön [S] 172 G1
Ulvsvåg [S] 192 C4
Umag [HR] 112 D1
Uman [UA] 206 E3
Umbertide [I] 116 A1
Umbukta [N] 190 E2
Umčari [YU] 154 H3
Umeå [S] 198 A6
Umfors [S] 190 E2
Umhausen [A] 72 C1
Umka [YU] 154 G3
Umurbey [TR] 146 B5
Umurbey [TR] 146 F4
Umurlu [TR] 144 E5
Uña [E] 98 C2
Unaðsdalur [IS] 194 C1
Unari [FIN] 196 D7
Uncastillo [E] 84 C5
Undenäs [S] 166 G5
Undersåker [S] 182 F2
Úněšov [CZ] 48 D4
Ungheni [MD] 206 D4
Unhošť [CZ] 48 F3
Unichowo [PL] 22 C3
Uničov [CZ] 50 C4
Uniejów [PL] 36 F4
Unirea [RO] 150 F1
Unna [D] 32 C4
Unnaryd [S] 162 C4
Unterach [A] 60 H5
Unterlüss [D] 18 G6
Unter Pfaffenhofen [D] 60 D4

Unter–Schleissheim [D] 60 E4
Unteruhldingen [D] 58 H4
Unterwasser [CH] 58 H5
Unterweissenbach [A] 62 C4
Unterwössen [D] 60 F5
Upavon [GB] 12 G4
Úpice [CZ] 50 B2
Uppad [S] 166 D6
Upper Chapel [GB] 12 F1
Upper Ruskoe [GB] 8 C5
Uppingham [GB] 14 E1
Upplands Väsby [S] 168 D2
Uppsala [S] 168 D1
Úras [I] 118 C6
Ura Vajgurore [AL] 128 B4
Urbánia [I] 110 H6
Urbino [I] 112 B6
Urçay [F] 56 C5
Urda [E] 96 F3
Urdos [F] 84 D4
Uriage–les–Bains [F] 68 H5
Uriz / Arze–Arce [E] 84 C4
Urjala [FIN] 176 F2
Urk [NL] 16 E3
Urla [TR] 144 C4
Urlingford [IRL] 4 E3
Urnäsch [CH] 58 H5
Urnes [N] 170 D1
Uroševac [YU] 150 C6
Ursus [PL] 38 B3
Ururi [I] 116 F6
Ury [F] 42 F5
Urziceni [RO] 206 D6
Urziçuţa [RO] 150 F2
Usagre [E] 94 H3
Uşak [TR] 144 G3
Ušče [YU] 150 B3
Usedom [D] 20 E4
Ushakovo [RUS] 22 G2
Uši [MK] 128 F2
Usingen [D] 46 C2
Usk [GB] 12 F2
Uskedal [N] 170 B5
Üsküdar [TR] 146 E3
Uslar [D] 32 F4
Usmate Velate [I] 70 G4
Usseglio [I] 70 C5
Ussel [F] 68 B2
Usseln [D] 32 D5
Usson–du–Poitou [F] 54 F5
Usson–les–Bains [F] 106 B6
Ustaoset [N] 170 E4
Ustaritz [F] 84 C2
Úštěk [CZ] 48 F2
Uster [CH] 58 G5
Ustibar [BIH] 152 E2
Ústí nad Labem [CZ] 48 F2
Ústí nad Orlicí [CZ] 50 B4
Ustiprača [BIH] 152 E1
Ustjužna [RUS] 204 E2
Ustka [PL] 22 B2
Ust'–Luga [RUS] 178 E6
Ustrem [BG] 146 A1
Ustroń [PL] 50 F5
Ustronie Morskie [PL] 20 H3
Ustrzyki Dolne [PL] 52 F5
Ustrzyki Górne [PL] 52 F6
Ustye [RUS] 200 H1
Ustyluh [UA] 38 G6
Ususău [RO] 76 H5
Utajärvi [FIN] 198 E4
Utåker [N] 170 B5
Utbjoa [N] 164 B1
Utebo [E] 90 E3
Utena [LT] 202 G4
Uthlede [D] 18 D4
Utiel [E] 98 D4
Utne [N] 170 C4
Utrecht [NL] 16 D5
Utrera [E] 100 G2
Utrine [YU] 76 E5
Utsjoki [FIN] 196 D3
Uttendorf [A] 72 F1
Uttendorf [A] 60 G4
Utti [FIN] 178 C3
Utting [D] 60 D4
Uttoxeter [GB] 10 E5
Utvängstorp [S] 162 C1

Utvik [N] 180 D5
Utvorda [N] 190 C4
Uukuniemi [FIN] 188 G5
Uurainen [FIN] 186 F4
Uusikaarlepyy / Nykarleby [FIN] 186 C1
Uusikaupunki / Nystad [FIN] 176 C3
Uusikylä [FIN] 178 B3
Uusi–Värtsilä [FIN] 188 G3
Uva [FIN] 198 F4
Uvac [BIH] 152 E1
Úvaly [CZ] 48 G4
Uvarná [S] 172 F5
Uyeasound [GB] 6 H3
Uzdowo [PL] 22 G5
Uzel [F] 26 A5
Uzerche [F] 66 G2
Uzès [F] 106 G3
Uzeste [F] 66 D4
Uzhorod [UA] 206 B3
Užice [YU] 150 A2
Uzunköprü [TR] 146 B3
Uzunkuyu [TR] 144 B4
Uzuntarla [TR] 146 G3
Užventis [LT] 202 E4

V

Vå [N] 164 E1
Vaajakoski [FIN] 186 G4
Vääkio [FIN] 198 F3
Vääksy [FIN] 178 A2
Vaala [FIN] 198 E4
Vaalajärvi [FIN] 196 D6
Vaalimaa [FIN] 178 D3
Väärinmaja [FIN] 186 E5
Vaas [F] 42 B6
Vaasa / Vasa [FIN] 186 B2
Vaassen [NL] 16 F4
Väätäiskylä [FIN] 186 E3
Vabalninkas [LT] 202 F3
Vác [H] 64 C5
Vacha [D] 46 F1
Váchartyán [H] 64 C6
Väckelsång [S] 162 E5
Väderstad [S] 166 G6
Vadheim [N] 170 C1
Vado Ligure [I] 108 H3
Vadsø [N] 196 E2
Vadstena [S] 166 G5
Vaduz [FL] 58 H6
Væggerløse [DK] 20 B1
Vafaïka [GR] 130 E3
Vafiohóri [GR] 128 G3
Vågaholmen [N] 190 D1
Vågámo [N] 180 G5
Vågan [N] 192 C6
Våge [N] 164 C6
Våge [N] 170 B3
Våge [N] 164 A1
Vägeva [EST] 200 E2
Vaggeryd [S] 162 D3
Vaggsvik [N] 192 D3
Vágia [GR] 134 B5
Vagioniá [GR] 140 E5
Vaglio Basilicata [I] 120 H4
Vagnhärad [S] 168 D4
Vagos [P] 80 B5
Vågsbygd [N] 164 D6
Vågsele [S] 190 G5
Vägsjöfors [S] 172 E5
Vågslid [N] 164 D1
Vågur [DK] 160 A3
Vahanka [FIN] 186 E3
Vái [GR] 140 H4
Vaiano [I] 110 F5
Vaiges [F] 40 H5
Vaihingen [D] 46 C6
Väike–Maarja [EST] 200 F1
Vailly [F] 56 C2
Vailly [F] 44 A2
Vainutas [LT] 202 D5
Vaison–la–Romaine [F] 106 H3
Vajszló [H] 76 A5

Vajza [AL] 128 B5
Vakarel [BG] 150 G5
Vakıfköy [TR] 144 F5
Vakiflar [TR] 146 C2
Vakijaur [S] 190 H1
Vaksdal [N] 170 B3
Valaajärvi [FIN] 196 D6
Vålådalen [S] 182 E2
Valandovo [MK] 128 G2
Valanída [GR] 132 F1
Valareña [E] 84 B6
Valašská Polanka [CZ] 50 E6
Valašské Meziříčí [CZ] 50 E5
Valbella [CH] 70 H1
Valberg [F] 108 E3
Vålberg [S] 166 E3
Valbiska [HR] 112 E2
Valbondione [I] 72 A4
Valbonè [AL] 150 B4
Valbonnais [F] 68 H5
Valcarlos / Luzaide [E] 84 C3
Val–Claret [F] 70 C4
Valdagno [I] 72 D6
Valdahon [F] 58 B5
Valdaj [RUS] 204 D3
Valdalen [N] 182 D5
Valdeganga [E] 98 C5
Valdeltormo [E] 90 G6
Valdemärpils [LV] 200 C4
Valdemarsvik [S] 168 C6
Valdemorillo [E] 88 F5
Valdemoro [E] 88 F6
Valdenoceda [E] 82 F4
Valdepeñas [E] 96 F5
Valdepeñas de Jaén [E] 102 E3
Valderas [E] 82 B5
Valderice [I] 126 B2
Valderöy [N] 180 C3
Valderrobres [E] 98 G1
Valdeverdeja [E] 96 C1
Val d'Isère [F] 70 C4
Val–d'Izé [F] 26 D6
Valdobbiádene [I] 72 E5
Valdoviño [E] 78 D1
Valea lui Mihai [RO] 206 B4
Valebø [N] 164 F2
Vale de Açor [P] 94 D3
Vale de Cambra [P] 80 C5
Vale de Lobos [P] 94 C5
Vale do Poço [P] 94 D4
Váleggio S Míncio [I] 110 E1
Valença do Minho [P] 78 B5
Valençay [F] 54 H3
Valence [F] 66 E6
Valence [F] 66 F6
Valence [F] 68 F5
Valence d'Albigeois [F] 106 C2
Valencia [E] 98 E4
Valencia de Alcántara [E] 86 F5
Valencia de Don Juan [E] 82 B5
Valencia de las Torres [E] 94 H3
Valencia del Ventoso [E] 94 G3
Valenciennes [F] 28 G4
Văleni [RO] 148 B1
Vălenii de Munte [RO] 206 C6
Valensole [F] 108 C4
Valentano [I] 114 G3
Valentigney [F] 58 C4
Valenza [I] 70 F6
Våler [N] 166 B2
Våler [N] 172 D4
Valeria [E] 98 B3
Valevåg [N] 170 B6
Valfábbrica [I] 116 A2
Valga [EST] 200 F4
Valgeristi [EST] 200 D2
Valguarnera Caropepe [I] 126 F3
Valimítika [GR] 132 G6
Valjevo [YU] 150 A1

Valjok [N] 196 C3
Valka [LV] 200 F4
Valkeakoski [FIN] 176 F2
Valkeala [FIN] 178 C2
Valkenburg [NL] 30 F4
Valkenswaard [NL] 30 E3
Valkininkai [LT] 24 H2
Valko / Valkom [FIN] 178 B4
Valkom / Valko [FIN] 178 B4
Vallada [E] 78 F4
Valladolid [E] 88 E2
Vallåkra [S] 156 H2
Vallata [I] 120 F3
Valldal [N] 180 E4
Valldemossa [E] 104 E4
Valle [LV] 200 E6
Valle [N] 164 D2
Vallecorsa [I] 120 C1
Valle de Abdalajís [E] 102 B4
Valle de Cabuérniga [E] 82 E3
Valle de la Serena [E] 96 A3
Valledoria [I] 118 C2
Vallehermoso [E] 100 B5
Vallelunga Pratameno [I] 126 D3
Vallen [S] 184 D1
Vallentuna [S] 168 E2
Valleraugue [F] 106 E2
Vallet [F] 54 C2
Valletta [M] 126 C6
Vallfogona de Ripollès [E] 92 E2
Vallo di Lucania [I] 120 F5
Valloire [F] 70 B5
Vallombrosa [I] 110 F5
Vallon–en–Sully [F] 56 C5
Vallon–Pont–d'Arc [F] 68 E6
Vallorbe [CH] 58 B6
Vallorcine [F] 70 C3
Vallouise [F] 70 B6
Valls [E] 92 C4
Vallset [N] 172 C4
Vallsta [S] 174 D1
Vallter Œ0 [E] 92 E2
Valmadrid [E] 90 E4
Valmiera [LV] 200 E4
Valmontone [I] 116 B6
Valmorel [F] 70 B4
Valognes [F] 26 D2
Valongo [P] 80 C4
Valøy [N] 190 C4
Valozhyn [BY] 202 H6
Valpaços [P] 80 E3
Valporquero de Torio [E] 78 H5
Valpovo [HR] 76 B6
Valras–Plage [F] 106 D5
Valréas [F] 106 H2
Vals [CH] 70 G2
Valset [N] 190 B6
Valsjöbyn [S] 190 E5
Vals–les–Bains [F] 68 E6
Valsøybotn [N] 180 G2
Val–Suzon [F] 56 G3
Valtessiníko [GR] 136 D2
Val Thorens [F] 70 B5
Valtiendas [E] 88 G3
Valtierra [E] 84 B5
Valtimo [FIN] 198 F5
Váltos [GR] 130 H1
Valtournenche [I] 70 D3
Valverde [E] 100 A6
Valverde de Júcar [E] 98 B3
Valverde del Camino [E] 94 F5
Valverde de Leganés [E] 94 F2
Valverde del Fresno [E] 86 G3
Vama Veche [RO] 148 G1
Vamberk [CZ] 50 B3
Vamdrup [DK] 156 C3
Våmhus [S] 172 G3
Vammala [FIN] 176 E2
Vámos [GR] 140 C4

Vámosmikola [H] 64 C5
Vámospércs [H] 64 H6
Vámosszabadi [H] 62 H6
Vampula [FIN] 176 E3
Vamvakoú [GR] 132 G2
Vanda / Vantaa [FIN] 176 H4
Vandel [DK] 156 C2
Vandellòs [E] 90 H6
Vandenesse [F] 56 E4
Vandoies / Vintl [I] 72 E2
Vändra [EST] 200 E2
Väne [LV] 200 C5
Vänersborg [S] 166 D5
Vangshylla [N] 190 C6
Vangsnes [N] 170 D2
Vangsvik [N] 192 D3
Vanhakylä [FIN] 186 B5
Vänjaurfräsk [S] 190 G5
Vânju Mare [RO] 150 E1
Vännacka [S] 166 D2
Vännäs [S] 190 H6
Vannes [F] 40 D5
Vansbro [S] 172 G4
Vanse [N] 164 C5
Vantaa / Vanda [FIN] 176 H4
Vanttauskoski [FIN] 196 D8
Vanvik [N] 164 C1
Vanvikan [N] 190 B6
Vanyarc [H] 64 D5
Vara [S] 166 E6
Varabla [EST] 200 D3
Varades [F] 40 G6
Varakļāni [LV] 200 F5
Varallo [I] 70 E4
Varanava [BY] 202 G6
Varangerbotn [N] 196 E2
Varaždin [HR] 74 F4
Varaždinske Toplice [HR] 74 F4
Varazze [I] 108 H3
Varberg [S] 160 H4
Varbola [EST] 200 D2
Varces [F] 68 H5
Várda [GR] 136 B1
Varde [DK] 156 B2
Vardim [BG] 148 C2
Vårdö [FIN] 176 B5
Vardø [N] 196 F2
Várdomb [H] 76 C4
Varduva [LT] 202 D3
Varel [D] 18 C4
Vareleİ [GR] 134 D5
Varena [LT] 24 G2
Varengeville–sur–Mer [F] 28 C4
Varenna [I] 70 G3
Varennes–en–Argonne [F] 44 D3
Varennes–sur–Allier [F] 56 D6
Vareš [BIH] 154 D4
Varese [I] 70 F4
Varese Ligure [I] 110 C3
Vårgårda [S] 162 B1
Vargön [S] 166 D5
Varhaug [N] 164 A4
Vári [GR] 138 D2
Varilhes [F] 84 H5
Váris [GR] 128 F6
Várkiza [GR] 136 H1
Varmahlíð [IS] 194 D3
Värmdö [S] 168 E3
Värmlandsbro [S] 166 E3
Värmskog [S] 166 E2
Varna [BG] 148 F3
Varna [YU] 154 F3
Värnamo [S] 162 D4
Varnany [BY] 202 H5
Varnhem [S] 166 F5
Varniai [LT] 202 E4
Varnja [EST] 200 F2
Varnsdorf [CZ] 48 G1
Városföld [H] 76 D3
Varovnik [BG] 148 F5
Varpaisjärvi [FIN] 198 F6
Várpalota [H] 76 B2
Varpanen [FIN] 178 C1

Varparanta [FIN] 188 E4
Várpslőd [H] 74 H2
Värriö [FIN] 196 E6
Vars [F] 108 E2
Vårșand [RO] 76 G3
Varsi [I] 110 C3
Varsseveld [NL] 16 F6
Vartdal [N] 180 C4
Vârtoapele [RO] 148 B1
Vârtopu [RO] 150 F1
Värtsilä [FIN] 188 G3
Varvara [BG] 148 A6
Varvara [BG] 148 G5
Varvará [GR] 130 C4
Varzi [I] 110 B2
Varzy [F] 56 E3
Vasa / Vaasa [FIN] 186 B2
Vasalemma [EST] 200 D1
Vasankari [FIN] 198 C5
Vasarapera [FIN] 196 F8
Vásárosnamény [H] 206 B3
Väse [S] 166 F3
Vasiliká [GR] 136 C2
Vasiliká [GR] 134 B3
Vasiliká [GR] 130 B5
Vasilikí [GR] 132 C5
Vasilikó [GR] 134 B5
Vasilikós [GR] 136 B2
Vasilishki [BY] 24 H3
Vasilkov [UA] 206 E2
Vaskelovo [RUS] 200 H6
Vaskelovo [RUS] 178 H3
Vaskio [FIN] 176 E4
Vaskivesi [FIN] 186 D5
Vasknarva [EST] 200 G2
Vasles [F] 54 E4
Vaslui [RO] 206 D5
Vassarás [GR] 136 E3
Vassbø [N] 164 B4
Vassbotten [S] 166 C4
Vassenden [N] 180 C6
Vassilítsi [GR] 136 D5
Vassmolösa [S] 162 F5
Vassy [F] 26 E4
Västansfors [S] 168 A1
Västemyrriset [S] 190 G5
Västerås [S] 168 B2
Västergärn [S] 168 F5
Västerhaninge [S] 168 E3
Västerrottna [S] 166 E1
Västervik [S] 162 G2
Vasto [I] 116 E5
Vasvár [H] 74 G2
Vasylivka [UA] 206 H4
Vát [H] 74 G1
Vatan [F] 54 H3
Vaterá [GR] 134 G3
Vathí [GR] 144 C6
Vathí [GR] 138 H4
Vathílakos [GR] 130 D2
Vathiý [GR] 134 B5
Vathýpetrou [GR] 140 E5
Vatland [N] 164 C5
Vatne [N] 164 D4
Vatne [N] 180 D3
Vatne [N] 164 B4
Vatnstraum [N] 164 E5
Vatólakkos [GR] 128 E6
Vatoúsa [GR] 134 G2
Vatra Dornei [RO] 206 C4
Vau [P] 94 B5
Vauclaix [F] 56 E3
Vaucouleurs [F] 44 D5
Vau i Dejës [AL] 128 B1
Vauldalen [N] 182 D3
Vauvenargues [F] 108 B4
Vauvert [F] 106 F4
Vauville [F] 26 D1
Vauvillers [F] 58 B3
Vawkavysk [BY] 24 G5
Vaxholm [S] 168 E3
Växjö [S] 162 E4
Våxtorp [S] 162 B6
Väylä [FIN] 196 D4
Vayrac [F] 66 H4
V. Bodarna [S] 160 H1
Veberöd [S] 158 C3
Veblungsnes [N] 180 E3
Vechta [D] 18 C6
Vecinos [E] 88 B3

Vecpiebalga [LV] 200 F5
Vecsés [H] 76 C1
Vecumnieki [LV] 200 E5
Vedavågen [N] 164 A2
Vedbaek [DK] 156 G2
Veddige [S] 160 H3
Vedea [RO] 148 C2
Vedelago [I] 72 E5
Vedersø Klit [DK] 160 B5
Vedum [S] 166 E6
Veendam [NL] 16 H2
Veenendaal [NL] 16 E5
Veere [NL] 16 B6
Vega de Espinareda [E] 78 F4
Vega de los Árboles [E] 96 G4
Vegadeo [E] 78 F2
Vega de Pas [E] 82 F3
Vega de Valcarce [E] 78 E4
Vegårshei [N] 164 F4
Vegas de Coria [E] 88 B4
Vegas del Condado [E] 78 H5
Vegger [DK] 160 D4
Veggli [N] 170 F5
Veghel [NL] 16 E6
Veglie [I] 122 G5
Vegusdal [N] 164 E4
Vehkajärvi [FIN] 176 G1
Vehmaa [FIN] 176 D4
Vehu [FIN] 186 E3
Veidnesklubben [N] 196 C2
Veinge [S] 162 B5
Veitshöchheim [D] 46 E4
Vejano [I] 114 H4
Vejbystrand [S] 162 B6
Vejen [DK] 156 B2
Vejer de la Frontera [E] 100 F5
Vejers Strand [DK] 156 A2
Vejle [DK] 156 C2
Vejprty [CZ] 48 D2
Velagiói [BIH] 154 B3
Vela Luka [HR] 152 A3
Velanídia [GR] 136 F5
Velbert [D] 30 H3
Velburg [D] 46 H6
Velbuzhdki Prolaz (Velbuzhdki Pateka) [Eur.] 150 E6
Veldemelen [N] 190 C5
Velden [A] 74 B3
Velden [D] 60 F4
Velden [D] 46 H4
Veldhoven [NL] 30 E2
Velebit [YU] 76 E5
Velefique [E] 102 G4
Velēna [LV] 200 F4
Velenje [SLO] 74 D4

Velešín [CZ] 62 C2
Velešta [MK] 128 D3
Velestínon [GR] 132 H2
Vélez–Blanco [E] 102 H3
Vélez–Málaga [E] 102 C5
Vélez–Rubio [E] 102 H3
Veličani [BIH] 152 C3
Velika Brusnica [BIH] 154 D2
Velika Drenova [YU] 150 C3
Velika Gorica [HR] 74 E6
Velika Kladuša [HR] 112 H2
Velika Kruša [YU] 150 B6
Velika Plana [YU] 150 C1
Velike Lašče [SLO] 74 C5
Velikije Luki [RUS] 204 C4
Veliki Preslav [BG] 148 E3
Veliki Šiljegovac [YU] 150 D3
Veliki Zdenci [HR] 74 G6
Veliko Orašje [YU] 150 C1
Veliko Türnovo [BG] 148 C3
Veli Losinj [HR] 112 E4
Velingrad [BG] 150 G6
Velipojë [AL] 128 A1
Veliz [RUS] 204 C4
Veljun [HR] 112 G2
Velká Bíteš [CZ] 50 B6
Velká Hled'sebe [CZ] 48 C4
Velká nad Veličkou [CZ] 62 H2
Velké Brezno [CZ] 48 F2
Velké Kapušany [SK] 64 H3
Velké Karlovice [CZ] 50 E6
Vel'ké Leváre [SK] 62 G3
Velké Losiny [CZ] 50 C4
Velké Meziříčí [CZ] 50 B6
Velké Němčice [CZ] 62 F2
Vel'ke Ripňany [SK] 64 A3
Vel'ké Uherce [SK] 64 B3
Velkua [FIN] 176 D4
Velký Folkmar [SK] 64 F2
Vel'ký Krtíš [SK] 64 D4
Vel'ký Meder [SK] 64 A5
Velký Újezd [CZ] 50 D5
Velletri [I] 116 A6
Vellinge [S] 158 B3
Velp [NL] 16 F5
Velpke [D] 34 A2
Vel. Trnovac [YU] 150 D5
Veltrusy [CZ] 48 F3
Velušina [MK] 128 E4
Velvary [CZ] 48 F3
Velvendós [GR] 128 F5
Velyka Lepetykha [UA] 206 G4
Velykyi Bereznyi [UA] 206 B3

Vemb [DK] 160 B5
Vemdalen [S] 182 F4
Vemhån [S] 182 G5
Vemmelev [DK] 156 F3
Vemmenaes [DK] 156 E4
Vena [S] 162 F3
Venabu [N] 170 H1
Venaco [F] 114 B4
Venafro [I] 120 D1
Venaria [I] 70 D5
Venčane [YU] 150 B1
Vence [F] 108 E4
Venda Nova [P] 80 D3
Vendargues [F] 106 F4
Vendas de Galizes [P] 86 E2
Vendas Novas [P] 86 C6
Vendays–Montalivet [F] 66 C1
Vendel [S] 174 F5
Vendelsö [S] 168 E3
Vendeuvre [F] 44 B6
Vendôme [F] 42 D6
Veneheitto [FIN] 198 E4
Veneskoski [FIN] 186 C3
Venetpalo [FIN] 198 D5
Venets [BG] 148 E2
Venets [BG] 148 E4
Venevere [EST] 200 F2
Venézia [I] 72 E6
Venlo [NL] 30 F3
Vennesla [N] 164 D5
Vennesund [N] 190 C4
Venosa [I] 120 H3
Venray [NL] 30 F2
Vent [A] 72 C2
Venta de Arraco [E] 84 D4
Venta de los Santos [E] 96 G6
Venta del Pobre [E] 102 H5
Venta El Alto [E] 94 G5
Ventas de Huelma [E] 102 D4
Ventimíglia [I] 108 F4
Ventnor [GB] 12 H5
Ventosa de Pisuerga [E] 82 D5
Ventspils [LV] 200 B4
Venus [RO] 148 G1
Venzone [I] 72 G4
Vepsä [FIN] 198 D4
Vera [E] 102 H5
Vera [N] 190 C6
Vera de Bidasoa / Bera [E] 84 B2
Verbania–Pallanza [I] 70 F3
Verberie [F] 42 G2
Verbicaro [I] 120 H6
Verbier [CH] 70 D3

VENÉZIA

IHT

Vercelli [I] 70 E5
Verch. Oselki [RUS] 178 H4
Verdalsøra [N] 190 C6
Verden [D] 18 E6
Verdens Ende [N] 164 H3
Verdikoússa [GR] 132 F1
Verdun [F] 44 D4
Verfeil [F] 106 A3
Vergato [I] 110 F4
Vérgi [GR] 130 B3
Vergiate [I] 70 F4
Vergína [GR] 128 G5
Vergt [F] 66 F3
Verhnedneprovsk [UA] 206 G3
Verín [E] 78 D6
Verket [N] 164 H2
Verkhnyaya Tulivaara [RUS] 198 G5
Verl [D] 32 D3
Verma [N] 180 F4
Vermenton [F] 56 E2
Vermeş [RO] 76 H6
Vermiglio [I] 72 C4
Vermosh [AL] 150 A5
Vermuntila [FIN] 176 C3
Vernazza [I] 110 C4
Vernet [F] 84 H3
Vernet–les–Bains [F] 92 F1
Verneuil [F] 26 H5
Vernio [I] 110 F5
Vernon [F] 42 E2
Verny [F] 44 E4
Véroia [GR] 128 G5
Verolanuova [I] 72 A6
Veroli [I] 116 C6
Verona [I] 72 C6
Verrabotn [N] 190 B6
Verrès [I] 70 D4
Verrières–de–Joux [F] 58 B6
Versailles [F] 42 F3
Versmold [D] 32 D3
Versoix [CH] 70 B2
Verteillac [F] 66 E2
Vertou [F] 54 C1
Vertus [F] 44 B4
Verucchio [I] 110 H5
Verviers [B] 30 E5
Vervins [F] 28 G5
Verwood [GB] 12 G5
Verzuolo [I] 108 F2
Verzy [F] 44 B3
Vesanka [FIN] 186 G4
Vesanto [FIN] 186 G2
Vescovato [I] 110 D1
Vése [H] 74 G4
Veselí nad Lužnicí [CZ] 48 G6
Veselí nad Moravou [CZ] 62 H2
Veselinovo [BG] 148 E3
Veselinovo [UA] 206 F4
Veshchevo [RUS] 178 F3
Vesivehmaa [FIN] 178 A2
Vesjegonsk [RUS] 204 F2
Veskoniemi [FIN] 196 D4
Vesoul [F] 58 B3
Vessingebro [S] 162 B4
Vestbjerg [DK] 160 E3
Vestby [N] 166 B2
Vestbygd [N] 164 B5
Vesterby [DK] 156 F4
Vester Egense [DK] 156 D2
Vester Egesborg [DK] 156 F4
Vesterø Havn [DK] 160 F3
Vestervig [DK] 160 B4
Vestfossen [N] 164 G1
Vestmanna [DK] 160 A1
Vestmarka [N] 166 D1
Vestnes [N] 180 E3
Vestone [I] 72 B5
Vestre Gausdal [N] 170 H2
Vestre Jakobselv [N] 196 E2
Veszprém [H] 76 A2
Veszprémvarsány [H] 76 A1
Vésztő [H] 76 G2
Veteli [FIN] 186 D1

Vetlanda [S] 162 E3
Vetralla [I] 114 H4
Vetren [BG] 148 C4
Vetrino [I] 148 F2
Vetriolo Terme [I] 72 D4
Vetschau [D] 34 F4
Vetsikko [FIN] 196 D3
Vettasjärvi [S] 192 F6
Veules–les–Roses [F] 28 B4
Veulettes–sur–Mer [F] 26 H2
Veurne (Furnes) [B] 28 F1
Vevey [CH] 70 C1
Vévi [GR] 128 E4
Veynes [F] 108 C2
Veyrier [F] 70 B3
Vézelay [F] 56 E3
Vézelise [F] 44 E6
Vézénobres [F] 106 F3
Vezzano [I] 72 C4
Viadana [I] 110 E2
Viais [F] 54 B2
Viana do Alentejo [P] 94 D2
Viana do Bolo [E] 78 E6
Viana do Castelo [P] 78 A6
Vianden [L] 44 F2
Viane [F] 106 C3
Vianen [NL] 16 D5
Vianne [F] 66 E5
Vias [F] 106 E4
Viborg [DK] 160 D5
Vibo Valentia [I] 124 D6
Vibraye [F] 42 C5
Viby [DK] 156 G3
Vic [E] 92 E3
Vic [F] 68 D2
Vič [SLO] 74 C3
Viča [YU] 150 B3
Vicchio [I] 110 F5
Vicdessos [F] 84 H5
Vic–en–Bigorre [F] 84 F3
Vicenza [I] 72 D6
Vic–Fezensac [F] 84 F2
Vichy [F] 68 D1
Vickan [S] 160 G3
Vico [F] 114 A4
Vico del Gargano [I] 116 H6
Vico Equense [I] 120 E4
Vicovaro [I] 116 B5
Vic–sur–Aisne [F] 28 F6
Vic–sur–Cère [F] 68 B4
Victoria [M] 126 C5
Vidago [P] 80 E3
Vidamlya [BY] 38 G2
Viðareiði [DK] 160 B1
Vidauban [F] 108 D5
Viddalba [I] 118 D2
Vide [P] 86 F2
Videbæk [DK] 156 B1
Videle [RO] 206 C6
Videseter [N] 180 E5
Vidigueira [P] 94 D2
Vidin [BG] 150 E2
Vidlin [GB] 6 H3
Vidsel [S] 198 A3
Vidzy [BY] 202 H4
Viechtach [D] 48 D6
Vieki [FIN] 198 G6
Viekšniai [LT] 200 C6
Viella [E] 84 G5
Vielsalm [B] 30 E6
Vienenburg [D] 32 H3
Vienne [F] 68 F3
Vieremä [FIN] 198 E6
Viersen [D] 30 G3
Vieru [RO] 148 C2
Vierumäki [FIN] 178 B2
Vierzehnheiligen [D] 46 G3
Viesīte [LV] 200 E6
Viesites [LV] 200 E6
Vieste [I] 116 H6
Vietasbygget [S] 192 E5
Vietri di Potenza [I] 120 G4
Vietri sul Mare [I] 120 E4
Vietsiluoto [FIN] 198 C3
Vieux–Boucau–les–Bains [F] 66 A6
Vievis [LT] 202 G5

Vif [F] 68 H5
Vig [DK] 156 F2
Vigeland [N] 164 C6
Vigévano [I] 70 F5
Vígla [GR] 132 D3
Vignale Monferrato [I] 70 E6
Vignanello [I] 114 H4
Vigneulles [F] 44 E4
Vignola [I] 110 E3
Vignory [F] 44 C6
Vigo [E] 78 B4
Vigo di Fassa [I] 72 D3
Viguera [E] 90 B1
Vihantasalmi [FIN] 178 C1
Vihanti [FIN] 198 D4
Vihiers [F] 54 D2
Vihren [BG] 130 B1
Vihtari [FIN] 188 E3
Vihtasuo [FIN] 198 G6
Vihti [FIN] 176 G4
Vihtijärvi [FIN] 176 G4
Vihtiläjärvi [FIN] 186 C6
Viiala [FIN] 176 F2
Viinijärvi [FIN] 188 E2
Viinikoski [FIN] 198 E3
Viinistu [EST] 178 B6
Viitaperä [FIN] 186 F2
Viitaniemi [FIN] 188 D1
Viitasaari [FIN] 186 G2
Viitna [EST] 200 E1
Vijküla [EST] 200 D3
Vijterna [EST] 200 C2
Vik [IS] 194 C6
Vik [N] 170 C2
Vik [N] 190 C3
Vik [N] 164 E5
Vik [S] 158 D3
Vika [S] 174 C4
Vikajärvi [FIN] 196 D7
Vikane [N] 166 B3
Vikanes [N] 170 B3
Vikarbyn [S] 172 H3
Vikebukt [N] 180 E3
Vikedal [N] 164 B1
Viken [S] 156 H1
Vikersund [N] 170 G5
Vikeså [N] 164 B4
Vikmanshyttan [S] 174 C5
Vikran [N] 192 E2
Viktring [A] 74 B3
Viladamat [E] 92 G3
Vila de Rei [P] 86 D3
Vila do Bispo [P] 94 A5
Vila do Conde [P] 80 B3
Vilafamés [E] 98 F3
Vila Flor [P] 80 E4
Vilafranca de Bonany [E] 104 E5
Vilafranca del Maestrat / Villafranca del Cid [E] 98 F2
Vilafranca del Penedès [E] 92 D4
Vila Franca de Xira [P] 86 B5
Vila Fresca de Azeitão [P] 86 B6
Vilagarcía de Arousa [E] 78 B3
Vila Joiosa, la– / Villajoyosa [E] 104 E2
Vilaka [LV] 200 G4
Vila Mea [P] 80 E3
Vilamor [E] 84 G6
Vilamoura [P] 94 C5
Vilāni [LV] 200 F5
Vila Nogueira de Azeitão [P] 86 B6
Vilanova d'Alcolea [E] 98 G3
Vilanova de Arousa [E] 78 B3
Vila Nova de Cerveira [P] 78 A5
Vila Nova de Famalicão [P] 80 C3
Vila Nova de Foz Côa [P] 80 E5
Vila Nova de Gaia [P] 80 B4

Vilanova de la Barca [E] 90 H4
Vila Nova de Milfontes [P] 94 B3
Vila Nova de Ourém [P] 86 D3
Vila Nova de Paiva [P] 80 D5
Vila Nova de São Bento [P] 94 E3
Vilanova i la Geltrú [E] 92 D5
Vila Pouca de Aguiar [P] 80 D3
Vila Praia de Âncora [P] 78 A5
Vila Real [P] 80 D4
Vila Real de Santo António [P] 94 D5
Vilar Formoso [P] 86 H2
Vila–rodona [E] 92 C4
Vilarouco [P] 80 E5
Vila–seca [E] 92 C5
Vilassar de Mar [E] 92 E4
Vila Velha de Ródão [P] 86 E4
Vila Verde [P] 78 B6
Vila Verde da Raia [P] 80 E3
Vila Verde de Ficalho [P] 94 E3
Vila Viçosa [P] 86 E6
Vilches [E] 102 F1
Vildbjerg [DK] 160 C6
Vilémov [CZ] 48 H4
Vilhelmina [S] 190 F5
Vília [GR] 134 B6
Viljakkala [FIN] 186 D6
Viljandi [EST] 200 E3
Viljolahti [FIN] 188 E4
Vilkaviškis [LT] 24 E1
Vilkija [LT] 202 F5
Villablino [E] 78 G4
Villacañas [E] 96 G2
Villacarrillo [E] 102 F1
Villacastín [E] 88 E4
Villach [A] 74 A3
Villacidro [I] 118 C6
Villada [E] 82 C5
Villa del Prado [E] 88 E6
Villa del Río [E] 102 D1
Villadiego [E] 82 E5
Villadossola [I] 70 E3
Villa Estense [I] 110 G2
Villafranca del Bierzo [E] 78 F5
Villafranca del Cid / Vilafranca del Maestrat [E] 98 F2
Villafranca de los Barros [E] 94 G3
Villafranca di Verona [I] 110 E1
Villafranca Montes de Oca [E] 82 F6
Villafranca Piemonte [I] 70 D6
Villafranca Tirrena [I] 124 B7
Villafranco del Guadalquivir [E] 100 G2
Villafrati [I] 126 D2
Villafruela [E] 88 G1
Villaggio Mancuso [I] 124 E5
Villagrains [F] 66 C4
Villagrande Strisaili [I] 118 E5
Villaharta [E] 96 C6
Villahermosa [E] 96 G5
Villahoz [E] 88 G1
Villaines–la–Juhel [F] 26 F6
Villajoyosa / Vila Joiosa, la– [E] 104 E2
Villala [FIN] 188 F4
Villalba Alta [E] 78 E2
Villalba Baja [E] 88 F5
Villalba de Guardo [E] 82 C4
Villalba de la Sierra [E] 98 C2

Villalcázar de Sirga [E] 82 D5
Villalgordo del Marquesado [E] 98 A3
Villa Literno [I] 120 D3
Villalón de Campos [E] 82 C6
Villalpando [E] 82 B6
Villamañán [E] 82 B5
Villamanín de la Tercia [E] 78 H5
Villamanrique de la Condesa [E] 94 F6
Villamar [I] 118 C6
Villamartín [E] 100 G3
Villamartín de Campos [E] 82 C6
Villamassargia [I] 118 B7
Villamayor de Santiago [E] 96 H2
Villamediana de Iregua [E] 82 H6
Villa Minozzo [I] 110 D3
Villandraut [F] 66 D4
Villandry [F] 54 F2
Villanova d'Asti [I] 70 D6
Villanova Monteleone [I] 118 B3
Villanúa [E] 84 D5
Villanubla [E] 88 E1
Villanueva de Alcardete [E] 96 H3
Villanueva de Argaño [E] 82 E5
Villanueva de Cañedo [E] 80 H6
Villanueva de Córdoba [E] 96 C5
Villanueva de Gállego [E] 90 E3
Villanueva de Huerva [E] 90 E4
Villanueva del Aceral [E] 88 E3
Villanueva de la Fuente [E] 96 H5
Villanueva de la Jara [E] 98 B4
Villanueva de la Reina [E] 102 E1
Villanueva del Arzobispo [E] 102 G1
Villanueva de la Serena [E] 96 B3
Villanueva de la Sierra [E] 88 A4
Villanueva de la Vera [E] 88 C5
Villanueva del Campo [E] 82 B6
Villanueva del Duque [E] 96 C5
Villanueva del Fresno [E] 94 F2
Villanueva de los Castillejos [E] 94 E5
Villanueva de los Infantes [E] 96 G5
Villanueva de los Infantes [E] 98 F3
Villanueva del Rey [E] 96 B5
Villanueva del Río y Minas [E] 94 H5
Villanueva de San Carlos [E] 104 H5
Villanueva de Sigena [E] 90 G4
Villány [H] 76 B5
Villapalacios [E] 96 H6
Villapiana Scalo [I] 122 D6
Villa Potenza [I] 116 C1
Villaputzu [I] 118 E6
Villaquejida [E] 82 B5
Villarcayo [E] 82 F4
Villard–de–Lans [F] 68 G5
Villardebelle [F] 106 B5
Villar de Cantos [E] 98 B3
Villar de Ciervo [E] 80 E6
Villar de Domingo García [E] 98 B1

Villardefrades [E] 88 D1
Villar del Arzobispo [E] 98 E3
Villar del Pozo [E] 98 B5
Villar del Rey [E] 86 F6
Villarejo de Salvanés [E] 96 G1
Villares del Saz [E] 98 B2
Villargordo del Cabriel [E] 98 C4
Villaricos [E] 104 A5
Villarluengo [E] 98 F1
Villarmayor [E] 80 G6
Villarquemado [E] 98 D1
Villarramiel [E] 82 C6
Villarreal de San Carlos [E] 88 A6
Villarrobledo [E] 96 H4
Villarroya de la Sierra [E] 90 C4
Villarrubia de los Ojos [E] 96 F3
Villars [CH] 70 C2
Villars [F] 108 E4
Villars–les–Dombes [F] 68 G2
Villars–sur–Var [F] 108 E4
Villarta [E] 98 C4
Villarta de San Juan [E] 96 F3
Villasalto [I] 118 D6
Villasana de Mena [E] 82 F4
Villa San Giovanni [I] 124 C7
Villa Santa Maria [I] 116 D5
Villa Santina [I] 72 G4
Villaseco de los Gamitos [E] 80 G6
Villasimíus [I] 118 D7
Villasor [I] 118 C6
Villasrubias [E] 86 H3
Villastar [E] 98 D2
Villatobas [E] 96 G2
Villatoro [E] 82 E6
Villatoya [E] 98 C4
Villavelayo [E] 90 A1
Villaverde del Río [E] 94 H5
Villaviciosa [E] 96 C6
Villaviciosa [E] 82 C2
Villa Vomano [I] 116 C3
Villé [F] 58 D2
Villebois–Lavalette [F] 66 E2
Villedieu–les–Poêles [F] 26 D4
Ville–en–Tardenois [F] 44 B3
Villefagnan [F] 54 E5
Villefontaine [F] 68 G3
Villefort [F] 68 D6
Villefranche [F] 108 F4
Villefranche–d'Albigeois [F] 106 C2
Villefranche–de–Conflent [F] 92 F1
Villefranche–de–Lauragais [F] 106 A4
Villefranche–de–Lonchat [F] 66 E3
Villefranche–de–Panat [F] 106 D2
Villefranche–de–Rouergue [F] 66 H5
Villefranche–du–Périgord [F] 66 F4
Villefranche–sur–Cher [F] 54 H2
Villefranche–sur–Saône [F] 68 F2
Villel [E] 98 D2
Villemur [F] 106 A2
Villena [E] 104 D1
Villenauxe–la–Grande [F] 42 H5
Villeneuve [F] 66 H5
Villeneuve [F] 106 G3
Villeneuve–de–Berg [F] 68 E6
Villeneuve–de–Marsan [F] 66 C6

Villeneuve–l'Archevêque [F] 42 H6
Villeneuve–Loubet [F] 108 E4
Villeneuve–sur–Allier [F] 56 D5
Villeneuve–sur–Lot [F] 66 E5
Villeneuve–sur–Yonne [F] 42 G6
Villeréal [F] 66 F4
Villers [F] 26 G3
Villers–Bocage [F] 26 E3
Villers–Bretonneux [F] 28 E5
Villers–Cotterêts [F] 42 H3
Villersexel [F] 58 C4
Villers–le–Lac [F] 58 C5
Villers–St–Georges [F] 42 H4
Villerville [F] 26 G3
Villeta Barrea [I] 116 D6
Villingen [D] 58 F3
Villoldo [E] 82 C5
Villorba [I] 72 E5
Vilnius [LT] 202 G5
Vilppula [FIN] 186 E5
Vils [D] 60 H3
Vilsbiburg [D] 60 F3
Vilseck [D] 46 H5
Vilshofen [D] 60 H3
Vilsund [DK] 160 C4
Vilusi [YU] 152 D3
Viluste [EST] 200 F3
Vilyeyka [BY] 204 B5
Vilyki Mosty [UA] 52 H3
Vimianzo [E] 78 B2
Vimieiro [P] 86 D6
Vimioso [P] 80 G4
Vimmerby [S] 162 F2
Vimoutiers [F] 26 G4
Vimpeli [FIN] 186 D2
Vimperk [CZ] 62 A2
Vina [YU] 150 D4
Vinac [YU] 154 C4
Vinádio [I] 108 E3
Vinaixa [E] 92 C4
Vinaròs [E] 92 A6
Vinay [F] 68 G4
Vinça [F] 92 F1
Vinchiaturo [I] 120 E1
Vinci [I] 110 E5
Vindbyholt [DK] 156 G4
Vindelgransele [S] 190 G4
Vindeln [S] 190 H5
Vinderup [DK] 160 C5
Vindsvik [N] 164 C2
Vinga [RO] 76 G5
Vingåker [S] 168 B4
Vingnes [N] 172 B2
Vinhais [P] 80 F3
Vinica [MK] 128 G1
Viničani [MK] 128 F2
Vinishte [BG] 150 F3
Vinje [N] 164 E1
Vinje [N] 170 C3
Vinjeøra [N] 180 G2
Vinkovci [HR] 154 E1
Vinliden [S] 190 G5
Vinnytsia [UA] 206 D3
Vinogradov [UA] 206 B3
Vinon–sur–Verdon [F] 108 C4
Vinslöv [S] 158 D1
Vinsternes [N] 180 F1
Vinstra [N] 170 H1
Vintjärn [S] 174 D3
Vintrosa [S] 166 G3
Viñuelas [E] 88 G5
Vinuesa [E] 90 B2
Vinzelberg [D] 34 B2
Vipiteno / Sterzing [I] 72 D2
Vira [HR] 152 A2
Vire [F] 26 E4
Vireši [LV] 200 F4
Virgen [A] 72 F2
Virgen de la Cabeza [E] 96 E6
Virginia [IRL] 2 E5
Virieu [F] 68 G4
Virieu–le–Grand [F] 68 H3

Vīrkby / Virkkala [FIN] 176 G5
Virkkala / Vīrkby [FIN] 176 G5
Virklund [DK] 156 C1
Virmutjoki [FIN] 178 E1
Virojoki [FIN] 178 D3
Virolahti [FIN] 178 D3
Virovitica [HR] 74 H5
Virpazar [YU] 152 E5
Virrat [FIN] 186 D4
Virsbo [S] 168 B1
Virsbo bruk [S] 168 B1
Virserum [S] 162 F3
Virtaniemi [FIN] 196 E4
Virtasalmi [FIN] 188 D4
Virton [B] 44 E2
Virtsu [EST] 200 D3
Virttaa [FIN] 176 E3
Viru–Jaagupi [EST] 200 F1
Virvoru [RO] 150 F1
Visaginas [LT] 202 H4
Visbek [D] 18 C6
Visby [DK] 156 B4
Visby [S] 168 G4
Visé [B] 30 E4
Višegrad [BIH] 152 E1
Visegrád [H] 64 C5
Viseu [P] 80 C6
Vishnyeva [BY] 202 H6
Vishovgrad [BG] 148 C3
Visiedo [E] 90 D6
Vişina Veche [RO] 148 A2
Viskafors [S] 162 B2
Viskinge [DK] 156 F2
Vislanda [S] 162 D5
Visočka Ržana [YU] 150 E4
Viso del Marqués [E] 96 F5
Visoka [YU] 150 A3
Visoko [BIH] 154 D4
Visp [CH] 70 E2
Vissefjärda [S] 162 F5
Visselhövede [D] 18 E6
Vissenbjerg [DK] 156 D3
Vissiniá [GR] 128 E5
Visso [I] 116 B2
Vistheden [S] 198 A3
Vištytis [LT] 24 D2
Visuvesi [FIN] 186 E5
Visz [H] 76 A3
Vităneşti [RO] 148 C1
Vitanovac [YU] 150 B3
Vitebsk [BY] 204 C4
Vitemölla [S] 158 D2
Viterbo [I] 114 H4
Vithkuq [AL] 128 C5
Vitigudino [E] 80 F6
Vitina [BIH] 152 B2
Vitis [A] 62 D3
Vitkovo [YU] 150 C3
Vitolište [MK] 128 F3
Vitomirica [YU] 150 B5
Vitoria–Gasteiz [E] 82 G5
Vitré [F] 26 D6
Vitry–le–François [F] 44 C5
Vitsand [S] 172 E5
Vittangi [S] 192 F5
Vitteaux [F] 56 G3
Vittel [F] 58 B2
Vittjärn [S] 172 D5
Vittória [I] 126 F5
Vittoriosa [M] 126 C6
Vittório Véneto [I] 72 E5
Vittsjö [S] 162 C6
Viù [I] 70 D5
Vivario [F] 114 B4
Viveiro [E] 78 E1
Vivel del Río Martín [E] 90 E6
Viver [E] 98 E3
Viverone [I] 70 E5
Viviers [F] 68 F6
Vivikonna [EST] 200 F1
Vivonne [F] 54 E4
Vize [TR] 146 C2
Vizille [F] 68 H5
Vižinada [HR] 112 D1
Vizovice [CZ] 50 E6
Vizzavona [F] 114 B4
Vizzini [I] 126 F4
Vjazma [RUS] 204 E4

Vlaardingen [NL] 16 C5
Vlachiótis [GR] 136 E4
Vlachokerasiá [GR] 136 E3
Vlachovo Březí [CZ] 48 E6
Vladičin Han [YU] 150 D5
Vladimirescu [RO] 76 G4
Vlagtweed [NL] 16 H3
Vlas [BG] 148 F4
Vlasenica [BIH] 154 E4
Vlašim [CZ] 48 G5
Vlaşin [RO] 148 C1
Vlasina Okruglica [YU] 150 E5
Vlasotince [YU] 150 D4
Vlissingen [NL] 16 B6
Vlochós [GR] 132 F2
Vlorë [AL] 128 A6
Vlotho [D] 32 E2
Vlychó [GR] 132 D5
Vočin [HR] 74 H6
Vöcklabruck [A] 62 A5
Vodice [HR] 112 H6
Voditsa [BG] 148 D3
Vodňany [CZ] 48 F6
Vodnjan [HR] 112 D2
Vodskov [DK] 160 E3
Voe [GB] 6 G3
Voerså [DK] 160 E3
Vogatsikó [GR] 128 E5
Voghera [I] 70 F6
Vohburg [D] 60 E2
Vohenstrauss [D] 48 C5
Vohma [EST] 200 C3
Võhma [EST] 200 E2
Vöhringen [D] 60 B4
Void [F] 44 D5
Voinka [UA] 206 G5
Voiron [F] 68 H4
Voise [F] 42 E4
Võiske [EST] 200 D3
Voitsberg [A] 74 D2
Voix [F] 108 C3
Vojakkala [FIN] 176 G3
Vojčice [SK] 64 G3
Vojens [DK] 156 C3
Vojlovica [YU] 154 H2
Vojnič [HR] 112 H1
Vojnik [SLO] 74 D4
Vojtanov [CZ] 48 C3
Voknavolok [RUS] 198 G3
Voláda [GR] 140 H2
Vólakas [GR] 130 C2
Volary [CZ] 62 B2
Volda [N] 180 C4
Volders [A] 72 D1
Volendam [NL] 16 E4
Volimés [GR] 136 A2
Volissós [GR] 134 G4
Volkach [D] 46 F4
Völkermarkt [A] 74 C3
Völklingen [D] 44 G4
Volkmarsen [D] 32 E5
Volkovija [MK] 128 D2
Voločisk [UA] 206 C2
Volodymyr–Volyns'kyi [UA] 38 H6
Volokolamsk [RUS] 204 E4
Vólos [GR] 132 H2
Volosovo [RUS] 178 G6
Volosovo [RUS] 200 G2
Volovo [BG] 148 C2
Volpiano [I] 70 D5
Volterra [I] 114 F1
Voltri [I] 110 A3
Voltti [FIN] 186 C2
Volturara Appula [I] 120 F1
Volvic [F] 68 C2
Volyně [CZ] 48 E6
Vónitsa [GR] 132 D4
Võnnu [EST] 200 F3
Voorschoten [NL] 16 C4
Voorst [NL] 16 F5
Vopnafjörður [IS] 194 G4
Võrå / Vöyri [FIN] 186 B2
Vorau [A] 74 E1
Vorbasse [DK] 156 B2
Vorchdorf [A] 62 B5
Vörden [D] 32 D1
Vordernberg [A] 62 C6
Vorderriss [D] 60 D6
Vordingborg [DK] 156 F4

Vorë [AL] 128 B3
Voreppe [F] 68 H4
Vorey [F] 68 E4
Vorinó [GR] 128 F3
Vormsund [N] 172 C5
Vorožba [UA] 204 D4
Vorsfelde [D] 32 H2
Voskopojë [AL] 128 C5
Voss [N] 170 C3
Vossijatskoje [UA] 206 E3
Votice [CZ] 48 G5
Votonósi [GR] 132 D1
Vouillé [F] 54 E4
Voukoliés [GR] 140 B4
Voúla [GR] 136 G1
Vouliagméni [GR] 136 G1
Vourkári [GR] 138 C2
Vourvouroú [GR] 130 C5
Voutás [GR] 134 A4
Vouvant [F] 54 C3
Vouvray [F] 54 G2
Vouzela [P] 80 C5
Vouziers [F] 44 C3
Voves [F] 42 E5
Vovoússa [GR] 132 D1
Voxna [S] 174 C2
Voynitsa [RUS] 198 G3
Voznesensk [UA] 206 F4
Vrå [DK] 160 E3
Vrå [S] 162 C5
Vráble [SK] 64 B4
Vračev Gaj [YU] 154 H2
Vračevšnica [YU] 150 B2
Vrådal [N] 164 E2
Vrahnéika [GR] 132 F6
Vrahtháliosen [N] 164 E2
Vråliosen [N] 164 E2
Vrana [HR] 112 E3
Vranduk [BIH] 154 D4
Vranino [BG] 148 G2
Vranja [HR] 112 E1
Vranje [YU] 150 D5
Vranjska Banja [YU] 150 D5
Vranov [SK] 64 G2
Vranov nad Dyjí [CZ] 62 E2
Vransko [SLO] 74 C4
Vrástama [GR] 130 C5
Vratarnica [YU] 150 E2
Vratnica [MK] 150 C6
Vratno [HR] 74 E4
Vratsa [BG] 150 G3
Vražogrnac [YU] 150 E2
Vrbanja [HR] 154 E2
Vrbas [YU] 76 D6
Vrbaška [BIH] 154 C2
Vrbnica [YU] 150 B6
Vrbnik [HR] 112 F1
Vrbno pod Pradědem [CZ] 50 D3
Vrboska [HR] 152 A2
Vrbové [SK] 62 H3
Vrbovec [HR] 74 F5
Vrbovsko [HR] 112 F1
Vrchlabí [CZ] 50 A2
Vrčin [YU] 154 G3
Vreden [D] 16 G5
Vrees [D] 18 C5
Vrelo [HR] 112 G5
Vrena [S] 168 C4
Vresse [B] 44 D1
Vretstorp [S] 166 G4
Vrgorac [HR] 152 B2
Vrhnika [SLO] 74 B5
Vrhpolje [BIH] 154 B3
Vrigstad [S] 162 D3
Vrin [CH] 70 G1
Vrínena [GR] 132 H3
Vrissoúla [GR] 132 C3
Vrlika [HR] 154 A4
Vrnjačka Banja [YU] 150 C3
Vron [F] 28 D3
Vrondoú [GR] 128 G6
Vrontádos [GR] 134 G4
Vroomshoop [NL] 16 G4
Vrosína [GR] 132 C2
Vrouhás [GR] 140 F4
Vroutek [CZ] 48 E3

Vrpolje [HR] 112 H6
Vrpolje [HR] 154 D1
Vršac [YU] 206 A5
Vršani [BIH] 154 E2
Vrsar [HR] 112 D2
Vrška Cuka [YU] 150 E2
Vrsi [BIH] 154 A3
Vrútky [SK] 50 F6
Vrův [BG] 150 E1
Vrýses [GR] 140 C4
Vsetín [CZ] 50 E6
V. Torsas [S] 162 D5
Vučitrn [YU] 150 C5
Vučkovci [BIH] 154 D2
Vuckovica [YU] 150 B2
Vught [NL] 16 E6
Vüglevtsi [BG] 148 C4
Vukovar [HR] 154 E1
Vukovec [HR] 74 F5
Vulcăneşti [MD] 206 D5
Vülchedrüm [BG] 150 F2
Vülchidol [BG] 148 F2
Vuojärvi [FIN] 196 D7
Vuokatti [FIN] 198 F5
Vuolenkoski [FIN] 178 B2
Vuolijoki [FIN] 198 E5
Vuollerim [S] 198 A2
Vuonislahti [FIN] 188 F1
Vuontisjärvi [FIN] 192 G4
Vuoriniemi [FIN] 188 F5
Vuostimo [FIN] 196 E7
Vuotner [S] 190 H3
Vuotsino [FIN] 196 E7
Vuotso [FIN] 196 D5
Vuottolahti [FIN] 198 E5
Vürbitsa [BG] 148 E3
Vürshets [BG] 150 F3
Vyartsilya [RUS] 188 G3
Vybor [RUS] 200 H4
Vyborg [RUS] 178 F3
Vyerkhnyadzvinsk [BY] 204 B4
Vyra [RUS] 178 H6
Vyritsa [RUS] 178 H6
Vyshgorodok [RUS] 200 G4
Vyskatka [RUS] 200 G1
Vyškov [CZ] 50 C6
Vyšná Revúca [SK] 64 C2
Vyšné Raslavice [SK] 52 D6
Vyšni Voloček [RUS] 204 E3
Vysokaye [BY] 38 F2
Vysoké Mýto [CZ] 50 B4
Vyšší Brod [CZ] 62 B3
Vytína [GR] 136 D2

W

Waabs [D] 18 F1
Waalwijk [NL] 16 D6
Wabern [D] 32 E5
Wąbrzeźno [PL] 22 E5
Wąchock [PL] 38 B6
Wachow [D] 34 D2
Wächtersbach [D] 46 D2
Wackersdorf [D] 48 C5
Waddington [GB] 10 G5
Wadebridge [GB] 12 C4
Wädenswil [CH] 58 F5
Wadlew [PL] 36 G5
Wadowice [PL] 50 G4
Wagenfeld [D] 32 E1
Wageningen [NL] 16 E5
Waging [D] 60 G5
Wagrain [A] 72 G1
Wagrowiec [PL] 36 D1
Wahlwies [D] 58 G4
Wahrenholz [D] 32 H1
Waiblingen [D] 58 H1
Waidhaus [D] 48 C5
Waidhofen an der Thaya [A] 62 D3
Waidhofen an der Ybbs [A] 62 C5
Waidring [A] 60 F6
Wainfleet all Saints [GB] 10 G6
Waischenfeld [D] 46 G4
Wakefield [GB] 10 F4

Walbeck [D] 34 A2
Walberswick [GB] 14 H3
Wałbrzych [PL] 50 B2
Walchensee [D] 60 D6
Walchsee [A] 60 F5
Walcourt [B] 28 H4
Wałcz [PL] 22 A5
Wald [CH] 58 G5
Wald–angelloch [D] 46 C5
Waldböll [D] 32 C6
Waldeck [D] 32 E5
Waldenbuch [D] 58 H1
Waldenburg [D] 48 C1
Waldfischbach [D] 44 H4
Waldheim [D] 34 D6
Waldkirch [D] 58 E3
Waldkirchen [D] 62 A3
Waldkraiburg [D] 60 F4
Waldmünchen [D] 48 C5
Waldowice [PL] 34 H2
Waldsassen [D] 48 C4
Waldshut [D] 58 F4
Walenstadt [CH] 58 H6
Wallasey [GB] 10 D4
Walldorf [D] 46 C5
Walldürn [D] 46 D4
Wallenfels [D] 46 H3
Wallersdorf [D] 60 G3
Wallerstein [D] 60 C2
Wallingford [GB] 14 D3
Walls [GB] 6 G4
Wallsbüll [D] 156 B4
Walsall [GB] 10 E6
Walsrode [D] 18 E6
Walten [GB] 6 F3
Walton–on–the–Naze [GB] 14 G4
Waltrop [D] 30 H2
Wambierzyce [PL] 50 B2
Wanderup [D] 18 E1
Wanfried [D] 32 G5
Wangen [D] 60 B5
Wangenbourg [F] 44 G6
Wangerooge [D] 18 C3
Wängi [CH] 58 G5
Wankendorf [D] 18 G2
Wantage [GB] 12 H3
Wanzleben [D] 34 B3
Warburg [D] 32 E4
Wardenburg [D] 18 C5
Ware [GB] 14 E3
Waregem [B] 28 G2
Wareham [GB] 12 G5
Waremme [B] 30 E4
Waren [D] 20 C4
Warendorf [D] 32 D3
Warin [D] 20 A4
Warka [PL] 38 C4
Warkworth [GB] 8 G5
Warlubie [PL] 22 E4
Warmbad Villach [A] 72 H3
Warmensteinach [D] 46 H4
Warminster [GB] 12 G4
Warnemünde [D] 20 B3
Warnsveld [NL] 16 F5
Warrenpoint [GB] 2 G4
Warrington [GB] 10 D4
Warsop [GB] 10 F5
Warstein [D] 32 D4
Warszawa [PL] 38 B3
Warta [PL] 36 F4
Warta Bolesławiecka [PL] 36 A6
Warth [A] 72 B1
Wartha [D] 32 G6
Warwick [GB] 12 H2
Wasbister [GB] 6 G1
Wasdale Head [GB] 10 D1
Washington [GB] 8 G6
Wasilków [PL] 24 G5
Wąsosz [PL] 36 C5
Wasselonne [F] 44 G6
Wassen [CH] 70 F1
Wassenaar [NL] 16 C4
Wassenberg [D] 30 F4
Wasseralfingen [D] 60 C2
Wasserbillig [L] 44 F2
Wasserburg [D] 60 F4
Wassertrüdingen [D] 46 F6
Wassy [F] 44 C5
Wasungen [D] 46 F1
Watchet [GB] 12 E3

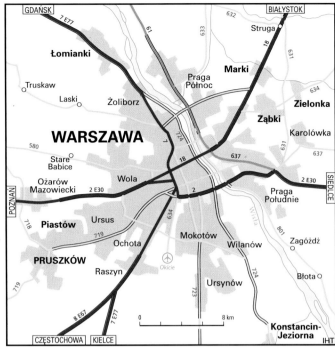

WARSZAWA

Łomianki · Truskaw · Laski · Żoliborz · Praga Północ · Marki · Zielonka · Ząbki · Karolówka · Stare Babice · Wola · Ożarów Mazowiecki · Piastów · Ursus · Ochota · Mokotów · Wilanów · Zagóżdż · PRUSZKÓW · Raszyn · Ursynów · Błota · Konstancin-Jeziorna

GDAŃSK · BIAŁYSTOK · POZNAŃ · SIEDLCE · CZĘSTOCHOWA · KIELCE

Waterford / Portlairge [IRL] 4 E5	Weiz [A] 74 D2	West Bromwich [GB] 10 E6
Watergrasshill [IRL] 4 D5	Wejherowo [PL] 22 D2	Westbury [GB] 12 G4
Waterloo [B] 30 C4	Welden [D] 60 C3	West Calder [GB] 8 E3
Waterlooville [GB] 12 H5	Wełdkowo [PL] 22 A3	Westende-Bad [B] 28 F1
Waterville [IRL] 4 A4	Well [NL] 30 F2	Westendorf [A] 60 F6
Watford [GB] 14 E4	Wellaune [D] 34 D5	Westenholz [D] 18 F6
Watten [F] 14 H6	Welle [D] 18 F5	Westensee [D] 18 F2
Wattens [A] 72 D1	Wellesbourne [GB] 12 H2	Westerdale [GB] 6 F3
Watton [GB] 14 G2	Wellin [B] 30 D6	Westerdale [GB] 10 G2
Wattwil [CH] 58 G5	Wellingborough [GB] 14 E2	Westerham [GB] 14 E5
Waulsort [B] 30 D6	Wellington [GB] 12 F4	Westerhever [D] 18 D2
Wavre [B] 30 D4	Wells [GB] 12 F4	Westerholt [D] 18 B3
Waxweiler [D] 44 F1	Wells [GB] 12 F1	Westerland [D] 156 A4
Wda [PL] 22 D4	Wells-next-the-Sea [GB] 10 H6	Westerlo [B] 30 D3
Wdzydze [PL] 22 D3	Wels [A] 62 B4	Westerstede [D] 18 C4
Węchadłów [PL] 52 B2	Welsberg / Monguelfo [I] 72 E3	Westkapelle [NL] 16 B6
Wedel [D] 18 F4	Welschofen / Nova Levante [I] 72 D3	West Kilbride [GB] 8 C3
Weener [D] 18 B5	Welshpool [GB] 10 C5	
Weert [NL] 30 E3	Weltenburg [D] 60 E2	
Weesen [CH] 58 G6	Welton [GB] 8 E6	
Weeze [D] 30 F2	Welwyn Garden City [GB] 14 E3	
Wegberg [D] 30 F3	Welzheim [D] 60 B2	
Weggis [CH] 58 F6	Wem [GB] 10 D5	
Węgliniec [PL] 34 H6	Wembury [GB] 12 D5	
Węgorzewo [PL] 24 C2	Wemding [D] 60 D2	
Węgorzyno [PL] 20 G5	Wemperhaardt [L] 30 F6	
Węgrów [PL] 38 D2	Wendover [GB] 14 D3	
Wegscheid [D] 62 A3	Wenecja [PL] 36 D1	
Wehr [D] 58 E4	Wengen [CH] 70 E1	
Wehr [D] 30 H6	Wenns [A] 72 C1	
Weichshofen [D] 60 F3	Wenvoe [B] 30 D5	
Weida [D] 48 C1	Weppersdorf [A] 62 F6	
Weiden [D] 48 C4	Werben [D] 34 C1	
Weidenberg [D] 46 H4	Werbomont [B] 30 E5	
Weigetschlag [A] 62 B3	Werdau [D] 48 C2	
Weikersheim [D] 46 E5	Werder [D] 34 D2	
Weil [D] 58 G1	Werdohl [D] 32 C5	
Weilburg [D] 46 C2	Werfen [A] 60 G6	
Weilheim [D] 60 D5	Werl [D] 32 C4	
Weimar [D] 32 D6	Werlte [D] 18 B6	
Weimar [D] 34 A6	Wermelskirchen [D] 30 H4	
Weinfelden [CH] 58 G4	Wernberg [D] 48 C5	
Weingarten [D] 60 B5	Werne [D] 32 C4	
Weinheim [D] 46 C4	Werneck [D] 46 E3	
Weinsberg [D] 46 D5	Werneuchen [D] 34 F2	
Weismain [D] 46 G3	Wernigerode [D] 32 H4	
Weissbriach [A] 72 G3	Wertach [D] 60 C5	
Weissenbach [A] 60 C6	Wertheim [D] 46 D4	
Weissenburg [D] 46 G6	Werther [D] 32 D3	
Weissenfels [D] 34 C6	Wertingen [D] 60 C3	
Weissenhorn [D] 60 B3	Wesel [D] 30 G2	
Weissenkirchen [A] 62 D4	Wesenberg [D] 20 C5	
Weissensee [D] 32 H5	Wesendorf [D] 32 H1	
Weissenstadt [D] 48 B3	Wesselburen [D] 18 E2	
Weisskirchen [A] 74 C2	Wessobrunn [D] 60 D5	
Weisswasser [D] 34 G5	West Bridgford [GB] 10 F5	
Weitendorf [D] 20 B3		
Weitra [A] 62 C3		

West Linton [GB] 8 E4	Wiehe [D] 34 B5	Willebroek [B] 30 C3
West Lulworth [GB] 12 G5	Wiek [D] 20 D1	Willemstad [NL] 16 C6
West Mersea [GB] 14 F4	Większyce [PL] 50 E3	Willerby [GB] 10 G4
Weston-super-Mare [GB] 12 F3	Wielbark [PL] 22 H5	Willingen [D] 32 D5
Westport [IRL] 2 C4	Wieleń [PL] 36 B1	Willisau [CH] 58 E5
West Sandwich [GB] 6 H3	Wielichowo [PL] 36 B3	Wilmslow [GB] 10 E4
West-Terschelling [NL] 16 E1	Wieliczka [PL] 52 A4	Wilnsdorf [D] 32 C6
Westward Ho! [GB] 12 D3	Wieliczki [PL] 24 D3	Wilster [D] 18 E3
West Wittering [GB] 14 D5	Wielogłowy [PL] 52 B5	Wilton [GB] 12 G4
Wetheral [GB] 8 E6	Wielowieś [PL] 50 F2	Wiltz [L] 44 E2
Wetherby [GB] 10 F3	Wieluń [PL] 36 F6	Wimborne Minster [GB] 12 G5
Wetter [D] 30 H3	Wien [A] 62 F4	Wimereux [F] 14 G6
Wetteren [B] 28 H2	Wiener Neustadt [A] 62 F5	Wincanton [GB] 12 G4
Wettringen [D] 16 H5	Wienhausen [D] 32 G1	Winchcombe [GB] 12 H2
Wetzikon [CH] 58 G5	Wierden [NL] 16 G4	Winchelsea [GB] 14 F6
Wetzlar [D] 46 C1	Wieruszów [PL] 36 E6	Winchester [GB] 12 H4
Wexford / Loch Garman [IRL] 4 F5	Wierzbica [PL] 38 B5	Windeck [D] 32 C6
Weyer-Markt [A] 62 C5	Wierzchowo [PL] 22 B4	Windermere [GB] 10 D2
Weyhausen [D] 32 G1	Wierzchucino [PL] 22 D1	Windisch [D] 48 C4
Weymouth [GB] 12 F5	Wies [D] 60 D5	Windischgarsten [A] 62 B6
Weyregg [A] 62 A5	Wiesau [D] 48 C4	Windsbach [D] 46 G5
Whaw [GB] 10 E2	Wieselburg [A] 62 D4	Windsor [GB] 14 D4
Wheddon Cross [GB] 12 E3	Wiesenburg [D] 34 C3	Winkleigh [GB] 12 E4
Whitby [GB] 10 G2	Wiesentheid [D] 46 F4	Winklern [A] 72 G2
Whitchurch [GB] 10 D5	Wiesloch [D] 46 C5	Winnenden [D] 60 A2
Whitegate [IRL] 4 D5	Wiesmath [A] 62 F6	Winnica [PL] 38 B2
Whitehall [GB] 6 G2	Wiesmoor [D] 18 C4	Winnigstedt [D] 32 H3
Whitehaven [GB] 8 D6	Wietze [D] 32 G1	Winnweiler [D] 46 B4
Whitehead [GB] 2 H3	Wigan [GB] 10 D4	Winschoten [NL] 16 H2
Whithorn [GB] 8 C5	Wigston Magna [GB] 10 F6	Winsen [D] 18 G5
Whiting Bay [GB] 8 C3	Wigton [GB] 8 E6	Winsen [D] 32 G1
Whitley Bay [GB] 8 G6	Wigtown [GB] 8 C5	Winsford [GB] 10 D4
Whitstable [GB] 14 F5	Wijhe [NL] 16 F4	Wińsko [PL] 36 C5
Whittlesey [GB] 14 F2	Wil [CH] 58 G5	Winslow [GB] 14 D3
Wiartel [PL] 24 C4	Wilczkowo [PL] 22 G3	Winsum [NL] 16 G2
Wick [GB] 6 F3	Wilczyska [PL] 52 C5	Winterberg [D] 32 D5
Wickham Market [GB] 14 G3	Wildalpen [A] 62 C6	Winterbourne Abbas [GB] 12 F5
Wicklow [IRL] 4 G4	Wildbad [D] 58 G1	
Wicko [PL] 22 C1	Wildenrath [D] 30 F4	Winterfeld [D] 34 B1
Widawa [PL] 36 F5	Wildeshausen [D] 18 D6	Wintermoor [D] 18 F5
Widnes [GB] 10 D4	Wildhaus [CH] 58 H5	Winterswijk [NL] 16 G5
Widoma [PL] 52 A3	Wildon [A] 74 D3	Winterthur [CH] 58 G4
Więcbork [PL] 22 C5	Wilfersdorf [A] 62 F3	Wintringham [GB] 10 G3
Wiedenbrück [D] 32 D3	Wilga [PL] 38 C4	Wipperfürth [D] 30 H4
Wiefelstede [D] 18 C5	Wilhelmsburg [A] 62 D5	Wippra [D] 34 A4
	Wilhelmshaven [D] 18 C4	Wisbech [GB] 14 F2
	Wilhering [A] 62 B4	Wischhafen [D] 18 E3
	Wilków [PL] 38 B4	Wisełka [PL] 20 F3

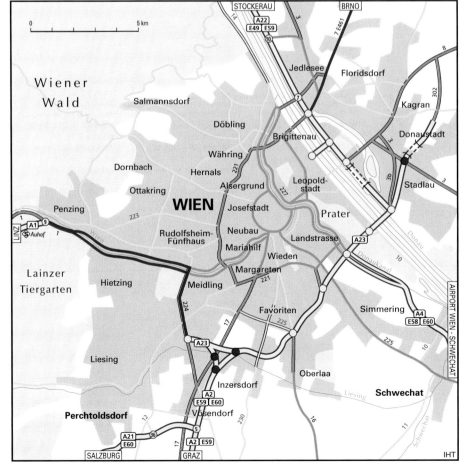

WIEN

Wiener Wald · Jedlesee · Floridsdorf · Salmannsdorf · Döbling · Kagran · Brigittenau · Donaustadt · Währing · Dornbach · Hernals · Leopold-stadt · Stadlau · Ottakring · Alsergrund · Penzing · Josefstadt · Prater · Rudolfsheim-Fünfhaus · Neubau · Landstrasse · Mariahilf · Wieden · Lainzer Tiergarten · Hietzing · Margareten · Meidling · Favoriten · Simmering · Liesing · Oberlaa · Schwechat · Inzersdorf · Perchtoldsdorf · Vösendorf

STOCKERAU · BRNO · LINZ · Auhof · AIRPORT WIEN - SCHWECHAT · SALZBURG · GRAZ

IHT

Wishaw [GB] 8 D3
Wiskitki [PL] 38 A3
Wisła [PL] 50 F5
Wišlica [PL] 52 B3
Wismar [D] 20 A3
Wišniowa [PL] 52 D4
Wissant [F] 14 G6
Wissembourg [F] 46 B6
Wissen [D] 32 C6
Wisznice [PL] 38 F4
Witham [GB] 14 F4
Witheridge [GB] 12 E4
Withernsea [GB] 10 H4
Witkowice [PL] 50 G1
Witkowo [PL] 36 E2
Witney [GB] 12 H3
Witnica [PL] 34 G2
Witostowice [PL] 50 C2
Wittdün [D] 18 D1
Witten [D] 30 H3
Wittenberge [D] 20 A6
Wittenburg [D] 18 H4
Wittichenau [D] 34 F5
Wittingen [D] 32 H1
Wittlich [D] 44 G2
Wittmund [D] 18 C4
Wittstock [D] 20 C5
Witzenhausen [D] 32 F5
Wiveliscombe [GB] 12 E4
Wiżajny [PL] 24 E2
Wizna [PL] 24 D5
Władysławowo [PL] 22 D1
Wleń [PL] 50 A1
Włocławek [PL] 36 G2
Włodawa [PL] 38 F4
Włoszczowa [PL] 50 H1
Woburn [GB] 14 E3
Wodzisław [PL] 52 B2
Wodzisław Šlaski [PL] 50 F4
Woerden [NL] 16 D5
Woerth [F] 44 H5
Wohlen [CH] 58 F5
Wojeiesów [PL] 50 B1
Wojnicz [PL] 52 C4
Woking [GB] 14 D4
Wokingham [GB] 14 D4
Wola Idzikowska [PL] 38 F6
Wola Rakowa [PL] 36 G4
Wolbórz [PL] 36 H5
Wolbrom [PL] 50 H3
Wołczyn [PL] 50 E1
Woldegk [D] 20 D5
Wolfach [D] 58 F2
Wolfegg [D] 60 B5
Wolfen [D] 34 C4
Wolfenbüttel [D] 32 H3
Wolfhagen [D] 32 E5
Wolframs-Eschenbach [D]
  46 F6
Wolfratshausen [D] 60 E5
Wolfsberg [A] 74 C3
Wolfsburg [D] 32 H2
Wolfstein [D] 44 H3
Wolgast [D] 20 E3
Wolhusen [CH] 58 E6
Wolin [PL] 20 F4
Wólka [PL] 52 A1
Wólka Dobryńska [PL] 38
  F3
Wólka Łabuńska [PL] 52 G2
Wolkenstein [D] 48 D2
Wolkenstein in Gardena /
  Selva di Val Gardena [I]
  72 E3
Wolkersdorf [A] 62 F4
Wöllersdorf [A] 62 E5
Wollin [D] 34 C3
Wolmirstedt [D] 34 B3
Wolnzach [D] 60 E3
Wołomin [PL] 38 C2
Wołów [PL] 36 C5
Wolsingham [GB] 8 F6
Wolsztyn [PL] 36 B3
Wolvega [NL] 16 F3
Wolverhampton [GB] 10 D6
Woodbridge [GB] 14 G3
Woodford [IRL] 2 C6
Woodstock [GB] 14 D3
Woolacombe [GB] 12 D3
Wooler [GB] 8 F5
Wooton Bassett [GB] 12 G3
Worb [CH] 58 D6

Worbis [D] 32 G5
Worcester [GB] 12 G2
Wörgl [A] 60 F6
Workington [GB] 8 D6
Worksop [GB] 10 F5
Workum [NL] 16 E2
Wörlitz [D] 34 C4
Wormerveer [NL] 16 D4
Wormhout [F] 14 H6
Worms [D] 46 C4
Worpswede [D] 18 E5
Wörrstadt [D] 46 B3
Wörth [D] 46 D4
Wörth [D] 60 F2
Wörth [D] 46 B6
Worthing [GB] 14 D5
Woźniki [PL] 50 G2
Wożuczyn [PL] 52 G2
Wragby [GB] 10 G5
Wrangle [GB] 10 G6
Wredenhagen [D] 20 C5
Wrexham [GB] 10 D5
Wriezen [D] 34 F2
Wróblew [PL] 36 F5
Wrocław [PL] 36 C6
Wronki [PL] 36 B2
Wroxham [GB] 14 G2
Wrząca Wielka [PL] 36 F3
Września [PL] 36 D3
Wschowa [PL] 36 B4
Wulfen [D] 30 H2
Wullowitz [A] 62 C3
Wünnenberg [D] 32 D4
Wunsiedel [D] 48 B3
Wunstorf [D] 32 F2
Wuppertal [D] 30 H3
Wurzbach [D] 48 B2
Würzburg [D] 46 E4
Wurzen [D] 34 D5
Wust [D] 34 C2
Wusterhausen [D] 34 D1
Wüstermarke [D] 34 E4
Wustrow [D] 20 C2
Wuustwezel [B] 30 D2
Wydminy [PL] 24 D3
Wygoda [PL] 52 D4
Wyk [D] 156 A5
Wymondham [GB] 14 G2
Wyrzysk [PL] 22 C6
Wyśmierzyce [PL] 38 B4
Wysokie Mazowieckie [PL]
  24 D6
Wysowa [PL] 52 C5
Wyszków [PL] 38 C2
Wyszogród [PL] 38 A2
Wyszyna [PL] 36 F3

Xàbia / Jávea [E] 104 F1
Xabier / Javier [E] 84 C4
Xanten [D] 30 G2
Xánthi [GR] 130 E2
Xàtiva [E] 98 E6
Xeraco [E] 98 F6
Xeresa [E] 98 E6
Xertigny [F] 58 C2
Xesta, Puerto de la- [E] 78
  E2
Xhoffraix [B] 30 F5
Xilopáriko [GR] 132 E2
Xiniáda [GR] 132 G3
Xíno Néro [GR] 128 F4
Xinzo de Limia / Ginzo de
  Limia [E] 78 C6
Xirokámbi [GR] 136 E4
Xirókambos [GR] 142 B2
Xixona / Jijona [E] 104 E2
Xodos / Chodos [E] 98 F2
Xubia [E] 78 D1
Xylaganí [GR] 130 F3
Xylókastro [GR] 132 H6

Yablanitsa [BG] 148 A4
Yağcılar [TR] 144 E1
Yagoda [BG] 148 C5

Yakoruda [BG] 150 G6
Yalakdere [TR] 146 F3
Yalıkavak [TR] 142 C2
Yalova [TR] 146 F3
Yalta [UA] 206 G6
Yamanlar [TR] 144 G4
Yambol [BG] 148 E5
Yamm [RUS] 200 G2
Yancıklar [TR] 146 C2
Yanguas [E] 90 C2
Yantarnyy [RUS] 22 G1
Yarbasan [TR] 144 F2
Yarcombe [GB] 12 F4
Yarımca [TR] 146 G3
Yarm [GB] 10 F2
Yarmouth [GB] 12 H5
Yasen [BG] 148 A3
Yasna Polyana [BG] 148 F5
Yassıören [TR] 146 E2
Yassıören [TR] 144 F1
Yatağan [TR] 142 D1
Yavorets [BG] 148 B4
Yavoriv [UA] 52 G3
Yaylabayır [TR] 144 E2
Yazıköv [TR] 142 C3
Ybbs an der Donau [A] 62
  D4
Ybbsitz [A] 62 C5
Ýdra [GR] 136 G3
Ydrefors [S] 162 F2
Yeadon [GB] 10 F3
Yecla [E] 104 D1
Yecla de Yeltes [E] 80 F6
Yeleğen [TR] 144 F4
Yelverton [GB] 12 D5
Yemel'yanovka [RUS] 198
  H5
Yemişendere [TR] 142 E1
Yemişli [TR] 144 F2
Yenice [TR] 146 C5
Yenice [TR] 144 F5
Yenice [TR] 146 D4
Yeniçiftlik [TR] 146 D3
Yenicöy [TR] 144 D3
Yenifoça [TR] 144 C3
Yenihisar [TR] 142 C2
Yeni Karpuzlu [TR] 130 H3
Yeniköy [TR] 146 E2
Yeniköy [TR] 146 C3
Yeniköy [TR] 130 H6
Yeniköy [TR] 144 F2
Yeniköy [TR] 146 F6
Yenikoy [TR] 146 D6
Yeniköy [TR] 146 G3
Yeniköy [TR] 146 F4
Yenipazar [TR] 144 E5
Yenipazar [TR] 146 H4
Yenişakran [TR] 144 C3
Yenişehir [TR] 144 F3
Yenişehir [TR] 146 G4
Yenne [F] 68 H3
Yeovil [GB] 12 F4
Yerkesik [TR] 142 E2
Yerville [F] 26 H3
Yesa / Esa [E] 84 C4
Yeşilçay [TR] 144 F2
Yeşilçay / Ağva [TR] 146
  G2
Yesilköy [TR] 144 F2
Yeşilova [TR] 144 H5
Yeşilyurt [TR] 144 F4
Yeşlköy [TR] 146 E3
Yeste [E] 102 H1
Yetholm [GB] 8 F4
Yevpatora [UA] 206 G5
Yiğitler [TR] 144 B1
Ylämaa [FIN] 178 E3
Yläne [FIN] 176 D3
Ylihärmä [FIN] 186 C2
Yli-Ii [FIN] 198 D3
Yli-Kärppä [FIN] 198 D2
Ylikiiminki [FIN] 198 D4
Yli-Lesti [FIN] 186 E1
Yli-Ii [FIN] 198 D3
Ylimarkku / Övermark [FIN]
  186 B4
Yli-Muonio [FIN] 192 G4
Yli-Nampa [FIN] 196 D7
Ylistaro [FIN] 186 C3
Ylitornio [FIN] 196 B8
Ylivieska [FIN] 198 D5

Ylöjärvi [FIN] 176 F1
Yngsjö [S] 158 D2
Yockenthwaite [GB] 10 E2
Yoğuntas [TR] 146 B1
Yolüstü [TR] 144 F5
Yordankino [BG] 150 G4
York [GB] 10 F3
Youghal [IRL] 4 D5
Youlgreave [GB] 10 E5
Yport [F] 26 G2
Yppäri [FIN] 198 C5
Ypres (Ieper) [B] 28 F2
Ýpso [GR] 132 B2
Ypsous [GR] 136 D2
Yset [N] 182 B4
Yssingeaux [F] 68 E4
Ystad [S] 158 D3
Yste brød [N] 164 B4
Ystradgynlais [GB] 12 E2
Ytre Arna [N] 170 B3
Ytre Enebakk [N] 166 B1
Ytterby [S] 160 G1
Ytterbyn [S] 198 C3
Ytterhogdal [S] 182 H5
Yttermalung [S] 172 F4
Yukhavichy [RUS] 200 H6
Yulga Urpala / Torf'anovka
  [RUS] 178 E3
Yundola [BG] 150 G6
Yunquera [E] 102 B4
Yuntdağ [TR] 144 C3
Yunuseli [TR] 146 F4
Yuratsishki [BY] 202 H6
Yürücekler [TR] 146 F5
Yverdon–les–Bains [CH] 58
  C6
Yvetot [F] 26 H3
Yvoir [B] 30 D5
Yvoire [F] 70 B2
Yxnerum [S] 168 B6

Z

Zaandam [NL] 16 D4
Žabalj [YU] 154 G1
Zabar [H] 64 E4
Žabari [YU] 150 C1
Zabierzów [PL] 50 H3
Zabki [PL] 38 B3
Zabkowice Šląskie [PL] 50
  C2
Zablače [HR] 112 H6
Žabljak [YU] 152 E2
Zabłudów [PL] 24 F6
Žabno [HR] 74 F5
Žabno [PL] 52 C3
Zabok [HR] 74 E5
Zabolottia [UA] 38 G4
Zabór [PL] 36 A4
Zăbrani [RO] 76 H5
Zábřeh [CZ] 50 C4
Zabrze [PL] 50 F3
Zabrzeź [PL] 52 B5
Zacháro [GR] 136 C3
Zadar [HR] 112 G5
Zadvarje [HR] 152 A2
Zadzyezhzha [BY] 200
  H6
Zafferana Etnea [I] 126
  G3
Zafirovo [BG] 148 E1
Zafra [E] 94 G3
Žaga [SLO] 72 H4
Żagań [PL] 34 H5
Zagare [LT] 200 D6
Zaglav [HR] 112 F5
Zaglavak [YU] 150 A2
Zagorá [GR] 132 H2
Zagórów [PL] 36 E3
Zagorye [RUS] 200 G1
Zagórz [PL] 52 E5
Zagreb [HR] 74 E6
Žagubica [YU] 150 D1
Zagvozd [HR] 152 B2
Zahara [E] 100 H3
Zahara de los Atunes [E]
  100 G5
Zahna [D] 34 D4
Zaiceva [LV] 200 G4

Zajas [MK] 128 D2
Zaječar [YU] 150 E2
Zakliczyn [PL] 52 C4
Zaklików [PL] 52 E1
Zakopane [PL] 50 H6
Zakroczym [PL] 38 B2
Zákros [GR] 140 H5
Zakrzewo [PL] 36 F1
Zákupy [CZ] 48 G2
Zákynthos [GR] 136 B2
Zalaapáti [H] 74 G3
Zalabaksa [H] 74 F3
Zalabér [H] 74 G2
Zalaegerszeg [H] 74 G3
Zalakomár [H] 74 G4
Zalalövö [H] 74 F3
Zalamea de la Serena [E]
  96 B4
Zalamea la Real [E] 94 F5
Zalaszántó [H] 74 G3
Zalaszentbalázs [H] 74 G3
Zălau [RO] 206 B4
Zaleščiki [UA] 206 C3
Zalewo [PL] 22 F4
Zalla [E] 82 G4
Zaltbommel [NL] 16 E6
Załuż [PL] 52 E5
Zalužnica [HR] 112 G3
Zamárdi [H] 76 A3
Zamarte [PL] 22 C4
Žamberk [CZ] 50 B4
Zambrana [E] 82 G5
Zambrów [PL] 24 D6
Zambujeira do Mar [P] 94
  B4
Zamora [E] 80 H5
Zamošč [PL] 52 F1
Zamošč [PL] 24 C6
Zamostne [PL] 22 D2
Zandvoort [NL] 16 D4
Zanglivéri [GR] 130 B4
Zaniemyšl [PL] 36 D3
Zante [LV] 200 C5
Zaorejas [E] 90 B5
Zaostrog [HR] 152 B3
Zapałów [PL] 52 F3
Zapfendorf [D] 46 G3
Zapolyarnyy [RUS] 196 F3
Zaporizhia [UA] 206 H3
Zaporozhskoye [RUS] 178
  H3
Záppeio [GR] 132 G2
Zapponeta [I] 120 H1
Zaprešič [HR] 74 E5
Zaprudy [BY] 38 H2
Zaragoza [E] 90 E4
Zárakes [GR] 134 D5
Zărand [RO] 76 H4
Zarasai [LT] 202 H4
Zarautz [E] 84 A2
Zaręby–Warchoły [PL] 38
  D1
Żarki [PL] 50 G2
Zárkos [GR] 132 F2
Zărneşti [RO] 206 C5
Žarnovica [SK] 64 B3
Żarnów [PL] 38 A6
Żarnowiec [PL] 50 H2
Zarós [GR] 140 E5
Żarów [PL] 50 B1
Zarrentin [D] 18 H4
Zarszyn [PL] 52 E5
Żary [PL] 34 H5
Zarza de Alange [E] 94 H2
Zarzadilla de Totana [E] 104
  B3
Zarza la Mayor [E] 86 G4
Zasa [LV] 200 F6
Zasieki [PL] 34 G4
Žaškov [UA] 206 E3
Žatec [CZ] 48 E3
Zator [PL] 50 G4
Zauchwitz [D] 34 D3
Zauczyn Poduchowny [PL]
  38 D3
Zavala [BIH] 152 C3
Zavet [BG] 148 D2
Zavidoviči [BIH] 154 D3
Zavlaka [YU] 154 F3
Zawada [PL] 36 A4
Zawadzkie [PL] 50 F2
Zawichost [PL] 52 D1

Zawidów [PL] 48 G1
Zawiercie [PL] 50 G2
Žažina [HR] 154 A1
Zbaszyń [PL] 36 B3
Zbąszynek [PL] 36 A3
Zblewo [PL] 22 D4
Zborov [SK] 52 D5
Zborowice [PL] 52 C4
Zbraslav [CZ] 48 F4
Zbraslavice [CZ] 48 H4
Zdar [CZ] 48 E3
Žd'ár nad Sázavou [CZ] 50
  B5
Zdiby [CZ] 48 F3
Zdice [CZ] 48 F4
Ždírec nad Doubrava [CZ]
  50 A5
Zdounky [CZ] 50 D6
Zdunje [MK] 128 D1
Zduńska Wola [PL] 36 F5
Zduny [PL] 36 D5
Zdziechowice [PL] 52 E1
Zdzieszowice [PL] 50 E3
Zebrák [CZ] 48 E4
Zebrzydowa [PL] 34 H6
Žednik [YU] 76 D5
Zeebrugge [B] 28 G1
Zefýría [GR] 138 D4
Żegiestów [PL] 52 C5
Zehdenick [D] 20 D6
Zeist [NL] 16 E5
Zeitz [D] 34 C6
Zelazno [PL] 22 D1
Zelechów [PL] 38 D4
Zelenika [YU] 152 D4
Zelenogorsk [RUS] 178 G4
Zelenogradsk [RUS] 202
  C5
Želetava [CZ] 50 A6
Železná Ruda [CZ] 48 D6
Železnik [YU] 154 G3
Železnogorsk [RUS] 204
  E6
Železný Brod [CZ] 48 H2
Željezovce [SK] 64 B5
Želin [SLO] 74 A5
Zelina [HR] 74 E5
Zèlio [GR] 132 H4
Zeliv [CZ] 48 H5
Żelkowo [PL] 22 C2
Zell [A] 62 A4
Zell [D] 44 G2
Zell [D] 58 E4
Zella–Mehlis [D] 46 G2
Zell am See [A] 72 F1
Zell am Ziller [A] 72 E1
Želnava [CZ] 62 B2
Zelów [PL] 36 G5
Zeltini [LV] 200 F4
Zeltweg [A] 74 C2
Zel'va [BY] 24 H5
Zelzate [B] 28 H1
Žemaičiu Naumiestis [LT]
  202 D5
Żembersee [SK] 64 C4
Zemblak [AL] 128 D4
Zeme [I] 70 F5
Zemen [BG] 150 F5
Zemite [LV] 200 C5
Zenica [BIH] 154 D4
Žepa [BIH] 154 E4
Zepče [BIH] 154 D3
Zerbst [D] 34 C3
Zerevna [BG] 148 D4
Zerf [D] 44 F3
Zerind [RO] 76 G3
Zermatt [CH] 70 D3
Zernez [CH] 72 B2
Zernien [D] 18 H6
Zerniki [PL] 36 C6
Zerqan [AL] 128 C2
Zestoa / Cestona [E] 84 A2
Zetel [D] 18 C4
Zeulenroda [D] 48 B2
Zeven [D] 18 E5
Zevenaar [NL] 16 F5
Zevenbergen [NL] 16 C6
Zevgaráki [GR] 132 E5
Zeybekçayırı [TR] 146 C6
Zeytindağı [TR] 146 E4
Zeytindağı [TR] 144 C3
Zgierz [PL] 36 G4

Zgórsko [PL] 52 C3
Zgorzelec [PL] 34 G6
Zhaludok [BY] 24 H4
Zhelenodorozhnyy [RUS] 24 B2
Zheleznitsa [BG] 150 F5
Zhovkva [UA] 52 H3
Zhuprany [BY] 202 H6
Zhydachiv [UA] 52 H5
Zhytomyr [UA] 206 E2
Ziákas [GR] 132 E1
Žiar nad Hronom [SK] 64 C3
Zicavo [F] 114 B5
Zickhusen [D] 20 A4
Zidani Most [SLO] 74 D5
Židlochovice [CZ] 62 F2
Ziębice [PL] 50 C2
Ziegenrück [D] 46 H2
Zielona Chocina [PL] 22 C4
Zielona Góra [PL] 34 H4
Zielonka [PL] 38 B3
Zieluń–Osada [PL] 22 G6
Zierikzee [NL] 16 B6
Ziersdorf [A] 62 E3
Zierzow [D] 20 A5
Ziesar [D] 34 C3
Ziethen [D] 20 D4
Žiežmariai [LT] 202 F5
Zijpe [NL] 16 C6
Žilina [SK] 50 F6
Zilupe [LV] 200 G5
Zimandu Nou [RO] 76 G4
Zimnicea [RO] 148 C2
Zimnitsa [BG] 148 E4
Zinal [CH] 70 D3
Zingst [D] 20 C2
Zinnowitz [D] 20 E3
Zinnwald–Georgenfeld [D] 48 E2
Zipári [GR] 142 C3
Zirc [H] 76 A2
Zirchow [D] 20 E4
Žiri [SLO] 74 B5
Zirl [A] 72 D1

Zíros [GR] 140 G5
Žirovnice [CZ] 48 G6
Zistersdorf [A] 62 F3
Žitište [YU] 154 G1
Žitkoviči [BY] 204 B6
Zitomisliči [BIH] 152 C2
Žitoradja [YU] 150 D4
Zítsa [GR] 132 C2
Zittau [D] 48 G1
Živaja [HR] 154 B1
Zivinice [BIH] 154 E3
Živogošče [HR] 152 B2
Zizers [CH] 70 H1
Zlatá Koruna [CZ] 62 B2
Zlatar [BG] 148 E3
Zlatar Bistrica [HR] 74 E5
Zlatarevo [GR] 128 H2
Zlatari [YU] 150 C3
Zlaté Hory [CZ] 50 D3
Zlaté Moravce [SK] 64 B4
Zlatitsa [BG] 148 A4
Zlatna Panega [BG] 148 A4
Zlatni Pyasŭtsi [BG] 148 G2
Zlatograd [BG] 130 E2
Žleby [CZ] 48 H4
Zliechov [SK] 64 B2
Zlín [CZ] 50 D6
Žljebovi [BIH] 154 E4
Žlobin [BY] 204 C6
Złocieniec [PL] 20 H5
Złoczew [PL] 36 F5
Zlonice [CZ] 48 F3
Zlot [YU] 150 D2
Złotoryja [PL] 36 B6
Złotów [PL] 22 B5
Złoty Stok [PL] 50 C3
Žlutice [CZ] 48 D3
Zlynka [RUS] 204 D6
Žmerinka [UA] 206 D3
Żmigród [PL] 36 C5
Žminj [HR] 112 D2
Znamenka [RUS] 204 E5
Znamenka [UA] 206 F3
Znamensk [RUS] 24 B1
Żnin [PL] 36 D1

Znojmo [CZ] 62 E3
Žodino [BY] 204 B5
Zoetermeer [NL] 16 C5
Zofingen [CH] 58 E5
Zogaj [AL] 150 B6
Zolder [B] 30 E4
Żółki [PL] 24 E5
Zołkiewka [PL] 38 E6
Zolotonoša [UA] 206 F2
Żółtki [PL] 24 E5
Zomba [H] 76 B4
Zóni [GR] 130 G1
Zonza [F] 114 B5
Zörbig [D] 34 C4
Zorge [D] 32 H4
Zorita [E] 96 B2
Zorneding [D] 60 E4
Zornitsa [BG] 148 E5
Żory [PL] 50 F4
Zossen [D] 34 E3
Zoutkamp [NL] 16 G2
Zoutleeuw [B] 30 D4
Zoúzouli [GR] 128 D6
Zovka [RUS] 200 G2
Žovten [UA] 206 E4
Zreče [SLO] 74 D4
Zrenjanin [YU] 154 G1
Zrze [YU] 150 B6
Zsadány [H] 76 G2
Zsana [H] 76 D4
Zschopau [D] 48 D2
Zubcov [RUS] 204 E4
Zubin Potok [YU] 150 B4
Zubiri [E] 84 B3
Zubrzyca Górna [PL] 50 H5
Zudar [D] 20 D2
Zuera [E] 90 E3
Zug [CH] 58 F5
Zuidhorn [NL] 16 G2
Zuidlaren [NL] 16 G2
Zújar [E] 102 F3
Żukowo [PL] 22 D2
Zülpich [D] 30 G5
Zumaia [E] 84 A2
Zumarraga [E] 82 H4

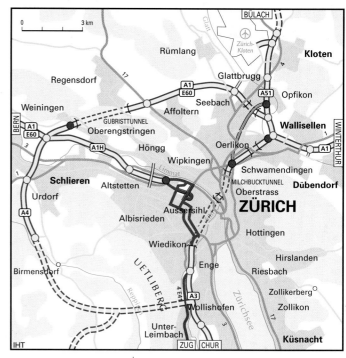

Zundert [NL] 30 D2
Zuoz [CH] 72 A3
Županja [HR] 154 E2
Žur [YU] 150 B6
Zuera [E]
Zürich [CH] 58 F5
Żurrieq [M] 126 C6
Zurzach [CH] 58 F4
Zusmarshausen [D] 60 C3
Züsow [D] 20 A3

Zutphen [NL] 16 F5
Zvarisht [AL] 128 C4
Zvezdel [BG] 130 F1
Zvezdets [BG] 148 F5
Zvolen [SK] 64 C3
Zvonce [YU] 150 E4
Zvornik [BIH] 154 E3
Zweibrücken [D] 44 G4
Zweisimmen [CH] 70 D1
Zwettl [A] 62 D3
Zwettl an der Rodl [A] 62 B3
Zwickau [D] 48 C2

Zwiefalten [D] 58 H3
Zwierzyniec [PL] 52 F2
Zwiesel [D] 60 H2
Zwijndrecht [NL] 16 D5
Zwingenberg [D] 46 D5
Zwoleń [PL] 38 C5
Zwolle [NL] 16 F4
Żychlin [PL] 36 G3
Żydowo [PL] 36 D2
Zyrardow [PL] 38 A3
Żywiec [PL] 50 G5
Żywocice [PL] 50 E3

1st edition January 2000

© Istituto Geografico De Agostini S.P.A. and
© Automobile Association Developments Ltd

Published by Istituto Geografico De Agostini S.P.A.
and Automobile Association Developments Limited whose registered office is Norfolk House, Priestly Road, Basingstoke,
Hampshire RG24 9NY. Registered number 1878835.

Published in the United States by IDG Books Worldwide, Inc.
An International Data Group Company 919 E. Hillsdale Blvd. Suite 400 Foster City, CA 94401.

ISBN 0.7645.6175.8

A CIP catalogue record for this book is available from The British Library.

Printed and bound in Italy by Printer Trento srl.

The contents of this atlas are believed to be correct at the time of the latest revision. However, the publishers cannot be held
responsible for loss occasioned to any person acting or refraining from action as a result of any material in this atlas, nor
for any errors, omissions or changes in such material.